Robert C Turner
Cornell University
219 Chestnut St
Ithaca NY

WORKS OF
FRED B. SEELY, M.S.

PUBLISHED BY

JOHN WILEY & SONS, Inc.

Advanced Mechanics of Materials
   xi + 331 pages. 6 by 9. 242 figures. Cloth.

Resistance of Materials
   Second Edition. xii + 436 pages. 6 by 9. 383 figures. Cloth.

By F. B. SEELY and N. E. ENSIGN

Analytical Mechanics for Engineers
   By Fred B. Seely, M.S., and Newton E. Ensign, M.A., Professor of Theoretical and Applied Mechanics, University of Illinois. Third Edition, Rewritten. xv + 450 pages. 6 by 9. 612 figures. Cloth.

ANALYTICAL MECHANICS FOR ENGINEERS

BY

FRED B. SEELY, M.S.
Professor of Theoretical and Applied Mechanics

AND

NEWTON E. ENSIGN, M.A. (Oxon.)
*Professor of Theoretical and Applied Mechanics
University of Illinois*

*THIRD EDITION
Eleventh Printing*

NEW YORK
JOHN WILEY & SONS, Inc.
LONDON: CHAPMAN & HALL, LIMITED

COPYRIGHT, 1921, 1933, 1941,
BY FRED B. SEELY
AND
NEWTON E. ENSIGN

All Rights Reserved
This book or any part thereof must not be reproduced in any form without the written permission of the publisher.

THIRD EDITION
Eleventh Printing, January, 1947

PRINTED IN THE U. S. A.

PREFACE TO THIRD EDITION

The principal changes in the third edition of this book consist of the addition of many new problems and figures; some reduction in the text discussion in the first three parts (Statics, Kinematics, and Kinetics), although the number of problems in these three parts has been increased considerably; more emphasis on variable forces in Part III (Kinetics); and the addition of a new chapter on mechanical vibrations in Part IV, which consists of a group of special topics somewhat more advanced than those treated in the first three parts.

The book has been completely reset, and many detailed changes in the presentation of the subject have been made for the purpose of giving special emphasis to various ideas, concepts, and principles that experience has shown are especially difficult for the student to grasp. Likewise, several rather comprehensive illustrative problems have been added, particularly in Statics and Kinetics, for the purpose of emphasizing the great importance of a general method of attack in applying the principles of mechanics to the solution of problems.

The lists of review questions and problems at the end of chapters—a feature that was introduced in the second edition—have been retained in this edition in response to many favorable comments on this feature of the book.

As in the previous editions, the aim in this revision has been to present the subject as an integrated whole and to encourage the student to seek the meaning and significance of detailed knowledge through its relation to the larger topic or the more general conditions.

The authors wish to express their appreciation of the many suggestions offered by those who have used the second edition of the book. These suggestions have been considered carefully in preparing the third edition.

F. B. SEELY.
N. E. ENSIGN.

URBANA, ILLINOIS,
December, 1940.

PREFACE TO FIRST EDITION

THIS book, as its name suggests, presents those principles of mechanics that are believed to be essential for the student of engineering.

Throughout the book the aim has been to make the principles of mechanics stand out clearly; to build them up as much as possible from common experience (the student's experience); to apply the principles to concrete problems of practical value; and to emphasize the physical rather than the mathematical interpretation of the principles. Important equations are printed in bold-faced type and the statements of the more important principles are italicized.

The book is divided into three parts; namely, Statics, Kinematics, and Kinetics. Statics is presented first because of its simplicity and its direct relation to the student's experience. However, in the first two chapters are developed certain concepts and elementary principles that are fully as important in kinetics as in statics, and the authors feel that it is essential to a satisfactory grasp of mechanics, as a whole, that sufficient time and care be taken to cause these elementary concepts and principles to crystallize in the student's mind before the more general principles and problems are studied. The equilibrium of the various types of force systems are treated both by the algebraic and by the graphical method. A large number of problems involving the equilibrium of the simpler structures and machines are given, and figures illustrating the structures and machines are used freely.

Although kinematics as herein developed is mainly a preliminary to kinetics, the authors' experience indicates that the kinematic properties of motion must be isolated and developed with care if they are to be used with success in the study of the kinetics of the motion.

Both kinematics and kinetics have been developed with regard for the increasing importance of dynamics to engineers. The geometric and physical conceptions and interpretations of the quantities in kinematics have been emphasized rather than the mathematical conceptions. A treatment of acceleration is given which, it is hoped, will help to overcome some of the difficulties frequently found in the use of this quantity. The treatment of kinetics has been restricted to the more common types of motion found in engineering practice, but these motions have been treated more fully than is usual in elementary texts on mechanics. This is particularly true of plane motion. D'Alembert's principle (involving inertia forces) has been used for each type of motion as a second method of solution. The methods of procedure used in the analysis of kinetics problems are strongly emphasized both in the general discussions and in the solutions of illustrative problems.

Illustrative problems are given at the end of the more important articles and many problems are offered for solution. Great care has been exercised in selecting problems that are of practical interest and yet are easily comprehended and are free from unimportant details so that the principles used in their solution will stand out clearly. The answers to about one-half of the problems are given.

Graphical methods of representation and of solution have been used frequently in all three parts of the book. A knowledge of elementary calculus is assumed although little use is made of it in the first four chapters.

The discussion of centroids (Chapter V) is developed directly from the principle of moments—a principle given much emphasis throughout the book.

Several special topics are discussed in Section 3 of Chapter IX. They may be omitted without interfering with the continuity of the book, or any one of the topics may be studied alone without studying the whole section. Further, if it is desired to reduce the time given to kinetics, the second method of analysis of the motion of rotation or of plane motion (which employs D'Alembert's principle and inertia forces) in Section 2 of Chapter IX may be omitted. And, in general, the last part of the material in any section or chapter may be omitted without interfering with the student's progress in the first part of the next section or chapter.

The authors wish to acknowledge their indebtedness to Professor A. N. Talbot for his interest in the book during its preparation and for his helpful suggestions on the treatment of certain important topics. The authors are also indebted to Professor G. A. Goodenough for valuable material in the treatment of Governors and to Professor O. A. Leutwiler for the data and figures for a number of valuable engineering problems.

URBANA, ILLINOIS,
December, 1920.

F. B. SEELY.
N. E. ENSIGN.

CONTENTS

	PAGE
Preface	v

PART I. STATICS

CHAPTER I. FUNDAMENTAL CONCEPTIONS AND DEFINITIONS

1. Introduction	1
2. Rigid Body	2
3. Conception of a Force	3
4. External Effects of a Force	3
5. Characteristics of a Force	4
6. Principle of Transmissibility	4
7. Measure of a Force. Units	4
8. Scalar and Vector Quantities. Vector Representation of a Force	5
9. Classification of Forces. Definitions	6
10. Parallelogram and Triangle Laws	7
11. Resolution of a Force	11
12. Moment of a Force	15
13. Principle of Moments. Varignon's Theorem	17
14. Couples	19
15. Characteristics of a Couple	20
16. Transformations of a Couple	21
17. Vector Representation of a Couple	23
18. Resolution of a Force into a Force and a Couple	24
19. Methods of Solution of Problems	27
20. Dimensional Equations	29

CHAPTER II. RESULTANTS OF FORCE SYSTEMS

21. Introduction	34

§ 1. *Collinear Forces*

22. Algebraic Method	34

§ 2. *Coplanar, Concurrent, Non-parallel Forces*

23. Graphical Methods	35
24. Algebraic Method	36

§ 3. *Coplanar, Non-concurrent, Parallel Forces*

25. Graphical Method	39
26. Principle of Moments	43
27. Algebraic Method	44

CONTENTS

§ 4. *Coplanar, Non-concurrent, Non-parallel Forces*

	PAGE
28. Graphical Methods	48
29. Principle of Moments	49
30. Algebraic Method	50

§ 5. *Non-coplanar, Concurrent, Non-parallel Forces*

31. Graphical Method	53
32. Algebraic Method	54

§ 6. *Non-coplanar, Non-concurrent, Parallel Forces*

33. Algebraic Method	55

§ 7. *Couples in Space*

34. Resultant of a System of Couples	58
35. Composition of Couples in Space by Means of Vectors	60

§ 8. *Non-coplanar, Non-concurrent, Non-parallel Forces*

36. Algebraic Method	61

CHAPTER III. EQUILIBRIUM OF FORCE SYSTEMS

§ 1. *Introduction*

37. Preliminary	64
38. Graphical Conditions of Equilibrium	65
39. Algebraic Conditions of Equilibrium	65
40. Free-Body Diagram	66

§ 2. *Collinear Forces*

41. Equations of Equilibrium	70

§ 3. *Coplanar, Concurrent, Non-parallel Forces*

42. Equations of Equilibrium	71

§ 4. *Coplanar, Non-concurrent, Parallel Forces*

43. Equations of Equilibrium	78

CONTENTS

§ 5. Coplanar, Non-concurrent, Non-parallel Forces

	PAGE
44. Equations of Equilibrium	83
45. Graphical Solution of a Typical Problem	88
46. Procedure in the Solution of Problems in Equilibrium	90

§ 6. Equilibrium of Trusses and Cables

47. Stresses in Trusses	95
48. Graphical Analysis of Trusses	101
49. Flexible Cables	104
50. The Parabolic Cable	104
51. The Catenary	107

§ 7. Non-coplanar, Concurrent, Non-parallel Forces

52. Equations of Equilibrium	111

§ 8. Non-coplanar, Non-concurrent, Parallel Forces

53. Equations of Equilibrium	114

§ 9. Non-coplanar, Non-concurrent, Non-parallel Forces

54. Equations of Equilibrium	116

CHAPTER IV. FRICTION

55. Friction Defined	121
56. Coefficient of Friction	122
57. Angle of Friction	123
58. The Laws of Friction	124
59. Types of Problems Involving Frictional Forces	125
60. Pivot Friction	132
61. The Screw	134
62. Belt Friction	136
63. Rolling Resistance	140

CHAPTER V. FIRST MOMENTS AND CENTROIDS

64. First Moment	144
65. Centroids	146
66. Planes and Lines of Symmetry	148
67. Centroids by Integration	148
68. Centroids of Composite Figures and Bodies	153
69. Theorems of Pappus and Guldinus	157
70. Center of Pressure	159
71. Graphical Method of Determining Centroids of Areas	161
72. Determination of Center of Gravity by Experiment	162

PART II. KINEMATICS

CHAPTER VI. MOTION OF A PARTICLE

	PAGE
73. Introduction	164
74. Vector Addition and Subtraction	164
75. Types of Motion	165
76. Linear Displacement	165
77. Angular Displacement	166
78. Relation between Linear and Angular Displacements	166
79. Linear Velocity and Speed	167
80. Angular Velocity	169
81. Relation between Linear and Angular Velocities	172
82. Components of Velocity	174
83. Linear Acceleration	177
84. Acceleration in Rectilinear Motion	178
85. Uniformly Accelerated Rectilinear Motion	182
86. Simple Harmonic Motion	186
87. Acceleration in Curvilinear Motion. Tangential and Normal Accelerations	190
88. Angular Acceleration	192
89. Uniformly Accelerated Circular Motion	193
90. Relation between Linear and Angular Accelerations	194
91. Axial Components of Acceleration	196
92. Relative Motion	199

CHAPTER VII. MOTION OF RIGID BODIES

93. Introduction	206
94. Translation	206
95. Rotation	207
96. Plane Motion	208
97. Instantaneous Center	215

PART III. KINETICS

CHAPTER VIII. FORCE, MASS, AND ACCELERATION

§ 1. *Preliminary Considerations. Kinetics of a Particle*

98. Introduction	220
99. The General Kinetics Problem	221
100. Characteristics of a Force System	221
101. Inertia and Mass	222
102. Newton's Laws	223
103. Mathematical Statement of Newton's Second Law. Units	224
104. Equations of Motion for a Particle	225
105. Procedure in the Solution of Problems in Kinetics	225
106. Inertia-Force Method for a Particle	231
107. Force Proportional to Displacement. Free Vibration	232

§ 2. *Kinetics of Bodies*

	PAGE
108. Introduction. Methods of Analysis	237
109. Motion of the Mass-Center of a System of Particles	239

Translation

110. Kinetics of a Translating Rigid Body	242

Rotation

111. Kinetics of a Rotating Rigid Body	249
112. Second Method of Analysis. Inertia-Force Method	256
113. Center of Percussion	262

Plane Motion

114. Kinetics of Plane Motion of a Rigid Body	264

CHAPTER IX. WORK AND ENERGY

115. Introduction	274

§ 1. *Work and Power*

116. Work Defined	275
117. Algebraic Expressions for Work Done by a Force	275
118. Work Done by a Couple	277
119. Work a Scalar Quantity. Sign and Units of Work	277
120. Graphical Representation and Calculation of Work	278
121. Work Done on a Body by a Force System	279
122. Power Defined	284
123. Special Equations for Power	285

§ 2. *Energy*

124. Energy Defined	287
125. Potential Energy	288
126. Kinetic Energy	290
127. Kinetic Energy of a Particle	291
128. Kinetic Energy of a Body	292
129. Non-mechanical Energy	296

§ 3. *Principle of Work and Energy*

130. Preliminary	297
131. Principle of Work and Kinetic Energy	298
132. Conservation of Energy	306

CONTENTS

§ 4. *Efficiency. Dissipation of Energy*

133. Efficiency Defined.. 307
134. Dissipation of Energy... 308
135. A Simple Dynamometer. Prony Brake.............................. 308

CHAPTER X. IMPULSE AND MOMENTUM
136. Preliminary.. 313

§ 1. *Impulse*

137. Impulse and Impact Defined. Units................................ 314
138. Components of Linear Impulse...................................... 315
139. Moment of Impulse. Angular Impulse.............................. 315

§ 2. *Momentum*

140. Momentum of a Particle Defined. Units............................ 317
141. Components of Momentum. Angular Momentum................... 318
142. Linear Momentum of a Body....................................... 319
143. Angular Momentum of a Rotating Rigid Body....................... 319
144. Angular Momentum of a Rigid Body Having Plane Motion............ 320

§ 3. *Principles of Impulse and Momentum*

145. Preliminary... 323
146. Principle of Linear Impulse and Linear Momentum.................. 323
147. Principle of Angular Impulse and Angular Momentum............... 324
148. Method of Analysis of the Motion of a Body by Means of Impulse and Momentum... 325
149. Conservation of Momentum.. 330
150. Impact.. 335
151. Impact of Two Translating Bodies.................................. 336

PART IV. SPECIAL TOPICS

CHAPTER XI. MECHANICAL VIBRATIONS

152. Introduction.. 339
153. Free Vibrations... 339
154. Simple Pendulum.. 345
155. Compound Pendulum.. 346
156. Free Torsional Vibration.. 347
157. Analysis of Free Vibrations by Principle of Work and Energy........ 352
158. Free Vibration with Viscous Damping.............................. 355
159. Forced Vibrations without Damping................................ 359
160. Vibration Reduction... 364

CHAPTER XII. BALANCING

161. Need for Balancing.. 369
162. Balancing of Rotating Masses...................................... 370
163. Several Masses in a Single Plane of Rotation....................... 371
164. Masses in Different Transverse Planes............................. 372

CONTENTS

Chapter XIII. The Gyroscope

165. The Problem Defined.. 378
166. Analysis of Forces in the Gyroscope.................................. 378
167. The Moment of the Gyroscopic Couple................................ 381
168. Gyroscopic Couple Found by Use of Principle of Impulse and Momentum. 383

Chapter XIV. Further Study of the Acceleration of a Point

169. Introduction... 390
170. Transverse and Radial Components of Acceleration.................... 390
171. Coriolis' Law.. 391

Chapter XV. Governors

172. The Action of Governors... 396
173. The Conical Pendulum.. 396
174. The Loaded Governor... 398
175. The Porter Governor... 399
176. The Centrifugal Shaft Governor...................................... 400
177. The Inertia Shaft Governor.. 401
178. Comparison of the Two Types of Governors........................... 402
179. Analysis of Forces in the Rites Inertia Governor.................... 402

Appendix. Second Moment. Moment of Inertia

§ 1. *Moments of Inertia of Areas*

180. Moment of Inertia of an Area Defined................................ 413
181. Polar Moment of Inertia... 414
182. Radius of Gyration.. 414
183. Parallel Axis Theorem for Areas..................................... 415
184. Moments of Inertia by Integration................................... 416
185. Moments of Inertia of Composite Areas............................... 421
186. Moments of Inertia of Areas by Graphical and Approximate Methods.... 424
187. Product of Inertia Defined.. 425
188. Axes of Symmetry.. 425
189. Parallel Axis Theorem for Products of Inertia....................... 426
190. Moments of Inertia with Respect to Inclined Axes.................... 428
191. Principal Axes.. 429

§ 2. *Moments of Inertia of Bodies*

192. Moment of Inertia of Mass Defined................................... 432
193. Radius of Gyration.. 433
194. Parallel Axis Theorem for Masses.................................... 433
195. Moments of Inertia with Respect to Two Perpendicular Planes......... 434
196. Moments of Inertia of Solids by Integration......................... 435
197. Moments of Inertia of Composite Bodies.............................. 440
198. Moments of Inertia of Bodies by Experimental Methods................ 443

ANALYTICAL MECHANICS FOR ENGINEERS

PART I. STATICS

CHAPTER I

FUNDAMENTAL CONCEPTIONS AND DEFINITIONS [1]

1. Introduction.—The term *mechanics* is used in a broad sense to denote the science which treats of the motion of bodies, rest being considered as a special case of motion. The science of mechanics constitutes a large part of our knowledge of the laws of the universe, including the laws relating to gases and liquids as well as the laws relating to solid bodies, and it takes a prominent place in the study of astronomy and physics as well as in the study of machines and structures which are involved in engineering practice.

The object of analytical mechanics as developed in this book is to determine the laws by which the motions of bodies (mainly solid bodies) are governed and to apply these laws to conditions met in engineering practice.

In the development of the laws of mechanics certain concepts are assumed to be fundamental, that is, no one of them can be expressed in terms of the others or in simpler terms. Such concepts grow out of our experiences, and other ideas and laws are derived from these condensed experiences.

The fundamental concepts involved in the laws of mechanics are: (1) force, which is made known to us through the tension and the compression of our muscles as a pull or a push, (2) bodies or inert material

---

[1] In this introductory chapter are considered certain concepts, definitions and principles which are used not only in the following pages but in the whole field of mechanics. The student is advised, therefore, to master thoroughly the contents of this chapter in order to have a sound foundation on which to build his knowledge of the subject.

(matter) on which forces act and without which forces cannot exist, (3) space, and (4) time. A more definite understanding of force and inert bodies can be obtained only after the laws of kinetics have been developed. To start with, however, it is necessary only to recognize the existence of these quantities.

In the process of the development of the laws of mechanics, considerable use is made of mathematics. It should be kept in mind, however, that mechanics is a physical science and that mathematics is used, mainly, to express and interpret physical laws.

For convenience, the study of mechanics is considered under three main divisions: namely, *Statics*, *Kinematics*, and *Kinetics*.

Statics is that branch of mechanics which treats of bodies that are acted on by balanced forces and hence are at rest or have uniform motion.

Kinematics is that branch of mechanics which treats of the motion of bodies without considering the manner in which the influencing factors (force and matter) affect the motion. It deals with the fundamental concepts of space and time, and the quantities, velocity and acceleration, derived therefrom. It is, therefore, sometimes called the *geometry of motion*. Kinematics forms an important part of the study of mechanics, not only because it treats of a part of the general kinetics problem in which forces are involved, but also because, in many problems which involve only motions of parts of a machine, the principles of kinematics, alone, are sufficient for the solution of the problem. Such problems are discussed in treatises on *kinematics of machinery*, in which subject the motion of such machine elements as valve gears, quick-return mechanisms, etc., are considered.

Kinetics is that branch of mechanics which treats of bodies which are acted on by unbalanced forces and, hence, have non-uniform or accelerated motions. In particular, it treats of the change of motion of bodies and the manner in which the change is related to the factors that affect it, namely, the actions of other bodies (forces), and the properties (inertia, etc.) of the bodies themselves. Frequently the term *dynamics* is used in technical literature to denote those subdivisions of mechanics with which the idea of motion is most closely associated, namely, kinematics and kinetics.

2. Rigid Body.—The bodies dealt with in this book are, in general, considered to be rigid. A rigid body is defined as a definite portion of matter the parts (particles) of which do not move relative to each other. Actual solid bodies are never rigid. The relative displacement (deformation) of their particles forms an important part of the study of *Strength of Materials*. But the theoretical laws which govern the motion of ideal rigid bodies may be used, usually with very small error, or with modifications, if necessary, to determine the motion of actual solid bodies.

3. Conception of a Force.—It was stated in Art. 1 that force is one of the fundamental concepts on which the subject of mechanics is built. A force is the action of one body on another body which changes or tends to change the state of motion of the body acted on. The idea of force, then, implies the mutual actions of two bodies, since one body cannot exert a force on another body unless the other offers a resistance to the one. A force, therefore, never exists alone. Forces always occur in pairs. Furthermore, as will be seen later when Newton's laws are discussed, the two forces are of equal magnitude and opposite sense.

Our conception of force comes mainly from our experiences in which we have been one of the bodies between which mutual actions have occurred. The resistance which is offered by one body to the action of another body arises out of the ability of a body (1) to resist a change of shape (rigidity) and (2) to resist change of motion (inertia). If a body is acted on by one force, only, a change of motion of the body will always take place; but if the body is acted on by two or more forces, it may be held at rest.

Although a single force never exists, it is convenient in the study of the motion of a body to think of a single force and to consider only the actions of other bodies on the body in question without taking into account the reactions of the body in question on the other bodies. However, the fundamental nature of force should be kept in mind.

4. External Effects of a Force.—When a force is applied to a rigid body the external effect on the body is either to change the motion of the body acted on, or to develop resisting forces (reactions) exerted on the given body by other bodies. Both the foregoing effects, of course, may be produced simultaneously. For example, consider a body falling freely under the action of gravity. The sole external effect of the force acting on the body (its weight) is to produce an acceleration g (32.2 ft. per sec.^{2} approximately). If the same body is placed on the floor of an elevator which is at rest, the sole external effect of the weight is to produce an upward reaction of the floor on the body. If now the elevator moves downward with an acceleration less than g, the effect of the weight is partly to cause an acceleration of the body (the same as that of the elevator) and partly to produce an upward pressure (reaction) of the floor on the body.

The internal effects of a force on a non-rigid or elastic body are to produce stress and deformation in the body on which the force acts. The internal effects of forces are discussed in books on *Strength of Materials*.

5. Characteristics of a Force.—From experience we learn that the external effects of a force on a rigid body depend on (1) the magnitude of the force, (2) the position of the line of action of the force in the body, and (3) the sense of the force, that is, the direction along the line of action. These three properties of a force are called its *characteristics*. A change in any one of them causes a change in the external effect of the force. A discussion of the exact manner in which these characteristics influence the change of motion of a body forms an important part of the study of kinetics, and their influence on the reactions developed in holding a body at rest is considered in the study of statics.

6. Principle of Transmissibility.—The external effect of a force on a rigid body does not depend on the point of application of the force. This fact, the truth of which is found in our experience, is formally expressed in the principle of transmissibility. This principle states that *the external effect of a force on a rigid body is the same for all points of application along its line of action.* It will be noted that the external effect, only, remains unchanged. The internal effect of a force (stress and deformation) may be greatly influenced by a change in the point of application along the line of action of the force.

7. Measure of a Force. Units.—Although we are conscious of forces of varying magnitudes, we are not able to compare the magnitudes with precision by means of our muscular sense. In order to express the magnitude of a force, some standard force must be selected as a unit in terms of which other forces may be expressed. The unit of force commonly used by the engineer is the earth-pull (weight) on an arbitrarily chosen body, as found at a specified or standard position on the earth's surface. Examples of such units are the pound, ton, kilogram, etc. The earth-pull on any body varies slightly with its position (altitude and latitude) on the earth. For most engineering calculations, however, the variation in the weight of a body may be neglected.[1]

There are two common methods used by the engineer for measuring a force, that is, for finding the number of units in a force: (1) by use of the spring balance in its various forms such as steam gages, certain forms of dynamometers, testing machines, etc.; (2) by use of a beam or lever balance or system of levers such as platform scales, screw type of testing machines, etc.

---

[1] The earth-pull on a body varies directly with g, the acceleration due to the earth-pull. The extreme variation in the value of g corresponding to a change in the position of the body on the earth's surface from a high altitude at the equator to the pole is 0.6 per cent. Within the United States the maximum variation is about 0.3 per cent.

SCALAR AND VECTOR QUANTITIES

(1) Owing to the fact that many materials possess nearly perfect elasticity, within limits, the unit of force may be considered to be the force required to produce a certain stretch or deflection of an elastic body. A properly graduated spring balance, therefore, furnishes one means of measuring any force in terms of the arbitrarily chosen unit of force.

(2) In the beam or lever balance, the force to be measured is applied at one end of a lever or system of levers and an arbitrarily selected body is placed at such a position on the other end of the lever that the earth-pull on the body balances the force. The arbitrarily selected body is a body on which the earth-pull at a standard location is the unit of force or some multiple thereof. The lever is so graduated that the number of units in the unknown force may be read off directly from the lever or beam.

Units of space (length), such as the foot, yard, mile, meter, etc., and units of time, such as the second, minute, hour, etc., are assumed to be familiar to the student.

8. Scalar and Vector Quantities. Vector Representation of a Force.—Quantities which possess magnitude only, as, for example, areas, volumes, etc., are called *scalar* quantities. Many quantities involved in the study of mechanics, however, have direction as well as magnitude. Any quantity which has direction, as well as magnitude, as an inherent property is called a *vector quantity*. Thus, as stated in Art. 5, the effect of a force depends on its direction as well as its magnitude, and hence force is a vector quantity. Other examples of vector quantities are velocity, acceleration, momentum, etc.

A vector quantity may be conveniently represented wholly or in part by means of a directed straight line. Any such line is called a *vector*. Thus, the direction of a force may be represented by a straight line drawn parallel to the action line of the force, the sense being represented by an arrow-head on the line, and the magnitude by the length of the line according to some convenient scale. If the magnitude and direction, only, are to be represented, the vector may be laid off along any line parallel to the action line of the force. Such a vector is called a *free vector*. If, in addition, the action line of the force is to be represented, the vector must be laid off along the line of action. Such a vector is called a *localized vector*. Further, if it is desired to represent the point of application of the force, the point of application may be taken as one end of the vector.

In dealing with the forces which act on a body it is frequently convenient to represent the forces by free vectors. The diagram in which are represented the free vectors is called the *vector diagram*. The diagram which represents the body and the action lines of the forces that act on the body is called the *space diagram*. Both diagrams as a rule play an important part in the complete solution of a problem and will be used frequently in the subsequent pages. In Fig. 1 is shown a wall bracket, the horizontal arm of which is acted on by three forces having points of application at 1, 2, and 3, the action lines being indicated as dashed lines and denoted by letters on the two sides of the lines as *ab*, *bc*, and *cd*, in the space diagram. The forces are represented in magnitude and direction in any convenient place by the vectors AB, BC, and CD, the lengths of the vectors representing the magnitudes of the forces according to a convenient scale. The direction of each vector is the same as that of the action line of the force which it represents, and the sense is indicated by the arrow-head.

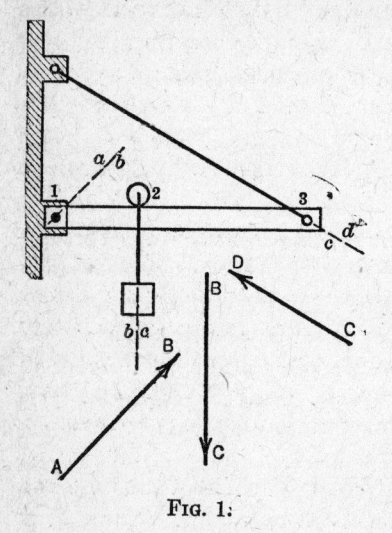

The notation used in the above illustration is known as Bow's notation and will be used frequently in the subsequent pages. According to this notation the action line of a force is denoted by two lower-case letters, one on each side of the action line, and the vector which represents the magnitude and direction of the force is denoted by the corresponding capital letters; the sense of the force may be indicated by the order of the letters (if an arrow-head is not used); thus the sense of the vector BA would be opposite to that of AB, etc.

FIG. 1.

9. Classification of Forces. Definitions.—Forces may be classified as surface forces and body forces, sometimes called forces of contact and forces at a distance according as the action of one body on another is exerted over a portion of the surfaces of two bodies that are in contact or is distributed throughout the materials of the bodies. The most important body force considered in mechanics is the earth-pull (weight). Magnetic forces are of the same class. A surface force becomes a concentrated force when the area over which the force is distributed is so small compared to the surface of the body acted on that it may be regarded as a point. This point is called the point of application of the force. The action line of a concentrated force is a line containing the point of application of the force and having the same direction as that of the force.

Any number of forces treated as a group constitute a *force system*. A force system is said to be *concurrent* if the action lines of all the forces intersect in a common point, and *non-concurrent* if the action lines do not intersect at a point. A force system is said to be *coplanar* when all the forces lie in the same plane, and *non-coplanar* when the forces do not lie in the same plane. A *parallel* force system is one in which the action lines of the forces are parallel, the senses of the forces not necessarily being the same, and a *non-parallel* system is one in which the action lines of the forces are not parallel. If the forces of a system have a common line of action the system is said to be *collinear*.

If a force system applied to a body produces no external effect on the body, the forces are said to *balance* or to be in *equilibrium*, and the body on which the forces act is also said to be in equilibrium. The forces which hold a body at rest are always in equilibrium. If a body is acted on by a force system which is not in equilibrium there always is a change in the motion of the body. Such a force system is said to be unbalanced or to have a resultant.

Two force systems are said to be *equivalent* if they will produce the same *external* effect when applied in turn to a given body. The *resultant* of a force system is the simplest equivalent system to which the system will reduce. The resultant of a force system is frequently a single force. For some force systems, however, the simplest equivalent system is composed of two equal, non-collinear, parallel forces of opposite sense, called a *couple*. And still other force systems reduce to a force and a couple as the simplest equivalent system.

The process of reducing a force system to a simpler equivalent system is called *composition*. The process of expanding a force or a force system into a less simple equivalent system is called *resolution*. A *component* of a force is one of the two or more forces into which the given force may be resolved. The *anti-resultant* or *equilibrant* of a force system is the simplest force system which will balance the given system.

10. Parallelogram and Triangle Laws. *Parallelogram Law.*—The parallelogram law is the fundamental principle on which the composition and resolution of forces is based. The law may be stated as follows: *If from a point vectors are drawn representing in direction and magnitude two concurrent forces, and if a parallelogram is constructed having these vectors as sides, the diagonal of the parallelogram drawn from the point to the opposite vertex of the parallelogram is a vector that represents in direction and magnitude the resultant of the two forces.*

For example, in Fig. 2(a) P and Q are two forces acting on a rigid body MN. If from any point O in Fig. 2(b) vectors OA and OB are laid off representing in magnitude and direction the forces P and Q, the vector OC represents in magnitude and direction (but not in line of action) the resultant, R,[1] of the two forces.

If the point O is taken as the intersection of the action lines of P and Q, as in Fig. 2(a), then the diagonal represents the line of action of the resultant as well as its magnitude and direction since the action line of the resultant of two concurrent forces must pass through the point of intersection of the action lines of the two forces. Thus by superimposing the vector diagram (Fig. 2b) on the space diagram (Fig. 2a) all three of the characteristics (magnitude, line of action, and sense) are determined. However, in many problems, it is more convenient to use the two diagrams separately, in which procedure the vector diagram determines the magnitude, direction, and sense of the resultant, and the space diagram determines one point on the action line of the resultant; the

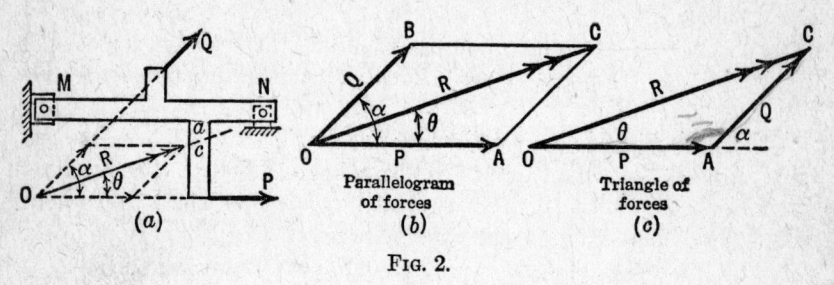

FIG. 2.

direction of the resultant and one point on its action line determine the line of action.

Triangle Law.—The triangle law is a corollary of the parallelogram law. The law may be stated as follows: *If vectors representing in magnitude and direction two concurrent forces be drawn in order and a triangle be constructed having these vectors as sides, the third side of the triangle (the vector drawn from the beginning of the first vector to the end of the second vector) represents the resultant of the two forces in magnitude and direction.* Thus in Fig. 2(c) if OA and AC are vectors representing P and Q in magnitude and direction, the vector OC (not CO) represents the resultant, R, of P and Q in magnitude and direction but not in line of action. The line of action ac of the resultant passes through O (Fig. 2a) as discussed under the parallelogram law. Although the triangle law is essentially the same as the parallelogram law, its extension to more than two forces, leading to the force polygon, frequently makes its use more convenient than that of the parallelogram law.

[1] The fact that a force is the resultant of two or more forces is frequently indicated by two arrow-heads on the vector representing the force. This fact will also be indicated sometimes by drawing the resultant force vector as a dashed line.

Algebraic Method.—Instead of determining the resultant of two concurrent forces graphically, from the parallelogram or the triangle of forces, it may be found algebraically. Thus by referring to Fig. 2(c) and making use of trigonometry, the magnitude and the direction of the resultant may be expressed by the equations:

$$R = \sqrt{P^2 + Q^2 + 2PQ \cos \alpha}$$

$$\tan \theta = \frac{Q \sin \alpha}{P + Q \cos \alpha}$$

where α is the angle between the action lines of P and Q and θ is the angle between the action lines of R and P.

Although it is not necessary to draw the parallelogram or triangle of forces to scale in determining the resultant by the algebraic method, the student should always make a free-hand sketch of the parallelogram or triangle of forces when using the above equations.

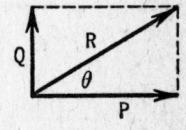

Fig. 3.

In a special case of considerable importance, namely that in which the action lines of the two forces are perpendicular ($\alpha = 90°$) as in Fig. 3, the above equations reduce to

$$R = \sqrt{P^2 + Q^2}$$

$$\tan \theta = \frac{Q}{P} \quad \text{or} \quad \cos \theta = \frac{P}{R}.$$

Another special case is that in which the two concurrent forces have the same direction (in this case the forces are said to be collinear). If the two collinear forces have the same sense ($\alpha = 0$), $R = P + Q$ and if the forces have opposite senses ($\alpha = 180°$), $R = P - Q$.

It should be noted that two equations are needed to determine the magnitude and the direction of the resultant force, whereas one vector diagram is sufficient for the same purpose.

ILLUSTRATIVE PROBLEM

Problem 1.—Two forces P and Q (Fig. 4a) act on a rigid body M. Find the resultant of the two forces. In other words, find the magnitude, line of action, and sense of the single force that will produce the same external effect on the body. (In this case the external effect of the forces is to develop reactions as A and B.)

Graphical Solution.—To determine the resultant of the two forces graphically, a vector diagram is drawn (Fig. 4b). The resultant is represented in magnitude and direction by the vector DE. The magnitude of the resultant is found, by measuring

10 FUNDAMENTAL CONCEPTIONS AND DEFINITIONS

DE to be 26.4 lb. and by use of a protractor the angle θ is found to be 41°, i.e., $\theta_x = 319°$. The information obtained from the vector diagram (unless superimposed on the space diagram) is not sufficient to determine the line of action of R. If, however, one point on the action line of R is found, this point and the direction already found determine the action line. For locating one point on the action line of R, the space diagram is used. Thus in Fig. 4(c) the point O in which the action lines ab and bc of P and Q intersect is one point on the action line of R. Hence if R

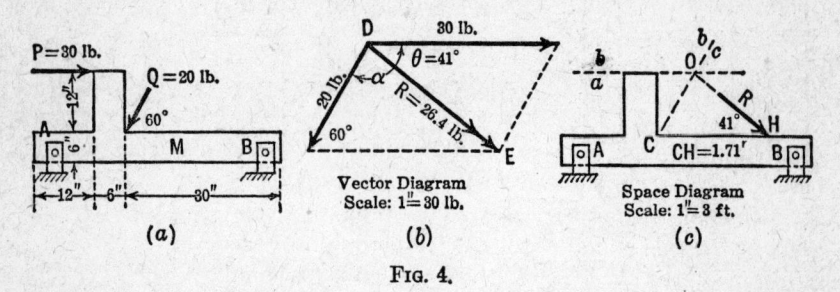

FIG. 4.

is applied to the body as indicated in Fig. 4(c), the external effect (reactions at A and B) would be the same as in Fig. 4(a). The position of the action line can be indicated by stating the distance from C to H which is found by measuring (to scale) to be 1.71 ft.

Algebraic Solution.—Referring to Fig. 4, we have:

$$R = \sqrt{30^2 + 20^2 - 2 \times 30 \times 20 \cos 60°} = \sqrt{700} = 26.4 \text{ lb.}$$

$$\frac{\sin \theta}{20} = \frac{\sin 60}{26.4} \qquad \sin \theta = \frac{17.32}{26.4} = 0.656$$

$$\therefore \quad \theta = 41° \quad \text{or} \quad \theta_x = 319°$$

$$CH = 1 \times \tan 30° + 1 \times \cot 41° = 0.577 + 1.150 = 1.73 \text{ ft.}$$

PROBLEMS

NOTE.—In the following problems in which the resultant of two forces is to be determined, as well as in subsequent problems in which the resultant of any system of forces is to be determined, the resultant should always be completely represented by a vector in the diagram.

2. Determine completely the resultant, R, of the two forces shown acting on the body in Fig. 5.

3. The forces P and Q in Fig. 6 are two of the forces of an unbalanced system acting on the body M, causing a change of motion of M along a horizontal plane indicated by the dotted line. The magnitudes of P and Q are 2 lb. and $\sqrt{5}$ lb., respectively. Replace P and Q by a single force, R, so that the change of motion of (external effect on) M will be the same as if P and Q were acting. (It is assumed the other forces acting on M are not changed when R replaces P and Q.)

Ans. $R = 1$ lb.; $\theta_x = 270°$.

4. When the semi-circle in Fig. 7 is drawn to full-size scale (1 ft. = 1 ft.), the vectors shown represent forces P and Q to a scale of 1 ft. = 10 lb. Determine completely the resultant of the two forces.

5. Two forces having magnitudes of 7 lb. and 3 lb., respectively, have the same point of application in a body. The action line of the 3-lb. force is horizontal and its

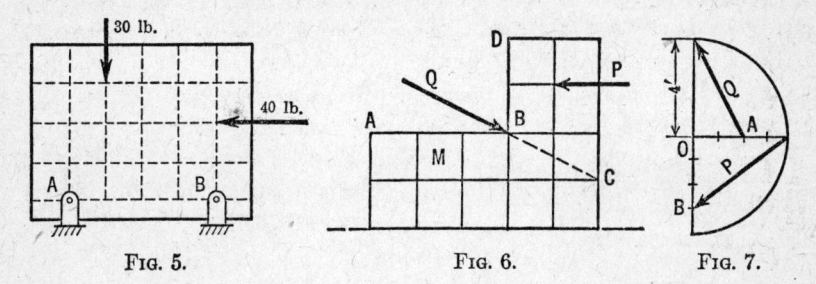

FIG. 5.   FIG. 6.   FIG. 7.

sense is to the right; the action line of the 7-lb. force makes an angle of 45° with the horizontal and its sense is upward to the left. Find the magnitude and direction of the resultant of the two forces.   *Ans.* $R = 5.31$ lb.; $\theta_x = 111° 28'$.

6. A force P of 10 lb. in the xy-plane passes through the origin and makes an angle of 30° with the x-axis. Another force Q of 8 lb. in the same plane passes through the point 0, 2 and makes an angle of 150° with the x-axis. Find the resultant of the two forces algebraically.

11. Resolution of a Force.—In the two preceding articles it was assumed that a body was acted on by two forces and a third force was found which if allowed to replace the two would have the same external

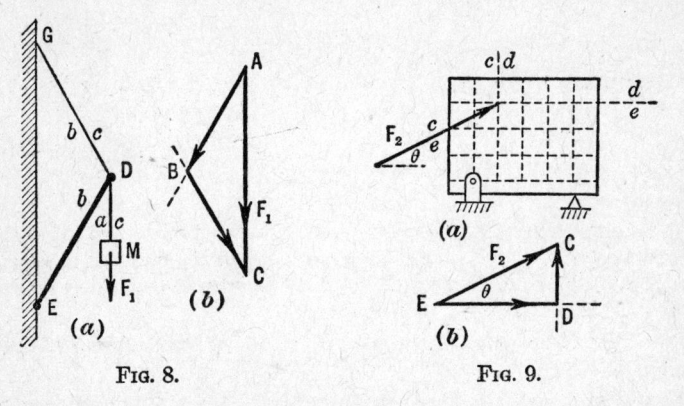

FIG. 8.   FIG. 9.

effect on the body. The reverse of this process, namely, the resolution of a force into two components, is also of great importance in mechanics. The resolution of a force may be accomplished by means of the parallelogram law or the triangle law, and the components may be found graphically or algebraically. For example, in Fig. 8(a) let F_1 be the weight of the body M, and let it be required to resolve F_1 into two components, one along the line DE and one along the line DG; the action lines of the components are represented, using Bow's notation, by ab and bc as shown in the space diagram (Fig. 8a) and similarly the action line of F_1 is indicated by ac.

The magnitudes and directions of the components are represented graphically by AB and BC in the triangle of forces (Fig. 8b). This triangle was constructed by laying off (to scale) AC equal to F_1 parallel to ac and by drawing from A a line parallel to ab and from C another line parallel to bc. The two lines intersect at B. Thus the components of F_1 are represented in magnitude and direction but not in action line by AB and BC. The action lines of the two components must intersect at a point on the action line of F_1.

The resolution of a force into two rectangular components is of special importance. The particular value of resolving into rectangular components lies in the fact that these components may be found from very simple algebraic expressions. Thus in Fig. 9(a) let it be required to resolve the force F_2 into two rectangular components having action lines cd and de. The triangle of forces shown in Fig. 9(b) was constructed in the same way as in Fig. 8(b). The horizontal and vertical components of F_2 or EC are represented in magnitude and sense by ED and DC, respectively.

The magnitudes of these components are expressed as follows:

$$ED = EC \cos \theta \quad \text{and} \quad DC = EC \sin \theta.$$

Or, in general, if F denotes a force which makes an angle θ_x with the x-axis, the x- and y-components of the force are:

$$F_x = F \cos \theta_x \quad \text{and} \quad F_y = F \sin \theta_x.$$

Hence, *the magnitude of the component of a force in a given direction (the other component being perpendicular thereto) equals the product of the magnitude of the force and the cosine of the angle which the force makes with the given direction.*[1]

It is frequently convenient to resolve a force into three rectangular

---

[1] In specifying the direction of a force by giving the angle it makes with a given line, the x-axis for instance, it is convenient to follow a definite convention, namely, to indicate the angle, θ_x, that the vector representing the force makes with the positive end of the x-axis, the angle being measured counter-clockwise from the positive end of the x-axis. For example, for a force directed upward to the right at an angle of 30° with the x-axis, $\theta_x = 30°$; if the sense of the force is reversed $\theta_x = 210°$.

components. This involves only a slight extension of the parallelogram law. Thus, the force F (Fig. 10), represented by OA, may be resolved into the two rectangular components OB and OC, and the component OC may be resolved further into two rectangular components OD and OE. The magnitudes of the components of F in the x-, y-, and z-directions, respectively, are

$$F_x = F \cos \theta_x \quad F_y = F \cos \theta_y$$
$$F_z = F \cos \theta_z,$$

in which θ_x, θ_y, θ_z are the angles which the force makes with the x-, y-, and z-directions, respectively.

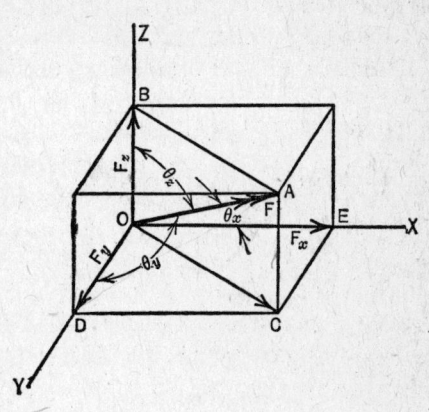

FIG. 10.

ILLUSTRATIVE PROBLEM

Problem 7.—In Fig. 11(a) are shown two forces P and Q[1] acting on a rigid body. Determine the resultant of the two forces (a) by resolving Q at point O into horizontal and vertical components, then finding the resultant of P and the horizontal component of Q, and finally combining this resultant with the vertical component of Q; and (b) by use of the equations of Art. 10.

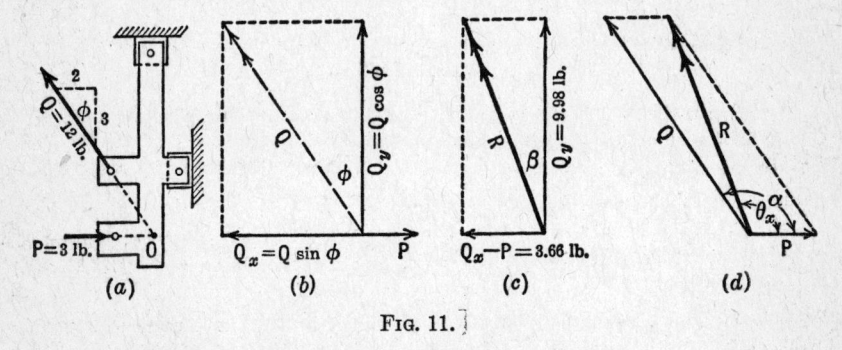

FIG. 11.

---

[1] In this problem the direction of the vector representing the force Q is denoted, not by indicating the angle that the vector makes with some specified line (the angle ϕ in Fig. 11(a), say), but by indicating the slope (or bevel) of the vector; the slope being denoted by the ratio of the vertical projection of any segment of the vector to the corresponding horizontal projection. This method of indicating the direction of a vector or line is frequently used in engineering problems; for, the function of the angle ϕ can be found without finding the angle itself. For instance in Fig. 11(a), $\tan \phi = 2/3$, and hence $\cos \phi = 3/\sqrt{13}$ and $\sin \phi = 2/\sqrt{13}$.

Solution.—(a) Referring to Fig. 11(b) we have

$$Q_x = -Q \sin \phi = -12 \times \frac{2}{\sqrt{13}} = -6.66 \text{ lb.}$$

$$Q_y = Q \cos \phi = 12 \times \frac{3}{\sqrt{13}} = 9.98 \text{ lb.}$$

The resultant of P and $Q_x = 3 - 6.66 = -3.66$ lb. Referring to Fig. 11(c), we have

$$R = \sqrt{(3.66)^2 + (9.98)^2} = 10.6 \text{ lb.}$$

$$\theta_x = 90° + \beta = 90° + \tan^{-1} \frac{3.66}{9.98} = 90° + 20° \, 10' = 110° \, 10'$$

The action line of R must of course pass through the point O (Fig. 11a). The method of procedure used here is of considerable importance in subsequent chapters.

(b) Referring to Fig. 11 we see that $\phi = \tan^{-1} \frac{2}{3} = 33° \, 40'$ and hence $\alpha = 90° + 33° \, 40'$. Therefore $\cos \alpha = -\sin 33° \, 40' = -0.554$ and $\sin \alpha = \cos 33° \, 40' = 0.832$. Hence from Art. 10 we have

$$R = \sqrt{P^2 + Q^2 + 2PQ \cos \alpha} = \sqrt{12^2 + 3^2 - 2 \times 12 \times 3 \times 0.554}$$

$$= \sqrt{113.11} = 10.6 \text{ lb.}$$

$$\tan \theta_x = \frac{Q \sin \alpha}{P + Q \cos \alpha} = \frac{12 \times 0.832}{3 - 12 \times 0.554} = -\frac{9.984}{3.648} = -2.73$$

$$\therefore \quad \theta_x = 110° \, 10'$$

PROBLEMS

8. Resolve the force R shown in Fig. 12 into two components, P acting along BC and Q having an action line that passes through D.

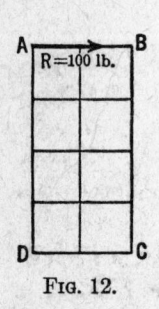

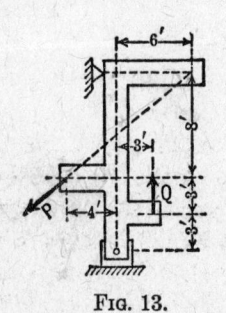

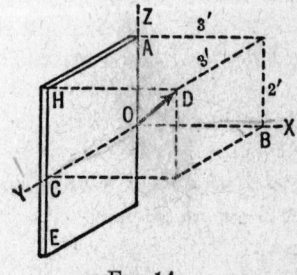

Ans. $P = 200$ lb.; $Q = 224$ lb.

Fig. 12. Fig. 13. Fig. 14.

9. The magnitudes of forces P and Q acting on the body as shown in Fig. 13 are 30 lb. and 40 lb., respectively. Find the resultant of the two forces by the first of the two methods used in Problem 7.

10. The vector OD in Fig. 14 represents a force of 50 lb. acting on the rigid body AE. Resolve the force into components along the lines OB, OC, and OA (F_x, F_y, and F_z). If the body AE were extended to include the point D would the external effect on the body be the same if these components were applied at D?

Ans. $F_x = 32.0$ lb.; $F_y = 32.0$ lb.; $F_z = 21.3$ lb.

11. A thin board in a vertical plane is 6 ft. long and 4 ft. high. The board is acted on by a force of 60 lb. along a line joining the upper left-hand corner, A, to a point, B, 2 ft. above the lower right-hand corner, the sense being downward to the right. Resolve the force into two components (a) parallel to the horizontal and vertical edges of the board, and (b) parallel to the vertical edges and along a line joining the lower left-hand corner to B. Show the first pair of components acting at A and the second pair acting at B.

12. If in Fig. 10 the magnitude of the force F is 100 lb. and the lengths of the edges OE, OD, and OB of the parallelopiped are 15 in., 12 in., and 9 in., respectively, what are the magnitudes of the components of F along the coordinate axes?

12. Moment of a Force.—The moment of a force about (with respect to) a line or axis that is perpendicular to the action line of the force is defined as the product of the magnitude of the force and the perpendicular distance from the action line of the force to the axis. Thus in Fig. 15, the moment of the force F about the axis YY is Fd. The physical significance of the moment of a force about an axis lies in the fact that it is a measure of the tendency of the force to turn the body on which the force acts about that axis.

Since the moment, Fd, of the force F about YY is also the product of F and its perpendicular distance from the point O in which YY intersects the plane in which F lies, Fd may also be regarded as the moment of the force about the point O in the plane of the force. In dealing later with coplanar force systems, moments of the forces will frequently be found with respect to points in the plane of the forces. However, the physical significance of a moment should be kept in mind, for in problems involving physical bodies moments about lines are to be considered. In Fig. 15 the point O is called the *moment-center* and the distance d the moment arm.

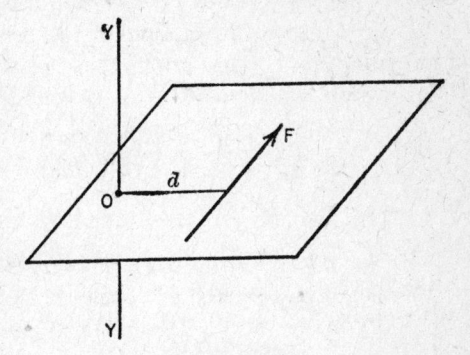

FIG. 15.

Sign and Units.—The sign of the moment of a force about a point in its plane is regarded as positive if the sense of rotation is counter-clockwise. Thus in Fig. 15, the moment of F about O is positive. Considering the moment of F about the axis YY (not the point O) the moment would be positive if viewed from the upper end of the YY axis and negative if viewed from the lower end. Later, in dealing with the moment of a force about an axis, it will be found convenient to select the axis as one of a set of coordinate axes and to regard the moment of a force about a coordinate axis as positive if the sense of rotation is counter-clockwise when viewed from the positive end of the axis.

Since the moment of a force is the product of force and a length, the dimensional expression for a moment is FL. Hence moments may be expressed in lb.-ft., lb.-in., etc.

Force not Perpendicular to Moment Axis.—The moment of a force about an axis that is not perpendicular to the action line of the force can be found by resolving the force into two components, one perpendicular to the moment-axis and one parallel to the axis, and then finding the moment of the perpendicular component which is equal to the moment of the given force, since the moment of the parallel component about the axis is zero. Thus in Fig. 16, the moment of F about the axis OZ is $M_z = F_y \times \overline{OA}$.

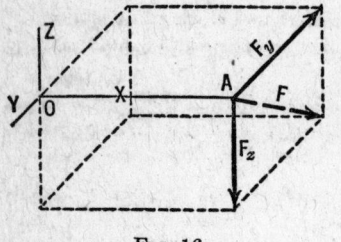

Fig. 16.

ILLUSTRATIVE PROBLEM

Problem 13.—Find the algebraic sum of the moments about the x-axis of the 30-lb. and 40-lb. forces shown in Fig. 17(a). Assume the unit of length in the figure to be one foot.

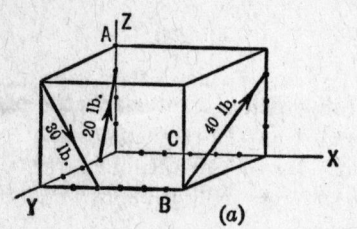

Fig. 17.

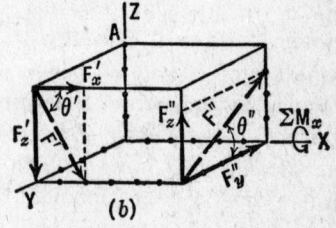

Solution.—First the 30-lb. and 40-lb. forces are resolved into rectangular components as indicated in Fig. 17(b). The magnitudes of the components are found to be as follows:

$$F'_x = 30 \cos \theta' = 30 \times 2/\sqrt{20} = 13.4 \text{ lb.}$$
$$F'_z = 30 \sin \theta' = 30 \times 4/\sqrt{20} = 26.8 \text{ lb.}$$
$$F''_y = 40 \cos \theta'' = 40 \times \tfrac{4}{5} = 32 \text{ lb.}$$
$$F''_z = 40 \sin \theta'' = 40 \times \tfrac{3}{5} = 24 \text{ lb.}$$

PRINCIPLE OF MOMENTS. VARIGNON'S THEOREM

Hence the moment M'_x of the 30-lb. force about the x-axis is $M'_x = F'_z \times 4 = 26.8 \times 4 = 107.2$ lb.-ft. counter-clockwise and hence positive and $M''_x = -F''_z \times 4 = -24 \times 4 = -96$ lb.-ft. clockwise and hence negative. The moments of F'_x and F''_y about the x-axis are zero.

$M_x = 107.2 - 96 = 11.2$ lb.-ft. counter-clockwise as indicated.

PROBLEMS

14. Determine the moment of the 20-lb. force in Fig. 17(a) about the x-axis.

15. Find the algebraic sum of the moments of the 30-lb. and 40-lb. forces in Fig. 17(a) about the y-axis. *Ans.* $M_y = 90.3$ lb.-ft.

16. A force of 20 lb. is exerted on the knob of a door as shown in Fig. 18. If the action line of the force lies in a plane perpendicular to the door, what is the moment of the force about the axis YY?

17. Calculate the moment about the x-axis of the force P of 50 lb. shown in the yz-plane in Fig. 19, (a) by making use of two rectangular components of P acting at

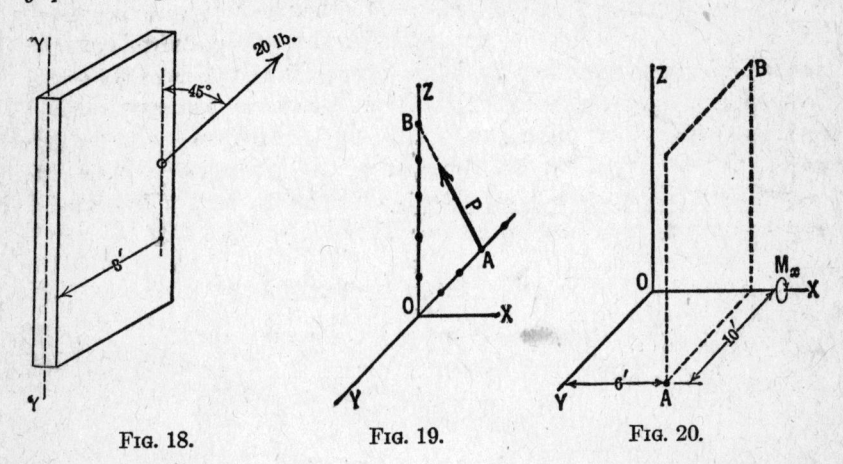

FIG. 18.   FIG. 19.   FIG. 20.

the point A, (b) by making use of two rectangular components of P acting at the point B, and (c) by finding the product of P and the perpendicular distance of P from the x-axis. Assume the unit of length in the figure to be one foot.

Ans. $M_x = 128.6$ lb.-ft.

18. If the force P in Fig. 7 has a magnitude of 40 lb. determine the moment of P with respect to point A.

19. A force P has a point of application at A (Fig. 20) in the xy-plane. The force lies in the plane AB which is parallel to the yz-plane. The moment of the force about the x-axis is 60 lb.-ft., having a negative sense as indicated; the y-component of the force is negative and has a magnitude of 8 lb. (a) Find the magnitude and direction of P. (b) Calculate the moment of P about the y-axis.

Ans. (a) $P = 10$ lb., $\theta_z = 53°\,8'$; (b) $M_y = 36$ lb.-ft.

13. Principle of Moments. Varignon's Theorem.

The principle of moments is of great importance in mechanics. It applies to lines, areas, volumes, etc., as well as to forces. As applied to forces the principle states that the moment of the resultant of any system of forces about any point or line is equal to the algebraic sum of the moments of the forces about the same point or line. It will be considered, however, at this point only in connection with two concurrent forces. The principle for this restricted case, which is known as Varignon's theorem, states that *the moment of the resultant of two concurrent forces about any point in their plane is equal to the algebraic sum of the moments of the two forces about the same point.*

The fact that the principle of moments for two concurrent forces is in agreement with the parallelogram law may be shown by deducing the principle from the parallelogram law as follows: In Fig. 21 let P and Q represent two forces concurrent at A, the resultant according to the parallelogram law being R. Let O be any moment-center in the plane of the forces. It is required to prove that

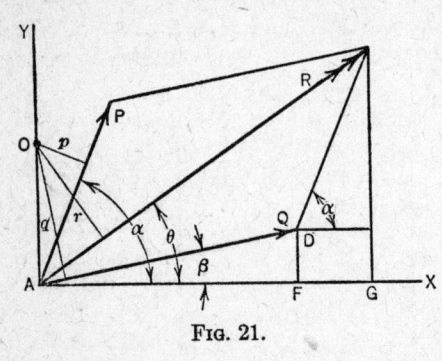

$$Rr = Pp + Qq$$

where p, q, and r are the moment-arms of P, Q, and R, respectively. Let a set of rectangular coordinate axes AX and AY be chosen as shown in the figure, AY passing through the moment-center O. Let α, β, and θ denote the angles which the action lines of P, Q, and R, respectively, make with the AX axis. From the figure it is seen that

$$\overline{AG} = \overline{FG} + \overline{AF}$$

that is, $$R \cos \theta = P \cos \alpha + Q \cos \beta.$$

By multiplying both sides of this equation by AO, the following equation is obtained: $$R \cdot \overline{AO} \cos \theta = P \cdot \overline{AO} \cos \alpha + Q \cdot AO \cos \beta.$$

Hence, $$Rr = Pp + Qq.$$

It is often convenient to obtain the moment of a force about a point in its plane (or about an axis through the point perpendicular to the plane) by resolving the force, at any point on its action line, into two rectangular components and finding the algebraic sum of the moments of the two components.

In finding the moment of a force about any axis that is not perpendicular to the action line of the force, it is convenient to select the moment-axis as one of a system of coordinate axes, and then to resolve the force into three rectangular components parallel to the coordinate axes and find the algebraic sum of the moments of the three components about the given axis.

PROBLEMS

20. In Fig. 5 determine the resultant of the 30-lb. and 40-lb. forces, and by the principle of moments find the perpendicular distance from A to the action line of the resultant. *Ans.* $R = 50$ lb.; $p = 1$ ft.

21. A rectangular board in a vertical plane is 6 ft. wide and 4 ft. high. At the upper left-hand corner are applied two forces; one force has a magnitude of 40 lb. and acts along the upper edge to the right, and the other force, P, is unknown in magnitude and acts along the left-vertical edge. The algebraic sum of the moments of the forces about the lower right-hand corner of the board is 340 lb.-ft. in a clockwise direction. Find the resultant of the two forces.

22. Find the moment about the x-axis, of a 100-lb. force applied at A in Fig. 17(a) and acting along AB towards B. Assume the dimensions to be in feet.
Ans. $M_x = 212$ lb.-ft.

23. In Fig. 6, P and Q have magnitudes of 20 lb. and 40 lb., respectively. Resolve Q into rectangular components at B and then find the algebraic sum of the moments, about A, of these two components and P.

24. In Fig. 7 the magnitudes of P and Q are 40 lb. and 120 lb., respectively. Find the algebraic sum of the moments, about O, of the two forces by resolving P into rectangular components at B, and Q into rectangular components at A, and then finding the algebraic sum of the moments, about O, of the four rectangular components. *Ans.* $\Sigma M_0 = 118.8$ lb.-ft.

25. If F in Fig. 10 is 80 lb. and the length of each of the edges of the parallelopiped is 4 ft., find the moment of F about the lower front edge of the parallelopiped.

26. A room is 20 ft. long, 15 ft. wide, and 12.5 ft. high. A rope is attached at one of the upper corners of the room and extends towards the center of the floor. A downward pull of 120 lb. is exerted on the rope. Find the magnitude of the moment of the force about one of the longer edges of the floor. *Ans.* $M = 636$ lb.-ft.

14. Couples.—Two equal parallel forces which are opposite in sense and are not collinear are called a *couple*. A couple cannot be reduced to any simpler force system. The fact that the only external effect of a couple is to produce or to prevent turning is obtained intuitively. The moment of a couple about any point in the plane of the couple (or any axis perpendicular to the plane of the couple) is defined as the algebraic sum of the moments of the forces of the couple about the point

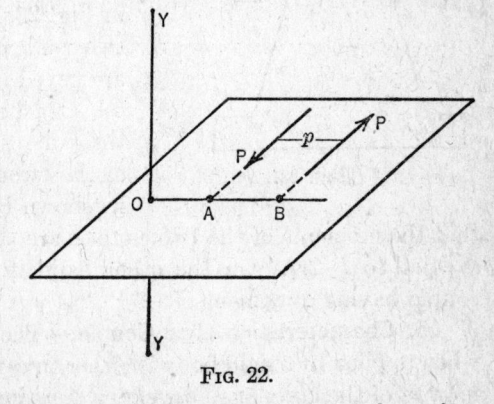

Fig. 22.

(or axis). From this definition it follows that the moment of a couple about any point in the plane of the couple (or axis perpendicular to its plane) is the product of the magnitude of either force of the couple and the perpendicular distance (moment-arm) between the action lines of the two forces. This statement may be proved as follows: In Fig. 22 let P, P be the two forces of a couple, and let O be any point in their plane and YY any axis perpendicular to their plane. The algebraic sum of the moments of the two forces about O (or YY) is

$$P \cdot \overline{OB} - P \cdot \overline{OA},$$

which may be written thus:

$$P(\overline{OB} - OA) = P \cdot AB = Pp.$$

The moment of a couple will be regarded as positive if the sense of rotation is counter-clockwise, and the units used in expressing the moment are the same as for the moment of a force (lb-ft., lb.-in., etc.).

In like manner the moment of the couple may be shown to be the same about any other point in the plane (or any other axis parallel to YY). Since the moment of a couple depends only on the product of either force of the couple and the arm of the couple, it follows that the turning effect of a couple on a rigid body about an axis in the body is the same for different magnitudes and lines of action of the forces, provided that the moment and sense of the couple remains constant, and the direction of the plane of the couple does not change. For example, in Fig. 23, if cords are wrapped around two pulleys, of radii r_1 and r_2, which are keyed together, and if equal weights are attached to the ends of the cords, the pulleys will rotate exactly the same as they would if forces F, F were applied as shown by the dotted lines, provided that the moments of the two couples are the same, that is if $W(r_2 - r_1)$ is equal to $F \cdot 2r_2$. On the other hand if motion is to be prevented a couple having a moment of $-(F \cdot 2r_2)$ would be required.

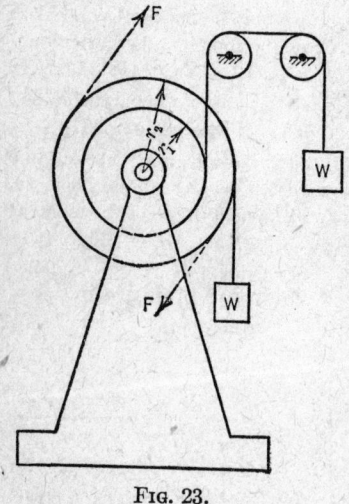

Fig. 23.

15. Characteristics of a Couple.—The external effect of a couple when applied to a rigid body is either to cause a change in the rotational motion of the body or to develop a resisting couple due to the actions of other bodies on the body in question. Both of the foregoing effects may of course be produced simultaneously. From experience we learn that the external effect of a couple depends on (1) the magnitude of the moment of the couple, (2) the sense or direction of rotation of the couple, and (3) the aspect of the plane of the couple, that is, the direction or slope of the plane (not its location). These three properties of a couple are called its *characteristics*. Since parallel planes have the same aspect it follows from what has been stated above that two couples which have the same moment and sense are equivalent if they lie in parallel planes. The fact that the external effect of a couple is independent of the position of the plane of the couple and depends only on the direction of the plane is amply verified by experience. Thus, in screwing a pipe into a joint by means of two pipe wrenches the forces applied at the end of the wrenches constitute a couple, and it is a matter of experience that the effort required is the same regardless of the position along the pipe at which the wrenches are applied.

16. Transformations of a Couple.—It should be noted that several modifications in a couple can be made without changing any of the

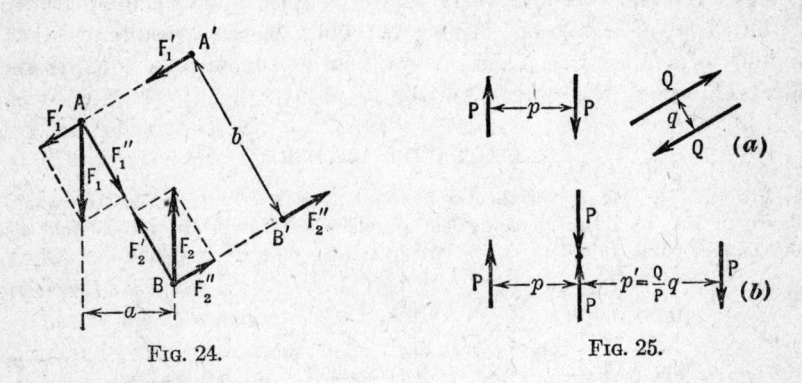

FIG. 24.

FIG. 25.

characteristics of the couple; namely, (a) a couple may be translated to a parallel position in its plane or to any parallel plane; (b) it may be rotated in its plane; and (c) the magnitude of the two forces of the couple and the distance between them may be changed provided that the product of either force and the distance between the two forces remains constant. Although our acceptance of the truth of these statements is a direct outgrowth of experience, it is of value to show that the transformations of a couple are in accordance with the parallelogram law and the principle of transmissibility.

For example, in Fig. 24 let a couple consist of the two equal forces F_1 and F_2 having a moment-arm a. The forces may be resolved at A and B, respectively, into components so that one component, F''_1, of F_1 is equal and opposite to, and collinear with, one component, F'_2, of F_2. These two components will therefore cancel, and hence the couple consisting of the forces F'_1 and F''_2 ($=F'_1$) having the moment-arm b is equivalent to the original couple. Further, the forces F'_1 and F''_2 may be applied at any points along their action lines, as at A' and B'.

It follows from the transformations of a couple that the resultant of any two couples in a plane (or in parallel planes) is a couple whose moment is the algebraic sum of the moments of the two couples. Consider for example the two couples Pp and Qq in Fig. 25(a). By means of transformation (c), the couple Qq may be replaced by an equivalent couple whose forces are each equal to P if the moment-arm is changed from q to p', where $p' = Qq/P$ since $Pp' = Qq$. If now this transformed couple is rotated and translated, it can be placed in the position shown in Fig. 25(b) so that the two collinear forces P,P will cancel, leaving as a resultant of the two couples a couple whose moment is $P(p + Qq/P) = Pp + Qq$, the sense of the resultant couple in this case being negative.

By the same procedure, this resultant couple could be combined with a third couple, and so on. Hence it follows that the resultant of any number of couples in a plane is a couple whose moment is equal to the algebraic sum of the moments of the couples.

ILLUSTRATIVE PROBLEM

Problem 27.—By use of the transformations of a couple, replace the couple shown in Fig. 26(a) by an equivalent couple whose forces are vertical and act through the points C and D.

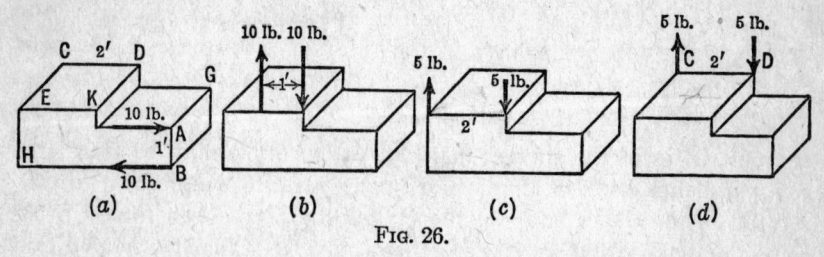

Fig. 26.

Solution.—The couple shown in Fig. 26(a) may be rotated through 90° in its plane and then translated (in its plane) into the position shown in Fig. 26(b) by use of transformations (b) and (a) of Art. 16. By use of transformation (c) the forces may be reduced from 10 lb. to 5 lb. and the arm increased from 1 ft. to 2 ft. as shown in Fig. 26(c). Finally by use of transformation (a) the couple in Fig. 26(c) may be translated into a parallel plane as shown in Fig. 26(d). The couple in Fig. 26(d) has the same moment, aspect, and sense as the couple in Fig. 26(a) and hence if applied to the body would produce the same external effect on the body as would the original couple.

PROBLEMS

28. Show by use of the transformations of a couple (applied in any order) that the couple consisting of two 20-lb. forces acting on the body at A and B in Fig. 27 may be replaced by the two 10-lb. forces at C and D without changing the external effect on the body.

29. In Fig. 27 let a couple having a clockwise moment of 60 lb.-ft. be applied to the body in the vertical face AD, the forces being vertical and having points of application at A and B. By use of the transformations of a couple, find an equivalent couple consisting of horizontal forces applied at E and C.

30. In Fig. 27 replace, by use of the transformations of a couple, the two couples shown by any equivalent couple and show this couple acting on the body.

FIG. 27.

31. A couple consisting of two horizontal forces of 20 lb. each and having a counter-clockwise sense acts on the body shown in Fig. 26(a). The forces act along the lines EK and HB, the distance EH being 1.5 ft. Transform the couple into an equivalent couple whose forces are vertical and act through C and D.

32. A couple having a clockwise moment of 40 lb-ft. consists of two forces acting along the lines CE and DK in Fig. 26(a). Transform the couple into an equivalent couple consisting of forces parallel to BH and acting at points A and G, the length of AG being 3 ft.

17. Vector Representation of a Couple.—In dealing with couples it is convenient to represent them by means of vectors. In order to represent a couple completely by a vector, all the characteristics of the couple must be represented. The moment of the couple may be represented to scale by the length of the vector. The aspect of the couple may be represented by drawing the vector perpendicular to the plane of the couple. The sense of the couple may be represented by an arrow-head on the vector, the usual convention being to direct the arrow-head away from the plane of the couple in the direction from which the rotation appears counter-clockwise. This method of representing the sense of a couple involves the so-called convention of the right-handed screw, since a right-handed screw having an axis perpendicular to the plane of the couple would move in the direction of the arrow if given a rotation which agrees in sense with that of the couple. Thus, in Fig. 28 the vector OA completely represents the couple Fd, provided that the length of OA represents to scale the product $F \cdot d$.

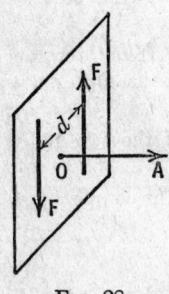

FIG. 28.

The fact that a couple can be completely represented by a vector is of considerable importance in problems involving the composition and resolution of couples. For example if two couples in different planes be represented by vectors and the resultant of these vectors be found by the parallelogram law, the resultant vector completely represents a couple that is the resultant of the two couples.

PROBLEMS

33. The steering wheel of an automobile, shown in Fig. 29, is 18 in. in diameter. Forces exerted by the driver's hands on the wheel constitute a couple which is represented by the vector AB. If the length of AB is 1.5 in. and the scale used is 1 in. = 60 lb.-in., represent the forces of the couple on the circumference of the wheel.

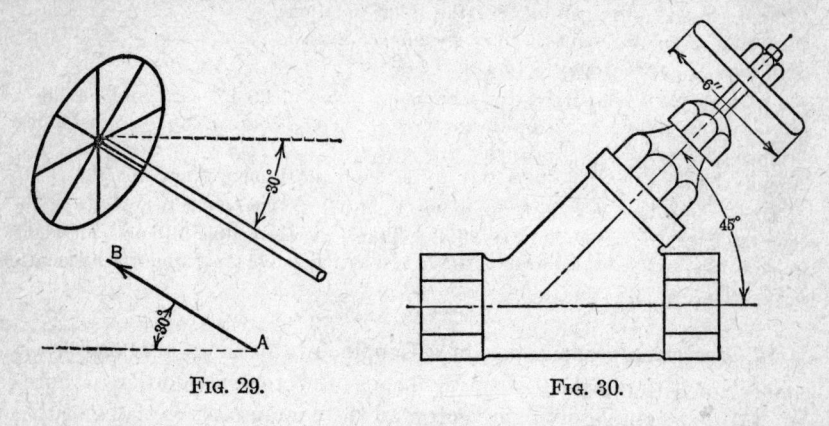

FIG. 29.   FIG. 30.

34. A couple having a moment of 60 lb.-in. is required to open the blow-off valve shown in Fig. 30. Represent the couple completely by a vector, using a scale of 1 in. = 24 lb.-in.

35. In Fig.17 (a) let a 30-lb. force be applied to the point C and act from C towards A. Represent by a vector the couple composed of this force and the 30-lb. force shown in the figure.

36. In Fig. 27 represent by a vector the couple consisting of the two 20-lb. forces.

37. If each force P in Fig. 22 is 60 lb. and p is 5 in., represent the couple by a vector.

18. Resolution of a Force into a Force and a Couple.—In many problems in mechanics it is convenient to resolve a force into a force parallel to the given force, and a couple in the plane of the force. Thus, in Fig. 31, let P represent a force acting on a body at A. Let two equal, opposite, and collinear forces P,P be introduced at any point O, each of the forces being parallel to the original force and of the same magnitude. The three forces are equivalent to the original one, since the two equal, opposite, and collinear forces have no external effect on the body. The force system may now be considered to be a force P acting at O (parallel to the given force and of the same magnitude and sense), and a couple, the moment of which is the same as the moment of the original force about O. The magnitudes and action lines of the forces of this couple, however, may be changed in accordance with the transformations of a couple discussed in Art. 16.

Since a force may be resolved into a force and a couple lying in the same plane, it follows conversely, that a force and a couple lying in the same plane may be combined into a resultant force in the plane, having the same magnitude, direction, and sense as the given force. For if a force P and a couple lie in the same plane, the couple

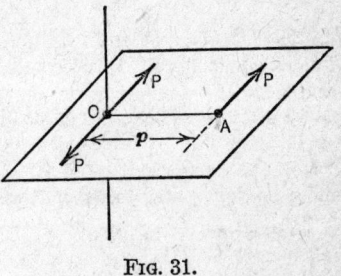

Fig. 31.

may be transformed into an equivalent couple consisting of two forces each equal to P, one of which is collinear with, and opposite in sense to, the given force. These last two forces cancel, leaving as a resultant of the system the remaining force P of the couple.

The sole effect, then, of combining a couple with a force is to move the action line of the force into a parallel position, leaving its magnitude and sense unchanged.

ILLUSTRATIVE PROBLEM

Problem 38.—In Fig. 32(a) is shown a body mounted on an axle O and acted on by a force P of 20 lb. at C. Resolve the force P into a force acting through O and a couple consisting of two horizontal forces acting at A and B.

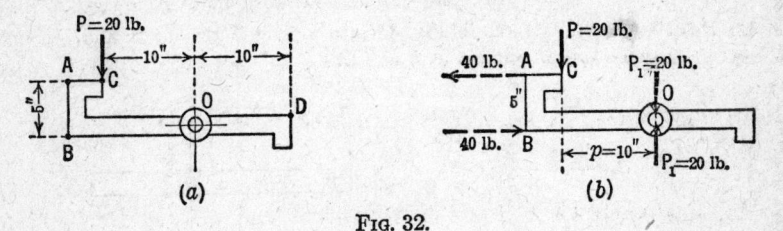

Fig. 32.

Solution.—By introducing two equal and opposite forces, P_1, P_1 acting at O and having the same magnitude as P, the external effect of P will not be changed. But the force system may now be considered to be a downward force P_1 (indicated by the dashed line) at O and a counter-clockwise couple having a moment $Pp = P_1 p = 20 \times 10 = 200$ lb.-in., the forces of which are represented by the full-lined vectors. This couple may be transformed, by rotating and translating the couple and by changing the magnitude of the forces and the moment-arm (without changing the moment of the couple), to the couple represented by the 40-lb. horizontal forces at A and B (Fig. 32b). Thus the three forces represented by dashed lines (the downward 20-lb. force at O and the couple consisting of the two 40-lb. forces acting at A and B) are equivalent to the original force P acting at C.

PROBLEMS

39. If the force P in Fig. 6 has a magnitude of 30 lb., find the force acting at C and the couple having horizontal forces acting through A and D that will replace P without changing the external effect on the body. The squares in the figure have sides 1 ft. long.

40. A gusset plate B (Fig. 33) is attached to another plate A by means of four rivets as shown. A force of 10,000 lb. at the point O (1.5 in. below the horizontal dotted line) is transmitted to the member A. Resolve this force into a force, acting along the horizontal dotted line, and a couple.

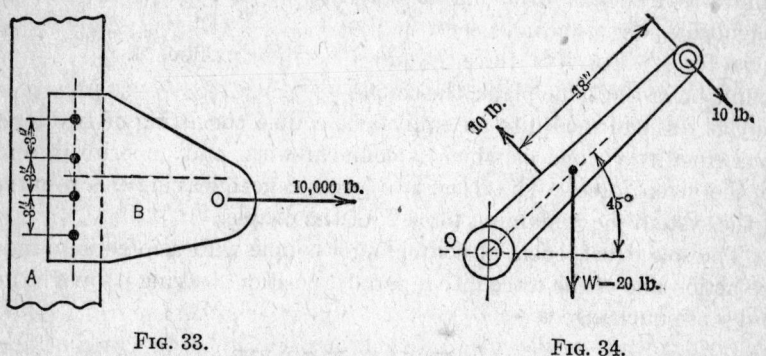

FIG. 33.   FIG. 34.

41. A body weighing 20 lb. is mounted on an axle O (Fig. 34) and is acted on by a couple as shown in the figure, in addition to its weight and the axle reaction at O (not shown). Replace the weight and the couple by an equivalent single force.

Ans. $R = 20$ lb. downward and 9 in. to right of W.

42. Resolve the 60-lb. force in Fig. 35 into a force acting at A and a couple whose forces are horizontal and act at B and C.

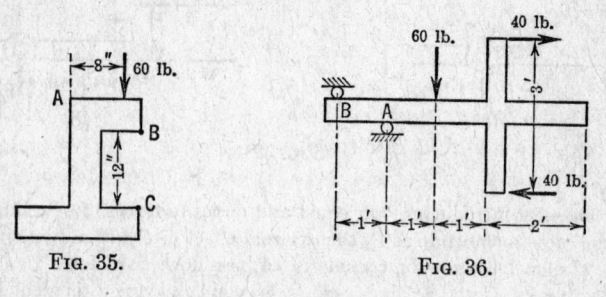

FIG. 35.   FIG. 36.

43. Replace the force and couple shown acting on the body in Fig. 36 by a force that will produce the same external effect (reactions at A and B). Show on the body the vector representing this force.

44. Replace the 30-lb. force in Fig. 5 by a force acting at A and a couple composed of horizontal forces acting at the upper left-hand corner of the body and at the point of application of the 40-lb. force, so that the reactions at A and B will be unchanged. The squares in the figure have sides 1 ft. long.

19. Methods of Solution of Problems. *Algebraic and Graphical Methods.*—In the analysis and solution of problems in mechanics, two general methods may be used, namely, algebraic and graphical methods. In the algebraic method of solution results are calculated, whereas in the graphical method results are obtained by measuring distances and angles in geometric constructions. Simple graphical methods have already been used in the preceding articles in connection with forces and couples. In general, either of the two methods may be used in the solution of a problem. Some problems, however, may be solved more easily by the algebraic method, whereas other problems yield more readily to the graphical method. The operations involved in the solution of a problem by the two methods are so different that one method of solution serves as an excellent check on the other method.

Method of Trial and Error.—A common engineering method used for computing an approximate result for an unknown quantity in an algebraic equation is called the method of trial and error or the method of successive approximations.

To illustrate the method, let it be required to compute the value of the independent variable x in the equation $y = 2x^3 - 3x^2$ corresponding to a known value of the dependent variable y. In the method of trial and error, a trial value (a first guess or first approximation) for x is substituted in the equation and the resulting value of y is computed. This value of y is compared to the known value of y and the error noted. If the first trial value of x gives a value for y different from the known value, a second trial value of x is used that will cause the corresponding computed value of y to approach closer to the known value of y. This method of successive approximations may be continued until the final trial value of x causes the corresponding computed value of y to differ from the known value as little as may be desired, and hence a value of x is found that approaches as closely as desired to the true value of x.

Frequently by plotting several trial values of the independent variable as abscissas and the corresponding computed values of the dependent variable as ordinates, and drawing a curve through the plotted points, a relatively small number of trial computations may be required for determining a final value having a specified or permissible error, since the trend of the curve thus obtained is an aid in choosing the successive trial values.

Degree of Accuracy.—In making computations it is important to keep in mind the degree of accuracy which should be obtained. The degree of accuracy desired will depend, in general, on two factors, namely:

(1) The degree of accuracy of the original data or quantities on which the computation is based, and

(2) The use which is to be made of the computed results.

The data on which many engineering computations are based are determined from experiments and hence are approximate values, the degree of approximation depending on the instruments and methods used, and on the care and skill of the observer. The computed results which are based on these values cannot have a greater degree of accuracy than that of the original data. In general a sum, difference, product, or quotient of two approximate values will not have a greater degree of accuracy than that of the less accurate of the two numbers. For example, if one numerical quantity is accurate to two significant figures and another quantity to three significant figures, the product of the two numbers will not be accurate to more than two significant figures, and hence more than two significant figures should not be retained in the result.

The degree of accuracy of results obtained by graphical methods depends on the care with which the graphical diagrams are constructed and on the scale (or scales) used in the construction. The scale should be sufficiently large to make it possible to obtain results whose accuracy is comparable to the accuracy of the original data.

ILLUSTRATIVE PROBLEM

Problem 45.—In the equation $y^3 = Ax^2 - Bx$, $y = 10$, $A = 16$, and $B = 50$. Compute by the method of trial and error, the value of x to three significant figures.

Solution.—The equation becomes $y^3 = 16x^2 - 50x$ and since the value of y is 10, a value of x must be found that will make the value of y^3 (or $16x^2 - 50x$) equal to 1000. As a first trial value let $x = 8$. The first trial computation then gives

$$y^3 = 16 \times 64 - 50 \times 8 = 624$$

This value of y^3 is too small; hence try $x = 9$ and we then obtain

$$y^3 = 16 \times 81 - 50 \times 9 = 846$$

This value of y^3 is still too small. By trying $x = 9.6$ we obtain

$$y^3 = 16 \times 92.2 - 50 \times 9.6 = 995$$

Thus x has a value slightly greater than 9.6. Assuming $x = 9.63$ as a fourth trial value of x, we find

$$y^3 = 16 \times 92.7 - 50 \times 9.63 = 1001.7$$

Further approximations will not change the value of the third significant figure and hence $x = 9.63$.

PROBLEMS

46. The equation $Q = 0.622 \sqrt{2g}(b - 0.2h)h^{3/2}$ is used to determine the quantity of water flowing per unit of time over a rectangular weir of width b when the height of water above the weir is h, g being the acceleration due to gravity (32.2 ft./sec.^{2}).

If Q equals 24.4 cu. ft. per sec. and b equals 3 ft., compute, by the method of trial and error, the value of h to three significant figures. NOTE: This formula is valid only when $0.2h$ is small compared with b. Hence the term $0.2h$ may be omitted and a trial value of h may be found by solving the resulting equation. This value of h may now be used in the term $0.2h$ and a second trial value of h may be obtained by solving the resulting equation. This process may be repeated.

Ans. $h = 1.48$ ft.

47. Find to three significant figures, by the method of trial and error, the value of x that will satisfy the equation $2x^3 + 3x = 20$.

48. In finding the diameter, d, of a pipe required to discharge a given quantity of water, the formula $d^5 = Ad + B$ is used. If $A = 15.5$ and $B = 400$, compute, by the method of trial and error, the value of d to three significant figures.

Ans. $d = 3.39$.

49. In Prob. 45, let $y = 5$, $A = 2$, and $B = 4$. Find to three significant figures the value of x, using the method of successive approximations.

20. Dimensional Equations.—In algebraic equations in which the variables represent physical quantities, all the terms of the equation must be of the same dimensions, or, to express the same idea in mathematical language, an algebraic equation which expresses a relation between physical quantities must be homogeneous. The use of this principle is of assistance in checking any equation for correctness, and in determining the specific units in which a result is expressed when computed from a given equation. For each of these purposes the given algebraic equation is replaced by a dimensional equation.

The dimensional equation corresponding to any algebraic equation is formed by replacing each term of the given equation by a term which indicates the kinds of fundamental quantities in which the term is expressed and which also indicates the degree of the corresponding quantities in each term.

The fundamental quantities used in engineering are force, mass, length, and time (F, M, L, and T). Hence, in an equation, a term which represents an area is replaced by L^2 in the dimensional equation since an area is the square of a length. A velocity is a length divided by time and hence is represented in the dimensional equation by LT^{-1}, and similarly for other quantities. It should be noted that in the dimensional equation only the kinds of fundamental quantities are indicated and not the specific units used in measuring these quantities, and also that the number of such units is not indicated. Hence, numerical constants in the algebraic equation do not appear in the dimensional equation.

For example, consider the equation $ad^2 + d^3 = v$, in which a represents an area, d a length, and v a volume. Since an area is the square of a length (L^2) and a volume is the cube of a length (L^3), the dimensional equation is $L^4 + L^3 = L^3$, and hence the given equation is incorrect.

Consider also the equation $P + kv = as$, in which P represents a force, k a weight (force) per unit volume, v a volume, a an area, and s a force per unit area. The dimensional equation then may be written:

$$F + \frac{F}{L^3} \cdot L^3 = L^2 \cdot \frac{F}{L^2}.$$

That is:

$$F + F = F,$$

and hence the equation is dimensionally correct.

Furthermore, consider the equation $E = \dfrac{Pl}{ae}$, in which P represents a force in pounds, l a length in inches, a an area in square inches, and e a length in inches. Let it be required to determine the units in which E is expressed. The dimensional equation is

$$E = \frac{F \times L}{L^2 \times L} = \frac{F}{L^2}.$$

Hence, in accordance with the units stated (pound and inch), E is expressed in pounds per square inch (lb./sq. in. or lb./in.^{2}).

Further use is made of dimensional equations in applying the results obtained in experimental investigations on models to their full-scale counter-parts. Space in this book, however, does not permit of the discussion of this subject, commonly referred to as dimensional analysis.

PROBLEMS

50. In the equation $s = \frac{1}{2}(u + v)t$, s is a length, u and v are lengths per unit time, and t is time. Is the equation dimensionally correct?

51. The equation $s = Mc/I$ is dimensionally correct. What are the dimensions of M if s is a force per unit area, c is a length, and I is a length to the fourth power?
Ans. FL.

52. In the equation $d^4 = Ad^2 + Bd$, if d is a length, what are the dimensions of A and B?

53. In the equation given in Prob. 46, what are the units in which Q is expressed if b and h are expressed in feet?

54. The equation $\theta = \omega t$ is dimensionally correct; ω is an angle (expressed in radians) per unit of time, and t is time. What are the dimensions of θ. NOTE: Since a radian is a length along the arc of a circle divided by the length of the radius, an angle expressed in radians has no dimensions.

Ans. θ is a dimensionless number.

55. Is the equation $x^3 + ax^2 + bx + ab/x = 0$ dimensionally correct if x, a, and b represent physical quantities? *Ans.* No.

REVIEW QUESTIONS AND PROBLEMS

NOTE: The following review questions and problems, as well as similar ones at the close of subsequent chapters, are meant to set before the student a definite review assignment of the essential parts of the theory and applications covered in the chapter, by the use of which the student may test for his own satisfaction his mastery of the subject.

56. Correct the following false statement: The resultant of two concurrent forces that act on a rigid body is a single force that will replace the two forces and produce the same internal effect on the body.

57. What properties of a force are represented in a vector diagram? What properties of a force are represented in a space diagram?

58. Is the following statement correct? In finding the resultant of two concurrent forces graphically, by use of a vector diagram and a space diagram (not superimposed), only one point on the action line of the resultant is located in the space diagram, this point being the intersection of the action lines of the two given forces.

59. Is it true that the action lines of any two components of a force must intersect on the action line of the force?

60. What is wrong with the following statement? If a force whose action line lies in the xy-plane and passes through the origin is resolved into two components, one of which lies along the x-axis, the other component must lie along the y-axis.

61. The following statement is indefinite and incomplete: The moment of a force with respect to an axis is the product of the component of the force that is perpendicular to the axis and the perpendicular distance from the axis to this component. Criticize the statement.

62. Part of the following statement is untrue; indicate the part that should be omitted. If the algebraic sum of the moments of two concurrent forces about a point O in their plane is zero, it follows from the principle of moments that (a) the resultant of the two forces is equal to zero and (b) the action line of the resultant passes through the point O.

63. Is the following statement correct? The moment of a couple is the product of one of the two forces and one-half the distance between the two forces.

64. Is the following statement correct? The moment of a couple about a point midway between the two forces of the couple is one-half as large as the moment of the same couple about a point on the action line of one of the forces.

65. Three of the five parts of the following statement are wrong. Correct the errors. If a force P acting on a rigid body is resolved into a force Q and a couple C, then Q must (1) have the same magnitude as P, (2) be perpendicular to P, (3) be opposite to P; and C must (4) have a moment equal to the product of P and the distance between P and Q, (5) have a sense the same as the sense of rotation of Q about a point on P.

66. The top of a table is 3 ft. wide and 5 ft. long. A string, attached to the table at the center of the top, extends towards a point, B, on one of the long edges 6 in. from a corner. A pull of 20 lb. is exerted on the string. Find the components of the pull parallel to the two edges of the table and draw a sketch showing the components acting on the top. *Ans.* 16 lb.; 12 lb.

67. In the preceding problem find, by the principle of moments, the moment of the 20-lb. force about the corner of the table nearest to the point B. Check the result by finding the moment-arm and calculating the moment of the 20-lb force directly. *Ans.* $M = 6$ lb.-ft.

68. A force P of 20 lb. acts as shown in Fig. 37. Resolve P into three components along the edges of the cube and find, by the principle of moments, the moment of P with respect to the axis YY. *Ans.* $M = 46.2$ lb.-ft.

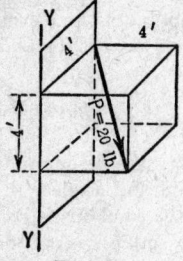

Fig. 37. 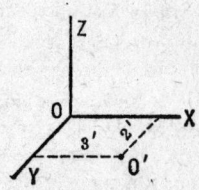   Fig. 38.

69. The point of application of a force P that is parallel to the xz-plane is at O' (Fig. 38). The moments of P with respect to the x-, y-, and z-axis are -20 lb.-ft., $+30$ lb.-ft., and $+40$ lb.-ft., respectively, the signs of the moments being in accordance with the convention stated in Art. 12. Find the force P and represent it by a vector in the figure. *Ans.* $P = 22.4$ lb.

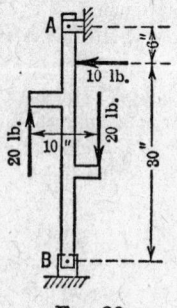

Fig. 39. 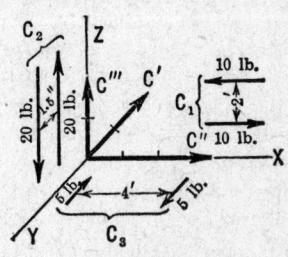   Fig. 40.

70. Replace the force and couple acting on the body AB in Fig. 39 by a single force that will produce the same reactions at A and B. Solve by use of the transformations of a couple.

Ans. A horizontal 10-lb. force to the left with action line 26 in. below A.

71. Do the vectors C', C'', and C''' in Fig. 40 correctly represent the couples C_1, C_2 and C_3? The vector C' lies along the y-axis.
Ans. Two of the vectors have the wrong sense.

72. The equation $\theta = Tl/EJ$ is dimensionally correct. What are the dimensions of J, if θ is an angle in radians, T is the moment of a force, l is a length, and E is a force per unit area? *Ans.* L^4.

CHAPTER II

RESULTANTS OF FORCE SYSTEMS

21. Introduction.—The determination of the resultants of various force systems as discussed in this chapter is of importance, mainly, (1) in the study of the conditions which the forces of a system satisfy when they hold a body in equilibrium (Statics, Chapter III), and (2) in the study of the laws by which the motions of bodies are governed (Part III, Kinetics).

(1) The equations of equilibrium for a given type of force system are obtained by expressing the conditions which the forces must satisfy in order that the resultant of the system shall be zero. Therefore the resultant to which a given type of force system reduces must be known before the conditions which are required to make the resultant equal to zero can be established. Furthermore, in dealing with forces in equilibrium it is frequently convenient to replace several of the forces of a balanced system by the resultant of the several forces and to deal with the resulting force system instead of the original system.

(2) The motion of a body is determined by the resultant of the forces which act on the body. In the study of the motions of physical bodies, therefore, a knowledge of the resultants of the various force systems and of methods of expressing the characteristics of resultants in terms of the forces of the system must be understood. The force systems to be considered in the following pages may be classified as follows:

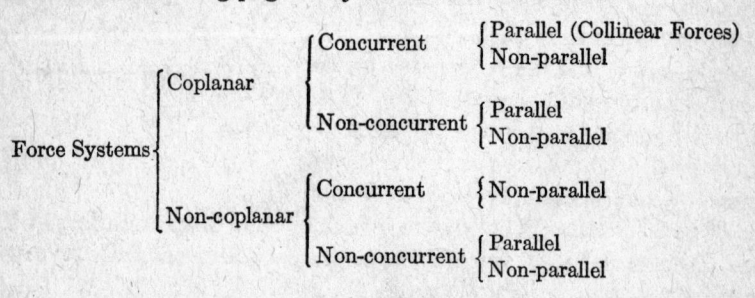

Force Systems
- Coplanar
  - Concurrent
    - Parallel (Collinear Forces)
    - Non-parallel
  - Non-concurrent
    - Parallel
    - Non-parallel
- Non-coplanar
  - Concurrent
    - Non-parallel
  - Non-concurrent
    - Parallel
    - Non-parallel

§ 1. COLLINEAR FORCES

22. Algebraic Method.—The resultant will be found first for two collinear forces, P and Q, having the *same* sense. It is a matter of experience that the two forces are equivalent to a single force which has a magnitude equal to $P + Q$ and a line of action and sense which are the same as the line of action and sense of the given forces. This proposition, moreover, follows directly from the parallelogram law (Art 10). Similarly, the resultant of two collinear forces P and Q having *opposite* senses (P being the larger of the two forces) is a force the magnitude of which is given by the equation $R = P - Q$, the sense of R being the same as that of the larger force P. Hence, the resultant of any two collinear forces is a single force having the same line of action as the given forces, the magnitude and sense being indicated by the algebraic sum of the forces. The extension of this method to any number of collinear forces may easily be made. Thus the resultant of two of the forces may be combined with a third force; the resultant thus obtained may then be combined with a fourth force, and so on, until the entire system is reduced to a single resultant force. Therefore the magnitude of the resultant of a collinear force system is given by the equation

$$R = \Sigma F.$$

The sense of R is determined by the sign of the ΣF.

§ 2. Coplanar, Concurrent, Non-parallel Forces

23. Graphical Methods. *First Method.*—The resultant of an unbalanced system of concurrent forces in a plane is a force which may be found by means of the parallelogram law. In Fig. 41 are shown three forces F_1, F_2, and F_3, which act on a body at the point O. The forces F_1 and F_2 may be combined into a force R_1 by means of the parallelogram law. Similarly R_1 and F_3 may be combined into a force R_2. R_2 then is the resultant of the given forces. By continuing this process, any number of concurrent forces may be combined into a single force. The order in which the forces are taken is immaterial. If the resultant force obtained by combining all except one of the forces of a concurrent system is equal to that one, collinear with it, and of opposite sense, the two forces cancel and hence the resultant of the given system is equal to zero.

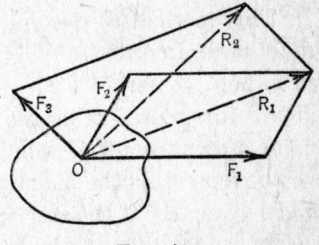

Fig. 41.

Second Method.—Another graphical method of determining the resultant of a system of concurrent forces in a plane involves the application of the triangle law. Consider, for example, the three forces F_1, F_2, and F_3 which act on a body and concur at a point O as shown in

Fig. 42(a). In order to determine the resultant of the three forces, draw from any arbitrary point A (Fig. 42b) a vector representing the magnitude and the direction of the force F_1; from the end of this vector draw another vector representing the magnitude and the direction of the force F_2. R_1, the resultant of F_1 and F_2, is represented in direction and magnitude by the vector drawn from A to the end of F_2. To find the resultant of R_1 and F_3, and hence of the three given forces, draw from the end of R_1 (or F_2) a vector representing F_3 in magnitude and in direction. The resultant of R_1 and F_3 is then represented in magnitude and in direction by the vector R_2 drawn from A to the end of F_3. It should be noted that this vector R_2 represents the magnitude and the direction, only, of the resultant of the given forces and not the action

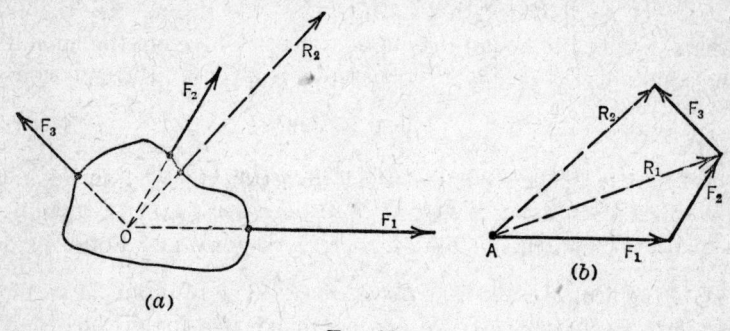

FIG. 42.

line of the resultant. The action line of the resultant must pass through the point O in the body at which the forces are concurrent.

This method of determining the resultant may be stated formally as follows: In order to find the resultant of a system of concurrent forces in a plane, construct a polygon (called a *force polygon*) the sides of which are vectors representing the given forces in magnitude and in direction; a line drawn from the beginning of the first vector to the end of the last vector represents the magnitude and the direction of the resultant of the given system. If the force polygon closes, that is, if the end of the last vector coincides with the beginning of the first vector, the resultant of the given system is equal to zero.

24. Algebraic Method.—In Fig. 43(a) is represented a coplanar force system which is concurrent. Each of the four forces of the system may be resolved into two components, one lying along the x-axis and one along the y-axis. The x-components of the forces constitute a collinear system the resultant of which is a force along the x-axis. The magnitude of this resultant is equal to ΣF_x. The y-components of the forces likewise constitute a collinear system the resultant of which is a force along the y-axis of magnitude ΣF_y. Since the system, by this method, is reduced to two forces, the resultant of the given system is the resultant of these two forces. If the magnitude of this resultant is

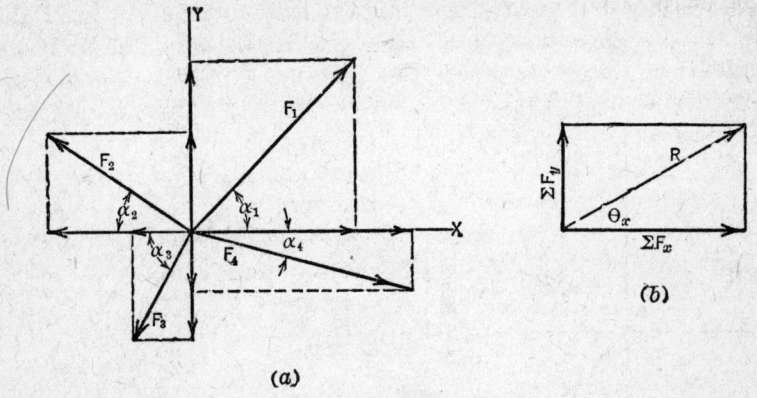

FIG. 43.

denoted by R and the direction which its action makes with the x-axis by the angle θ_x as shown in Fig. 43(b), the resultant may be found from the equations:

$$R = \sqrt{(\Sigma F_x)^2 + (\Sigma F_y)^2},$$

$$\tan \theta_x = \frac{\Sigma F_y}{\Sigma F_x}.$$

The direction of the resultant could also be determined from the equation

$$\cos \theta_x = \frac{\Sigma F_x}{R} \quad \text{or} \quad \sin \theta_x = \frac{\Sigma F_y}{R}.$$

The action line of the resultant must, of course, pass through the point of concurrence of the forces. If $\Sigma F_x = 0$ and $\Sigma F_y = 0$, the resultant of the system is zero.

ILLUSTRATIVE PROBLEM

Problem 73.—Find the resultant of the system of concurrent forces shown in Fig. 44(a).

Algebraic Solution:

$$\Sigma F_x = 20 \cos 30° - 30 \cos 60° - 10 \cos 45° + 25 \cos 45°$$
$$= 17.32 - 15 - 7.07 + 17.67 = 12.92 \text{ lb.}$$

$$\Sigma F_y = 20 \cos 60° + 30 \cos 30° - 10 \cos 45° - 25 \cos 45°$$
$$= 10 + 25.98 - 7.07 - 17.67 = 11.24 \text{ lb.}$$

$$R = \sqrt{(12.92)^2 + (11.24)^2} = 17.1 \text{ lb.} \quad \text{(Fig. 44b)}$$

and
$$\theta_x = \tan^{-1}\frac{11.24}{12.92} = 41°.$$

Graphical Solution:

To determine the resultant of the system graphically, a force polygon $ABCDE$ is constructed as shown in Fig. 44(c), using a scale of 1 in. = 30 lb. The resultant is represented by the vector AE. The magnitude of the resultant, R, is found, by

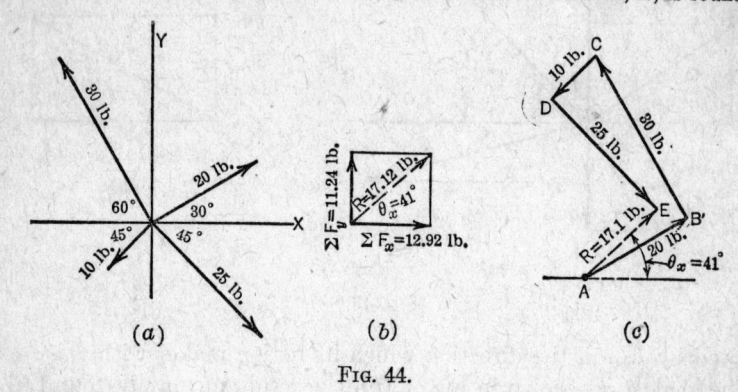

FIG. 44.

measuring the length of AE, to be 17.1 lb., and the angle which the resultant makes with the x-axis is found by use of a protractor to be 41°. The action line of R, of course, passes through the origin.

PROBLEMS

74. Figure 45 represents a body acted on by four forces. Determine completely the resultant of the four forces by the graphical method and check the results by the algebraic method.

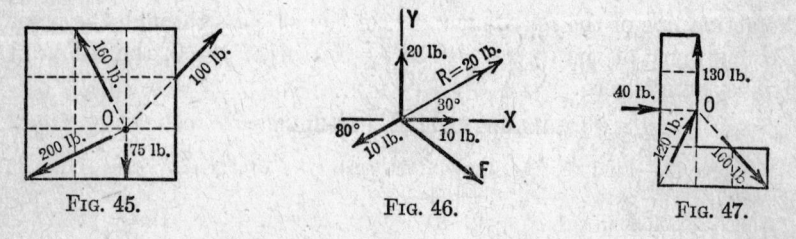

FIG. 45. FIG. 46. FIG. 47.

75. In Fig. 46, R is the resultant of the other four forces shown. Find the magnitude and direction of the force F algebraically.

Ans. $F = 16.7$ lb.; $\theta_x = 342° 35'$.

76. The body represented in Fig. 47 is acted on by four forces as shown. Replace the four forces by a single force that will have the same external effect on the body. Solve by the algebraic method. *Ans.* $R = 234$ lb.; $\theta_x = 45° 20'$.

COPLANAR, NON-CONCURRENT, PARALLEL FORCES 39

In the following three problems the forces are concurrent at the origin. The values of F are the magnitudes of the forces and the values of θ_x are the angles which the action lines of the forces make with the positive end of the x-axis, the angles being measured in a counter-clockwise direction. In each problem it is required to find the resultant of the forces specified.

77.	F	100 lb.	60 lb.	40 lb.	50 lb.
	θ_x	30°	135°	240°	330°
78.	F	20 lb.	10 lb.	15 lb.	5 lb.
	θ_x	0°	45°	120°	270°
79.	F	25 lb.	10 lb.	30 lb.	40 lb.
	θ_x	0°	30°	135°	240°

Ans. $R = 11.3$ lb.; $\theta_x = 228°\ 10'$.

80. The moment, about the point O, of the resultant of the three forces shown in Fig. 48 is 140 lb.-ft., counter-clockwise. Find, by the algebraic method, the magnitude of P, and the resultant of the three forces.

Ans. $P = 20$ lb.; $R = 28.6$ lb.; $\theta_x = 114°\ 45'$.

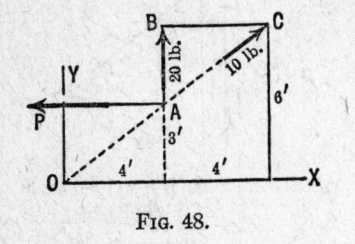

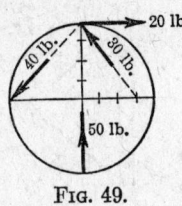

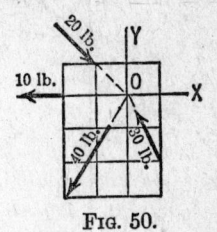

FIG. 48.   FIG. 49.   FIG. 50.

81. Find, by the graphical method, the resultant of the four forces shown in Fig. 49.

82. Find, by the graphical method, the resultant of the four forces shown in Fig. 50.   *Ans.* $R = 37.6$ lb.; $\theta_x = 213°\ 10'$.

§3. COPLANAR, NON-CONCURRENT, PARALLEL FORCES

25. Graphical Method.—Let a system of parallel forces F_1, F_2, and F_3, having action lines ab, bc, and cd (Fig. 51a) act on a body. It is required to find the resultant of the forces. The resultant of a coplanar parallel force system may be a force or a couple; the case in which the resultant is a force will be considered first. By means of the parallelogram law F_1 may be resolved into two components F'_1 and F'''_1 at any point, A_1, on the action line of F_1 as shown in (c) of Fig. 51. Furthermore, F_2 may be resolved at the point B_2 into components F''_2 and F'''_2 so that F'''_2 is equal and opposite to F'_1 and collinear with it. Similarly, F_3 may be resolved into components F'_3 and F'''_3 so that F'''_3 and F'_2 are equal, opposite, and collinear. Since the two pairs of equal, opposite, and collinear forces cancel, the six forces into which the original system was resolved are now reduced to the two forces F'''_1 and F'_3, and the resultant of the given system is the resultant, R, of these two forces. The action line of R will, of course, pass through the point of intersection, A', of the action lines of F'''_1 and F'_3. The magnitude and direction of R may be found by means of the parallelogram law as shown in Fig. 51(c).

A more convenient graphical method, especially when a relatively large number of forces is involved, makes use of two diagrams as discussed in the next paragraph.

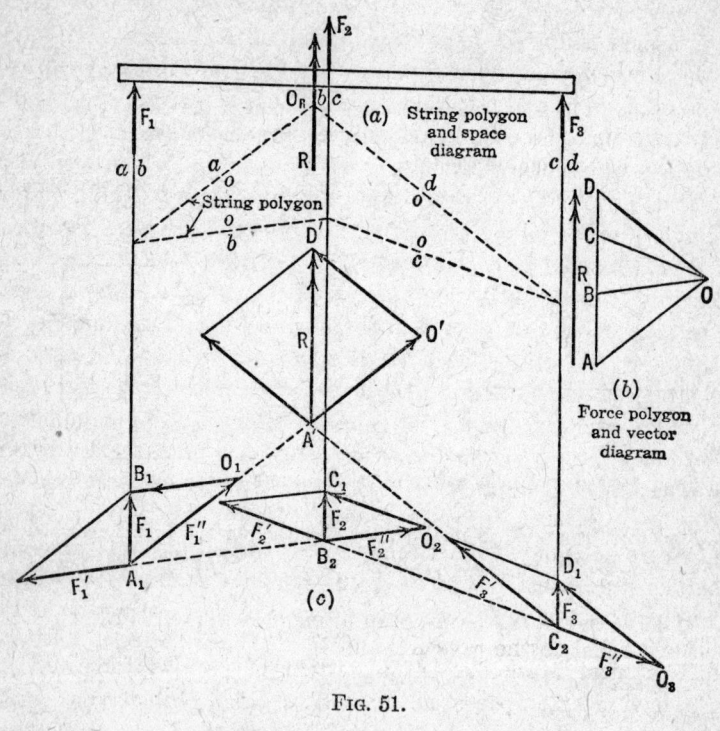

FIG. 51.

Force and String Polygons.—The resultant of the force system here considered is a force (a parallel force system for which the resultant is a couple will be considered later). The magnitude, direction, and sense (but not action line) of the resultant force may be found by drawing first a force polygon (Fig. 51b), and then one point on the action line of the resultant force may be obtained in the space diagram by drawing a string or funicular polygon (Fig. 51a). These diagrams are explained in the following paragraphs, but it is important to observe that all the facts necessary for an understanding of the two diagrams have already been brought out in the explanation of Fig. 51(c).

COPLANAR, NON-CONCURRENT, PARALLEL FORCES

The force polygon is constructed as follows: On a line parallel to the action lines of the forces are laid off, to scale (Fig. 51b), vectors AB, BC, and CD which represent the given forces in magnitude and direction, the sense of each force being indicated by the order of the letters according to Bow's notation (Art. 8); the vector AD drawn from the beginning of the first vector to the end of the last vector represents the magnitude, direction and sense (but not action line) of the resultant force. Now if one point on the action line of the resultant force can be found, this point together with the direction of the resultant determines its line of action. A point on the line of action of the resultant force may be found as follows: From any arbitrarily chosen point O (Fig. 51b) lines are drawn to the points A, B, C, and D. These lines are called *rays* and the point O is called the *pole*. The complete diagram composed of the rays and the line $ABCD$ is frequently called the *vector diagram* or *force polygon*, although the line $ABCD$ is sometimes called the force polygon. From the triangle law it follows that, by this construction, the force AB (Fig. 51b) is resolved into two components represented in magnitude and direction (but not in action line) by the rays AO and OB. Similarly, the rays BO and OC represent the magnitude and direction of the components of BC, etc. The lines of action of AO and OB must, of course, intersect on the action line ab of AB; similarly the forces BO and OC must intersect on bc, etc. The action lines of the components represented by the rays are called *strings* and, of course, the strings are drawn in the space diagram; the diagram having strings as its sides is called the *string polygon* or *funicular polygon*.

The string polygon which is constructed for the purpose of locating one point on the action line of the resultant force is drawn as follows: From any point on ab in the space diagram (Fig. 51a) strings ao and ob are drawn parallel to the rays AO and OB. From the point of intersection of ob and bc the string bo (which will coincide with string ob) and the string oc are drawn. From the intersection of oc and cd are drawn co and od. Since by this construction ob and bo, the action lines of the equal and opposite forces OB and BO, are collinear the two forces OB and BO, if laid off along their action lines as was done in Fig. 51(c), will cancel; similarly for OC and CO. The system then is reduced to two forces represented in magnitude and direction by the rays AO and OD and in action line by the strings ao and od; and the point of intersection of ao and od (O_R in Fig. 51a) must be one point on the action line of the resultant. In Fig. 51(c) the equal and opposite forces were laid off as vectors along their action lines, and it will be noted that Fig. 51(c) would be obtained if the triangle of forces for each force in Fig. 51(b) were superimposed on the string polygon in Fig. 51(a) and the corresponding parallelogram of forces completed. For example the triangle $A_1O_1B_1$ in Fig. 51(c) is the triangle AOB in Fig. 51(b) superimposed on Fig. 51(c), etc. Likewise the triangle $A'O'D'$ in Fig. 51(c) is the triangle AOD in Fig. 51(b) superimposed on Fig. 51(c).

If the force polygon closes, that is, if D (Fig. 51b) coincides with A, the rays AO and OD represent two forces which are equal in magnitude and which have parallel action lines and opposite senses. The resultant in this case is a couple provided that the string polygon does not close. If, however, the string polygon also closes, that is, if ao and od coincide, the two forces AO and OD will balance and the resultant of the given system will be equal to zero.

In constructing the force and string polygons any point may be taken for the pole and the string polygon may be started at any point on the action line of any one of the forces. A change in the positions of these points has the effect, only, of locating a different point on the action line of the resultant if the resultant of the system is a force. If the resultant of the system is a couple, the effect is to change both the magnitude of the forces constituting the resultant couple and the length of its moment-arm. The couples will be equivalent, however; that is, they will have the same moment and sense.

ILLUSTRATIVE PROBLEM

Problem 83.—Find by the graphical method the resultant of the four parallel forces shown in Fig. 52(a), the scale used in the space diagram being 1 in. = 2 ft.

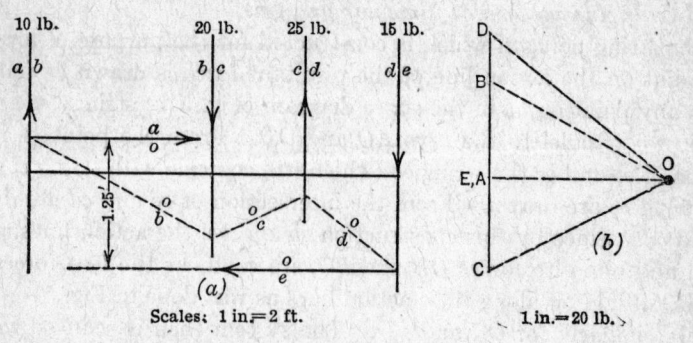

FIG. 52.

Solution.—The force polygon $ABCDE$ is drawn to a scale of 1 in. = 20 lb. as shown in Fig. 52(b). Since the force polygon closes, the resultant is not a force and hence, if the force system has a resultant, it is a couple. In constructing the rays (Fig. 52b) it is convenient to take the pole O so that the force represented by OA has an integral value. OA here represents to scale 20 lb. The string polygon in Fig. 52(a) is constructed according to the method described in Art. 25. The resultant is a couple consisting of the two 20-lb. forces AO and OE. The arm as scaled from the string polygon is 1.25 ft. Hence the moment of the resultant couple is -25 lb.-ft., the minus sign indicating a clockwise direction of rotation.

26. Principle of Moments.—The principle of moments as discussed in Art. 13 for the special case of two concurrent forces may be extended to all force systems. Briefly, the principle states that the moment of the resultant of a force system is equal to the algebraic sum of the moments of the forces of the system. The principle is of great importance in the determination, by the algebraic method, of (*a*) the action line of the resultant of a system of forces when the resultant is a force, and (*b*) the moment and sense of the resultant of the force system when the resultant is a couple. A formal statement and proof of the principle of moments will not be given for each of the force systems considered since the method of proof is substantially the same for all the force systems. As applying to a system of parallel forces in a plane the principle may be stated formally as follows: *The moment of the resultant of any system of coplanar, non-concurrent, parallel forces about any point in the plane of the forces is equal to the algebraic sum of the moments of the forces about the same point.*

In demonstrating the truth of this statement use will be made of the diagrams (*a*) and (*b*) in Fig. 51, and of the methods of the preceding article. The given system of three forces (Fig. 51) was replaced by another system of six forces which were represented in magnitude and in direction by the rays of the force polygon and in line of action by the strings of the string polygon. Four of these forces occur in pairs, the two forces of each pair being collinear, equal in magnitude, and opposite in sense. Obviously, the sum of the moments of the two forces of each pair with respect to any point in their plane is equal to zero. For any moment-center in the plane, by use of Varignon's theorem, the following relations may be written,

$$\text{moment of } AB = \text{moment of } AO + \text{moment of } OB,$$
$$\text{`` `` } BC = \text{`` `` } BO + \text{`` `` } OC,$$
$$\text{`` `` } CD = \text{`` `` } CO + \text{`` `` } OD.$$

If the two sides of the above equations are added, the result obtained may be stated as follows:

The sum of the moments of the forces of the system

$$= \text{moment of } AO + \text{moment of } OD,$$

since the remaining terms on the right side of the equations cancel in pairs. But AO and OD are the components of the resultant force of the system, and hence, by Varignon's theorem, the sum of the moments of *AO* and *OD* is equal to the moment of the resultant of the system. Hence, the proposition is proved for a parallel force system in which the resultant is a force.

If the resultant of the force system is a couple, that is, if the forces *AO* and *OD* are parallel, equal, and opposite as in Fig. 52, the proposition also holds, since the sum of the moments of *AO* and *OD* is equal to the moment of the resultant couple.

27. Algebraic Method.—A system of coplanar parallel forces is shown in Fig. 53, the forces being parallel to the *y*-axis. In the graphical determination of the resultant of such a system it was seen that the resultant was either a force or a couple. If the resultant is a force, *R*, its action line is parallel to the action lines of the forces of the system and its magnitude and sense are indicated by the algebraic sum of the forces, that is, $R = \Sigma F$. In order to locate the line of action of the resultant force, the principle of moments will be applied. For convenience the origin, *O*, will be taken as the center of moments. The moment of *R* then with respect to *O* is equal to the algebraic sum of the moments of the forces with respect to the same point. If the distance from the action line of *R* to the *y*-axis is denoted by $\bar{x}$, the moment of *R* with respect to the origin is equal to $R\bar{x}$. Furthermore, if the algebraic sum of the moments of the forces of the system with respect to the origin is denoted by $\Sigma(Fx)$ or ΣM_0, the principle of moments may be expressed by the equation $R\bar{x} = \Sigma M_0$. The resultant, then, if a force, is parallel to the *y*-axis and is determined by the following equations:

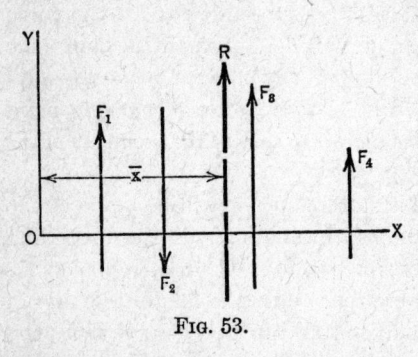

$$R = \Sigma F,$$

$$R\bar{x} = \Sigma M_0.$$

The sign of $\bar{x}$ may be determined by inspection, since the resultant force must lie on that side of the moment-center which will make the sense of its moment agree with that of the moment of the system.

If the resultant of all except one of the forces of the system is equal to that one and of opposite sense, ΣF then equals zero and the resultant is a couple, the moment of which, according to the principle of moments, is equal to the algebraic sum of the moments of the forces of the system.

Hence, if the resultant of a coplanar parallel force system is a couple the moment, C, of the couple may be determined from the expression

$$C = \Sigma M,$$

the aspect of the couple, of course, is the same as that of the plane of the forces and the sense is indicated by the sign of the algebraic summation.

If both ΣF and ΣM equal zero the resultant is equal to zero.

ILLUSTRATIVE PROBLEMS

Problem 84.—Figure 54 represents a beam resting on two supports and carrying four loads as indicated. Find the resultant of the loads.

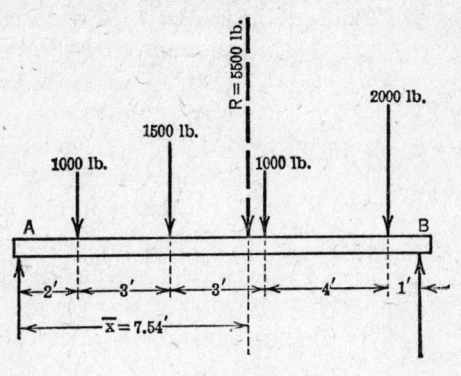

FIG. 54.

Solution.—

$R = \Sigma F = -1000 - 1500 - 1000 - 2000 = -5500$ lb. (downward)

In order to locate the action line of the resultant, the point A will be selected as the moment-center. Thus:

$$R\bar{x} = \Sigma M_A = -1000 \times 2 - 1500 \times 5 - 1000 \times 8 - 2000 \times 12$$
$$= -41{,}500 \text{ lb.-ft. (clockwise)}$$

Therefore

$$\bar{x} = \frac{41{,}500}{5500} = 7.54 \text{ ft.}$$

Hence a single load of 5500 lb. at a point 7.54 ft. from A as shown will produce the same external effect (reactions at A and B) as the four given forces. R, being a downward force, must lie to the right of A since the moment of R about A must agree in sense with that of ΣM_A and hence must be clockwise.

Problem 85.—An arm mounted on an axle at O (Fig. 55) is acted on by the four forces represented by the vectors shown as full lines. Determine the resultant of the forces.

Solution.—

$$R = \Sigma F = 15 + 15 - 20 - 10 = 0.$$

Therefore the resultant is not a force, but is a couple, C, the moment of which may be found by taking moments about O (any other point could have been selected). Thus,

$$C = \Sigma M_o = 20 \times 10 - 15 \times 6 - 10 \times 5 + 15 \times 12 = 240 \text{ lb.-in.}$$

Since the sign of ΣM_o is positive, the sense of C is counter-clockwise. Hence any couple having a counter-clockwise moment of 240 lb.-in. will produce the same

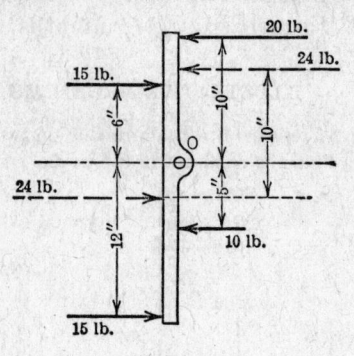

FIG. 55.

external effect on the arm (change in the rotational motion) as the four given forces. One such couple having forces equal to 24 lb. is shown in the figure.

PROBLEMS

86. Three forces which act vertically downward are spaced at one-foot intervals. Reading from left to right, the magnitudes of the forces are 1 lb., 2 lb., and 3 lb. Determine the resultant of the forces algebraically.

Ans. $R = -6$ lb., $1\frac{1}{3}$ ft. to right of 1-lb. force.

87. In Fig. 56 are shown five forces acting on a beam. Find algebraically the resultant of the five forces.

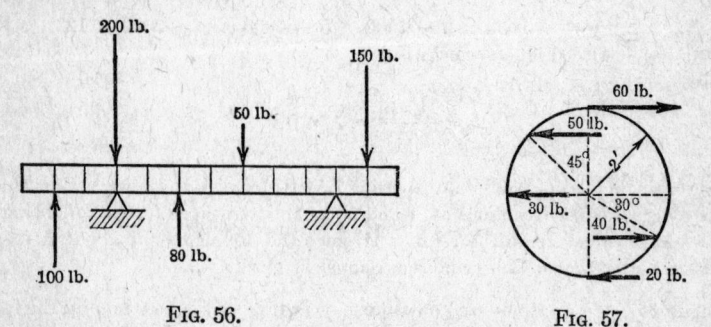

FIG. 56.   FIG. 57.

88. Solve the preceding problem graphically by use of a force polygon and a string polygon.

89. Determine the resultant of the forces shown in Fig. 57.

PROBLEMS

90. Determine the resultant of the forces acting on the body as shown in Fig. 58. Solve algebraically and check the result by use of the transformations of a couple (see Art. 18). *Ans.* $R = 20$ lb. to right and 1 ft. above 20-lb. force.

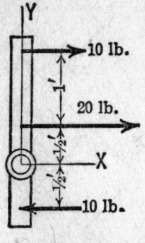

Fig. 58.

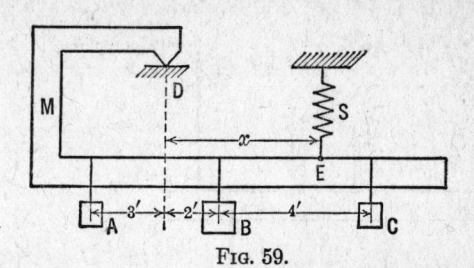

Fig. 59.

91. Three bodies A, B, and C are hung on a frame M as shown in Fig. 59. The frame is supported at D by a fixed plane and at the point E by the spring S. The resultant of the four forces consisting of the earth-pulls (weights) of A, B, and C and the pull P of the spring on M is a force of 70 lb. acting vertically downward through the point D. Find the value of P and the horizontal distance x. The weights of A, B, and C are 20 lb., 80 lb., and 20 lb., respectively.
Ans. $P = 50$ lb.; $x = 4.4$ ft.

92. Determine the resultant of the five forces shown in Fig. 60. Each space represents 1 ft.

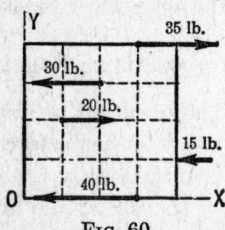

Fig. 60.

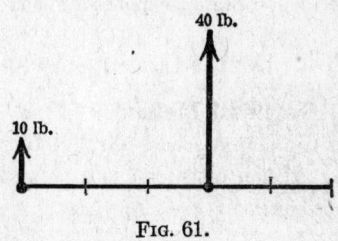

Fig. 61.

93. The 40-lb. force shown in Fig. 61 is the resultant of the 10-lb. force and a force P not shown. Determine P completely by means of a force polygon and a string polygon, and check the result by the algebraic method.
Ans. $P = 30$ lb. upward and 1 ft. to right of 40-lb. force.

In each of the following three problems find the resultant of the force system. The forces in each problem are parallel to the y-axis. The values of F given are the magnitudes of the forces (expressed in pounds), and the values of x are the distances of the action lines of the forces from the y-axis (expressed in feet).

94. F	$+10$	-20	$+25$	-15	
x	-2	$+1$	$+3$	$+4$	
95. F	-10	$+5$	-20	$+15$	
x	-2	$+1$	$+3$	$+5$	
96. F	$+40$	-60	$+80$	-70	$+10$
x	0	$+4$	$+9$	$+12$	$+14$

Ans. $C = -220$ lb.-ft.

97. A bar 10 ft. long is acted on by the forces shown in Fig. 62. Find the simplest equivalent force system.

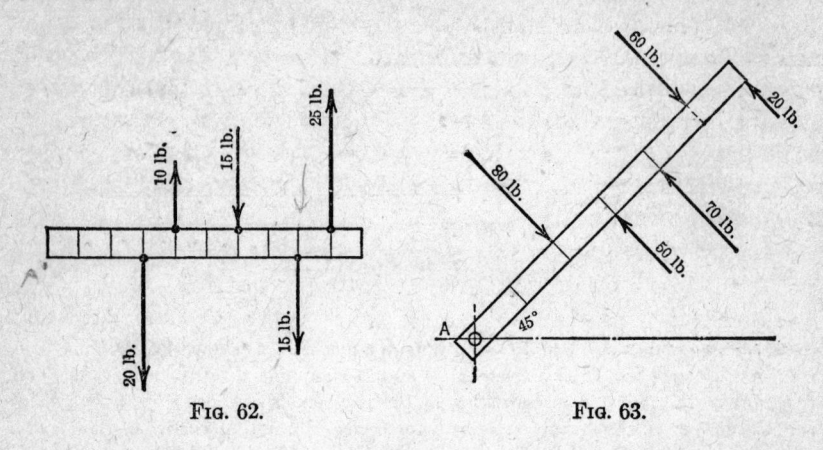

Fig. 62.

Fig. 63.

98. A bar 6 ft. long is hinged at A (Fig. 63) and is acted on by five forces as shown. Determine the resultant of the five forces by use of a force polygon and a string polygon. *Ans.* $C = 90$ lb.-ft.

99. A force of 10 lb. acts along the y-axis, the sense of the force being positive. Resolve the force into components P and Q along the lines $x = 1$ and $x = 3$.

§ 4. Coplanar, Non-concurrent, Non-parallel Forces

28. Graphical Methods. *First Method.*—The resultant of a system of non-concurrent, non-parallel forces in a plane is either a force or a couple. If the resultant is a force it may be determined by use of the parallelogram law. In Fig. 64 are shown three non-concurrent, non-parallel forces F_1, F_2, and F_3 acting on a body. The forces F_1 and F_2 may be combined into a resultant force R_1. R_1 and F_3 may be combined into a force R_2 which is the resultant of the given system of forces.

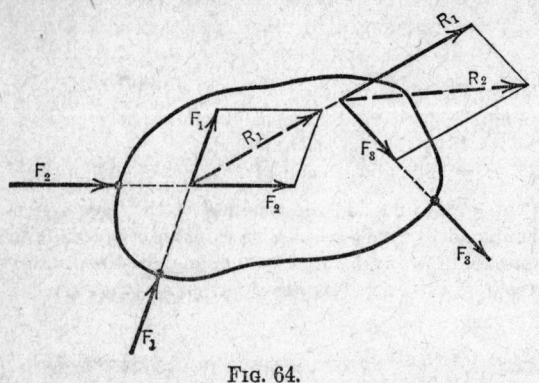

Fig. 64.

If the resultant obtained by combining all except one of the forces of such a system is equal to that one and is parallel to it and of opposite sense, the two forces constitute a couple. Furthermore, if the action lines of these two forces are collinear the forces cancel and the resultant of the system is equal to zero.

Second Method.—The resultant of a system of non-concurrent, non-parallel forces in a plane may also be found by the construction of a force polygon and a funicular polygon. The method of construction of these polygons is the same as that described in connection with a system of parallel forces (Art. 25) and will not here be discussed in detail for the non-parallel force system. The method will be illustrated, however, by the following problem.

ILLUSTRATIVE PROBLEM

Problem 100.—A beam 9 ft. long is acted on by four forces as shown in Fig. 65. Determine the resultant of the forces by use of the force and string polygons.

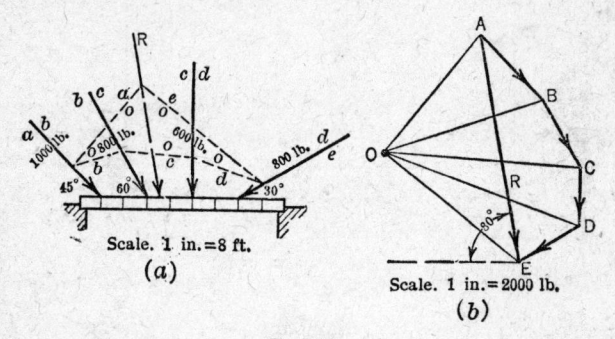

FIG. 65.

Solution.—The force polygon as shown in Fig. 65(b) is constructed by laying off the vectors AB, BC, CD, and DE which represent the magnitudes and the directions of the given forces. The closing side AE of the polygon represents the resultant force in magnitude and in direction. By measuring AE to scale the magnitude of the resultant force is found to be 2450 lb. and the line AE is found to make an angle of 80° with the horizontal, as indicated in Fig. 65(b).

In Fig. 65(a) is shown the string polygon in which one point on the action line of the resultant is found, namely, the intersection of oa and oe. Therefore the action line of the resultant passes through this point and is parallel to AE. By measurement the action line is found to intersect the beam at a point 3.6 ft. from the left end of the beam. Hence, if the four forces were replaced by a single force, R, of 2450 lb. as shown in Fig. 65(a), the reactions at the ends of the beam (external effects) would be unchanged.

29. Principle of Moments.—The algebraic sum of the moments of the forces of a coplanar, non-concurrent, non-parallel force system about any point in the plane of the forces is equal to the moment of the resultant of the system about the same point. The proof is identical with that given for a system of parallel forces (Art. 26), and the **principle**

will be used, in the algebraic method, for finding the action line of the resultant force or the moment of the resultant couple similar to the way it was used for parallel forces.

30. Algebraic Method.—The resultant of a system of non-concurrent, non-parallel forces in a plane is either a force or a couple. If the resultant is a force it may be determined as follows: In Fig. 66(a) is represented a body acted on by four forces F', F'', F''', and F''''. Let each force be replaced by its x- and y-components. The original force system is now resolved into two systems of parallel forces. According to Art. 27 the resultant of the components in the x-direction is a force

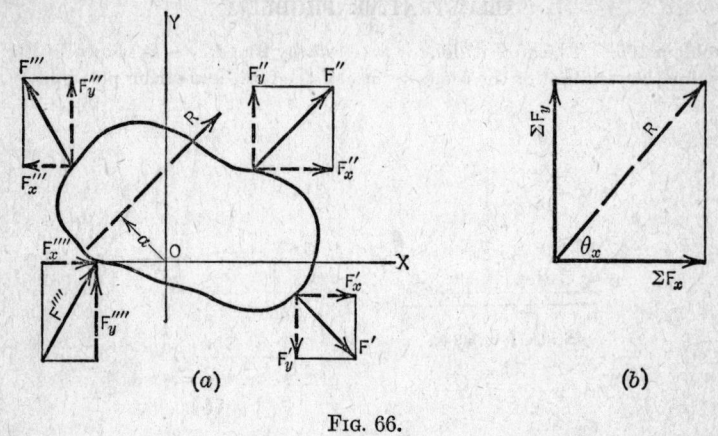

FIG. 66.

parallel to the x-axis whose magnitude is ΣF_x, and whose sense is indicated by the sign of ΣF_x; the sense is assumed to be positive in Fig. 66(b). Similarly, the resultant of the components in the y-direction is a force parallel to the y-axis whose magnitude is ΣF_y. Hence, the magnitude and the direction of the resultant of these two forces (which is also the resultant of the original forces) may be found from the equations

$$R = \sqrt{(\Sigma F_x)^2 + (\Sigma F_y)^2} \quad \text{and} \quad \tan \theta_x = \frac{\Sigma F_y}{\Sigma F_x} \text{ (Fig. 66b),}$$

in which θ_x is the angle which the action line of R makes with the x-axis. In order to obtain the position of the line of action of the resultant force R, the principle of moments may be used. The principle is expressed by the equation $Ra = \Sigma M_o$, in which a (Fig. 66a) is the perpendicular distance from the moment-center, O, to the action line of the resultant, and ΣM_o is the algebraic sum of the moments of the forces with respect to O.

Hence, if the resultant of a coplanar, non-concurrent, non-parallel system of forces is a force, it may be determined completely by the equations

$$R = \sqrt{(\Sigma F_x)^2 + (\Sigma F_y)^2},$$
$$\tan \theta_x = \frac{\Sigma F_y}{\Sigma F_x},$$
$$Ra = \Sigma M_o.$$

The sense of the moment of R (sign of Ra) must, of course, agree with that of ΣM_o. If, for instance, the sign of ΣM_o is negative, and R has the direction and sense as indicated in Fig. 66(b), the position of the action line of R is indicated in Fig. 66(a).

If both ΣF_x and ΣF_y are equal to zero the resultant is not a force and hence is a couple the moment C of which, according to the principle of moments, is the algebraic sum of the moments of the forces of the system; that is:

$$C = \Sigma M.$$

The center about which the moments of the forces are taken may be any point in the plane of the forces since the moment of a couple is the same about all points in the plane. The sense of rotation of the resultant couple is indicated by the sign of the algebraic summation, and the aspect of the couple, of course, is the same as that of the plane of the forces.

If ΣF_x and ΣF_y are equal to zero and ΣM is also equal to zero, the resultant is equal to zero.

ILLUSTRATIVE PROBLEM

Problem 101.—Find the resultant of the system of four forces which act on the body represented in Fig. 67(a). Each space represents 1 ft.

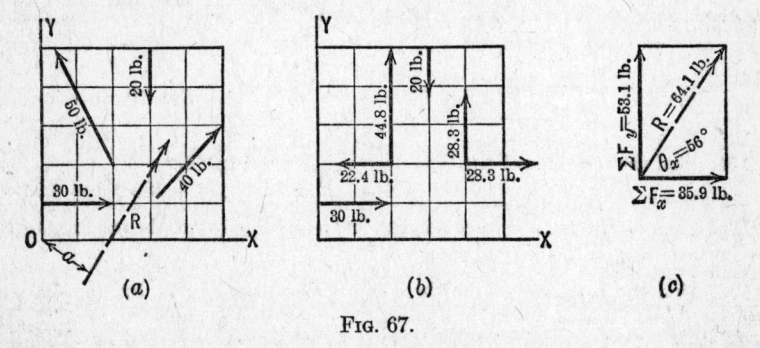

Fig. 67.

Solution.—In finding the moments of the 40-lb. and 50-lb. forces about O it will be convenient to resolve the forces at any point on their action lines into horizontal and vertical components as shown in Fig. 67(b) and find the algebraic sum of the moments of the two components of each force about O. The solution may be put in tabular form as follows:

F	$\cos\theta_x$	$\sin\theta_x$	$F_x = F\cos\theta_x$	$F_y = F\sin\theta_x$	M_o
50	$-\dfrac{1}{\sqrt{5}}$	$\dfrac{2}{\sqrt{5}}$	-22.4	44.8	134.4
20	0	-1	0.0	-20.0	-60.0
30	1	0	30.0	0.0	-30.0
40	$\dfrac{1}{\sqrt{2}}$	$\dfrac{1}{\sqrt{2}}$	28.3	28.3	56.6
			$\Sigma F_x = 35.9$	$\Sigma F_y = 53.1$	$\Sigma M_o = 101.0$

Therefore

$$R = \sqrt{(35.9)^2 + (53.1)^2} = 64.1 \text{ lb.},$$

$$\theta_x = \tan^{-1}\frac{53.1}{35.9} = 56°, \quad a = \frac{101}{64.1} = 1.57 \text{ ft.}$$

Alternative Method.—Since the given system may be replaced by two parallel force systems as shown in Fig. 67(b), the problem could have been solved by finding the magnitude, line of action, and sense of the resultant of each of the parallel systems. The resultant of the given system then is the resultant of these two resultants.

PROBLEMS

102. Find, by the algebraic method, the resultant of the three forces shown in Fig. 68. *Ans.* $R = 32.8$ lb.; $\theta_x = 340°\,30'$; $a = 5.28$ ft.

103. Solve Prob. 101 graphically by use of a force polygon and a string polygon.

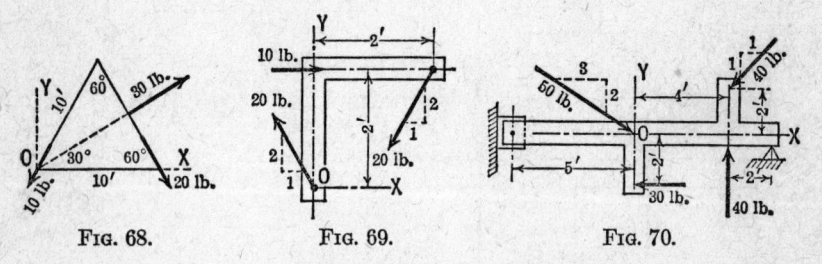

Fig. 68.   Fig. 69.   Fig. 70.

104. Find the resultant of the three forces shown in Fig. 69.
Ans. $R = 7.9$ lb.; $\theta_x = 180°$; $a = 4.8$ ft.

105. Find, by the use of a force polygon and a string polygon, the resultant of the four forces acting on the body as shown in Fig. 70.

106. Find the resultant of the three forces shown in Fig. 71 by the following method: (1) Resolve each force into a force through O and a couple (Art. 18); (2) find the resultant of the concurrent forces at O (Art. 24) and the resultant of the system of couples (Art. 16); and (3) by use of the transformations of a couple (Art. 16), combine the resultant of the concurrent forces and the resultant of the couples into a single force. *Ans.* $R = 35.4$ lb.; $\theta_x = 40°\,15'$; $a = 1.45$ ft.

NON-COPLANAR, CONCURRENT, NON-PARALLEL FORCES

107. Find the resultant of the four forces shown in Fig. 72.

108. Replace the four forces shown in Fig. 73 by the simplest force system that will produce the same external effect on the body on which the forces act.

Ans. $R = 41.5$ lb.; $\theta_x = 142° 25'$; $a = 0.96$ ft.

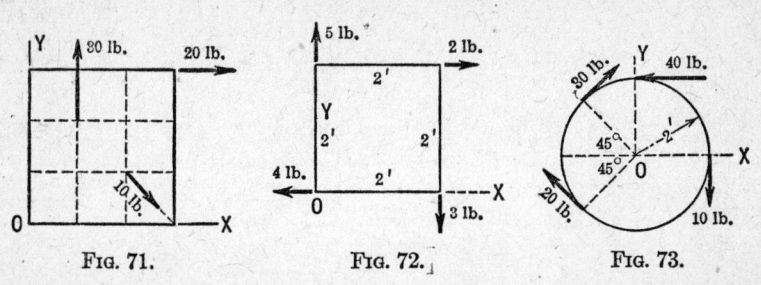

FIG. 71.   FIG. 72.   FIG. 73.

109. The forces of a coplanar system are specified below, the magnitudes of the forces being expressed in pounds and the coordinates x and y of a point on the action line in feet. θ_x denotes the angle that the action line of any force makes with the positive end of the x-axis, the angle being measured counter-clockwise.

F	20	15	10	15
x, y	0, 2	0, 2	4, 2	6, 2
θ_x	0°	45°	90°	135°

Find the resultant of the system.

110. Find algebraically the resultant of the five forces shown in Fig. 74.

Ans. $R = 5.83$ lb.; $\theta_x = 42° 40'$; $a = 3.22$ ft.

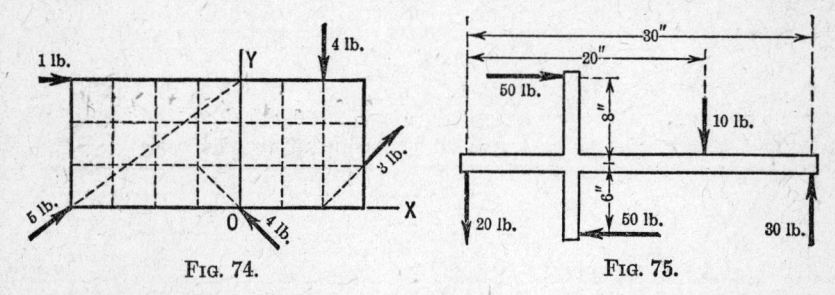

FIG. 74.   FIG. 75.

111. Solve the preceding problem by use of a force polygon and a string polygon.

112. In Fig. 75, assume that the 20-lb. force is removed and show by means of a force polygon and a string polygon that the resultant of the remaining four forces is a force equal to the 20-lb. force and collinear with it but of opposite sense.

§ 5. NON-COPLANAR, CONCURRENT, NON-PARALLEL FORCES

31. Graphical Method.—The resultant of a system of non-coplanar, concurrent forces is a force (acting through the point of concurrence of the forces) that may be found by constructing a force polygon as was done in finding the resultant of a system of coplanar, concurrent forces.

The line drawn from the beginning of the first vector to the end of the last vector of the polygon is a vector that represents the resultant of the system in magnitude and direction. The force polygon, however, is not a plane polygon and, hence, the graphical method of determining the resultant of this system or of any non-coplanar force system is not convenient. Graphical methods, therefore, will not be discussed in connection with any of the non-coplanar force systems.

32. Algebraic Method.—Before discussing the method of determining the resultant of any number of non-coplanar, concurrent forces, the special case of three concurrent forces having action lines which are mutually perpendicular will be considered. In Fig. 76 are represented three such forces, P, Q, and S, the action lines of the forces being taken as the coordinate axes. The forces P and Q may be combined into a single force (represented by the vector OA) the magnitude of which is $\sqrt{P^2 + Q^2}$. The resultant of this force and the force S is also the resultant of the given system of three forces and is represented by the vector OB, its magnitude being $\sqrt{P^2 + Q^2 + S^2}$. Hence the magnitude of the resultant, R, of the three forces and the angles θ_x, θ_y, and θ_z which the line of action of the resultant makes with the coordinate axes may be found from the equations.

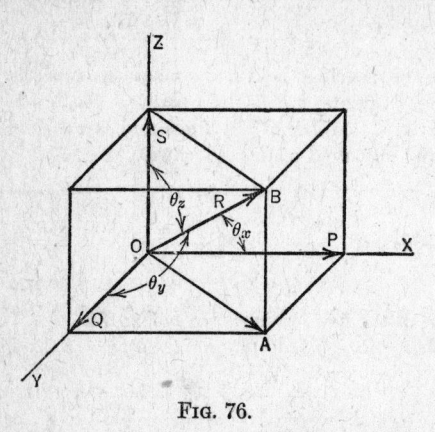

Fig. 76.

$$R = \sqrt{P^2 + Q^2 + S^2},$$

$$\cos \theta_x = \frac{P}{R}, \quad \cos \theta_y = \frac{Q}{R}, \quad \cos \theta_z = \frac{S}{R}.$$

In finding the resultant of any number of non-coplanar, concurrent forces by the algebraic method it will be convenient to take the point of concurrence of the forces as the origin of a set of rectangular axes. Each force of the system may be resolved into components along the coordinate axes (Art. 11). The system is thus replaced by three collinear systems each of which may be replaced by a single force (Art. 22). Thus, the resultant of the components along the x-axis is a single force along the x-axis, the magnitude of which is expressed by ΣF_x. Similarly, the y-components may be replaced by a single force of magnitude ΣF_y along the y-axis, etc. (Fig. 77). These three forces may be combined into a single force which is the resultant of the given system and which is completely defined by the following equations:

$$R = \sqrt{(\Sigma F_x)^2 + (\Sigma F_y)^2 + (\Sigma F_z)^2},$$

$$\cos \theta_x = \frac{\Sigma F_x}{R},$$

$$\cos \theta_y = \frac{\Sigma F_y}{R},$$

$$\cos \theta_z = \frac{\Sigma F_z}{R},$$

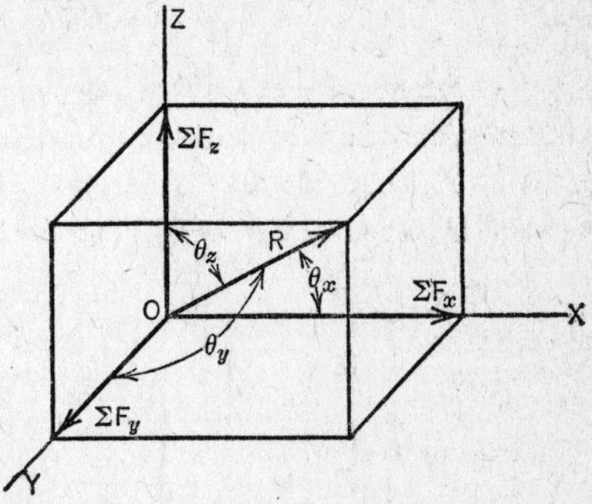

where θ_x, θ_y, and θ_z are the angles which the action line of the resultant makes with the coordinate axes as shown in Fig. 77.

Fig. 77.

PROBLEMS

In the following problems the forces are concurrent at the origin. F denotes the magnitude of a force and x, y, z are the coordinates of a point on the action line of a force. It is required to find the resultants of the systems.

113. F 10 lb.   20 lb.   15 lb.
   x,y,z 1, 2, 1   2, 2, 3   3, 1, 2

114. F 100 lb.   150 lb.   50 lb.   200 lb.
   x,y,z 2, 2, 1   3, 2, −2   −4, −3, −5   3, −2, 4

115. F 10 lb.   30 lb.   20 lb.
   x,y,z 1, 2, 1   1, 4, 2   2, 3, 3

Ans. $R = 59.0$ lb.; $\theta_x = 71°\ 5'$; $\theta_y = 37°\ 2'$; $\theta_z = 59°\ 32'$.

§ 6. Non-coplanar, Non-concurrent, Parallel Forces

33. Algebraic Method.—The resultant of a system of non-coplanar, parallel forces is, in general, a force parallel to the system whose magnitude and sense are found from the algebraic sum of the forces ($R = \Sigma F$). In determining the resultant of such a system by the algebraic method it is convenient to select coordinate axes so that one axis is parallel to the forces. In Fig. 78 is shown a system of parallel forces referred to such a set of axes. The line of action of the resultant force is found by applying the principle of moments. Thus, if the algebraic sum of the moments of the forces with respect to the x-axis be denoted by ΣM_x and the distance of the resultant from the x-axis be denoted by $\bar{y}$, then the principle of moments is expressed by the equation

$R\bar{y} = \Sigma M_x$. In a similar manner, $R\bar{x} = \Sigma M_y$. The resultant, if a force, will then be completely defined by the following equations:

$$R = \Sigma F,$$
$$R\bar{x} = \Sigma M_y$$
$$R\bar{y} = \Sigma M_x$$

If the resultant R_1 of all except one (P, say) of the forces of a non-coplanar, parallel system is equal to P, of opposite sense, and not collinear with P, then R and P form a couple which is the resultant of the system. (In this case $\Sigma F = 0$). The resultant couple will, of course, lie in a plane parallel to the forces of the system (parallel to the z-axis in Fig. 78). According to the principle of moments, the moment C_x of the resultant couple with respect to the x-axis is equal to the algebraic sum of the moment of the forces of the system with respect to the x-axis, that is, $C_x = \Sigma M_x$. Similarly, $C_y = \Sigma M_y$. C_x and C_y are couples (components of the resultant couple) which lie in (or parallel to) the yz and xz planes, respectively. The moment of the resultant couple is given by the expression $C = \sqrt{C_x^2 + C_y^2}$ which follows from the vector representation of couples (Art. 17) and the use of the parallelogram law. Hence the moment of the resultant couple is

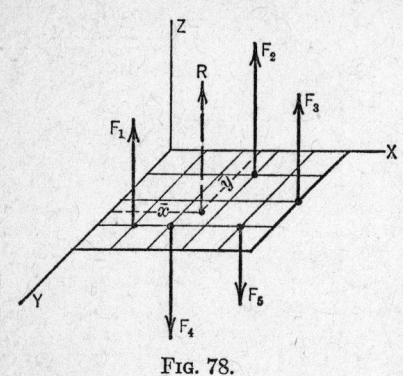

$$C = \sqrt{(\Sigma M_x)^2 + (\Sigma M_y)^2}$$

Fig. 78.

ILLUSTRATIVE PROBLEM

Problem 116.—Find the resultant of the system of parallel forces shown in Fig. 79. Each space in the figure represents 1 ft.

Solution:

$R = \Sigma F = 10 + 15 - 20 - 30 = -25$ lb.

$\Sigma M_x = 20 \times 2 + 30 \times 3 - 10 \times 1 - 15 \times 1 = 105$ lb.-ft.

$\Sigma M_y = 10 \times 1 + 15 \times 3 - 20 \times 2 - 30 \times 5 = -135$ ft.-lb.

$\therefore \bar{x} = \dfrac{135}{25} = 5.4$ ft.

and

$\bar{y} = \dfrac{105}{25} = 4.2$ ft.

Hence the resultant is a downward force of 25 lb. as shown in Fig. 79.

Caution.—Care must be exercised in finding $\bar{x}$ and $\bar{y}$. For instance, in the above example if the value of ΣM_x (+105 lb.-ft.) be divided by R (−25 lb.) the quotient is −4⅕ ft., which is *not* the value of $\bar{y}$, since a downward force of 25 lb. in this position would have a moment of −105 lb.-ft. with respect to the x-axis. The magnitudes of $\bar{x}$ and $\bar{y}$ should be obtained by dividing the magnitudes of ΣM_y and ΣM_x by the

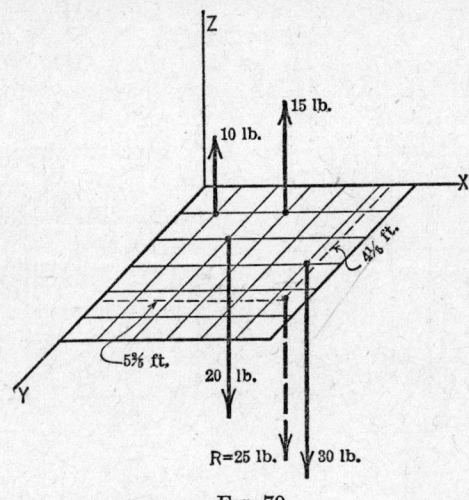

FIG. 79.

magnitude of R, and their signs should be determined by inspection. The signs of $\bar{x}$ and $\bar{y}$, of course, must be such that the moment of the resultant will have the same sense of rotation as is indicated by the algebraic sum of the moments of the forces of the system.

PROBLEMS

117. A board 6 ft. square is acted on by five forces as shown in Fig. 80. Determine the resultant of the forces.

Ans. $R = +10$ lb.; $\bar{x} = +2.5$ ft.; $\bar{y} = +3.5$ ft.

118. A table 5 ft. square carries four concentrated loads as shown in Fig. 81. Find the resultant of the four loads.

Find the resultant of each of the following systems of forces which are parallel to the z-axis. The values of x and y, expressed in feet, are the coordinates of the points where the action lines of the forces intersect the xy-plane.

119.	F	20 lb.	10 lb.	25 lb.	−15 lb.	−10 lb.
	x,y	1, 3	3, 2	6, 6	2, 5	6, 4

Ans. $R = +30$ lb.; $\bar{x} = +3.67$ ft.; $\bar{y} = +3.83$ ft.

120.	F	20 lb.	−15 lb.	30 lb.	−10 lb.
	x,y	1, 1	1, 4	4, 2	2, 2

121. Assume in Fig. 80 that a downward force of 40 lb. acting at the point $x = 1$, $y = 2$ is substituted for the 15-lb. force and the other forces remain as shown. Find the resultant of the system.

Ans. $R = -15$ lb.; $\bar{x} = -2$ ft.; $\bar{y} = +2$ ft.

122. Assume in Fig. 80 that the 10-lb. force is removed from the system of forces shown. Find the resultant of the remaining four forces.

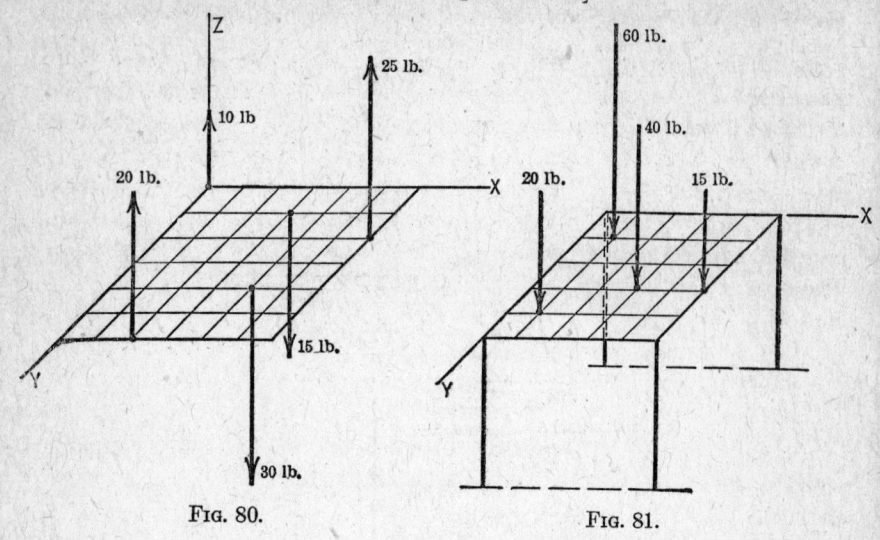

FIG. 80.

FIG. 81.

§ 7. COUPLES IN SPACE

34. Resultant of a System of Couples. *Proposition.*—*The resultant of any number of couples is a couple.*

Proof.—It is sufficient to prove this proposition for two couples, only, since if two couples can be combined into a single resultant couple this

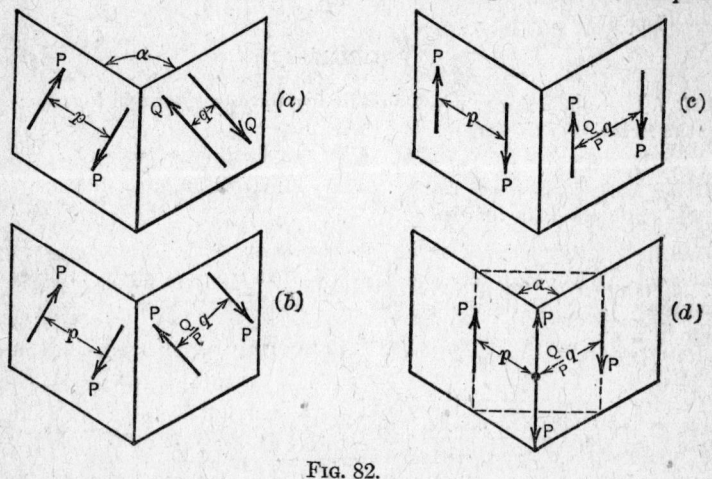

FIG. 82.

couple can be combined with a third couple in exactly the same way, and so on. Thus, consider the two couples Pp and Qq in planes making an angle α with each other as shown in Fig. 82(a). The forces Q, Q of the couple Qq can be made equal to P, P if the arm be changed to $\dfrac{Qq}{P}$ (Art. 16) as shown in Fig. 82(b). Each couple can then be rotated in its plane until the forces of the couples are parallel to the line of intersection of the two planes (Art. 16) as shown in Fig. 82(c). Now let the two couples be translated until one force of each couple lies in the line of intersection of the two planes. This translation can always be made so that the two forces in this line are opposite in sense and hence will cancel, thereby leaving a couple the forces of which are P, P (Fig. 82d). The arm of this couple (as found by use of trigonometry) is

$$\sqrt{p^2 + \frac{Q^2 q^2}{P^2} - 2\frac{Qqp}{P}\cos\alpha}.$$

Special Cases.—I. If the angle α equals 90°, that is, if the planes of the couples are perpendicular (Fig. 83), the moment, C, of the resultant couple is

$$C = P\sqrt{p^2 + \frac{Q^2}{P^2}q^2} = \sqrt{(Pp)^2 + (Qq)^2}$$

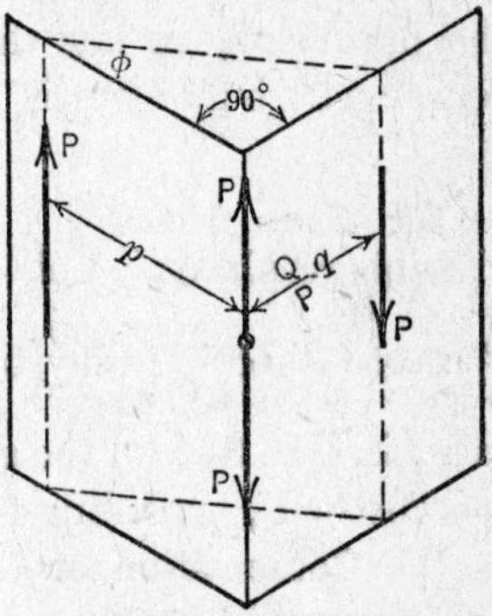

That is, the moment of the resultant couple is the square root of the sum of the squares of the moments of the two couples. The plane of the resultant couple makes an angle ϕ (Fig. 83) with the plane of the couple Pp such that

FIG. 83.

$$\tan\phi = \frac{\frac{Q}{P}q}{p} = \frac{Qq}{Pp},$$

and the sense of rotation of the resultant couple is indicated in Fig. 83.

II. If α equals 180°, the couples are in the same or in parallel planes and hence have the same aspect. The moment of the resultant couple then is

$$C = P\sqrt{p^2 + \frac{Q^2}{P^2}q^2 + 2p\frac{Q}{P}q} = P\left(p + q\frac{Q}{P}\right) = Pp + Qq.$$

That is, the moment of the resultant couple is the algebraic sum of the moments of the two couples, and its aspect, of course, is the same as that of each of the couples, the sense of rotation being indicated by the sign of the algebraic summation.

Parallelogram Law Applied to Couples.—It is frequently convenient to represent couples by vectors (see Art. 17) and to use the parallelogram law for the composition and resolution of couples. The method will here be illustrated for Case I above; namely, for couples lying in two planes that are perpendicular to each other. For example in Fig. 84(a), couple C_z, which lies in (or parallel to) the xy-plane and has a moment only about the z-axis, is represented by the vector that is also denoted as C_z, in Fig. 84(b). Similarly C_x is a vector representing the couple C_x. By the parallelogram law the vector C (Fig. 84b) represents the resultant couple whose moment is

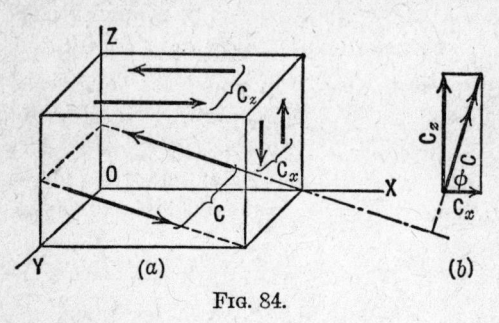

$$C = \sqrt{C_x^2 + C_z^2}$$

This resultant couple must lie in a plane perpendicular to the vector C whose direction may be found from the relation $\tan \phi = \dfrac{C_z}{C_x}$ as indicated in Fig. 84 and the sense of rotation is determined by the arrow on the vector C, according to the convention stated in Art. 17.

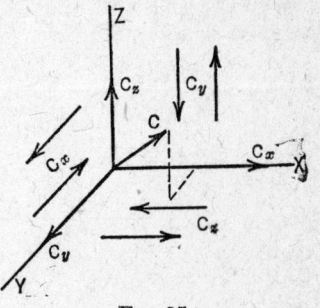

35. Composition of Couples in Space by Means of Vectors.—In order to combine a system of couples in space into a single resultant couple, each couple can first be resolved into three component couples by representing the couple by a vector, C, drawn for convenience from the origin of a set of rectangular axes, as shown in Fig. 85. The vector can then be resolved into components C_x, C_y and C_z along the coordinate axes. These vector components represent couples lying in the yz-, zx-, and xy-planes, respectively. In this way, then each of the couples of the system may be resolved into three component couples lying in the three coordinate planes and represented completely by vectors along the coordinate axes. The couples lying in the yz-plane may now be combined into a single couple lying in the yz-plane and represented by a vector along the x-axis. This vector is of course the resultant of the x-components of the vectors that represent the couples of the original system and may be designated by ΣC_x. In a similar manner the systems of couples lying in the zx- and xy-planes may be replaced by equivalent couples lying in the respective planes and represented by vectors ΣC_y and ΣC_z along the y- and z-axes. The original system of couples is thus reduced to three couples lying in the coordinate planes and the resultant of the system is the resultant of these three couples and is represented by a vector which is the resultant of the three vectors ΣC_x, ΣC_y and ΣC_z. This resultant is $\sqrt{(\Sigma C_x)^2 + (\Sigma C_y)^2 + (\Sigma C_z)^2}$. But since ΣC_x is equal to ΣM_x, the sum of the moments about the x-axis of the forces constituting the original system of couples, the moment of the resultant couple may be expressed by the equation

$$C = \sqrt{(\Sigma M_x)^2 + (\Sigma M_y)^2 + (\Sigma M_z)^2}$$

The aspect of the resultant couple may be defined by the angles ϕ_x, ϕ_y and ϕ_z which the vector representing the couple makes with the coordinate axes. Thus

$$\cos \phi_x = \frac{\Sigma M_x}{C}, \quad \cos \phi_y = \frac{\Sigma M_y}{C}, \quad \cos \phi_z = \frac{\Sigma M_z}{C}$$

§ 8. Non-coplanar, Non-concurrent, Non-parallel Forces

36. Algebraic Method.—The resultant of a system of non-coplanar, non-concurrent, non-parallel forces is a force (whose action line may be made to pass through any arbitrary point) and a couple. In order to find the resultant force and couple, each force of the system may be resolved into an equal parallel force through any point (taken for convenience as the origin of a system of coordinate axes) and a couple (Art. 18). Thus the given system may be replaced by two systems; (1) a system of non-coplanar, concurrent forces through the origin having the same magnitudes and directions as the forces of the original system; and (2) a system of non-coplanar couples. The resultant of the concurrent force system is a force through the origin which may be completely defined by the equations of Art. 32. The resultant of the system of couples is a couple which may be completely defined by the equations of Art. 35. The resultant force and resultant couple together constitute the resultant of the system. In special cases the resultant couple may vanish, leaving the force as a resultant of the system. Again in special cases the resultant force may vanish leaving the couple as the resultant of the system. If the resultant force and the resultant couple both vanish, the resultant of the system is zero.

REVIEW QUESTIONS AND PROBLEMS

123. Correct the error in each of the following statements: (*a*) A ray is a line in the vector diagram that represents the magnitude and action line of a component of one of the forces in the given force system. (*b*) A string (or funicular) polygon is drawn in the space diagram in order to obtain the direction of the resultant force of a coplanar force system.

124. If the resultant of a coplanar force system is a couple, how is the magnitude of each of the forces of the couple determined graphically by use of a force polygon and a string polygon? How is the moment-arm determined?

125. The force polygon for a given coplanar, non-concurrent, parallel force system closes. Which of the following conclusions can be drawn? (*a*) The resultant of the system is zero. (*b*) The resultant is a couple. (*c*) The resultant may be zero or a couple.

126. In finding, by the algebraic method, the resultant of a coplanar, non-concurrent force system, what information about the resultant is found by applying the principle of moments (*a*) when the resultant is a force and (*b*) when the resultant is a couple?

127. If it is known that the resultant of a coplanar force system is a force and that the algebraic sum of the moments of the forces about a point in the plane of the forces is zero, what can be said about the resultant force?

128. A force system consisting of two couples acts on a body. (*a*) If the force system has a resultant, must it be a couple? (*b*) If the system has no resultant must the two couples lie in the same plane?

129. Given two systems of forces that lie in the same plane, one of the systems being concurrent and the other non-concurrent. For each force in the concurrent system there is a corresponding force in the non-concurrent system having the same magnitude, direction, and sense. Which two of the following statements concerning the resultants of the two systems are correct? (*a*) If the resultant of the concurrent system is a force, the resultant of the non-concurrent system is an equal parallel force. (*b*) If the resultant of the concurrent system is zero, the resultant of the non-concurrent system is also zero. (*c*) If the resultant of the concurrent system is zero, the resultant of the non-concurrent system is a couple. (*d*) If the resultant of the concurrent system is zero, the resultant of the non-concurrent system is either zero or a couple.

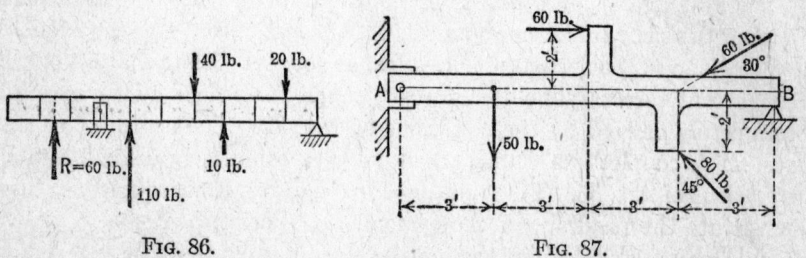

FIG. 86.

FIG. 87.

130. Show that the force R in Fig. 86 is the resultant of the other four forces acting on the body.

131. Replace the four forces acting on the bar AB (Fig. 87) by a single force that will produce the same reactions at A and B. Solve by the algebraic method. Represent the resultant force by a vector in the diagram.

Ans. $R = 53.9$ lb.; $\theta_x = 205°\ 47'$; $a = 2.67$ ft.

132. Solve the preceding problem by use of a force and a string polygon.

133. Determine the resultant of the three forces shown in Fig. 88. Each side of the triangle is 2 ft. in length. Ans. $C = 17.3$ lb.-ft.

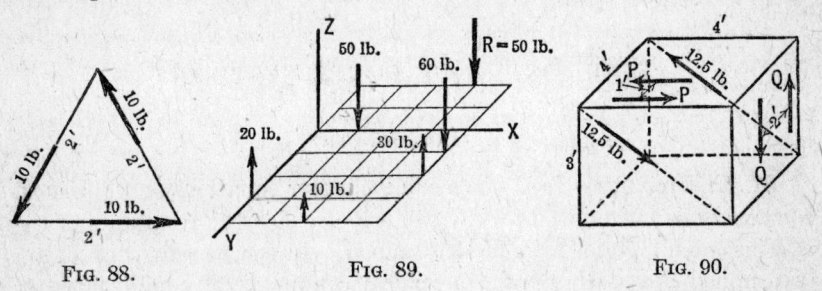

FIG. 88.   FIG. 89.   FIG. 90.

134. Show that the force R in Fig. 89 is the resultant of the other five parallel forces shown.

135. The values of P and Q in Fig. 90 are 40 lb. and 15 lb., respectively. Represent each of the two couples by a vector and, by the parallelogram law, determine the vector that represents the resultant couple. Would the couple consisting of the two 12.5-lb. forces shown in Fig. 90 have the same external effect on the body as would the two given couples?

CHAPTER III

EQUILIBRIUM OF FORCE SYSTEMS

§ 1. Introduction

37. Preliminary.—In the preceding chapter equations and graphical constructions were developed by the use of which the resultants of the various force systems may be determined. In the present chapter are determined the algebraic and graphical conditions of equilibrium for the various force systems, that is, the conditions which the forces of the various systems must satisfy in order that the resultants of the systems shall be equal to zero. These conditions may be expressed by means of algebraic equations which the forces must satisfy, called the *equations of equilibrium,* or by stating the conditions which graphical diagrams involving the forces, such as force and string polygons, must satisfy. Diagrams which satisfy these conditions are sometimes called *equilibrium diagrams* or *equilibrium polygons.*

Many problems in engineering practice involve bodies which are in equilibrium under the action of a system of forces as, for example, a bridge, roof-truss, crane, etc. In such problems certain characteristics of the forces acting on the body may be unknown, as, for example, the magnitude or the direction of one or more of the forces. If the number of unknown characteristics in a force system that is in equilibrium is not greater than the number of equations of equilibrium for that system, the system is said to be *statically determinate* and all the unknown characteristics may be found from the equations of equilibrium for the system.

If the number of unknown characteristics in a force system is greater than the number of equations of equilibrium for that particular force system, the force system is said to be *statically indeterminate,* as, for example, the forces which act on a horizontal beam which rests on three or more supports and carries known vertical loads. The beam is in equilibrium under the action of a system of coplanar, parallel forces all of which are known except the three upward reactions of the supports. As is shown in Art. 43, there are only *two* independent equations of equilibrium for such a force system, and hence the three reactions cannot be found from the equations of equilibrium alone. The force system is therefore statically indeterminate.

38. Graphical Conditions of Equilibrium.—In the previous chapter it was shown that the resultant of an unbalanced force system in a plane is either a force or a couple. Furthermore, it was shown that if the resultant is a force, it is represented in magnitude and in direction by the closing side of the force polygon, and that if the resultant is a couple, the two forces of the couple act along the first and last strings of the string polygon. Hence, if the force polygon closes, the resultant cannot be a force but may be a couple. If, however, the string polygon also closes, that is, if the first and last strings along which the two forces of the couple act are collinear, the two forces cancel and hence the resultant couple vanishes. There are, then, two conditions which the forces of a coplanar force system must satisfy if they have no resultant, that is, if the forces are in equilibrium.

(1) The force polygon must close. If this condition is satisfied the resultant cannot be a force.

(2) The string or funicular polygon must close. If this condition is satisfied the resultant cannot be a couple.

39. Algebraic Conditions of Equilibrium.—The two conditions which the graphical diagrams for a balanced force system must satisfy, as stated in the preceding article, may also be expressed algebraically. Thus, if the force polygon closes, the projections (components) of the forces on any line also form a closed polygon, as shown in Fig. 91, and since these components are collinear their vector sum is the same as their algebraic sum. Hence, the fact that the force polygon for the components closes may be expressed by stating that the algebraic sum of the components of the forces in any direction is equal to zero.

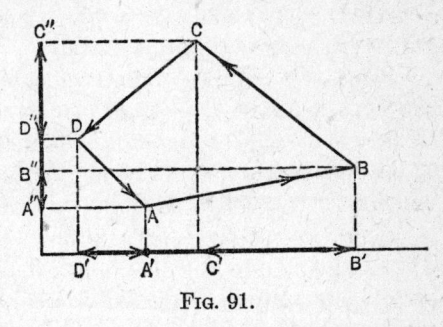

Fig. 91.

If the string or funicular polygon closes, the resultant cannot be a couple, since the first and last strings of the funicular polygon are collinear and hence the algebraic sum of the moments, about any point, of the two equal and opposite forces which act along these strings is equal to zero. But the algebraic sum of the moments of these two forces is equal to the algebraic sum of the moments of the forces of the system. Therefore, the statement that the funicular polygon must close is equivalent to the statement that the algebraic sum of the moments of the forces of the system must equal zero. Hence the algebraic conditions of equilibrium are:

(1) The algebraic sum of the components of the forces in any direction must equal zero.

(2) The algebraic sum of the moments of the forces about any point must equal zero.

An infinite number of equations could be written in accordance with these conditions by taking different directions of resolution and different moment centers, but not all of the equations would be independent. The number of independent equations is different for the various force systems, as will be discussed in the succeeding articles, but for any force system the independent equations of equilibrium are the equations which are necessary and sufficient to ensure that the resultant of that particular force system shall be equal to zero.

If a given body is in equilibrium under the influence of a system of forces some of which are unknown, wholly or in part, these unknowns may be found by applying the equations of equilibrium which apply to that particular system of forces.

If the number of unknowns in a system of forces which is in equilibrium is equal to the number of independent equations of equilibrium for that particular system, the determination of all the unknowns involves the use of all the equations of equilibrium. Frequently, however, it is not required to determine all the unknowns in such a system, for a single unknown only may be required, as, for example, the magnitude of a certain force, the line of action and sense of which is known. In such cases the unknown may frequently be found by using only one of the equations of equilibrium. In applying the equilibrium equations, the work may be materially simplified by properly selecting the directions of resolution and the moment axes or moment centers.

Before applying the equations of equilibrium to any system of forces which holds a body in equilibrium it is important to have a clear idea of the forces which act on the body. For this purpose it is necessary to construct a free-body diagram which will be explained in the following article.

40. Free-Body Diagram.—A *free-body diagram is a diagram in which are shown an isolated (free) body and all the forces exerted by other bodies on the given body.* It does not show the forces exerted by the given body on other bodies. It is important to note that *all* the forces acting on the body considered must be shown; the student is likely to overlook and omit a force from the free-body diagram. On the other hand it must be remembered that a force cannot exist unless there is a body to exert the force; the student frequently shows a force in the free-body diagram when there is no body present to exert the force shown. The number of forces in the free-body diagram is determined by noting the number of bodies that exert forces on the given body; these forces may be either forces of contact or body forces, the most important body force being the earth-pull on (or weight of) a body.

The word *free* in the name "free-body diagram" emphasizes the idea that all the bodies exerting forces on the given body are removed or withdrawn and are replaced by the forces they exert; it is considered undesirable to show both the bodies *and* the forces exerted by them. However, it is sometimes convenient to indicate, by light-weight dotted lines, the faint outlines of the bodies removed, in order to make more evident the geometry and dimensions involved in the problem.

Types of Reaction Involved.—In drawing a free-body diagram of a given body, certain assumptions are frequently made as to the nature of the forces (reactions) exerted by other bodies on the given body. The more common assumptions are the following: (a) If a surface of contact at which a force is applied by one body to another body has only a small degree of roughness, it may be assumed to be smooth (frictionless), and hence the action (or reaction) of the one body on the other is directed normal to the surface of contact. (One method of indicating a smooth surface is shown at point B in Fig. 94); (b) A body that possesses only a small degree of bending stiffness, such as a cord, rope, chain, etc., may be considered to be perfectly flexible, and hence the pull of such a body on any other body is directed along the axis of the flexible body.

Further, in drawing the free-body diagram of a body, if one of the forces acting on the body is unknown in direction, as well as in magnitude (such as a pin reaction in a pin-connected structure), it is frequently convenient to show two rectangular components of the force instead of the single force, and thus deal with two forces each being known in direction but unknown in magnitude. After solving for the two rectangular components their resultant, which is the original force, may be found both in magnitude and in direction.

Method of Showing an Internal Force in the Free-Body Diagram.—The term "given body" used in the definition of a free-body diagram may mean any definite portion of material and frequently is taken as a portion, only, of a physical object such as an eye-bar in a bridge or a connecting rod in a gas engine. Likewise, the given body may be taken as a group of physical bodies joined together (considered as one body), such as the whole bridge or the whole engine.

The forces in a free-body diagram, however, are external forces, that is, forces exerted by other (outside) bodies on the given body. The question then arises: How can a portion of a physical body be considered as the body in a free-body diagram when such a diagram involves only external forces? The method is as follows: Let a plane be assumed to pass through the body severing from the body that portion of it which is to be considered in the free-body diagram. This severed portion is now considered as the "free" body, and the force (or forces) that was exerted on it at the severed (or cut) section by the other part of the body (before the severed portion was removed) is now external to the severed portion and will be shown in the free-body diagram of the severed portion together with all the original external forces that act on this severed portion.

Most of the ideas discussed in this article are illustrated in the following problem.

ILLUSTRATIVE PROBLEM

Problem 136.—A homogeneous cylinder weighing 100 lb. and having a radius of 1 ft. rests between two smooth planes OA and OB, as shown in Fig. 92(a).

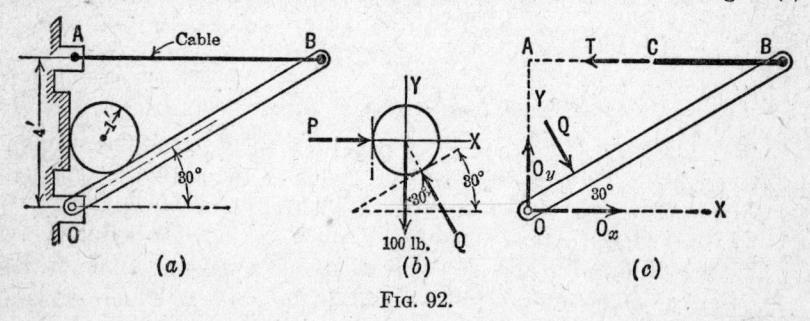

Fig. 92.

Member OB is attached to the vertical wall at O by a smooth pin. Similarly the horizontal cable is attached at A and B by smooth pins. The weights of OB and AB may be assumed to be negligible. Draw a free-body diagram of (a) the cylinder and (b) the bar OB with one-half of the cable AB attached (considered as one body).

Solution.—(a) The cylinder is acted on by three (and only three) bodies; namely, the earth, the vertical plane and the bar OB. There will be, therefore, three (and only three) forces in the free-body diagram. Further, since all the surfaces of contact are assumed to be smooth, the force P exerted by the vertical wall on the cylinder will be normal to the wall and hence horizontal as shown in Fig. 92(b); for the same reason Q, the force exerted by the bar OB on the cylinder, is normal to OB. Figure 92(b) is then the free-body diagram of the cylinder since it shows the cylinder alone or free from the other bodies (even though the bodies of contact are shown faintly as dotted lines) with all the forces acting on it. It will be observed that the forces whose magnitudes are unknown are represented by dashed-line vectors, and the forces whose magnitudes are known by solid-line vectors; this method or some other convenient method (such as representing the unknown forces by colored lines) for distinguishing between known and unknown forces is very desirable.

PROBLEMS 69

(b) The body for which a free-body diagram is required is shown as OBC in Fig. 92(c). A plane is assumed to have been passed through the cable at its midpoint C, and the force exerted at the severed section (or cut section) by the left half (that has been removed) on the body OBC is shown as T; this force acts along the cable since the cable is assumed to be flexible. There are, then, three bodies acting on OBC; namely, the left half of the cable, the cylinder, and the pin at O. Hence there are three (and only three) forces acting on the body OBC; namely, the force T, the force Q perpendicular to OB (equal and opposite to Q in Fig. 92b); and the pressure of the pin at O; this pin pressure is unknown in direction as well as in magnitude, for although it is directed normal to the surfaces of contact since the pin is smooth, the point (or line) of contact on the two surfaces is unknown. It will be convenient to replace the pin pressure by its two components O_x and O_y as shown in Fig. 92(c). It should be noted that the force at O is denoted by the same letter as the point, and that the components of the force are denoted by subscripts on the letter. This has the disadvantage of using a letter for two purposes but is otherwise convenient. Another convenient notation is to denote the horizontal component of a force (or component parallel to the x-axis) at a point $(O$, say) as H_o and the vertical component (or component parallel to the y-axis) as V_o. Another convention is to designate the reaction at a point $(O$, say) by R_o. This latter method has the disadvantage of requiring two subscripts to denote a component of a force. For example, the x-component of a force at O would be designated by $(R_o)_x$ or R_{ox}. Some consistent and convenient notation is highly desirable in designating forces in free-body diagrams, especially for problems involving many forces.

PROBLEMS

137. A cylinder weighing 100 lb. is supported by a flexible cable and a smooth inclined plane as shown in Fig. 93. Consider as a free body the cylinder and one-half of the attached cable, and draw the free-body diagram of this body.

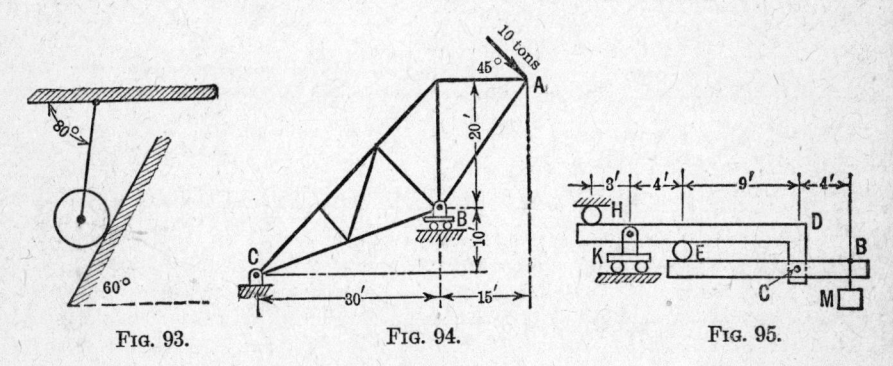

FIG. 93.   FIG. 94.   FIG. 95.

138. In Fig. 94 is shown a truss supported by a smooth pin at C and a smooth surface at B. Draw a free-body diagram of the whole truss, considered as a free body. Neglect the weight of the truss.

139. In Fig. 95, two bars HD and EB are connected by a smooth pin at C. At H and E are smooth rollers, and the surface at K is smooth. A body M weighing 100 lb. is attached to the bar EB by a flexible cable. Draw a free-body diagram of (a) the two bars and the roller at E, considered as one body; (b) the bar EB, the cable, and the attached body M, considered as one body; and (c) the bar HD. Neglect the weights of the bars.

§ 2. COLLINEAR FORCES

41. Equations of Equilibrium.—A system of collinear forces is in equilibrium if the forces of the system satisfy either of the following equations:

or
$$\Sigma F = 0 \quad \ldots \ldots \ldots \ldots \quad (A)$$
$$\Sigma M_A = 0 \quad \ldots \ldots \ldots \ldots \quad (B)$$

where A is any point not on the action line of the forces.

Proof.—As shown in Art. 22, if a collinear force system is not in equilibrium, the resultant of the force system is a force having the same action line as the forces and having a magnitude, R, which is given by the equation, $R = \Sigma F$. If the forces of the system satisfy the equation $\Sigma F = 0$, the resultant is not a force and therefore the system is in equilibrium. The equation $\Sigma M_A = 0$ is also sufficient to ensure equilibrium, for if the forces of the system satisfy this equation, the resultant force must, in accordance with the principle of moments, pass through the point A. But this is impossible since the resultant force, if there be one, has the same line of action as the forces and hence cannot pass through A.

Therefore, if either one of the equations (A) and (B) is satisfied, the resultant is equal to zero and hence there is but one independent equation of equilibrium for a collinear force system.

ILLUSTRATIVE PROBLEM

Problem 140.—Two men pull on the ends of a rope with forces of 100 lb. each (Fig. 96a). What is the tensile stress in the rope?

Solution.—Suppose the rope to be divided into two parts A and B as shown in Fig. 96(b). Consider as a free body the part A. The forces acting on A are two in number, namely, the 100-lb. force and the force exerted by B on A. The latter is the internal stress required. Let this stress be denoted by S. The equation of equilibrium then becomes:

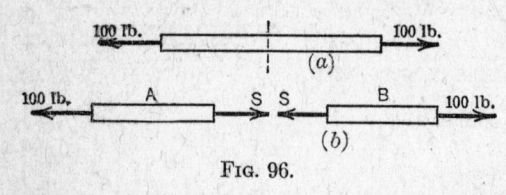

$$\Sigma F = S - 100 = 0.$$

Therefore
$$S = 100 \text{ lb.}$$

FIG. 96.

Obviously, B could have been taken as the free body and the same result would have been obtained.

It should be noted that while S is an internal force (stress) when the rope as a whole is considered, it becomes an external force acting on part A when A is considered as a free body.

Two-Force Member.—If a body or a member of a structure is held in equilibrium by *two* forces only, the two forces must be equal, opposite, and collinear. If the body on which the two forces act is of prismatic form such as a straight bar or a cable and the forces are applied at the ends of the member, the internal stress in the member is numerically equal to each of the applied forces and is collinear with them as was found in Prob. 140. Such a member is called a *two-force member*.

Examples of two-force members will be encountered in many subsequent problems, especially in determining stresses in pin-connected, pin-loaded trusses. Stresses in members that are acted on by more than two forces are considered in the subject of Resistance of Materials.

§ 3. Coplanar, Concurrent, Non-parallel Forces

42. Equations of Equilibrium.—A system of coplanar, concurrent forces is in equilibrium if the forces of the system satisfy the following equations:

$$\left. \begin{array}{l} \Sigma F_x = 0 \\ \Sigma F_y = 0 \end{array} \right\} \qquad \ldots \ldots \ldots \quad (A)$$

where x and y denote any two non-parallel lines in the plane. It is convenient, however, to take as the two lines a set of rectangular axes with the point of concurrence of the forces as origin.

Proof.—In Art. 24 it was shown that if a concurrent system of forces in a plane is not in equilibrium the resultant is a force whose components are equal to ΣF_x and ΣF_y. If, then, the forces of the system satisfy the equation $\Sigma F_x = 0$ the resultant cannot have a component along the x-axis, and if the equation $\Sigma F_y = 0$ is satisfied the resultant cannot have a component along the y-axis. Therefore, if both of these equations are satisfied, the resultant cannot be a force and hence the system must be in equilibrium. There are, then, only two independent equations of equilibrium for a coplanar, concurrent system of forces.

Another set of independent equations which, if satisfied by the forces of a coplanar, concurrent force system, are sufficient to ensure equilibrium may be expressed as follows:

$$\left. \begin{array}{l} \Sigma F_x = 0 \\ \Sigma M_A = 0 \end{array} \right\} \qquad \ldots \ldots \ldots \quad (B)$$

where x denotes any line in the plane (taken for convenience as one of two rectangular axes through the point of concurrence of the forces) and A is any point in the plane not on the y-axis.

Proof.—If the forces of the system satisfy the equation $\Sigma F_x = 0$, the resultant cannot have a component along the x-axis, that is, the resultant, if there be one, must lie along the y-axis. If the equation $\Sigma M_A = 0$ is satisfied, the resultant, if there be one, must pass through the point A in accordance with the principle of moments. It is impossible for a force to satisfy these two conditions simultaneously and hence, if both the equations are satisfied by the forces of the system, the system is in equilibrium.

A third set of equations of equilibrium for a coplanar, concurrent force system is as follows:

$$\left.\begin{array}{l}\Sigma M_A = 0 \\ \Sigma M_B = 0\end{array}\right\} \quad \ldots \ldots \ldots \ldots (C)$$

where A and B are any two points in the plane of forces, provided that the line joining A and B does not pass through the point at which the forces are concurrent. The proof that these equations are sufficient to ensure equilibrium will be left to the student.

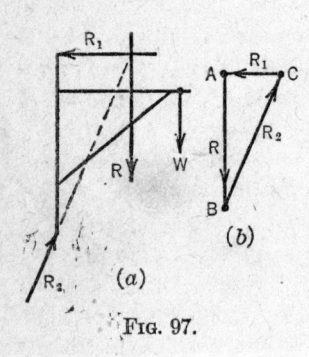

Three Forces in Equilibrium.—If three coplanar, non-parallel forces are in equilibrium the forces must be concurrent. In order that the three forces shall be in equilibrium, the resultant of any two of the forces must be a force which is collinear with the third force, of equal magnitude, and of opposite sense. But the resultant of the two forces will have the same line of action as the third force only if the two intersect on the action line of the third force in which case the three forces are concurrent. This principle is of considerable importance, as it simplifies the solution of many problems. Consider, for example, the crane shown in Fig. 97(a). The forces acting on the crane are the reaction R_1 at the upper end (assumed to be horizontal), the load W, the weight of the crane (not shown), and the reaction R_2 at the lower end, the direction of the latter force being unknown. The load W and the weight of the crane may be replaced by a single resultant force, R, and the system will then consist of three forces, R_1, R_2, and R. Since the three forces must be concurrent, R_2 must pass through the point of intersection of R_1 and R, and hence its action line is determined as indicated by the dotted line. The magnitudes of the reactions R_1 and R_2 may now be determined by drawing the force polygon (Fig. 97b). The force polygon is constructed by drawing AB to represent the known force R and by drawing from A and B lines parallel to R_1 and R_2, respectively, which intersect at C. The reaction R_1 is represented by CA, and R_2 is represented by BC.

Convention Concerning Direction and Sense of an Unknown Force.—In many problems that involve the equilibrium of force systems, the action line of one (or more) of the forces may be known but the magnitude and sense may be unknown. In many cases the sense of such a force is evident by inspection and the force may be shown in the free-body diagram with the proper sense. If, however, it is not obvious by inspection, the sense may be assumed, and if on solving for the unknown force its sign is found to be positive, the assumed sense is correct; if the sign is negative the sense is opposite to that assumed.

Again, in some problems in equilibrium, only a point on the line of action of a force is known, the direction, sense and magnitude of the force being unknown. In this case it will generally be convenient to represent the force in the free-body diagram by means of its two components parallel to the coordinate axes; the direction of each component is then known, but the sense and magnitude are unknown. If the sense of either or both of the components is evident by inspection, the component (or components) should be shown in the free-body diagram with the proper sense. If, however, the sense of a component is not evident it may be shown as having a positive sense and if on solving for the component the sign is found to be positive, the sense is positive as assumed; if the sign is negative the sense is opposite to that assumed.

ILLUSTRATIVE PROBLEMS

Problem 141.—A body is held in equilibrium by a system of three concurrent forces as shown in Fig. 98. Find the values of P and θ.

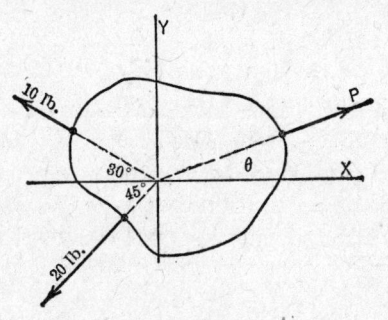

Fig. 98.

Solution.—The equations of equilibrium are:

$$\Sigma F_x = P \cos \theta - 10 \cos 30° - 20 \cos 45° = 0,$$
$$\therefore P \cos \theta = 8.66 + 14.14 = 22.80 \text{ lb.} \quad \quad \quad \quad \quad (1)$$

74 EQUILIBRIUM OF FORCE SYSTEMS

$$\Sigma F_y = P \sin \theta + 10 \sin 30° - 20 \sin 45° = 0,$$
$$\therefore P \sin \theta = 14.14 - 5.00 = 9.14 \text{ lb.} \quad \ldots \ldots \ldots \quad (2)$$

By dividing (2) by (1), θ may be obtained. Thus

$$\tan \theta = \frac{9.14}{22.80} = 0.401, \qquad \therefore \theta = 21° 50'.$$

By squaring and adding (1) and (2), P may be obtained. Thus

$$P^2 = (22.80)^2 + (9.14)^2 = 603.5, \qquad \therefore P = 24.5 \text{ lb.}$$

Problem 142.—Figure 99(a) represents a lower panel point of a pin-connected Pratt truss. The stresses in two of the members are 1000 lb. and 3000 lb. as shown. Find the stresses, P and Q, in the other members.

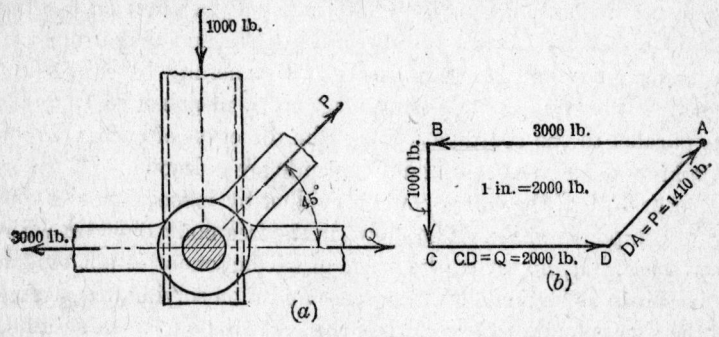

Fig. 99.

Algebraic Solution.—

$$\Sigma F_x = Q + P \cos 45° - 3000 = 0, \quad \ldots \ldots \ldots \quad (1)$$
$$\Sigma F_y = P \sin 45° - 1000 = 0 \quad \ldots \ldots \ldots \quad (2)$$

From (2)

$$P = \frac{1000}{\sin 45°} = 1414 \text{ lb.}$$

Substituting in 1,

$$Q = 3000 - 1414 \cos 45°$$
$$= 3000 - 1000 = 2000 \text{ lb.}$$

*Graphical Solution.—*The problem may be solved graphically by constructing a closed force polygon as shown in Fig. 99(b). The polygon is constructed as follows: Vectors AB and BC are drawn to represent the 3000-lb. and 1000-lb. forces, respectively. A line is then drawn from C parallel to the direction of the force Q and a line is drawn from A parallel to the direction of the force P. These lines intersect at D. Q is then represented by CD and P by DA. The magnitudes of Q and P are found by measuring, according to the scale indicated, to be 2000 lb. and 1410 lb., respectively.

Problem 143.—Two bodies A and B (Fig. 100) weighing 200 lb. and 50 lb., respectively, are held in equilibrium on smooth rods by a connecting flexible cable that makes an angle θ with the horizontal. Find the reactions of the rods on the bodies, the tensile stress in the cable, and the angle θ.

ILLUSTRATIVE PROBLEMS

Solution.—A free-body diagram of body A and a small part of the attached cable, considered as one body, is shown in Fig. 100(b). This body is acted on by a coplanar, concurrent force system consisting of the force T exerted by the part of the cable removed (and hence is the tensile stress in the cable), the reaction R_A of the rod, and the earth-pull of 200 lb. There are three unknown quantities in the diagram; namely, the magnitude and direction of T and the magnitude of R_A (T, θ, and R_A), and since there are only two equations of equilibrium for a coplanar concurrent force system, all three of the unknown quantities cannot be found, that is, the force system is statically indeterminate. Therefore a free-body diagram of the body B is drawn

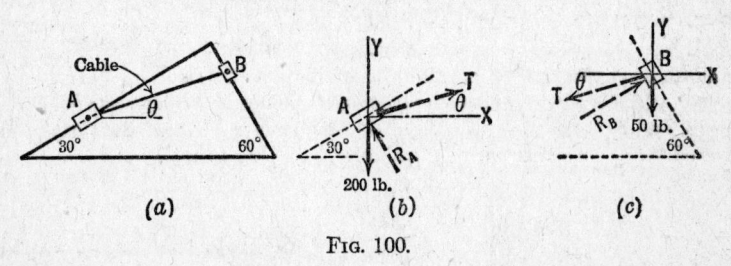

FIG. 100.

(Fig. 100c), to see if the force system acting on B is statically determinate. If this system is found to be statically determinate, the value of T could be found and this value used for the force T in the force system acting on body A, thus making the force system acting on body A statically determinate.

The force system acting on B, however, is also found to be statically indeterminate since three unknown quantities (T, θ, and R_B) are involved. However, since the forces T in Fig. 100(b) and T in Fig. 100(c) are identical (except in sense) it is seen that in the two force systems there are only four unknown quantities (T, θ, R_A, R_B) and these may be found from the four equations of equilibrium (two for each of the force systems) that can be written. Applying the equations of equilibrium we have, then

For A $\begin{cases} \Sigma F_x = T \cos \theta - R_A \sin 30° = 0 \quad \ldots \ldots \ldots \quad (1) \\ \Sigma F_y = T \sin \theta + R_A \cos 30° - 200 = 0 \quad \ldots \ldots \quad (2) \end{cases}$

For B $\begin{cases} \Sigma F_x = - T \cos \theta + R_B \cos 30° = 0 \quad \ldots \ldots \ldots \quad (3) \\ \Sigma F_y = - T \sin \theta + R_B \sin 30° - 50 = 0 \quad \ldots \ldots \quad (4) \end{cases}$

Eliminating R_A from (1) and (2), we find

$$T \cos (30° - \theta) = 100 \quad \ldots \ldots \ldots \quad (5)$$

Eliminating R_B from (3) and (4), we find

$$T \sin (30° - \theta) = 43.3 \quad \ldots \ldots \ldots \quad (6)$$

Dividing (6) by (5), we have $\tan (30° - \theta) = 0.433$
Hence
$$30° - \theta = \tan^{-1} 0.433 = 23° 25', \quad \therefore \theta = 6° 35'$$

Substituting the value of θ in (5) we find $T = 109$ lb.
Substituting the values of T and θ in (1) and (3) we find

$$R_A = 216 \text{ lb. and } R_B = 125 \text{ lb.}$$

PROBLEMS

144. A sphere weighing 100 lb. rests against two smooth planes that form a V-shaped trough. The right-hand plane makes an angle of 30° with the horizontal, and the angle between the two planes is 105°. Find the reactions of the planes on the sphere.

145. A sphere which weighs 40 lb. is held on a smooth inclined plane by means of a flexible cord which is attached to a ceiling as shown in Fig. 93. Determine the pressure R of the plane against the sphere and the tension T in the cord.
Ans. $R = 7.39$ lb.; $T = 36.9$ lb.

146. A body weighing 60 lb. is held in equilibrium on a smooth horizontal surface by two flexible cords which pass over frictionless pulleys and carry suspended weights of 30 lb. and 50 lb. as shown in Fig. 101. Find the reaction of the surface on the body and the angle θ that one cord makes with the horizontal.

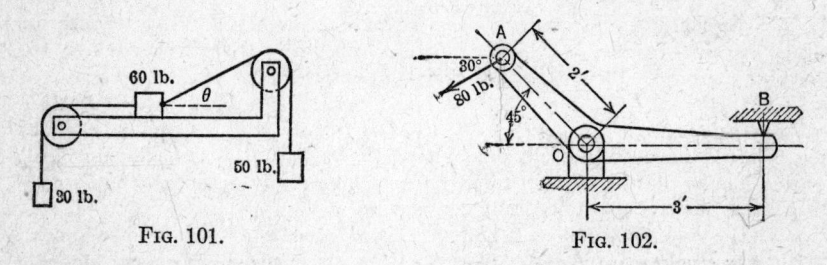

FIG. 101.   FIG. 102.

147. In Fig. 102 is shown a bell-crank mounted on a smooth pin at O and subjected to a force of 80 lb. at A as shown, causing the bell-crank to press against a smooth stop at B. Find the pin pressure at O and the reaction at B. Solve graphically, observing that three non-parallel forces in equilibrium must be concurrent.
Ans. $R_o = 115$ lb.; $\theta_x = 52° 50'$; $R_B = 51.5$ lb.

148. A body weighing 100 lb. is suspended from a ceiling by a string 4 ft. long. At the mid-point of the string is attached another string by means of which a horizontal force of 50 lb. is applied. Find the tension in the upper half of the string and its inclination to the horizontal.

149. The truss shown in Fig. 94 is supported by smooth rollers at B and by a smooth pin at C. A load of 10 tons is applied at A as shown. Find the reactions of the pins at B and C on the truss. Solve algebraically by use of equations (B) of Art. 42, observing that three non-parallel, coplanar forces that are in equilibrium must be concurrent. In applying the equations of equilibrium, assume the x-axis to be horizontal and choose the point C as the moment-center.
Ans. $R_B = 17.7$ tons; $R_C = 12.7$ tons.

150. A uniform beam weighing W lb. rests with its ends on two smooth planes that make angles of 30° and 60° with the horizontal. The planes intersect in a horizontal line and the angle between the planes is 90°. Find the inclination of the beam to the horizontal.

151. In Fig. 103, when r is zero, the tension in the spring S is 50 lb. The modulus of the spring is 58 lb. per in. Find the tension T in the spring in pounds when

$r = 3$ in. and also find the pulls P, P required to cause this spring tension. What is the total stretch s of the spring?

Ans. $T = 94.1$ lb.; $P = 23.5$ lb.; $s = 1.62$ in.

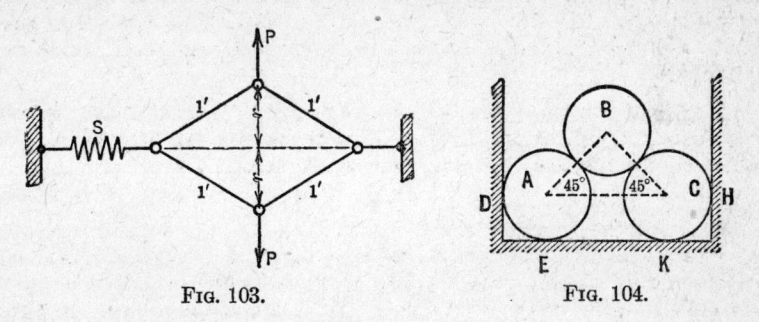

Fig. 103.   Fig. 104.

152. In Fig. 104 are shown three smooth homogeneous cylinders whose radii are equal. If each cylinder weighs 100 lb., what are the pressures on cylinder A of the vertical and horizontal surfaces at D and E, respectively.

Ans. $R_D = 50$ lb.; $R_E = 150$ lb.

153. A body weighing 20 lb. is held in equilibrium by four cords as shown in Fig. 105. What are the stresses in cords A, B, and C? Solve by use of equations (A) of Art. 42.

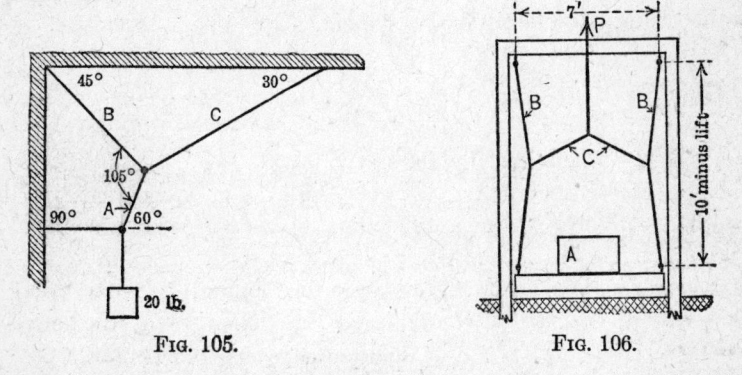

Fig. 105.   Fig. 106.

154. A body A rests on a platform (Fig. 106). The platform is suspended from the top cross-bar of a frame by two ropes B, B. The mid-points of the ropes are connected by another rope C. At the center of the rope C a vertical pull P is exerted by a man standing on the cross-bar. Before the pull P is applied, the ropes B, B are vertical and 10 ft. long and the rope C is horizontal and 7 ft. long. The body A is placed at the center of the platform and the weight of A and the platform is 2000 lb. What force P must the man exert to support the platform (a) 1 in. above its original position; (b) 5 in. above its original position? Solve graphically using scales 1 in. = 2 ft. and 1 in. = 200 lb.   Ans. (a) $P = 335$ lb.;   (b) $P = 1155$ lb.

155. In the cone clutch shown in Fig. 107, the force P acting vertically on the bell-crank as shown produces a normal pressure at the surface of contact of the clutch of 15 lb. per sq. in. If $\theta = 12\frac{1}{2}°$, find the force P and the reaction R on the bell-crank of the smooth pin at the fixed point of the bell-crank. Disregard friction between the two parts of the clutch.

Ans. $P = 196$ lb.; $R = 416$ lb.; $\theta_x = 208° 5'$.

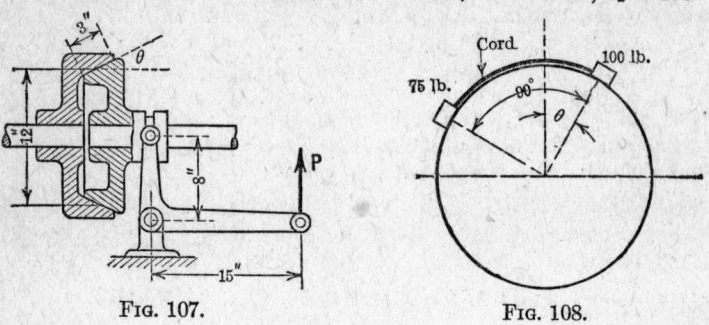

Fig. 107.   Fig. 108.

156. Two bodies weighing 75 lb. and 100 lb. rest on a smooth cylinder and are connected by a cord as shown in Fig. 108. Find the reactions of the cylinder on the bodies, the tension in the cord, and the value of θ.

§ 4. Coplanar, Non-concurrent, Parallel Forces

43. Equations of Equilibrium.—A coplanar, parallel force system is in equilibrium if the forces of the system satisfy the equations

$$\left.\begin{array}{l}\Sigma F = 0 \\ \Sigma M_A = 0\end{array}\right\} \quad \cdots\cdots\cdots \quad (A)$$

where A is any point in the plane of the forces.

Proof.—According to Art. 27, the resultant of a coplanar, parallel force system which is not in equilibrium is either a force or a couple. If the resultant is a force, the magnitude, R, is expressed by the equation $R = \Sigma F$, and if the resultant is a couple the moment, C, is expressed by the equation $C = \Sigma M$. If the forces of the system satisfy the equation $\Sigma F = 0$, the resultant is not a force and if the equation $\Sigma M_A = 0$ is satisfied the resultant is not a couple. Hence, if both equations are satisfied the resultant of the force system can be neither a force nor a couple and therefore the system is in equilibrium. Two equations, then, are necessary and sufficient to ensure that the forces are in equilibrium. In other words, there are only two independent equations of equilibrium for a system of parallel forces in a plane.

Another set of equations of equilibrium for a system of coplanar, parallel forces may be written as follows:

$$\left.\begin{array}{l}\Sigma M_A = 0 \\ \Sigma M_B = 0\end{array}\right\} \quad \cdots\cdots\cdots \quad (B)$$

ILLUSTRATIVE PROBLEMS

Problem 157. A load of 1200 lb. is applied to a beam AB as shown in Fig. 109(a). The left end of the beam is carried by a smooth roller resting on a second beam CD. Find the reactions on the second beam at C and D.

Solution.—The free-body diagrams for the two beams are shown in Fig. 109(b) and 109(c). Considering the beam AB as a free body and using the equation $\Sigma M_A = 0$, we have

$$\Sigma M_A = 1200 \times 9 - R_B \times 12 = 0, \quad \therefore R_B = 900 \text{ lb.}$$

There is, then, a load of 900 lb. acting on the beam CD at B. Next considering the beam CD as a free body, the two reactions R_C and R_D may be found by applying either set of equilibrium equations of Art. 43. Thus, using the equations $\Sigma M_C = 0$ and $\Sigma M_D = 0$, the two reactions may be found as follows:

$$\Sigma M_C = R_D \times 10 - 900 \times 6 = 0, \quad \therefore R_D = 540 \text{ lb.}$$
$$\Sigma M_D = -R_C \times 10 + 900 \times 4 = 0, \quad \therefore R_C = 360 \text{ lb.}$$

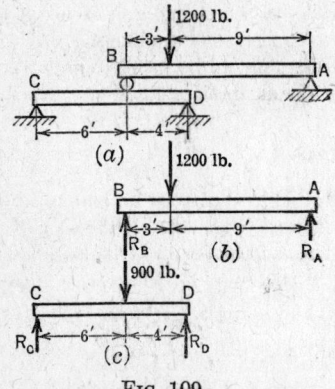

Fig. 109. 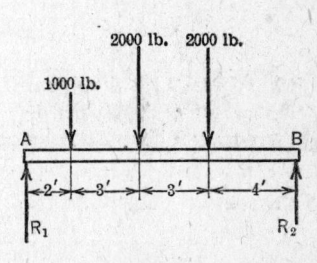   Fig. 110.

Problem 158.—A beam 12 ft. long carries three loads as shown in Fig. 110. Find the reactions at the ends of the beam. Solve algebraically and graphically.

Algebraic Solution.—

$$\Sigma M_B = -12R_1 + 1000 \times 10 + 2000 \times 7 + 2000 \times 4 = 0,$$
$$12R_1 = 32{,}000, \quad \therefore R_1 = 2667 \text{ lb.}$$
$$\Sigma M_A = 12R_2 - 1000 \times 2 - 2000 \times 5 - 2000 \times 8 = 0,$$
$$12R_2 = 28{,}000, \quad \therefore R_2 = 2333 \text{ lb.}$$

In order to check the results the equation $\Sigma F = 0$ may be applied. Thus,

$$2667 + 2333 - 1000 - 2000 - 2000 = 0.$$

Graphical Solution.—In order to determine the reactions by the graphical method, a force and a funicular polygon are constructed as shown in Fig. 111. Since the forces are in equilibrium the two polygons must close. The three known forces are represented by AB, BC, and CD. The right reaction will be represented by DE, the position of the point E being as yet unknown. Obviously the left reaction will be represented by EA since the force polygon must close. The strings oa, ob, oc, and od of the funicular polygon are drawn parallel to the corresponding rays. Since the string oe must intersect the string oa on ea and since oe must also intersect the string

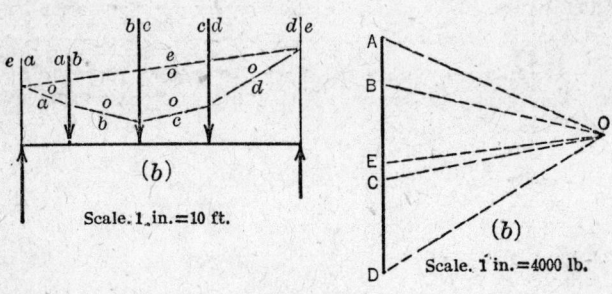

FIG. 111.

od on de, the position of the string oe is determined. The direction of the ray OE is now determined also, since it must be parallel to the string oe. Hence E is the point where a line drawn through O parallel to oe intersects the line AD. The magnitudes of DE and EA are found, from the diagram, to be 2330 lb. and 2670 lb., which agree closely with the values found by the algebraic method of solution.

PROBLEMS

159. A beam 14 ft. long carries a concentrated load of 1000 lb. and a uniformly distributed load of 200 lb. per linear foot as shown in Fig. 112. If the weight of the beam is neglected find the reactions at the ends of the beam.

Ans. $R_1 = 1136$ lb.; $R_2 = 1264$ lb.

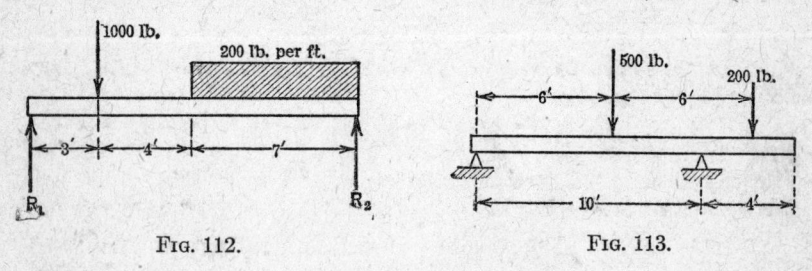

FIG. 112. FIG. 113.

160. The beam shown in Fig. 113 weighs 10 lb. per linear foot. Find the reactions due to the weight of the beam and the loads shown.

161. A bar 8 ft. long is held in equilibrium by the three forces shown in Fig. 114 and two forces acting along the lines ef and de. Find the magnitudes and senses of the two forces.

PROBLEMS

162. A beam 8 ft. long rests on two horizontal supports and is loaded as shown in Fig. 115. If the weights of the beams are neglected, find the reactions R_1 and R_2 at the points of support. Solve by two methods; (a) by considering the entire system of beams as a free body, and (b) by considering each of the beams as a free body. *Ans.* $R_1 = 5714$ lb.; $R_2 = 2286$ lb.

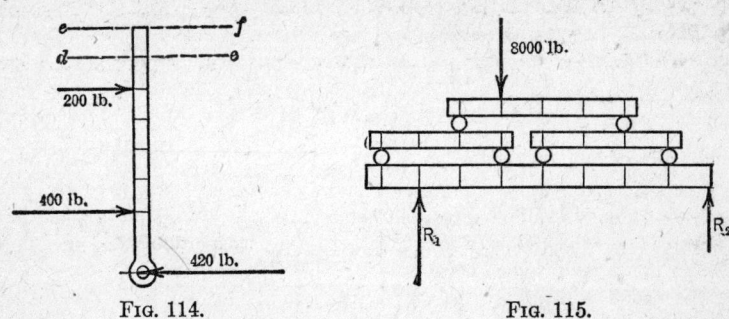

FIG. 114.   FIG. 115.

163. A rigid frame M (Fig. 116) is supported by a smooth pin at O and has attached to it by flexible cords bodies weighing 20 lb. and 40 lb. at points A and B, respectively. Determine the reaction of the pin on the frame and the angle of inclination of AB with the horizontal. Neglect the weight of the frame.
Ans. $R_O = 60$ lb.; $\theta = 45°$.

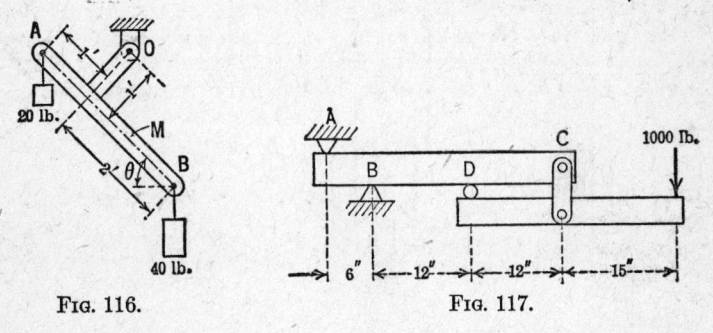

FIG. 116.   FIG. 117.

164. In Fig. 117 find the reactions at A and B. Also find the reactions at C and D on the upper member.
Ans. $R_A = 6500$ lb.; $R_B = 7500$ lb.; $R_C = 2250$ lb.; $R_D = 1250$ lb.

165. In Fig. 118 the beam CE is supported by a smooth pin at E and a smooth roller at D. The beam AB is supported by a smooth pin at A and a smooth roller between the two beams. Find the reaction of the pin at E on the beam CE. Neglect the weights of the beams.

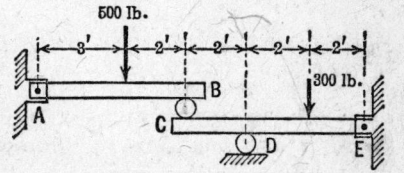

FIG. 118.

166. A block and tackle which is attached to a stake driven in the ground is used in moving a car by the method shown in Fig. 119. If the holding power of the stake is limited, which of the two arrangements shown is preferable, that shown in

82   EQUILIBRIUM OF FORCE SYSTEMS

(a) or (b)? If the force that must be applied to the car to cause it to move is 800 lb., find the value of the force P required to move the car in each of the two arrangements. Find also the tension T in the cable connected to the stake in each case.

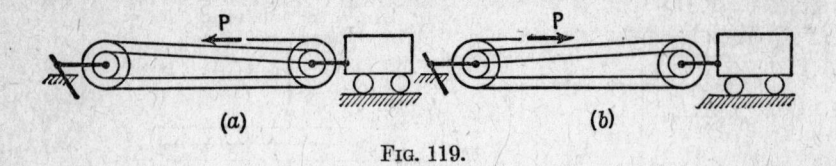

FIG. 119.

167. In Fig. 120 is represented a differential chain hoist. Two sheaves of radii r_1 and r_2 are fastened together and a continuous chain passes around the small sheave, then around a movable pulley of diameter $r_1 + r_2$, and then around the larger sheave. Neglecting the resistance due to friction, find the relation between the applied force F and the load W which it will hold in equilibrium. $\quad$ *Ans.* $F = \dfrac{W(r_1 - r_2)}{2r_1}$.

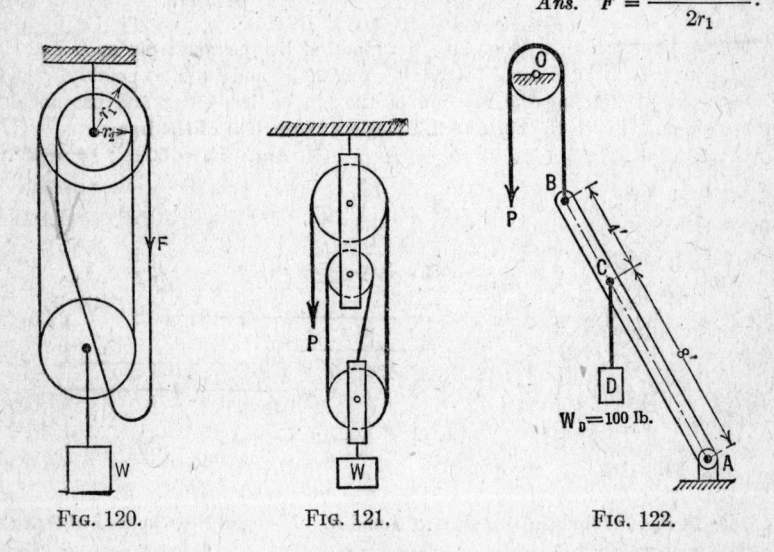

FIG. 120.   FIG. 121.   FIG. 122.

168. In Fig. 121 what force P is required to hold in equilibrium a weight W of 2 tons?

169. In Fig. 122 is shown a uniform bar AB supported by a smooth pin at A and a flexible cord which is attached at B and passes over a pulley that is supported by a smooth pin at O. A body D weighing 100 lb. is attached to the bar at C by a flexible cord. If the bar weighs 10 lb. per ft. of length what force P must be applied to hold the bar in equilibrium in the position shown? $\quad$ *Ans.* $P = 126.7$ lb.

§ 5. Coplanar, Non-concurrent, Non-parallel Forces

44. Equations of Equilibrium.—A system of coplanar, non-concurrent, non-parallel forces is in equilibrium if the forces of the system satisfy the equations,

$$\left.\begin{array}{r}\Sigma F_x = 0 \\ \Sigma F_y = 0 \\ \Sigma M_A = 0\end{array}\right\} \quad \dots \dots \dots \quad (A)$$

where x and y denote the coordinate axes and A is any point in the plane of the forces.

Proof.—If a system of coplanar, non-concurrent, non-parallel forces is not in equilibrium, the resultant of the system is either a force having components equal to ΣF_x and ΣF_y or a couple having a moment equal to ΣM_A (Art. 30). If the forces of the system satisfy the equation $\Sigma F_x = 0$, the resultant, if a force, must be parallel to the y-axis. If the equation $\Sigma F_y = 0$ is satisfied, the resultant, if a force, must be parallel to the x-axis. A force cannot be parallel to both the x- and y-axes and hence, if the first two equations are satisfied, the resultant of the system cannot be a force. If the equation $\Sigma M_A = 0$ is satisfied, the resultant cannot be a couple. Therefore, if the forces of the system satisfy the three equations, the force system is in equilibrium.

Another set of independent equations of equilibrium for a non-concurrent, non-parallel system of forces in a plane may be written as follows:

$$\left.\begin{array}{r}\Sigma F_x = 0 \\ \Sigma M_A = 0 \\ \Sigma M_B = 0\end{array}\right\} \quad \dots \dots \dots \quad (B)$$

where x denotes any line or axis in the plane of the forces and A and B are any two points in the plane, provided that the line AB is not perpendicular to the x-axis.

A third set of equilibrium equations for the force system here considered may be written as follows:

$$\left.\begin{array}{r}\Sigma M_A = 0 \\ \Sigma M_B = 0 \\ \Sigma M_C = 0\end{array}\right\} \quad \dots \dots \dots \quad (C)$$

where A, B, and C are any three non-collinear points in the plane of the forces.

It will be left to the student to prove that either set of equations (B) or (C) is sufficient and necessary to ensure the equilibrium of a coplanar, non-concurrent, non-parallel system of forces.

Any one of the above sets of equations, therefore, may be used to determine the unknown quantities in a coplanar, non-concurrent, non-parallel force system which is in equilibrium, provided there are not more than three such unknowns.

Choice of Moment-Centers and of Directions of Resolution.—In applying the equations of equilibrium to a system of coplanar, non-concurrent, non-parallel forces in which the magnitudes (and senses) of three forces are unknown, the solution may frequently be simplified by selecting the moment-centers and the directions of resolution in a particular way. For example, in Fig. 123 is represented a portion of a roof-truss which is

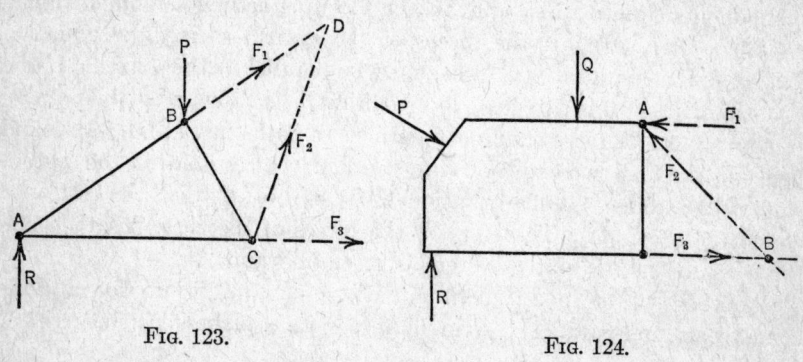

FIG. 123.   FIG. 124.

held in equilibrium by the five forces shown, of which P and R are known completely and F_1, F_2, and F_3 are unknown in magnitude. By selecting C, the intersection of the two unknown forces F_2 and F_3, as a moment-center and applying the equilibrium equation $\Sigma M_C = 0$, the force F_1 may be found from the one equation. Likewise by choosing D as a moment-center and applying a second equation of equilibrium, $\Sigma M_D = 0$, the force F_3 may be found directly. Similarly, F_2 may be found by selecting A as the moment-center and applying the third equilibrium equation, $\Sigma M_A = 0$. Thus by the proper selection of moment-centers each of the three equations involves one unknown quantity only.

As another example, consider a body which is held in equilibrium by the six forces shown in Fig. 124, all of which are completely known except F_1, F_2, and F_3, which are unknown in magnitude. The forces F_1 and F_3 are parallel. By selecting B as the moment-center, the force F_1 may be found from one equation, namely, $\Sigma M_B = 0$. Likewise, F_3 may be found from the single equation $\Sigma M_A = 0$, where A is the intersection of the two forces F_1 and F_2. Further, F_2 may be found from the single equation $\Sigma F_y = 0$ provided that the y-direction is chosen perpendicular to the forces F_1 and F_3.

ILLUSTRATIVE PROBLEMS

Problem 170.—The wall bracket shown in Fig. 125(a) consists of a horizontal member AB, which is attached to the wall at A by means of a smooth pin, and a rod CB, which is attached to the member AB at B and to the wall at C by means of smooth pins. Find the tension, T, in the rod and the pin reaction, R, at A if the weights of the members are neglected.

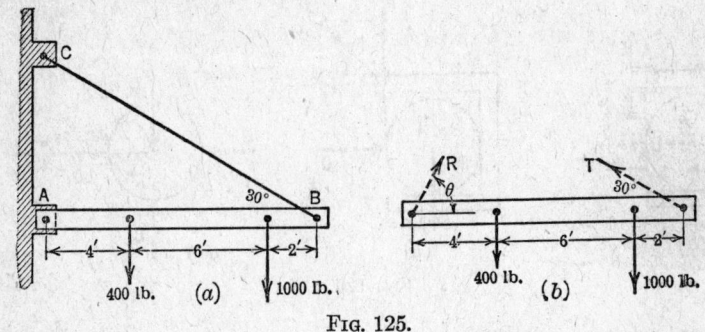

FIG. 125.

Solution.—A free-body diagram of the horizontal member is shown in Fig. 125(b). There are three unknown quantities in the force system, namely, T, R, and θ. Applying the three equations of equilibrium we have

$$\Sigma M_A = T \times 12 \sin 30° - 1000 \times 10 - 400 \times 4 = 0, \quad \ldots \quad (1)$$

$$\therefore T = 1930 \text{ lb}.$$

$$\Sigma F_x = R \cos \theta - T \cos 30° = 0,$$

$$\therefore R \cos \theta = 1930 \cos 30° = 1670 \text{ lb}. \quad \ldots \ldots \ldots \ldots (2)$$

$$\Sigma F_y = R \sin \theta + T \sin 30° - 400 - 1000 = 0,$$

$$\therefore R \sin \theta = 1400 - 1930 \sin 30° = 435 \text{ lb}. \quad \ldots \ldots \ldots (3)$$

By solving equations (2) and (3) the following results are obtained,

$$R = 1730 \text{ lb.}; \quad \theta = 14° 35'.$$

Problem 171.—A smooth cylinder weighing 120 lb. is supported as shown in Fig. 126. The pin at A connecting the frame M to the vertical wall is smooth and the weight of M may be neglected. Find the reaction of the pin at A on M, and the pressures on the cylinder at B, C, and D.

Solution.—The frame M and the cylinder, treated as one body, will first be taken as a free body. The free-body diagram for this body is shown in Fig. 126(b), in which the components of the pin reaction A are used instead of A itself; there are three unknown forces (indicated by heavy dashed-line vectors). Since the force system involved is coplanar, non-concurrent, and non-parallel, there are three equations of equilibrium and hence all three unknown forces can be found. Thus applying one set of equilibrium equations to the force system in Fig. 126(b), we have

$$\Sigma M_A = 120 \times 3 - 4D = 0 \qquad \therefore D = 90 \text{ lb.}$$

$$\Sigma F_y = A_y - 120 = 0 \qquad \therefore A_y = 120 \text{ lb.}$$

$$\Sigma F_x = A_x - D = 0 \qquad \therefore A_x = 90 \text{ lb.}$$

Hence, $A = \sqrt{120^2 + 90^2} = 150 \text{ lb.}, \quad \theta_x = \tan^{-1}\dfrac{120}{90} = 53° \, 10'.$

FIG. 126.

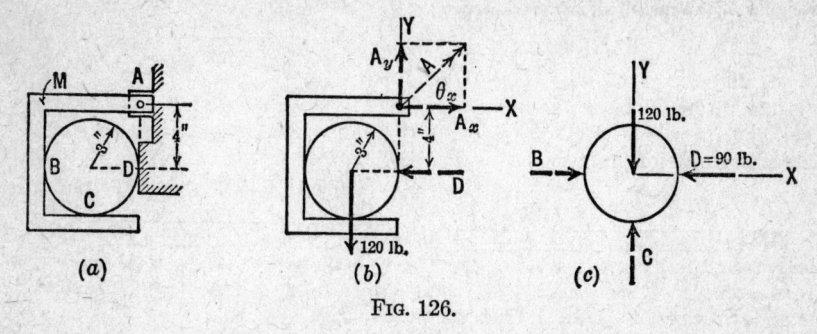

In order to find the pressures on the cylinder at B and C, a free-body diagram of the cylinder is drawn; this is shown in Fig. 126(c) in which the force D is now known. There are two unknown forces B and C and since the force system is coplanar and concurrent there are two equations of equilibrium and, hence, the two unknowns can be found. Thus

$$\Sigma F_x = B - 90 = 0, \qquad \therefore B = 90 \text{ lb.}$$

$$\Sigma F_y = C - 120 = 0, \qquad \therefore C = 120 \text{ lb.}$$

PROBLEMS

172. In Fig. 127, AB is a bar 6 ft. long and of negligible weight. C is a smooth drum. Determine the tension in the cable and the horizontal and vertical components of the pin reaction at A on AB.

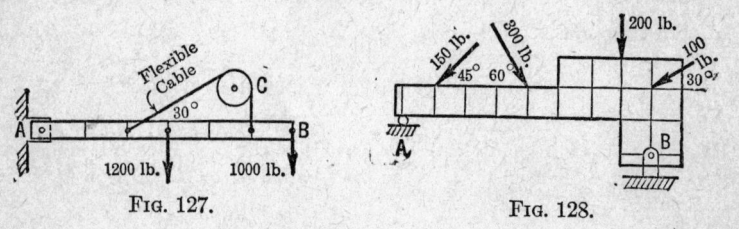

FIG. 127.

FIG. 128.

173. Find the reactions at A and B on the body shown in Fig. 128. Each division on the body is 1 ft. long. *Ans.* $A = 258 \text{ lb.}; B = 360 \text{ lb.}; \theta_x = 83° \, 12'.$

PROBLEMS

174. The bar shown in Fig. 129 is connected to a fixed support by a smooth pin at A and rests on a smooth surface at B. Find the reaction at B and the magnitude and direction of the pin pressure on AB at A.

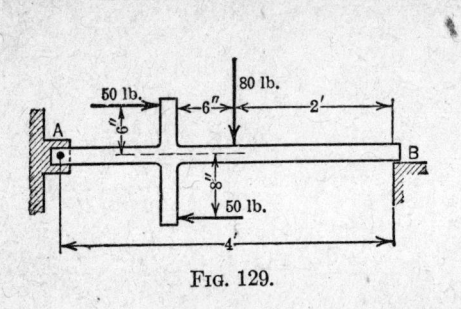

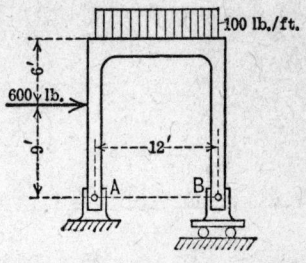

FIG. 129.

FIG. 130.

175. In Fig. 130 is shown a frame subjected to a horizontal load of 600 lb. and a uniformly distributed vertical load of 100 lb. per ft. Find the reaction at B and the horizontal and vertical components of the reaction at A.

Ans. $B = 1050$ lb.; $A_x = -600$ lb.; $A_y = 150$ lb.

176. A bar (Fig. 131) leans against a smooth vertical post and rests with its lower end on a smooth horizontal plane, slipping of the lower end being prevented by the cord as shown. If the weight of the bar is neglected, find the reaction of the plane at A and of the post at B and also find the tension in the cord.

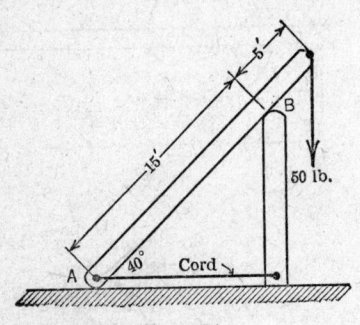

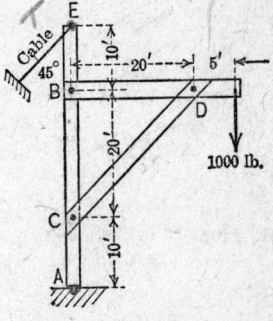

FIG. 131.

FIG. 132.

177. Find the pull of the cable at E on the crane shown in Fig. 132. Find also the horizontal and vertical components of the reaction at A due to the 1000-lb. load.

Ans. $T = 884$ lb.; $A_x = 625$ lb.; $A_y = 1625$ lb.

178. The truss in Fig. 133 is loaded as shown. Find the reaction at D and the magnitude and direction of the pin reaction at G, neglecting the weight of the truss. Are the reactions in a rigid structure influenced by the way in which the loads are transmitted to the supports? For example, if the 6000-lb. load were applied at F and the 1500-lb. load applied at E, would the reactions be altered? Or if the truss were replaced by a solid (weightless) block would the reactions be altered?

179. In Fig. 134 find the reaction on the truss at G and the horizontal and vertical components of the reaction at H due to the loads shown.

$$\text{Ans.} \quad G = 13{,}860 \text{ lb.}; \; H_x = 12{,}000 \text{ lb.}; \; H_y = -1730 \text{ lb.}$$

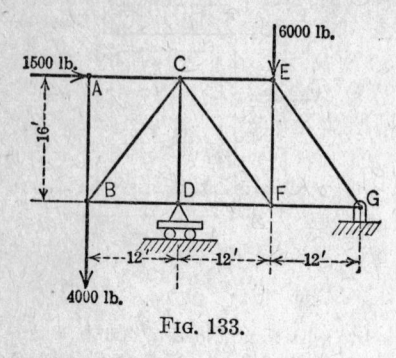

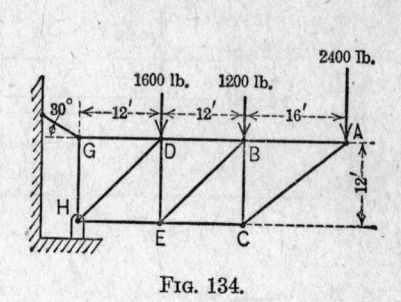

FIG. 133.

FIG. 134.

180. The weight of the cylinder B in Fig. 135 is 200 lb. Assuming that all surfaces of contact are smooth and that the weight of the bar AC is negligible, find all forces acting on the bar.

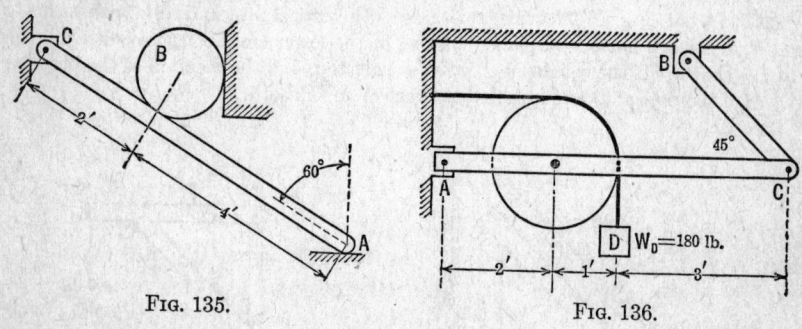

FIG. 135.

FIG. 136.

181. Find the reactions of the smooth pins at A and C on the bar AC of the pin-connected frame shown in Fig. 136. Neglect the weights of the members.

$$\text{Ans.} \quad A = 269 \text{ lb.}; \; \theta_x = 26° 35'; \; C = 84.8 \text{ lb.}$$

45. Graphical Solution of a Typical Problem.—Any problem which involves a balanced, non-concurrent, non-parallel force system in a plane, in which not more than three characteristics of the forces are unknown may be solved graphically as well as algebraically. A graphical method of solution making use of force and string polygons, for one typical problem will here be discussed. In the force system considered, all of the forces will be assumed to be known completely except two, the action line of one of these two being known and also one point on the action line of the other. The three unknown characteristics, then, are the magnitude of one of the two forces and the magnitude and the direction of the other.

PROBLEMS 89

As an example of such a force system, consider the forces acting on the beam shown in Fig. 137(a) which is supported by a smooth surface at the left end and a smooth pin at the right end. The unknown elements are the magnitude of the vertical reaction at the left end of the beam and the magnitude and the direction of the reaction at the right end of the beam.

The force and string polygons are shown in Fig. 137. In constructing the force polygon AB, BC, and CD are first drawn to represent the three known forces (Fig. 137b). Since the magnitude of the force DE is unknown the location of E is not known, but it must lie in a vertical

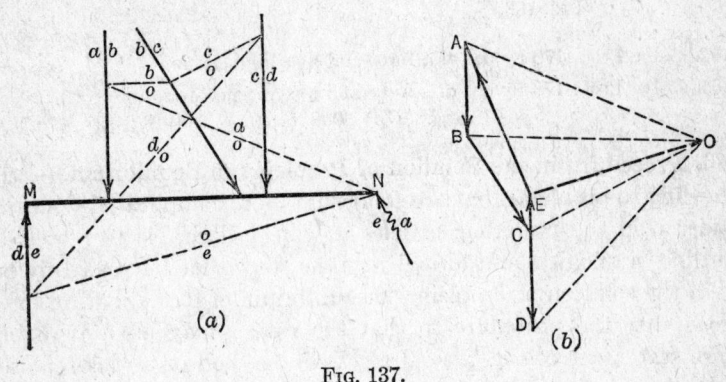

FIG. 137.

line through D. The rays OA, OB, OC, and OD are then drawn from O, after which the string polygon is constructed (Fig. 137a). Since the point N is the only known point on the action line of the force EA, the string polygon must be started at this point. The strings oa, ob, oc, and od are drawn as shown. Since the string oe must intersect od on de and must also intersect oa on ea, its position is determined. The ray OE must be parallel to the string oe. Hence E is the point of intersection of a vertical line through D and a line through O parallel to oe. DE then represents the left reaction, and the right reaction is represented in magnitude and in direction by EA.

PROBLEMS

182. The Fink truss shown in Fig. 138 is subjected to wind loads as indicated, the loads being perpendicular to the upper chord AD. The truss rests on a smooth plate at the left end, and hence the reaction at that end is vertical. Determine completely, by use of a force and a string polygon, the reactions R_1 and R_2.

Ans. $R_1 = 3460$ lb.; $R_2 = 3460$ lb.; $\theta = 30°$.

183. Find graphically the reactions of the supports on the pins at A and I of the truss shown in Fig. 139, due to the loads indicated.

184. Find by means of a force and a string polygon the reactions at A and B on the bar shown in Fig. 87.   Ans. $A = 49.8$ lb.; $\theta_x = 13° 15'$; $B = 12$ lb.

Fig. 138.

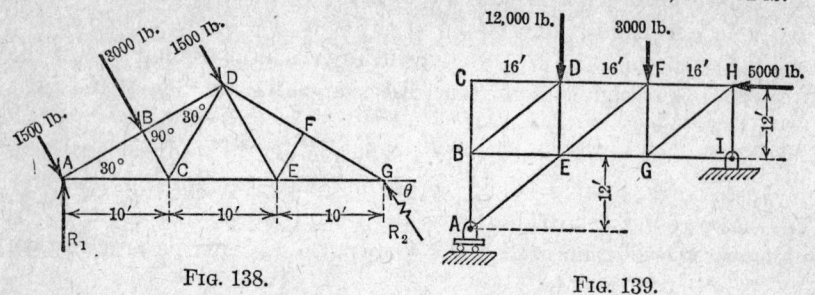

Fig. 139.

185. Solve Prob. 170 by use of a force and a string polygon.

186. Solve Prob. 178 by use of a force and a string polygon.

Ans. $D = 8000$ lb.; $G = 2500$ lb.; $\theta_x = 126° 52'$.

46. Procedure in the Solution of Problems in Equilibrium.—Before proceeding to problems that are somewhat more complicated than those considered in the preceding articles it will be desirable to review and to outline in a logical and formal way the steps that have already been used in the solution of problems of equilibrium of forces, and to extend or generalize the procedure so that the reader may have available a concise statement of the general algebraic method of attack for use in the solution of all problems in the equilibrium of forces. The main steps in the procedure may be stated as follows:

1. Determine carefully (a) what is given in the problem and (b) what is required in the problem. Many of the student's difficulties arise from failure to observe this preliminary step. To make the given and the required quantities definite they should be listed or in some other way isolated.

2. Draw a complete free-body diagram of the body, or of part of the body, or of a group of the bodies, on which are acting the forces required to be found. It will be found helpful to show all unknown forces in color or as dashed lines and known forces in black or as solid lines, thereby further emphasizing what is known and what is unknown. Further, it is desirable to show coordinate axes in each free-body diagram particularly if the directions of these axes are not the same in the several diagrams.

3. Observe the type of force system shown in the free-body diagram, and write the equations of equilibrium for this type of force system.

4. Then observe whether or not there are a sufficient number of equations of equilibrium to solve for all the unknown forces. If so (that is, if the force system is statically determinate), apply the equations and solve for *all* the unknown forces. If the force system is statically indeterminate, one or more (but not all) of the unknown forces may sometimes be found; but in order to reduce the number of unknown forces so that the force system becomes statically determinate the following step is necessary.

5. Draw a complete free-body diagram of one of the other bodies, or of part of

ILLUSTRATIVE PROBLEM

a body, or of a group of the bodies on which are acting one (or more) of the unknown forces that acts on the first free body and apply the equations of equilibrium to the forces in this second free-body diagram. This force system does not necessarily have to be statically determinate since a solution giving *all* the unknown forces in it is *not* required; only those particular forces that will make the force system in the first free-body diagram statically determinate are required. In some problems more than one additional free-body diagram must be used in order to determine a sufficient number of forces to make the forces in the first free-body diagram statically determinate.

6. Return now to the first free-body diagram and its equations of equilibrium and complete the solution, making use, of course, of any additional equations other than equations of equilibrium that apply to the problem such as the defining equation for coefficient of friction ($F' = \mu N$), etc.

The procedure is illustrated in the solution of the following problem.

ILLUSTRATIVE PROBLEM

Problem 137.—Find the pull of the tie rod AB and the x- and y-components of the pin pressure of D on the member EH of the frame shown in Fig. 140. The cylinder C has a radius of 1 ft. and weighs 100 lb. Assume that there is no friction at surfaces of contact of the various members. Neglect the weight of all members of the frame, and also neglect the width of members EH and FG in calculating distances.

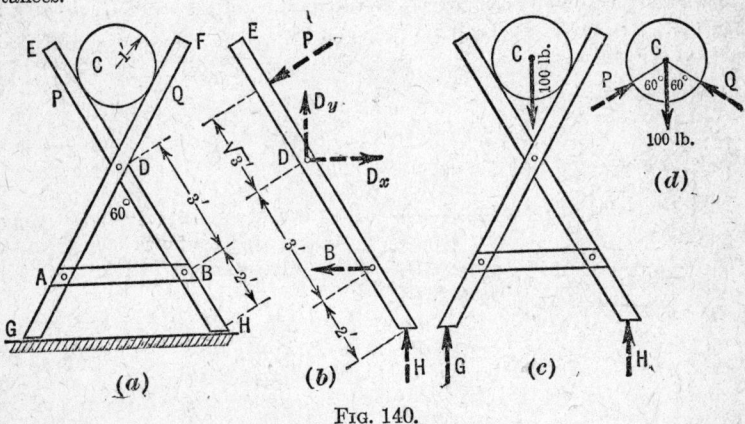

FIG. 140.

Solution.—The forces required are acting on EH, and therefore a free-body diagram of EH is drawn as shown in Fig. 140(b). All five forces are unknown, and there are three equations of equilibrium for the type of force system involved. Therefore, the forces P and H must be found by considering the equilibrium of one or more of the other bodies or group of bodies before the three required forces can be found. H may be found by considering the equilibrium of all the bodies, treated as one body, as shown in Fig. 140(c). The three forces constitute a parallel system for which there are two equations of equilibrium. Without formally applying these equations, it is obvious by inspection of Fig. 140(c) that

$$G = H = \frac{100}{2} = 50 \text{ lb.}$$

Furthermore, P (reversed in sense) is a force acting on the cylinder C. Therefore, by drawing a free-body diagram of C as shown in Fig. 140(d) and applying the two equations of equilibrium for the concurrent force system we have:

$$\Sigma F_x = P \cos 30° - Q \cos 30° = 0, \qquad \therefore P = Q$$

$$\Sigma F_y = P \sin 30° + Q \sin 30° - 100 = 0,$$

or

$$\Sigma F_y = 2P \sin 30° - 100 = 0, \qquad \therefore P = 100 \text{ lb.}$$

Now returning to Fig. 140(b), P and H may be put in as known forces; then by writing the three equations of equilibrium we may find B, D_x, and D_y as follows:

$$\Sigma M_D = -B \times 3 \cos 30° + 50 \times 5 \sin 30° + 100 \times \sqrt{3} = 0, \quad \therefore B = 115 \text{ lb.}$$

$$\Sigma F_y = D_y - 100 \sin 30° + 50 = 0, \qquad \therefore D_y = 0.$$

$$\Sigma F_x = D_x - B - 100 \cos 30 = 0, \qquad \therefore D_x = 201 \text{ lb.}$$

PROBLEMS

188. In Prob. 187, instead of drawing a free-body diagram of EH alone, draw a free-body diagram of EH and C considered as one body, and then from Fig. 140(c) and (d) find H and Q, respectively. Now return to the free-body diagram of EH and C and find D_x, D_y, and B.

189. Find the x- and y-components of the reaction of the pin C on member BE in Fig. 141. The pulley at D is frictionless and has a diameter of 2 ft. Neglect the weights of the members. *Ans.* $C_x = 3000$ lb., $C_y = -4000$ lb.

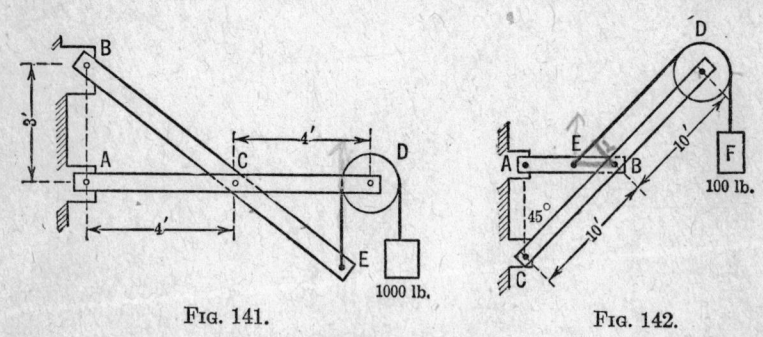

FIG. 141.   FIG. 142.

190. Find the x- and y-components of the reaction of the pin at A on the member AB in Fig. 142. The drum D is frictionless and has a radius of 2 ft. Neglect the weights of the members.

191. In Fig. 143, find the reaction of the pin at C and of the roller at D on member M, assuming the weight of E to be 200 lb. and neglecting the weights of the other bodies.

192. Find the magnitudes of the reactions of the pins at A, B, and C on the member AC of the frame shown in Fig. 144.

Ans. $A = 500$ lb.; $B = 4950$ lb.; $C = 4030$ lb.

193. In the hydraulic crane shown in Fig. 145 the weight of the boom ABC is 500 lb., as shown in the figure, and the weights of the members AD and BD may

PROBLEMS 93

be neglected. In raising the boom the hydraulic pressure from the cylinder transmits a pressure P to the pin at D. Neglecting the frictional resistance, find the value of P required to raise the boom when loaded as shown. Find also the stresses

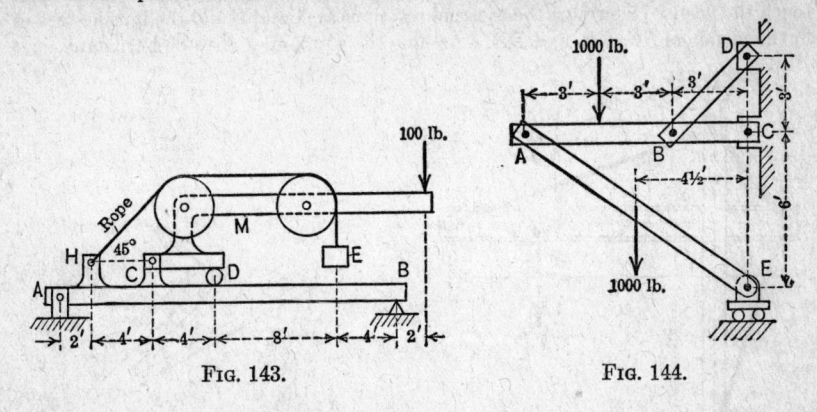

FIG. 143.

FIG. 144.

in BD and AD and the pressures of the rolls at A and at D against the vertical post.
 Ans. $P = 2500$ lb.; $D = A = 5540$ lb.; $DB = 6550$ lb. tension;
 $AD = 760$ lb. compression.

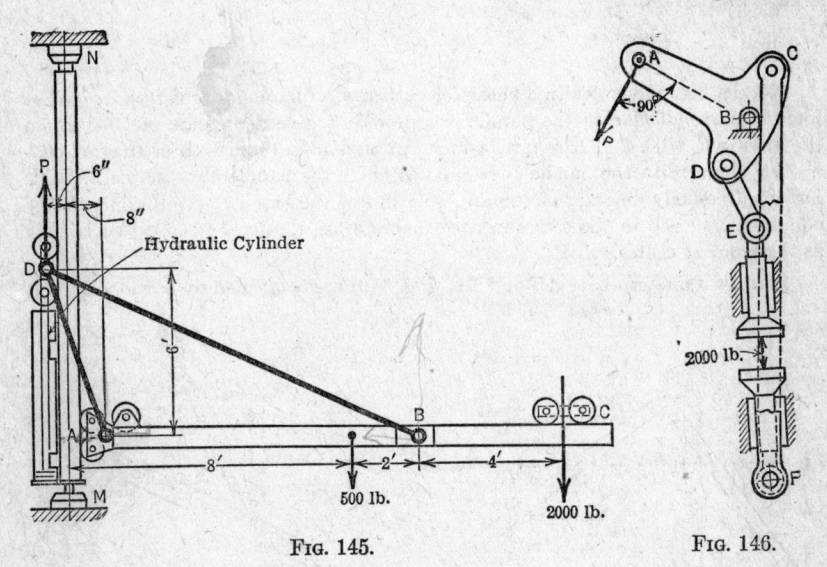

FIG. 145.

FIG. 146.

194. The power press shown in Fig. 146 has the following dimensions: $AB = 2.5$ ft. $BC = BD = 1$ ft. $DE = 1.3$ ft. $FC = 8$ ft. The points B, E, and F are on the same vertical line. The line CBD makes an angle of 60° with the horizontal and the line AB makes an angle of 30° with the horizontal. What force P is required to cause a pressure of 2000 lb. between the jaws of the press if friction be neglected?
 Ans. $P = 1065$ lb.

195. In the crane shown in Fig. 147, the post AE weighs 1600 lb. and the member CH weighs 1200 lb. The remaining members are cables the weights of which may be neglected. The member CH passes through a slot in the post AE and does not touch the post. Determine the external reactions at A and E and the tensile stresses in the members BC, CD, and DH. Assume the reaction at E to be horizontal.

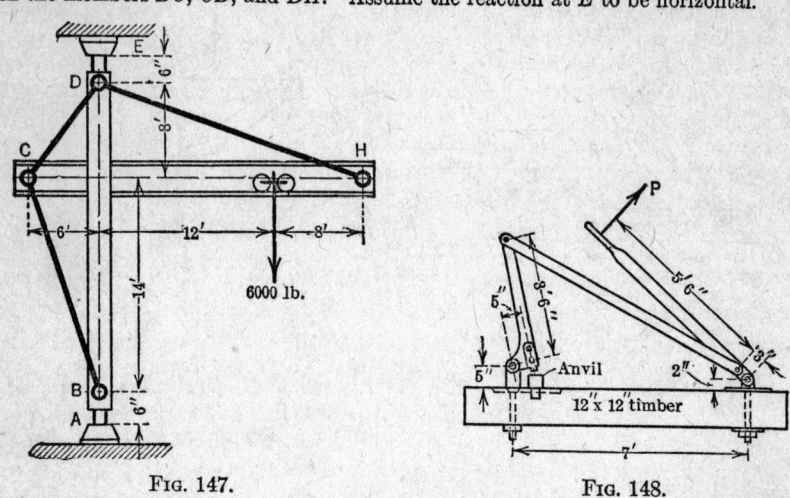

FIG. 147.

FIG. 148.

196. In Fig. 148 is shown a shear for cutting steel bars in a repair yard. What force P perpendicular to the handle is required to give a pressure of 7000 lb. on the anvil when the 3 ft 6 in. arm is vertical, assuming the length of the bar connecting the arm to the handle is such as to make the handle also vertical. Hint: Draw a free-body diagram of the arm and also of the handle, and in applying the equation $\Sigma M = 0$ to the forces in each diagram use the fixed point on each body as the moment center. *Ans.* $P = 34$ lb.

197. Two uniform bars AB and BC (Fig. 149) are connected by a smooth pin at

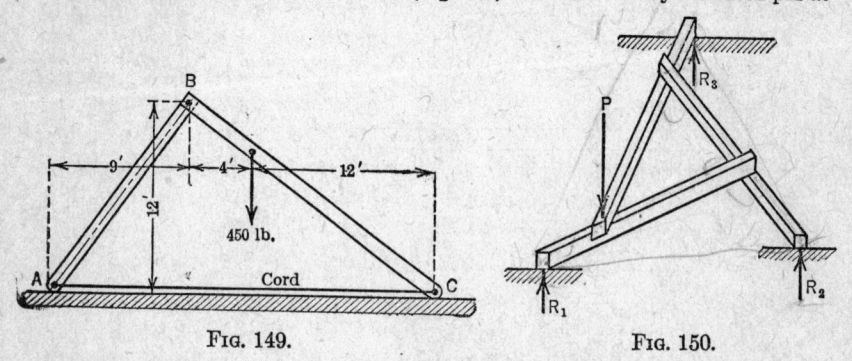

FIG. 149.

FIG. 150.

B and their lower ends rest on a smooth horizontal surface, slipping on the surface being prevented by a cord which connects the ends A and C. The weight of AB is 120 lb. and the weight of BC is 180 lb. The bar BC also carries a concentrated load of 450 lb. as shown. Find the reactions of the surface, the tension in the cord, and the pin reaction at B on either bar.

Ans. $R_A = 372$ lb.; $R_C = 378$ lb.; $T = 234$ lb.; $R_B = 344$ lb.

198. Three rods each of length l rest on each other (Fig. 150) in such a way as to form a central equilateral triangle each side of which is $\frac{2}{3}l$. A load P is applied at one corner as shown. Find the reactions R_1, R_2, and R_3 in terms of P. Neglect the weights of the rods. Hint: The force system shown in Fig. 150 is a non-coplanar, parallel system, for which the equations of equilibrium have not yet been discussed. It will be necessary, therefore, to consider as free bodies the three rods separately and to apply the equations of equilibrium for the coplanar, parallel force systems involved. *Ans.* $R_1 = \frac{9}{13}P$; $R_2 = \frac{3}{13}P$; $R_3 = \frac{1}{13}P$.

§ 6. Equilibrium of Trusses and Cables

47. Stresses in Trusses.—Important examples of coplanar force systems in equilibrium are met in the analysis of the internal forces (stresses) in trusses. In determining the stresses in trusses, only those trusses will here be considered for which the following assumptions may be made:

(1) The members of the truss lie in one plane and the external forces acting on the truss lie in the same plane, and hence the forces involved in the determination of the stresses in members of the truss form coplanar systems.

(2) The members of the truss are rigid and are connected at their ends by means of smooth pins that fit perfectly to the members.

(3) The applied loads and reactions on the truss act only on the pins, that is, at the ends of the members.

(4) The weights of the members are neglected, since the stresses due to the weights are assumed to be small in comparison with the stresses due to other loads.

It follows from (3) and (4) that each member is a two-force member (see Art. 41), which means that the stress in each member is directed along the member and is equal to the pin pressure at either end. (See Fig. 96 and Prob. 140.) The stress in the member is a tensile stress if the pin pressures at the ends act outward or away from the member, or tend to pull the member apart, and a compressive stress if the pin pressures act toward the member.

The usual methods of indicating the kind of stress (tension or compression) in a member is to indicate a tensile stress by a plus sign or by the letter T, and a compressive stress by a negative sign or by the letter C.

In the analysis of the stresses in a pin-connected, pin-loaded structure algebraically, by use of the equations of equilibrium two methods may be used: namely, the *method of joints* and the *method of sections*. In both methods a section is passed through the structure to obtain the part of the structure that is to be taken as the free body, but the difference in the methods lies chiefly in the type of force system acting on the portion of the structure that is considered as the free body. In the first method a *concurrent* force system is involved and in the second method a *non-concurrent*, non-parallel system is dealt with.

Method of Joints.—In determining the stresses in the members of a pin-connected, pin-loaded truss by the method of joints, a section is passed through the truss cutting members that are attached to a common pin; one such section is indicated as aa in Fig. 151(a). The portion thus severed from the truss by this section (consisting of the pin and attached parts of the members) is then treated as a free body in equilibrium under the action of any known external forces that act on this body (such as the reaction at A) in Fig. 151(a) and the forces (stresses) exerted at the cut sections by the other portions of the members. A free-body diagram for the joint A in Fig. 151(a) is shown in Fig. 151(b).

It will be noted that the method of joints involves the equilibrium of a *concurrent* force system, and since there are two equations of equilibrium for such a force system, the section passed through the truss must not cut more than two members in which the stresses are unknown. (It is assumed that all external loads and reactions are known.)

Instead of selecting the free body as discussed above, it is sometimes convenient to treat the pin alone as the free body in equilibrium under the actions of the pressures of the members on the pin and any known loads or reactions, as shown in Fig. 151(c). As already noted the stress in each member is numerically equal to the pin pressure at either end of the member so that the two free-body diagrams lead to the same solution.

In determining the stresses in all members of a truss by the method of joints, the equations of equilibrium must be applied to the joints in turn and in such an order that not more than two unknown stresses occur in each free body diagram. Thus, if the stress in a single member near the center of the truss is required, it is usually necessary to start at the end of the truss and consider the equilibrium of the joints in order until a joint is reached which involves the particular member. By the method of sections, discussed in the next paragraph, the stress in a single member may frequently be found by use of one free-body diagram and by the use of only one equation of equilibrium.

Method of Sections.—In determining the stresses in the members of a pin-connected, pin-loaded truss, by the method of sections, a section is passed through the truss cutting members that are not attached to a common pin; two such sections are indicated as bb and cc in Fig. 151(a). The part of the truss on either side of this section is then treated as a

EQUILIBRIUM OF TRUSSES AND CABLES

free body in equilibrium under the action of the known external forces that act on that part and the forces (stresses) which the members of the other part exert, at the cut sections, on the part considered as the free

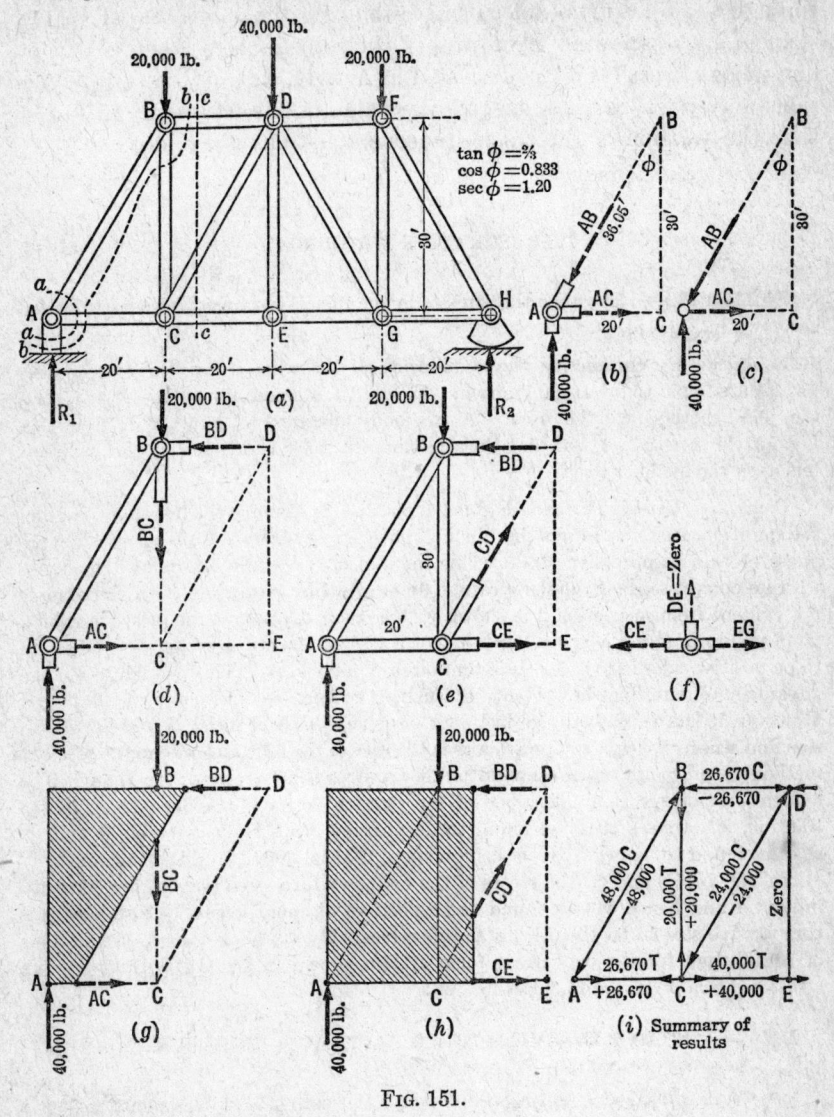

FIG. 151.

body. Free-body diagrams are shown in Fig. 151(d) and (e) for the portions of the truss to the left of sections bb and cc, respectively, in Fig. 151(a).

It will be noted that the method of sections involves the equilibrium of a *non-concurrent, non-parallel* force system, and since there are three equations of equilibrium for such a force system, the section passed through the truss must not cut more than three members in which the stresses are unknown. By a proper choice of moment centers and of directions of resolution, as discussed in Art. 44, each of the three equations may often be made to give the value of one unknown stress and thus the solution of three simultaneous equations is avoided.

ILLUSTRATIVE PROBLEM

Problem 199.—Determine the stresses in the members of the Howe truss loaded as shown in Fig. 151(a).

Solution.—By considering the equilibrium of the whole truss, the reactions R_1 and R_2 are found to be 40,000 lb. each. To find the stresses in members AB and AC the joint method will be used. A free-body diagram of joint A is shown in Fig. 151(b); it will be noted that the stress in a member is denoted by the same letters as is the member itself.

Convention Used in Designating Kind of Stress.—In drawing the free-body diagram the question arises as to whether an unknown stress should be shown as a tensile stress or as a compressive stress. One method of procedure is to show the stress with its correct sense if the sense can be determined by inspection (or if the sense is not evident from inspection it is shown with a sense that seems the most plausible). If an unknown stress is shown with its correct sense the stress will always be found to be positive whether the stress is tension or compression. This procedure has the advantage of requiring the student to visualize the forces as they act in the structure. However, it has a disadvantage in that a positive sign does not always indicate tension and a negative sign compression as is the case in the following method. Another method of procedure is to show all unknown stresses as tension even though it is evident from inspection that some of the stresses are compression. Then, in the solution, all stresses that are found to be positive are tension as assumed and all stresses found to be negative are compression, that is, opposite to that assumed.

In Fig. 151(b) and (c) the senses of the unknown forces AB and AC are correctly indicated and hence will be found to be positive although one of the stresses is a compressive stress and the other a tensile stress. By applying one set of equations of equilibrium for the concurrent force system shown in Fig. 151(b) and (c), the stresses AB and AC are found as follows:

$$\Sigma M_B = -40,000 \times 20 + AC \times 30 = 0 \qquad \therefore AC = 26{,}670 \text{ lb. } T.$$

$$\Sigma F_y = -AB \cos \phi + 4000 = 0 \qquad \therefore AB = \frac{40{,}000}{0.833} = 48{,}000 \text{ lb. } C.$$

To find the stresses in members BC and BD let a section bb be passed (Fig. 151a) through the truss. The forces acting on the part of the truss to the left of this section form a non-concurrent force system (Fig. 151d) and all three stresses could be found from the three equations of equilibrium. But since the stress in AC has already been found, only two of the three equations need be applied. Thus

$$\Sigma M_C = -40{,}000 \times 20 + BD \times 30 = 0 \qquad \therefore BD = 26{,}670 \text{ lb. } C.$$

$$\Sigma F_y = 40{,}000 - 20{,}000 - BC = 0 \qquad \therefore BC = 20{,}000 \text{ lb. } T.$$

In a similar manner the stresses in CD and CE may be found by the method of sections. By considering the part of the truss to the left of the section cc (Fig. 151e) the stresses in these two members may be found. Thus

$$\Sigma M_D = -40{,}000 \times 40 + 20{,}000 \times 20 + CE \times 30 = 0$$
$$\therefore CE = 40{,}000 \text{ lb. } T$$
$$\Sigma F_y = 40{,}000 - 20{,}000 + CD \cos \phi = 0$$
$$\therefore CD = -20{,}000 \times \sec \phi = -20{,}000 \times 1.20 = -20{,}000 \text{ lb. } C.$$

It will be noted that all the stresses except CD (Fig. 151e) are assumed to act in the correct directions, and hence are found to be positive whether they are tensile or compressive. The stress in CD is assumed to be tension and hence the negative sign indicates that it is compression.

In considering the equilibrium of the forces which act on the pin E (Fig. 151f), it is evident that the stress DE is zero, and that CE equals EG. Furthermore, since the truss is symmetrical with respect to the center line DE and the loads are also symmetrical with respect to this line, it is obvious that the stresses in the members of the right half of the truss are equal to the stresses in the corresponding members of the left half.

It is well to note that the stresses in the members of a truss are *internal* forces in considering the whole truss as a free body but the stresses in members that are cut by a given section passed through the truss are *external* forces with respect to the portion on either side of that section. Therefore, the portion of the truss on one side of the section may be considered to be a weightless rigid body of *any shape* provided the (external) forces acting on it have the same relative positions (and the same magnitude, of course) as in the actual body. Thus the free-body diagrams in Fig. 151(d) and (e) could be replaced by Fig. 151(g) and (h).

Summary of Results.—The results are summarized in Fig. 151(i) where the kind of stress (tension or compression) in each member is indicated by the sign + or − before the value of the stress, as well as by the letter T or C after the value of the stress. A third method of indicating the kind of stress makes use of arrows on each member which show the directions of the pressures of the member on the pins at its ends (not the pressures of the pins on the member); thus a compressive stress is represented by an arrow at each end of the member directed towards the pin at the end. Similarly a tensile stress is indicated by arrows directed toward the center of the member, that is, away from each pin.

PROBLEMS

200. In Fig. 151(a) let it be assumed that the stresses in AB and BC have been found to be 48,000 lb. $C.$ and 20,000 lb. $T.$, respectively. Pass a section cutting the members AB, BC, CD, and CE and then draw a free-body diagram of the portion of the truss to the left of this section and solve for the two unknown stresses.

201. In the Fink truss shown in Fig. 152, BC is perpendicular to AD and B is the mid-point of AD. Find the stresses in the members BC, BD, CD, and CE.
  Ans. $BC = -1730$ lb.; $AB = -6000$ lb.; $CD = +1730$ lb.; $CE = +3465$ lb.

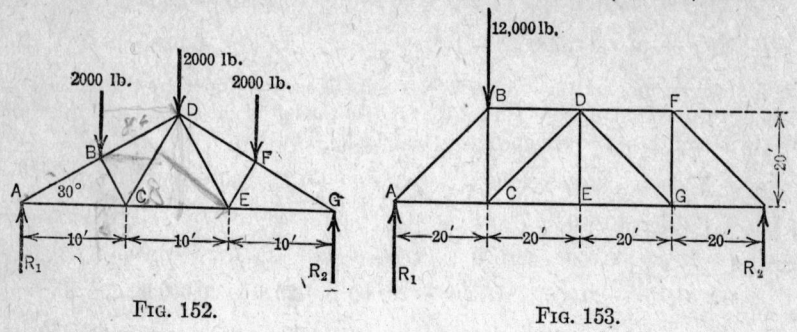

Fig. 152.

Fig. 153.

202. Find the stresses in the members DF, DG, and FG of the Howe truss shown in Fig. 153.

203. Find, by the method of sections, the stresses in members CE, CF, and DF of the pin-connected structure shown in Fig. 154.
  Ans. $CE = +8000$ lb.; $CF = -5655$ lb.; $DF = -4000$ lb.

204. Find the stresses in members BD, CD, and CE of the truss shown in Fig. 155.

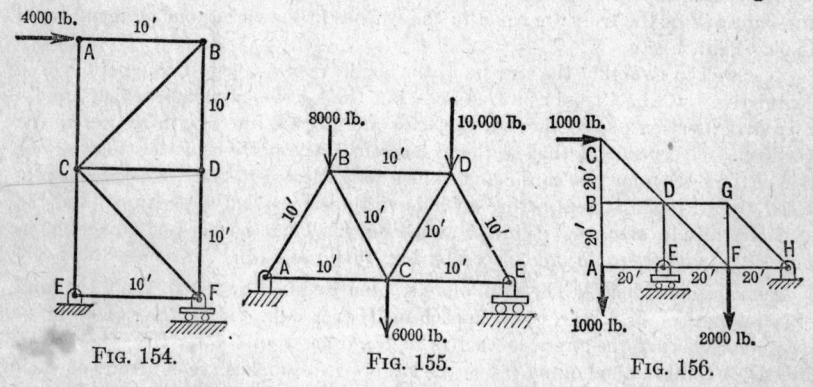

Fig. 154.

Fig. 155.

Fig. 156.

205. Find, by the method of joints, the stresses in the members BC and CD of the pin-connected truss shown in Fig. 156. Find, by the method of sections, the stresses in DG, DF, and EF.
  Ans. $BC = 1000$ lb.; $CD = -1415$ lb.; $DG = -1500$ lb.; $DF = 707$ lb.; $EF = 0$.

206. Find the stresses in the members BD, BE, and CE of the truss shown in Fig. 134. Note that it is not necessary to determine the reactions at H and G to solve the problem.

207. Find, by the method of sections, the stresses in the members BC, BE, and AE of the truss shown in Fig. 157.

208. Find the stresses in the members AC, BC, and BD of the truss shown in Fig. 158.
  Ans. $AC = 0$; $BC = 1465$ lb.; $BD = -4000$ lb.

GRAPHICAL ANALYSIS OF TRUSSES 101

209. The truss shown in Fig. 159 is supported at A and E. Find the stresses in the members BD, CD, and CE.

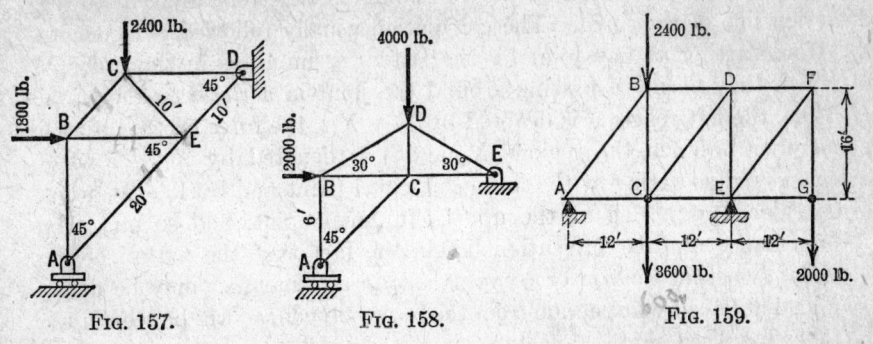

FIG. 157.   FIG. 158.   FIG. 159.

210. In the truss shown in Fig. 133 find the stresses in EG, CE, CF, and DF. Would the truss be improved by omitting the member CB and adding a member AD?

48. Graphical Analysis of Trusses.—The graphical method of analysis of a truss is sometimes simpler than the algebraic method. This is particularly true when the form of the truss is such that a considerable amount of calculation is necessary to determine the directions and moment-arms of the forces involved. The graphical method consists essentially in constructing the force polygon for the concurrent forces at each joint and superimposing these polygons. The method will be explained in detail with reference to the Howe truss shown in Fig. 160(a). The truss is assumed to be subjected to known equal loads

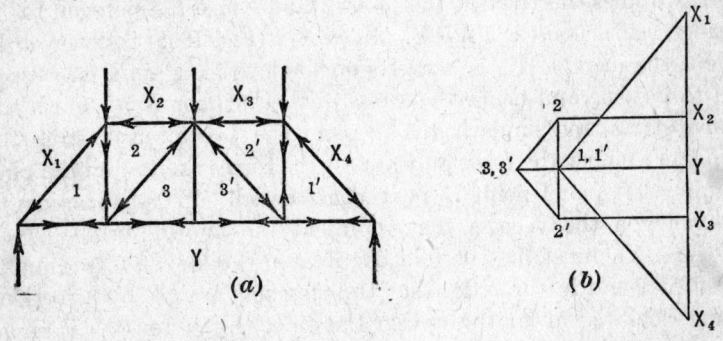

FIG. 160.

at the upper panel points, and hence the reactions at the ends of the truss are each equal to one-half of the sum of the loads.

Convention Used in Designating Stresses in Members.—It is convenient to use the Bow system of notation (Art. 8). In this system, the regions on either side of the action line of a force (either external or internal) are denoted by numbers or letters as shown in Fig. 160(a), and the force is denoted by the two numbers or letters adjacent to the action line of the force. The convention usually followed is to denote a force acting at any joint by the letters or numbers in the order in which they occur in passing around the joint in a *clockwise* direction. Thus, the left reaction is denoted by $Y - X_1$; the force exerted by the member between the regions X_1 and 1 is denoted by $X_1 - 1$ when considered as acting at the lower-left panel point and by $1 - X_1$ when considered as acting at the upper-left panel point, and so on. The importance of this convention lies in the fact that the nature of the stress (whether tension or compression) in any member may be determined at once by inspection from the force polygon, as will be seen in the following discussion.

The force polygon (Fig. 160b) for the truss in Fig. 160(a) is constructed as follows: First consider the three concurrent forces acting on the pin at the lower-left panel point; as previously explained, these forces are equal to the stresses in the members that exert the forces on the pin. Of these three forces the left reaction $Y - X_1$ is completely known and the directions of the other two, $X_1 - 1$ and $1 - Y$, are known. Since the three forces are in equilibrium their force polygon must close. This polygon is constructed by first laying off to scale the vector YX_1 that represents the force $Y - X_1$, since the force polygon must be started with the known force, and then drawing from X_1 a line $X_1 1$ parallel to $X_1 - 1$ and from Y a line $Y1$ parallel to $Y - 1$. These two lines intersect in the point 1 and hence the polygon for the lower-left panel point is $YX_1 1Y$. Since $X_1 1$ (Fig. 160b) is downward to the left, the member $X_1 - 1$ exerts on the lower-left pin a force downward to the left and hence the stress in the member $X_1 - 1$ is a compressive stress, and similarly the stress in $1 - Y$ is a tensile stress.

In like manner the force polygon for the forces exerted on the pin at the upper-left panel point is next constructed. In constructing this force polygon the vectors that represent the known forces ($1 - X_1$ and $X_1 - X_2$) must first be laid off because the known forces must be laid off first and in the order that the members are cut by a section in passing clockwise around the pin. But since the vector $1X_1$ is already in the diagram it is only necessary to lay off to the same scale the vector $X_1 X_2$; then from X_2 a line $X_2 2$ is drawn parallel to $X_2 - 2$, and from 1 a line 1 2 is drawn parallel to $1 - 2$. The polygon for this panel point then is $1X_1 X_2 21$. From the convention noted above it is evident that the stress in $X_2 - 2$ is a compressive stress and that in $2 - 1$ is a tensile stress. In a similar manner the remaining joints are considered and the entire polygon shown in Fig. 160(b) is completed; the length of any line in the polygon represents to scale the magnitude of the stress in the corresponding member.

It should be noted that the joints must be taken in such order that at no joint are there more than two unknown forces; otherwise it would be impossible to complete the polygon for the joint.

ILLUSTRATIVE PROBLEM

Problem 211.—Find the stresses in the members of the truss shown in Fig. 161(a). The members $X_1 - 1$ and $2 - 3$ are parallel, and the members $X_1 - 2$ and $Y - 1$ are parallel.

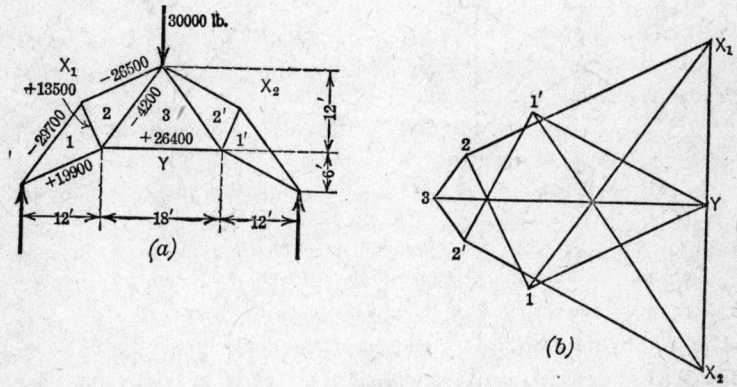

Fig. 161.

Solution.—The force polygon for the forces acting on the pins (that is, for the stresses in the members) is drawn to scale in Fig. 161(b). The magnitude of the stresses is found by measuring the lengths of the lines in the force polygon and the kind of stress in each member is determined by the convention explained in Art. 48. The magnitudes of the stresses are shown on the members in Fig. 161(a), the plus or minus sign indicating whether the stress in the member is tension or compression.

PROBLEMS

212. Find, by the graphical method, the stresses in the members of the truss shown in Fig. 162, the value of P being 10,000 lb.

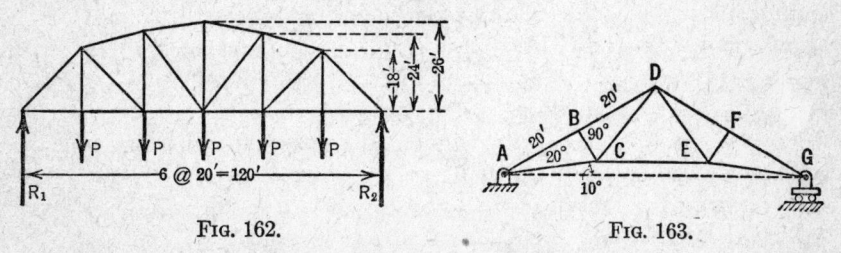

Fig. 162. Fig. 163.

213. A total wind pressure of 4000 lb. acts on the upper cord ABD of the truss shown in Fig. 163, the pressure being normal to the surface. Assuming that this pressure is equivalent to a load of 2000 lb. at B (normal to ABD) and loads of 1000 lb. each at A and D, determine the reactions at A and G by either the algebraic or graphical method and then find the stresses in the members of the truss by the graphical method.

214. Determine graphically the stresses in the members of the truss shown in Fig. 164 due to the 2000-lb. load.

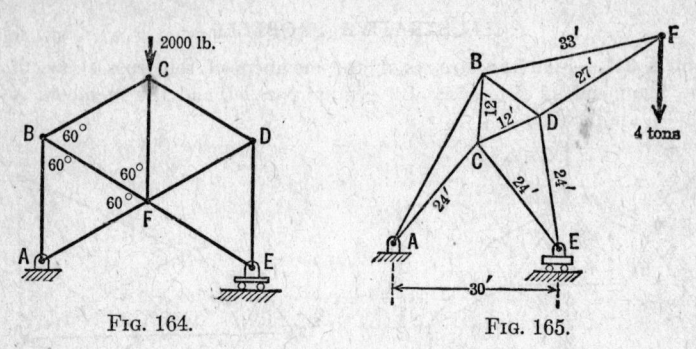

FIG. 164.

FIG. 165.

215. The members of the crane shown in Fig. 165 are connected by smooth pins. Find by the graphical method the stresses in the members due to the 4-ton load.

216. Find, by the graphical method, the stresses in the truss shown in Fig. 152.

217. Find, by the graphical method, the stresses in the truss shown in Fig. 138.

218. Find graphically the stresses in all of the members of the truss shown in Fig. 139.

49. Flexible Cables.—In the following two articles the equilibrium of flexible cables or cords will be discussed. A cable is said to be perfectly flexible when it can offer no resistance to bending. A flexible cable, then, can transmit a stress only along its axis; that is, the stress at any point of a flexible cable is tangent to the curve assumed by the cable. Although physical cables and cords are not perfectly flexible the resistance they offer to bending is generally so small that it can be neglected without serious error. In the discussion of cables it will be assumed that the cables are perfectly flexible and inextensible.

50. The Parabolic Cable.—If a flexible cable is suspended from two points and carries a load that is distributed uniformly horizontally (Fig. 166), the curve assumed by the cable is a parabola, as will presently be shown. In the present discussion the points from which the cable is suspended will be assumed to be in the same horizontal plane. An example of a cable carrying a load which closely approximates that above indicated is the cable of a suspension bridge, since the weight of the roadway is distributed uniformly horizontally and the weights of the cable and hangers are small in comparison with the weight of the roadway and therefore may be neglected. Another example is that of a tightly stretched cable (that is, one in which the sag is small as compared with the span) which carries no load except its own weight, as, for example, the cable of an electric transmission line, a telegraph wire, etc. In this case the load carried by the cable (its weight) is distributed uniformly along the curve assumed by the cable, but since the sag is small the horizontal projection of an arc of the curve is approximately equal to the length of the arc, and hence the load is distributed approximately uniformly in the horizontal direction.

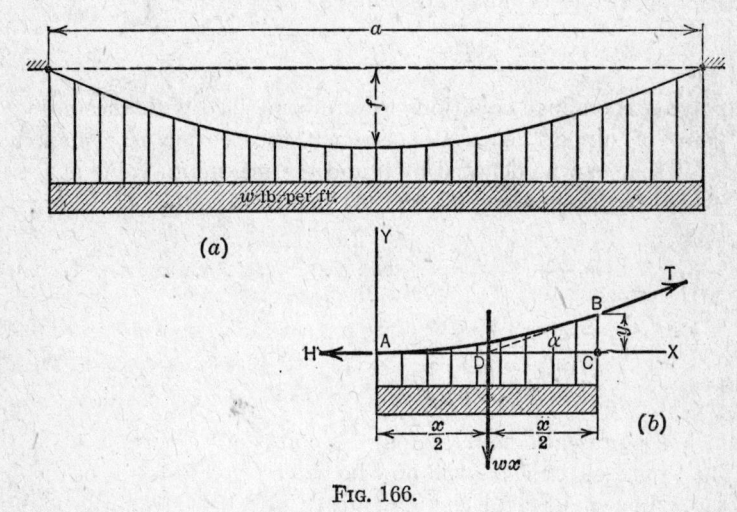

FIG. 166.

In the solution of problems involving the parabolic cable, use is made of the equation of the curve assumed by the cable (parabola) and of equations which express relations between the span, sag, length of the cable, tension, etc. In order to determine the equation of the parabola a portion AB of the cable will be considered as a free body (Fig. 166b). A, the lowest point of the cable, will be taken as the origin of coordinates, and the tension at this point will be denoted by H. The tension at any point, B, will be denoted by T. The portion of cable AB, then, is in equilibrium under the action of the three forces H, T, and the vertical load wx which acts through the point D midway between A and C. Since these three forces are in equilibrium they must be concurrent, and hence the action line of T passes through D. The equations of equilibrium are:

$$\Sigma F_x = T \cos \alpha - H = 0, \quad \cdots \cdots \quad (1)$$

$$\Sigma F_y = T \sin \alpha - wx = 0 \quad \cdots \cdots \quad (2)$$

Eliminating T from (1) and (2), we have

$$\tan \alpha = \frac{wx}{H}, \quad \text{but} \quad \tan \alpha = \frac{2y}{x}.$$

Hence

$$\frac{2y}{x} = \frac{wx}{H}, \quad \text{or} \quad y = \frac{wx^2}{2H} \quad \cdots \cdots \quad (3)$$

The curve, then, is a parabola with its vertex at A and its axis vertical. Eliminating α from (1) and (2), we have

$$T = \sqrt{H^2 + w^2 x^2} \quad \cdots \cdots \quad (4)$$

In applying the above equations we are concerned with the tension at the point of support since at this point the tension is a maximum. Hence, if the span be denoted by a and the maximum value of y (that is, the sag) by f, equations (3) and (4) reduce to

$$f = \frac{wa^2}{8H}, \quad \cdots \cdots \cdots \quad (5)$$

and

$$T = \frac{1}{2} wa \sqrt{1 + \frac{a^2}{16 f^2}}, \quad \cdots \cdots \quad (6)$$

in which T represents the tension at the points of support.

The length of the cable will now be determined in terms of the span and sag. In any curve the length of an arc is obtained from the equation

$$s = \int \sqrt{1 + \left(\frac{dy}{dx}\right)^2} dx.$$

From equation (3), $\dfrac{dy}{dx} = \dfrac{wx}{H}$. Hence, if the length of the cable be denoted by l, we have

$$l = 2 \int_0^{\frac{a}{2}} \sqrt{1 + \frac{w^2 x^2}{H^2}}\, dx.$$

Substituting for H from equation (5), this equation becomes

$$l = 2 \int_0^{\frac{a}{2}} \sqrt{1 + \frac{64 f^2 x^2}{a^4}}\, dx.$$

The exact expression for l, obtained from this integral, involves a logarithmic function and is difficult to apply. A simpler expression for l

may be obtained by expanding the expression under the integral into a series and integrating the series term by term. This method leads to the following equation:

$$l = a\left[1 + \frac{8}{3}\left(\frac{f}{a}\right)^2 - \frac{32}{5}\left(\frac{f}{a}\right)^4 + \cdots\right] \quad \ldots \quad (7)$$

Since the sag ratio f/a is generally small, the series converges rapidly and it is sufficient in most practical computations to use only the first two or three terms of the series to obtain a close approximation to the value of l.

ILLUSTRATIVE PROBLEM

Problem 219.—The horizontal load carried by each cable of a suspension bridge is 1000 lb. per ft. The span of the bridge is 800 ft. and the sag is 50 ft. Determine the tensions at the ends and at the middle of the cable and also find the length of the cable.

Solution.—From equations (5) and (6),

$$H = \frac{1000 \times (800)^2}{8 \times 50} = 1,600,000 \text{ lb.}$$

and

$$T = \frac{1}{2} \times 1000 \times 800 \sqrt{1 + \frac{(800)^2}{16 \times (50)^2}} = 1,650,000 \text{ lb.}$$

The length of the cable may be determined by using equation (7). Thus

$$l = 800\left[1 + \frac{8}{3}\left(\frac{50}{800}\right)^2 - \frac{32}{5}\left(\frac{50}{800}\right)^4\right] = 808.24 \text{ ft.}$$

PROBLEMS

220. A telegraph wire weighing 0.1 lb. per ft. is stretched between two poles 150 ft. apart. The tension in the wire at the insulators (which are in the same horizontal plane) is 500 lb. Find the sag, assuming that the weight of the wire is uniformly distributed horizontally. Find also the length of the wire.

Ans. $f = 0.562$ ft.; $l = 150.005$ ft.

221. Each cable of a suspension bridge carries a load of 1200 lb. per ft. uniformly distributed along the horizontal. The span is 1000 ft. and the sag is 50 ft. Find the maximum stress in the cable and the length of the cable.

222. A cable 100 ft. in length is suspended from two points in a horizontal plane which are 99 ft. apart. If the cable carries a load that is uniformly distributed along the horizontal what is the sag of the cable? *Ans.* $f = 6.10$ ft.

51. The Catenary.—The curve assumed by a flexible cable of uniform cross-section which is suspended from two points, and which carries no load except its own weight (Fig. 167), is called a catenary. The load which causes a cable to assume the form of a catenary, then, differs from that which causes the form of a parabola in that the load is distributed uniformly along the cable in the former case, whereas in the latter case the load is distributed uniformly horizontally.

The discussion of the catenary is of practical importance only for cables in which the sag ratio is large, since for a small sag ratio the curve assumed by a cable may be regarded with small error as being a parabola, as discussed in the preceding article.

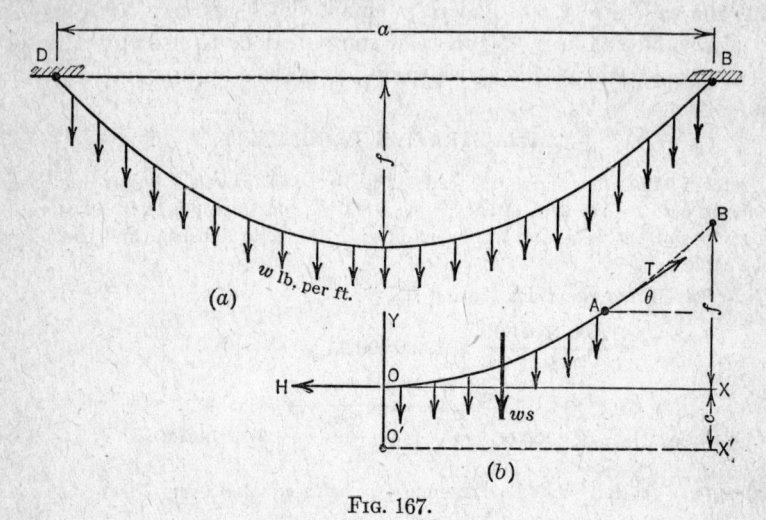

FIG. 167.

In order to determine the equation of the catenary and also to find certain important relations between such quantities as the sag, span, length of cable, tension, etc., the equilibrium of a portion, OA, of the cable (Fig. 167) will be considered, O being the lowest point of the cable and A any other point. The point O will be taken as the origin of coordinates, the weight of the cable per unit of length will be denoted by w, and the length of the arc OA will be denoted by s. The portion, OA, of the cable is in equilibrium under the influence of three forces, namely, the tension H at the point O, the tension T at the point A, and the weight ws. The angle which T makes with the horizontal will be denoted by θ. The equations of equilibrium for the concurrent force system are:

$$\Sigma F_x = T \cos \theta - H = 0, \quad \therefore \quad T \cos \theta = H \quad . \quad . \quad (1)$$

$$\Sigma F_y = T \sin \theta - ws = 0, \quad \therefore \quad T \sin \theta = ws \quad . \quad . \quad (2)$$

From (1) and (2) we have

$$\tan \theta = \frac{ws}{H} = \frac{s}{c} \quad \text{where} \quad \frac{H}{w} = c \text{ (a constant)}.$$

THE CATENARY

Hence
$$s = c \tan \theta \quad \text{or} \quad s = c\frac{dy}{dx} \quad \ldots \ldots \ldots \quad (3)$$

This equation is the intrinsic equation of the catenary. The cartesian equation will now be found. In any curve,
$$\frac{ds}{dy} = \sqrt{1 + \left(\frac{dx}{dy}\right)^2}.$$

Hence, from (3), the following equation is obtained:
$$\frac{ds}{dy} = \sqrt{1 + \frac{c^2}{s^2}} = \frac{\sqrt{s^2 + c^2}}{s}.$$

Therefore
$$dy = \frac{s\,ds}{\sqrt{s^2 + c^2}}.$$

Integrating,
$$y + A = \sqrt{s^2 + c^2}$$

where A is a constant of integration. If now the origin is transferred to O', where $OO' = c$, then $y = c$ when $s = 0$ and hence $A = 0$. The last equation, therefore, becomes
$$y = \sqrt{s^2 + c^2} \quad \ldots \ldots \ldots \quad (4)$$

Eliminating y from (3) and (4),
$$dx = \frac{c\,ds}{\sqrt{c^2 + s^2}}.$$

Integrating this equation,
$$x + B = c \log_e (s + \sqrt{s^2 + c^2}).$$

Since $s = 0$ when $x = 0$, $B = c \log_e c$, and hence the last equation becomes
$$x = c \log_e \frac{s + \sqrt{s^2 + c^2}}{c} = c \log_e \frac{y + s}{c} \quad \ldots \ldots \quad (5)$$

Equation (5) can also be written in the form,
$$\sqrt{s^2 + c^2} + s = ce^{x/c} \quad \ldots \ldots \ldots \quad (6)$$

By inverting each side of (6) and rationalizing the denominator of the left side, the following equation is obtained:
$$\sqrt{s^2 + c^2} - s = ce^{-x/c} \quad \ldots \ldots \quad (7)$$

Adding (6) and (7) and using (4),

$$y = \frac{c}{2}(e^{x/c} + e^{-x/c}) = c \cosh \frac{x}{c} \quad \ldots \quad (8)$$

This is the cartesian equation of the catenary. Subtracting (7) from (6), we have

$$s = \frac{c}{2}(e^{x/c} - e^{-x/c}) = c \sinh \frac{x}{c} \quad \ldots \quad (9)$$

Squaring and adding (1) and (2), we have

$$T^2 = H^2 + w^2 s^2 = w^2 c^2 + w^2 s^2 = w^2 y^2.$$

Hence

$$T = wy \quad \ldots \quad (10)$$

In summarizing, then, the following important properties of the catenary may be stated:

(1) The horizontal component of the stress at any point is constant and equal to wc.
(2) The vertical component of the stress at any point is equal to ws.
(3) The total stress T at any point is equal to wy.

In engineering problems which involve the catenary we are concerned particularly with the tension at the points of support, since at these points the tension is a maximum. Hence, in the above formula, T will be regarded as the tension at the points of support and the values of x, y, and s will be regarded as the values of the variables at these points. Therefore, if the length of the cable be denoted by l, the span by a, and the sag by f, then the values of x, y, and s in the above equations become $a/2$, $f + c$, and $l/2$, respectively.

The formulas of Art. 50 are generally used when the sag is small, since they are much easier to apply and the results obtained are sufficiently accurate for practical purposes. When the sag is large compared with the span, however, the above formulas should be used.

Since the relations between the quantities as expressed by the above equations are complicated, many of the problems which involve the catenary can be solved only by trial.

ILLUSTRATIVE PROBLEM

Problem 223. A cable weighing 4 lb. per ft. is stretched between two points in the same horizontal plane. The length of the cable is 600 ft. and the tension at the points of support is 2000 lb. Find the sag and also the distance between the points of support.

NON-COPLANAR, CONCURRENT, NON-PARALLEL FORCES

Solution.—From equation (10)

$$y = \frac{T}{w} = \frac{2000}{4} = 500 \text{ ft.}$$

From equation (4)

$$c = \sqrt{y^2 - s^2} = \sqrt{(500)^2 - (300)^2} = 400 \text{ ft.}$$

Hence

$$f = y - c = 500 - 400 = 100 \text{ ft.}$$

From equation (5)

$$x = c \log_e \frac{\sqrt{s^2 + c^2} + s}{c} = 400 \log_e \frac{\sqrt{(300)^2 + (400)^2} + 300}{400}$$

$$= 277.2 \text{ ft.}$$

Hence

$$a = 2x = 554.4 \text{ ft.}$$

PROBLEMS

224. A cable 100 ft. long is suspended between two points which are in the same horizontal plane and 80 ft. apart. What is the sag at the mid-point of the cable?
Ans. $f = 26.54$ ft.

225. A cable weighing 2 lb. per ft. is stretched between two points in the same horizontal plane which are 150 ft. apart. If the sag is 5 ft. what is the length of the cable and the tension at the points of support? *Ans.* $l = 150.44$ ft.; $T = 1130$ lb.

§ 7. Non-coplanar, Concurrent, Non-parallel Forces

52. Equations of Equilibrium.—A non-coplanar, concurrent, non-parallel system of forces is in equilibrium if the algebraic sums of the components of the forces along any three non-coplanar lines through the point of concurrence of the forces are equal to zero. As a matter of convenience the three lines will be taken as a set of rectangular axes through the point of concurrence, in which case the equations of equilibrium may be written:

$$\Sigma F_x = 0, \quad \Sigma F_y = 0, \quad \Sigma F_z = 0.$$

Proof.—If a concurrent system of forces in space is not in equilibrium, the resultant of the system is a force (Art. 32). If the forces of the system satisfy the equation $\Sigma F_x = 0$, the resultant, if there be one, must lie in the yz-plane. In order to satisfy the equation $\Sigma F_y = 0$, the resultant must lie in the xz-plane, and in order to satisfy the equation $\Sigma F_z = 0$, the resultant must lie in the xy-plane. It is impossible for a force to lie in the three planes simultaneously, and hence, if the forces of the system satisfy the above equations, the resultant cannot be a force and, therefore, the system must be in equilibrium.

ILLUSTRATIVE PROBLEM

Problem 226. The wall bracket (Fig. 168) is composed of two flexible cables, AC and BC, and a stiff rod DC, which is pin-connected at D and C. The points A, B, and C lie in a horizontal plane and A, B, and D lie in a vertical plane, D being vertically beneath E, the mid-point of AB. Find the stresses in the three members due to the 100-lb. load shown.

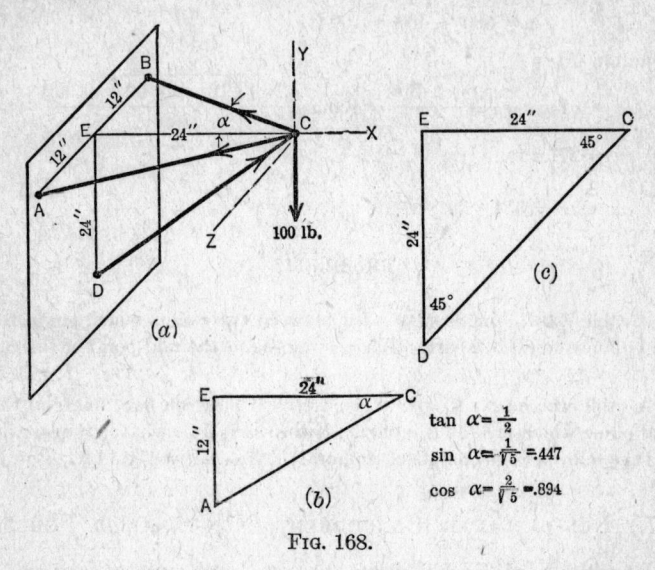

FIG. 168.

Solution.—The pin C is in equilibrium under the action of the 100-lb. load and the reactions of the three members, these reactions being equal to the stresses in the corresponding members. The forces acting on the pin at C are shown in Fig. 168a. By selecting axes as indicated and applying the equations of equilibrium, the following equations are obtained:

$$\Sigma F_y = DC \cos 45° - 100 = 0, \qquad \therefore DC = 141.4 \text{ lb.}$$

$$\Sigma F_z = AC \sin \alpha - BC \sin \alpha = 0, \qquad \therefore AC = BC.$$

$$\Sigma F_x = DC \cos 45° - AC \cos \alpha - BC \cos \alpha = 0,$$

$$\therefore DC \cos 45° = 2AC \cos \alpha,$$

and

$$BC = AC = \frac{DC \cos 45°}{2 \cos \alpha} = \frac{141.4 \times 0.707}{2 \times 0.894} = 55.9 \text{ lb.}$$

Hence there is a compressive stress of 141.4 lb. in the rod DC and a tensile stress of 55.9 lb. in each of the cables BC and AC.

PROBLEMS

227. In Fig. 169, AC and AB are flexible cables attached to pins at points B and C in the xy-plane and AE is a stiff pole connected to a fixed support at E by a smooth pin. Find the stresses in AB, AC, and AE due to the 1000-lb. load shown.

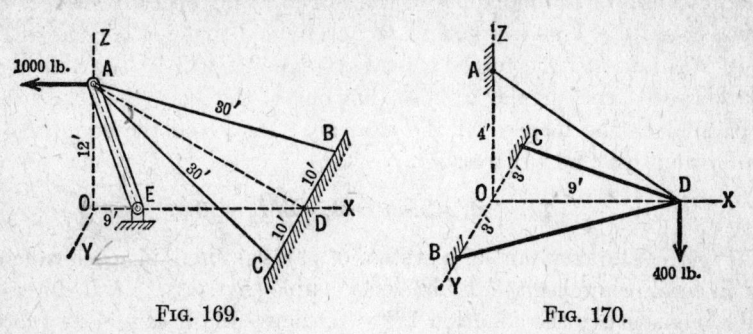

Fig. 169.

Fig. 170.

228. In Fig. 170, AD is a flexible cable and BD and CD are stiff members. The members are attached to a smooth pin at D and to the wall at A, B, and C by smooth pins. Find the stresses in AD, BD, and CD due to the 400-lb. load shown.

Ans. $AD = 985$ lb.; $BD = CD = 475$ lb.

229. Figure 171 represents a stiff-leg derrick. The member AC lies in the xz-plane and the members BD and BE lie in vertical planes making angles of 45° with the xz-plane. The weight carried is such as to produce a tensile stress of 5000 lb. in the member BC. Find the stresses in the members AC, BD, and BE.

Ans. $AC = 5670$ lb.; $BE = BD = 4910$ lb.

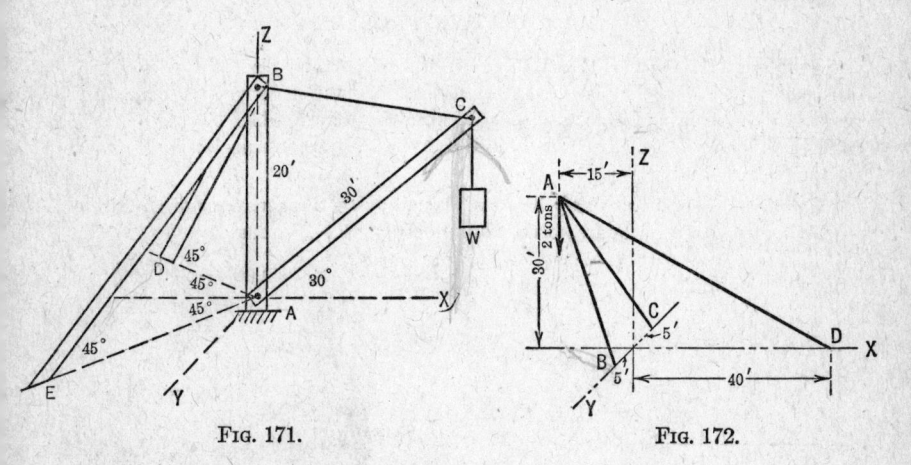

Fig. 171.

Fig. 172.

230. Find the stresses in the legs AB and AC of the shear-legs derrick shown in Fig. 172 and also the tension in the guy AD. Neglect the weights of the members.

§ 8. Non-coplanar, Non-concurrent, Parallel Forces

53. Equations of Equilibrium.—A system of parallel forces in space is in equilibrium if the algebraic sum of the forces is zero and if the algebraic sum of the moments of the forces with respect to each of the two non-parallel lines is equal to zero, provided that neither one of the lines is parallel to the forces of the system. It will be convenient to select a set of rectangular axes so that one of the axes (the z-axis, say) is parallel to the forces. If the axes are so selected the equations of equilibrium may be written:

$$\Sigma F = 0, \quad \Sigma M_x = 0, \quad \Sigma M_y = 0.$$

Proof.—The resultant of a system of parallel forces in space which is not in equilibrium is either a force or a couple (Art. 33). If the forces of the system satisfy the equation $\Sigma F = 0$, the resultant cannot be a force. If the resultant is a couple it must lie in a plane parallel to the xz-plane in order that the forces shall satisfy the equation $\Sigma M_x = 0$, and in order that the forces shall satisfy the equation $\Sigma M_y = 0$ the resultant must lie in a plane parallel to the yz-plane. A plane, however, cannot be parallel to both the xz- and yz-planes, and hence, if the two moment equations are satisfied, the resultant cannot be a couple. Therefore, if the forces of the system satisfy the three above equations, the force system is in equilibrium.

ILLUSTRATIVE PROBLEM

Problem 231.—In Fig. 173, ABC represents a triangular plate, the sides of which are each 2 ft. in length. It is held in a horizontal position by vertical cords at the vertices. A weight of 200 lb. is suspended from the point E which lies on the median AD, the distance DE being 6 in. Find the stresses in the cords neglecting the weight of the plate.

Solution.—The stresses may be found by applying the equations of equilibrium to the forces shown in the free-body diagram of the plate. Thus

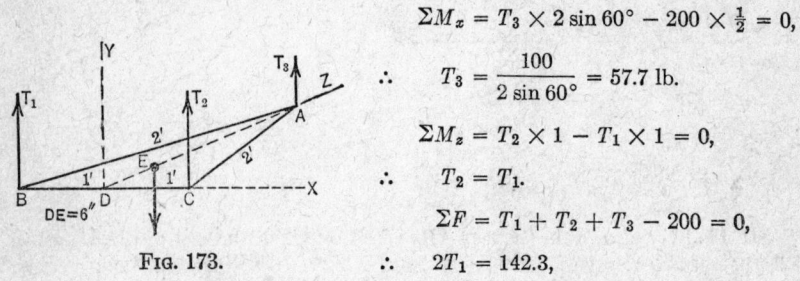

$$\Sigma M_x = T_3 \times 2 \sin 60° - 200 \times \tfrac{1}{2} = 0,$$

$$\therefore T_3 = \frac{100}{2 \sin 60°} = 57.7 \text{ lb.}$$

$$\Sigma M_z = T_2 \times 1 - T_1 \times 1 = 0,$$

$$\therefore T_2 = T_1.$$

$$\Sigma F = T_1 + T_2 + T_3 - 200 = 0,$$

$$\therefore 2T_1 = 142.3,$$

and

$$T_1 = T_2 = 71.15 \text{ lb.}$$

Fig. 173.

PROBLEMS

232. In Fig. 174, the side of each square is 1 ft. long. If the four parallel forces shown are in equilibrium, what are the magnitudes of P_1, P_2, and P_3?

233. The system of non-coplanar parallel forces shown in Fig. 175 is in equilibrium. The side of each square is 1 ft. Find the magnitudes of P_1, P_2, and P_3.
Ans. $P_1 = 300$ lb.; $P_2 = 233$ lb.; $P_3 = 533$ lb.

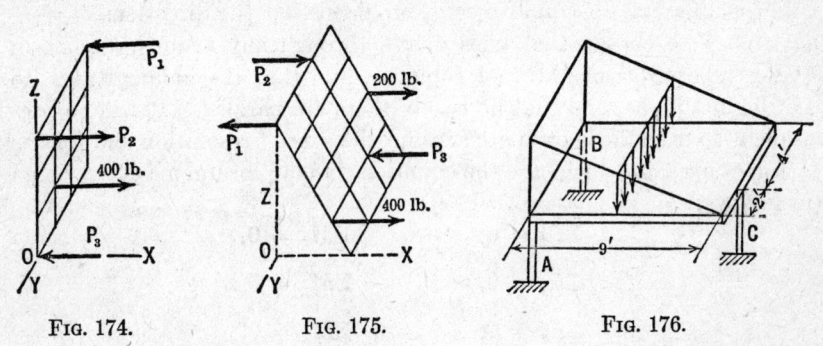

FIG. 174.   FIG. 175.   FIG. 176.

234. A horizontal plate shown in Fig. 176 rests on three posts A, B, and C. Material of uniform density is piled on the plate at a depth increasing uniformly from zero at the right edge of the plate to a maximum at the left edge. If the total weight of the material is 1000 lb., find the pressures of A, B, and C on the plate due to the weight of the material. As will be shown later, the resultant weight of the material acts at a distance of $\frac{2}{3}$ the width of the plate from the edge where the depth of the material is zero.

235. A square table weighing 50 lb. stands on four legs at the mid-points of the sides. Find the greatest weight that can be placed on one corner of the table without causing it to overturn. *Ans.* $W = 50$ lb.

236. The crank-pin pressures, P_1 and P_2, on the crank shaft shown in Fig. 177 are 6000 lb. and 4800 lb., respectively. Find the bearing reactions R_1 and R_2 (Fig. 177b) and the resisting moment Qq required for equilibrium of the shaft.

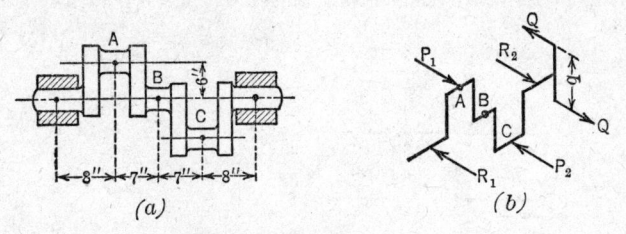

FIG. 177.

237. A uniform circular plate weighing 200 lb. is supported in a horizontal position at three points on its circumference. Find the reactions at the supports if the points divide the circumference into arcs of 90°, 135°, and 135°.
Ans. $R_1 = 82.8$ lb.; $R_2 = R_3 = 58.6$ lb.

§ 9. Non-coplanar, Non-concurrent, Non-parallel Forces

54. Equations of Equilibrium.—A system of non-coplanar, non-concurrent, non-parallel forces is in equilibrium if the algebraic sum of the components of the forces in each of three directions is equal to zero and if the algebraic sum of the moments of the forces with respect to each of three axes is equal to zero, provided that the directions of resolution are so chosen that lines drawn through any arbitrary point in these three directions are not coplanar, and that the moment axes do not lie in a plane, and that no two of them are parallel. It will be convenient to take the coordinate axes for the axes of resolution and for the moment axes, in which case the equations of equilibrium may be written as follows:

$$\Sigma F_x = 0, \qquad \Sigma M_x = 0,$$
$$\Sigma F_y = 0, \qquad \Sigma M_y = 0,$$
$$\Sigma F_z = 0, \qquad \Sigma M_z = 0.$$

Proof.—The resultant of a non-concurrent, non-parallel system of forces in space is, in general, a force and a couple (Art. 36). If the forces of the system satisfy the first three equations, the resultant force must vanish, and if the last three equations are satisfied the couple must vanish. If, therefore, the forces of the system satisfy the six equations the force system is in equilibrium.

ILLUSTRATIVE PROBLEM

Problem 238.—Figure 178 represents a windlass used in lifting weights. The end bearings will be regarded as smooth, and the force P applied to the crank will be assumed to be perpendicular to the axis of the cylinder and also perpendicular to the crank. Find the value of P required to hold the 450-lb. weight, and also find the reactions at the bearings, assuming that the crank is inclined 30° to the vertical.

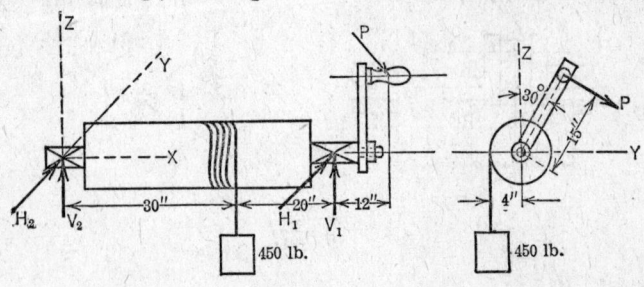

Fig. 178.

Solution.—The coordinate axes will be taken as shown in the figure. There are four forces acting on the windlass, namely, the weight of 450 lb., the force P, and the reactions at the bearings. Since the bearing reactions are unknown in direction as well as in magnitude it will be convenient to resolve them into horizontal and vertical components; H_1, V_1 and H_2, V_2, as indicated in the figure. Applying the equations of equilibrium to the system of forces acting on the windlass we have:

$$\Sigma F_y = P \cos 30° + H_1 + H_2 = 0 \quad \ldots \ldots \ldots \quad (1)$$

$$\Sigma F_z = V_1 + V_2 - P \sin 30° - 450 = 0 \quad \ldots \ldots \quad (2)$$

$$\Sigma M_x = 15P - 450 \times 4 = 0 \quad \ldots \ldots \ldots \quad (3)$$

$$\Sigma M_y = P \sin 30° \times 62 + 450 \times 30 - 50V_1 = 0 \quad \ldots \ldots \quad (4)$$

$$\Sigma M_z = 50H_1 + P \cos 30° \times 62 = 0. \quad \ldots \ldots \ldots \quad (5)$$

The solution of these equations gives the following values:

$P = 120$ lb., $H_1 = -128.8$ lb., $V_1 = 344.4$ lb., $H_2 = 24.92$ lb., $V_2 = 165.6$ lb.

PROBLEMS

239. In Fig. 179 is shown a vertical shaft AD that weighs 100 lb. and is supported by a smooth step bearing at D and a smooth journal bearing at B. Pulleys having a diameter of 1 ft. and a weight of 40 lb. each are keyed to the shaft at A and C. To the pulley at A are applied two forces parallel to the x-axis and to the pulley at C are applied two forces parallel to the y-axis as shown. If the shaft is in equilibrium, find the magnitudes of P and the x-, y-, and z-components of the bearing reactions at B and D.

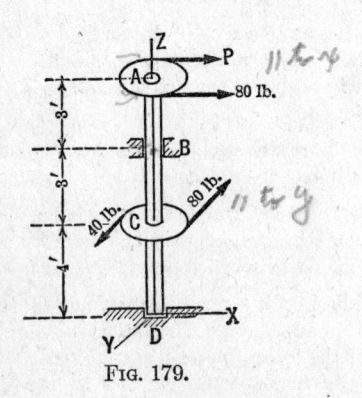

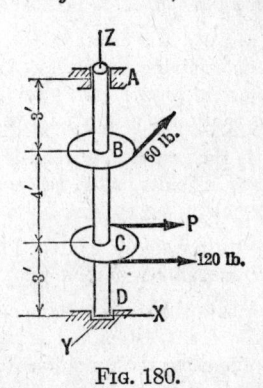

Ans. $P = 200$ lb.; $B_x = -400$ lb.; $B_y = 22.9$ lb.; $B_z = 0$; $D_x = 120$ lb.; $D_y = 17.1$ lb.; $D_z = 180$ lb.

FIG. 179.

FIG. 180.

240. In Fig. 180 is shown a vertical shaft AD that weighs 80 lb. and is supported by a smooth step bearing at D and a smooth journal bearing at A. A pulley weighing 10 lb. and having a diameter of 1 ft. is keyed to the shaft at B. To this pulley a force of 60 lb. is applied parallel to the y-axis. A pulley weighing 40 lb. and having a diameter of 1 ft. is keyed to the shaft at C. To this pulley two forces P and 120 lb. are applied parallel to the x-axis. If the shaft is in equilibrium, find the magnitudes P and the x-, y-, and z-components of the bearing reactions at D and A.

REVIEW QUESTIONS AND PROBLEMS

241. Is the following statement correct? A force system is in equilibrium when the forces of the system have no resultant.

242. If a coplanar, non-concurrent force system is in equilibrium, what two graphical conditions must the forces satisfy? Explain.

243. Prove that, if the forces of a coplanar, parallel system satisfy the equations $\Sigma M_A = 0$ and $\Sigma M_B = 0$, the forces must be in equilibrium; make clear the restriction on the choice of the points A and B.

244. What is meant by a statically indeterminate force system?

245. What is wrong with the following statement? A free-body diagram is a diagram showing the body and some (but not all) of the forces that the body exerts on other bodies.

246. Given the following equations of equilibrium for a coplanar, non-concurrent, non-parallel force system:

$$\Sigma F_x = 0, \quad \Sigma M_A = 0, \quad \Sigma M_B = 0.$$

(a) What are the restrictions placed on the selection of the points A and B? (b) What conclusion can be drawn regarding the resultant of the given force system if the forces of the system satisfy the first of these equations? (c) What conclusions can be drawn regarding the resultant if the forces satisfy the first two equations? (d) If they satisfy all three equations?

247. What is the essential difference between two-force members and members that are acted on by more than two forces? Which of these two classes of members occurs in a pin-connected pin-loaded truss?

248. Correct the errors in the following statement: If the method of joints is used in determining the stresses in members of a pin-connected, pin-loaded truss, non-concurrent force systems are involved and hence the unknown stresses in three members that meet at any joint can be found.

249. Is the graphical method of determining stresses in trusses (Art. 48) based on the method of joints or the method of sections?

250. Is the following statement correct? In determining stresses in trusses algebraically by the method of sections, each section used may cut more than three members but cannot cut more than three members in which the stresses are unknown.

251. Write the six equations of equilibrium for a non-coplanar, non-concurrent, non-parallel force system and show what equations of equilibrium are obtained from these by imposing the conditions (a) that the forces are coplanar; (b) that they are non-coplanar but parallel; (c) that they are non-coplanar but concurrent; (d) that they are coplanar and parallel.

252. In Fig. 181, A and B are smooth cylinders weighing 100 lb. each. Find the pressure, R, of one cylinder on the other and the pressures of the vertical walls on the cylinders at points C and D.   *Ans.* $R = 115.5$ lb.; $C = D = 57.7$ lb.

253. In Fig. 182, D is a cylinder weighing 100 lb. Find the reaction of the pin at B on the member AB. Assume all surfaces smooth and neglect the weights of AB and BC.   *Ans.* $B = 25$ lb.

REVIEW QUESTIONS AND PROBLEMS   119

254. In the crane shown in Fig. 183, assume that the weights of *AD* and *CH* are negligible and that the pin at *C* is smooth. Find the reaction of the pin at *C* on the member *CH* and find also the stress in the rod *BE*.

Ans. *C* = 4070 lb.; *BE* = 3555 lb.

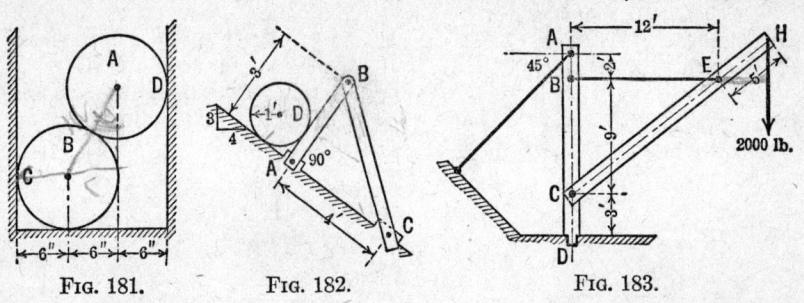

Fig. 181.   Fig. 182.   Fig. 183.

255. Find, by the method of sections, the stresses in the members *CE*, *DE*, and *DF* of the Howe truss shown in Fig. 184.

Ans. *CE* = −2000 lb.; *DE* = −2500 lb.; *DF* = 4000 lb.

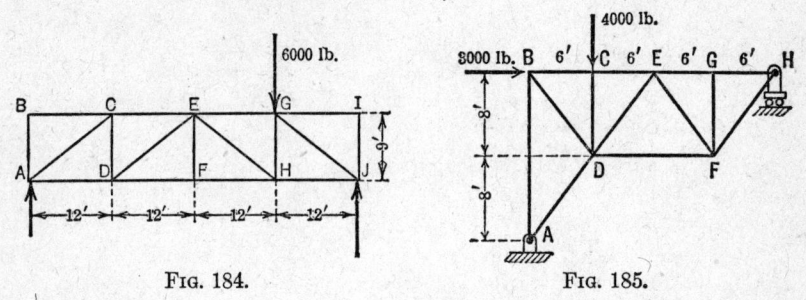

Fig. 184.   Fig. 185.

256. In Fig. 185 is shown a pin-connected, pin-loaded truss. Find the stresses in *GH* and *FH* due to the loads shown, using the method of joints. Find the stresses in *CE*, *DE*, and *DF* by the method of sections.

Ans. *GH* = −2250 lb.; *FH* = 3750 lb.; *CE* = −6750 lb.; *DE* = 3750 lb.; *DF* = 4500 lb.

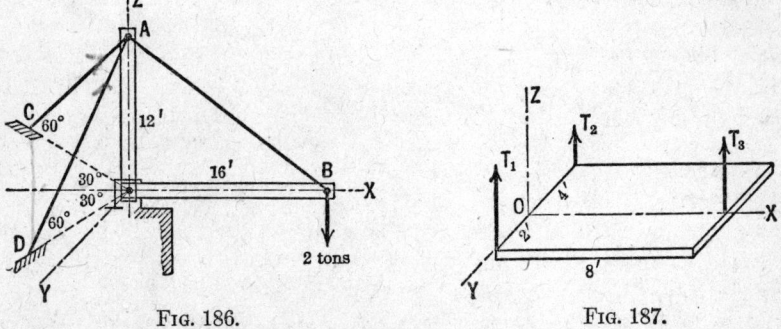

Fig. 186.   Fig. 187.

257. Find the stresses in all members of the truss shown in Fig. 184 by the graphical method.

120 EQUILIBRIUM OF FORCE SYSTEMS

258. In the derrick shown in Fig. 186, find the stresses in the flexible cables AB, AC, and AD due to the 2-ton load. The points C and D where the cables are attached lie in the xy-plane.   *Ans.* $AB = 6665$ lb.; $AC = AD = 6160$ lb.

259. The plate shown in Fig. 187 lies in a horizontal plane and is suspended by three flexible vertical cables which exert pulls T_1, T_2, and T_3 on the plate as shown. If the weight of the plate is 100 lb. per sq. ft. of area, find the stresses in the cables.
Ans. $T_1 = 800$ lb.; $T_2 = 1600$ lb.; $T_3 = 2400$ lb.

CHAPTER IV

FRICTION

55. Friction Defined.—If two bodies slide or tend to slide on each other, the resisting force tangent to the surface of contact which one body offers to the other is defined as *friction*.

Friction is of great importance in engineering practice. Since it always opposes motion, it is an undesirable and expensive factor in the operation of many machines and in such cases is reduced as much as practicable by means of lubricants. In other machines it becomes a very desirable and useful element, as in various forms of brakes, friction drives, etc. In fact, many of our normal physical activities, such as walking, would be impossible without the aid of friction.

If the resistance between two bodies prevents motion of one body relative to the other, the resistance is called *static friction*; the frictional resistance between two bodies which move relative to each other is called *kinetic friction*. If the friction is static, the amount of friction developed is just sufficient to maintain equilibrium with the other forces acting on the body. That is, static friction is an adjustable force, the magnitude of which is determined from the equations of equilibrium for all the forces which act on the body. Thus, let Fig. 188 represent a body in equilibrium on a rough horizontal plane under the action of a horizontal force P, which tends to move

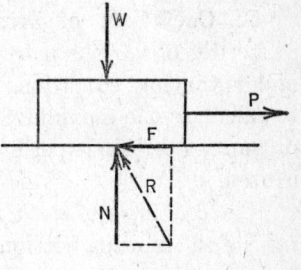

FIG. 188.

the body, the reaction, R, of the plane, and the weight, W, of the body. Let the reaction R be resolved into two components F and N parallel and perpendicular, respectively, to the plane. The component F along, or tangent to, the plane is the frictional force as defined above. The component N is called the *normal pressure* and R is called the *total reaction*. Since the body is in equilibrium, the equation of equilibrium $\Sigma F_x = 0$ must be satisfied, and hence F is equal to P; the equation $\Sigma F_y = 0$ must also be satisfied, and hence $N = W$. If the force P is gradually increased, F must increase in the same ratio in order to maintain a condition of equilibrium. There is a definite limit, however, to the amount of frictional resistance that can be developed, and when the value of P exceeds this limiting value motion will ensue. The limiting or maximum value of the frictional force is called *limiting friction* and is denoted by F'. Its value depends on the normal pressure and on the roughness of the surfaces of contact.

In Fig. 188 it was seen that the frictional force F was equal to the applied force P and that the normal pressure N was equal to W, the weight of the body. However, the student should not make the mistake of assuming that in all cases in which one body tends to slide over another F is equal to P or to the component of P parallel to the plane, and that N is equal to W; it is important to note that in all cases both the static friction and the normal pressure are determined by the conditions of equilibrium for *all* the forces acting on the body. Consider, for example, the body shown in Fig. 189 and assume that motion of the body is impending up the plane under the influence of the applied force P and the other forces acting on the body. By applying the equations of equilibrium, $\Sigma F_x = 0$ and $\Sigma F_y = 0$, it is seen that $F' = P \cos \theta - W \sin \alpha$ and $N = W \cos \alpha - P \sin \theta$.

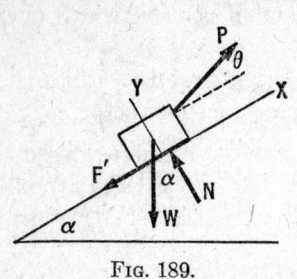

Fig. 189.

56. Coefficient of Friction.—In order to compare the frictional properties of various pairs of materials or of the same pair of materials under varying conditions of their surfaces of contact, and in order to calculate the maximum frictional force corresponding to any normal pressure, a certain experimental constant, called the *coefficient of friction*, is used.

The *coefficient of static friction* for any two surfaces is defined as the ratio of the limiting friction to the corresponding normal pressure. Thus, if the coefficient of static friction is denoted by μ, it may be expressed as follows:

$$\mu = \frac{F'}{N} \quad \text{or} \quad F' = \mu N.$$

It is important to note that F' in the above equation is the maximum friction which the surfaces can develop, that is, the friction corresponding to impending motion. Thus the maximum frictional force which any two surfaces can develop is equal to μN.

The value of μ must be determined experimentally, and, as stated above, it is a constant for any two materials for a definite condition of the surfaces of contact. It varies considerably, however, for different conditions of the surfaces, and it varies widely for different pairs of materials, as is shown in the following table, which gives the values of the coefficient of friction for dry surfaces as determined by Morin and others.

COEFFICIENT OF STATIC FRICTION

Wood on wood	0.25 to 0.50
Metal on wood	.20 to .60
Metal on metal	.15 to .30
Metal on leather	.30 to .60
Wood on leather	.25 to .50
Stone on stone	.40 to .65
Metal on stone	.30 to .70
Earth on earth	.25 to 1.00

If two surfaces move relative to each other, the ratio of the friction developed to the corresponding normal pressure is defined as the *coefficient of kinetic friction*. The value of the coefficient of kinetic friction for two surfaces is influenced by more factors than is the value of the coefficient of static friction. A brief discussion of the influencing factors is given in Art. 58. For values of the coefficient of kinetic friction for various conditions of rubbing surfaces the reader is referred to Goodman's "Mechanics Applied to Engineering."

57. Angle of Friction.—The *angle of static friction* for two surfaces is defined as the angle between the directions of the total reaction and the normal pressure *when motion is impending*. Thus in Fig. 190, if the force P is just large enough to develop the limiting friction, the angle which R, the reaction of the plane on the body, makes with the normal pressure, N, is the angle of static friction and is denoted by ϕ.

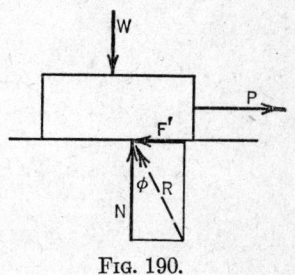

Fig. 190.

Since the components of R, parallel and perpendicular respectively to the plane, are F' and N, it is evident from the figure that $\tan \phi = \dfrac{F'}{N}$.

But since the ratio $\dfrac{F'}{N}$ is defined as the coefficient of static friction, μ, the following important relation may be written:

$$\mu = \tan \phi,$$

that is, *the coefficient of static friction is equal to the tangent of the angle of static friction.*

If the two surfaces move relative to each other, then the angle between the total reaction and the normal pressure is called the *angle of kinetic friction*. Its value is somewhat less than the angle of static friction, since the frictional force after motion ensues becomes less than the limiting friction. The relation $\mu = \tan \phi$ also holds for kinetic friction, the value of μ for kinetic friction being somewhat less than for static friction. The angle of friction (for both static and kinetic friction) is convenient to use particularly in the solution of problems by graphical methods.

Angle of Repose.—If a body rests on an inclined plane, as shown in Fig. 191, and is acted on by no forces except its weight and the reaction of the plane, and if α, the angle of inclination of the plane to the horizontal, is such that motion of the body impends down the plane, the angle α is defined as the *angle of repose*.

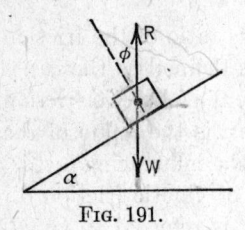

Since the body is in equilibrium under the action of the two forces R, the reaction of the plane, and W, the weight of the body, these forces must be equal, opposite, and collinear. Hence the reaction R is vertical. Furthermore, the angle which R makes with the normal to the plane is ϕ, the angle of friction. It is evident from the figure that the angles α and ϕ are equal. The angle of repose for two surfaces can be found easily by experiment, after which the coefficient of friction for the surfaces may be found from the relation $\mu = \tan \phi = \tan \alpha$.

Fig. 191.

58. The Laws of Friction.—One of the earliest contributions to our knowledge of the laws of friction was made by Coulomb, who published, in 1781, the results of experiments on the friction of plane dry surfaces. Later experiments by Morin confirmed, in the main, the results obtained by Coulomb. The results of the experiments of Morin on dry surfaces, published in 1831, may be stated as follows:

1. The friction between two bodies when motion is impending (limiting friction) is proportional to the normal pressure; that is, the coefficient of friction is independent of the normal pressure.

2. The coefficient of static friction is independent of the area of contact.

3. The coefficient of kinetic friction is less than the coefficient of static friction and is independent of the relative velocity of the rubbing surfaces.

Although these laws are probably correct for the conditions under which the tests were made, they must be modified in order to apply to friction which is developed under conditions quite different from those found in the experiments. The pressures used in the experiments of Morin varied from ¾ lb. per sq. in. to 100 lb. per sq. in. It has been found in later experiments that for pressures less than ¾ lb. per sq. in. the value of the coefficient of static friction increases somewhat. For very great pressures the coefficient also increases. The highest velocity used in Morin's experiments was 10 ft. per sec. For greater velocities than this it has been found in later experiments that the coefficient of kinetic friction decreases with the velocity. The experiments of Jenkin show that for extremely low velocities (the lowest velocity measured was 0.0002 ft. per sec.) there is an increase in the coefficient of kinetic friction. These experiments indicate that the value of the coefficient of kinetic friction gradually increases as the velocity decreases and passes without discontinuity into that of static friction.

From experiments made by Tower, Goodman, Thurston, and others, on lubricated surfaces, it has been found that the laws of friction for lubricated surfaces are almost the reverse of those stated for dry surfaces. For example, it is found that the friction of two surfaces is almost independent of the nature of the surfaces and of the normal pressure so long as there is a film of lubricant between the surfaces. Again, for lubricated surfaces, it is found that the friction is materially affected by the temperature, which is not true in the case of dry surfaces.

59. Types of Problems Involving Frictional Forces.—In the following problems there are two general types: (1) In one type a body is in equilibrium under the action of a force system one (or more) of which is a frictional force, but motion of the body is impending; in other words, the frictional force developed is the limiting friction and can therefore be expressed as $F' = \mu N$. It is important to note that such a problem is a problem in equilibrium and is no different from those treated in the preceding chapter, for, the equations of equilibrium apply to *all* the forces acting on the body (including friction forces and the normal pressures). But in addition to the relationship that must exist among *all* the forces as expressed in the equations of equilibrium there is a special relationship between two of the forces that act on the body, namely, $F' = \mu N$. This equation then is used together with the equations of equilibrium to effect a solution of some of the unknown forces. If more than one pair of rubbing surfaces are involved there will, of course, be more than one equation of the type $F' = \mu N$.

(2) In the other type of problem a body is acted on by a force system one (or more) of which is a frictional force but it is not known whether the body is in equilibrium under the action of the applied forces because it is not known whether the frictional force (or forces) required

for equilibrium can be developed on the surfaces of contact. One method of attacking such a problem is first to assume the body to be in equilibrium and then find the frictional force and corresponding normal pressure required (with the other forces) to hold the body in equilibrium by applying the equations of equilibrium. This magnitude of the frictional force is then compared to the value of the limiting friction, $F' = \mu N$, and if it is less than F' the body will be in equilibrium and the frictional force will have the value found from the equilibrium equations, but if it is greater than F' the body will not be in equilibrium, and hence the problem is one of kinetics instead of statics.

ILLUSTRATIVE PROBLEMS

Problem 260.—A lift shown in Fig. 192 slides on a vertical shaft having a square cross-section 2 in. on a side. Find the greatest distance, x, from the edge of the shaft at which a load W can be placed and still cause the lift to slide on the shaft. Neglect the weight of the lift and use 0.2 for the coefficient of friction.

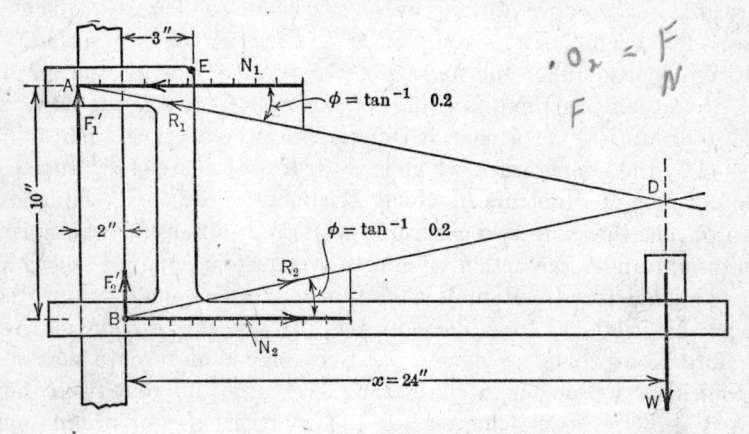

Fig. 192.

Graphical Solution.—Since motion impends, the angle between the reaction R_1 and the normal pressure N_1 of the shaft at A is equal to the angle of friction; that is, the tangent of the angle is equal to 0.2. Hence, by laying off ten spaces along the normal and two spaces perpendicular to the normal, as shown in Fig. 192, the action line of R_1 is determined. In a similar manner the action line of R_2 is found. Now the three forces R_1, R_2 and W must be concurrent in order to be in equilibrium (Art. 42) and hence, W must pass through the intersection of R_1 and R_2. Now the intersection of these two forces can never be nearer to the shaft than the point D, since the angle ϕ cannot be greater than $\tan^{-1} 0.2$. The distance, x, of D from the shaft is found by measurement to be 24 in.

Algebraic Solution.—The five forces, F'_1, N_1, F'_2, N_2, and W which hold the lift in equilibrium as shown in the free-body diagram (Fig. 192) form a coplanar, non-concurrent force system and hence there are three equations of equilibrium as follows:

$$\Sigma F_x = N_2 - N_1 = 0. \quad \ldots \ldots \ldots \ldots \ldots (1)$$

$$\Sigma F_y = -W + 0.2N_1 + 0.2N_2 = 0. \quad \ldots \ldots \ldots (2)$$

$$\Sigma M_B = -Wx + 10N_1 - 2 \times 0.2N_1 = 0, \quad \ldots \ldots (3)$$

in which

$$0.2N_1 = F'_1 \text{ and } 0.2N_2 = F'_2.$$

From (1) and (2) we have

$$W = 0.4N_1 = 0.4N_2.$$

By substituting this value of W in (3) the equation obtained is

$$-0.4N_1 \cdot x + 10N_1 - 0.4N_1 = 0,$$

whence

$$x = 24 \text{ in.}$$

Problem 261. A body weighing 80 lb. rests on a plane inclined 20° to the horizontal as shown in Fig. 193(a). The coefficient of friction between the body and plane is 0.30. If a horizontal force P of 20 lb. is applied to the body will it slide? If so, will it slide up or down the plane? If the body does not slide what is the magnitude and sense of the frictional force developed?

Solution.—First it will be assumed that the body is in equilibrium and that the frictional force F acts downward along the plane; in other words it is assumed that the body would slide up the plane if no frictional force existed. The free-body diagram would then be as shown in Fig. 193(a). Using one of the equations of equilibrium we have

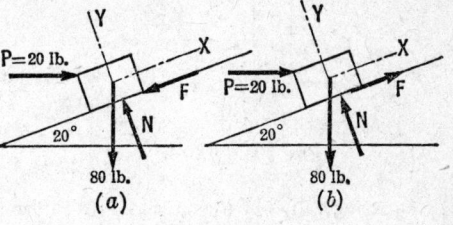

FIG. 193.

$$\Sigma F_x = 20 \cos 20° - 80 \sin 20° - F = 0$$

$$\therefore F = 20 \times 0.940 - 80 \times 0.342 = -8.56 \text{ lb.}$$

Since the sign of F is negative, or in other words, since the x-component of the weight of the body is greater than the x-component of P, the direction of F is up instead of down the plane. Hence if the body slides, it must slide down the plane. If it does not slide down it must be held in equilibrium by the forces shown in Fig. 193(b).

Applying the equations of equilibrium to this force system, we have

$$\Sigma F_x = F + 20 \times 0.940 - 80 \times 0.342 = 0 \qquad \therefore F = +8.56 \text{ lb.}$$
$$\Sigma F_y = N - 20 \times 0.342 - 80 \times 0.940 = 0 \qquad \therefore N = 82.04 \text{ lb.}$$

The maximum value that F can have is

$$F' = \mu N = 0.3 \times 82.04 = 24.6 \text{ lb.}$$

and since a frictional force of only 8.56 lb. is needed to hold the body in equilibrium, the body will *not* slide and the frictional force developed is 8.56 lb. directed up the plane.

128   FRICTION

Problem 262.—Figure 194(a) represents a cotter joint. The angle α equals 15° and the angle of friction for all rubbing surfaces is 12°. What is the value of the force P required to overcome the 1000-lb. force applied on part A?

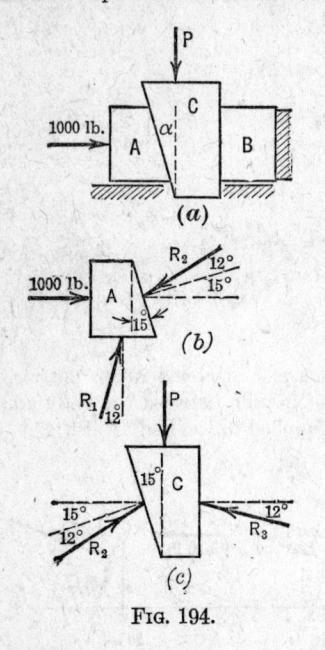

Solution.—Free-body diagrams of the block A and the cotter pin C are shown in Fig. 194(b) and 194(c), respectively. The equations of equilibrium for the two blocks may be written as follows:

For A

$$\Sigma F_x = 1000 + R_1 \sin 12° - R_2 \cos 27° = 0, \quad (1)$$

$$\Sigma F_y = R_1 \cos 12° - R_2 \sin 27° = 0. \quad (2)$$

For C

$$\Sigma F_x = R_2 \cos 27° - R_3 \cos 12° = 0, \quad (3)$$

$$\Sigma F_y = R_2 \sin 27° + R_3 \sin 12° - P = 0. \quad (4)$$

By eliminating R_1 from (1) and (2), the equation obtained is,

$$R_2 = \frac{1000 \cos 12°}{\cos 39°}. \quad (5)$$

By eliminating R_3 from (3) and (4) the following equation is obtained:

Fig. 194.

$$R_2 = \frac{P \cos 12°}{\sin 39°}. \quad (6)$$

By equating values of R_2 in (5) and (6) the value of P may be found. Thus

$$\frac{P \cos 12°}{\sin 39°} = \frac{1000 \cos 12°}{\cos 39°}.$$

Therefore

$$P = 1000 \tan 39° = 810 \text{ lb.}$$

Problem 263.—In Fig. 195 assume that W and α are known; assume also that the coefficient of friction μ (and hence also the angle of friction ϕ) is known. Find, in terms of θ and the known quantities, the value of P that will make motion impend up the plane. Show also that P will be a minimum when $\theta = \phi$, and find the minimum value of P.

Solution.—The body is in equilibrium and hence the equations of equilibrium may be applied to the system of forces acting on it. In addition to the required force P, the forces acting on the body are the weight, W, of the body, and the reaction of the plane. The latter force will be resolved into components N, perpendicular to the plane, and F' (equal to μN), parallel to the plane, as shown in the free-

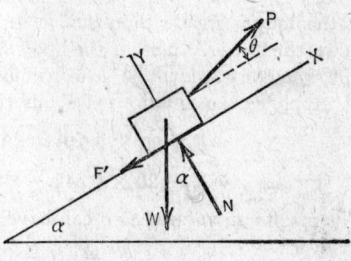

Fig. 195.

body diagram. If the x-axis be taken parallel to the plane and the y-axis perpendicular to the plane, the equations of equilibrium may be written as follows:

$$\Sigma F_x = P \cos \theta - \mu N - W \sin \alpha = 0,$$
$$\Sigma F_y = N + P \sin \theta - W \cos \alpha = 0.$$

Eliminating N from the two equations we have:

$$P = \frac{W(\sin \alpha + \mu \cos \alpha)}{\cos \theta + \mu \sin \theta}.$$

If $\tan \phi$ be substituted for μ this may be written:

$$P = W \frac{\sin(\alpha + \phi)}{\cos(\theta - \phi)}.$$

If the values of W, α, and ϕ are specified, P may be regarded as a function of θ. The value of P is a minimum when θ is equal to ϕ, since this value of θ makes $\cos(\theta - \phi)$ a maximum; the minimum value of P, then, is $W \sin(\alpha + \phi)$. If the force P is applied parallel to the plane its value becomes $W \dfrac{\sin(\alpha + \phi)}{\cos \phi}$.

PROBLEMS

264. A block weighing 100 lb. rests on a plane inclined 30° to the horizontal. If the coefficient of static friction is 0.3, will a horizontal force of 50 lb. start the body up the plane?

265. In Fig. 196 what must be the magnitude of a horizontal force, P, to cause motion to impend? The coefficient of static friction for both pairs of rubbing surfaces is 0.2. Bodies A and B weigh 150 lb. each and the force exerted on A and B by the spring S is 200 lb. Is the action line of the force P shown correctly in the figure?   *Ans.* $P = 80$ lb.

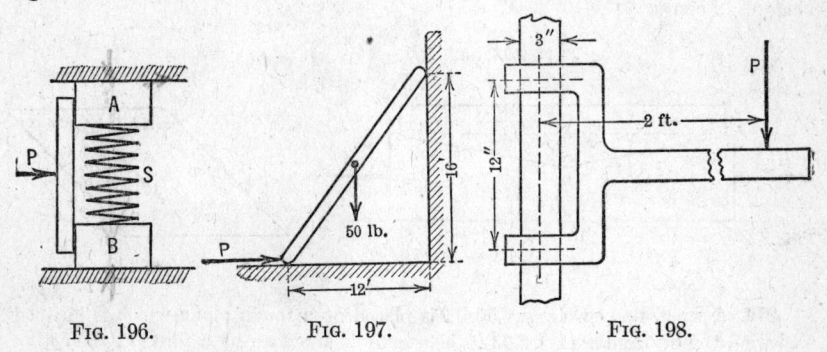

Fig. 196.   Fig. 197.   Fig. 198.

266. The uniform ladder shown in Fig. 197 weighs 50 lb. The coefficient of friction for the ladder and vertical wall is 0.25, and for the floor and ladder 0.5. Find the horizontal force P which will cause motion to impend to the right.

267. A load, P, of 80 lb. is applied to the arm (Fig. 198) at a distance of 2 ft. from the axis of the shaft. If $\mu = 0.15$ will the arm slide on the shaft?   *Ans.* Yes.

268. If the angle θ in Fig. 101 is 45° when motion impends, what is the coefficient of friction for the 60-lb. body and the horizontal plane? Assume the pulleys to be frictionless.

269. If the weight W in Prob. 260 is 500 lb. and x is 24 in., what vertical force P applied at E will be just sufficient to start the lift up? *Ans.* $P = 862$ lb.

270. A body weighing 200 lb. rests on a plane inclined 30° to the horizontal and is acted on by a force of 120 lb. as shown in Fig. 199. The coefficient of friction for the body and plane is 0.3. Find the friction between the body and plane.

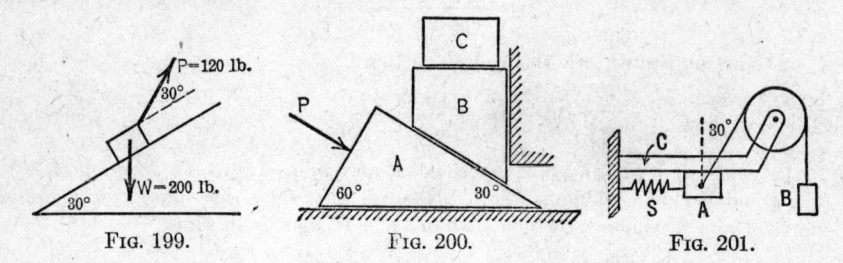

FIG. 199. FIG. 200. FIG. 201.

271. In Fig. 200 body C weighs 1000 lb. The coefficient of friction between A and the horizontal surface is 1/10. Disregard the friction between A and B and between B and the vertical surface. What is the least value of P that will raise the body C assuming the weights of A and B to be negligible? *Ans.* $P = 831$ lb.

272. In Fig. 201, body A has been pulled to the right into the position shown where it is held in equilibrium by its weight, the tension in the spring S, the tension in the cord connecting it to B, and the reaction of the member C. The weights of A and B are 20 lb. and 100 lb., respectively, and the coefficient of friction for A and C is 0.5. Find the tension in the spring. *Ans.* $T = 16.7$ lb.

273. The load of 100,000 lb. (Fig. 202) is raised by applying forces P, P to the wedges. What is the required value of P if the coefficient of friction is 0.2 for all surfaces of contact?

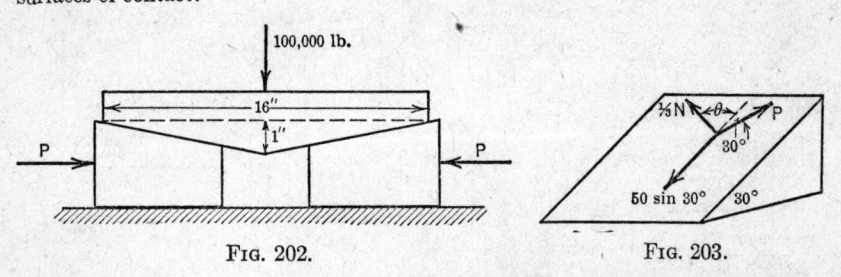

FIG. 202. FIG. 203.

274. A small body weighing 50 lb. is placed on a rough plane which is inclined 30° with the horizontal (Fig. 203). The body is acted on by a force P, the action line of which lies in the plane and makes an angle of 30° with the line of greatest slope in the plane. If the coefficient of friction is ⅓, find the value of P that will just start the block in motion, and find the direction in which the block will begin to move. *Ans.* $P = 14.4$ lb.

275. A homogeneous rectangular prism, the dimensions of which are 1 ft. by 1 ft. by 2 ft., stands on end on a flat square board, the edges of the base of the prism being parallel to the edges of the board. The coefficient of friction for the board and prism is 0.2. If one side of the board is gradually raised will the prism slide or tip?

276. A horizontal pull is exerted on one handle of a desk drawer a distance x from the center line of the drawer. The drawer has a length L parallel to the direction of pull. Show that the maximum value x can have and still allow the drawer to open is $L/2\mu$, where μ is the coefficient of friction for each side of the drawer. Assume that when motion impends the friction and the normal pressure on each side are concentrated at the front or back edge of the drawer and that friction on the bottom of the drawer is negligible.

277. A crown friction drive as indicated in Fig. 204 is used on screw power presses, motor trucks, etc. The cast-iron disk B rotates at 1000 r.p.m. and drives the crown wheel C which is faced with leather-fiber. The diameter of C is 20 in. and the value of μ is 0.35. If a turning moment of 100 ft.-lb. is transmitted to the crown-wheel shaft when slipping impends, what is the normal pressure between the disk and the crown wheel? What is the pressure on the bearings at A and D?

Ans. $N = 343$ lb; $A = 257$ lb.; $D = 86$ lb.

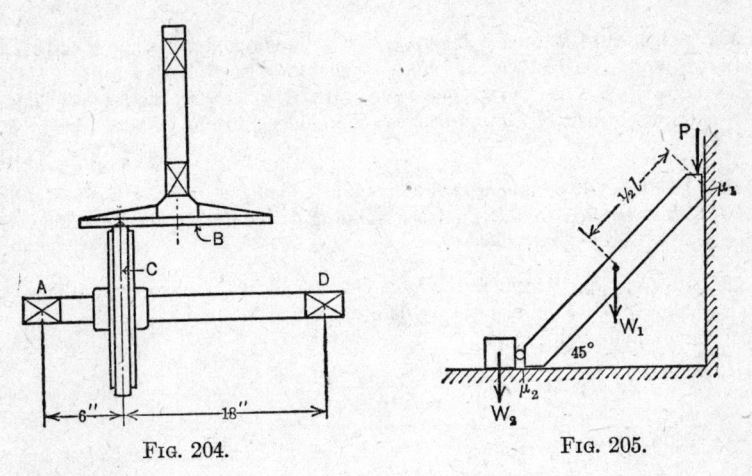

Fig. 204.   Fig. 205.

278. The weights of the bodies in Fig. 205 are $W_1 = 60$ lb. and $W_2 = 30$ lb. The coefficients of friction are $\mu_1 = \frac{1}{4}$ and $\mu_2 = \frac{1}{3}$. What is the least value of P that will cause the bodies to move?

279. Two bodies weighing 50 lb. and 100 lb. rest on an inclined plane and are connected by a cord which is parallel to the line of greatest slope. The body weighing 50 lb. is below the one weighing 100 lb., and the coefficient of friction for the 50-lb. body is $\frac{1}{5}$ and that for the 100-lb. body is $\frac{1}{4}$. Find the inclination of the plane to the horizontal and the tension in the cord, when motion impends.

Ans. $\theta = 13°\,7'$; $T = 1.61$ lb.

280. A cone clutch as shown in Fig. 206 is used to connect two shafts. If the normal pressure between the two surfaces of contact is 15 lb. per sq. in. and the coefficient of friction is 0.25, what is the maximum torque the clutch can transmit? Assume that the frictional force has a mean arm of 6 in. and that $\theta = 12.5°$.

Ans. $T = 2545$ lb.-in.

281. In Fig. 207, find the least value of P that will prevent the 800-lb. weight from descending and turning the wheel and axle D. Assume the axle to be smooth and disregard the weight of the wheel and axle. Assume the coefficient of friction between AC and D to be 0.3 and the thickness of the bar AC to be negligible.

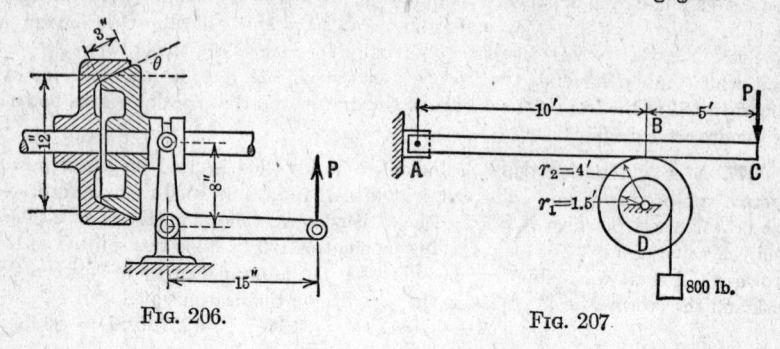

Fig. 206.

Fig. 207.

282. A ladder 14 ft. long is inclined 60° to the horizontal, its upper end resting against a smooth vertical wall and its lower end on a rough horizontal plane. The center of gravity is 6 ft. from the lower end. If the ladder is on the point of slipping, what is the coefficient of friction between the ladder and horizontal surface?

Ans. $\mu = 0.247$.

283. In Prob. 262 assume that A is fixed instead of B and that a horizontal force of 1000 lb. is applied to B. Find the value of P required to make motion of B impend.

284. In Prob. 263 determine the force P that will just prevent motion down the plane when $\alpha > \phi$. Find also the value of θ for which P is a minimum and determine the minimum value of P.

Ans. $P = \dfrac{W \sin (\alpha - \phi)}{\cos (\theta + \phi)}$; $\theta = -\phi$; $P = W \sin (\alpha - \phi)$.

285. In Prob. 263 determine the force P that will just start the body down the plane when $\alpha < \phi$. Find also the value of θ for which P is a minimum and determine the minimum value of P.

Ans. $P = \dfrac{W \sin (\phi - \alpha)}{\cos (\theta + \phi)}$; $\theta = -\phi$; $P = W \sin (\phi - \alpha)$.

286. A body weighing W lb. rests on a rough plane inclined at an angle θ to the horizontal. What horizontal force must be applied in order to start the body up the plane if the angle of friction is ϕ? Express the force in terms of W, θ, and ϕ and also in terms of W, θ, and μ.

Ans. $P = W \tan (\theta + \phi) = W \dfrac{\sin \theta + \mu \cos \theta}{\cos \theta - \mu \sin \theta}$.

60. Pivot Friction.—In Fig. 208 is shown a step bearing. Let it be required to find the expression for the frictional moment developed on the flat end of the shaft as it turns in its bearing. The assumption will

PIVOT FRICTION

be made that the coefficient of friction, μ, for the rubbing surfaces is constant, and that the pressure on the bearing is uniformly distributed. Let the total axial load be denoted by W, the radius of the shaft by r, and the bearing area by A.

Obviously the frictional moment cannot be found by obtaining the total frictional force F' from the equation $F' = \mu N$ and then multiplying this force by the moment-arm, for the resultant of the frictional forces is not a force but a couple. However, the frictional force dF' on any small (differential) part dA of the area may be found from the equation $dF' = \mu dN$, where dN is the normal pressure on the differential area, and the moment of this frictional force may be found by multiplying the force by its moment-arm ρ which of course varies with the position of dA. Hence we are here dealing with a continuously varying quantity and the total or resultant frictional moment M_F must be thought of as a summation of the products $(\rho \cdot dF')$ which involves the method of the calculus. Thus

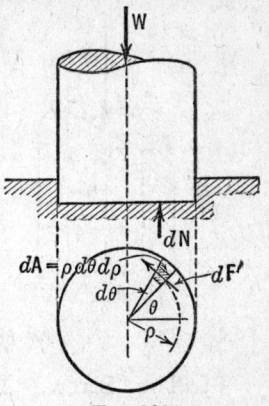

Fig. 208.

$$M_F = \int \rho dF' = \int \rho \mu dN,$$

But

dN = pressure per unit area times the area dA

$$= \frac{W}{\pi r^2} dA = \frac{W}{\pi r^2} \rho d\rho d\theta.$$

Therefore

$$M_F = \frac{\mu W}{\pi r^2} \int_0^r \int_0^{2\pi} \rho^2 d\rho d\theta = \frac{2}{3} \mu W r.$$

NOTE: The student should note well the method used in the above analysis. This method, which makes use of the calculus, will frequently be used in subsequent articles in dealing with many different types of problems in which continuously varying quantities are encountered, such as a pressure distributed non-uniformly over an area, the moment of the mass of a body about an axis through the body, etc.

PROBLEMS

287. Show that the frictional moment for the hollow flat pivot (Fig. 209a) or the collar bearing (Fig. 209b) is

$$M_F = \frac{2}{3} \mu W \frac{(r_2^3 - r_1^3)}{r_2^2 - r_1^2}.$$

134   FRICTION

288. The weight of the vertical shaft and the rotating parts of a turbine is 100,000 lb. and the diameter of the shaft is 10 in. Assuming the coefficient of friction to be 0.015 and the bearing to be a flat-ended pivot, find the frictional moment.

289. Find the moment of the friction on a collar bearing, when subjected to a pressure of 6000 lb., if the radii of the collar are 3.5 in. and 4.5 in. and the coefficient of friction is 0.025.

Ans. $M_F = 603$ lb.-in.

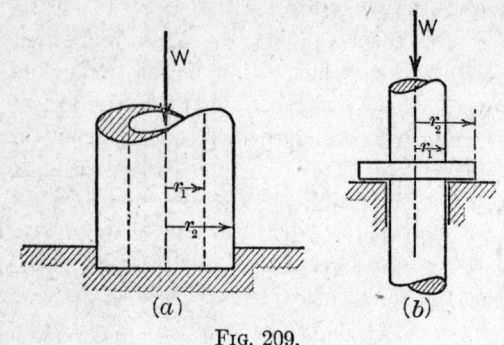

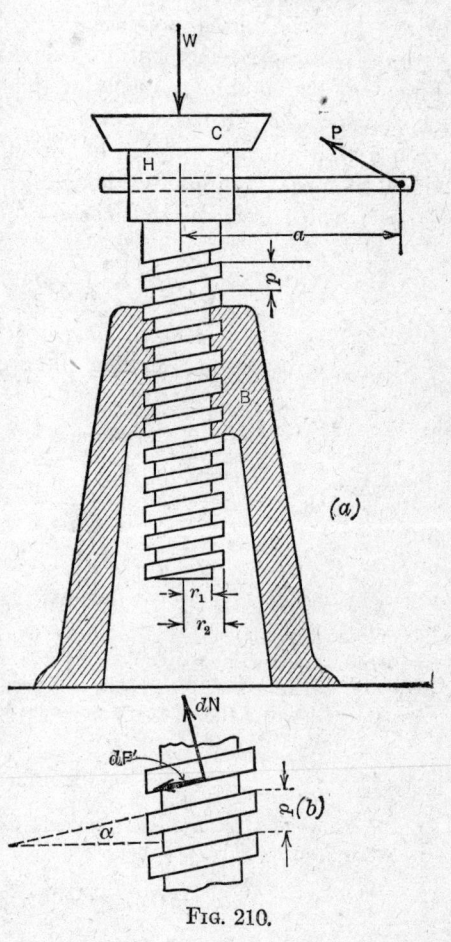

FIG. 209.

61. The Screw.—A screw is, in effect, an inclined plane wound around a cylinder. Screws are made with square threads and with triangular threads, but square-threaded screws, only, will be considered here. Fig. 210(a) shows a jack-screw with square threads which is used in raising or lowering heavy loads. The radius of the base of the thread is denoted by r_1 and the outer radius by r_2; α is called the *pitch angle* and p is called the *pitch* of the screw. Let it be required to find the force, P, which, when applied at the end of the lever of length a, is just sufficient to raise the load W. The forces which hold the screw in equilibrium are: the force P; the pressure of the cap, C, on the head, H; and the reaction of the nut, B, on the screw. The latter is distributed over the area of the threads in contact with the nut. If the friction between the cap and the

FIG. 210.

head of the screw is neglected, the pressure of the cap on the head of the screw will be a vertical force equal to W; the problem will be solved on this assumption. Two of the six equilibrium equations which apply to this type of force system will be sufficient for the solution of the problem, namely, $\Sigma F_z = 0$ and $\Sigma M_z = 0$, where z is taken as the axis of the screw. The reaction between the nut and the thread of the screw on an element of area dA will be denoted by dR. This force may be resolved into components dN normal to the thread and dF' parallel to the thread as shown in Fig. 210(b). In taking moments about the axis of the thread it will be sufficiently accurate to consider the moment-arm of dF' to be equal to the mean radius of the thread, $\frac{1}{2}(r_1 + r_2)$, which will be denoted by r. The equilibrium equations stated above, then, become:

$$\Sigma F_z = \Sigma dN \cos \alpha - \Sigma dF' \sin \alpha - W = 0,$$

$$\Sigma M_z = Pa - \Sigma r dN \sin \alpha - \Sigma r dF' \cos \alpha = 0.$$

Since $dF' = \mu dN$, these equations may be written:

$$\cos \alpha \Sigma dN - \mu \sin \alpha \Sigma dN - W = 0, \quad \ldots \quad (1)$$

$$Pa - r \sin \alpha \Sigma dN - \mu r \cos \alpha \Sigma dN = 0. \quad \ldots \quad (2)$$

By eliminating ΣdN from (1) and (2) the equation obtained is,

$$Pa = Wr \frac{\sin \alpha + \mu \cos \alpha}{\cos \alpha - \mu \sin \alpha}.$$

By substituting $\tan \phi$ for μ this equation may be written in the form

$$Pa = Wr \tan (\phi + \alpha) \quad \ldots \quad \ldots \quad (A)$$

If the pitch angle α is large and the angle of friction is small, the load W will cause the screw to run down unless a force is applied to prevent it. The force P required to hold the load is found by a method of analysis similar to that used above, the only difference being that the sense of the frictional force is reversed. The least value of P required to prevent the screw from running down is given by the equation

$$Pa = Wr \tan (\alpha - \phi). \quad \ldots \quad \ldots \quad (B)$$

If $\alpha = \phi$ in the above equation, the force P reduces to zero, that is, the load will be held by friction alone. If $\alpha < \phi$, a force is required (the sense of which is opposite to that in the two cases above considered) to lower the load. The value of the force required to lower the load is given by the equation

$$Pa = Wr \tan (\phi - \alpha). \quad \ldots \quad \ldots \quad (C)$$

PROBLEMS

290. The mean diameter of the screw of a square-threaded jack-screw is 1.8 in. The pitch of the thread is 0.4 in. and the coefficient of friction for the screw and nut is 0.12. What force must be applied at the end of a lever 18 in. long to raise a weight of 5000 lb.? What force is required to lower the weight? *Ans.* 48.1 lb.; 12.4 lb.

291. A weight of 1000 lb. is lifted by applying a couple, Pd, to the hand wheel of the apparatus shown in Fig. 211. The diameter, d, of the hand wheel is 20 in.; the mean diameter of the screw is 1.5 in.; the pitch of the thread is $\frac{1}{8}$ in.; and the coefficient of friction is 0.15. Find the values of the forces of the couple when the value of θ is 15°.

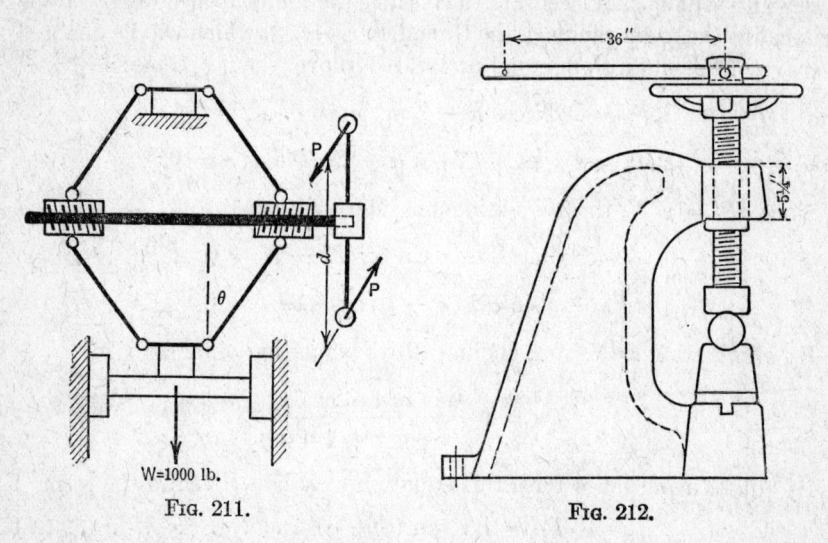

FIG. 211.

FIG. 212.

292. The shaft-straightening hand press shown in Fig. 212 is used for bending or straightening $3\frac{1}{2}$-in. steel shafts. What force, P, applied at the end of a 36-in. lever is required to produce a pressure, Q, of 24,000 lb. on the shaft? The threads have a mean diameter of 2 in. and there are four threads per inch. Consider friction between the screw and nut only, and use a value of 0.2 for the coefficient of friction.
Ans. $P = 161$ lb.

62. Belt Friction.—Belt friction is important in the transmission of power by belt and rope drives and in resisting large loads by means of band brakes, capstans, etc. If a belt, rope, or steel band passes over a *smooth* cylinder or pulley that offers resistance to turning, no difference in the tensions in the belt, rope, or band on the two sides of the pulley can be developed since a difference in the tensions requires that there be friction on the surface of contact between the belt and pulley. If the cylinder or pulley is *rough*, however, the tensions will not, in general, be equal. In the present article the relation between the tensions in the belt, on the two sides of a rough pulley, *when the belt is about to slip*, will be determined. It is evident that the greater tension must be just large enough to overcome the smaller tension in addition to the friction between the belt and the pulley. In Fig. 213(a) is represented a belt on a pulley, the angle of contact being α and the belt tensions being T_1 and T_2. Let T_1 be the greater tension, and let it be assumed that the belt is about to slip on the pulley. The normal pressure between the belt and the pulley per unit length of belt, that is, the intensity of pressure at any point, will be denoted by p, and the tension in the belt at

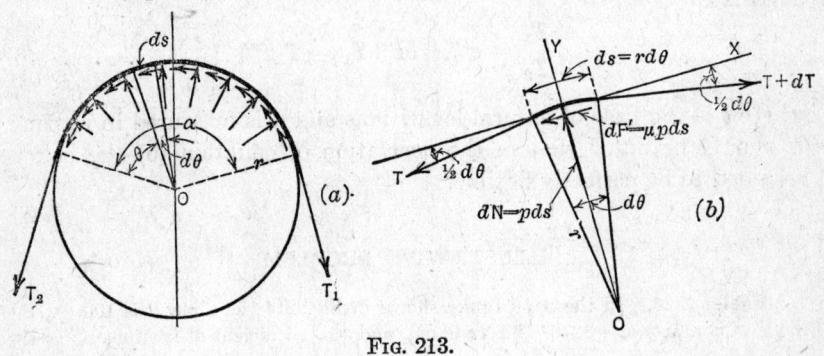

FIG. 213.

the same point will be denoted by T. Fig. 213(b) is a free-body diagram of an element of belt of length ds. The forces acting on this element are the tensions T and $T + dT$ at the ends, and the reaction of the pulley. The latter force may be resolved into a component, $dN = pds$, normal to the face of the pulley and a frictional component, $dF' = \mu pds$, tangent to the face of the pulley. The equations of equilibrium may be applied as follows:

$$\Sigma F_x = (T + dT) \cos \frac{d\theta}{2} - T \cos \frac{d\theta}{2} - \mu pds = 0. \quad (1)$$

$$\Sigma F_y = pds - (T + dT) \sin \frac{d\theta}{2} - T \sin \frac{d\theta}{2} = 0. \quad (2)$$

Since $\frac{d\theta}{2}$ is small, $\cos \frac{d\theta}{2}$ is approximately equal to unity and $\sin \frac{d\theta}{2}$ is approximately equal to $\frac{d\theta}{2}$. The term $dT \sin \frac{d\theta}{2}$ is a small quantity of the second order and may be neglected. By using these approximations, equations (1) and (2) become

$$dT - \mu pds = 0, \quad \quad (3)$$

$$pds - Td\theta = 0. \quad \quad (4)$$

Eliminating pds from equations (3) and (4), we have

$$\frac{dT}{T} = \mu d\theta. \qquad \ldots \ldots \ldots (5)$$

By integrating equation (5) the relation between T_1 and T_2 may be found as follows:

$$\int_{T_2}^{T_1} \frac{dT}{T} = \int_0^\alpha \mu d\theta, \quad \text{or} \quad \log_e \frac{T_1}{T_2} = \mu\alpha.$$

That is

$$\frac{T_1}{T_2} = e^{\mu\alpha}, \quad \text{or} \quad T_1 = T_2 e^{\mu\alpha} \quad \ldots \ldots (6)$$

where e is the base of natural logarithms and α is measured in radians. It should be noted that in the derivation of equation (6) the belt is assumed to be perfectly flexible.

ILLUSTRATIVE PROBLEM

Problem 293.—In the band brake shown in Fig. 214 the force P is 100 lb., the angle of contact, α, is 270° ($\frac{3}{2}\pi$ radians), and the coefficient of friction, μ, for the band and the brake wheel is 0.2. If the brake wheel rotates in a counter-clockwise direction find the tensions in the band and the frictional moment developed.

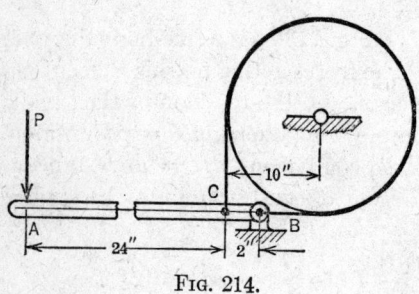

Solution.—Since the operating lever ACB is in equilibrium the equation $\Sigma M_B = 0$ may be applied, from which the band pull at C, that is, the tension T_2, is found. Thus

$$\Sigma M_B = 100 \times 26 - T_2 \times 2 = 0,$$
$$\therefore\ T_2 = 1300 \text{ lb.}$$

Fig. 214.

Since T_2 is now known, the tension T_1 may be found from the belt-friction formula. Thus

$$T_1 = T_2 \times e^{\mu\alpha} = 1300 \times (2.718)^{0.2 \times 3/2 \pi}$$
$$\log T_1 = \log 1300 + 0.3\pi \log 2.718$$
$$= 3.114 + 0.942 \times 0.434 = 3.522. \quad \therefore\ T_1 = 3330 \text{ lb.}$$

Frictional moment $= (T_1 - T_2) \times 10 = 2030 \times 10 = 20{,}300$ lb.-in.

PROBLEMS

294. A body weighing 2000 lb. is suspended by means of a rope wound 1½ turns around a drum. If the coefficient of friction is 0.3 what force must be exerted at the other end of the rope to hold the body?   *Ans.* $T_2 = 118$ lb.

295. A rope passes over a horizontal circular beam making 1½ complete turns around the beam. What is the greatest weight on one end of the rope that can be supported by a force of 1000 lb. applied to the other end of the rope if the coefficient of static friction is 0.3?

296. A body weighing 500 lb. is raised by means of a rope which passes over a round beam, the angle of contact being 180°. If the coefficient of friction is 0.4, what is the least force P which will raise the body? What is the least force P which will hold the body? *Ans.* $P = 1755$ lb.; $P = 142$ lb.

297. A body having a weight, W, of 1 ton is suspended by means of a wire rope which passes over two fixed drums, as shown in Fig. 215. If the coefficient of friction for the rope and drums is 0.3, what force, P, will be required (a) to hold the body; (b) to start the body upwards?

298. A rope is wound twice around a post. If a pull of 50 lb. at one end of the rope will just support a force of 6000 lb. at the other end, what is the coefficient of friction? *Ans.* $\mu = 0.38$.

299. A boat is brought to rest by means of a rope which is wound around a capstan. If a force of 4000 lb. is exerted by the boat and a pull of 100 lb. is exerted on the other end of the rope, find the number of turns the rope makes around the capstan, assuming the value of μ to be 0.25.

300. In Fig. 216 is represented a band brake, the angle of contact of the band on the brake wheel being 180°. If the coefficient of friction is 0.2, find the frictional moment developed (a) when the brake wheel rotates clockwise; (b) when the brake wheel rotates counterclockwise. *Ans.* (a) 157 lb.-ft.; (b) 84 lb.-ft.

Fig. 215.

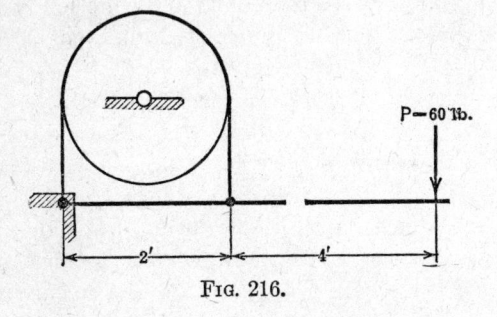

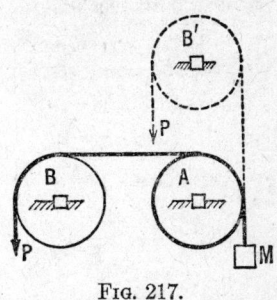

Fig. 216.   Fig. 217.

301. A body, M (Fig. 217), weighing 500 lb. is suspended by a rope that makes 1¼ turns around a fixed cylindrical drum A and then extends horizontally to another fixed drum B as shown. A downward force P applied at the end of the rope is just sufficient to prevent M from descending. (a) If the coefficient of friction for the rope and each drum is 0.20, find the value of P. (b) If the drum B were placed in position B' would the value of P be less? If so how much less?

302. In Fig. 218 what is the value of P if it just prevents downward motion of

140   FRICTION

the 2000-lb. weight? The rope makes one complete turn around the post. The drum turns in a frictionless bearing, and μ for the post and rope is $1/\pi$.

Ans. $P = 271$ lb.

303. Solve the preceding problem assuming that the drum B cannot turn and that μ for the rope and drum is $2/\pi$.

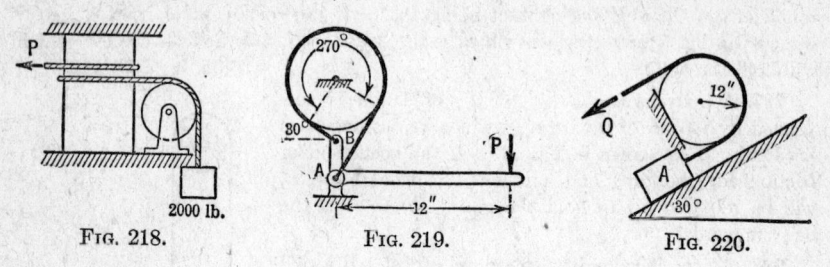

FIG. 218.   FIG. 219.   FIG. 220.

304. A frictional resisting moment of 760 lb.-in. is exerted on the drum in Fig. 219 by the band brake when a load P of 10 lb. is applied as shown. Find the value of the coefficient of friction for the band and drum. Assume the radius of the drum to be 4 in. and the drum to be rotating counter-clockwise. *Ans.* $\mu = 0.367$.

305. In Fig. 220, Q is a force applied at one end of a flexible belt that passes around a fixed drum. The body A weighs 200 lb. The coefficient of friction for the belt and drum is $1/\pi$ and for the body A and the plane 0.2. Find the value of Q that will cause A to have impending motion (*a*) up the plane and (*b*) down the plane.

Ans. (*a*) $Q = 366$ lb.; (*b*) $Q = 24.1$ lb.

63. Rolling Resistance.—If a rigid wheel or roller which carries a vertical load rests on a *rigid* horizontal surface, a horizontal force, however small, will cause the wheel or roller to roll on the surface. If a wheel rolls over a *yielding* surface, however, a resistance to the motion is encountered owing to the fact that the surface immediately in front of the wheel is being deformed.

In Fig. 221 is shown a wheel carrying a vertical load W. Let P be a horizontal force which causes the center of the wheel to move with a constant velocity. Since the surface on which the wheel rolls deforms under the wheel, the pressure between the wheel and the surface is distributed over the area of contact. The resultant pressure or reaction of the surface on the wheel then passes through some point, B, in the area of contact as shown in the figure. Since the velocity of the wheel is constant, the three forces acting are in equilibrium and hence the

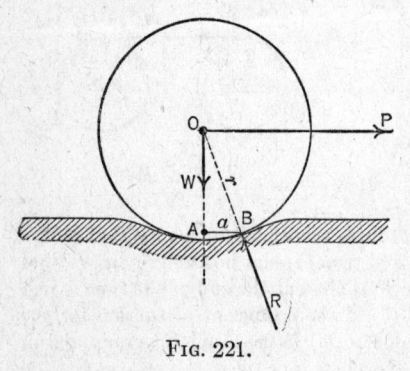

FIG. 221.

reaction, R, of the surface on the wheel must pass through O, the center of the wheel. Taking moments about B we have

$$\Sigma M_B = W \times AB - P \times OA = 0.$$

Since the depression is usually small, OA is approximately equal to r, the radius of the wheel. By using this approximation and denoting AB by a, the value of P is found to be

$$P = \frac{Wa}{r}.$$

The horizontal component of the reaction R is equal to P and is called the *rolling friction* or *rolling resistance*; the distance a is sometimes called the *coefficient of rolling resistance*. However, since a is a linear quantity and not a pure number it is not a true coefficient. The value of a is generally expressed in inches. The laws of rolling resistance are not well known, and there is need of further investigation on the subject. It was assumed by Coulomb that the coefficient of rolling resistance is independent of the radius of the wheel. Tests by Dupuit indicate that the coefficient varies as the square root of the diameter. Whether the conclusion of the latter is correct or not, it seems reasonable to assume that the value of the coefficient depends on the diameter of the wheel. The values of the coefficient of rolling resistance given by various investigators are not in close agreement and should be used with caution.

COEFFICIENTS OF ROLLING RESISTANCE
(Due to Coulomb and Goodman)

	a (inches)	
Lignum vitæ on oak	0.0195	
Elm on oak	0.0327	
Steel on steel	0.007	to 0.015
Steel on wood	0.06	to 0.10
Steel on macadam road	0.05	to 0.20
Steel on soft ground	3.0	to 5.0
Pneumatic tires on good road	0.02	to 0.022
Pneumatic tires on mud road	0.04	to 0.06
Solid rubber tire on good road	0.04	
Solid rubber tire on mud road	0.09	to 0.11

PROBLEMS

306. The rolling resistance for the wheels of a freight car is 3 lb. per ton. If the diameter of the car wheels is 33 in., what is the coefficient of rolling resistance?

Ans. 0.025 in.

307. An oak beam which carries a load of 5000 lb. rests on elm rollers the diameters of which are 6 in. The rollers rest on a horizontal track. What horizontal force is required to move the load if the weight of the beam is neglected?

308. What is the rolling resistance of a wagon wheel on a macadam road if the diameter of the wheel is 4 ft. 6 in.? Assume the coefficient of rolling resistance to be 0.2 in. *Ans.* 14.8 lb. per ton.

REVIEW QUESTIONS AND PROBLEMS

309. Show that the angle of static friction is equal to the angle of repose.

310. Show that the coefficient of static friction is equal to the tangent of the angle of friction.

311. A body rests on an inclined plane. Is the friction of the plane on the body necessarily equal to the product of the normal pressure of the plane and the coefficient of friction?

312. Correct the error in the following statement: The angle between the total reaction and the normal pressure is always equal to the angle of friction.

313. If relative motion between two bodies is impending and additional forces are applied to the bodies causing an increase in the normal pressure, does the angle of friction also increase?

314. If a body rests on a plane and motion of the body is impending what are two ways of representing the action of the plane on the body in a free-body diagram?

315. Correct the error in each of the following statements: (*a*) The coefficient of friction for two surfaces of contact is the ratio of the normal pressure to the limiting friction. (*b*) The angle of friction is the angle between the action lines of the limiting friction and the normal pressure. (*c*) The normal pressure of a plane on a body that slides or tends to slide on the plane is always equal to the component of the weight of the body in a direction normal to the plane. (*d*) The coefficient of static friction for a given pair of rubbing surfaces is not a constant for that pair of surfaces because the limiting friction developed varies with the normal pressure.

316. In obtaining the expression for the frictional moment on a flat pivot bearing, why is the moment obtained by first getting the moment of the frictional force on an elementary area dA and then finding the sum of all such moments rather than by finding the resultant of the frictional forces and then getting the moment of this resultant?

317. In Fig. 222 what is the greatest weight A can have without causing the cylinder B to turn? The coefficient of friction for the cylinder and the horizontal plane is 0.25 and the vertical surface is smooth. The weight of the cylinder is 120 lb.

Ans. $W = 120$ lb.

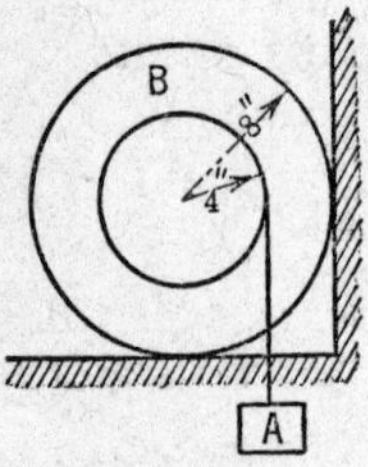

Fig. 222. 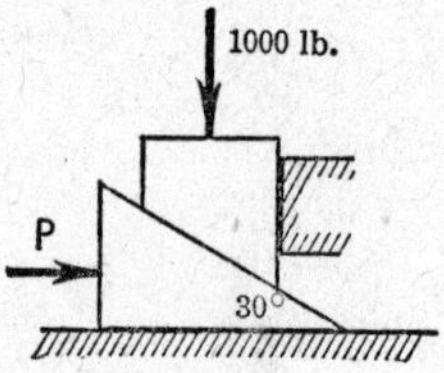   Fig. 223. 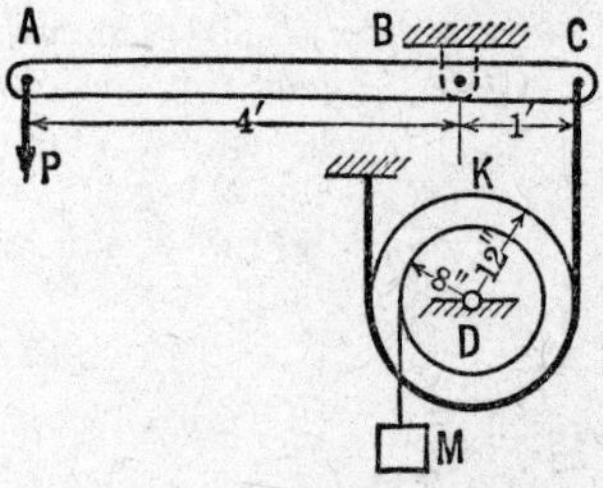   Fig. 224.

318. In Fig. 223, the coefficient of friction for the wedge and horizontal surface is 0.25 and all other surfaces are smooth. Find the least value of P that will raise the 1000-lb. load. *Ans.* $P = 827$ lb.

319. A band brake (Fig. 224) prevents the wheel, K, and drum, D, from being turned by the weight of the body, M, which is attached to a rope that is wound around the drum, D. What is the greatest weight M can have if a force P of 20 lb. applied as shown to the arm AC will just prevent the drum from turning? The friction of the drum bearing and of the pin at B may be neglected. The coefficient of friction for the band and wheel K is 0.40. *Ans.* $W = 300$ lb.

320. A rectangular block of wood 10 in. $\times$ 10 in. $\times$ 20 in. stands on end on a horizontal floor. The block weighs 40 lb. and the coefficient of friction for the block and floor is 0.20. A horizontal force P is applied to the block through the center of the upper base and perpendicular to one side of the block. If the force P is gradually increased until motion of the block ensues will it slide or overturn? What is the value of P when the block starts to move? *Ans.* Will slide; $P = 8$ lb.

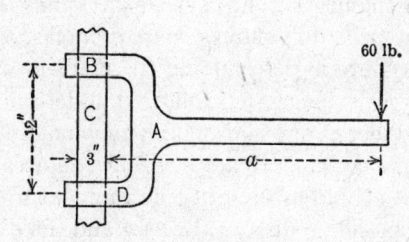

Fig. 225.

321. In Fig. 225 the coefficient of friction between A and the vertical post is 0.2. Find the distance a of the 60-lb. load from the post when A is on the point of sliding down the post. *Ans.* $a = 28.5$ in.

322. Two bodies A and B rest upon a plane inclined 30° to the horizontal and are connected by a cord parallel to the plane. The lower body, A, weighs 50 lb. and B weighs 200 lb. If the coefficient of static friction between A and the plane is 0.25 and between B and the plane is 0.7, will the bodies slide down the plane? Find the tension in the cord. *Ans.* No; $T = 14.2$ lb.

CHAPTER V

FIRST MOMENTS AND CENTROIDS

64. First Moment.—In the preceding chapters, moments of forces about points or axes have frequently been considered. In the analysis of many problems in engineering, however, expressions are frequently met which represent moments of volumes, masses,[1] areas, or lines. Since the mathematical procedure in determining the moment of a volume, mass, or line is precisely the same as that followed in determining the moment of an area, the further discussion of first moments and centroids will, for the most part, be confined to areas. Since an area, unlike a concentrated force, is a distributed quantity its moment about a line or axis cannot be defined as the product of the area and the distance of the area from the axis (similar to the manner in which the moment of a force was defined), since the different parts of the area are at different distances from the axis and hence *the distance of the area from the axis* is indefinite and meaningless. The area may, however, be thought of as being made up of very small (differential) elements and the moment of an element of area (dA) about an axis can then be defined as the product of the area of the element and the distance of the element from the axis. The moment of an area about a line or axis in the plane of the area may then be defined as the algebraic sum of the moments of the elements of area about the axis. Thus the moments about the x- and the y-axes of an area in the xy-plane (denoted by Q_x and Q_y, respectively) may be defined by the equations

$$Q_x = \int y dA \quad \text{and} \quad Q_y = \int x dA.$$

In a similar way the moment of an area, volume, mass, etc., with respect to a *plane* may be defined.

The moment thus defined is frequently called the *first moment* when it is desired to distinguish it from the moment of inertia (or second moment), since the distances of the various elements of area from the

---

[1] The term *mass* cannot be defined completely nor its physical significance discussed until the laws of motion of physical bodies are treated. (See Art. 101.) As here used it is sufficient to think of mass as the inert material or matter of which bodies are composed, the quantitative expression of which is the volume of the body times a density factor.

144

ILLUSTRATIVE PROBLEMS

axis or plane with respect to which moments are taken enter into the expression for the first moment to the first power and into the expression for the moment of inertia or second moment to the second power. The first moment of an area is frequently called the *statical moment* of the area. Second moments will be considered in the Appendix.

Sign, Dimensions, and Units.—The sign of the moment of an element of an area about an axis may be positive or negative according as the coordinate of the element is positive or negative. Likewise, the moment of an area about an axis may be positive, negative, or zero according as the sum of the positive moments of the elements of the area is larger than, smaller than, or equal to the sum of the negative moments of the elements.

Furthermore, the dimensional expression for the moment of a line is length squared (L^2) expressed in such units as inch^2, foot^2, etc. Similarly, the dimensions of the moments of an area and of a volume are, respectively, length cubed (L^3) and length to the fourth power (L^4).

ILLUSTRATIVE PROBLEMS

Problem 323.—Find the moments about the x- and y-axes of the area (Fig. 226) bounded by the curve $y^2 = x^3$, the x-axis, and the line $x = a$. What are the numerical values of the moments if $a = 2$ in.?

Solution. First Method.—By taking as the element of area $dA = dx\,dy$, the moments of the area about the x- and y-axes may be found as follows:

$$Q_x = \int y\,dA = \int_0^a \int_0^{x^{3/2}} y\,dy\,dx = \int_0^a [\tfrac{1}{2}y^2]_0^{x^{3/2}}\,dx = \int_0^a \tfrac{1}{2}x^3\,dx = \frac{1}{8}a^4$$

$$Q_y = \int x\,dA = \int_0^{a^{3/2}} \int_{y^{2/3}}^a x\,dx\,dy = \int_0^{a^{3/2}} [\tfrac{1}{2}x^2]_{y^{2/3}}^a\,dy = \tfrac{1}{2}\int_0^{a^{3/2}} (a^2 - y^{4/3})\,dy$$

$$= \tfrac{1}{2}[a^2 y - \tfrac{3}{7}y^{7/3}]_0^{a^{3/2}} = \tfrac{1}{2}[a^{7/2} - \tfrac{3}{7}a^{7/2}] = \frac{2}{7}a^{7/2}$$

Second Method.—The moments of the area about the x- and y-axes may also be found by selecting as the elements of area $dA = (a - x)dy$ and $dA = y\,dx$, respectively. Thus

$$Q_x = \int_0^{a^{3/2}} y(a - x)\,dy = \int_0^{a^{3/2}} y(a - y^{2/3})\,dy$$

$$= [\tfrac{1}{2}ay^2 - \tfrac{3}{8}y^{8/3}]_0^{a^{3/2}} = \tfrac{1}{2}a^4 - \tfrac{3}{8}a^4 = \frac{1}{8}a^4$$

and

$$Q_y = \int_0^a xy\,dx = \int_0^a x \cdot x^{3/2}\,dx = \tfrac{2}{7}[x^{7/2}]_0^a = \frac{2}{7}a^{7/2}$$

When $a = 2$ in., $Q_x = 2$ in.^{3} and $Q_y = 3.23$ in.^{3}

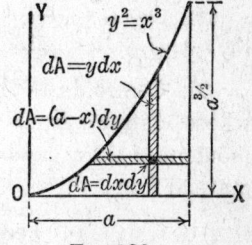

FIG. 226.

FIRST MOMENTS AND CENTROIDS

Problem 324.—Find the moment, about the x-axis, of the mass of one-half of the homogeneous rim of a wheel (Fig. 227) in which the thickness of the rim is negligible compared to the radius r. The moment of the mass of the rim may be assumed to be the same as the moment of the semi-circular arc (line) times a density factor.

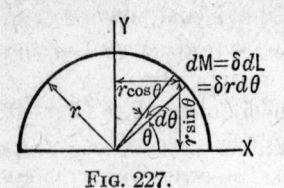

Fig. 227.

Solution.—The element of mass dM, expressed in polar coordinates, is the product of a density factor δ (mass per unit length of arc) and the length $dL = rd\theta$ of the element of the arc. Hence, the moment of the mass of the rim about the x-axis is

$$Q_x = \int y\, dM = \int_0^\pi r \sin\theta \cdot \delta r d\theta = \delta r^2 \int_0^\pi \sin\theta\, d\theta$$

$$= -\delta r^2 [\cos\theta]_0^\pi = 2\delta r^2 = \frac{2}{\pi} Mr$$

where $M = \pi r \delta$ is the mass of the rim.

PROBLEMS

325. Find the moment of the area of a triangle of base b and altitude h, about the base of the triangle. *Ans.* $Q = \frac{1}{6}bh^2$.

326. The bending moment at any point in a beam that supports a uniformly distributed load is represented by the corresponding ordinate to a parabola whose equation is $y = C_1 x - C_2 x^2$ which is represented by the curve in Fig. 228. The moment of the area under this curve with respect to the x-axis is used in obtaining the stress in the beam. If $C_1 = 500$ and $C_2 = 50$ find the moment with respect to the x-axis of the area under the curve (a) by the first method used in Prob. 323; (b) by the second method used in Prob. 323.

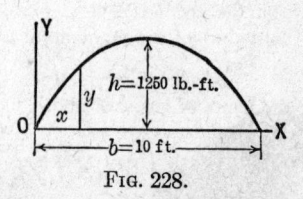

Fig. 228.

327. Find the moment about the x-axis of the area of the upper half of the circle $x^2 + y^2 = r^2$. *Ans.* $Q_x = \frac{2}{3}r^3$.

328. Find the moment of the volume of a right circular cone about the base. Express it in terms of r, the radius of the base, and h, the altitude of the cone.

329. Find the moment about the y-axis of the area bounded by the curve $x^2 = y$ and the lines $x + y = 0$ and $x = 6$. *Ans.* $Q_y = 396$.

330. Find the moment about the x-axis of the area bounded by the curve $y^2 = 4x$ and the lines $x = 4$ and $y = 2$.

331. Find the moment of the volume of a hemisphere, of radius r, with respect to the base of the hemisphere. *Ans.* $Q = \frac{1}{4}\pi r^4$.

65. Centroids.—The centroid of an area is the point in the area whose distance from any axis multiplied by the area is equal to the moment of the area about the axis. This definition expressed in mathematical form is

$$A\bar{x} = \int x\, dA \quad \text{and} \quad A\bar{y} = \int y\, dA \quad \ldots \quad (1)$$

Where A is the area and $\bar{x}$ and $\bar{y}$ (called centroidal distances) are the co-ordinates of the centroid with respect to the y- and x-axes, respectively.

If the centroidal distances $\bar{x}$ and $\bar{y}$ for an area are known, the moment of the area can usually be found more conveniently from the expression $A\bar{x}$ than from $\int x dA$. The centroidal distances for many geometric forms of lines, areas, volumes and masses are given in engineering handbooks, and it is important that the method of applying equations (1) for determining the centroidal distances of such geometric forms as are illustrated in the next article be well understood.

Since $A\bar{x}$ would, by definition, be the moment of the area, A, if all the area were located (concentrated) at a point whose distance from the axis is $\bar{x}$, equation (1) may be interpreted as follows: The centroid of an area is a point at which the whole area may be conceived to be concentrated so that the moment of the concentrated area about any axis is equal to the moment of the actual distributed area about the same axis.

Mass-Center.—Although the term centroid as defined above has been used in connection with masses as well as with volumes, areas, and lines, it is sometimes used in a restricted sense as applying only to geometrical figures (volumes, areas, and lines), in which no idea of mass is involved, and the term *mass-center* or *center of mass* is used to denote that point of a physical body where the mass could be conceived to be concentrated so that the moment of the concentrated mass about any axis or plane would be equal to the moment of the distributed mass of the body about the same axis or plane. Hereafter, then, with reference to physical bodies the terms centroid and mass-center will be regarded as synonymous. It should be noted that the centroid of a geometrical solid (volume) coincides with the centroid (or mass-center) of a homogeneous physical solid (body) provided the two solids are congruent.

Center of Gravity.—Another term closely associated with centroid and mass-center is center of gravity. The *center of gravity* of a body is generally defined as that point in a body through which the weight of the body acts, regardless of the position (or orientation) of the body. Now the weight of a body is merely the resultant of the parallel forces exerted on the particles of the body by the earth, and if the body is reorientated the weights of those particles which move nearer to the earth are increased and the weights of those particles which move farther from the earth are decreased. Hence, in considering two different positions of the body, two different force systems are involved, and strictly speaking, there is in general no one point in the body through which the resultant weight acts regardless of the position of the body. In other words, the center of gravity in general does not exist. From a practical viewpoint, however, the variation in the weights of the particles due to a change in the position of the body are extremely small and may be entirely disregarded, in which case the weights of the particles are proportional to their masses and hence the center of gravity as above defined coincides exactly with the mass-center, and hence the terms mass-center and center of gravity as applied to a physical body are usually regarded as synonymous and will be so used hereafter. The fundamental significance of the two terms should, however, be kept in mind, for in finding the mass-center of a body, the moment of a mass system is involved; and in finding the center of gravity, the moment of a force system is involved.

By way of summary, then, the x-coordinate, $\bar{x}$, of the centroid of a line of length L, an area A, a volume V, or a mass M may be found from the following equations, respectively:

$$L\bar{x} = \int x dL; \quad A\bar{x} = \int x dA; \quad V\bar{x} = \int x dV; \quad M\bar{x} = \int x dM$$

and the y- and z-coordinates may be found from similar equations.

66. Planes and Lines of Symmetry.—If a geometrical figure (volume, area, or line) is symmetrical with respect to a given plane or axis, the centroid of the figure lies in the given plane or axis. This statement is evident from the fact that the moments of the parts of the figure on the opposite sides of the plane or axis are numerically equal but of opposite sign. If a figure is symmetrical with respect to each of two planes or lines, the centroid of the figure lies in the line of intersection of the two planes or at the point of intersection of the two axes. If the figure has three planes of symmetry, the centroid coincides with the point of intersection of the three planes. The foregoing statements apply also to the centroids of the masses of homogeneous physical solids which are symmetrical with respect to one or more planes. The centroids of many simple figures may be partially or completely determined from symmetry. It is well to note that axes of symmetry are always centroidal axes, but centroidal axes are not always axes of symmetry.

67. Centroids by Integration.—In determining the centroid of a volume, mass, area, or line by the method of integration, from the equations of Art. 65, it is possible to select the element of volume, area, etc., in various ways and to express the element in terms of either cartesian or polar coordinates. The resulting integral may be a single, a double, or a triple integral, depending on the way the element is selected. The integral, of course, is a definite integral, the limits of integration depending on the boundary curve or surface of the figure or body. In any case the element of volume, mass, area, or line must be taken so that:

ILLUSTRATIVE PROBLEMS

1. All points of the element are the same distance from the line or plane about which moments are taken; otherwise, the distance from the line or plane to the element will be indefinite. Or so that:

2. The centroid of the element is known, in which case the moment of the element about the moment-axis or plane is the product of the element and the distance of its centroid from the axis or plane.

The centroids of some of the common figures (lines, areas, and volumes) will be found in the following illustrative problems.

ILLUSTRATIVE PROBLEMS

Find, by the method of integration, the centroids of the following figures with respect to the axes indicated.

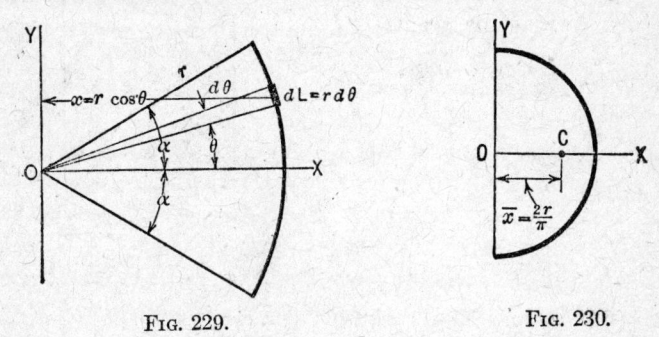

FIG. 229.　　　　FIG. 230.

Problem 332.—Arc of a Circle.—The radius which bisects the arc will be taken as the x-axis (Fig. 229). By symmetry the centroid lies on this axis. Hence $\bar{y} = 0$. If r denotes the radius of the arc and 2α the subtended angle, then, in terms of polar coordinates, the element of arc, dL, and its distance x from the y-axis are $dL = rd\theta$ and $x = r\cos\theta$. Thus, the element of arc is selected in accordance with the first of the above rules, and $\bar{x}$ may be found as follows:

$$L\bar{x} = \int x\,dL = \int_{-\alpha}^{+\alpha} r\cos\theta \cdot r d\theta = r^2 \int_{-\alpha}^{+\alpha} \cos\theta\, d\theta = 2r^2 \sin\alpha.$$

Therefore
$$\bar{x} = \frac{2r^2 \sin\alpha}{L} = \frac{2r^2 \sin\alpha}{2r\alpha} = \frac{r\sin\alpha}{\alpha}.$$

If the arc is a semicircle, that is, if $\alpha = 90° = \dfrac{\pi}{2}$ radians, $\bar{x} = \dfrac{2r}{\pi}$ (Fig. 230). That is, the distance of the centroid of a semi-circular arc from the center of the circle is slightly less than two-thirds of the radius of the circle.

Problem 333.—Area of a Triangle. *First Method.*—In accordance with the first of the above rules the elements of area will be taken as strips parallel to the base of the triangle (Fig. 231). Since each element is bisected by the median drawn from the vertex opposite the base, the centroid of each element, and hence of the entire area, lies on this median. If x denotes the width of the strip, the area of the strip is $dA = xdy$. Thus

$$A\bar{y} = \int xy\,dy.$$

From similar triangles, the relation between x and y is $x = \dfrac{b}{h}(h - y)$.
Hence

$$A\bar{y} = \frac{b}{h}\int_0^h (h - y)y\,dy = \tfrac{1}{6}bh^2.$$

Therefore

$$\bar{y} = \frac{\tfrac{1}{6}bh^2}{\tfrac{1}{2}bh} = \frac{1}{3}h.$$

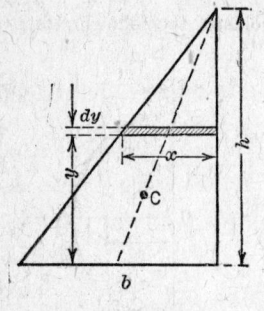

FIG. 231. 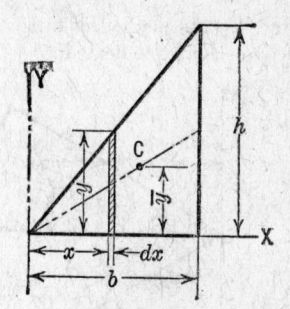   FIG. 232.

The centroid of a triangle area, then, is on a median and at a distance of one-third of the altitude from the base.

Second Method.—In accordance with the second of the above rules the element of area will be taken as a vertical strip as shown in Fig. 232. The moment of the element is $dA \cdot \dfrac{y}{2}$ or $y\,dx \cdot \dfrac{y}{2}$. Since $y = \dfrac{h}{b}x$, we have

$$A\bar{y} = \int_0^b \frac{y}{2} y\,dx = \frac{h^2}{2b^2}\int_0^b x^2\,dx = \tfrac{1}{6}h^2b,$$

$$\bar{y} = \frac{\tfrac{1}{6}bh^2}{\tfrac{1}{2}bh} = \frac{1}{3}h.$$

Problem 334.—*Sector of a Circle. First Method.*—The element of area will be selected in accordance with the first of the above rules as indicated in Fig. 233. Since the area is symmetrical with respect to the x-axis, the centroid lies on this axis and hence $\bar{y} = 0$. The value of $\bar{x}$ may then be found from the equation

$$A\bar{x} = \int x\,dA = \int_0^r \int_{-\alpha}^{+\alpha} \rho \cos\theta \cdot \rho\,d\rho\,d\theta = \tfrac{2}{3}r^3 \sin\alpha.$$

Therefore

$$\bar{x} = \frac{\tfrac{2}{3}r^3 \sin\alpha}{A} = \frac{\tfrac{2}{3}r^3 \sin\alpha}{r^2\alpha} = \frac{2}{3}\frac{r \sin\alpha}{\alpha}.$$

Second Method.—In accordance with the second of the above rules, the element of area will be selected as a triangle, as indicated in Fig. 234. The area of the triangle is $\frac{1}{2}r^2 d\theta$ and the distance of its centroid from the y-axis is $\frac{2}{3}r \cos \theta$. Hence, the

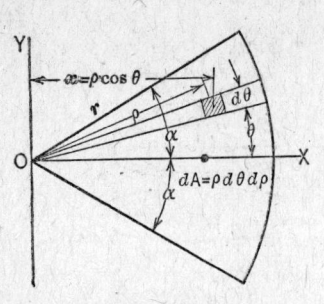

FIG. 233.

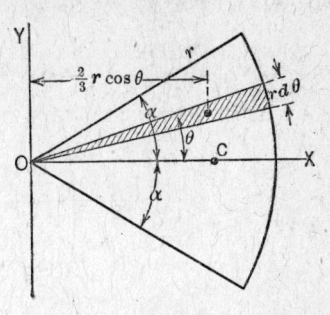

FIG. 234.

moment of the triangle with respect to the y-axis is $\frac{1}{3}r^3 \cos \theta d\theta$ and $\bar{x}$ is obtained from the equation

$$A\bar{x} = \int_{-\alpha}^{+\alpha} \frac{1}{3}r^3 \cos \theta d\theta = \frac{2}{3}r^3 \sin \alpha.$$

Therefore

$$\bar{x} = \frac{\frac{2}{3}r^3 \sin \alpha}{r^2 \alpha} = \frac{2}{3}\frac{r \sin \alpha}{\alpha}.$$

If $\alpha = 90° = \frac{\pi}{2}$ radians (Fig. 235), that is, if the sector is a semi-circular area, $\bar{x} = \frac{4r}{3\pi}$.

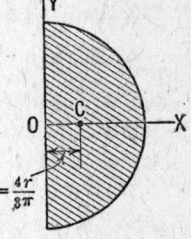

FIG. 235.

PROBLEMS

335. Find the x- and y-coordinates of the centroid of the parabolic segment shown in Fig. 236. Select the element of area dA as indicated in the figure.

Ans. $\bar{x} = \frac{3}{5}a$; $\bar{y} = \frac{3}{8}b$.

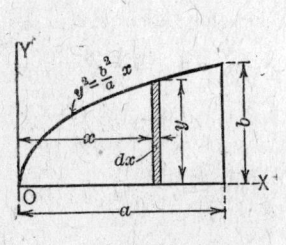

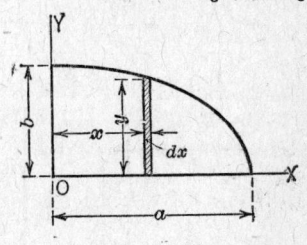

FIG. 236.

FIG. 237.

336. Find the x- and y-coordinates of the centroid of the area of the quadrant of the ellipse $\frac{x^2}{a^2} + \frac{y^2}{b^2} = 1$ shown in Fig. 237. Select the element of area dA as indicated in the figure.

Ans. $\bar{x} = \frac{4a}{3\pi}$; $\bar{y} = \frac{4b}{3\pi}$.

337. Find the x-coordinate of the centroid of the volume of the right circular cone shown in Fig. 238. Select the element of volume dV as indicated in the figure.

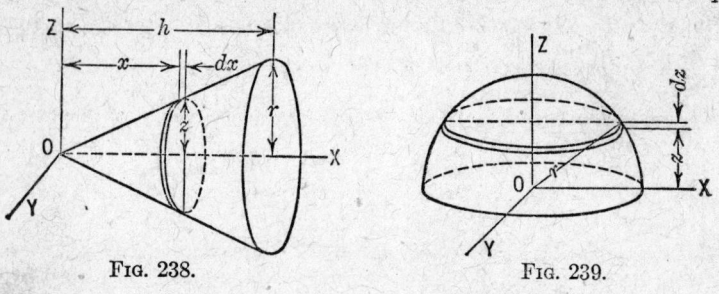

Ans. $\bar{x} = \frac{3}{4}h$.

Fig. 238.   Fig. 239.

338. Find the z-coordinate of the centroid of the volume of the hemisphere shown in Fig. 239. Select the element of volume dV as indicated in the figure.

Ans. $\bar{z} = \frac{3}{8}r$.

339. Find the y-coordinate of the centroid of the area under the sine curve $y = \sin x$ between ordinates corresponding to $x = 0$ and $x = \pi$. Ans. $\bar{x} = \dfrac{\pi}{8}$.

340. A pulley having a thin rim is 2 ft. in diameter. How far from the center of the pulley is the mass-center of one-half of the rim?

341. Find the y-coordinate of the centroid of the area included between the x-axis, the curve $y^2 = x^3$, and the line $x = a$. Ans. $\bar{y} = \frac{5}{16}a^{3/2}$.

342. A sector having a central angle of 120° is removed from a circular area of radius r. Find the centroid of the remaining area.

343. Show that the centroid of the surface of a right circular cone is on the axis of the cone at a distance of $\frac{2}{3}h$ from the apex, where h is the altitude of the cone.

344. The radius of the base of a right circular cone is 5 in. and its height is 2 ft. Locate the centroid of (a) the volume of the cone; (b) the curved surface area of the cone.

345. Locate the centroid of the area included between the y-axis, the line $y = b$, and the parabola $y^2 = \dfrac{b^2 x}{a}$ as shown in Fig. 240. Select the element of area as shown in the figure.

Ans. $\bar{x} = \frac{3}{10}a$; $\bar{y} = \frac{3}{4}b$.

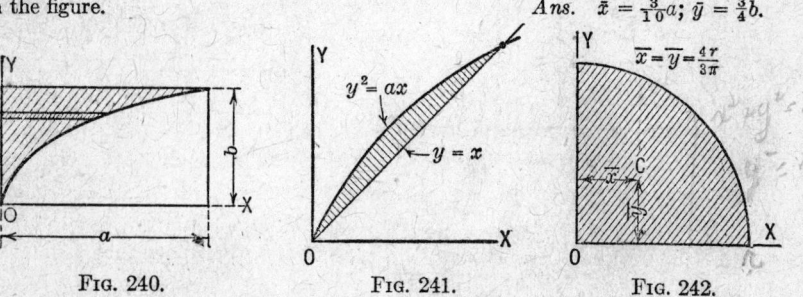

Fig. 240.   Fig. 241.   Fig. 242.

346. Find the centroid of the area (Fig. 241) included between the curve $y^2 = ax$ and the line $y = x$.

CENTROIDS OF COMPOSITE FIGURES AND BODIES 153

347. Show that the centroidal distances for the area of a quadrant of a circle of radius r (Fig. 242) are $\bar{x} = \bar{y} = \dfrac{4r}{3\pi}$.

348. Find the coordinates of the centroid of the area bounded by the ellipse $\dfrac{x^2}{25} + \dfrac{y^2}{16} = 1$, the line $x = 5$, and the line $y = 4$.

349. Find the centroid of the area bounded by the curve $y = x^3$, the x-axis, and the line $x = a$. *Ans.* $\bar{x} = \tfrac{4}{5}a;\ \bar{y} = \tfrac{2}{7}a^3$.

350. Find the centroid of the area bounded by the parabola $x^2 = \dfrac{a^2}{b} y$, the line $x = a$, and the x-axis.

351. A paraboloid is generated by rotating the parabola $y^2 = px$ about the x-axis. Locate the centroid of the volume included between the paraboloid and the plane $x = a$. *Ans.* $\bar{x} = \tfrac{2}{3}a$.

352. Find the y-coordinate of the centroid of the area bounded by the curve $y^2 = 4x$ and the lines $x = 4$ and $y = 2$.

353. Find the y-coordinate of the centroid of the area bounded by the parabolas $y^2 = ax$ and $x^2 = ay$. *Ans.* $\bar{y} = \tfrac{9}{20}a$.

354. The area included between the x-axis, the curve $y^2 = x^3$, and the line $x = a$ is rotated about the x-axis. Find the centroid of the volume generated.

355. Find the position of the mass-center of a hemisphere in which the density at any point varies directly as the distance of the point from the base.
Ans. $\bar{y} = \tfrac{8}{15}r$.

356. Find the mass-center of a right circular cone in which the density at any point varies directly as the distance of the point from the base.

357. The density at any point of a slender rod of length l varies directly as the distance of the point from one end of the rod. Show that the mass-center of the rod is $\tfrac{2}{3}l$ from that end.

68. Centroids of Composite Figures and Bodies.

As noted in Art. 65, if the centroid of a line, area, volume, or mass is known, the moment with respect to an axis or plane is most easily found by multiplying the line, area, volume, or mass by the distance of the centroid from the axis or plane. Thus, if a given line, area, volume, or mass can be divided into parts, the centroids of which are known, the moment of the whole line, area, etc., may be found without integrating, by obtaining the algebraic sum of the moments of the parts into which the line, area, volume, or mass is divided, the moment of each part being the product of that part and the distance of its centroid from the line or plane. Thus, for example, in the case of a composite area, if a_1, a_2, a_3, etc., denote the parts into which the area A is divided, and x'_0, x''_0, x'''_0, etc., denote the x-coordinates of the centroids of the respective parts, then

$$(a_1 + a_2 + a_3 + \cdots)\bar{x} = a_1 x'_0 + a_2 x''_0 + a_3 x'''_0 + \cdots,$$

or
$$\Sigma a \cdot \bar{x} = \Sigma(ax_0),$$
Hence,
$$A\bar{x} = \Sigma(ax_0), \text{ and similarly, } A\bar{y} = \Sigma(ay_0).$$

From similar equations the centroid of a composite line, volume, or mass may be found.

ILLUSTRATIVE PROBLEMS

Problem 358.—Locate the centroid of the T-section shown in Fig. 243.

Solution.—If axes be selected as indicated it is evident from symmetry that $\bar{x} = 0$. By dividing the given area into areas a_1 and a_2 and by taking moments about the bottom edge of the area, $\bar{y}$ may be found as follows:

$$A\bar{y} = \Sigma(ay_0),$$

$$\bar{y} = \frac{12 \times 1 + 12 \times 5}{6 \times 2 + 6 \times 2} = 3 \text{ in.}$$

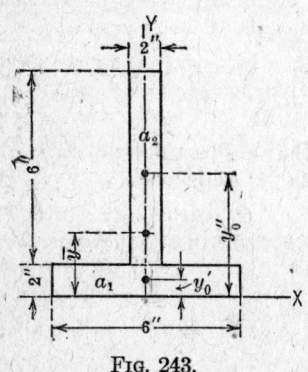

FIG. 243. 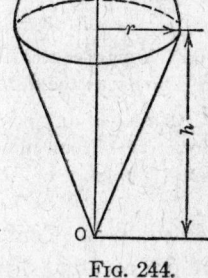   FIG. 244.

Problem 359.—Locate the centroid of the volume of the cone and hemisphere shown in Fig. 244, the values of r and h being 6 in. and 18 in., respectively.

Solution.—The axis of symmetry will be taken as the y-axis. From symmetry then $\bar{x} = 0$. By taking the x-axis through the apex of the cone as shown, the equation $V\bar{y} = \Sigma(vy_0)$ becomes

$$(\tfrac{1}{3}\pi r^2 h + \tfrac{2}{3}\pi r^3)\bar{y} = \tfrac{1}{3}\pi r^2 h \times \tfrac{3}{4}h + \tfrac{2}{3}\pi r^3(h + \tfrac{3}{8}r).$$

That is
$$\tfrac{1}{3}\pi r^2(h + 2r)\bar{y} = \tfrac{1}{3}\pi r^2(\tfrac{3}{4}h^2 + 2rh + \tfrac{3}{4}r^2).$$

Therefore
$$\bar{y} = \frac{\tfrac{3}{4}h^2 + 2rh + \tfrac{3}{4}r^2}{h + 2r}$$

$$= \frac{\tfrac{3}{4} \times (18)^2 + 2 \times 6 \times 18 + \tfrac{3}{4} \times (6)^2}{18 + 2 \times 6} = 16.2 \text{ in.}$$

PROBLEMS

360. A rectangular area 6 in. wide and 12 in. high has cut from it a semi-circular area the diameter of which coincides with one long side of the rectangle. Find the centroid of the remaining area.

361. From an area 6 in. square is cut out an isosceles triangle whose base coincides with one side of the square. If the centroid of the remaining area is at the vertex of the triangle, what is the altitude of the triangle?   *Ans.* $h = 3.8$ in.

362. Locate, with respect to the axes shown, the centroid of the shaded area in Fig. 245.

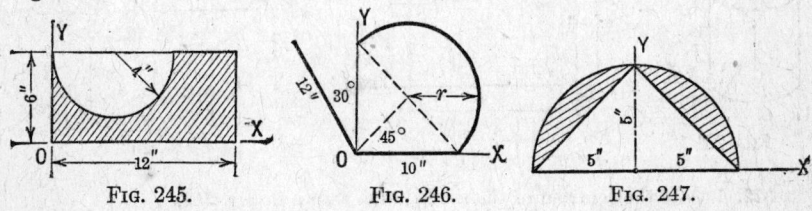

FIG. 245.   FIG. 246.   FIG. 247.

363. A wire is bent in the form shown by the heavy line in Fig. 246. Locate the centroid (or mass-center) of the wire.   *Ans.* $\bar{x} = 4.42$ in.; $\bar{y} = 5.52$ in.

364. Find the centroid of the shaded area shown in Fig. 247.

365. A triangular corner whose area is 25 sq. in. is cut from a square 10 in. on a side. What are the dimensions of the triangle if the centroid of the remaining area is 4 in. from one side of the square?   *Ans.* $8\frac{1}{3}$ in. $\times$ 6 in.

366. The area of an isosceles triangle having an altitude h and a base b is divided into two areas by a line parallel to the base and distant $h/2$ therefrom. Find the distance from the base to the centroid of each of the two areas.

367. Locate, with respect to the axes shown, the centroid of the shaded area in Fig. 248.   *Ans.* $\bar{x} = 3.61$ in.; $\bar{y} = 5.24$ in.

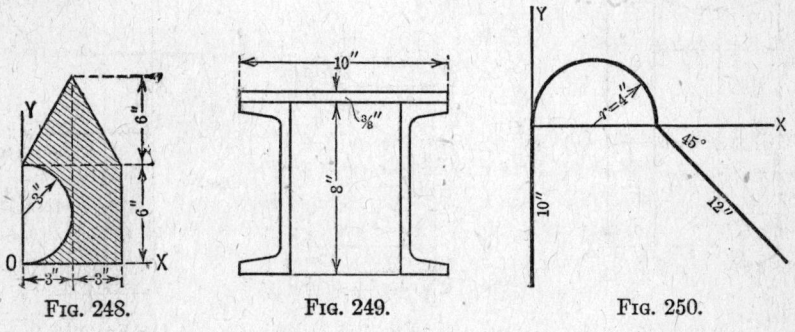

FIG. 248.   FIG. 249.   FIG. 250.

368. Fig. 249 represents the cross-section of the end post of a bridge. The area of each channel section is 4.78 sq. in. Find the distance from the top of the cover plate to the centroid of the section.

369. A slender steel rod is bent in the form shown in Fig. 250. Locate the centroid of the rod with respect to the axes shown.

Ans. $\bar{x} = 5.70$ in.; $\bar{y} = -1.99$ in.

370. In Fig. 244 let $h = 12$ in. and $r = 4$ in. Find the y-coordinate of the centroid of the lateral area of the cone and hemisphere.

371. In Fig. 251 find the z-coordinate of the centroid of the lateral area of the cylinder and cone. *Ans.* $\bar{z} = 4.79$ in.

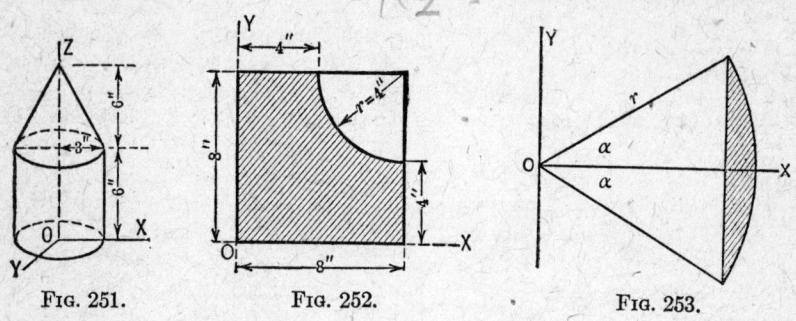

Fig. 251.   Fig. 252.   Fig. 253.

372. Locate the centroid of the shaded area shown in Fig. 252.

373. Locate the centroid of the segment of a circle as shown in Fig. 253. In the expression for $\bar{x}$ make $\alpha = \dfrac{\pi}{2}$, and see if the result agrees with the result found in Prob. 334 for a semi-circle.

374. In Fig. 254 is represented a homogeneous solid which consists of a hemisphere and a right circular cylinder from which a cone is removed. Locate the centroid of the solid with respect to the axes indicated.   *Ans.* $\bar{z} = 6.45$ in.

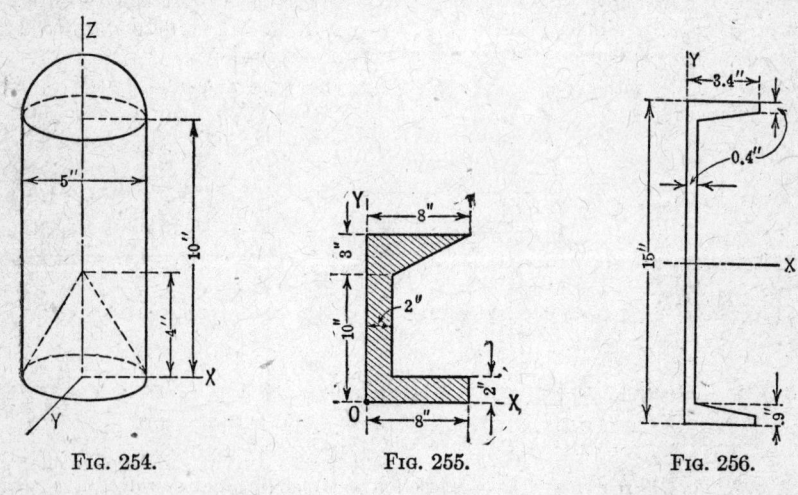

Fig. 254.   Fig. 255.   Fig. 256.

375. Locate, with respect to the axes shown, the centroid of the shaded area in Fig. 255.

376. Find the centroid of the area of the channel section shown in Fig. 256.
Ans. $\bar{x} = 0.79$ in.

377. The radii of the upper and lower bases of the frustum of a right circular cone are r_1 and r_2 and the altitude is a. Find the distance of the centroid of the volume above the lower base.

378. Three particles of equal mass are placed at the vertices of a triangle. Show that the mass-center of the particles coincides with the centroid of the area of the triangle.

379. Two homogeneous spheres A and B, connected by a rod, are mounted on a vertical axis as shown in Fig. 257. The weights of the spheres are 20 lb. and 60 lb., respectively, and the weight of the rod is 10 lb. How far from the axis is the center of gravity of the three bodies?

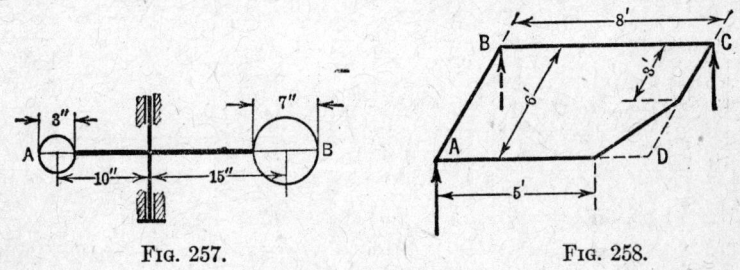

FIG. 257.   FIG. 258.

380. If the top of the table (Fig. 258) weighs 40 lb. per sq. ft., find the reaction of the floor on each of the three legs at the corners A, B, and C. Neglect the weights of the legs.   Ans. $A = 810$ lb.; $B = 127.5$ lb.; $C = 802.5$ lb.

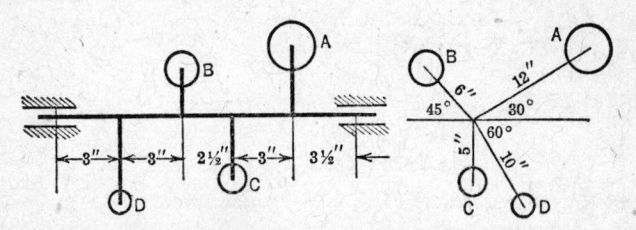

FIG. 259.

381. Four bodies A, B, C, and D are carried by a rotating shaft as shown in Fig. 259. The weights of the bodies are 20, 15, 10, and 8 lb., respectively, and the distances of their centers of gravity from the axis of the shaft are 12, 6, 5, and 10 in., respectively. Find the center of gravity of the four bodies when in the positions shown.

69. Theorems of Pappus and Guldinus.

—I. The area of a surface of revolution generated by revolving a plane curve about any non-intersecting axis in its plane is equal to the product of the length of the curve and the length of the path described by the centroid of the curve.

Proof.—Let the curve AB (Fig. 260) be revolved about OX. The area of the surface generated is given by the equation

$$A = \int 2\pi y \cdot dL = 2\pi \int y dL = 2\pi \bar{y} \cdot L,$$

where $\bar{y}$ is the distance of the centroid of the curve from OX and L is the length of the curve.

II. The volume of the solid generated by revolving any plane area about any non-intersecting line in its plane is the product of the area and the length of the path described by the centroid of the area.

Proof.—Let the plane area A (Fig. 261) be rotated about the axis OX. Each elementary area dA will generate a circular ring the volume of

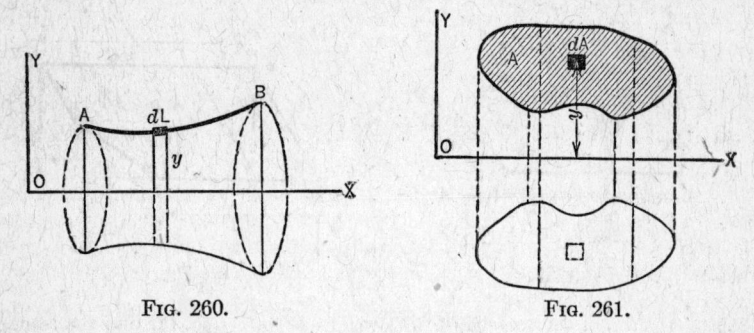

FIG. 260.

FIG. 261.

which is $2\pi y dA$ and hence the entire volume generated is given by the equation

$$V = \int 2\pi y dA = 2\pi \int y dA = 2\pi \bar{y} \cdot A,$$

where $\bar{y}$ is the distance of the centroid of the area from OX.

ILLUSTRATIVE PROBLEMS

Problem 382.—Show that the area of the surface of a hemisphere generated by rotating the quadrant of a circle (shown in Fig. 262) about the x-axis is $2\pi r^2$.

Solution.—

$$A = L \cdot 2\pi \bar{y} = \frac{2\pi r}{4} \times 2\pi \times \frac{2r}{\pi} = 2\pi r^2 \text{ (see Prob. 332)}.$$

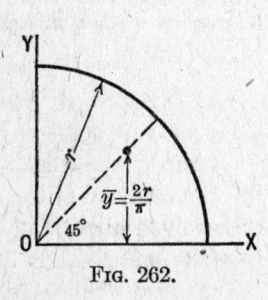

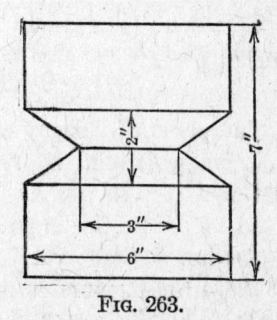

FIG. 262.

FIG. 263.

Problem 383.—A V-shaped groove is turned out of a cylinder as indicated by Fig. 263. Find the volume of the material removed.

Solution.—The distance of the centroid of the triangle, which generates the volume, from the axis of the cylinder is 2.5 in. and the area of the triangle is 1.5 sq. in. Hence

$$V = A \cdot 2\pi \bar{x} = 1.5 \times 2\pi \times 2.5 = 23.55 \text{ cu. in.}$$

PROBLEMS

Solve the following problems by the theorems of Pappus and Guldinus:

384. Find, in terms of the radius, the surface area and the volume of a sphere.

385. An area in the xy-plane is bounded by the lines $x = 0$, $x = 6$, $y = 6$, and $2y = x$. Find the x-coordinate of the centroid of the area. Find also the volume of the solid generated by rotating the area about the y-axis.

Ans. $\bar{x} = 2\frac{2}{3}$ in.; $V = 452$ cu. in.

386. Find the lateral surface and the volume of a cone. Express the results in terms of the radius of the base and the altitude of the cone.

387. The center of a circle which lies in the xy-plane and has a radius r is at a distance a from the y-axis. The solid generated by rotating the circle about the y-axis is a torrus (or anchor ring) provided a is greater than r. Find the surface area and the volume of the solid. *Ans.* $A = 4\pi^2 ar$; $V = 2\pi^2 ar^2$.

388. Find the lateral area of the solid generated by revolving the square shown in Fig. 264 about the y-axis through an angle of 90°. *Ans.* $A = 603$ sq. in.

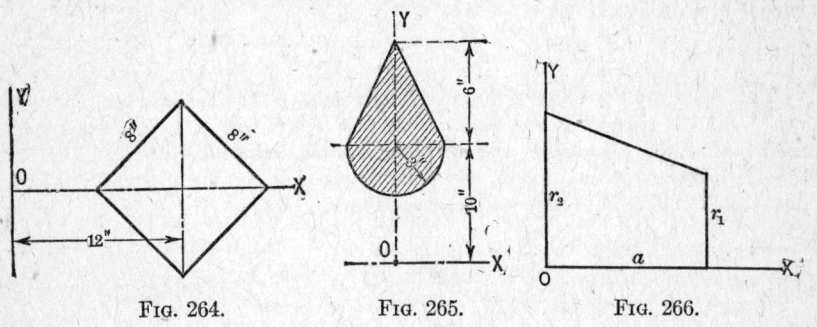

Fig. 264.   Fig. 265.   Fig. 266.

389. Find the volume generated by revolving the shaded area shown in Fig. 265 about the x-axis.

390. Find the volume of the ellipsoid generated by revolving the right half of the ellipse, $\dfrac{x^2}{a^2} + \dfrac{y^2}{b^2} = 1$, about the y-axis. *Ans.* $V = \frac{4}{3}\pi a^2 b$.

391. Find the y-coordinate of the centroid of the trapezoid shown in Fig. 266. Determine the volume of the frustum of a cone generated by revolving the trapezoid about the x-axis.

70. Center of Pressure.—A point closely associated with the center of gravity is the *center of pressure*. If a pressure is distributed over a given plane area the center of pressure is that point in the area at which the resultant pressure acts. If the pressure is uniformly distributed over the area, the center of pressure coincides with the centroid of the area. If the pressure on the area is produced by the weight of material placed on the area, the center of pressure is that point in the area vertically below the center of gravity of the material. The center of pressure is of special importance in the study of *hydraulics*.

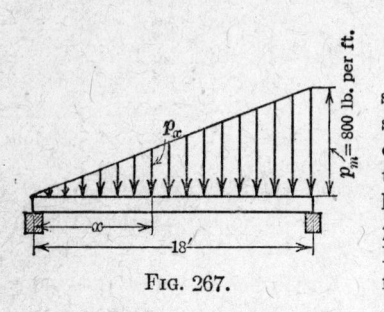

ILLUSTRATIVE PROBLEM

Problem 392.—Gravel is piled on a floor so that the pressure on the beams which support the floor increases in the direction of the beams as shown in Fig. 267. The intensity of pressure varies from zero at the left end of the beam to a maximum of $p_m = 800$ lb. per linear foot at the right end. Find the total pressure on the floor. Also find the position of the center of pressure.

FIG. 267.

Solution.—Let the intensity of pressure at any distance x from the left end of the beam be p_x lb. per ft. This pressure may be assumed to be constant over a length dx and hence the pressure over this length is $dP = p_x dx$. But $p_x = \dfrac{x}{l} \cdot p_m$. Therefore the total pressure on the beam is

$$P = \int p_x dx = \int_0^l \frac{x}{l} p_m dx = \frac{p_m}{2} \times l = 7200 \text{ lb.}$$

Hence, the total pressure of the gravel (its weight) is the same in magnitude as it would be if the gravel were spread uniformly to a depth equal to one-half that of the maximum depth. The total pressure, however, would then act at the center of the beam, whereas, according to the above distribution, the center of pressure is at a distance $\bar{x}$ from the left end of the beam such that

$$P\bar{x} = \int x dP,$$

$$\left(\frac{p_m}{2} \times l\right) \bar{x} = \int_0^l \frac{x}{l} p_m dx \, x = \frac{p_m l^2}{3}.$$

Therefore

$$\bar{x} = \frac{2}{3} l.$$

This result might have been obtained, without taking the above detailed steps, from the fact that the gravel may be conceived to be concentrated in a plane (of triangular shape), the position of the center of gravity of the gravel then being the same as that of the centroid of the triangular area, and as noted above the center of pressure is vertically beneath the center of gravity.

PROBLEMS

393. A beam is loaded with brick piled so as to produce the distribution of pressure as indicated in Fig. 268. Find the center of pressure on the beam.

394. A beam 10 ft. long is subjected to a pressure that varies as the ordinate to the parabola $y^2 = 1000x$ as indicated in Fig. 269, where y is the pressure in pounds per linear foot, and x is the distance in feet from the left end of the beam. Find the reactions R_1 and R_2. *Ans.* $R_1 = 267$ lb.; $R_2 = 400$ lb.

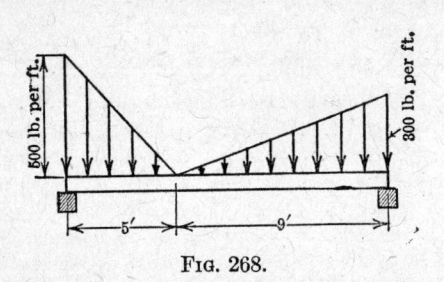

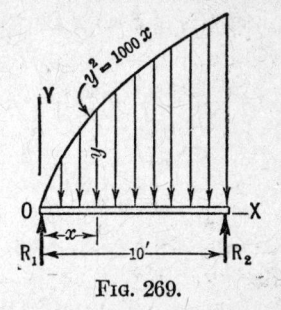

FIG. 268.   FIG. 269.

395. The vertical side of a tank is 8 ft. wide and 6 ft. deep. The tank is filled with water. Locate the center of pressure of the water on the side of the tank. The pressure at any point in the water is proportional to the depth of the point below the free surface, and is the same in all directions.

396. A rectangular grain bin is 6 ft. wide and 12 ft. long. The depth of grain across one 6-ft. end is 4 ft., and the depth increases uniformly to 6 ft. at the opposite end. Find the resultant pressure on the bottom of the bin and also find the center of pressure, assuming the weight of the grain to be 40 lb. per cu. ft.
Ans. $P = 14,400$ lb.; $\bar{x} = 6.4$ ft.

397. A semi-circular plate that is supported around its semi-circumferential boundary is subjected to a vertical load (not shown) that produces a uniform pressure along the support as shown in Fig. 270. Find in terms of r the distance, $\bar{x}$, of the center of pressure from the straight edge of the plate. If a pressure is uniformly distributed along a line how is the center of pressure related to the centroid of the line?

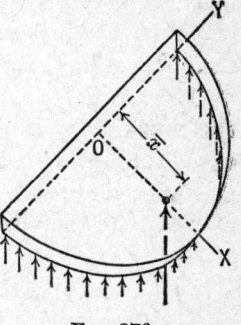

FIG. 270.

71. Graphical Method of Determining Centroids of Areas.—If the boundary of an area is an irregular curve which cannot be represented by an equation, the centroid cannot be determined by the method of integration. In such cases, however, the centroid may be determined by a graphical method which makes use of the force and string polygons. The irregular area is drawn to scale and is then divided into a large number of narrow strips parallel to one coordinate axis, the areas of which can be determined or estimated closely. These strips of area are then thought of as having weight and are replaced by a parallel force system in which the magnitude of each force is numerically equal to the area of the corresponding strip and acts vertically downward through the center of the strip. Now by use of a force and a string polygon, a point on the action line of the resultant of the parallel force system is found as in Art. 25 and the centroid of the area lies on a vertical line through this point. The distance of this line from the coordinate axis that is parallel to the strips gives one coordinate of the centroid. By dividing the area into strips parallel to the other coordinate axis and repeating the process the other coordinate of the centroid is found.

72. Determination of Center of Gravity by Experiment.—When a body is irregular in shape, the center of gravity cannot be determined by the method of integration since the limits of the integral cannot be determined. The center of gravity of such a body, however, may be determined by the following experimental methods.

Method of Suspension.—If a body be suspended by a cord the center of gravity is on the (vertical) line coinciding with the axis of the cord. This statement follows from the fact that the two forces which hold the body in equilibrium (the upward tension in the cord and the downward earth-pull) must be equal, opposite, and collinear, and the earth-pull or weight of the body of course acts through the center of gravity of the body. Hence if a body be suspended from each of two points, the center of gravity will be located in each of two lines in the body and hence is at the point of intersection of the two lines.

Method of Balancing.—If a body be balanced on a knife-edge the center of gravity of the body will be in a vertical plane through the knife-edge. Hence if the body be balanced on a knife-edge in three different positions, three such planes in the body will be located, and the center of gravity of the body is the point in which the three planes intersect.

REVIEW QUESTIONS AND PROBLEMS

398. Define the moment of a line about a coordinate axis (*a*) in words and (*b*) by a mathematical expression.

399. What is the value of the moment of the surface area of a right circular cone that has a base of radius r and an altitude h about a plane in which the axis of the cone lies.

400. What are the dimensions of the moment of an area about an axis? Of a volume about a plane?

401. What is the value of the moment of the area of the base of a right circular cone about a plane parallel to the base and passing through the vertex of the cone? The known quantities are the radius, r, of the base and the altitude, h, of the cone.

402. Correct the following statement: The centroid of a plane area is a point in the area whose distance from a given axis divided by the area is equal to the moment of the area with respect to the axis.

403. In finding centroids of lines, areas, and volumes by the method of integration, what are the two general ways in which the element of the line, area, or volume may be selected?

REVIEW QUESTIONS AND PROBLEMS 163

404. Explain why the following statement is indefinite and meaningless: The centroid of a volume is a point at which the whole volume may be thought of as being located or concentrated.

405. In Fig. 271 show, by integration, that the moments of the areas A and B with respect to the x-axis are each equal to $\frac{1}{4}ab^2$.

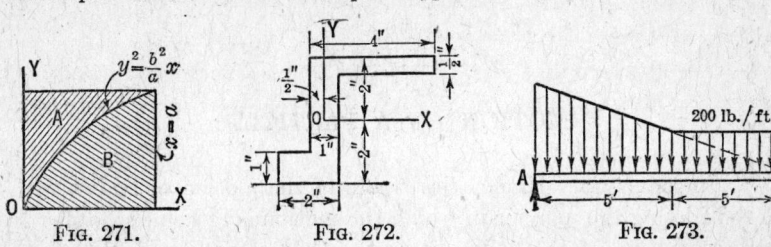

FIG. 271.   FIG. 272.   FIG. 273.

406. Find, without integrating, the x- and y-coordinates of the centroid of the area shown in Fig. 272. *Ans.* $\bar{x} = 0.308$ in.; $\bar{y} = 0.173$ in.

407. The beam AB (Fig. 273) is subjected to a pressure that varies as indicated. How far from A is the center of pressure? *Ans.* $\bar{x} = 4.33$ ft.

408. An isosceles triangle whose two equal sides are each c and whose base is b is rotated 360° about the base. Find by the theorems of Pappus and Guldinus the surface area generated by the sides of the triangle and the volume generated by the area of the triangle.

Ans. $A = \pi c \sqrt{4c^2 - b^2}$; $V = \dfrac{\pi b}{12}(4c^2 - b^2)$.

409. A homogeneous cube each edge of which is b in. long rests on a horizontal plane. On top of the cube is placed a homogeneous right circular cone having a base of diameter b in. and an altitude of b in., the base of the cone resting on the upper face of the cube. Find the distance of the center of gravity of the two bodies above the horizontal plane. *Ans.* $0.65b$.

PART II. KINEMATICS

CHAPTER VI

MOTION OF A PARTICLE

73. Introduction.—Kinematics treats of the motion of bodies without considering the manner in which the motion is influenced, either by the forces acting on the bodies or by the character of the bodies themselves. That is, the bodies are treated as geometric solids and not as physical bodies. When the geometric solids are endowed with physical properties, we are led to a study of force, energy, momentum, etc., that is, to a study of Kinetics (Part III).

Kinematics deals with the relation between distance, time, velocity, and acceleration. In order to build up the fundamental conceptions which are involved in the study of the motion of bodies, the kinematics of a particle (material point) will be treated first. A particle is a part of a body the dimensions of which are negligible compared with its range of motion. Bodies are made up of particles, and the study of the motion of bodies is largely a study of the motion of their particles.

The study of the motion of bodies will, for the most part, be restricted to rigid bodies, and the motions considered will be limited mainly to translation, rotation, and plane motion.

74. Vector Addition and Subtraction.—In discussing the motion of a point in terms of the vector quantities displacement, velocity, and acceleration, the addition and the subtraction of vectors are involved. According to the parallelogram (or triangle) law, the *sum* of two vectors, such as OA and OB in Fig. 274, is the diagonal OC of the parallelogram shown in the figure. The *difference* of the two vectors OA and OB is the other diagonal, BA, of the parallelogram. This fact is also in accordance with the triangle law since the difference between two quantities is the quantity that must be added to one of the two quantities to make the resulting quantity equal to the other. Thus the vector BA (not AB) must be added to the vector OB to make the resulting vector equal to OA.

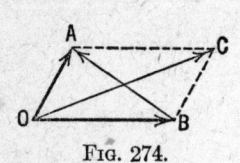

The symbols ↔ and → will be used to denote vector addition and

Fig. 274.

subtraction, respectively. Hence the above statements, with reference to Fig. 274, may be expressed as follows:

$$OC = OA \leftrightarrow OB \quad \text{and} \quad BA = OA \rightarrow OB$$

It will be observed that the vector difference, BA, between OA and OB may also be obtained by reversing the sense (changing the sign) of vector OB and adding it to OA, which is analogous to the rule for algebraic subtraction. It should also be noted that the difference between OB and OA is AB (not BA). That is, $OB \rightarrow OA = AB$.

75. Types of Motion.—The motion of a particle along a straight-line path is called *rectilinear* motion. The motion of a particle along a curved path is called *curvilinear* motion. If the moving particle describes equal distances along its path in equal periods of time, however small, the motion is said to be *uniform*. If unequal distances are described by the moving point in equal periods of time, the motion is said to be *non-uniform* or *variable*.

Thus, if the crank shaft of a steam engine revolves at a constant number of revolutions per minute, the crosshead of the engine has a non-uniform rectilinear motion, the crank pin has a uniform curvilinear motion, and any intermediate point on the connecting rod has a non-uniform, curvilinear motion.

76. Linear Displacement.—The linear displacement of a moving point is defined as the change of position of the point. The position of a moving point, at any instant, may be specified in a number of ways, as, for example, by stating the rectangular coordinates or the polar coordinates of the point. Thus, in Fig. 275 the position, at any instant, of the point M as it travels along the curve from B to C may be specified by the rectangular coordinates (x, y) or by the polar coordinates (ρ, θ). The displacement Δc of the point as it moves from the position (x_1, y_1) or (ρ_1, θ_1) to the position (x_2, y_2) or (ρ_2, θ_2) is the straight line BC, that is, the vector drawn from B to C. This displacement may be expressed as the *vector sum* of its x- and y-components by the vector equation

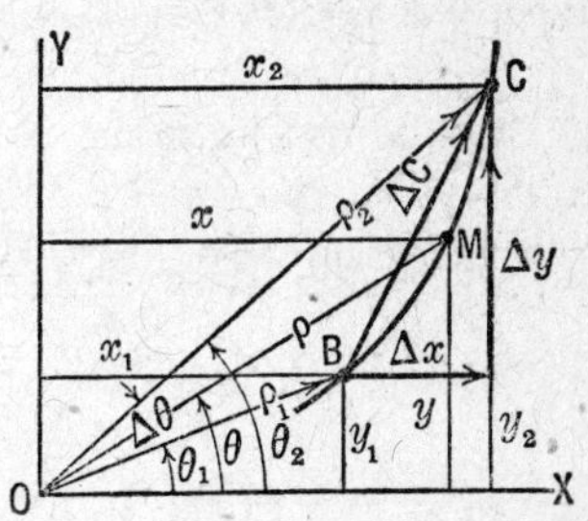

$$\Delta c = \Delta x \leftrightarrow \Delta y.$$

Fig. 275.

The *magnitude* and *direction* of Δc may be expressed by the two scalar equations

$$\Delta c = \sqrt{(\Delta x)^2 + (\Delta y)^2}, \quad \tan \phi = \frac{\Delta y}{\Delta x}.$$

The displacement Δc may be expressed also as the *vector difference* of the radius vectors to the two positions of the moving point. Thus

$$\Delta c = \rho_2 \rightarrow \rho_1,$$

that is, Δc is the directed distance which must be added to ρ_1 to give ρ_2. Or, in other words, ρ_2 is the vector sum of ρ_1 and Δc.

The unit of displacement is any convenient unit of length, such as the inch, foot, mile, etc. It will be noted, however, that displacement is a *directed* distance or length, that is, a vector quantity. Displacements, therefore, may be combined and resolved according to the parallelogram (or triangle) law like forces and other vector quantities. It is important to note that by one of the above equations the displacement, Δc, is expressed as the *vector sum* of two directed distances, whereas by the other equation it is expressed as the *vector difference* of two directed distances.

If the displacement of the particle is decreased indefinitely, the point C (Fig. 275) will approach the point B and, in the limit, the chord Δc becomes coincident with the tangent to the path at B. Therefore, the direction of motion of the particle at any point on its path is tangent to the path at that point.

77. Angular Displacement.—The angular displacement of a line that moves in a plane is the change in the angle that the moving line makes with any fixed line or axis in the plane. The angular displacement of a moving point with respect to a given point or pole is the angular displacement of the line joining the moving point to the pole. Thus, in Fig. 275, the angular displacement, $\Delta\theta$, of M relative to O, corresponding to the linear displacement, Δc, is

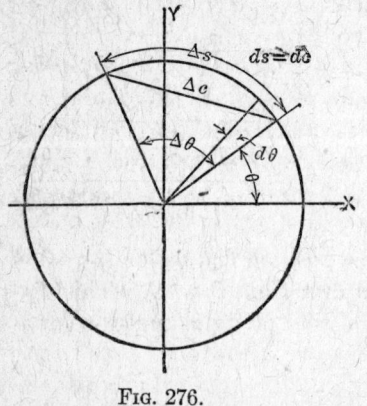

$$\Delta\theta = \theta_2 - \theta_1.$$

It is important to note that the angular displacement of a point depends upon the reference point or pole selected. If the point moves on a circular arc, the center of the circle is usually taken as the pole. The unit of angular displacement may be any convenient angular measure, such as the degree, revolution, radian, etc.

Fig. 276.

78. Relation between Linear and Angular Displacements.—If a point moves counter-clockwise along a circular path of radius r, the linear displacement, dc (Fig. 276), corresponding to an indefinitely small angular displacement $d\theta$ may be considered to be coincident with the arc ds, which is subtended by the angle $d\theta$. Since the arc of a circle is the product of the radius and the central angle, when the angle is measured in radians, the relation between the linear and angular displacements may be expressed by the equation

$$ds = rd\theta.$$

For a large angular displacement $\Delta\theta$, the corresponding linear displacement Δc is *not* equal to $r\Delta\theta$. The distance Δs along the arc, however, *is* expressed by $r\Delta\theta$.

If the moving point does not travel on a circular path, but on a path having a variable radius of curvature, the equation $ds = rd\theta$ may be used, provided that r is the radius of curvature of the path at the given position of the point and that $d\theta$ is measured with respect to the center of curvature as the pole.

If, however, the pole is not chosen as the center of curvature of the path (Fig. 277), the displacement may then be expressed in terms of its two components parallel and perpendicular, respectively, to the radius vector as follows:

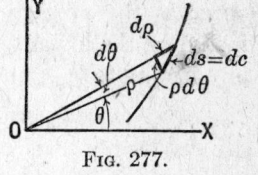

$$ds = \rho d\theta \leftrightarrow d\rho,$$

Fig. 277.

in which ρ is the radius vector to the point and *not* the radius of curvature of the path at that point. The components $\rho d\theta$ and $d\rho$ are called the *transverse* and *radial* components of displacement.

79. Linear Velocity and Speed.—The linear velocity of a moving particle is the time rate at which the particle is changing position, or, more briefly, the time rate of linear displacement. The direction of the velocity of the moving particle at a given point on its path is tangent to the path at that point (Art. 76). Velocity, like displacement, possesses both magnitude and direction and, therefore, is a vector quantity. The magnitude of the velocity of a point is called the *speed* of the point. Speed, therefore, is a scalar quantity. It may be defined as the time rate of describing distance (not the time rate of *displacement*). Although the terms velocity and speed are frequently used interchangeably, it is important to associate with the word *velocity* the two properties which it possesses, for a change in the direction of a velocity is fully as important in the laws of motion of physical bodies as is a change in the speed.

If a point has a *uniform* motion along any path, the speed, v, of the point is the ratio of any distance, Δs, described by the point, to the corresponding interval of time, Δt. Thus

$$v = \frac{\Delta s}{\Delta t}.$$

It will be noted that if a particle has uniform motion, whether rectilinear or curvilinear, the speed of the particle is constant. The velocity, however, is constant only in the case of uniform *rectilinear* motion, since in any curvilinear motion the velocity of the particle continually changes direction.

If the motion of the point is non-uniform, the above equation does not give the speed of the point at each instant in the interval, but gives only the average speed for the time interval, Δt. The instantaneous speed is the average speed over an indefinitely small period of time including the instant, or, expressed in mathematical form, the speed at any instant is

$$v = \underset{\Delta t \doteq 0}{\text{Limit}} \frac{\Delta s}{\Delta t} = \frac{ds}{dt}. \quad \ldots \ldots \quad (1)$$

The direction of v, as already noted, is tangent to the path at the point on the path where the moving particle is located at the instant. In order to find the value of v by differentiation, as indicated in equation (1), s must be expressed in terms of t.

The unit of velocity may be any convenient unit of length per unit of time; such as, foot per second (ft./sec.), mile per hour (mi./hr.), centimeter per second (cm./sec.), etc.

If v is expressed as a function of t, the displacement Δs along the path in any time interval $t_2 - t_1$ may be found by integrating v with respect to t. Thus from equation (1)

$$ds = v\,dt$$

Integrating,

$$\int_{s_1}^{s_2} ds = \int_{t_1}^{t_2} v\,dt$$

That is,

$$s_2 - s_1 = \Delta s = \int_{t_1}^{t_2} v\,dt \quad \ldots \ldots \quad (2)$$

It should be noted that Δs denotes the distance the point moves along its path and not the *linear displacement* of the point unless the path of the point is a straight line.

Distance-Time and Speed-Time Curves.—It is convenient to interpret equations (1) and (2) graphically. Thus let a distance-time (s–t) curve be constructed by plotting a series of points, the rectangular coordinates of each point being simultaneous values of s and t (Fig. 281). The slope to this curve is represented by ds/dt; but $v = ds/dt$, and hence it follows that the slope at any point of the (s–t) curve represents to some scale (depending on the scales used in plotting the curve) the speed of the moving point at the corresponding instant.

Similarly, if the relation between v and t is shown graphically by plotting a speed-time (v–t) curve for the moving point as shown in Fig. 278, the area under this curve between the ordinates v_2 and v_1 represents to some scale (depending on the scales used in plotting the curve) the displacement Δs of the point along its path in the corresponding time interval $t_2 - t_1$. This is evident from a consideration of equation (2) and Fig. 278.

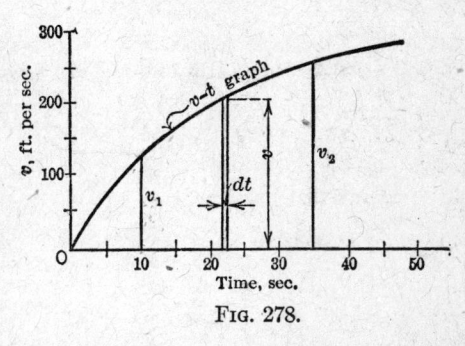

FIG. 278.

80. Angular Velocity.—The angular velocity of a moving line is defined as the time rate of angular displacement of the line. The angular velocity of a moving point with respect to a given point or pole is the angular velocity of the line joining the moving point to the pole. If equal angular displacements occur in equal time intervals, however small, the motion is said to be uniform, and the angular velocity, ω, is expressed as the ratio of any angular displacement, $\Delta \theta$, to the time interval, Δt, during which the displacement occurs. Thus

$$\omega = \frac{\Delta \theta}{\Delta t}.$$

If unequal angular displacements occur in equal time intervals, the motion is said to be non-uniform or variable. For such a motion the above equation gives the average angular velocity during the time interval Δt. When the angular velocity varies during the interval, its value at any instant is the average velocity over an indefinitely small time interval including the instant. Or, expressed mathematically, the instantaneous angular velocity is

$$\omega = \underset{\Delta t \doteq 0}{\text{Limit}} \frac{\Delta \theta}{\Delta t} = \frac{d\theta}{dt} \quad \dots \dots \dots \quad (1)$$

In order to determine the angular velocity from the above equation, θ must be expressed in terms of t.

The relation between θ and t and between ω and t may be shown graphically by curves similar to those discussed in the preceding article.

The unit of angular velocity is any convenient unit of angular displacement per unit of time, such as degree per second (deg./sec.), revolution per minute (r.p.m.), radian per second (rad./sec.), etc.

ILLUSTRATIVE PROBLEMS

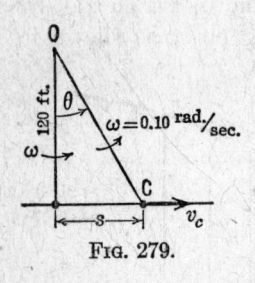

Problem 410.—In Fig. 279, C is a car (considered as a point) moving on a straight road and O is an observer in a tower directly over the road. If the car moves so that its angular velocity with respect to the observer is constant and equal to 0.10 rad./sec., find the linear velocity of the car when its position is such that θ is 0°, 30°, and 60°.

FIG. 279.

Solution.—From Fig. 279 it is seen that $s = 120 \tan \theta$ and since $v = ds/dt$ we have

$$v = \frac{d(120 \tan \theta)}{dt} = 120 \sec^2 \theta \frac{d\theta}{dt} = 120 \sec^2 \theta \times \omega = 12 \sec^2 \theta$$

$= 12 \times 1 = 12$ ft./sec. when $\theta = 0°$

$= 12 \times \frac{4}{3} = 16$ ft./sec. when $\theta = 30°$

$= 12 \times 4 = 48$ ft./sec. when $\theta = 60°$.

Problem 411.—The length of the crank, OA, of a steam engine (Fig. 280) is denoted by r and the length of the connecting rod, BA, is denoted by l. If the crank turns with constant angular velocity, ω, determine the velocity of the crosshead, B, in terms of r, l, ω, and the angle, θ, which the crank makes with the horizontal.

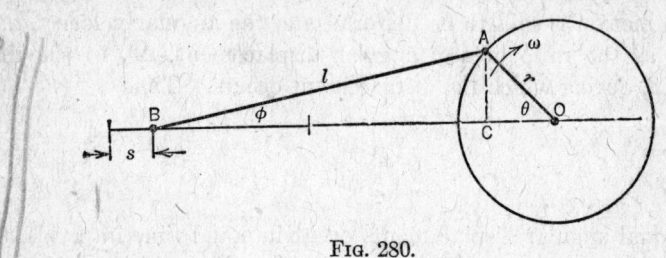

FIG. 280.

Solution.—The displacement, s, of the crosshead from its extreme position may be determined in terms of θ, and since $\theta = \omega t$, s may also be expressed as a function of t, since ω is known. Thus

$$s = l + r - l \cos \phi - r \cos \theta.$$

But

$$AC = l \sin \phi = r \sin \theta,$$

and

$$l \cos \phi = \sqrt{l^2 - l^2 \sin^2 \phi} = \sqrt{l^2 - r^2 \sin^2 \theta}.$$

By expanding the last expression by the binomial theorem and using only the first two terms of the expansion, since r/l is generally small, the last equation may be written, with a close degree of approximation,

$$l \cos \phi = l - \frac{r^2}{2l} \sin^2 \theta.$$

Therefore

$$s = r - r \cos \theta + \frac{r^2}{2l} \sin^2 \theta.$$

Hence

$$v = \frac{ds}{dt} = r \sin \theta \frac{d\theta}{dt} + \frac{r^2}{l} \sin \theta \cos \theta \frac{d\theta}{dt}$$

$$= r\omega \left(\sin \theta + \frac{r}{l} \sin \theta \cos \theta \right) = r\omega \left(\sin \theta + \frac{r}{2l} \sin 2\theta \right).$$

PROBLEMS

412. A point moves along a straight line according to the law $s = t^3 + 4t^2 + 2t$, where s and t are expressed in feet and seconds, respectively. Find (a) the velocity of the point at the end of 2 sec., (b) the displacement during the third second, and (c) the average velocity during the fourth second.

Ans. (a) $v = 30$ ft./sec.; (b) $\Delta s = 41$ ft.; (c) $v_{av} = 67$ ft./sec.

413. A point moves along a straight line according to the law $v = 3t^2 + 4t + 2$, where v and t are expressed in feet per second and seconds, respectively. If $s = 20$ ft. when $t = 2$ sec., what is the value of s when $t = 3$ sec.?

414. A point moves on a circle whose radius is 5 ft. according to the law $s = 3t^2 + 8/t$, where s and t are expressed in feet and seconds, respectively. Find the angular velocity of the point relative to the center of the circle when $t = 2$ sec.

Ans. $\omega = 2$ rad./sec.

415. A point moves on a circle according to the law $\omega = t^3 + 4t + 2$, where ω is the angular velocity in radians per second relative to the center of the circle and t is expressed in seconds. If $\theta = 10$ radians when $t = 2$ sec., what is the value of θ when $t = 3$ sec.?

416. The speed-time curve for the rectilinear motion of a certain point is shown in Fig. 278. The scales are: 1 in., vertically, equals 200 ft./sec., and 1 in., horizontally, equals 20 sec. If the area under the curve between the ordinates corresponding to $t = 10$ sec. and $t = 35$ sec. is 1.2 sq. in., how far does the point travel in the interval?

Ans. $\Delta s = 4800$ ft.

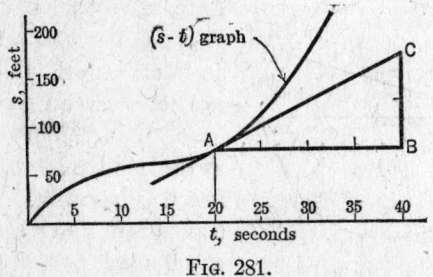

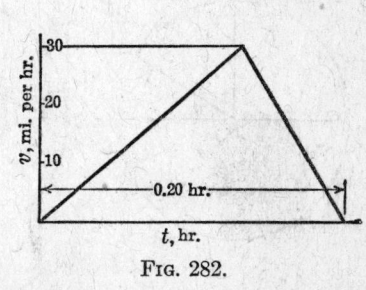

Fig. 281.

Fig. 282.

417. In Fig. 281 is shown the $(s - t)$ curve for a point moving on a straight line. What is the velocity of the point when $t = 20$ sec.?

418. Two railway stations are connected by a straight track. A train starts from rest at one station and after 12 min. comes to rest at the other station. The $(v-t)$ curve for the motion is shown in Fig. 282. Find the distance between the stations.

419. The crank OA (Fig. 283) rotates with a constant angular velocity ω about O. Find, by use of equation (1) of Art 79, the linear velocity of B in terms of r, θ, and ω.

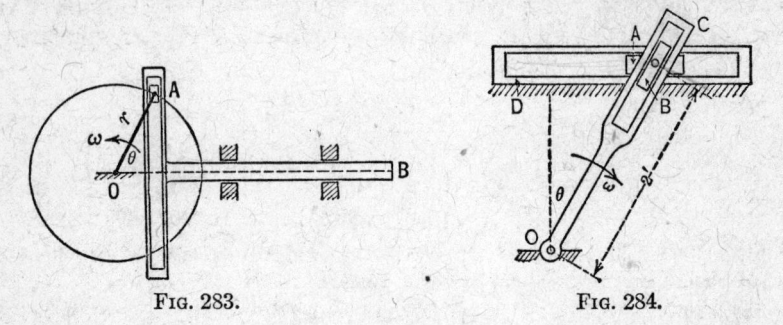

$$Ans. \quad v = -r\omega \sin \theta.$$

FIG. 283.   FIG. 284.

420. In Fig. 284 the blocks A and B are pinned together. Block A slides in a horizontal slot in D, and B slides in a slot in OC as OC rotates about O. When OC is in the position shown ($\theta = 30°$), the angular velocity ω is 20 rad./sec. Find, by equation (1) of Art. 79, the linear velocity of block A.

421. If in Fig. 284, the linear velocity of block A is 30 ft./sec. when $\theta = 30°$, find by use of equation (1) of Art. 80 the angular velocity of OC.

$$Ans. \quad \omega = 13.0 \text{ rad./sec.}$$

422. A point starts from rest at the origin and moves along the x-axis in such a way that the velocity at any instant is proportional to the elapsed time after starting. If $s = 8$ ft. when $t = 2$ sec., find the values of s and v when $t = 3$ sec.

423. A ship is sailing due east at a constant speed of 20 mi./hr. At a given instant a second ship which is sailing due north at a constant speed of 15 mi./hr. is 125 mi. directly south of the first ship. When will the distance between the two ships be a minimum? Find the minimum distance. $Ans.$ $t = 3$ hr.; $s = 100$ mi.

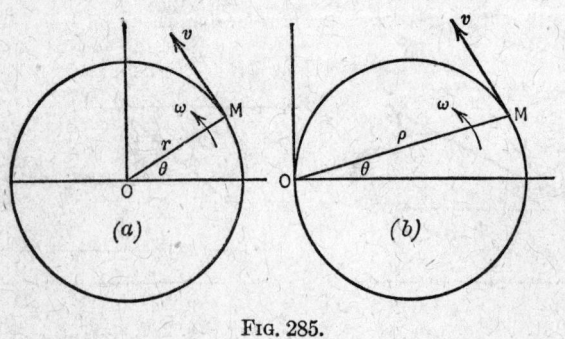

81. Relation between Linear and Angular Velocities.—If a point moves on a circular path the relation between its linear and angular velocities may be found as follows: Let a point M move on a circular path of radius r (Fig. 285a); let v be the linear velocity of the point at any instant and let ω be the

FIG. 285.

angular velocity of the point, with respect to the center of the circle, at the same instant. By definition,

$$v = \frac{ds}{dt} \text{ and } \omega = \frac{d\theta}{dt}.$$

But the distance ds traversed in the time dt may be expressed in terms of the corresponding angular displacement $d\theta$, by the equation $ds = r d\theta$ (Art. 78). Therefore

$$v = \frac{r d\theta}{dt} = r\omega. \quad \ldots \ldots \ldots \quad (1)$$

Hence, at any instant, the linear velocity of a point moving on a circle is the product of its angular velocity (with respect to the center of the circle) and the radius of the circle, where the angular velocity ω is expressed in *radians* per unit of time.

If the particle does not move on a circular path, the equation $v = \omega r$ is also true if r is the radius of curvature of the path at the given position of the particle, and if ω is the angular velocity of the particle with respect to the center of curvature as the pole.

Furthermore, if the point moves on a curve of any form and the center of curvature is not taken as the pole (Fig. 285b), then the term $\rho\omega$, where ρ denotes the radius vector to the point, gives one component only of the linear velocity, as is shown in the next article.

PROBLEMS

424. A flywheel 6 ft. in diameter rotates at 120 r.p.m. Find the linear velocity, in feet per second, of a point on its circumference.   *Ans.* $v = 37.7$ ft./sec.

425. A rod 4 ft. long rotates in a horizontal plane about a vertical axis through one end of the rod, so that the linear velocity of its mid-point is 60 ft. per sec. Find the angular velocity of the rod, in r.p.m.

426. A disk, A (Fig. 286), rotating with an angular velocity ω_1 of 30 r.p.m. turns (without slipping) another disk, B, by means of friction at their surfaces of contact. A drum, D, is attached to the disk, B, and turns with it, thereby raising the body, C. The radii r_1, r_2, and r_3 are 6 in., 10 in., and 4 in., respectively. Find the velocity of C in ft. per sec.
   Ans. $v_C = 0.63$ ft./sec.

427. In Fig. 204 the disk B rotates at 200 r.p.m. and turns (without slipping) the wheel C by means of the frictional force on the circumference of C. The distance from the center line of B to the point of contact between B and C is 8 in., and the diameter of C is 20 in. What is the angular velocity of C, in r.p.m.?

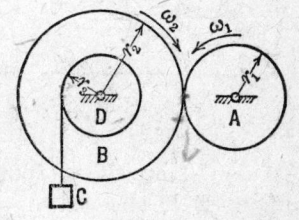

Fig. 286.

428. A rigid body composed of two disks of different diameters (Fig. 287) turns about the center O with a constant angular velocity of 80 r.p.m. If $r_1 = 2$ ft. and $r_2 = 3$ ft., what is the velocity of body A and of body B? A unwinds from the large disk as B winds up on the small disk. How far will A and B travel in 6 sec.?

Ans. $v_A = 25.1$ ft./sec.; $v_B = 16.8$ ft./sec.; $\Delta s_A = 150.8$ ft.; $\Delta s_B = 100.5$ ft.

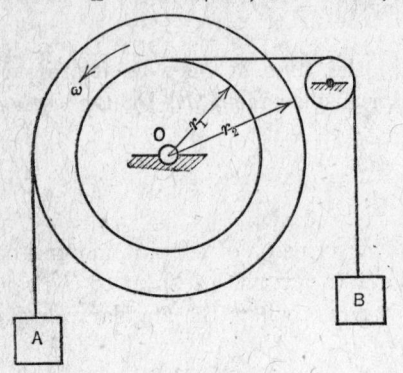

FIG. 287. 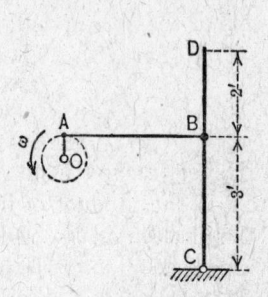   FIG. 288.

429. The rod CD (Fig. 288) is made to oscillate by the crank OA and connecting rod AB. The angular velocity ω of the crank is 90 r.p.m. In the position shown AB is perpendicular to OA and to CD. The length of OA is 6 in. Find the angular velocity of the rod CD and the linear velocity of D.

82. Components of Velocity.—It is frequently convenient to find the velocity of a moving point by determining its components, or to deal with the components of the velocity instead of the total velocity.

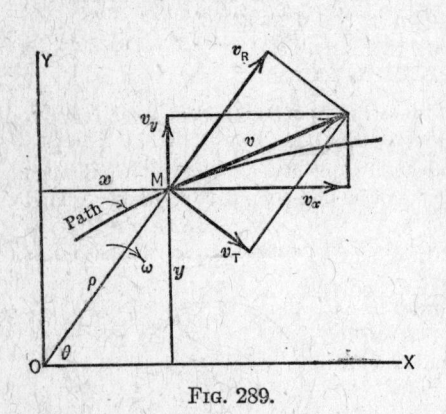

Two sets of components only are here determined; namely, the axial components (v_x and v_y), parallel, respectively, to the x- and y-axes, and the radial and transverse components (v_R and v_T), parallel and perpendicular, respectively, to the radius vector (Fig. 289).

FIG. 289.

Thus, since the component, in any direction, of the linear velocity of a point is the time rate of the component displacement of the point in the given direction, the axial components of the velocity v of the moving point M (Fig. 289) are given by the expressions

$$v_x = \frac{dx}{dt} \quad \text{and} \quad v_y = \frac{dy}{dt}, \quad \ldots \ldots \quad (1)$$

or, if the coordinates, x and y, of the particle change uniformly, then

$$v_x = \frac{\Delta x}{\Delta t} = \frac{x_2 - x_1}{t_2 - t_1} \quad \text{and} \quad v_y = \frac{\Delta y}{\Delta t} = \frac{y_2 - y_1}{t_2 - t_1}.$$

Likewise, at any instant, the transverse and radial components of velocity, v_T and v_R, are expressed as follows:

$$v_T = \frac{\rho d\theta}{dt} \quad \text{and} \quad v_R = \frac{d\rho}{dt}, \quad \ldots \quad (2)$$

in which $\rho d\theta$ and $d\rho$ are the components of displacement in the transverse and radial directions during the time interval dt, as shown in Art. 78, and ω is the angular velocity of the point with reference to the pole O. It will be noted that when O is chosen as the center of curvature of the path the transverse component of the velocity becomes the total velocity, tangent to the path, v_R then being equal to zero.

Since the pole O may be arbitrarily chosen, the components v_T and v_R are different for different positions of the pole or origin, whereas v_x and v_y are independent of the origin and depend on the directions only of the coordinate axes.

In obtaining the radial and transverse components of velocity, the graphical method of solution is frequently preferable to the algebraic method which makes use of Eq. (2) above. The graphical method is illustrated in Prob. 431.

ILLUSTRATIVE PROBLEMS

Problem 430.—If the angular velocity of the oscillating arm OM (Fig. 290) is 40 r.p.m. when $\theta = 30°$, find, by use of Eq. (2) above, the radial and transverse components of the velocity of the block A, referred to O as the pole. Also find the total velocity of A.

Solution.—From Fig. 290 the value of ρ is

$$\frac{20}{12 \cos \theta} = \frac{5}{3} \sec \theta \text{ ft.}$$

and

$$\omega = \frac{d\theta}{dt} = \frac{40 \times 2\pi}{60} = \frac{4\pi}{3} \text{ rad./sec.}$$

Hence

$$v_R = \frac{d\rho}{dt} = \frac{5}{3} \sec \theta \tan \theta \frac{d\theta}{dt}$$

$$= \frac{5}{3} \sec \theta \tan \theta \, \omega$$

$$= \frac{5}{3} \times \frac{2}{\sqrt{3}} \times \frac{1}{\sqrt{3}} \times \frac{4}{3}\pi = 4.65 \text{ ft./sec. when } \theta = 30°.$$

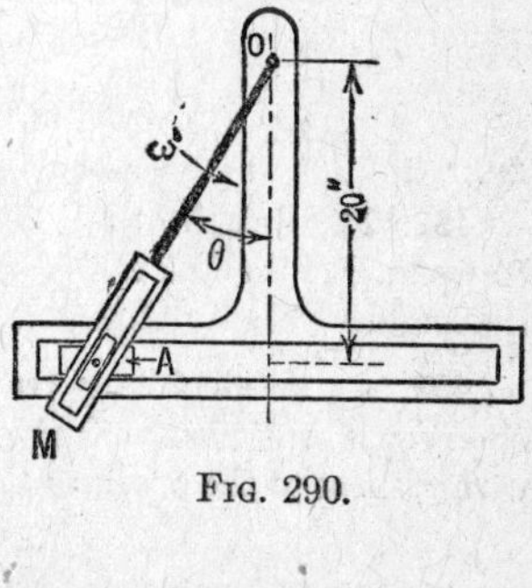

Fig. 290.

Also

$$v_T = \rho \frac{d\theta}{dt} = \frac{5}{3} \sec \theta \times \omega$$

$$= \frac{5}{3} \times \frac{2}{\sqrt{3}} \times \frac{4\pi}{3} = 8.06 \text{ ft./sec. when } \theta = 30°.$$

$$v_A = \sqrt{4.65^2 + 8.06^2} = 9.31 \text{ ft./sec.}$$

The student should show v_R, v_T and v as vectors in Fig. 290.

Problem 431.—In the quick-return mechanism shown in Fig. 291, $OO_1 = 18$ in. and the crank $OA = 8$ in. If the angular velocity of the crank is 40 r.p.m., what is the velocity of the block A? Find graphically the component of the velocity of A perpendicular to the rocker arm O_1M (the transverse component) in the position shown. Find also the angular velocity of O_1M.

Solution.—The block moves on the circular path of radius $r = 8$ in. Let ω denote the angular velocity of A with reference to the pole O and ω_1 the angular velocity of A with reference to the pole O_1 (that is, let ω_1 denote the angular velocity of O_1A, or ρ). The direction of the velocity of A is tangent to the circle and its magnitude is

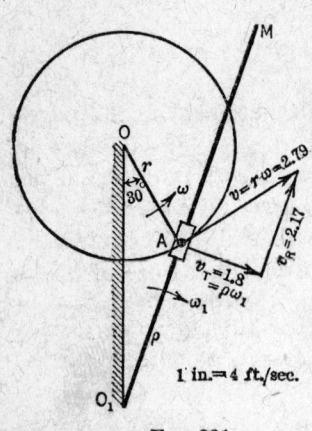

FIG. 291.

$$v = \omega r = \frac{40 \times 2\pi}{60} \times \frac{8}{12} = 2.79 \text{ ft./sec.}$$

By resolving v, graphically, into its transverse and radial components as shown in the figure, the following values are found:

$$v_T = 1.8 \text{ ft./sec.} \quad \text{and} \quad v_R = 2.17 \text{ ft./sec.}$$

But

$$v_T = \omega_1 \rho = \omega_1 \times O_1A.$$

By measuring, O_1A is found to be 11.7 in.
Therefore

$$\omega_1 = \frac{1.8 \times 12}{11.7} = 1.84 \text{ rad./sec.} = 17.6 \text{ r.p.m.}$$

PROBLEMS

432. The link BC (Fig. 292) is 2 ft. long and has an angular velocity, ω_1, of 50 r.p.m. If the link BA is perpendicular to BC, at the instant considered, what is the angular velocity of the crank OA if OA is 9 in. long?

433. An automobile is traveling at 30 miles per hour on a straight road. An observer is stationed at O (Fig. 293). Find the angular velocity of the automobile with respect to the observer (*a*) when the automobile is at A, (*b*) when at B.

Ans. (*a*) $\omega = 0.44$ rad./sec.; (*b*) $\omega = 0.352$ rad./sec.

434. In Fig. 294. A is a block that revolves about O with an angular velocity

ω = 60 r.p.m. O_1M is a rod that is pivoted at O_1 and passes through a slot in A.

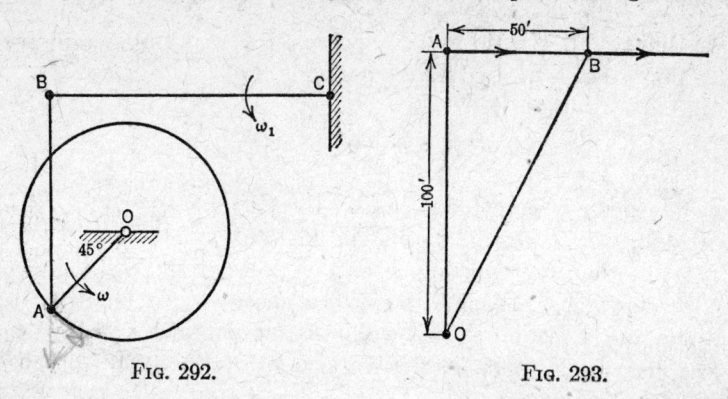

Fig. 292.

Fig. 293.

The lengths of OA and OO_1 are 12 in. and 6 in., respectively. Find, graphically, the radial and transverse components of velocity of A with respect to O_1 as a pole.

435. The cam shown in Fig. 295 revolves about the axis O, causing the roller A to change its x-coordinate at the rate of 4 in. per second when $\theta = 30°$. Find the angular velocity of the bell-crank AO_1B if O_1A is 18 in. *Ans.* ω = 4.24 r.p.m.

436. In Prob. 420, find the radial and transverse components of the velocity of the block B with respect to O as a pole.

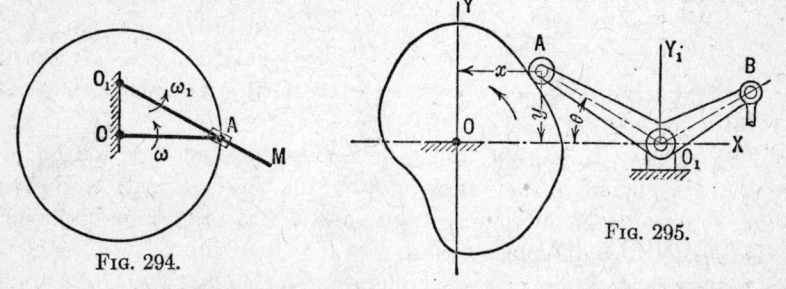

Fig. 294.

Fig. 295.

437. A point moves on the curve $y^2 = 9x$ according to the law $x = 4t^2 + 1$, x and y being measured in feet and t in seconds. Find the magnitude and direction of the velocity of the point when $t = 2$ sec. *Ans.* $v = 17.0$ ft./sec.; $\theta_x = 20°$.

438. A point moves in the xy-plane according to the law $v_x = 4t^3 + 4t$, $v_y = 4t$. If $x = 1$ and $y = 2$ when $t = 0$, what is the equation of the path of the point?

439. A point moves in the xy-plane according to the law $x = t + \dfrac{1}{t}$, $y = t - \dfrac{1}{t}$, x and y being measured in feet and t in seconds. Show that the path of the point is a hyperbola and find the magnitude and direction of the velocity of the point when $t = \frac{1}{2}$ sec. *Ans.* Path $x^2 - y^2 = 4$; $v = 5.82$ ft./sec.; $\theta_x = 121°$.

83. Linear Acceleration.—The linear acceleration of a moving point, at any instant, is defined as the time rate of change of the linear velocity of the point at the instant. If the change in the velocity in time Δt

be denoted by Δv, the average acceleration for the time interval is $\dfrac{\Delta v}{\Delta t}$, and the limit of this ratio as Δt approaches zero is the instantaneous acceleration. Or, expressed mathematically,

$$a = \underset{\Delta t \doteq 0}{\text{Limit}} \frac{\Delta v}{\Delta t}.$$

Since velocity is a vector quantity, the change, Δv, in the velocity may be due to a change in the magnitude, only, of the velocity as in rectilinear motion with varying speed; or to a change in the direction only, as in curvilinear motion with constant speed; or to a change in both magnitude and direction as in curvilinear motion with varying speed. The acceleration of a point having various types of motion will be considered in the following articles.

The unit of linear acceleration is any unit of linear velocity per unit of time, such as foot per second per second (ft./sec.^{2}), mile per hour per second (mi./hr./sec.), etc.

84. Acceleration in Rectilinear Motion.—In Fig. 296 let a point move so that its velocity changes in magnitude only. That is, let the point move on a straight line path with varying speed. Let v_1 be the velocity at one instant and let v_2 be the velocity after the time interval Δt. If the velocity changes uniformly, the magnitude of the acceleration is the ratio of any change in the velocity, Δv, to the time interval, Δt, during which the change Δv occurs. Since v_2 and v_1 have the same direction, Δv is the algebraic difference of v_2 and v_1 as well as the vector difference. Hence, the magnitude of the acceleration for uniformly accelerated, rectilinear motion is

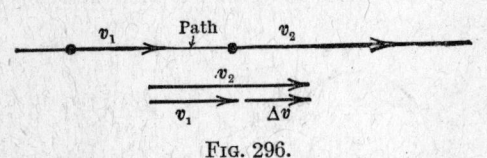

$$a = \frac{\Delta v}{\Delta t} = \frac{v_2 - v_1}{t_2 - t_1}. \qquad \ldots \ldots \ldots (1)$$

Fig. 296.

If the velocity of the moving point in Fig. 296 does not change uniformly, then equation (1) gives only the average acceleration during the period Δt. When the acceleration varies from instant to instant, its value at any instant is the average acceleration during a very small time interval including the instant. Or, expressed mathematically, the instantaneous acceleration for rectilinear motion is

$$a = \underset{\Delta t \doteq 0}{\text{Limit}} \frac{\Delta v}{\Delta t} = \frac{dv}{dt}. \qquad \ldots \ldots \ldots (2)$$

ACCELERATION IN RECTILINEAR MOTION

In order to find a from the above equation, v must be expressed in terms of t. Since $v = \dfrac{ds}{dt}$, the above expression may also be written

$$a = \frac{dv}{dt} = \frac{d^2s}{dt^2}. \quad \ldots \ldots \ldots (3)$$

The direction of the acceleration of the particle is the same as that of the change of velocity, Δv, but Δv is parallel to v, that is, along the path. If v_2 is smaller than v_1, the sense of Δv is negative, that is, opposite to that of v, and hence the acceleration then is negative. A negative acceleration is sometimes called a *deceleration*.

By dividing numerator and denominator of the right side of equation (2) by ds, another form of expressing a is obtained, namely,

$$a = v \frac{dv}{ds}.$$

If a is expressed as a function of t, the change of speed in any time interval $t_2 - t_1$ may be found by integrating a with respect to t. Thus from equation (2)

$$dv = a\, dt$$

Integrating,

$$\int_{v_1}^{v_2} dv = \int_{t_1}^{t_2} a\, dt$$

That is,

$$v_2 - v_1 = \Delta v = \int_{t_1}^{t_2} a\, dt. \quad \ldots \ldots (4)$$

Speed-Time and Acceleration-Time Curves.—It is convenient to interpret equations (2) and (4) graphically. The relation between v and t for the rectilinear motion of a point may be shown graphically by plotting a speed-time (v–t) curve, the coordinates of any point on which represent simultaneous values of v and t. The slope of this curve at any point is represented by $\dfrac{dv}{dt}$. But $a = \dfrac{dv}{dt}$, and hence the slope of the (v–t) curve at any point represents to some scale (depending on the scales used in plotting the curve) the acceleration of the moving point at the corresponding time. Thus if the rectilinear motion of a point is represented by the (v–t) curve in Fig. 297, the acceleration of the point when $t = 15$ sec. (corresponding to point A on the v–t curve) is $\dfrac{2 \times 20}{4 \times 5} = 2$ ft./sec.^{2}

180   MOTION OF A PARTICLE

Similarly, if an acceleration-time (a–t) curve for the rectilinear motion of a point is plotted as indicated in Fig. 298, the area under the curve between the ordinates a_2 and a_1 represents to some scale (depending

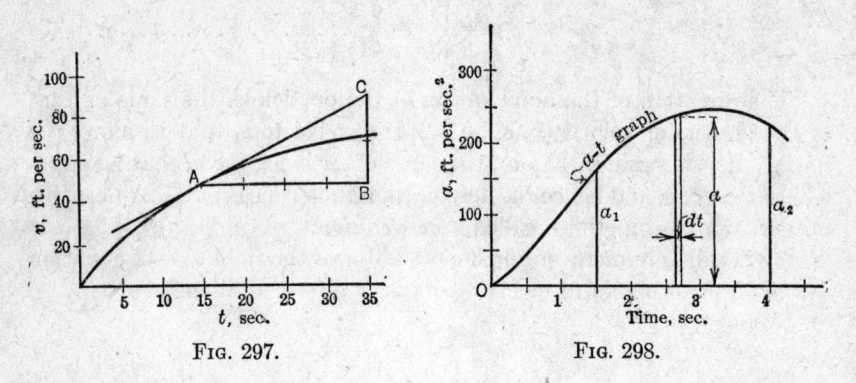

FIG. 297.

FIG. 298.

on the scales used in plotting the curve) the change in speed in the corresponding time interval $t_2 - t_1$ as is obvious from a consideration of equation (4) and Fig. 298.

ILLUSTRATIVE PROBLEMS

Problem 440.—In Prob. 410 find the acceleration of the car when $\theta = 30°$.

Solution.—The velocity of the car corresponding to any value of θ was found to be 12 sec.^{2} θ and hence

$$a = \frac{dv}{dt} = \frac{d}{dt}(12 \sec^2 \theta) = 24 \sec^2 \theta \tan \theta \, \omega$$

$$= 2.4 \sec^2 \theta \tan \theta$$

$$= 2.4 \times \frac{4}{3} \times \frac{1}{\sqrt{3}} = 1.85 \text{ ft./sec.}^2 \text{ when } \theta = 30°.$$

Problem 441.—Find by use of equation (3) of Art. 84 the acceleration of the crosshead of a steam engine in terms of r, l, θ, and ω as defined in Prob. 411.

Solution.—From Prob. 411 we have

$$v = r\omega \left(\sin \theta + \frac{r}{l} \sin \theta \cos \theta \right).$$

Hence

$$a = \frac{dv}{dt} = r\omega \left[\cos \theta + \frac{r}{l}(\cos^2 \theta - \sin^2 \theta) \right] \frac{d\theta}{dt}$$

$$= r\omega^2 \left(\cos \theta + \frac{r}{l} \cos 2\theta \right).$$

It may be noted that when the ratio of r to l is small, the second term in the above expression becomes small, and hence the acceleration is approximately $r\omega^2 \cos \theta$ and therefore the motion of the crosshead is approximately a simple harmonic motion (Art. 86).

PROBLEMS

442. In Prob. 412 find the acceleration of the point when $t = 2$ sec.

443. A point moves along a straight line according to the law $a = 12t^2 + 6$. If $s = 12$ and $v = 0$ when $t = 0$, what is the value of s when $t = 2$?   *Ans.* $s = 40$.

444. In Prob. 419 find the acceleration of B in terms of r, θ, and ω. Find also the numerical value of a if $r = 2$ ft., $\omega = 4$ rad./sec., and $\theta = 60°$.

445. In Prob. 420 find the linear acceleration of the block A when $\theta = 30°$, assuming ω to be constant and equal to 20 rad./sec.   *Ans.* $a = 1067$ ft./sec.^{2}

446. In Fig. 299 are shown the $(v\text{-}t)$ curves for three different rectilinear motions of a point. Draw the $(s\text{-}t)$ and $(a\text{-}t)$ curves for the motions represented in each of the diagrams.

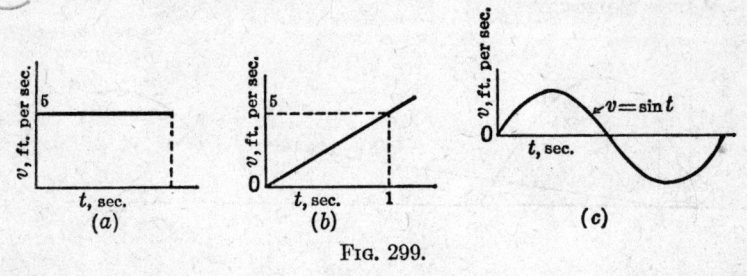

FIG. 299.

447. At a given point on the $(v\text{-}t)$ curve shown in Fig. 299(c) for the rectilinear motion of a point, the tangent to the curve makes an angle of 30° with the horizontal. If the scales used in plotting the curve are 1 in. = 20 ft./sec. and 1 in. = 2 sec., what is the acceleration of the point at the corresponding time?
Ans. $a = 5.77$ ft./sec.^{2}

448. The scales used in plotting an acceleration-time curve are: 1 in. = 200 ft./sec.^{2} and 1 in. = 2 sec. If the area under the curve between the ordinates corresponding to $t = 1.5$ sec. and $t = 4$ sec. is 1.3 sq. in., what is the speed at the end of 4 sec. if the speed at the end of 1.5 sec. is 20 ft./sec.?

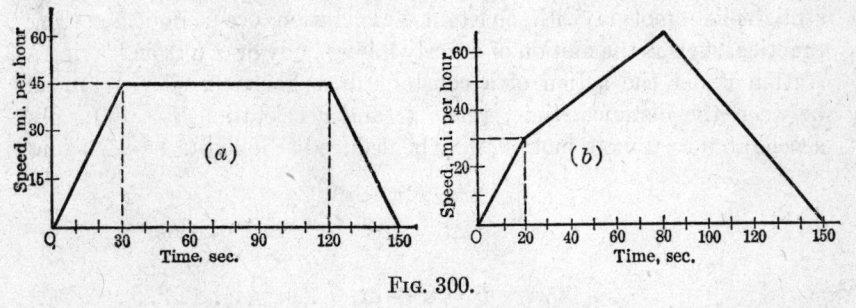

FIG. 300.

449. Two railway stations are connected by two straight parallel tracks. Two trains A and B start from rest at one station and reach the second station in 150 sec. The speed-time curve for A is shown in Fig. 300(a) and that for B in Fig. 300(b).

Draw the acceleration-time curve for each train, and find the distance between the two stations. Find also the maximum speed of B.

Ans. Distance = 1.5 mi.; v_{max} = 64.62 mi./hr.

450. A point starts from rest and moves on a straight line so that its acceleration at any instant is proportional to the time after starting ($a = kt$). If v = 10 ft./sec. when t = 2 sec., find the acceleration and velocity of the point when t = 4 sec.

451. A point starts at the origin and moves along the x-axis. The initial velocity of the point is 20 ft./sec. to the left and the acceleration of the point is constant and equal to 10 ft./sec.^{2} to the right. Find the equation of the (s–t) curve for the motion.

Ans. $s = 5t^2 - 20t$.

452. A point starts at the origin and moves along the y-axis with constant acceleration. When t = 2 sec. $y = -8$ ft. and when t = 4 sec., y = 16 ft. Find (a) the initial velocity of the point, (b) the acceleration of the point, (c) the linear displacement during the first three seconds, and (d) the distance traveled by the point in the first three seconds.

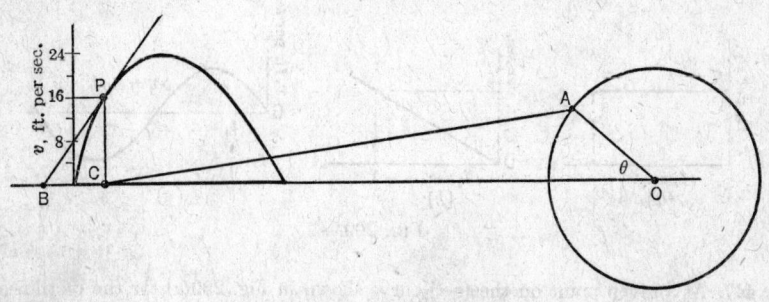

FIG. 301.

453. In Fig. 301 is shown the speed-displacement graph for the crosshead, C, of a steam engine. If the scale of abscissas is 1 in. = 1.75 ft. and if BC measures 0.33 in., what is the acceleration of the crosshead in the position shown. How may the position of C be found for which C has zero acceleration?

Ans. a = 443 ft./sec.^{2}

85. Uniformly Accelerated Rectilinear Motion.—Many examples of straight-line motion with constant acceleration occur in engineering practice, such as the motion of a freely falling body or of a train leaving a station under the action of a constant draw-bar pull. The relations between the distance, time, velocity, and acceleration, for uniformly accelerated rectilinear motion, may be deduced as follows: By definition,

$$a = \frac{\Delta v}{\Delta t} = \frac{v - u}{t},$$

or

$$v = u + at, \quad \ldots \ldots \ldots \quad (1)$$

in which u and v are the initial and final velocities, respectively, corresponding to the time interval Δt or simply t. Equation (1) may also be obtained from the (v–t) curve shown in Fig. 302. The slope of the curve represents the acceleration of the moving point. Hence $a = \text{slope} = \dfrac{v-u}{t}$.

Since the velocity increases or decreases uniformly, the average velocity is $\dfrac{u+v}{2}$ and the distance, s, traveled in time t is

$$s = \frac{u+v}{2} \cdot t \quad\quad\quad\quad (2)$$

$$= \frac{u+u+at}{2} \cdot t$$

$$= ut + \tfrac{1}{2}at^2. \quad\quad\quad\quad (3)$$

Fig. 302.

This equation also follows from the fact that s is represented by the area under the (v–t) curve (Fig. 302). The rectangular part of the area is expressed by ut and the triangular part by $\tfrac{1}{2}at^2$. Hence $s = ut + \tfrac{1}{2}at^2$. By eliminating t from equations (1) and (3), the following equation is obtained:

$$v^2 = u^2 + 2as. \quad\quad\quad\quad (4)$$

The motion of a freely falling body is a special case of uniformly accelerated rectilinear motion, in which the acceleration is usually denoted by g and is approximately equal to 32.2 ft./sec.^{2}

ILLUSTRATIVE PROBLEM

Problem 454.—A projectile is fired from a gun with an initial velocity u making an angle θ with the horizontal (Fig. 303). Find (a) the time of flight to reach the level from which it started, (b) the range on a horizontal plane through the point of projection, (c) the greatest height reached, and (d) the equation to the path of the projectile. The actual motion of a projectile is influenced by a number of conditions such as rotation of the projectile due to rifling of the gun barrel, wind velocity, air resistance, etc. The motion of the projectile under ideal conditions (in a vacuum and without rotation) will here be considered.

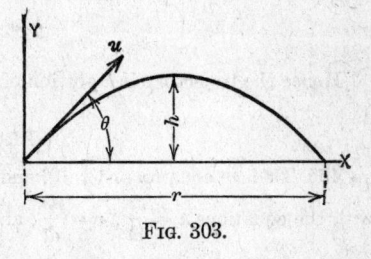

Fig. 303.

Solution.—The motion of the projectile may be assumed to be a combination of two simultaneous motions, namely, a uniform horizontal (rectilinear) motion with a constant velocity of $u \cos \theta$ and a uniformly accelerated vertical (rectilinear) motion with a constant acceleration which is downward and equal to g ($a_y = -g = -32.2$ ft./sec.²). Let v denote the velocity after any time t. Then we may write

$$a_x = \frac{v_x - u_x}{t} = 0 \quad \text{or} \quad v_x = u_x = u \cos \theta, \quad \ldots \ldots \ldots \quad (1)$$

and

$$a_y = \frac{v_y - u_y}{t} = -g \quad \text{or} \quad v_y = u_y - gt = u \sin \theta - gt. \ldots \ldots \quad (2)$$

The horizontal displacement, x, in any time interval t is

$$x = u \cos \theta \cdot t, \ldots \ldots \ldots \ldots \ldots \quad (3)$$

and the vertical displacement, y, in any time interval t is the average velocity times the time interval. Hence

$$y = u \sin \theta \cdot t - \tfrac{1}{2} gt^2. \ldots \ldots \ldots \ldots \quad (4)$$

Time of Flight.—Since y equals zero when the projectile reaches the x-axis, the time of flight, t_r, as found from equation (4), is

$$t_r = \frac{2u \sin \theta}{g}. \ldots \ldots \ldots \ldots \ldots \quad (5)$$

Range.—The range, r, equals the value of x in equation (3) when $t = t_r$. Therefore

$$r = \frac{u^2 \sin 2\theta}{g}. \ldots \ldots \ldots \ldots \ldots \quad (6)$$

Time to Reach Greatest Height.—When the projectile reaches its greatest height, $v_y = 0$. Hence, the time, t_h, required for the projectile to reach its greatest height, as found from equation (2), is

$$t_h = \frac{u \sin \theta}{g}. \ldots \ldots \ldots \ldots \ldots \quad (7)$$

Greatest Height.—The greatest height, h, will be given by y in equation (4) when t has the value t_h. Hence

$$h = \frac{u^2 \sin^2 \theta}{2g}. \ldots \ldots \ldots \ldots \ldots \quad (8)$$

The equation of the path of the projectile (called the trajectory) may be obtained by eliminating t from equations (3) and (4), which gives the following equation:

$$y = x \tan \theta - \frac{gx^2}{2u^2 \cos^2 \theta}. \ldots \ldots \ldots \quad (9)$$

Hence the trajectory is a portion of a parabola with its axis vertical.

PROBLEMS

455. Deduce equations (1), (3), and (4) of Art. 85 by calculus methods, starting with the equations $a = \dfrac{dv}{dt}$, $v = \dfrac{ds}{dt}$, and $a = v\dfrac{dv}{ds}$, respectively.

456. A train is moving on a straight track at a speed of 50 mi./hr. toward a station at which it must stop. If the brakes can retard the train at the rate of 1.5 ft./sec. each second, how far from the station should the brakes be applied?

Ans. $s = 1795$ ft.

457. A bullet leaves the muzzle of a gun with a velocity of 2000 ft./sec. The acceleration of the bullet while traveling in the barrel is not constant but in order to obtain an approximate value of the acceleration, it will be assumed to be constant. Find the acceleration of the bullet and the time required to travel the length of the barrel if the length of the barrel is 3 ft.

458. The brakes are set on a train running at 30 mi./hr., when $\frac{1}{2}$ mi. from a station. The train slows down uniformly, coming to rest at the station. Find the acceleration, and the time in stopping. *Ans.* $a = 0.366$ ft./sec.^{2} $t = 120$ sec.

459. If the maximum allowable speed of an elevator is 800 ft./min. and if it acquires this speed uniformly in a distance of 12 ft., what acceleration does it have?

460. A train in starting is uniformly accelerated and attains a speed of 60 mi./hr. in 5 min. After running for a certain period of time at this speed, the brakes are applied and it stops at a uniform rate in 4 min. If the total distance traveled is 10 mi. find the total time. *Ans.* $t = 14.5$ min.

461. If the cam A (Fig. 304) moves to the left, changing its velocity uniformly 5 in./sec. each second, what is the acceleration of the rod B (a) before the pin comes in contact with the cam and (b) while it is in contact with the cam?

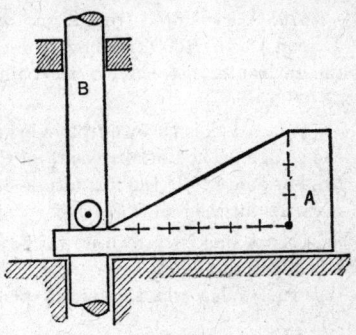

FIG. 304.

462. The speed-time curve for the rectilinear motion of a point is shown in Fig. 305. Find (a) the acceleration of the point during the period between 10 sec. and 20 sec., (b) between 30 sec. and 60 sec., and (c) the distance traveled by the point in 70 sec. *Ans.* (a) $a = 0$; (b) $a = -0.5$ ft./sec.^{2}; (c) $s = 775$ ft.

FIG. 305.

463. A bullet is projected upward at an angle of 60° with the horizontal with a velocity of 2000 ft./sec. Find the range and time of flight.

464. A point starts from rest and moves along a straight line so that $v = 2\sqrt{s}$ where v is the velocity of the point in feet per second and s is the displacement of the point in feet. Does the point have a uniform or non-uniform acceleration? Determine the displacement, velocity, and acceleration of the point at the end of 5 sec.
Ans. $s = 25$ ft.; $v = 10$ ft./sec.; $a = 2$ ft./sec.^{2}

465. A bag of sand is thrown out of a balloon that is rising with a velocity of 4 ft./sec. If the bag reaches the ground in 6 sec., how high above the ground was the balloon when the sand was thrown out?

466. A stone is dropped into a well and the splash is heard 2 sec. later. Assuming the velocity of sound to be 1100 ft./sec. how far is it to the surface of the water?
Ans. 60.6 ft.

467. A shot is fired from a gun on the top of a cliff 400 ft. high, with a velocity of 768 ft./sec., the angle of elevation of the gun being 30°. Find the range on a horizontal plane through the base of the cliff.

468. A stone is projected from the surface of the earth vertically upwards with a velocity of 100 ft./sec. Four seconds later a second stone is projected vertically upwards with a velocity of 50 ft./sec. At what distance above the earth will the two stones meet? *Ans.* $s = 37.6$ ft.

469. A train starts from a station with a uniform acceleration and attains a speed of 40 mi./hr. in 2 min. It runs for 11 min. at this speed and then reduces its speed uniformly during the next 3 min. and stops at the next station. Find the distance between the two stations.

470. A shell fired from a gun with an initial velocity of 1000 ft./sec. strikes a balloon that is 1000 ft. above the earth. If the angle of projection is 45°, what is the horizontal distance x of the balloon from the gun? Assume $g = 32$ ft./sec.^{2}
Ans. $x = 1035$ ft. or 30,200 ft.

471. A ball is thrown from a bridge at a height of 150 ft. above the water beneath the bridge. The initial velocity of the ball is directed upward at an angle of 60° with the horizontal. If the magnitude of the initial velocity is 100 ft./sec. find the time required for the ball to reach the water. How far above the bridge does the ball rise?

472. A ball is thrown upward at an angle of 45° with the horizontal. It strikes a vertical wall 100 ft. away at a point 10 ft. above the level from which the ball was thrown. What was the initial speed of the ball? *Ans.* $u = 59.8$ ft./sec.

86. Simple Harmonic Motion.—If the velocity of a point does not vary uniformly, the acceleration is not constant, and hence the equations of Art. 85 do not apply. One special case of rectilinear motion with variable acceleration is simple harmonic motion. A *simple harmonic motion* is defined as the motion of a point in a straight line such that the acceleration of the point is proportional to the distance, x, of the point from some fixed origin, O, in the line and is directed toward O. Or, expressed mathematically,

$$a = \frac{d^2x}{dt^2} = -kx, \quad \ldots \ldots \ldots \quad (1)$$

where k is a constant and the negative sign indicates that the sense of the acceleration is opposite to that of the displacement x (Fig. 306), that is, a is negative when x is positive, and positive when x is negative.

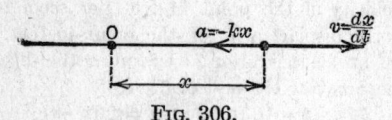

Fig. 306.

One example of a simple harmonic motion is the motion of a weight attached to the lower end of a helical spring (the upper end being fixed) which is allowed to vibrate freely. The motion of the crosshead of a steam engine closely approximates a harmonic motion if the ratio of the length of the connecting rod to that of the crank is large. The motion of an oscillating pendulum also approximates closely a simple harmonic motion if the arc through which the pendulum swings is small. In fact many of the vibrational motions so common and important in engineering problems may be assumed without serious error to be simple harmonic motions.

If a point moves with constant speed in a circular path, the motion of the projection of the point on a diameter of the circle is a simple harmonic motion. This statement may be proved as follows: In Fig. 307 let M be a point moving on a circle of radius r with constant speed v_M, and angular velocity ω. If t is the time required for M to move from A to its given position, then

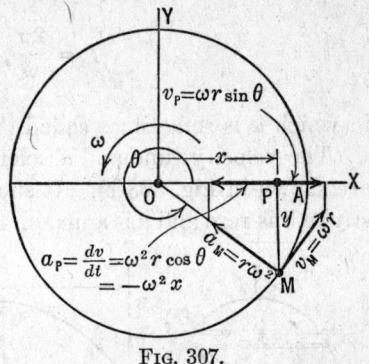

FIG. 307.

$$\theta = \omega t, \quad \text{and} \quad x = r \cos \theta = r \cos \omega t. \quad \ldots \quad (2)$$

Hence the velocity of P, the projection of M, is

$$v = \frac{dx}{dt} = -\omega r \sin \omega t = -\omega y, \quad \ldots \quad (3)$$

and

$$a = \frac{d^2 x}{dt^2} = -\omega^2 r \cos \omega t = -\omega^2 x. \quad \ldots \quad (4)$$

Therefore, the motion of P is harmonic and the constant k in equation (1) is here equal to ω^2. It should here be noted that if P were the projection of M on the vertical diameter, the expression for the acceleration of P would be defined by the equation $a = -\omega^2 r \sin \omega t$ as in Fig. 308.

This method of generating a simple harmonic motion is a convenient one for studying certain features of the motion. From the definition it follows that a simple harmonic motion is a periodic motion. It is convenient to study a periodic motion by means of the displacement-time, velocity-time, and acceleration-time curves.

For example, in Fig. 308(a) let a simple harmonic motion of the point B be generated by the mechanism shown. The motion of B is, of course, the same as that of the projection of C on the vertical diameter. A displacement-time (s–t) curve for the motion of B is shown in Fig. 308(b). The time to complete one cycle of the motion is called the *period* of the motion, and one complete cycle is called an *oscillation*. In Fig. 308(b) the period is denoted by T. The amplitude of the motion is one-half of the length of the path and is denoted by A. The *frequency* is the number of complete cycles or oscillations per unit of time and is denoted by f. It will be observed that since the motion of B is the same as the motion of the projection of C on a vertical diameter, we may write

$$T = \frac{2\pi}{\omega}, \quad \text{and} \quad f = \frac{\omega}{2\pi} \quad \ldots \ldots \quad (5)$$

in which ω is sometimes called the circular frequency.

The velocity-time and acceleration-time curves for the motion of B are shown in Fig. 308(c). It should be noted that at either end of the stroke, v is zero and a is a maximum and that at the center of the stroke a

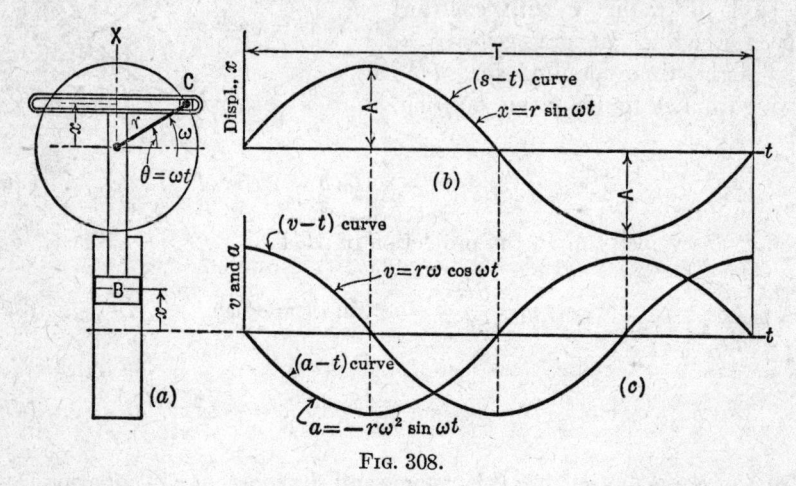

FIG. 308.

is zero and v is a maximum. Particular attention should be called to the fact that when v is equal to zero a is a maximum; the student is likely to make the mistake of reasoning that $a = \dfrac{dv}{dt}$ and hence when $v = 0$, a must also be zero. In certain types of rectilinear motion, including simple harmonic motion, the velocity may be changing rapidly through its zero value and hence $\dfrac{dv}{dt}$ may be large when $v = 0$. Or to state the same idea in mathematical language, the first derivative of a function is not necessarily equal to zero when the function is equal to zero.

ILLUSTRATIVE PROBLEM

Problem 473.—A body having a weight W is supported by a helical spring as shown in Fig. 309. The body is pulled down a distance of 4 in. from its equilibrium position OX and is then released, allowing it to oscillate about the equilibrium position with a simple harmonic motion. The weight of the body and the stiffness of the

PROBLEMS   189

spring are such that the acceleration of body for any value of y is $a = \dfrac{d^2y}{dt^2} = -60y$. Find the amplitude A and the period T of the motion. Find also the maximum velocity and maximum acceleration of the body.

Solution.—The amplitude is obviously $A = 4$ in. The value of ω in equation (4) is $\sqrt{60} = 7.75$ rad./sec. and hence

$$T = \frac{2\pi}{7.75} = 0.81 \text{ sec.}$$

The maximum values of v and a occur when the values of x and y in equations (3) and (4) are maximum, that is, when x and y are each equal to 4 in. Hence the maximum values of v and a are

$$v_{max.} = 4\omega = 4 \times 7.75 = 31.0 \text{ in./sec.} = 2.58 \text{ ft./sec.}$$

$$a_{max.} = 4\omega^2 = 4 \times (7.75)^2 = 240 \text{ in./sec.}^2 = 20 \text{ ft./sec.}^2$$

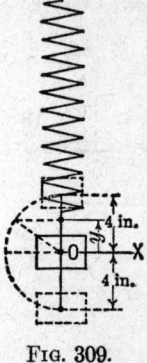

Fig. 309.

PROBLEMS

474. A point moves along a straight line so that its distance s from a fixed point in the line is $s = b \sin pt$ where b and p are constants and t is the time. Find the velocity and acceleration of the point in terms of b, p, and t. If $b = 2$ ft. and $p = \frac{1}{4}$ rad./sec., find the velocity and acceleration of the point when $t = 3$ sec.

Ans. $v = bp \cos pt$; $a = -bp^2 \sin pt$; $v = 0.366$ ft./sec.; $a = -0.085$ ft./sec.^{2}

475. If the body in Prob. 473 is pulled down 3 in. instead of 4 in. and then released, what will be the period and the frequency of the motion?

476. A point moves with a simple harmonic motion the amplitude of which is 10 in. If the period is 2 sec., determine the maximum velocity and maximum acceleration.   *Ans.* $v = 2.62$ ft./sec.; $a = 8.22$ ft./sec.^{2}

477. In Fig. 310 the body C is raised by the pressure of the roller A on the cam B as the crank OA rotates at a constant angular velocity ω of 20 r.p.m. The length of OA is 16 in. What is the acceleration of C (a) when $\theta = 30°$, and (b) when $\theta = 60°$?

478. The maximum velocity of a point which has a simple harmonic motion is 10 ft./sec. and the period is $\frac{1}{8}$ sec. Determine the amplitude of the motion and the maximum acceleration.   *Ans.* $r = 0.53$ ft.; $a = 188$ ft./sec.^{2}

479. The drivers of a Mikado locomotive are 60 in. in diameter and the length of the crank is 15 in. If the speed of the locomotive is 30 mi./hr., determine the maximum velocity and the maximum acceleration of the crosshead and piston relative to the engine frame, assuming that the connecting rod is so long that the motion of the crosshead is harmonic.

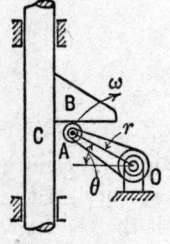

Fig. 310.

480. A point moves with a simple harmonic motion such that its speed is 90 in./sec. when it is 4 in. from the center of its path and 80 in./sec. when it is 6 in. from the center. Determine the period and the amplitude of the motion. Determine also the maximum velocity and the maximum acceleration of the point.

Ans. $T = 0.68$ sec.; $A = 10.56$ in.; $v = 97.5$ in./sec.; $a = 897$ in./sec.^{2}

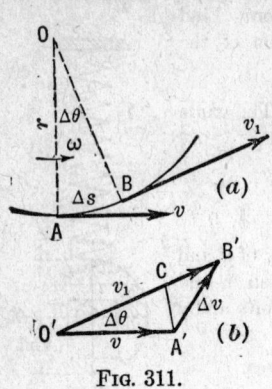

87. Acceleration in Curvilinear Motion. Tangential and Normal Components of Acceleration.

—Let a point move with varying speed along the curved path shown in Fig. 311(a) and let it be required to find the magnitude and direction of the linear acceleration of the moving point, at the instant it is at any point A on the path, from the equation

$$a = \operatorname*{Limit}_{\Delta t \doteq 0} \frac{\Delta v}{\Delta t}.$$

FIG. 311.

Let the time required for a small displacement AB (or Δs) be denoted by Δt, and let the velocities at A and B be denoted by v and v_1, respectively. Also let the radius of curvature at A be denoted by r and the angular displacement with respect to the center of curvature, O, be denoted by $\Delta\theta$. Now if, in Fig. 311(b), $O'A'$ and $O'B'$ be laid off to represent in direction and magnitude v and v_1 respectively, the change in velocity, Δv, is represented by the vector $A'B'$ (Art. 74). The average acceleration during the time interval Δt is therefore $\dfrac{A'B'}{\Delta t}$, and the instantaneous acceleration at A is the limit of this ratio as Δt (and also Δs and $\Delta\theta$) approaches zero. If, in Fig. 311(b), $O'C$ is laid off equal to $O'A'$ (or v), $A'B'$ may be expressed as the vector sum of $A'C$ and CB', and hence the acceleration may be expressed as the vector sum of two component accelerations as follows:

$$a = \operatorname*{Limit}_{\Delta t \doteq 0} \frac{A'B'}{\Delta t} = \operatorname*{Limit}_{\Delta t \doteq 0} \frac{A'C \nrightarrow CB'}{\Delta t}$$

$$= \operatorname*{Limit}_{\Delta t \doteq 0} \frac{A'C}{\Delta t} \nrightarrow \operatorname*{Limit}_{\Delta t \doteq 0} \frac{CB'}{\Delta t}.$$

Since $A'C$ would represent the change in the velocity if the velocity were constant in magnitude and changed only in direction, and since the length of CB' represents the change in the magnitude, only, of the velocity, it is evident that the first of the two components is the acceleration due to a change in the direction, only, of the velocity, and the second component is the acceleration due to a change in the magnitude, only, of the velocity.

The direction and magnitude of each of these two component accelerations defined by the last two terms of the above equation will now be found.

ACCELERATION IN CURVILINEAR MOTION

The direction of the first of the two components is the limiting direction of $A'C$ as Δt (and $\Delta\theta$) approaches zero. As $\Delta\theta$ approaches zero, the angle $O'A'C$ approaches 90° and hence in the limit $A'C$ is perpendicular to $O'A'$ (or v), and therefore the first term represents the component of acceleration normal to the path at A. This component is toward the center of curvature and is denoted by a_n. Similarly, the direction of the second component is the limiting direction of CB' as $\Delta\theta$ approaches 0 and therefore is in the direction of $O'A'$ (or v). Hence the second term represents the component of acceleration tangent to the path at A and is denoted by a_t.

The magnitudes of a_n and a_t may be found as follows:

$$a_n = \underset{\Delta t \doteq 0}{\text{Limit}} \frac{A'C}{\Delta t} = \underset{\Delta t \doteq 0}{\text{Limit}} \frac{2v \sin \frac{1}{2}\Delta\theta}{\Delta t}$$

$$= v \underset{\Delta t \doteq 0}{\text{Limit}} \frac{\Delta\theta}{\Delta t} = v \frac{d\theta}{dt} = v\omega,$$

where ω is the angular velocity of the point relative to the center of curvature O. And since $v = r\omega$, a_n may also be expressed as $r\omega^2$ or v^2/r.

The magnitude of the tangential component is

$$a_t = \underset{\Delta t \doteq 0}{\text{Limit}} \frac{CB'}{\Delta t} = \underset{\Delta t \doteq 0}{\text{Limit}} \frac{v_1 - v}{\Delta t} = \frac{dv}{dt},$$

and since $v = \frac{ds}{dt}$, a_t may also be expressed as $\frac{d^2s}{dt^2}$.

Summarizing; the two following important theorems may be stated:

I. When the velocity, v, of a particle changes in magnitude, an acceleration is produced the value of which is $\frac{dv}{dt}$; its direction at any instant is parallel to that of the velocity, that is, tangent to the path at the point at which the particle is located at the instant. Thus

$$a_t = \frac{dv}{dt} = \frac{d^2s}{dt^2}.$$

II. When the velocity, v, of a particle changes in direction, an acceleration is produced the value of which is $v\omega = \omega^2 r = \frac{v^2}{r}$; its direction, at any instant, is perpendicular to the velocity, towards the center of curvature of the path, at the point where the particle is located at the instant. Thus

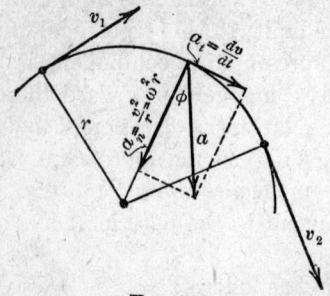

$$a_n = v\omega = \omega^2 r = \frac{v^2}{r}.$$

The total acceleration of a point that moves on a curved path with varying speed is the resultant, or vector sum, of the normal and tangential components of acceleration as shown in Fig. 312. The magnitude and direction of the acceleration may be found from the following equations:

Fig. 312.

$$a = a_n +\!\!+ a_t = \sqrt{a_n^2 + a_t^2}$$

$$\tan \phi = \frac{a_t}{a_n}$$

ILLUSTRATIVE PROBLEM

Problem 481.—A point P moves clockwise on a circular path of radius 2 ft. The angular velocity of the point with respect to the center of the circle is proportional to the square of the time after starting, that is $\omega = kt^2$ where k is a constant and ω and t are expressed in radians per second and seconds, respectively. If the speed of the point is 64 ft./sec. when $t = 2$ sec., what is the linear velocity and the linear acceleration of P when $t = \frac{1}{2}$ sec. Assume P to be at the top of the circle when $t = \frac{1}{2}$ sec.

Solution.—The linear velocity is $v = r\omega = 2\omega = 2kt^2$, and since $v = 64$ ft./sec. when $t = 2$ sec., we have

$$64 = 2k \times 4 \quad \text{or} \quad k = 8 \quad \therefore \ v = 16t^2$$

Hence when $t = \frac{1}{2}$ sec.,

$$v_P = 16 \times (\tfrac{1}{2})^2 = 4 \text{ ft./sec.}$$

And the tangential and normal components of the acceleration of P are

$$(a_P)_t = \frac{dv}{dt} = \frac{d}{dt}(16t^2)$$

$$= 32t = 16 \text{ ft./sec.}^2 \text{ when } t = \tfrac{1}{2} \text{ sec.}$$

$$(a_P)_n = \frac{v^2}{r} = \frac{4^2}{2} = 8 \text{ ft./sec.}^2 \text{ when } t = \tfrac{1}{2} \text{ sec.}$$

$$\therefore \ a_P = \sqrt{16^2 + 8^2} = 17.9 \text{ ft./sec.}^2$$

Also $\tan \phi = \tfrac{8}{16}$ $\quad \therefore \ \phi = 26° 34'.$

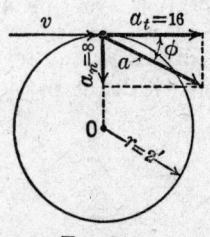

Fig. 313.

88. Angular Acceleration.—The angular acceleration of a line is the time rate of change of the angular velocity of the line. The angular

UNIFORMLY ACCELERATED CIRCULAR MOTION

acceleration of a moving point with respect to a fixed point or pole is the angular acceleration of the line joining the moving point to the pole. If the angular velocity, ω, of the point changes uniformly, the angular acceleration, α, is expressed by the ratio of any change, $\Delta\omega$, in the angular velocity to the corresponding time interval, Δt. Thus

$$\alpha = \frac{\Delta\omega}{\Delta t} = \frac{\omega_2 - \omega_1}{t_2 - t_1}.$$

If the angular velocity of the point does not change uniformly, the acceleration at any instant is the average acceleration during an indefinitely small time interval including the instant. Or, expressed mathematically the instantaneous angular acceleration is

$$\alpha = \underset{\Delta t \doteq 0}{\text{Limit}} \frac{\Delta\omega}{\Delta t} = \frac{d\omega}{dt}.$$

And since $\omega = \dfrac{d\theta}{dt}$, the above expression may also be written,

$$\alpha = \frac{d\omega}{dt} = \frac{d^2\theta}{dt^2}.$$

In order to find α from the above equations, ω and θ must be expressed in terms of t. The relations between θ, t, ω, and α may be shown graphically by diagrams similar to those used in Arts. 84 and 85 for s, t, v, and a.

The unit of angular acceleration is any convenient unit of angular velocity per unit of time; such as, degree per second per second (deg./sec.^{2}), revolution per minute per second (rev./min./sec.), radian per second per second (rad./sec.^{2}), etc.

89. Uniformly Accelerated Circular Motion.—Many problems involving the motion of a point on a circular path with constant angular acceleration occur in engineering practice. The following relations between the angular displacement, angular velocity, angular acceleration, and time may be deduced in a manner similar to that used in Art. 84:

$$\omega = \omega_0 + \alpha t \quad \ldots \ldots \ldots \ldots \quad (1)$$

$$\theta = \frac{\omega_0 + \omega}{2} \cdot t \quad \ldots \ldots \ldots \quad (2)$$

$$\theta = \omega_0 t + \tfrac{1}{2}\alpha t^2 \quad \ldots \ldots \ldots \quad (3)$$

$$\omega^2 = \omega_0^2 + 2\alpha\theta, \quad \ldots \ldots \ldots \quad (4)$$

where ω_0 and ω denote the initial and final angular velocities, respectively, corresponding to any time interval t, and θ and α denote the angular displacement and angular acceleration, respectively. The derivation of the above equations will be left to the student.

90. Relation between Linear and Angular Accelerations.—The relation between the linear and angular accelerations of a point that moves on a circular path may be found as follows: In Fig. 314 let a point move on the circular path shown, O being the center of the path and r the radius. If the magnitude of the velocity of the point changes (assumed to increase) there is, at any instant during the change, a tangential acceleration given by the equation

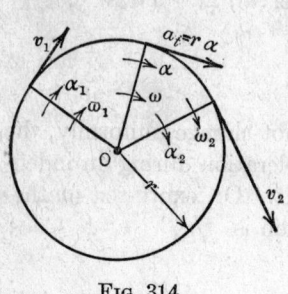

FIG. 314.

$a_t = \dfrac{dv}{dt}$. But $v = r\omega$ and therefore $a_t = \dfrac{d}{dt}(r\omega) = r\dfrac{d\omega}{dt}$. And since $\dfrac{d\omega}{dt}$ is the angular acceleration α of the point at the instant, we have

$$a_t = r\alpha.$$

Therefore the tangential acceleration, at any instant, of a point moving on a circular path is equal to the product of the radius of the circle and the angular acceleration of the point about the center of the circle at the same instant.

If the particle does not move on a circular path, the equation is also true provided that r is the radius of curvature of the path at the given position of the particle and that α is the angular acceleration of the particle with reference to the center of curvature.

The normal acceleration, $r\omega^2$, of the particle (not shown in the above diagram), unlike the tangential acceleration, is independent of the angular acceleration. It depends on the angular velocity at the instant, and not on the rate at which the angular velocity is changing at the instant.

PROBLEMS FOR ARTICLES 86 TO 89

482. A particle moves on a circular path according to the law $\theta = 3t^2 + 2t$ where θ and t are measured in radians and seconds, respectively. What is the angular velocity and the angular acceleration of the particle at the end of 4 sec.?

483. A point moves on a circle according to the law $s = t^3 + 2t^2$, s and t being measured in feet and seconds, respectively. If the acceleration of the point is $16\sqrt{2}$ ft./sec.^{2} when $t = 2$ sec., what is the radius of the circle? *Ans.* $r = 25$ ft.

484. Derive equations (1) and (3) of Art. 89 by calculus methods, starting with the equations $\alpha = \dfrac{d\omega}{dt}$ and $\omega = \dfrac{d\theta}{dt}$.

PROBLEMS FOR ARTICLES 86 TO 89

485. A bell-crank operated by a cam (see Fig. 295) rotates so that its angular acceleration α follows the law $\alpha = 4t^2 + 6$. If its initial angular velocity is 2 rad./sec., what is the angular velocity of the bell-crank at the end of 0.5 sec.?
Ans. $\omega = 5.17$ rad./sec.

486. A rod 3 ft. long is rotated in a horizontal plane about a vertical axis through one end of the rod so that the angular velocity increases uniformly from 10 to 40 r.p.m. in 3 sec. Find the tangential acceleration of the mid-point of the rod.

487. A quarter-mile track is made up of two straight parallel sides connected at the ends by two semi-circles, each having a radius of 100 ft. A boy runs the quarter mile in 50 sec. at uniform speed. What is the acceleration of the boy (a) when on the straight track and (b) when on the curved portion?
Ans. $a = 0$; $a = 6.97$ ft./sec.^{2}

488. A flywheel 8 ft. in diameter turns so that its angular velocity changes uniformly from 100 r.p.m. to 40 r.p.m. during a period of 4 sec. Find the tangential acceleration of a point on the rim during the 4-sec. period. Find the total acceleration of a point on the rim at the end of the period.

489. Two pulleys are connected so that they turn together about the center O (Fig. 315), causing the weight A to unwind and the weight B to wind up. If the angular velocity of the points M and P change uniformly from 10 r.p.m. to 60 r.p.m. during a period of 2 sec., find: (a) the tangential acceleration of each of the two points at any instant during the 2 sec.; (b) the acceleration of A and of B; (c) the total acceleration of M at the beginning, and of P at the end, of the 2-sec. period. Assume that M at the beginning of the 2-sec. period and P at the end of the period are in the positions shown.
Ans. $(a_M)_t = a_A = 1.96$ ft./sec.^{2}; $(a_P)_t = a_B = 2.62$ ft./sec.^{2};
$a_M = 2.12$ ft./sec.^{2}; $a_P = 39.5$ ft./sec.^{2}

490. As the drum (Fig. 316) turns, the weight A is wound up with decreasing speed. If its speed decreases 20 ft./sec. each second, what is the angular acceleration

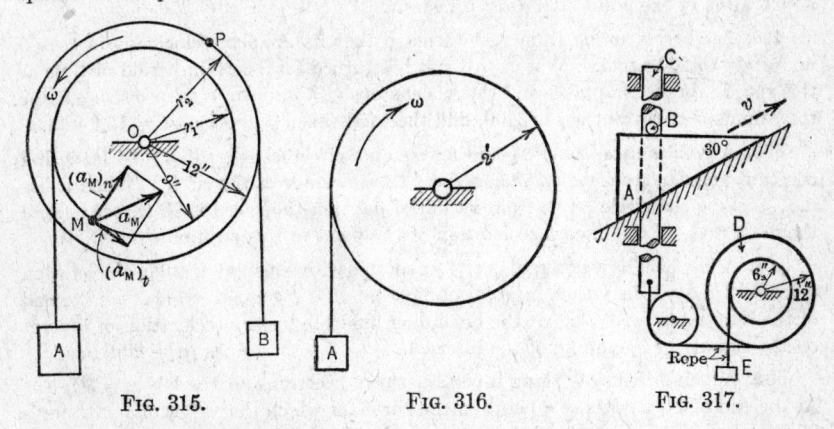

FIG. 315. FIG. 316. FIG. 317.

of a point on the rim of the drum? What is the tangential component of the acceleration of a point on the rim?

491. If at a certain instant the velocity of A in Fig. 317 is 4 in./sec. and is changing uniformly at the rate of 5 in./sec.², find the linear acceleration of C, the angular acceleration of the drum D, and the linear acceleration of E.

Ans. $a_C = 2.5$ in./sec.²; $\alpha = 0.208$ rad./sec.²; $a_E = 0.104$ ft./sec.²

492. A train, while traveling on a curve of ¼-mi. radius, changes its speed uniformly from 20 mi./hr. to 30 mi./hr. in 20 sec. What is the total acceleration of the train at the beginning and at the end of the 20-sec. period?

493. What is the angular acceleration, with respect to the center of the curve, of the train having the motion described in Prob. 492? *Ans.* $\alpha = 0.000555$ rad./sec.²

494. A point moves on a circular path having a radius of 2 ft. If its speed changes uniformly from 100 ft./min. to 240 ft./min. during a period of 3 sec., what are the tangential and normal accelerations (*a*) at the beginning of the period, (*b*) at the end of the period?

495. If in Fig. 288 the angular velocity of the crank OA is 6 rad./sec. and the angular acceleration is 9 rad./sec.², what is the angular acceleration of CD? Find also the tangential and normal components of the linear acceleration of the point D. Assume the length of OA to be 6 in.

Ans. $\alpha_{CD} = 1.5$ rad./sec.²; $a_t = 7.5$ ft./sec.²; $a_n = 5$ ft./sec.²

496. A point starts from rest and moves on a circle whose radius is 400 ft. in such a way that the rate of change of speed at any instant is proportional to the time after starting. If $v = 18$ ft./sec. when $t = 3$ sec., find the magnitude of the velocity and of the acceleration at the end of 8 sec.

497. A point moves on a circle with a constant angular acceleration, with respect to the center, of 2 rad./sec.² At a certain instant the angular velocity is 30 r.p.m. Find the angular velocity of the point after it has made 50 revolutions.

Ans. $\omega = 340$ r.p.m.

498. The total acceleration of a point on the rim of a pulley, at a given instant, is 40 ft./sec.² in a direction making an angle of 20° with the radius to the point. If the radius of the pulley is 18 in. what are the angular velocity and the angular acceleration of the point at the given instant?

499. A wheel starting from rest turns so that its angular velocity is increased uniformly to 200 r.p.m. in 6 sec. After it has turned for a certain period of time at this speed a brake is applied and the wheel stops at a uniform rate in 5 sec. If the total number of revolutions is 3100, find the total time. *Ans.* $t = 15.6$ min.

500. A point starts from rest and moves on a circle whose radius is 64 ft. with a constant angular acceleration with respect to the center of the circle. When it has moved along the circle 32 ft. from its initial position the speed is 32 ft./sec. Find the magnitude of the linear acceleration of the point in this position.

501. A flywheel having a radius of 4 ft. rotates with constant angular acceleration through 2 radians in a time interval of ⅔ sec. If the angular velocity at the end of the interval is twice that at the beginning, find the linear acceleration of a point on the rim at the beginning of the interval. *Ans.* $a = 20$ ft./sec.²

502. A point P moves along a certain curve according to the law $s = 3t^2 + 2$. At the end of 2 sec., P is at a point on the curve for which the radius of curvature is 27 ft. Find the magnitude of the linear acceleration of P at that instant.

91. Axial Components of Acceleration.

In Art. 87 the acceleration of a point was determined as the vector sum of the components of acceleration tangent and normal, respectively, to the path of the point. It is sometimes more convenient, however, to determine the acceleration of a point as the vector sum of the components of acceleration, a_x and a_y, parallel to the coordinate axes.

Since the component, in a given direction, of the acceleration of a point is the rate of change of the component of the velocity of the point in the given direction the axial components of acceleration (Fig. 318) are

$$a_x = \frac{dv_x}{dt} \quad \text{and} \quad a_y = \frac{dv_y}{dt}.$$

And since $v_x = \dfrac{dx}{dt}$ and $v_y = \dfrac{dy}{dt}$, we have

$$a_x = \frac{d^2x}{dt^2} \quad \text{and} \quad a_y = \frac{d^2y}{dt^2}.$$

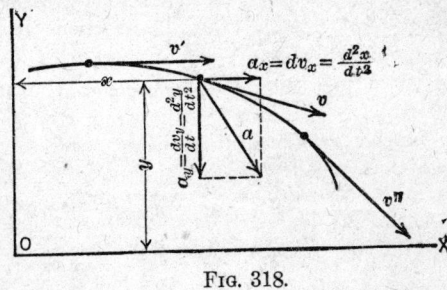

Fig. 318.

In order to determine the axial components from the above equations v_x (or x) and v_y (or y) must be expressed in terms of t, unless v_x and v_y change uniformly, in which case

$$a_x = \frac{\Delta v_x}{\Delta t} = \frac{v''_x - v'_x}{t_2 - t_1} \quad \text{and} \quad a_y = \frac{\Delta v_y}{\Delta t} = \frac{v''_y - v'_y}{t_2 - t_1},$$

where v' and v'' are the velocities at the beginning and end of the time interval $\Delta t (= t_2 - t_1)$.

It is important to note that, although the component of velocity in a given direction may be zero, it does not necessarily follow that the component of acceleration of the point in that direction is zero. For example, a ball thrown horizontally from a window has no vertical velocity just as it leaves the window, that is, $v_y = 0$, but the ball has an acceleration, the vertical component of which is $a_y = 32.2$ ft./sec.^{2} In other words, v_y is changing through its zero value at the rate of 32.2 ft./sec.^{2} Likewise, the velocity of the crosshead of a steam engine is zero at the end of the stroke, but its acceleration, $\dfrac{dv}{dt}$, has a large value as the velocity changes through its zero value; also a point moving on a circular path has no velocity component normal to the path, but there is a normal acceleration the magnitude of which, as shown in Art. 87 and also in the following illustrative problem, is $\dfrac{v^2}{r}$.

ILLUSTRATIVE PROBLEM

Problem 503.—A point moves with constant speed on a circle of radius r as indicated in Fig. 319. Let the directions parallel and perpendicular to the velocity v at B be denoted by x and y, respectively. Derive expressions for a_x and a_y, the rates of change in the x- and y-directions of the velocity, as the point moves from A to C. From these expressions find the accelerations in the x- and y-directions when the point is at B.

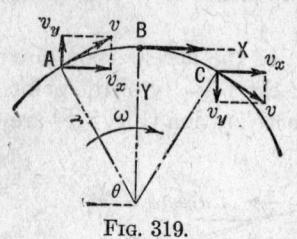

FIG. 319.

Solution.—When the moving point is at A, the components of its velocity in the x- and y-directions are $v_x = v \sin \theta$ and $v_y = -v \cos \theta$. Hence the x- and y-components of acceleration of the point are

$$a_x = \frac{dv_x}{dt} = \frac{d}{dt}(v \sin \theta) = v \cos \theta \frac{d\theta}{dt} = v\omega \cos \theta$$

$$a_y = \frac{dv_y}{dt} = \frac{d}{dt}(-v \cos \theta) = v \sin \theta \frac{d\theta}{dt} = v\omega \sin \theta.$$

Now when the point is at B, $\cos \theta = 0$ and $\sin \theta = 1$, and hence

$$a_x = 0 \quad \text{and} \quad a_y = v\omega = r\omega^2 = \frac{v^2}{r}.$$

PROBLEMS

504. A ball is thrown from a room through an open window. As the ball passes over the window sill its velocity is 40 ft./sec. in a horizontal direction. What is the radius of curvature of the path of the ball at this point?   *Ans.* $r = 49.7$ ft.

505. Find the magnitude and direction of the acceleration of the point whose motion is described in Prob. 439 when $t = \frac{1}{2}$ sec.

506. A point moves along the curve $y = \dfrac{x^3}{240}$ according to the law $x = t^2$, x and y being expressed in ft. and t in sec. Find the magnitude and direction of the acceleration of the point when $t = 2$ sec.   *Ans.* $a = 2.83$ ft./sec.^{2}; $\theta_x = 45°$.

507. A point starts from rest and moves in the xy-plane in such a way that the x-component of its acceleration is proportional to the time after starting, and the y-component of its acceleration is constant and equal to 3 ft./sec.^{2} If the linear acceleration of the point is 5 ft./sec.^{2} when $t = 4$ sec., find the linear velocity when $t = 6$ sec.

508. A particle starts from the point $x = 0$, $y = 3$ and moves in the xy-plane according to the law $v_x = 4 \cos t$, $v_y = -3 \sin t$. Find the equation to the path of the particle and determine the acceleration when $t = \dfrac{\pi}{4}$.

Ans. $\dfrac{x^2}{16} + \dfrac{y^2}{9} = 1$; $a = 3.53$ ft./sec.^{2}

509. A particle moves on the path $xy = 4$ according to the law $x = 2t^2$. (a) Find the x- and y-components of the velocity and of the acceleration when $t = 2$.

(b) Determine the total acceleration by combining the components graphically.
(c) Find the tangential and normal components graphically by resolving the total acceleration in the tangential and normal directions.

92. Relative Motion.

In the preceding articles, the motion of a particle is defined or described with reference to a point or a set of axes assumed to be fixed. All points and bodies, however, are in motion, but in most practical problems it is convenient to consider the earth to be fixed. Therefore a set of axes passing through any point on the earth will be regarded as a fixed reference frame. The motion of a particle described with reference to a point on the earth is called its *absolute* motion. The motion of a particle described with reference to a point that is moving with respect to the earth is called its *relative* motion. It will be observed that the absolute motion of a particle is its relative motion with respect to the earth.

In considering the motion of two moving particles, the motion of one particle relative to the other particle is often required. The relation between the absolute and relative motions of two particles A and B (assumed, for convenience, to be moving in a plane) may be expressed by an important theorem which may be stated in two forms as follows:

I. *The absolute displacement, velocity, or acceleration of A is the geometric or vector sum of the relative displacement, velocity, or acceleration, respectively, of A with respect to B and the absolute displacement, velocity, or acceleration, respectively, of B.*

II. *The relative displacement, velocity, or acceleration of A with respect to B is the vector difference of the absolute displacement, velocity, or acceleration, respectively, of A and the absolute displacement, velocity, or acceleration, respectively, of B.*

This theorem may be expressed in the form of equations as follows:

$$s_A = s_{\frac{A}{B}} + \!\!\!+\, s_B \quad \text{or} \quad s_{\frac{A}{B}} = s_A \rightarrow s_B.$$

$$v_A = v_{\frac{A}{B}} + \!\!\!+\, v_B \quad \text{or} \quad v_{\frac{A}{B}} = v_A \rightarrow v_B.$$

$$a_A = a_{\frac{A}{B}} + \!\!\!+\, a_B \quad \text{or} \quad a_{\frac{A}{B}} = a_A \rightarrow a_B.$$

where s_A denotes the absolute displacement of A, s_B denotes the absolute displacement of B, and $s_{\frac{A}{B}}$ denotes the relative displacement of A with respect to B, and similarly for velocities and accelerations.

Relative Displacement.—As applying to displacements, the above theorem is nearly self-evident. To illustrate, let A and B be two particles which have the same initial position as shown in Fig. 320. Let the point A be given a displacement $s_A = AA_1$, and the point B a displacement $s_B = BB_1$. The displacement of A relative to B, then, is represented in direction and magnitude by the vector B_1A_1, and it is evident that

$$s_{A} = s_A \nrightarrow s_B \quad \text{or} \quad s_A = s_A \rightarrow s_B \:. \quad . \quad . \quad . \quad . \quad (1)$$
$$\overline{B} \qquad\qquad\qquad \overline{B}$$

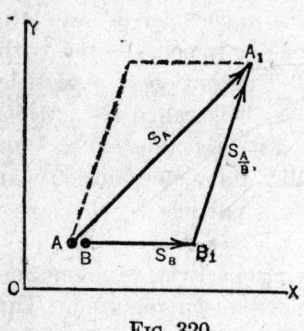

FIG. 320. 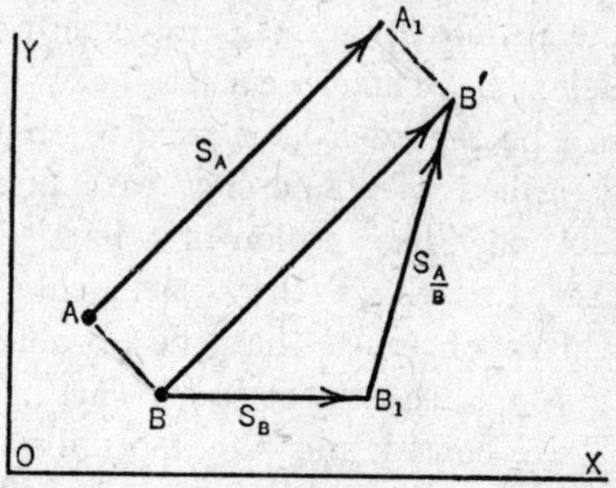   FIG. 321.

If the points A and B do not have the same initial position, the reasoning is changed but little, the final conclusion being the same as stated above as will be evident from a study of the diagram in Fig. 321.

ILLUSTRATIVE PROBLEM

Problem 510.—The current in a river with parallel sides is 4 mi./hr. A motor boat starting from one side keeps headed perpendicular to the sides and moves at a rate (relative to the water) of 6 mi./hr. If the river is 1 mi. wide, what is the absolute displacement of the boat after reaching the other side?

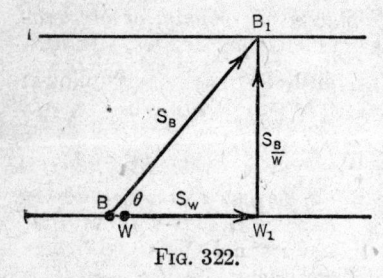

Solution.—Let B (Fig. 322) represent the boat and W the water that is in contact with the boat when the boat starts. Then

$$s_B = s_W \nrightarrow s_B\:.$$
$$\overline{W}$$

The displacement of the water while the boat is moving across is

$$s_W = WW_1 = \tfrac{2}{3} \text{ mi.}$$

FIG. 322.

After the boat has reached the other side its displacement relative to the water (now at W_1) is

$$s_B = W_1B_1 = 1 \text{ mi.}$$
$$\overline{W}$$

Therefore

$$s_B = 1 \nrightarrow \tfrac{2}{3} = \sqrt{(1)^2 + (\tfrac{2}{3})^2} = 1.2 \text{ mi.}$$

and

$$\tan\theta = \frac{s_B/\overline{W}}{s_W} = \frac{3}{2}. \quad \therefore \theta = 56° 20'.$$

Relative Velocity.—The above theorem, as applying to the velocities of two moving particles, may be proved by making use of an important principle of kinematics, namely, that the relative motion of two particles is not affected by any motion that they have in common. If, then, equal velocities are imposed on the motions of two particles, the relative velocity of one with respect to the other will not be changed. Further, if the velocities imposed cause the velocity of one particle to become zero, the resulting velocity of the other particle is then by definition its velocity relative to the one. It may be noted that the relative velocity of one point with respect to another point is the velocity that the first point would appear to have to an observer moving with the second point.

FIG. 323.

Let A and B (Fig. 323) be any two moving particles (assumed to move in a plane), let the absolute velocity, v_A, of A be represented by AA_1, and let BB_1 represent the absolute velocity, v_B, of B. Let a velocity equal to v_B but reversed in direction be given to each point. The velocity of the point B will then be zero and hence the resulting velocity of the point A is the velocity of A relative to B. Hence it is evident from the diagram that

$$v_A = v_{A \over B} + v_B \quad \text{or} \quad v_{A \over B} = v_A \rightarrow v_B \quad \ldots \quad (2)$$

The above method could also be used in finding the relation between the absolute and relative displacements of two particles, as expressed in equation (1).

ILLUSTRATIVE PROBLEM

Problem 511.—In the shaper mechanism shown in Fig. 324, let A be the sliding block and let B be the point on the rocker arm O_1BM which is coincident with A at the instant. The distance OO_1 is 20 in. and θ is 30°. If $\omega = 20$ r.p.m. and $r = \frac{1}{2}$ ft., find v_B, the absolute velocity of B, and $v_{A \over B}$, the relative velocity of A with respect to B.

Solution.—Since the block A moves on a circular arc at constant speed, its velocity is given in magnitude by the equation

$$v_A = \omega r = \frac{20 \times 2\pi}{60} \times \frac{1}{2} = 1.05 \text{ ft./sec.}$$

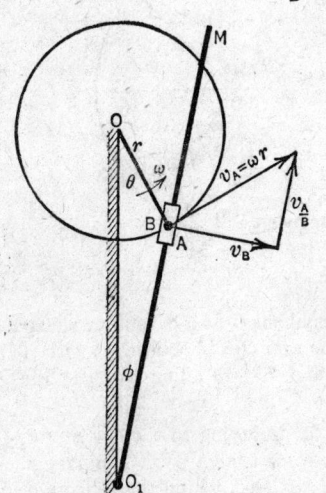

FIG. 324.

and its direction is perpendicular to r, as shown in Fig. 324. The direction of the absolute velocity of B is perpendicular to O_1BM and its magnitude is unknown. Likewise, the direction of the velocity of A relative to B is known since it is along (parallel to) the rocker arm. By applying the equation

$$v_A = v_{\frac{A}{B}} +\!\!\!\!+ v_B,$$

the magnitudes of $v_{\frac{A}{B}}$ and v_B are determined by the intersection of the lines that represent their directions. By scaling off the magnitudes, the following values are found:

$$v_{\frac{A}{B}} = 0.70 \text{ ft./sec.} \quad \text{and} \quad v_B = 0.79 \text{ ft./sec.}$$

In the illustrative Prob. 431 the method of solving this problem by use of radial and transverse components of velocity is given.

PROBLEMS

512. Two trains A and B travel on parallel straight tracks. The speed of A is 40 mi./hr. and that of B is 50 mi./hr. in the same direction. What is the velocity of A relative to B? Of B relative to A?

Ans. $v_{\frac{A}{B}} = -10$ mi./hr.; $v_{\frac{B}{A}} = 10$ mi./hr.

513. A train A travels with a velocity $v_A = 40$ mi./hr. and another train B travels with a velocity $v_B = 50$ mi./hr. in the directions shown in Fig. 325. What are the magnitude and the direction of the relative velocity of B with respect to A?

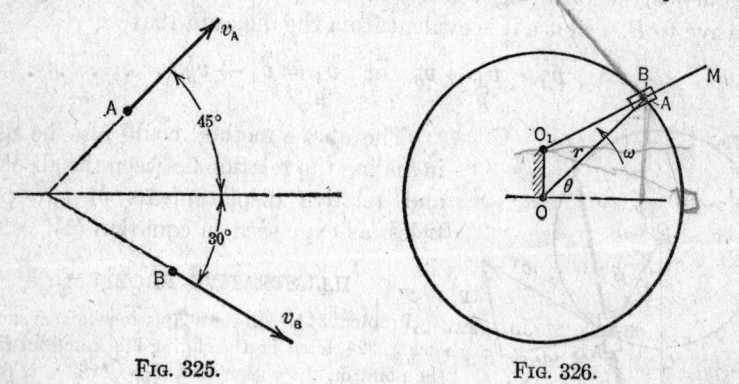

Fig. 325.   Fig. 326.

514. In Fig. 326, let A be a block which revolves about O at a constant angular velocity $\omega = 30$ r.p.m. and let B be the point on the arm O_1BM coincident with A at the instant. If $r = OA = 9$ in., $OO_1 = 3$ in., and $\theta = 45°$, find the absolute velocity of B. *Ans.* $v_B = 2.27$ ft./sec.

515. A point A moves along the parabola $y^2 = 9x$ according to the law $x = t^2$, x and y being expressed in ft., and t in sec. At the same time a point B moves to the right along the x-axis with a constant velocity of 8 ft./sec. Find the velocity of A relative to B when $t = 2$ sec.

516. A car A is moving north on a straight road at a speed of 60 mi./hr. and at the same time another car B is moving southeast on a straight road at a speed of 30 mi./hr. Find the velocity of B relative to A.

$$Ans.\ v_{\underset{A}{B}} = 84.0 \text{ mi./hr.}; \quad \theta_x = 284° 38'.$$

517. If, in Fig. 288, $\omega = 120$ r.p.m. and $OA = 0.5$ ft., what is the velocity of D relative to A?

518. Solve Prob. 420 by use of the principle of relative motion. See solution of Prob. 511.

519. A point P moves on a circle with constant speed. A and B are the projections of P on any two perpendicular diameters of the circle. Prove that for all positions of P the magnitude of the velocity of A relative to B is constant and equal to the speed of P.

Relative Acceleration.—In order to prove the above theorem as it relates to accelerations, it will be assumed that the relative acceleration of two particles is not changed if equal additional velocities and accelerations be given the two particles. This is similar to the assumption made in the discussion of relative velocities. Consider, then, two particles A and B which move along paths as indicated in Fig. 327. Assume that a velocity equal and opposite to the velocity of $B(-v_B)$ is imposed on each particle (not shown at A in Fig. 327). Assume also that accelerations equal to the acceleration of B but of opposite sense are imposed on the two particles. This will not change the relative motion of A with respect to B. Imposing a velocity of $-v_B$ and an acceleration of $-a_B$ on the particle B will make its position fixed. Now since, by definition, the acceleration of A relative to B is the acceleration that A would have if B were fixed, it follows that the resulting acceleration of A after imposing the acceleration $-a_B$ on A is the acceleration of A relative to B. Hence, as indicated in Fig. 327,

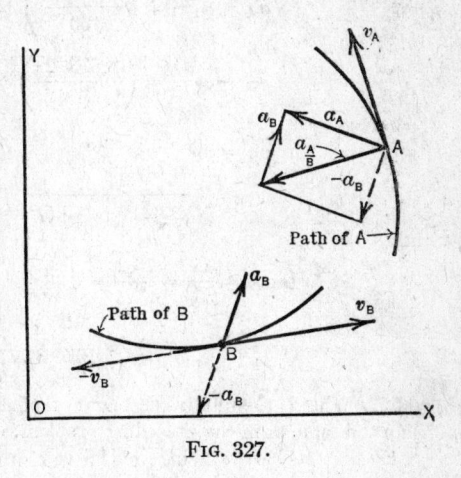

Fig. 327.

$$a_A = a_{\underset{B}{A}} +\!\!\!\!\!+ a_B \quad \text{or} \quad a_{\underset{B}{A}} = a_A \rightarrow a_B. \quad \cdots \quad (3)$$

which are in accordance with the principle stated at the beginning of this article.

ILLUSTRATIVE PROBLEM

Problem 520.—Two friction disks (Fig. 328) rotate with constant angular velocities. Let A and B be points on the circumferences of the large and small disks, respectively. If $\omega_1 = 40$ r.p.m., $r_1 = 9$ in., and $r_2 = 3$ in., find the magnitude and the direction of the acceleration of A relative to B.

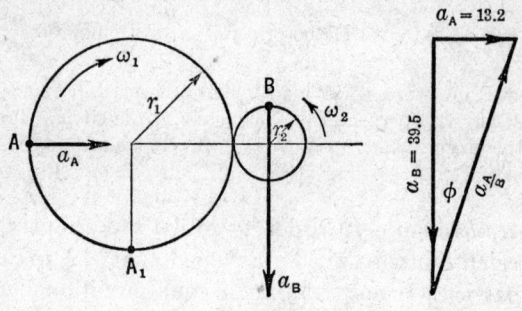

FIG. 328.

Solution.—

$$\omega_1 r_1 = \omega_2 r_2. \quad \therefore \omega_2 = \frac{\omega_1 r_1}{r_2} = \frac{40 \times 9}{3} = 120 \text{ r.p.m.,}$$

$$a_A = \omega_1^2 r_1 = \left(\frac{40 \times 2\pi}{60}\right)^2 \times \frac{9}{12} = 13.2 \text{ ft./sec.}^2,$$

$$a_B = \omega_2^2 r_2 = \left(\frac{120 \times 2\pi}{60}\right)^2 \times \frac{3}{12} = 39.5 \text{ ft./sec.}^2$$

Therefore

$$a_{\frac{A}{B}} = a_A \rightarrow a_B$$

$$= \sqrt{(13.2)^2 + (39.5)^2} = 41.5 \text{ ft./sec.}^2,$$

and

$$\tan \phi = \frac{a_A}{a_B} = \frac{13.2}{39.5} = 0.33. \quad \therefore \phi = 18° 25'.$$

PROBLEMS

521. What is the relative acceleration of A_1 (Fig. 328) with respect to B, the data being the same as in the preceding problem? *Ans.* $a_{\frac{A_1}{B}} = 52.6$ ft./sec.^{2}

522. Two trains A and B travel in the same direction on parallel tracks; A increases its speed uniformly 10 mi./hr./min. and B decreases its speed uniformly 5 mi./hr./min. What is the relative acceleration of A with respect to B?

523. An automobile, A, is traveling on a straight road, increasing its speed at the rate of 300 ft./min./sec. when in the position shown (Fig. 329). At the same time another automobile, B, is traveling in a circular path increasing its speed at the rate of 5 ft./sec.^{2} Its speed when in the position shown is $v_B = 12$ mi./hr., and the radius of the circular path is 40 ft. What is the relative acceleration of A with respect to B? Ans. $a_{\frac{A}{B}} = 12.3$ ft./sec.^{2}; $\theta_x = 41°41'$.

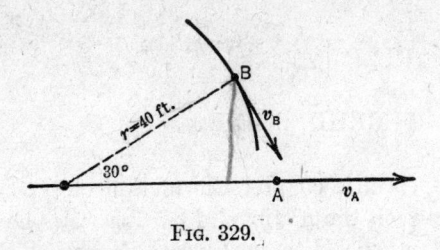

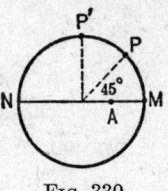

FIG. 329.

FIG. 330.

524. A point P (Fig. 330) moves on a circle of 2-ft. radius with a constant speed of 4 ft./sec. Another point A moves at the same time on the horizontal diameter from M toward N with a constant acceleration of 10 ft./sec.^{2} towards N. Find the acceleration of P relative to A (a) when P is in the position shown, (b) when P is in position P'.

525. In Fig. 317 assume the velocity of C to be 2 ft./sec. upward and the acceleration to be 2 ft./sec.^{2} upward. Find the acceleration of A relative to E.
Ans. $a_{\frac{A}{E}} = 3.61$ ft./sec.^{2}; $\theta_x = 16°5'$.

526. In Fig. 325 assume that v_A is increasing uniformly at the rate of 4 ft./sec.^{2} and that v_B is decreasing uniformly at the rate of 2 ft./sec.^{2} Find the acceleration of B relative to A.

527. Two points A and B move counter-clockwise with constant speeds on a circle of radius 2 ft. that lies in a vertical plane. At a given instant A is at the right end of the horizontal diameter and B is at the upper end of a vertical diameter. If the speed of A is 4 ft./sec. and the acceleration of A relative to B is 10 ft./sec.^{2}, what is the speed of B? Ans. $v_B = 3.46$ ft./sec.

528. A point P moves on a circular path of radius r. The angular velocity of P relative to the center of the circle is constant. Points A and B are the projections of P on the horizontal and vertical diameters, respectively, of the circle. Show that for all positions of P the magnitude of the acceleration of A relative to B is constant and equal to the magnitude of the acceleration of P.

529. A particle P moves along the curve $y = \dfrac{x^3}{240}$ according to the law $x = t^2$, x and y being measured in feet and t in seconds. The projections of P on the x- and y-axes are A and B, respectively. Find the magnitude and direction of the acceleration of A relative to B when $t = 2$ sec.

CHAPTER VII

MOTION OF RIGID BODIES

93. Introduction.—In the preceding chapter the motion of a point or particle and the relation between the motions of two particles have been considered. In engineering problems in general, however, the motion of bodies, not particles, must be considered. In some problems, the dimensions of the body may be small in comparison with its range of motion, and hence the body may be treated as a particle without introducing a serious error. In such problems, the methods and equations of the preceding chapter apply directly to the motion of the body. In general, however, the motion of bodies as met in engineering practice is such that the various points of a body have different motions.

The object of this chapter is to analyze certain common types of motion of a rigid body so that the displacement, velocity, and acceleration, both linear and angular, of any point in the body may be found from the methods and equations developed in the preceding chapter. The motions considered are *translation*, *rotation*, and *plane motion*.

94. Translation.—*Translation* of a rigid body is a motion such that no straight line in the body changes direction; that is, each straight line remains parallel to its initial direction. Hence, all points in the body move along parallel paths and have, at any instant, the same velocity and acceleration. If the particles move on curved paths the motion is called *curvilinear* translation, as, for example, the motion of the parallel rod of a locomotive. If the particles move on straight-line paths the motion is called *rectilinear* translation. The body may have a uniformly or non-uniformly accelerated motion. Hence a point in a translating body may have any of the motions treated in the preceding chapter. Furthermore, since all particles in the body have the same displacement in any time interval and have, at any instant, the same velocity and acceleration, the displacement, velocity, and acceleration of the body are described by the displacement velocity, and acceleration of *any* particle of the body.

PROBLEMS

530. The crank OA in Fig. 331 rotates with a constant angular velocity ω of 20 r.p.m., causing the jointed frame $CDFE$ to oscillate. In the position shown AB

and *DF* are horizontal and *OA*, *CD* and *EF* are vertical. The length of *OA* is 6 in. and the length of *CD* and of *EF* is 4 ft. *B* is the mid-point of *CD*. Find the acceleration of *G*, the mid-point of *DF*, in the position shown. *Ans.* $a_G = 1.10$ ft./sec.^{2}

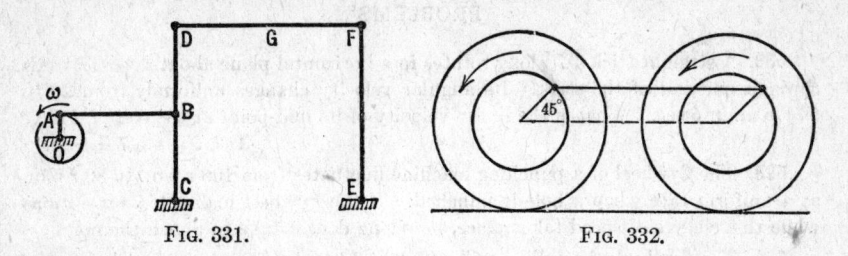

FIG. 331.   FIG. 332.

531. A locomotive is running on a straight track at a constant speed of 40 mi./hr. The diameter of the drivers is 6 ft. and the radius of the crank-pin circle is 15 in. What is the magnitude and the direction of the velocity and of the acceleration of the parallel rod, relative to the engine frame, when the rod is in the position shown in Fig. 332? What is the absolute velocity and the absolute acceleration for the same position?

95. Rotation.—*Rotation* of a rigid body is a motion such that one line in the body (or body extended) remains fixed in space while all points of the body not on the line describe circular paths having centers on the fixed line. The fixed line is called the *axis of rotation*, and the plane in which the mass-center of the body moves is called the *plane of motion*. The point of intersection of the axis of rotation and the plane of motion is called the *center of rotation*. It will be noted that any line parallel to the plane of motion changes direction. This motion is sometimes called a *pure rotation* in contrast to rotation in plane motion (Art. 96) in which all lines in the plane of motion change direction but no line perpendicular to the plane of motion remains fixed.

The motion of a body having rotation cannot be defined or described by stating the *linear* displacement, velocity, and acceleration of any point in the body, as was the case for translation, since all points in the body do not have the same linear motion. However, the *angular* displacements, velocities, and acceleration, respectively, about the axis of rotation, are the same for all particles in the body. Hence the motion of a rotating rigid body may be described by the angular motion, about the axis of rotation, of any point in the body not on the axis of rotation. Thus all the equations in the preceding chapter dealing with the angular motion of a point moving on a circular path, in which the radius vector is the radius of the circle, apply to the motion of a rotating rigid body, as well as to each point in the body. The linear displacement, velocity, and acceleration of any point may also be found from the equations in the preceding chapter, that deal with the linear motion of a point moving on a circular path.

PROBLEMS

532. A straight stick 4 ft. long rotates in a horizontal plane about a vertical axis through one end of the stick. Its angular velocity changes uniformly from 20 to 50 r.p.m. in 5 sec. What is the linear velocity of its mid-point at the end of 2 sec.?
Ans. $v = 6.7$ ft./sec.

533. The flywheel of a punching machine fluctuates from 100 r.p.m. to 80 r.p.m. at a uniform rate when a hole is punched. If the flywheel makes 1½ revolutions while this change of speed takes place, how long does it take to punch the hole?

534. The flywheel of a rolling-mill engine is 14 ft. in diameter. Just before the steel is fed in the rolls the speed of the flywheel is 90 r.p.m. As the steel enters the rolls the speed decreases uniformly during ½ sec., before the governor can operate. If the angular acceleration (negative) of the flywheel is 20 r.p.m. per sec., what is the decrease in the speed of the flywheel, expressed in revolutions per minute? *Ans.* $\Delta\omega = 10$ r.p.m.

535. A rod AB which is 2 ft. long rotates clockwise about a horizontal axis that passes through the mid-point of AB and is perpendicular to AB. When AB is in a horizontal position its angular velocity is 2 rad./sec. and its angular acceleration is 4 rad./sec.^{2} Find the relative velocity and relative acceleration of A with respect to B. Assume A to be the left end of the rod.

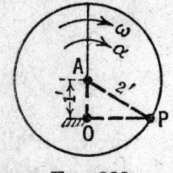

FIG. 333.

536. The circular disk in Fig. 333 rotates about an axis through O perpendicular to the plane of the disk. If $\omega = 2$ rad./sec. and $\alpha = 4\sqrt{3}$ rad./sec.^{2}, find the linear acceleration of A relative to P. *Ans.* $a_{\frac{A}{P}} = 16$ ft./sec.^{2}; $\theta_x = 30°$.

96. Plane Motion.

—*Plane motion* of a rigid body is a motion such that each point in the body remains at a constant distance from a fixed plane. The motion of the connecting rod of a steam engine is an example of plane motion. The wheels of a locomotive running on a straight track also have plane motion. The plane in which the mass-center of the body moves is called the *plane of motion*. It is evident that a pure rotation is always a special case of plane motion, whereas a translation may or may not be a plane motion.

In plane motion, in general, a straight line in the body lying in the plane of motion changes direction and, hence, the body rotates, but not about a fixed axis. The body, therefore, has angular motion, and its angular displacement, velocity, and acceleration are the same as that of any straight line in the body, in the plane of motion, since all such lines have the same angular motion if the body is rigid. The angular motion of the body, therefore, may be studied by means of the same equations that apply to the rotation of a rigid body about a fixed axis.

Rotation, however, is only one part of the motion of a rigid body having plane motion (except in a special case as noted in the next article). Plane motion of a rigid body may be resolved into two component motions, a rotation and a translation, according to the following theorem:

> Plane motion of a rigid body, at any instant, is a combination of: (1) a pure rotation of the body, about an axis (perpendicular to the plane of motion) passing through any point B in the body, with an angular velocity and acceleration the same as that which the body has at the instant; and (2) a translation of the body which gives to each point the same linear velocity and acceleration that the point B has at the instant.

The point B is called the *base point*. It is evident that all points except the base point have two motions: a rotation about the base point, and a motion the same as that of the base point. From the analysis of the motion according to the above theorem, the displacement, velocity, and acceleration of any point, A, in the body may be found from the equations developed in Art. 92 of the preceding chapter.

To arrive at the above theorem, consider the motion of the connecting rod of a steam engine (Fig. 334). Let P denote the position of the crosshead and Q that of the crank pin. When the crank moves from position OQ to position OQ_1 the connecting rod moves from position PQ to position P_1Q_1. This change of position can be given the rod by first rotating the rod about P, until it becomes parallel to its new position, and then giving the rod a translation such that each point receives a displacement equal to PP_1. By this combination of motions the point P moves along its actual path but any other point does not travel in its actual path. The point Q, for example, moves along the path $QQ'Q_1$ instead of its actual circular path QQ_1. However, as the change of position is made smaller and smaller, the path $QQ'Q_1$ approaches the circular path QQ_1 and, in the limit, as the two motions are generated simultaneously, each point is made to move on its actual path by successive combinations of a proper rotation and a proper translation. The rotation, at any instant, must give the body its actual angular velocity and acceleration at the instant, since the translation does not influence the angular motion of the body. The translation must give all points of

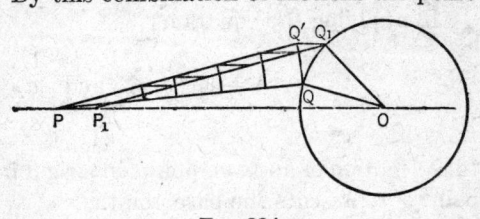

Fig. 334.

the body the same motion that the base point has at the instant, since the base point receives its total motion from the translation.

By the above method, the rod is given a rectilinear translation, since the point P moves on a straight-line path. If, however, another base point is chosen, as, for example, the point Q, the change of position from PQ to P_1Q_1 may then be made by: (1) a rotation about Q (Fig. 335); and (2) a curvilinear translation giving to each point the same motion that Q has. By this combination of a rotation and a translation the point P is made to take the path $PP'P_1$ instead of its actual path PP_1, but, reasoning as above, if the change of position is made smaller and smaller, the path $PP'P_1$ approaches the path PP_1 and, in the limit, as the two motions are imposed simultaneously, each point in the body is given its exact motion at any instant. Likewise, any other point in the body may be selected as the base point. And the plane motion of any other rigid body may be treated in like manner. Hence, a plane motion of a rigid body may be considered, at any instant, as a combination of a rotation of the body about any base point in the body, with an angular velocity and acceleration equal to the angular velocity and acceleration that the body has at the instant, and a translation of the body that gives to each point the same linear velocity and acceleration that the base point has at the instant.

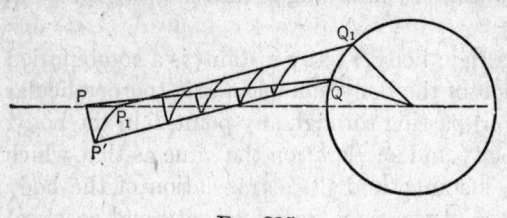

FIG. 335.

In applying the equations

$$v_P = v_{P\over Q} \mathrel{+\mkern-10mu+} v_Q \quad \text{and} \quad a_P = a_{P\over Q} \mathrel{+\mkern-10mu+} a_Q$$

to the motion of any two points in a rigid body having plane motion, the point Q represents the base point.

Since any two points in a rigid body remain a fixed distance apart, the relative velocity of either point with respect to the other is perpendicular to the line joining the two points. This is not true, however, of the relative acceleration, since it is made up of a tangential and a normal component, the normal component having a direction along the line joining the two points. The principles discussed in this article are involved in the solution of the following problem.

ILLUSTRATIVE PROBLEMS

Problem 537.—A circular disk of radius r rolls without slipping on a horizontal straight track. If v_0 and a_0 denote the linear velocity and linear acceleration of the center, O, of the disk, and ω and α denote the angular velocity and angular acceleration of the disk, show that $v_0 = r\omega$ and $a_0 = r\alpha$.

Solution.—The angular displacement of the disk (Fig. 336) corresponding to any linear displacement OO' (or s) of its center is the angle θ through which the radius OB turns in moving from the position OB to $O'B'$. Hence from the figure we have

$$s = AB' = \text{arc } AB = r\theta,$$

and therefore

$$v_O = \frac{ds}{dt} = r\frac{d\theta}{dt} = r\omega$$

and

$$a_O = \frac{d^2s}{dt^2} = r\frac{d^2\theta}{dt^2} = r\alpha.$$

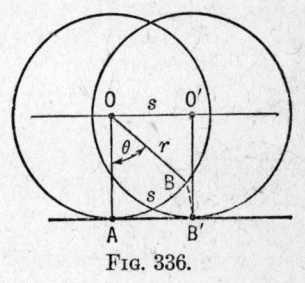

Fig. 336.

Problem 538.—A cylinder whose radius is 2 ft. (Fig. 337) rolls without slipping down an inclined plane with an angular acceleration of 6 rad./sec.^{2} At a given instant the angular velocity is 3 rad./sec. Find the linear velocity and linear acceleration of the point A at the instant.

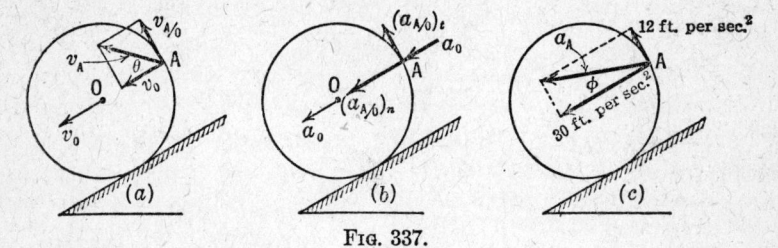

Fig. 337.

Solution.—The velocity of O is $v_O = r\omega = 2 \times 3 = 6$ ft./sec. parallel to the inclined plane. The velocity of A may be found from the equation $v_A = v_{A/O} + \!\!+\, v_O$ in which $v_{A/O} = \omega r = 6$ ft./sec. perpendicular to OA, as shown in Fig. 337(a), since O and A are points on a rigid body. It should be noted that $v_{A/O}$ is the velocity that A receives owing to the rotational component of the plane motion of the cylinder, using O as the base point, and v_O is the velocity that A receives due to the translational component of the plane motion. Hence the magnitude and direction of the velocity are given by the equations

$$v_A = v_{A/O} + \!\!+\, v_O = \sqrt{(6)^2 + (6)^2} = 8.48 \text{ ft./sec.}$$
$$\tan \theta = \tfrac{6}{6} = 1 \qquad \therefore \ \theta = 45°$$

The acceleration of A may be found from the equation $a_A = a_{A/O} + \!\!+\, a_O$. The acceleration $a_{A/O}$ is the acceleration given to the point A by the rotational component of the plane motion of the cylinder, and a_O is the acceleration given to A by the translational component of the plane motion. It is convenient to replace $a_{A/O}$ by its normal and tangential components as shown in Fig. 337(b). Hence

$$a_A = a_{A/O} \nrightarrow a_O = (a_{A/O})_n \nrightarrow (a_{A/O})_t \nrightarrow a_O$$
$$= 2 \times 9 \nrightarrow 2 \times 6 \nrightarrow 2 \times 6$$
$$= \sqrt{(30)^2 + (12)^2} = 32.3 \text{ ft./sec.}^2$$
$$\tan \phi = \tfrac{12}{30} = 0.4 \qquad \therefore \phi = 21° 48'.$$

Problem 539.—A 50-h.p. engine has a cylinder 10 in. in diameter and a stroke of 10 in. The engine runs at a constant speed of $\omega = 300$ r.p.m. The ratio of the length of the connecting rod to that of the crank is 5. Find the velocity and the acceleration of the crosshead when the crank angle is 30°.

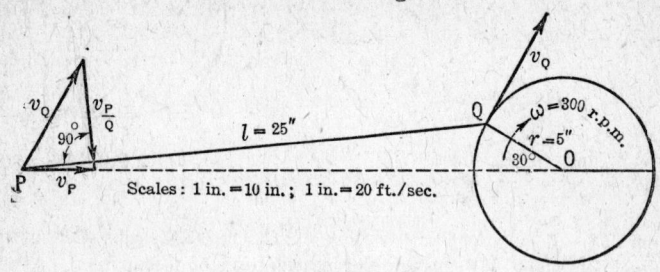

FIG. 338.

Solution.—Let P be the crosshead and Q the crank pin. Then in Fig. 338 PQ represents 25 in. and OQ or r represents 5 in., according to the scale used. The velocity of P may be found from the equation

$$v_P = v_{P \over \overline{Q}} \nrightarrow v_Q.$$

Six elements are involved in the equation, namely, three magnitudes and three directions, four of which must be found before the equation can be used to determine the other two. The direction of the velocity of Q is perpendicular to OQ, and its magnitude is

$$v_Q = \omega r = \left(\frac{300 \times 2\pi}{60} \right) \times \frac{5}{12} = 13.1 \text{ ft./sec.}$$

The direction of $v_{P \over \overline{Q}}$ is perpendicular to the line joining P and Q, and its magnitude is unknown. The direction of v_P is horizontal. Hence by laying off v_Q to a convenient scale in the proper direction from P, and by drawing a line from the end of v_Q, perpendicular to the connecting rod, until it intersects a horizontal line through P, the magnitudes of $v_{P \over \overline{Q}}$ and v_P are determined by the intersection. By scaling off the values of $v_{P \over \overline{Q}}$ and v_P, the following results are found:

$$v_{P \over \overline{Q}} = 11.4 \text{ ft./sec. and } v_P = 7.7 \text{ ft./sec.}$$

If the plane motion of the connecting rod is thought of as a combination of a rotation and a translation, $v_{P \over \overline{Q}}$ is the velocity which P is given by the rotation of the rod about Q, and v_Q is the velocity given to P by the translation of the rod. The two velocities produce the resultant velocity v_P.

The acceleration of P is given by the equation

$$a_P = a_{\frac{P}{Q}} + \!\!+ a_Q.$$

For convenience, $a_{\frac{P}{Q}}$ will be replaced by its tangential and normal components.

Hence

$$a_P = \left(a_{\frac{P}{Q}}\right)_t + \!\!+ \left(a_{\frac{P}{Q}}\right)_n + \!\!+ a_Q.$$

Eight elements are involved in the equation, namely, four magnitudes and four directions, six of which must be found before the graphical construction representing the equation can be completed. a_Q is directed from Q toward O, and its magnitude is

$$a_Q = \omega^2 r = \left(\frac{300 \times 2\pi}{60}\right)^2 \times \frac{5}{12} = 412 \text{ ft./sec.}^2$$

a_P is known in direction, being parallel to PO (horizontal), since v_P changes in magnitude only. $\left(a_{\frac{P}{Q}}\right)_n$ is directed from P toward Q, and its magnitude is

$$\left(a_{\frac{P}{Q}}\right)_n = \frac{\left(v_{\frac{P}{Q}}\right)^2}{PQ} = \frac{(11.4)^2}{\frac{25}{12}} = 62.4 \text{ ft./sec.}^2$$

$\left(a_{\frac{P}{Q}}\right)_t$ has a direction perpendicular to PQ. The two unknown elements are, therefore, the magnitudes of a_P and $\left(a_{\frac{P}{Q}}\right)_t$.

In Fig. 339, starting at P, the vectors are laid off to a convenient scale. Thus a_Q and $\left(a_{\frac{P}{Q}}\right)_n$ (both of which are completely known) are drawn, and then, from the end of $\left(a_{\frac{P}{Q}}\right)_n$, a line is drawn that represents the direction of $\left(a_{\frac{P}{Q}}\right)_t$, that is, it is drawn perpendicular to PQ. The intersection of this line with the line PO (which

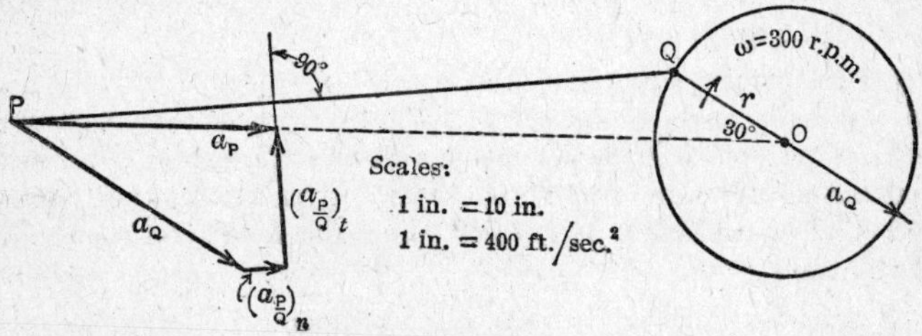

Scales:
1 in. = 10 in.
1 in. = 400 ft./sec.²

FIG. 339.

represents the direction of a_P) determines the lengths of the vectors that represent $\left(a_{\frac{P}{Q}}\right)_t$ and a_P. By scaling off the values, the following results are obtained:

$$\left(a_{\frac{P}{Q}}\right)_t = 200 \text{ ft./sec.}^2 \quad \text{and} \quad a_P = 404 \text{ ft./sec.}^2$$

PROBLEMS

540. If A and B are any two points in the plane of motion of a body that has plane motion, and C is a point midway between A and B, show that the velocity and acceleration of C may be expressed in terms of the velocities and accelerations of A and B as follows:

$$v_C = \tfrac{1}{2}(v_A \mathrel{+\!\!\!+} v_B), \quad \text{and} \quad a_C = \tfrac{1}{2}(a_A \mathrel{+\!\!\!+} a_B).$$

541. In Fig. 340, one end A of a bar AB that is 5 ft. long moves downward along OM and the other end B moves along ON. When the bar is horizontal the velocity of A is 10 ft./sec. Find the linear velocity of B and the angular velocity of the bar at this instant. *Ans.* $v_B = 5.77$ ft./sec.; $\omega = 2.31$ rad./sec.

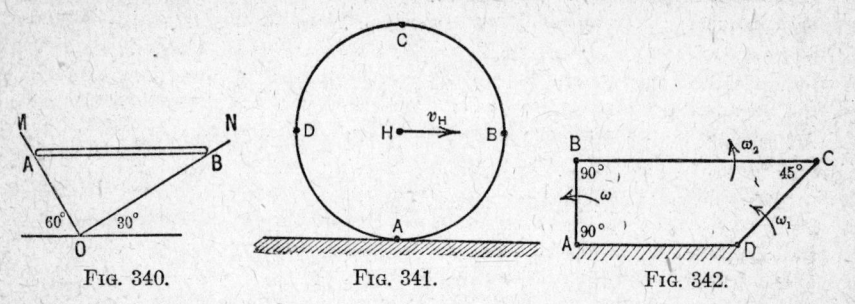

Fig. 340.   Fig. 341.   Fig. 342.

542. A wheel 4 ft. in diameter rolls, without slipping, on a horizontal track (Fig. 341). The velocity of its center, at a given instant, is 4 ft./sec. to the right, and the acceleration of the center is 6 ft./sec.^{2} in the same direction. Find the velocities and the accelerations of the points A and B.

543. In Fig. 342 $\omega = 4$ rad./sec., $AB = 0.5$ ft., and $BC = 1.5$ ft. Find the angular velocity ω_1 of DC and the angular velocity ω_2 of BC.
Ans. $\omega_1 = 4$ rad./sec., $\omega_2 = 1.33$ rad./sec.

544. An elliptical disk whose principal axes are 8 in. and 6 in. long rolls clockwise, without slipping, on a straight line, the plane of the disk being vertical. When the major axis is vertical the angular velocity of the disk is 2 rad./sec. If A is the forward end of the minor axis and B is the upper end of the major axis, find the velocity of A relative to B.

545. A circular disk whose diameter is 4 ft. rolls, without slipping, on a straight horizontal track, the plane of the disk being vertical. The center of the disk moves with a constant acceleration of 12 ft./sec.^{2} At a given instant the acceleration of the highest point of the disk is 30 ft./sec.^{2} Find the velocity of the center of the disk at that instant. *Ans.* $v = 6$ ft./sec.

546. A disk whose radius is 3 ft. rolls, without slipping, in the xy-plane and along the x-axis to the right. The angular velocity of the disk is 2 rad./sec. and its angular acceleration is 4 rad./sec.^{2} Find the linear acceleration of the point whose coordinates with respect to a set of rectangular axes through the center of the disk are $x = 2, y = -1$.

547. A circular disk 4 ft. in diameter rolls, without slipping, to the right on a straight horizontal track. The angular velocity of the disk is 2 rad./sec. and the angular acceleration is 4 rad./sec.², both clockwise. Find the acceleration of the point on the disk 1 ft. below, and 1 ft. to the right of the center of the disk.

Ans. $a = 0$.

548. The horizontal bar AB (Fig. 343) rotates about a vertical axis YY with an angular velocity of 30 r.p.m. in the clockwise direction. At the same time the horizontal bar CD, which is 2 ft. long, rotates with an angular velocity (relative to AB) of 60 r.p.m. in the clockwise direction. If $CB = BD$, what is the magnitude of the linear velocity of C, (a) when CD is parallel to AB with C between A and B, (b) when CD is perpendicular to AB, and (c) when CD is parallel to AB with D between A and B.

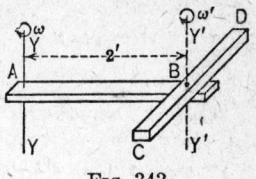

FIG. 343.

549. If the bar AB shown in Fig. 343 rotates about YY with an angular velocity of 2 rad./sec. and an angular acceleration of 5 rad./sec.², and at the same time CD rotates with a constant angular velocity (relative to AB) of 3 rad./sec., what are the magnitudes of the accelerations of C and D when CD is perpendicular to AB? Assume that the velocities and acceleration are all clockwise and that $CB = BD = 1$ ft. as in Prob. 548. *Ans.* $a_C = 19.8$ ft./sec.²; $a_D = 35.1$ ft./sec.²

550. One end A of a line AB 4 ft. in length moves along the positive end of the x-axis to the right and the other end B moves downward along the y-axis. When the angle between AB and the x-axis is $60°$ $v_A = 10\sqrt{3}$ ft./sec. and $a_A = 50$ ft./sec.² to the right. Find the velocity and acceleration of B.

551. In addition to the data given in Prob. 543 (Fig. 342) assume that ω is increasing at the rate of 4 rad./sec. each second. Find the angular accelerations of DC and BC. *Ans.* $\alpha_{BC} = 2.22$ rad./sec.²; $\alpha_{CD} = 6.67$ rad./sec.²

552. Find, by the graphical method, the velocity and the acceleration of the point C of the four-link mechanism described in Prob. 553 (Fig. 345). Use the following scales: 1 in. = 1 ft.; 1 in. = 2 ft./sec.; and 1 in. = 10 ft./sec.²
Ans. $v_C = 1.54$ ft./sec.; $a_C = 55.5$ ft./sec.²

97. Instantaneous Center.

—It was shown in the previous article that a plane motion of a rigid body may be considered, at any instant, as a rotation, about an axis through any point in the body, combined with a translation. However, by choosing a particular axis in the body (or its extension), the motion of the body, at any instant, becomes one of rotation only, that is, no translation need be combined with the rotation to produce the actual motion of the body. This axis is called the *instantaneous axis of rotation* or the *instantaneous axis of zero velocity*. Its intersection with the plane of motion is called the *instantaneous center of rotation* or the *instantaneous center of zero velocity*.

In order to show how the instantaneous center may be located, assume A and B in Fig. 344 to be any two points in the plane of motion whose velocities v_A and v_B are known in direction. Let lines through A and B perpendicular to v_A and v_B, respectively, intersect at O. The point O is the instantaneous center, as will now be shown. The velocity of O is the vector sum of $v_{O \atop \overline{A}}$, the velocity of O relative to A, and v_A. Since the body is rigid, $v_{O \atop \overline{A}}$ is perpendicular to OA, and since v_A is also perpendicular to OA, it follows that the velocity of O, if not zero, must be perpendicular to OA. Similarly the velocity of O, considered as a point on OB, if not zero, must be perpendicular to OB. Hence, v_O is zero since it cannot be perpendicular to OA and OB at the same time. In order to locate the instantaneous center, then, it is necessary to know the directions, only, of the velocities of any two points in the plane of motion.

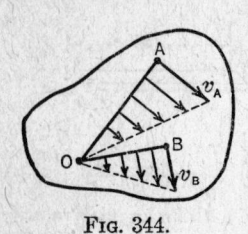

Fig. 344.

If, then, A and O are two points in the rigid body having plane motion, A being any point, and O the instantaneous center, the velocity of A is found as follows:

$$v_A = v_{A \atop \overline{O}} + \!\!\!\!+\, v_O = v_{A \atop \overline{O}} + \!\!\!\!+\, 0 = \omega \cdot OA.$$

Similarly, the velocity of B is $\omega \cdot OB$, and hence the velocities of A and B vary as their distances from the instantaneous center. Or, expressed in equational form,

$$\frac{v_A}{v_B} = \frac{\omega \cdot OA}{\omega \cdot OB} = \frac{OA}{OB}.$$

It should be noted that the instantaneous center is the center of zero velocity and *not* of zero acceleration. In the case of the motion of rotation of a rigid body about a fixed axis, which is a special case of plane motion, the axis of rotation is also the instantaneous axis and it has zero acceleration as well as zero velocity since it is at rest. In the general case of plane motion, however, the instantaneous center changes its position in the body and also in space. Although the velocity of the point in the body, coinciding with the instantaneous center at a given instant, is zero, the velocity is changing through its zero value and hence the point has an acceleration. Therefore in the equation

$$a_A = a_{A \atop \overline{O}} + \!\!\!\!+\, a_O,$$

in which A is any point and O is the instantaneous center, a_O is not zero. Hence the absolute acceleration, at any instant, of a point in a rigid body having plane motion cannot be found by considering the body to be rotating about a *fixed* axis through the instantaneous center of zero velocity, as may be done in determining the velocity of any point of the body.

ILLUSTRATIVE PROBLEM

Problem 553.—The four-link mechanism, $ABCD$, shown in Fig. 345 has the following dimensions: $AB = 6$ in.; $BC = 3$ ft.; $DC = 2$ ft.; $AD = 4$ ft.; $\theta = 45°$. Find the instantaneous center for the link BC. If the crank AB rotates at a constant angular velocity $\omega = 10$ rad./sec., find the angular velocities, ω_2, of the link DC, and ω_3 of the link BC. Also find the linear velocity, v_H, of H, the midpoint of BC.

Solution.—The instantaneous center for the link BC is O, the point of intersection of the lines AB and DC extended. By scaling off the lengths of OB, OC, and OH, the following values are found:

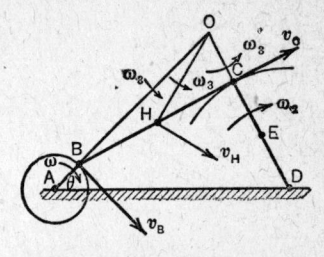

FIG. 345.

$$OB = 3.1 \text{ ft.} \quad OC = 0.96 \text{ ft.} \quad OH = 1.72 \text{ ft.}$$

The velocity of B, considered as a point on AB, is

$$v_B = \omega \times AB = 10 \times \tfrac{6}{12} = 5 \text{ ft./sec.}$$

Therefore the angular velocity of B, considered as a point on BC, is

$$\omega_3 = \frac{v_B}{OB} = \frac{5}{3.1} = 1.61 \text{ rad./sec.}$$

and the angular velocities, about O, of all points on BC are the same. The linear velocity of C is, therefore,

$$v_C = \omega_3 \times OC = 1.61 \times 0.96 = 1.54 \text{ ft./sec.}$$

And

$$v_H = \omega_3 \times OH = 1.61 \times 1.72 = 2.77 \text{ ft./sec.}$$

Therefore

$$\omega_2 = \frac{v_C}{DC} = \frac{1.54}{2} = 0.77 \text{ rad./sec.}$$

PROBLEMS

554. Using the data of Prob. 553, find the magnitude and the direction of the velocity of the point E (Fig. 345) on link DC midway between D and C?

Ans. $v_E = 0.77$ ft./sec. perpendicular to DC.

555. In Prob. 543, find the instantaneous center of BC and determine ω_2 by the instantaneous center method.

556. Using the data of Prob. 542, find by the instantaneous center method the velocities of the points B, C, and D in Fig. 341.

Ans. $v_B = 5.66$ ft./sec.; $v_C = 8$ ft./sec.; $v_D = 5.66$ ft./sec.

557. In Fig. 346, AB rotates about A with an angular velocity of $3\sqrt{3}$ rad./sec. and C moves along a horizontal line. When C is vertically beneath A, find the instantaneous center of rotation of CB and determine the linear velocity of P, the mid-point of CB.

558. A disk A (Fig. 347) rolls, without slipping, on a horizontal rail. Another disk B is attached to A and turns with it. The velocity of the center of disk A is 10 ft./sec. to the right. Find the velocity of the point M and of the point P.

Ans. $v_M = 3.33$ ft./sec.; $v_P = 16.7$ ft./sec.

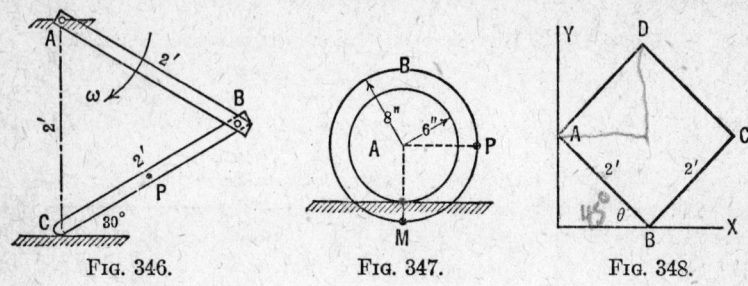

FIG. 346. FIG. 347. FIG. 348.

559. In Fig. 348, $ABCD$ is a board 2 ft. square. A moves downward on the y-axis with a velocity of 4 ft./sec. and B moves on the x-axis. Find the velocities of C and D when $\theta = 45°$. Solve algebraically by the method of instantaneous centers.

560. Find the velocities of C and D in Prob. 559 when $\theta = 30°$. Solve graphically. Ans. $v_C = 2.84$ ft./sec.; $v_D = 4.32$ ft./sec.

561. Locate the instantaneous center of the connecting rod of the steam-engine mechanism described in Prob. 539. Find the angular velocity of the connecting rod, the linear velocity of the crosshead, and the linear velocity of a point on the connecting rod midway from the crosshead to the crank pin.

Ans. $\omega_2 = 5.47$ rad./sec.; $v_P = 7.70$ ft./sec.; $v_M = 9.12$ ft./sec.

REVIEW QUESTIONS AND PROBLEMS

562. Point out and correct the error in each of the following statements:

(a) The linear velocity of a point is the time rate of change of the linear displacement of the point.

(b) The total linear acceleration of a point moving on any curved path is defined as the rate of change of the speed of the point and is expressed mathematically by the equation $a = \dfrac{dv}{dt}$.

(c) If a point moves on a circular path, the velocity is tangent to the path and hence can have no component towards the center of the circle; therefore, there can be no acceleration towards the center of the circle.

(d) The angular velocity of a point moving in a plane is the same with respect to all points in the plane.

(e) In uniformly accelerated rectilinear motion, the velocity of the moving point is constant.

(f) The tangential acceleration of a point moving on a curved path is equal to the product of the angular velocity of the point with respect to the center of curvature and the radius of curvature.

(g) Simple harmonic motion of a point is a periodic motion in a straight line such that the velocity of the point is proportional to the displacement of the point from a fixed origin in the line and is directed away from the origin.

REVIEW QUESTIONS AND PROBLEMS

563. Starting with the defining equation for the linear acceleration of a point, prove that the tangential and normal components of the acceleration are $a_t = \dfrac{dv}{dt}$ and $a_n = \omega^2 r = \dfrac{v^2}{r}$.

564. Prove that in uniformly accelerated rectilinear motion $s = ut + \tfrac{1}{2}at^2$.

565. Derive and interpret the equation $v_A = v_{A \overline{B}} \mathbin{+\mkern-8mu+} v_B$.

566. Define each of the following motions of a body: (a) translation, (b) rotation, and (c) plane motion.

567. If a rigid bar is given a plane motion, explain why the velocity of one end relative to the other end must be in a direction perpendicular to the length of the bar. Is the acceleration of one end relative to the other end perpendicular to the bar?

568. When plane motion of a rigid body is regarded as a combination of a rotation and a translation, state what angular velocity and angular acceleration are assumed to be given to the body in the rotational motion and what linear velocity and linear acceleration are assumed in the translational motion.

569. Define instantaneous center of rotation. If the directions of the velocities of any two points in the plane of motion of a body which has plane motion are known, how may the instantaneous center of rotation be found? Explain.

570. A point moves on a circular path having a radius of 20 ft. The angular velocity of the point with respect to the center of the circle changes uniformly from 1 rad./sec. to 5 rad./sec. in ½ sec. Find the total linear acceleration of the point at the middle of this ½-sec. period and represent it as a vector, assuming the point to be at the top of the circle at the instant. *Ans.* $a = 241$ ft./sec.^{2}

571. A car moves on the circular track shown in Fig. 349 at a constant speed of 30 mi./hr. If the radius of the track is 352 ft., find by three different methods the x-component of acceleration of the car when $\theta = 30°$. *Ans.* $a_x = 4.76$ ft./sec.^{2}

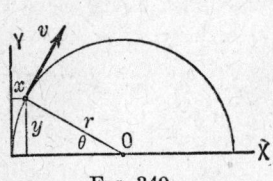

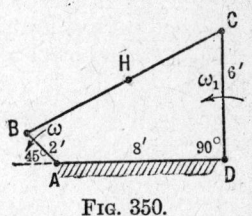

FIG. 349.   FIG. 350.

572. In the four-link mechanism shown in Fig. 350, the angular velocity ω of AB is 5 rad./sec. Find the linear velocity of C and the angular velocity of CD. Show, by means of a sketch, how the velocity of H, the mid-point of BC, may be found graphically by means of the instantaneous center.

Ans. $v_C = 10.5$ ft./sec.; $\omega_1 = 1.75$ rad./sec.

PART III. KINETICS

CHAPTER VIII

FORCE, MASS, AND ACCELERATION

§ 1. Preliminary Considerations. Kinetics of a Particle

98. Introduction.—*Kinetics* is that branch of mechanics which treats of the laws in accordance with which the motion of physical bodies takes place.

A *change* in the state of motion of a body always occurs when an *unbalanced* force system acts on the body, the unbalanced part (resultant) of the force system being the cause of the change in the motion. Experience teaches that the change of motion of the body is influenced both by the characteristics (Art. 5) of the resultant of the forces acting on the body and by the nature of the body itself. For example, different force systems acting, in turn, on the same body do not produce the same change of motion of the body. Further, the same force system applied to different bodies does not produce the same change in the motion of all of the bodies.

Although experience suggests that relations exist between the force system acting on a body, the properties of the body, and the change in the motion of the body, it required the work of many eminent men and a period of several centuries before definite and complete fundamental relations between these three factors were finally established. The laws expressing these relations were formulated by Sir Isaac Newton (1642–1727) and are known as Newton's laws of motion.

Newton's fundamental laws, however, apply directly only to the motion of a particle under the action of a single force, whereas in engineering practice the motion of a body (system of particles) under the action of a system of forces must be considered. The body may be rigid or non-rigid, and the force system acting on the body may produce any type of motion. The bodies treated hereafter, however, will, for the most part, be regarded as rigid, and the motions treated will, in general, be restricted to translation, rotation, and plane motion.

99. The General Kinetics Problem.—In each type of motion the general character of the kinetics problem is the same; namely, a physical body is acted on by a force system that has a resultant, which causes a change in the motion of the body, and in each problem it is required to deduce, by the use of Newton's laws, the equations expressing the definite relations between (1) the resultant of the force system, (2) the kinetic properties (mass, moment of inertia, etc.) of the body, and (3) the change of motion of the body, so that the motion of a given body produced by a given force system may be determined, or the force system required to produce a given motion may be found. The equations which express these relations are called the *equations of motion* for the body.

These three elements or factors which are involved in the equations of motion of bodies may be considered briefly before stating Newton's laws and before deriving the equations which express the relations between these three factors. Change of motion is measured by acceleration, which in turn may be expressed in terms of distance, time, and velocity, as discussed in Chapter VI. The characteristics of the resultant of a force system have also been considered, in Chapter II, and need only be reviewed briefly at this point (see next article) to show their connection with the general problem in kinetics. The property of the body (mass) which enables it to have an influence in determining its own motion, however, needs to be discussed at greater length (see Art. 101).

100. Characteristics of a Force System.—The only part of a force system that influences the motion of a body is the unbalanced part (resultant) of the force system. The forces which produce the types of motion considered in this chapter are coplanar and hence, the resultant of the forces is either a force or a couple (Art. 28). If the resultant is a force, the characteristics of the resultant which influence the motion of the body on which the force system acts are (1) its magnitude, (2) the position of its action line in the body, and (3) its sense (Art. 5). If, however, the resultant is a couple, the characteristics of the resultant which influence the motion of the body on which the force system acts are (1) the moment of the couple, (2) the sense of the couple, and (3) the aspect or direction of the plane of the couple (Art. 15).

Now the equations of motion of a body must be sufficient in number to take account of the influence of all the characteristics of the resultant of the force system as mentioned above. This may be done, for the types of motion considered in this chapter, by means of three equations. These three equations will contain the algebraic sum of the x-components of the forces acting on the body, the algebraic sum of the y-components, and the algebraic sum of the moments of the forces about some axis in the body (Art. 30).

101. Inertia and Mass.—The property of a body by virtue of which it offers resistance to any change in its motion, and thereby makes the body itself a factor in determining the motion which unbalanced forces impress upon it, is called *inertia*. All physical bodies are inert or possess inertia, but different bodies possess different amounts of inertia. That is, all bodies influence their own motion according to the same law but not to the same degree. In other words, all bodies do not offer the same resistance to being accelerated at a given rate.[1]

The quantitative measure of the inertia of a body, that is, the resistance the body offers to being accelerated at a given rate, is called the *mass* of the body, and is found, like other properties of bodies, by experiment. This may be done as follows:

Let a given body be acted on by a single force F_1, and let the resulting acceleration be a_1. In like manner let forces F_2, F_3, etc., be applied in turn to the body and let the resulting accelerations be a_2, a_3, etc. The results of such an experiment show that

$$\frac{F_1}{a_1} = \frac{F_2}{a_2} = \frac{F_3}{a_3} = \cdots \text{a constant} = C \text{ (say)}.$$

Or, in general, if any force F applied to the body causes an acceleration a

$$\frac{F}{a} = C. \qquad (1)$$

Now since C is the measure of the resistance, F, that the body offers to being accelerated at a rate a, it is proportional to the mass, M, of the body since the mass of a body is defined as a measure of the resistance the body offers to being accelerated at a given rate. Hence, $C = kM$, where k is a constant. Then equation (1) becomes

$$\frac{F}{a} = kM. \qquad (2)$$

In the above experiment, it was found that the ratio of any impressed force to the corresponding acceleration had a constant value C. Now if

---

[1] The way in which bodies resist motion is analogous to the manner in which elastic materials, such as steel, resist being stretched. Each material, within limits, resists according to the same law (stretch is proportional to stress), but some materials resist to a greater degree, that is, some materials are stiffer than others, which means that some materials require a greater force to produce a given stretch than do other materials, just as some bodies require a greater force to produce a given acceleration than do other bodies.

the body is allowed to fall freely under the influence of its weight W, the resulting acceleration is found to be g (32.2 ft./sec.^{2}), and hence

$$\frac{W}{g} = \frac{F}{a} = C. \qquad (3)$$

From equations (2) and (3) we have, then,

$$\frac{W}{g} = kM. \qquad (4)$$

If units for W, g, and M are so chosen that k in equation (4) equals unity (as will be discussed in Art. 103), then the number of units of mass in the body may be found from its weight by the equation

$$M = \frac{W}{g}.$$

102. Newton's Laws.—Newton established his laws of motion from a study of the motion of planets. Since the dimensions of a planet are negligible in comparison with the range of its motion, Newton's laws apply directly only to a particle, that is, to a body all points of which may be considered at any instant to have the same acceleration. In most cases of motion of bodies, however, the accelerations of different particles of the body are not the same, and hence Newton's laws do not apply directly to bodies. Bodies, however, may be considered to be made up of particles, and thus Newton's laws may be extended to bodies.

Newton's laws may be stated as follows:

First Law.—If no force acts on a particle, the particle remains at rest or continues to move with uniform velocity in a straight line.

Second Law.—If a force acts on a particle the particle is accelerated; the direction of the acceleration is the same as that of the force and its magnitude is directly proportional to the force and inversely proportional to the mass of the particle.

Third Law.—There are mutual actions between any two particles of a system (body) such that the action of the one on the other is equal, collinear, and opposite to that of the other on the one.

1. The first law implies that a particle has inertia, that is, it resists having its motion changed. It implies that a force must act on the particle if its motion (velocity) is changed either in direction or in magnitude, that is, if an acceleration is produced.

2. The second law is a quantitative one. It states what the magnitude and the direction of the force must be in order to produce a given acceleration of a given particle, and shows that although a particle

cannot, of itself, change its state of motion it does nevertheless influence the change of motion caused by the force, by regulating or governing the manner in which the acceleration shall take place; namely, that it shall be always inversely proportional to the mass of the particle.

3. In the second law, it is assumed that a single particle is acted upon by a single force. But the third law brings out the fact that a single force does not exist. The special significance of the third law lies in the fact that by its use Newton's second law, which applies only to a single particle under the influence of a single force, may be extended to a system of particles (body) acted on by a system of forces.

103. Mathematical Statement of Newton's Second Law. Units.—Newton's second law may be expressed mathematically by the equation

$$F = kma,$$

in which a is the acceleration of the particle of mass m, F is the single force acting on the particle, and k is a constant factor the value of which depends upon the units used to express the other quantities (F, m, and a) in the equation. In general the mass of a body will be denoted by M and that of a particle of the body by m or dM.

It is convenient to use a system of units in which k in the above equation is unity. Such a system of units is sometimes called a *kinetic system*. Thus, a kinetic system of units is one in which a unit force acting on a unit mass causes a unit acceleration. Now, in engineering problems, the units of force and acceleration are chosen arbitrarily, and hence the unit of mass is a derived unit—derived from the units of force and acceleration, since, if a kinetic system of units is used, $m = F/a = W/g$. A system of units in which the unit of mass is a derived unit is frequently called a *gravitational* system.

Thus, if one pound is chosen as the unit of force and one foot per second per second as the unit of acceleration, as is usual in engineering calculations, then since $M = W/g$, the number of units of mass in a body is the weight of the body in pounds divided by the acceleration of gravity, g, in feet per second per second (32.2). Thus a body weighing g (32.2) pounds has one unit of mass; this fact has suggested the name *g-pound* or *geepound* for this unit of mass. However, no name has gained general acceptance, although the name *slug* (from sluggishness which suggests inertia) has gained rather wide acceptance and will be employed in the subsequent pages. It is also frequently referred to as the *engineer's unit of mass*. In using a special name such as slug, it is important to keep in mind that the unit of mass is not an arbitrarily chosen unit but is derived from the units of force and acceleration.

PROCEDURE IN THE SOLUTION OF PROBLEMS IN KINETICS

In another system of units used considerably in electrical engineering, the units of mass, length, and time are chosen arbitrarily and the unit of force is the derived unit. Such a system is frequently called an *absolute* system of units. If one gram is chosen as the unit of mass, one centimeter as the unit of length, and one second as the unit of time, a unit force is a force that gives an acceleration of one centimeter per second per second to a mass of one gram. This force is called a *dyne*.

104. Equations of Motion for a Particle.—In Fig. 351, a particle of mass m is acted on by any system of forces F_1, F_2, F_3, etc., which give to the particle an acceleration a. It is required to find the equations that express the relations between the forces acting on the particle, the mass of the particle, and the acceleration of the particle. Let R denote the resultant of the forces acting on the particle and let θ_x, θ_y, θ_z denote the angles that R makes with the x-, y-, and z-axes, respectively. From Newton's second law we have $R = ma$. Multiplying each side of this equation by $\cos \theta_x$, we have

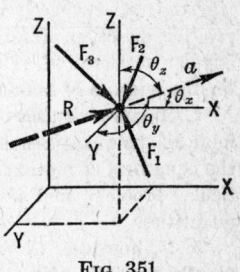

Fig. 351.

$$R \cos \theta_x = ma \cos \theta_x \quad \text{or} \quad R_x = ma_x.$$

But R_x may also be expressed in terms of the forces acting on the particle by the equation $R_x = \Sigma F_x$, and hence we have $\Sigma F_x = ma_x$. Similarly, equations may be obtained by expressing in two ways the y- and z-components of the resultant of the forces acting on the particle. Hence the equations of motion for a particle are:

$$\Sigma F_x = ma_x,$$
$$\Sigma F_y = ma_y,$$
$$\Sigma F_z = ma_z.$$

105. Procedure in the Solution of Problems in Kinetics.—In solving problems in kinetics, it is important to follow a rather definite procedure as outlined below. This procedure will be followed in the solution of the problems immediately following this article, in which the bodies are treated as particles, as well as in the solution of problems involving rigid bodies having various types of motion, which will be considered later. The main steps in the solution are as follows:

1. Determine carefully (*a*) what is given in the problem and (*b*) what is required in the problem. The quantities involved in this step may frequently be indicated by means of an illustrative sketch. Failure to carry out this step is a common cause of difficulty in the solution of problems.

2. Draw a complete free-body diagram of the body whose motion is under consideration (see Art. 40 for discussion of free-body diagram). That is, show the body

and all the forces exerted on it by other bodies. This diagram is of particular importance in determining the left-hand member of each of the equations of motion for the body.

3. Write all the equations of motion for the body and select the axes to be used in applying these equations. These axes should be shown in the free-body diagram. Frequently, by a proper choice of axes, the problem may be solved without using all the equations of motion. As a rule, it is convenient to select one axis parallel to the acceleration of the particle and to make the positive direction of the axis agree with the sense of the acceleration. Likewise when dealing with rotational motion, the positive direction of rotation will usually be made to agree with the sense of the angular acceleration of the body. The positive directions are chosen in this way for the purpose of making the right hand sides of the equations of motion positive.

4. Observe whether there are a sufficient number of equations of motion to determine all the quantities desired. If there are not, write any equations in addition to the equations of motion (such as kinematics equations, etc.) that apply to the particular problem, and if possible solve the equations and determine the unknown quantities.

5. If, however, there are still more unknowns than there are equations it is usually possible, when several bodies are involved in the motion, to select another body (or group of bodies) in the system on which is acting one (or more) of the forces that acts on the first body, and to treat the motion of this second body by the procedure outlined above and then to solve the two sets of equations simultaneously.

NOTE.—In the problems which follow, the assumption is made that the bodies having the motions described may be considered to be particles without introducing serious errors in the analysis of the motion. In the solution of the following illustrative problems, the steps in the above procedure are emphasized.

ILLUSTRATIVE PROBLEMS

Problem 573.—In Fig. 352, A and B are bodies suspended from the ends of a flexible, inextensible, weightless rope that passes over a smooth cylindrical surface. The weight of A is 40 lb. and the weight of B is 30 lb. Find the tensile stress in the rope.

Solution.—Since the cylindrical surface is frictionless and the rope is flexible, the force (stress) T in the rope has the same value on each side of the cylinder. Furthermore, since the rope does not stretch, the bodies A and B have accelerations that are equal in magnitude. The unknown force T, therefore, is a force acting on each of the two bodies. A free-body diagram of B is shown in Fig. 352, the axes being chosen in accordance with step 3 of Art. 105. There is one equation of motion only for this body; namely,

$$\Sigma F_y = ma_y \quad \text{or} \quad T - 30 = \frac{30}{32.2} a \quad \ldots \ldots \ldots (1)$$

Since there are two unknown quantities in this equation, T can not be found. Hence in accordance with step 5 of Art. 105 a free-body diagram of A is drawn (which also involves the force T). For this body there is also one equation of motion, namely,

$$\Sigma F_y = ma_y \quad \text{or} \quad 40 - T = \frac{40}{32.2} a \quad \ldots \ldots \ldots (2)$$

ILLUSTRATIVE PROBLEMS

The solution of the two simultaneous equations (1) and (2) gives the following results:

$$T = 34.3 \text{ lb.} \quad \text{and} \quad a = 4.60 \text{ ft./sec.}^2$$

Problem 574.—A small body weighing 4 lb. is attached to one end of a string 5 ft. long and is made to revolve as a conical pendulum with a constant angular velocity, ω, so that the string is inclined 30° to the vertical as shown in Fig. 353. What are the tension, T, in the string and the linear velocity, v, of the body?

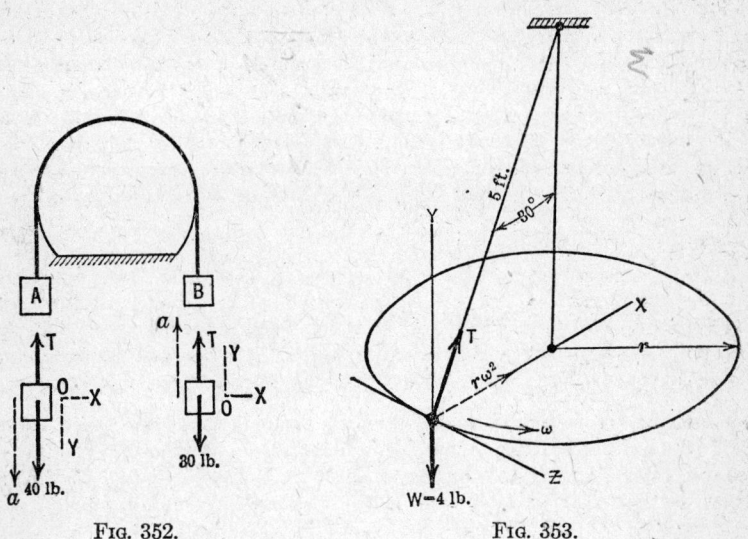

Fig. 352.　　　　　Fig. 353.

Solution.—The body moves on a circular path in a horizontal plane under the influence of two forces T and W as shown in the free-body diagram (Fig. 353). The acceleration of the body is $r\omega^2$, or $\dfrac{v^2}{r}$, toward the center of the circle. The equations of motion are:

$$\Sigma F_x = ma_x = \frac{W}{g} r\omega^2 = \frac{W}{g} \frac{v^2}{r}, \quad \ldots \ldots \ldots \quad (1)$$

$$\Sigma F_z = ma_z = \frac{W}{g} r\alpha = 0, \text{ since } \alpha = 0, \quad \ldots \ldots \quad (2)$$

$$\Sigma F_y = ma_y = 0, \text{ since } a_y = 0. \quad \ldots \ldots \ldots \quad (3)$$

From (1),
$$T \cos 60° = \frac{4}{32.2} \times \frac{v^2}{5 \sin 30°} \quad \ldots \ldots \ldots \quad (4)$$

From (3),
$$T \cos 30° - 4 = 0. \quad \therefore \quad T = 4.62 \text{ lb.} \quad \ldots \ldots \quad (5)$$

By substituting this value of T in (4), the value of v may be found. Thus

$$4.62 \cos 60° = \frac{4}{32.2} \times \frac{v^2}{5 \sin 30°}.$$

Hence
$$v^2 = \frac{4.62 \times 0.5 \times 32.2 \times 5 \times 0.5}{4} = 46.3.$$

Therefore
$$v = 6.8 \text{ ft./sec.}$$

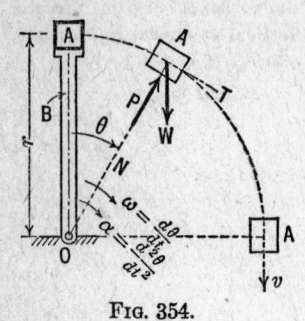

Problem 575.—In Fig. 354, A is a small block attached to the end of a vertical rod B whose lower end is connected to a smooth horizontal pin at O. The rod and block are given a very small displacement and then allowed to rotate about the pin at O. If the weight of the rod B is negligible, show that the velocity of A is $\sqrt{2gr}$ when B reaches a horizontal position.

Solution.—The only forces acting on A are its weight W and the reaction of the bar B, denoted by P. A free-body diagram of A is shown in Fig. 354. The equations of motion for A are

Fig. 354.

$$\Sigma F_t = ma_t \quad \text{or} \quad W \sin \theta = \frac{W}{g} r \frac{d^2\theta}{dt^2} \quad \cdots \quad (1)$$

$$\Sigma F_n = ma_n \quad \text{or} \quad W \cos \theta - P = \frac{W}{g} r \left(\frac{d\theta}{dt}\right)^2 \quad \cdots \quad (2)$$

From equation (1)
$$\frac{d^2\theta}{dt^2} = \frac{g}{r} \sin \theta. \quad \cdots \quad (3)$$

Multiplying each side of equation (3) by $\frac{d\theta}{dt}$, we have

$$\frac{d\theta}{dt} \frac{d^2\theta}{dt^2} = \frac{g}{r} \sin \theta \frac{d\theta}{dt}. \quad \cdots \quad (4)$$

Integrating equation (4) with respect to t, we have

$$\frac{1}{2}\left(\frac{d\theta}{dt}\right)^2 = -\frac{g}{r} \cos \theta + C$$

Since
$$\frac{d\theta}{dt} = 0 \quad \text{when } \theta = 0, \quad C = \frac{g}{r}$$

Hence
$$\omega = \frac{d\theta}{dt} = \sqrt{\frac{2g}{r}(1 - \cos \theta)}$$

When
$$\theta = \frac{\pi}{2}, \quad \omega = \sqrt{\frac{2g}{r}}$$

Hence
$$v = r\omega = r\sqrt{\frac{2g}{r}} = \sqrt{2gr}.$$

It will be noted that the body A would attain the same velocity if, starting from rest, it were to fall freely through a vertical distance r.

PROBLEMS

576. A box weighing 16.1 lb. rests on the floor of an elevator. If the elevator starts up with an acceleration of 8 ft./sec.^{2}, what is the pressure on the floor of the elevator? *Ans.* $P = 20.1$ lb.

577. A man weighing 150 lb. stands in an elevator weighing 2000 lb. If the tension in the hoisting cable is 2700 lb., with what acceleration will the elevator ascend? What will be the pressure of the man on the floor of the elevator?

578. A balloon weighing 400 lb. has a vertical component of acceleration of 2 ft./sec.^{2} upward. The horizontal wind pressure causes the balloon to travel in a direction making an angle of 30° with the vertical. Find the horizontal component of the acceleration of the balloon and the horizontal wind pressure.
Ans. 1.15 ft./sec.^{2}; 14.35 lb.

579. A body weighing 120 lb. is attached to the lower end of a rope and is lowered with a constant acceleration by means of the rope. If the greatest pull the rope can resist is 80 lb., what is the least acceleration the body can have?

580. In Fig. 355 the bodies A, B, and C weigh 10 lb., 20 lb., and 30 lb., respectively. The cord connecting B and C passes over a weightless, frictionless pulley. The coefficient of friction between A and B and the plane is 0.2. Find the acceleration of the bodies and the tension in the cord connecting A and B.
Ans. $a = 12.9$ ft./sec.^{2}; $T = 6$ lb.

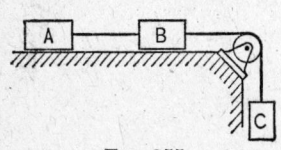

FIG. 355. 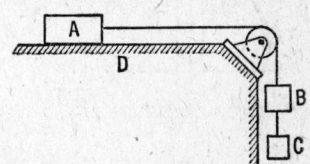   FIG. 356.

581. In Fig. 356, A weighs 40 lb., B weighs 20 lb., and C weighs 10 lb. The coefficient of friction for A and D is ¼. If the weights of the cord and pulley are negligible and the pulley turns in smooth bearings, find the tension in the cord between A and B, and in the cord between B and C. Find also the acceleration of A, B, and C.

582. Boxes are sent from the street into the basement of a store by means of an inclined plane. The plane is 20 ft. long and makes an angle of 30° with the floor. The boxes are given an initial velocity, v_0, of 10 ft./sec. Assuming that the coefficient of friction for the box while on the incline is 0.4, what is the velocity, v, of the box as it reaches the bottom of the incline, and how many seconds does it take to reach the bottom? *Ans.* $v = 17.3$ ft./sec.; $t = 1.47$ sec.

583. A man who is just strong enough to lift a 150-lb. weight when standing on the ground can lift a 200-lb. weight from the floor of an elevator when the elevator is going down with a certain acceleration. What is the acceleration? What weight can the man lift from the floor when the elevator is going up with the same acceleration?

584. A box is projected up an inclined plane, which makes an angle of 20° with the horizontal, with an initial velocity of 2400 ft./min. If the coefficient of friction is 0.2, how far up the plane does the box travel before coming to rest? Will the box remain at rest? If not, how long does it take it to reach the bottom of the incline?
Ans. $s = 46.9$ ft.; No; $t = 4.35$ sec.

585. A 3-ton cage descending a shaft with a speed of 9 yd./sec. is brought to rest with a uniform acceleration in a distance of 18 ft. What is the tension in the cable while the cage is coming to rest?

586. An automobile that weighs 3000 lb. is accelerated uniformly on a level road from 10 mi./hr. to 40 mi./hr. in 6 sec. Calculate the force exerted on the tires by the road, neglecting air resistance. *Ans.* $F = 683$ lb.

587. A body weighing 8 lb. and resting on a smooth horizontal plane is acted on by a horizontal force which causes the body to move along a straight line. If the distance s traveled by the body in time t is $s = 20t^2$ where s is expressed in feet and t in seconds, find the magnitude of the force.

588. In Fig. 357, A is a small ball that weighs 4 lb. and B is a block that weighs 12 lb. A is attached to B at O by a weightless, flexible cord. A force, P, is applied to B increasing very slowly until it reaches a value of 8 lb. after which it remains constant. Find the value of θ. assuming the plane on which B slides to be smooth.
Ans. $\theta = 26° 34'$.

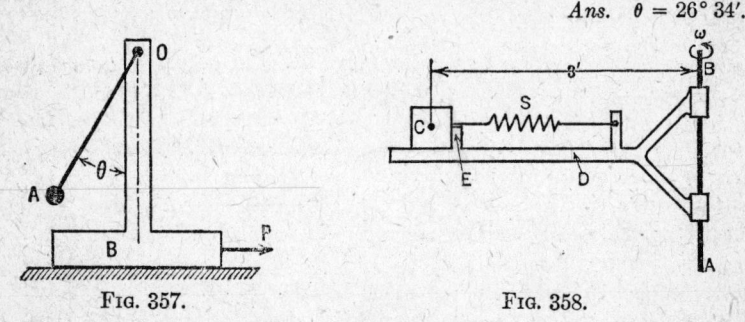

FIG. 357.

FIG. 358.

589. A body C weighing 10 lb. rests upon a frame D (Fig. 358) which rotates about a vertical axis AB. When the frame is not rotating, the tension in the spring, S, is 20 lb. If the angular velocity of the frame is 30 r.p.m. and the friction under C is neglected, what is the pressure against the stop at E?

590. A small body, A, weighing 4 lb. (Fig. 359) rotates in a vertical plane about a horizontal axis through O, to which it is attached by means of a weightless cord 2 ft. long. If the tension in the cord is 6 lb. when $\theta = 30°$, what is the velocity of A?
Ans. $v = 6.39$ ft./sec.

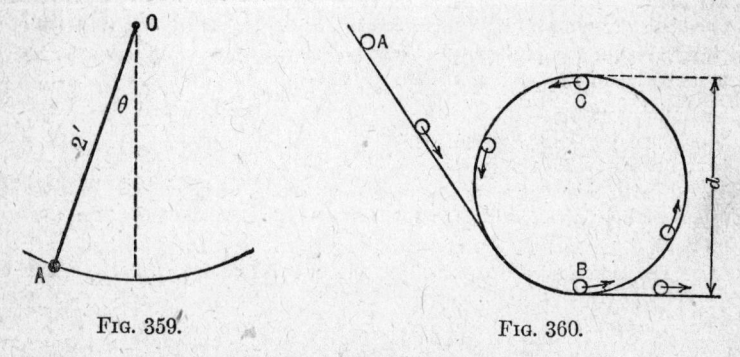

FIG. 359.

FIG. 360.

591. In "looping the loop" (Fig. 360), show that, if friction is neglected, the minimum value of the velocity of the car when at C is $\sqrt{\dfrac{gd}{2}}$ if the car does not leave the track.

592. A small body weighing 12 lb. rests on an inclined surface (Fig. 361) which is revolved about a vertical axis with a constant angular velocity of 20 r.p.m. If the

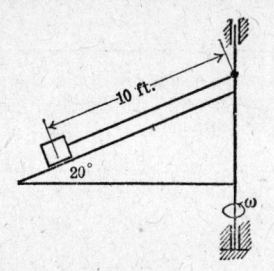

FIG. 361. 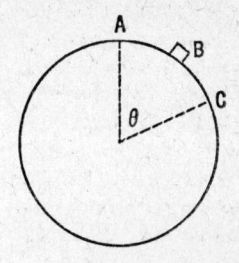   FIG. 362.

body is attached to the axis of rotation by a cord as shown in the figure, and if friction between the body and plane is neglected, find the tension, T, in the cord.

Ans. $T = 18.5$ lb.

593. In Fig. 362, B is a small body that starts from rest at A and slides on the surface of a smooth sphere until it leaves the surface at C. Find the angle θ.   *Ans.* $\theta = \cos^{-1} \frac{2}{3} = 48° 11'$.

594. Find the velocity of the body A in Prob. 575 when it reaches its lowest position.

595. In Fig. 363, the body A is attached to a flexible rope and is raised by winding the rope on a reel. The reel turns at a constant angular velocity of ω rad./sec. If the weight of A is W lb., the diameter of the rope is d in., and the weight of the rope is neglected, find the tension in the rope. Assume that A moves only vertically.

Ans. $T = W\left(1 + \dfrac{\omega^2 d}{2\pi g}\right)$.

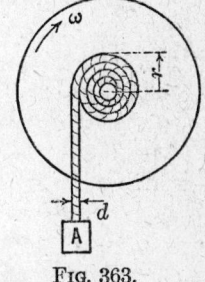

FIG. 363.

106. Inertia-Force Method for a Particle.—As pointed out in Art. 104, the resultant of all the forces that act on a particle having a mass m and an acceleration a is a force having a magnitude ma and a direction the same as that of a. Furthermore, since the forces acting on a particle constitute a concurrent system, the action line of the resultant passes through the particle. Therefore, if a force equal to this resultant but of opposite sense is assumed to act on the particle in addition to the actual forces acting on the particle, the particle will be in equilibrium and hence the equations of equilibrium may be applied to this force system. The reversed resultant (ma) force is called the *inertia force* for the particle. The resultant (ma) force is called the effective force for the particle and hence the inertia force is sometimes called the reversed effective force. It will be observed that the introduction of the inertia force transforms the kinetics problem to an equivalent statics problem

ILLUSTRATIVE PROBLEM

Problem 596.—Solve Prob. 574 by the inertia-force method.

Solution.—The resultant R of all the forces acting on the particle (effective force for the particle) is

$$R = ma = \frac{4}{32.2} \times \frac{v^2}{r} = \frac{4}{32.2} \times \frac{v^2}{2.5} = \frac{v^2}{20.1}$$

and is directed toward O the center of the circle. If a force equal but opposite to R is assumed to act on the body as shown in Fig. 364 in addition to T and W, the three forces would be in equilibrium and hence the equations of equilibrium for a concurrent force system may be applied to the forces, thus

$$\Sigma F_y = T \cos 30° - 4 = 0 \quad \therefore T = 4.62 \text{ lb.}$$

$$\Sigma F_x = 4.62 \sin 30 - \frac{v^2}{20.1} = 0$$

Hence

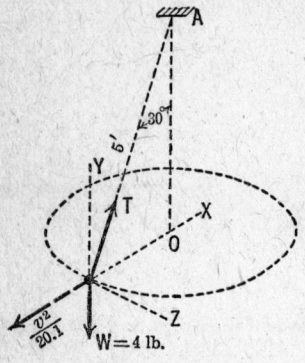

$$v^2 = 46.4 \quad \text{or} \quad v = 6.8 \text{ ft./sec.}$$

Fig. 364.

PROBLEMS

597. Solve Prob. 592 by the inertia-force method.

598. Solve Prob. 589 by the inertia-force method.

599. The bodies A and B (Fig. 365) and the frame on which they rest rotate about the vertical axis with a constant angular velocity of 40 r.p.m. The weights of A and B are 48 lb. and 32 lb., respectively. Find the pressure of the stop E on B, neglecting the friction between A and B and the frame. Ans. $R_E = 26.1$ lb.

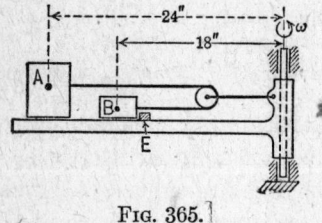

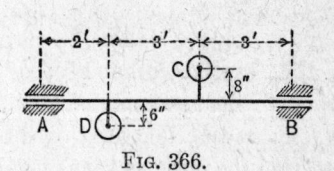

Fig. 365. Fig. 366.

600. The shaft AB and the balls C and D (Fig. 366) rotate at a constant angular velocity of 100 r.p.m. The weights of C and D are 8 lb. and 12 lb., respectively. Find the reactions of the bearings at A and B on the shaft when the balls are in the position shown, neglecting the weight of the shaft and also of the rods connecting the balls to the shaft.

107. Force Proportional to Displacement. Free Vibration.—Many problems in kinetics deal with a body having a periodic or vibrational motion (such as a simple harmonic motion) under the action of a resultant force that varies as some function of the displacement of the body. Such a force is usually applied to the body by means of a spring (or its

equivalent), which exerts a force directly proportional to the displacement of the body. It is the purpose of this article to study briefly the periodic rectilinear motion of a body acted on by a resultant force whose magnitude is proportional to the displacement of the body from some fixed point in its path.

In Fig. 367 a small body whose weight is W is suspended from one end of a helical spring, thereby causing a displacement of the lower end of the spring equal to δ_{st} when the body and spring are in static equilibrium. A downward pull is then exerted on the body causing the displacement x_0 of the body from its equilibrium position; the pull is suddenly released and the body undergoes a periodic (up and down) motion under the action of the earth-pull (weight) and the force exerted by the spring. The main features of this periodic or vibrational motion are to be investigated.

After the downward pull is released and the displacement from the position of static equilibrium has attained any value x, the forces acting on the body are as shown in Fig. 367, where k is the force required to stretch the spring a unit length and is called the *spring constant*. Thus the spring constant may be defined by the equation $k = \dfrac{W}{\delta_{st}}$. Or, in a somewhat more general form, it may be defined as the force that tends to restore the body to its initial equilibrium position divided by the corresponding displacement of the body.

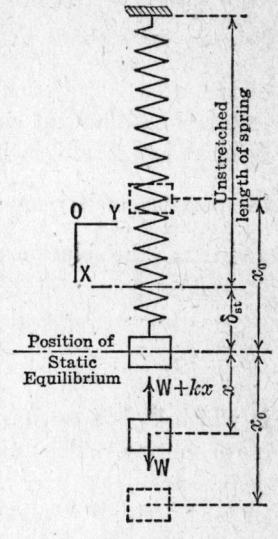

Fig. 367.

If, in Fig. 367, the positive direction for x is downward, the equation of motion, $\Sigma F_x = ma_x$, may be written as follows:

$$-(W + kx) + W = \frac{W}{g} a_x = \frac{W}{g} \frac{d^2x}{dt^2}. \quad \ldots \quad (1)$$

Hence

$$\frac{d^2x}{dt^2} = -\frac{kg}{W} x \quad \ldots \ldots \quad (2)$$

in which $\dfrac{kg}{W}$ is a constant. Eq. (2) shows that the motion of the body is a simple harmonic motion (see Art. 86) since the acceleration is a constant times the displacement and has a direction opposite to that of the displacement. Eq. (2) is the differential equation for the free or natural vibration of a particle.

It will be noted by reference to Art. 86 that the constant $\frac{kg}{W}$ in Eq. (2) corresponds to ω^2 in the equation $a = \frac{d^2x}{dt^2} = -\omega^2 x$ which was obtained by considering that the simple harmonic motion was the projection of a uniform circular motion on the diameter of the circle, ω being the angular velocity of the point on the circular path. In Art. 86 the solution of the equation $\frac{d^2x}{dt^2} = -\omega^2 x$ was found to be $x = r \cos \omega t$ and hence the solution of Eq. (2) is

$$x = C_1 \cos \sqrt{\frac{kg}{W}}\, t \quad \ldots \ldots \quad (3)$$

in which C_1 is a constant whose value depends on the initial conditions of the motion. Thus, since the body was started in motion by giving it a displacement x_0 from its equilibrium position and then releasing it without initial velocity we have $x = x_0$ when $t = 0$, and hence by substituting these values in Eq. (3) we find that $C_1 = x_0$. Therefore, the equation

$$x = x_0 \cos \sqrt{\frac{kg}{W}}\, t \quad \ldots \ldots \quad (4)$$

expresses the relation between the displacement x and the time t for the free vibration of a particle. It is important to note that in Eq. (4), x is measured from the equilibrium position of the body; or in other words the body oscillates about its equilibrium position.

The two properties or characteristics of the motion that are of particular significance are the amplitude and the period (or frequency) of the motion.

The amplitude, denoted by A, is the maximum value that x in Eq. (4) can have. This value is x_0 since the maximum value of $\cos \sqrt{\frac{kg}{W}}\, t$ is unity.

The period of oscillation or of vibration, denoted by T, is the time required for the moving body to make one oscillation, that is, one complete cycle. Hence the period of vibration is the time required for $\cos \sqrt{\frac{kg}{W}}\, t$ to pass through all of its values and return to the same value it had at the beginning of the period. Thus T is the value of t in the equation $\sqrt{\dfrac{kg}{W}}\,t = 2\pi$. Hence

$$T = 2\pi \sqrt{\dfrac{W}{kg}} = 2\pi \sqrt{\dfrac{\delta_{st}}{g}}. \quad \ldots \ldots \quad (5)$$

It will be observed that the period of oscillation depends only on the spring constant and the weight of the body; the period varies directly as $\sqrt{W}$ and inversely as $\sqrt{k}$. For example, a stiff spring (having a large value of k) and a light weight (small value of W) will have a short period of vibration and a flexible spring and a large weight will have a long period of vibration.

The frequency, f, of vibration is the number of complete cycles per unit of time and hence

$$f = \dfrac{1}{T} = \dfrac{1}{2\pi}\sqrt{\dfrac{kg}{W}} = \dfrac{1}{2\pi}\sqrt{\dfrac{g}{\delta_{st}}}. \quad \ldots \ldots \quad (6)$$

Equations (5) and (6) show that the natural period and frequency of vibration can be calculated from one measurable quantity alone; namely, the static elongation of the spring caused by the weight W of the body.

It is important to observe that the above equations apply only to free vibrations; namely, to the periodic motion of a body acted on only by its weight and a force exerted by a spring (or system of springs) such that the force is proportional to the displacement of the body and acts always to restore the position of the body to its equilibrium position. Thus the motion of the body described by the above equations does not occur in a resisting medium such as a liquid, which would produce a damped vibration rather than a free vibration. Nor is the motion a forced vibration in which an additional (periodic) force is applied to the body as it vibrates. In a forced vibration if the period of the impressed force is the same as that of the free or natural period of vibration of the system, the theoretical amplitude of the vibration becomes exceedingly large. This condition is known as *resonance* and is, of course, a condition to be avoided in parts of machines and structures. On the other hand it is a condition that we often intuitively create when we wish to build up a large amplitude as, for example, in jumping on a spring board in order to execute a high dive. We create the same condition in causing a tree to fall after it has been chopped almost through at the base, by pushing repeatedly with our hand on the tree trunk with a force that has the same frequency as that of the free oscillations of the tree. Damped and forced vibrations, including the condition of resonance, are discussed briefly in Chapter XI.

ILLUSTRATIVE PROBLEM

Problem 601.—A machine that weighs 800 lb. rests on a platform that weighs 200 lb. The platform and machine are supported by four springs, one at each corner of the platform, the four springs being alike. An additional downward force of 100 lb. is applied at the center of the platform and compresses each spring ¼ in. If the 100-lb. force is suddenly removed what will be the frequency and amplitude of the resulting vibratory motion assuming that the motion of the platform is a translation only?

Solution.—The restoring force in the system and hence the spring constant k is

$$k = \frac{100}{\frac{1}{4}} = 400 \text{ lb./in.}$$

The frequency, f, according to Eq. (6) is

$$f = \frac{1}{2\pi}\sqrt{\frac{kg}{W}} = \frac{1}{2\pi}\sqrt{\frac{400 \times (12 \times 32.2)}{1000}}$$

$$= 1.98 \text{ oscillations per sec.}$$

It should be noted that since k is expressed in pounds per *inch*, g must be expressed in *inches* per second per second.

The amplitude of the oscillations is the value of x_0 which is ¼ in.

PROBLEMS

602. A vertical, helical spring, one end of which is attached to a fixed point is stretched 2 in. by a weight of 20 lb. suspended from its lower end. The 20-lb. weight is lifted 2 in. so that the spring has its unstretched length and the weight is then suddenly released. What will be the amplitude and frequency of the resulting motion?

Ans. $A = 2$ in.; $f = 2.21$ cycles per sec.

603. A uniform bar weighing 60 lb. is supported by two helical springs as shown in Fig. 368. When the bar is pulled down 3 in. from its equilibrium position and then released, the frequency of the resulting motion is 2.21 cycles per sec. What is the spring constant for each spring, assuming that the two springs are alike and that the bar has a motion of translation only?

604. Each of the springs on which a car is mounted carries a load of P lb. and deflects vertically 3 in. under this load. What will be the frequency of the vertical oscillations of the car if a vertical force gives the springs an additional deflection and is then removed?

Ans. $f = 1.81$ cycles per sec.

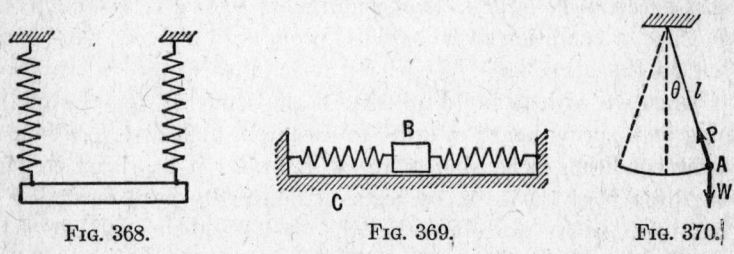

Fig. 368.   Fig. 369.   Fig. 370.

605. A body, B (Fig. 369), weighing 16 lb. is held in equilibrium by two springs in which there are equal initial tensile stresses. The body is displaced horizontally

2 in. from its equilibrium position and is then released causing the body to oscillate on the smooth surface C. The spring constant for each spring is 20 lb. per in. What is the frequency of oscillation of B?

606. A simple pendulum (Fig. 370) consists of a small body, A, of weight W lb. attached to a weightless string of length l. The body (and string) is deflected a small angle θ from its vertical position and is then released. Let it be assumed that the body moves in a straight line path since the angle θ is small. Show that the period of oscillation is $T = 2\pi \sqrt{\dfrac{l}{g}}$. HINT: The restoring force is $P \sin \theta$ or $P\theta$ (approximately) since θ is small and, the spring constant is $k = \dfrac{P\theta}{l\theta} = \dfrac{P}{l}$. Also $P \cos \theta = W$ and for small values of θ, $P = W$, approximately.

§ 2. KINETICS OF BODIES

108. Introduction. Methods of Analysis.—As pointed out in the preceding section, the general character of a problem in kinetics of bodies may be stated as follows: A physical body is acted on by a force system that has a resultant which causes a change in the motion of the body, and relations are required between (1) the resultant of the external force system, (2) the properties of the body (mass, moment of inertia, etc.), and (3) the change in the motion of the body. For each of the types of motion of rigid bodies treated in this section, the equations which express the relations between the three factors or elements in the problem (equations of motion) are found by the same procedure or series of steps, as follows:

1. The body is considered to be composed of particles, and, from the motion of the body, the acceleration, a, of any particle in the body is found, both in magnitude and in direction. This step involves the use of the facts and equations developed in the study of kinematics.

2. From the acceleration, a, of any particle and its mass, m, the force required to produce the acceleration is found, both in magnitude and in direction, by applying Newton's second law. This force, R, is called the *effective force* for the particle and, in accordance with Newton's second law, may be expressed by the equation $R = ma$, the direction of R being the same as that of a. Since R is the resultant of the actual forces acting on the particle, it may also be expressed in terms of the actual forces. Thus, by expressing the resultant of the forces acting on the particle in two ways: (1) in terms of m and a and (2) in terms of the actual forces acting on the particle, the relation between the forces acting on the particle, the mass of the particle, and the acceleration of the particle may be found.

It should be noted that some (most) of the particles of a body are acted on by internal forces only (in addition to their weights), that is, by the neighboring particles of the body, and some of the particles (located where the external forces are applied to the body) are acted on by both internal and external forces.

3. The magnitude and the direction of the effective force for each particle of the body having been determined, in terms of the mass and acceleration of the particle, the resultant of the effective forces for all the particles of the body is found completely by the same methods as were used in Chapter II for finding the resultant of a given system of forces. The effective forces for bodies having the motions considered in this section may be assumed to form a coplanar force system. Therefore, the characteristics of the resultant of the effective forces, in general, may be expressed by writing three equations (Art. 30) involving the summations of the x-components of the effective forces, of the y-components of the effective forces, and of the moments of the effective forces about some axis.

4. In the preceding step, the resultant of the forces acting on all the particles is expressed in terms of the effective (ma) forces; it may also be expressed in terms of the actual forces which include all the internal forces and all the external forces. But in obtaining the summations of the x- and of the y-components, and of the moments of these forces, the internal forces drop out of the expressions since they occur in collinear pairs, the forces of each pair being equal and opposite (Newton's third law). Therefore,

> The resultant of the effective forces for the particles of a body is identical with the resultant of the external forces which act on the body. Or,
>
> The resultant of the effective forces for all the particles of a body, if reversed and assumed to act on the body with the external forces, will hold the body in equilibrium.

The principle stated in the two forms above is known as D'Alembert's principle. It will be noted, therefore, that D'Alembert's principle in the second form makes it possible to reduce a problem in kinetics to an equivalent problem in statics by introducing a force (or forces) which may be found completely from the motion of the body by means of the first three steps outlined above.

Note on Limitations on Equations of Motion.—In the above discussion the body considered was assumed to be symmetrical with respect to the plane of motion. Thus the effective force system was equivalent to a coplanar system in the plane of motion, and the external force system was likewise assumed to lie in the plane of motion. When these conditions are satisfied three equations are sufficient to determine completely the motion of the body. It will be found that the kinetics problems most frequently encountered in engineering practice in connection with the translation, rotation, or plane motion of rigid bodies can be solved by use of the three equations obtained for the particular type of motion involved, on the basis of the above assumptions.

For the most general type of motion of a rigid body, however, there are six equations of motion, and hence if one (or more) of the above assumptions is not satisfied, more than the three equations referred to above are needed for a complete solution although even then much useful information may often be obtained from the three equations alone.

Furthermore, in certain problems in which the external forces do not lie in the plane of motion and hence do not satisfy one of the above assumptions, a complete solution may be made by using the inertia-force method, since this method then becomes equivalent to using one or more of the six equations of motion in addition to the three equations that are obtained by assuming that all the above-mentioned conditions are satisfied.

109. Motion of the Mass-Center of a System of Particles.

The steps outlined in the preceding article will be used first to deduce an important principle of kinetics, which is applicable to the motion of any mass-system (rigid or non-rigid) moving in any way, called the *principle of the motion of the mass-center*.

Let a system of particles (Fig. 371) whose masses are denoted by m', m'', m''', etc., move in any way under the action of any force system

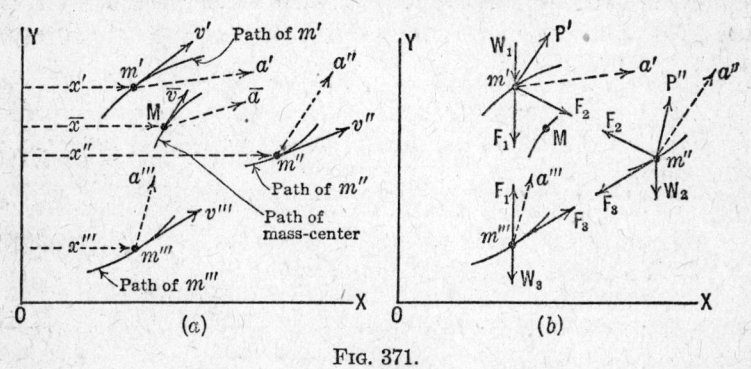

FIG. 371.

The principle of the motion of the mass-center expresses the relation between the external forces acting on this mass-system, the mass M of the whole system, and the acceleration of one point in the system, namely, the mass-center of the system. The principle may be deduced as follows:

In Fig. 371(a) only three particles are shown, and for convenience the particles are assumed to move in a plane. The forces that act on each particle and give the particle its acceleration are shown in Fig.

371(b). The forces acting on any particle consist of the forces exerted by other particles of the system (internal forces such as F_1 and F_2 acting on the particle of mass m') and any forces exerted by bodies that are not a part of the mass-system whose motion is being considered (external forces). The internal forces occur, of course, in equal, opposite, and collinear pairs. For example, in Fig. 371(b) the particle of mass m' is acted on by two external forces, namely, the earth pull W_1 (weight of the particle) and the force P', and by two internal forces F_1 and F_2.

Step 1. The acceleration of each particle is here assumed to be known; a', a'', a''', etc., are the accelerations of m', m'', m''', etc.

Step 2. The resultant of the forces acting on any particle is equal to ma and acts through the particle in the direction of the acceleration a of the particle; and the component of the resultant in any direction x is ma_x, etc.

Step 3. The x-component of the resultant of all the forces acting on all the particles then is

$$R_x = m'a'_x + m''a''_x + m'''a'''_x + \cdots \quad \ldots \quad (1)$$

Step 4. The x-component of the resultant of all the forces acting on all the particles may also be expressed in terms of the actual forces acting on all the particles, which are made up of forces external to the mass-system and the internal actions and reactions between the particles. Hence

$$R_x = (\Sigma F_x)_{\text{external}} + (\Sigma F_x)_{\text{internal}} = m'a'_x + m''a''_x + m'''a'''_x + \cdots \quad (2)$$

But by Newton's third law $(\Sigma F_x)_{\text{internal}} = 0$ since the internal forces occur in pairs of equal, opposite, and collinear forces, and hence letting ΣF_x refer to external forces only, we have

$$\Sigma F_x = m'a'_x + m''a''_x + m'''a'''_x \quad \ldots \ldots \quad (3)$$

To evaluate the right-hand side of this equation for any body (mass-system) would, in general, be an endless task since the acceleration of each particle of the body would have to be found.

It can be proved, however, that the right-hand side of the equation is equal to the product of the mass, M, of the whole system and the x-component of the acceleration, $\bar{a}$, of the mass-center of the system. In Fig. 371(a) the x-coordinates of the particles are denoted by x', x'', x''', etc., and the x-coordinate of the mass-center by $\bar{x}$. From the definition of mass-center we have then

$$m'x' + m''x'' + m'''x''' + \cdots = M\bar{x} \quad \ldots \ldots \quad (4)$$

But, since the system of particles is in motion, the x-coordinates of the particles vary with respect to time. Hence, differentiating the above equation with respect to t we have

$$m' \frac{dx'}{dt} + m'' \frac{dx''}{dt} + m''' \frac{dx'''}{dt} + \cdots = M \frac{d\bar{x}}{dt} \quad \ldots \quad (5)$$

or

$$m'v'_x + m''v''_x + m'''v'''_x + \cdots = M\bar{v}_x \quad \ldots \quad (6)$$

This equation expresses an important principle concerning the momentum of the system of particles and will be used later in Chapter X.

Differentiating Eq. (5) with respect to t we obtain

$$m' \frac{d^2 x'}{dt^2} + m'' \frac{d^2 x''}{dt^2} + m''' \frac{d^2 x'''}{dt^2} + \cdots = M \frac{d^2 \bar{x}}{dt^2} \quad \ldots \quad (7)$$

or,

$$m'a'_x + m''a''_x + m'''a'''_x + \cdots = M\bar{a}_x \quad \ldots \quad (8)$$

Therefore Eq. (3) may be written

$$\Sigma F_x = M\bar{a}_x$$

In a similar way equations involving the components in the y- and z-directions may be found. Hence the equations that express the relations between the external forces acting on any system of particles, the mass of the system, and the acceleration of the mass-center of the system are:

$$\left. \begin{array}{l} \Sigma F_x = M\bar{a}_x \\ \Sigma F_y = M\bar{a}_y \\ \Sigma F_z = M\bar{a}_z \end{array} \right\} \quad \ldots \ldots \ldots \quad (9)$$

If the resultant of the external forces acting on the system of particles is a force, denoted by R, the above three equations are equivalent to the single equation

$$R = M\bar{a}, \quad \ldots \ldots \ldots \ldots \quad (10)$$

where M is the mass of the system and $\bar{a}$ is the acceleration of the mass-center of the system.

The principle expressed either by equations (9) or by equation (10) is sometimes called the *principle of motion of the mass-center*; it simplifies the solution of many problems and is of great importance in the study of kinetics. The principle may be stated in words as follows:

> If an unbalanced external force system acts on a body (whether rigid or not), the resultant of the external force system, if a force, has a magnitude which is equal to the product of the mass of

the body and the acceleration of the mass-center of the body, and the direction of the resultant force is the same as that of the acceleration of the mass-center.

It should be noted, however, that the action line of the resultant force does not, in general, pass through the mass-center of the body.

Translation

110. Kinetics of a Translating Rigid Body.—The equations of motion for a translating rigid body may be found by applying the four steps outlined in Art. 108. In Fig. 372(a) is shown a body that is assumed to have a motion of translation when acted on by the external forces P, W, N, etc. It will further be assumed that the body is symmetrical with respect to the plane of motion and that the forces lie in the plane of motion. (See note in Art 108.) For convenience, the particles of which the body is composed may be regarded as small cubes.

Acceleration of Any Particle.—Since the body has a motion of translation, all the particles have the same acceleration a.

Effective Force for Any Particle.—By Newton's second law, the resultant of the forces (not shown) that act on any particle of mass m and give it its acceleration a is equal to ma and is in the direction of a. This resultant force is the effective force for the particle. Thus, the effective forces $m_1 a$, $m_2 a$, etc. (Fig. 372a), constitute a system of parallel forces.

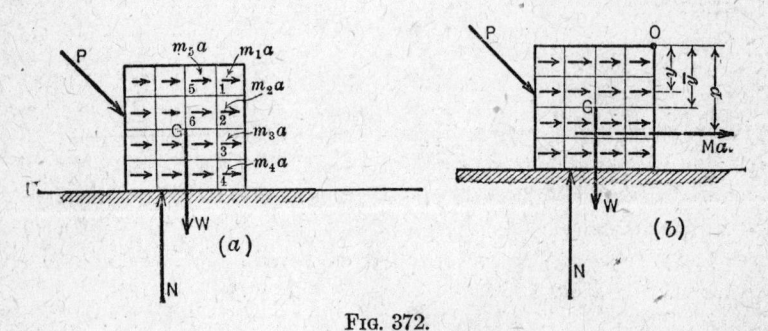

Fig. 372.

Resultant of the Effective Forces.—The resultant of the effective forces is a force and may be found by the methods of Chapter II. Thus, the magnitude of the resultant is equal to $\Sigma ma = a \Sigma m = Ma$, where M is the mass of the body; and the direction of the resultant is the same as that of the acceleration a of the body. The action line may be found by use of the principle of moments (Art. 26). Thus, if y (Fig. 372b) is the distance from any point O to the effective force ma for any particle, and p is the distance from O to the action line of the resultant of the effective forces, we have

$$Ma \cdot p = \Sigma(ma \cdot y) = a\Sigma my \quad \ldots \quad (1)$$

or,

$$p = \frac{\Sigma my}{M} = \frac{M\bar{y}}{M} = \bar{y} \quad \ldots \quad (2)$$

where $\bar{y}$ is the vertical distance of the mass-center from O. Hence the resultant passes through the mass-center, G, of the body as shown in Fig. 373(a) and is not in the position shown in Fig. 372(b).

Summarizing: If a rigid body has a motion of translation, the resultant of the effective forces is a force of magnitude Ma, through the mass-center of the body, and in the direction of the acceleration a of the body.

Relation between Effective Forces and External Forces.—Since, by D'Alembert's principle, the resultant of the external forces is identical with the resultant of the effective forces, the resultant of the external forces is also a force (R, say) of magnitude Ma in the direction of a and it passes through the mass-center (G) of the body. Since the resultant passes through G, its moment (and hence also the sum of the moments of the external forces) about G is zero. This fact may be expressed by the equation $\Sigma\bar{T} = 0$, where $\bar{T}$ denotes the moment of an external force about G. The resultant of the external forces is defined, then, by the equations

$$\left. \begin{array}{l} R = Ma \\ \Sigma\bar{T} = 0 \end{array} \right\} \quad \ldots \quad (3)$$

Letting x and y denote any two perpendicular axes in the plane of motion, each side of the first of the above equations may be resolved into components in the x- and y-directions. Thus, $R_x = Ma_x$ and $R_y = Ma_y$. But the components of the resultant R of the external forces may also be expressed in terms of the forces. Thus, $R_x = \Sigma F_x$ and hence $\Sigma F_x = Ma_x$. Similarly $\Sigma F_y = Ma_y$. Hence the first equation in (3) above may be replaced by two equations. The equations of motion, then, that express the relations between the external forces that act on the body, the mass of the body, and the acceleration of the body, may be written

$$\left. \begin{array}{l} \Sigma F_x = Ma_x \\ \Sigma F_y = Ma_y \\ \Sigma\bar{T} = 0 \end{array} \right\} \quad \ldots \quad (4)$$

It should be noted that the first two of these equations could have been obtained directly from equations (9) of Art. 109 since they apply to any type of motion.

Alternative Method. Inertia-Force Method.—Since the resultant (Ma) of the effective forces (Fig. 373a) is identical with the resultant

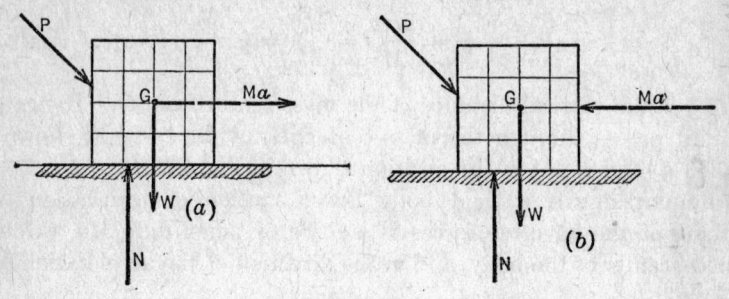

FIG. 373.

of the external forces, it is obvious that, if a force equal to Ma and having the same action line as Ma, but of opposite sense, were added to the actual external forces (P, W, N, etc.) as shown in Fig. 373(b), the system of forces so constituted would hold the body in equilibrium and hence would satisfy the equations of equilibrium:

$$\Sigma F_x = 0, \quad \Sigma F_y = 0, \quad \Sigma M = 0.$$

This additional (imaginary) force is sometimes called the *reversed effective force* or *inertia force* for the body. It is to be noted that the introduction of the inertia force has the effect of transforming the kinetics problem into an equivalent problem in statics. Methods of solution of problems by use of the equations of motion and by the inertia-force method will be illustrated in the following problems.

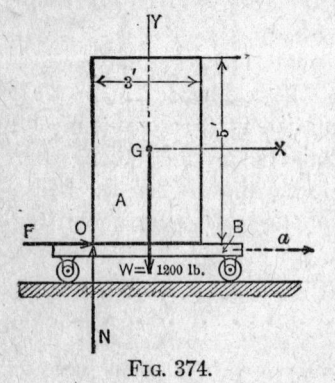

NOTE.—In analyzing and solving problems in kinetics of bodies, the same general procedure should be followed as was outlined in Art. 105.

ILLUSTRATIVE PROBLEMS

Problem 607.—The dimensions of block A (Fig. 374) are 3 ft. by 3 ft. by 5 ft. and the weight of the block is 1200 lb. The block rests on a carriage, B, which is given an acceleration a in the direction shown. If the friction between the block and carriage is sufficient to prevent slipping, what is the maximum acceleration that the carriage can have without causing the block to tip over?

FIG. 374.

Solution.—The block has a motion of translation under the action of two forces, namely, the weight, W, and the reaction, R, of the carriage. For convenience the latter force, which acts at O when the block is on the point of tipping, will be resolved into the normal pressure, N, and the frictional force, F, as indicated in the figure. The equations of motion for the block are

$$\Sigma F_x = M a_x. \quad \ldots \quad (1), \qquad \Sigma F_y = M a_y. \quad \ldots \quad (2), \qquad \Sigma \overline{T} = 0. \quad \ldots \quad (3)$$

Since the x-axis is chosen in the direction of the acceleration of the body, it follows that $a_x = a$ and $a_y = 0$.

From (1),
$$F = \frac{1200}{32.2} a. \quad \ldots \ldots \ldots \ldots \ldots \ldots \quad (4)$$

From (2),
$$N - 1200 = 0, \quad \ldots \ldots \ldots \ldots \ldots \quad (5)$$

From (3),
$$\tfrac{5}{2} F - \tfrac{3}{2} N = 0. \quad \ldots \ldots \ldots \ldots \ldots \quad (6)$$

By solving these equations, we find
$$F = 720 \text{ lb.} \quad \text{and} \quad a = 19.32 \text{ ft./sec.}^2$$

Inertia-Force Method.—If the inertia force (reversed effective force) for the body is assumed to act on the body with the external forces, the body may be assumed to be in equilibrium (D'Alembert's principle) and hence the equations of equilibrium may be applied to the force system thus formed.

The inertia force for the translating block A is
$$Ma = \frac{1200}{32.2} a.$$

Its direction is opposite to that of a and its action line passes through the mass-center of the block. Therefore, the forces acting on the block as shown in Fig. 375 will hold the block in equilibrium. The equations of equilibrium for the force system (Art. 44) are:

$$\Sigma F_x = F - \frac{1200}{32.2} a = 0,$$

$$\Sigma F_y = N - 1200 = 0,$$

$$\Sigma M_o = \frac{1200}{32.2} a \times \frac{5}{2} - 1200 \times \frac{3}{2} = 0.$$

The solution of the equations leads to the same results as were found by the first method of solution.

It should be noted that in obtaining the moments of the forces in the above equilibrium equation ($\Sigma M_o = 0$), the moment-center O may be taken as any point in the plane of the forces, whereas the moments of the forces in the third equation of motion ($\Sigma \overline{T} = 0$) used in the first method of solution *must* be taken about the mass-center of the body.

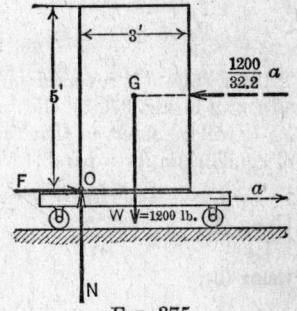

FIG. 375.

Problem 608.—The parallel rod of a locomotive (Fig. 376a) weighs 400 lb. The crank length, r_1, is 15 in., and the radius, r_2, of the drivers is 3 ft. If the speed of the engine is 50 mi./hr., what is the reaction of the pin at each end of the rod when the rod is in its lowest position?

Solution.—All particles of the rod have the same acceleration at any instant. When the rod is in its lowest position, the acceleration of each particle with reference to the engine frame is directed vertically upwards, its value being $\omega^2 r_1$. The angular velocity, ω, is

$$\omega = \frac{v}{r_2} = \frac{5280 \times 50}{60 \times 60} \times \frac{1}{3} = 24.44 \text{ rad./sec.}$$

The resultant of the effective forces acts through the mass-center, and its magnitude is

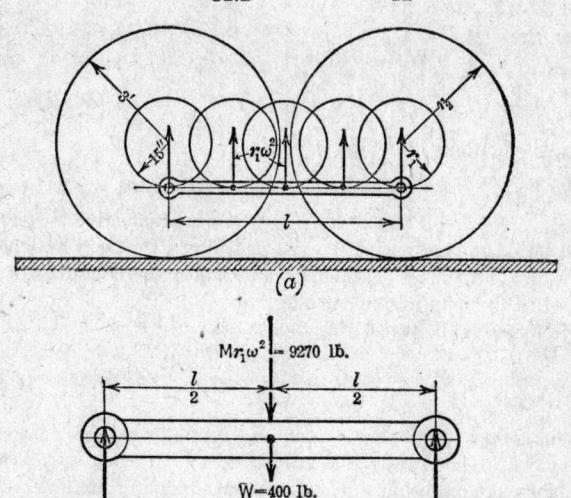

$$Ma = M\omega^2 r_1 = \frac{400}{32.2} \times (24.44)^2 \times \frac{15}{12} = 9270 \text{ lb.}$$

Fig. 376.

If this resultant is reversed and assumed to act on the body with the external forces, as shown in Fig. 376(b), the forces will be in equilibrium.

It will be observed that the forces form a parallel force system. The equations of equilibrium for a parallel force system (Art. 43) are,

$$\Sigma F = 0. \quad . \quad . \quad (1), \qquad \Sigma M = 0. \quad . \quad . \quad (2)$$

Using (1),
$$R_1 + R_2 - 9270 - 400 = 0.$$

Using (2),
$$R_1 \times l - (9270 + 400) \times \frac{l}{2} = 0.$$

Whence
$$R_1 = R_2 = 4835 \text{ lb.}$$

PROBLEMS

609. In Prob. 607, assume the acceleration of the cart and block to be 10 ft./sec.² Determine the position of the action line of the normal pressure N.

Ans. 0.724 ft. from left edge.

PROBLEMS

610. The sliding door shown in Fig. 377 weighs 160 lb. If the force P is 60 lb., what is the acceleration of the door and what are the reactions at A and B, assuming the friction of the rollers to be negligible?

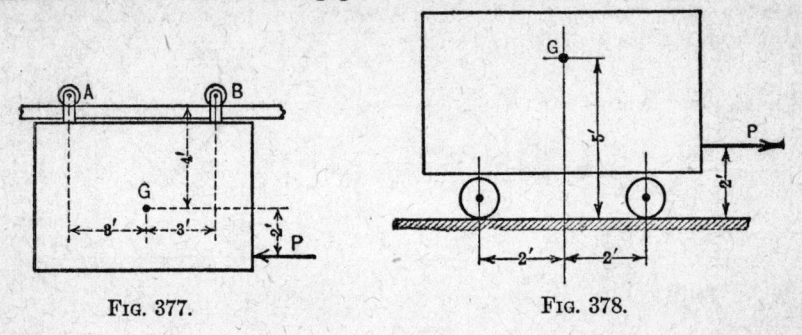

Fig. 377.   Fig. 378.

611. A small car (Fig. 378) with its load weighs 800 lb. and the center of gravity, G, of the total weight is 5 ft. from the track. A force P of 120 lb. is applied to the car as shown. Neglecting the friction on the track, find the acceleration of the car and the reactions of the track on each pair of wheels. What would be the reactions on the wheels if the force P acted through the point G?

Ans. $a = 4.83$ ft./sec.^{2}; $R_1 = 310$ lb.; $R_2 = 490$ lb.; $R_1 = R_2 = 400$ lb.

612. A homogeneous cube represented in Fig. 379 weighs 96.6 lb. The forces shown cause the body to have a motion of translation with an acceleration a in the direction indicated. If all forces are in the plane of motion what are the values of P, θ, and a?

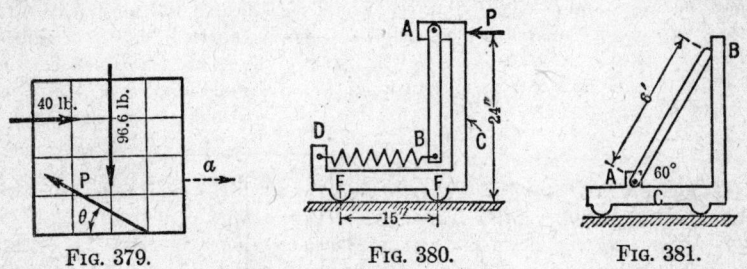

Fig. 379.   Fig. 380.   Fig. 381.

613. In Fig. 380, a uniform bar AB weighing 64.4 lb. is connected by a smooth pin at A to the frame C which weighs 128.8 lb. DB is a spring of negligible weight. When a horizontal force P is applied to the frame as shown, the system slides to the left on a smooth horizontal surface with an acceleration of 6 ft./sec.^{2} Find the magnitude of P. If the mass-center of the system is 18 in. above the surface and 3 in. to the left of F, find the reaction of the surface on the frame at E and F.

Ans. $P = 36$ lb.; $R_E = 53.0$ lb.; $R_F = 140.2$ lb.

614. In Prob. 613 determine the tension in the spring, assuming the bar AB to be vertical when the system is moving with an acceleration of 6 ft./sec.^{2}

615. In Fig. 381, AB is a uniform bar that weighs 120 lb. It is attached to the frame C by a smooth pin at A and rests against a smooth surface at B. What horizontal acceleration to the right must be given to the frame to cause the pressure on the bar at B to be zero?

Ans. $a = 18.6$ ft./sec.^{2}

616. In Fig. 382, a block has attached to it a uniform bar AC whose weight is 130 lb. The bar is held in a vertical position by a smooth pin at A and a flexible cord BD. If the block is moved to the right with a velocity that increases uniformly from 10 ft./sec. to 60 ft./sec. in 5 sec., what is the stress in the cord and pressure of the pin at A on the bar?

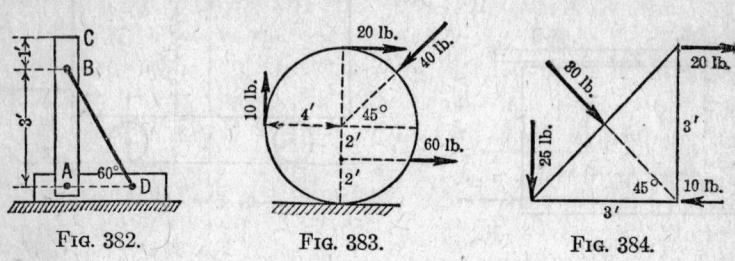

FIG. 382.   FIG. 383.   FIG. 384.

617. A homogeneous thin circular disk having a radius of 4 ft. rests on a smooth horizontal plane. If the four forces shown in Fig. 383 are applied to the disk in addition to its weight and the reaction of the plane, show that the disk will slide without rolling. If the acceleration of the disk is 8 ft./sec.^{2}, find the weight of the disk and the reaction of the plane.   *Ans.* $W = 208$ lb.; $N = 226$ lb.

618. One half of a homogeneous cube represented in Fig. 384 is acted on by the four forces shown, in addition to its weight which is 40 lb. The forces lie in the plane of symmetry of the body. Prove that the forces give a motion of translation to the body and find the magnitude of the acceleration of the body.

619. Bodies A and B (Fig. 385) are connected by a flexible, inextensible cord that passes over a weightless, frictionless pulley C. A weighs 644 lb. and the coefficient of friction between A and the plane is 0.2. What is the greatest weight B can have if A slides up the plane without overturning? Find the acceleration of A.
Ans. $W = 1340$ lb.; $a = 16.2$ ft./sec.^{2}

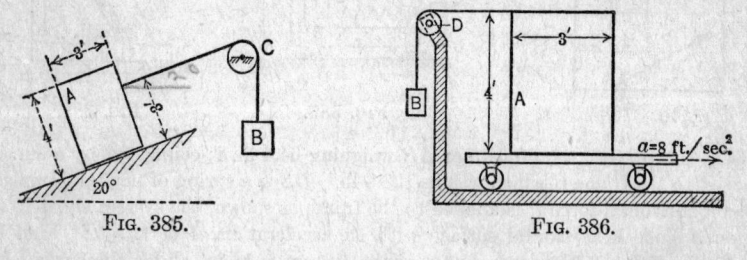

FIG. 385.   FIG. 386.

620. The dimensions of body A (Fig. 386) are 3 ft. by 2 ft. by 4 ft. and its weight is 1000 lb. Assuming that the body will not slip on the carriage, what is the maximum weight that B may have without causing A to tip over when the acceleration of the carriage is 8 ft. per sec.^{2}? The pulley D is assumed to be frictionless and weightless.

621. In Prob. 620 assume the weight of B to be 100 lb. and the acceleration of A to be 8 ft./sec.^{2} Locate the action line of the normal pressure of the carriage on A.
Ans. 0.504 ft. from left edge.

Rotation

111. Kinetics of a Rotating Rigid Body.—The equations of motion for a rigid body that rotates about a fixed axis may be found by the method outlined in Art. 108. But since the equations of motion of the mass-center (Art. 109) apply to any body having any type of motion, they may be used for the motion of rotation here considered. However, it will be necessary to derive an additional equation of motion which involves the moments of the external forces that act on the body.

In applying the equations of motion of the mass-center let Fig. 387 represent a rigid body that rotates about a fixed axis through O under the influence of an unbalanced force system (the weight W, the force P_1, and the reaction P of the axis). It will be assumed that the body is symmetrical with respect to the plane of motion and that the forces lie in the plane of motion (see note in Art. 108). At any instant all particles of the body have the same angular velocity ω and the same angular acceleration α about the axis of rotation. The linear velocity v and the linear acceleration a of any particle, however, vary as the distance r of the particle from the axis of rotation. Let G denote the mass-center of the body and $\bar{r}$ its distance from O. Furthermore, let axes ON and OT normal and tangent, respectively, to the path of the mass-center be selected as axes of reference. The normal and tangential components of the acceleration $\bar{a}$ of the mass-center are $\bar{a}_n = \bar{r}\omega^2$ and $\bar{a}_t = \bar{r}\alpha$ directed as shown in Fig. 387. Hence the equations of Art. 109 when applied to a rotating rigid body with axes chosen as in Fig. 387 become $\Sigma F_n = M\bar{r}\omega^2$ and $\Sigma F_t = M\bar{r}\alpha$. These two equations take account of the effect on the motion of the body of the magnitude and sense of the resultant of the external forces if the resultant is a force. But the effect of the action line of the resultant force (or the effect of the moment of the resultant couple, if the resultant is a couple) must also be included in the equations of motion. This latter effect is taken account of by means of a moment equation which is derived by use of the steps in Art. 108 as follows:

The resultant of all of the forces acting on any particle of mass m (the effective force for the particle) is ma and may be resolved into

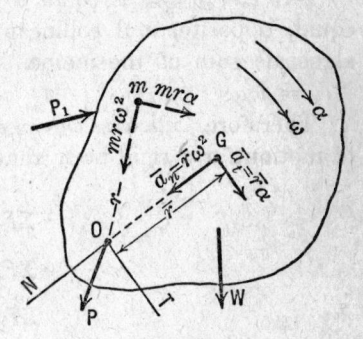

Fig. 387.

components $mr\omega^2$ and $mr\alpha$ as shown in Fig. 387. The moment about O of the effective force is $mr^2\alpha$ since the component $mr\omega^2$ passes through O. Hence the algebraic sum of the moments of all the effective forces about the axis of rotation is equal to $\Sigma mr^2\alpha = \alpha\Sigma mr^2 = I_o\alpha$, where I_o denotes the moment of inertia of the body with respect to the axis of rotation (see Appendix for discussion of moment of inertia).

Now the sum of the moments of the effective forces for all the particles is equal to the sum of the moments of all the forces acting on all of the particles of the body, and these forces include all the external forces impressed on the body and all the internal forces exerted by the particles on each other. Hence we may write

$$(\Sigma T_o)_{\text{external}} + (\Sigma T_o)_{\text{internal}} = I_o\alpha$$

But $(\Sigma T_o)_{\text{internal}}$ is equal to zero since the internal forces occur in equal, opposite, and collinear pairs. Hence letting ΣT_o denote the algebraic sum of the moments of the external forces only, we have $\Sigma T_o = I_o\alpha$.

Therefore, *with axes chosen as shown in Fig. 387*, the three equations of motion for a rigid body that rotates about a fixed axis are

$$\left.\begin{array}{l} \Sigma F_n = M\bar{r}\omega^2 \\ \Sigma F_t = M\bar{r}\alpha \\ \Sigma T_o = I_o\alpha \end{array}\right\} \quad \cdots \cdots \cdots \quad (1)$$

It should be noted that equations (1) are not sufficient for the complete analysis of all problems involving the rotation of a rigid body since in the preceding discussion it was assumed that the body was symmetrical with respect to the plane of motion and that the external forces were in the plane of motion. If these conditions are not satisfied additional equations involving moments about axes perpendicular to the axis of rotation are needed. Equations (1), however, are sufficient for most problems encountered in engineering practice. Furthermore, as pointed out at the end of Art. 108, for certain problems in which the external forces do not lie in the plane of motion the inertia-force method gives a complete solution.

If the body rotates about an axis through the mass-center, that is, if the points O and G coincide, then the right-hand members of the first two of the above equations become zero, since $\bar{r} = 0$. The directions of the n- and t-axes then become indeterminate, and hence any two perpendicular axes in the plane of motion may be used as reference axes.

ILLUSTRATIVE PROBLEMS

Denoting any two such axes by x and y, the above equations become

$$\left.\begin{array}{l}\Sigma F_x = 0 \\ \Sigma F_y = 0 \\ \Sigma \overline{T} = \overline{I}\alpha\end{array}\right\}, \quad \ldots \ldots \ldots \quad (2)$$

in which $\Sigma \overline{T}$ is the algebraic sum of the moments of the external forces about the axis of rotation (now through the mass-center) and $\overline{I}$ is the moment of inertia of the body about the axis of rotation.

It is evident from equations (2) that the resultant of the external forces acting on a body that rotates about an axis through its mass-center is a couple whose moment is $\overline{I}\alpha$.

ILLUSTRATIVE PROBLEMS

Problem 622.—Two spherical balls are connected by a light, slender, rigid rod and made to rotate in a horizontal plane about a vertical axis midway between the balls by a couple F, F in a plane perpendicular to the y-axis as shown in Fig. 388. Each sphere is 12 in. in diameter and weighs 64.4 lb. What is the moment of the couple if the rod and spheres acquire an angular velocity of 30 r.p.m. in 4 sec., starting from rest? If one of the two forces of the couple is applied 9 in. from the axis of rotation and the other force is the reaction of the axis, what is the magnitude of each force?

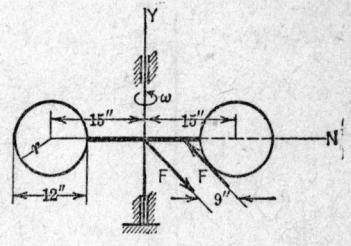

Fig. 388.

Solution.—Since the two spheres have a motion of rotation about an axis through the mass-center of the spheres, the equations of motion are:

$$\Sigma F_x = 0. \quad \ldots \quad (1), \qquad \Sigma F_y = 0. \quad \ldots \quad (2), \qquad \Sigma \overline{T} = \overline{I}\alpha. \quad \ldots \quad (3)$$

Letting the moment of the couple be denoted by C and the mass of each sphere by M we have, from (3),

$$\Sigma \overline{T} = C = \overline{I}\alpha = 2(\tfrac{2}{5}Mr^2 + Md^2)\alpha$$

$$= 2\left[\frac{2}{5} \times \frac{64.4}{32.2} \times \left(\frac{6}{12}\right)^2 + \frac{64.4}{32.2} \times \left(\frac{15}{12}\right)^2\right]\alpha = 6.65\alpha.$$

But, by definition,

$$\alpha = \frac{\omega - \omega_0}{t} = \frac{30 \times 2\pi}{60 \times 4} = 0.785 \text{ rad./sec.}^2$$

Therefore

$$C = 6.65 \times 0.785 = 5.23 \text{ lb.-ft.}$$

But

$$C = F \times \tfrac{9}{12}. \qquad \therefore \quad F = 5.23 \div \tfrac{9}{12} = 6.97 \text{ lb.}$$

Problem 623.—In Fig. 389, CD represents a brake for regulating the descent of the suspended body A. B is the drum from which the cable attached to A unwinds as A descends. The radius, r_1, of the drum is 6 ft. The radius, r_2, of the brake wheel is 7 ft. The radius of gyration, k_0, of the rotating parts (drum and brake wheel) about the axis of rotation is 4 ft. The rotating parts weigh 2000 lb. and the body A weighs 1000 lb. The coefficient of brake friction is ¼. If friction on the axle of the rotating parts is neglected, find the acceleration, a, of the body A, the tension, P, in the cable, and the horizontal and vertical components, R_1 and R_2, of the axle reaction, assuming the force at C to be 100 lb. Consider the cable to be flexible and neglect its weight.

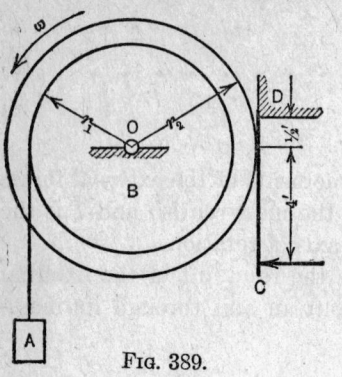

Fig. 389.

Solution.—Three bodies are to be considered: (1) the brake CD which is in equilibrium, (2) the drum and the brake wheel which have a motion of rotation, and (3) body A which has a motion of translation. The free-body diagram for each body is shown in Fig. 390. The brake CD is held

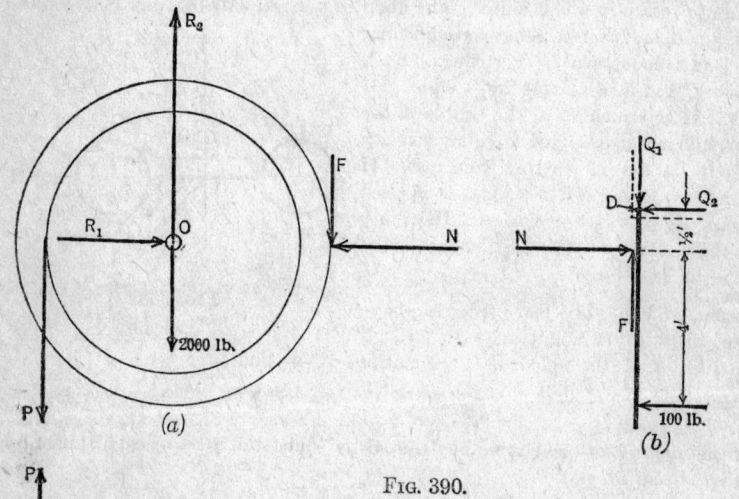

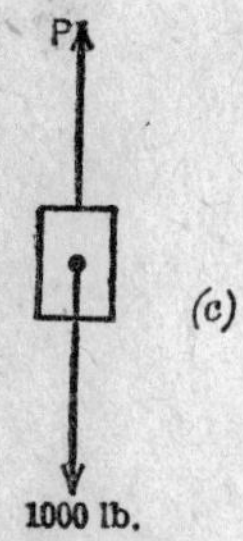

Fig. 390.

in equilibrium by a coplanar, non-concurrent force system for which the equations of equilibrium are:

$$\Sigma F_x = 0, \quad \Sigma F_y = 0, \quad \Sigma M_D = 0. \quad \ldots \quad (1)$$

The last equation only is needed in this problem since not all the forces acting on the brake are required.

The equations of motion for the drum and brake wheel are:

$$\Sigma F_x = 0. \ \ldots \ (2), \quad \Sigma F_y = 0. \ \ldots \ (3), \quad \Sigma \overline{T} = \overline{I}\alpha. \ \ldots \ (4)$$

In addition to these equations the defining equation of the coefficient of friction must be used, namely,

$$F = \mu N. \quad \ldots \quad \ldots \quad \ldots \quad \ldots \quad (5)$$

ILLUSTRATIVE PROBLEMS 253

One equation of motion only is needed for body A, namely,

$$\Sigma F_y = M a_y. \qquad (6)$$

Further, since the total acceleration of body A is in the y-direction and since it has the same magnitude as the tangential acceleration, a_t, of a point on the circumference of the drum, we may write:

$$a_y = a = a_t = r_1 \alpha. \qquad (7)$$

Applying the equations we have:

From (1),
$$-100 \times 4.5 + 0.5N = 0. \quad \therefore \quad N = 900 \text{ lb.}$$

From (5),
$$F = \tfrac{1}{4} \times 900 = 225 \text{ lb.}$$

From (2),
$$R_1 - N = 0. \quad \therefore \quad R_1 = N = 900 \text{ lb.}$$

From (4),
$$6P - 225 \times 7 = \frac{2000}{32.2} \times 4^2 \times \alpha. \qquad (8)$$

From (6),
$$1000 - P = \frac{1000}{32.2} \times a_y. \qquad (9)$$

Substituting $\dfrac{a}{r_1}$ from (7) for α in (8) and replacing a_y in (9) by a from (7), we have:

$$6P - 225 \times 7 = \frac{2000}{32.2} \times 16 \times \frac{a}{6},$$

and

$$1000 - P = \frac{1000}{32.2} a.$$

And, from (3),
$$R_2 - P - 225 - 2000 = 0.$$

These last three equations contain the three required quantities. The solution of the equations gives

$$a = 12.54 \text{ ft./sec.}^2, \quad P = 609 \text{ lb.}, \quad R_2 = 2834 \text{ lb.}$$

Problem 624.—A slender uniform bar (Fig. 391a) is free to rotate in a vertical plane about a smooth pin at O. The bar is held at rest with the free end vertically above O and is then released, allowing the bar to rotate. The bar is 2 ft. long and

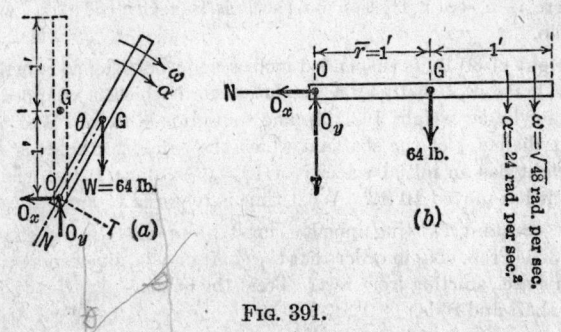

Fig. 391.

weighs 64 lb. (a) Find the angular velocity, ω, of the bar for any angular displacement θ. (b) Find the horizontal and vertical components of the pin reaction on the bar when θ = 90°. Use $g = 32$ ft./sec.^{2}

Solution.—The forces acting on the bar when the angular displacement is θ are shown in Fig. 391(a). The equations of motion for the bar are

$$\Sigma F_n = M\bar{r}\omega^2 \quad \ldots \quad (1) \qquad \Sigma F_t = M\bar{r}\alpha \quad \ldots \quad (2), \qquad \Sigma T_0 = I_0\alpha \quad \ldots \quad (3)$$

From equation (3) we have

$$64 \sin\theta = \frac{1}{3} \times \frac{64}{32} \times 4 \times \frac{d^2\theta}{dt^2}$$

Hence

$$\frac{d^2\theta}{dt^2} = 24 \sin\theta$$

Multiplying each side of this equation by $\dfrac{d\theta}{dt}$ and then integrating the resulting equation with respect to t we have

$$\frac{1}{2}\left(\frac{d\theta}{dt}\right)^2 = -24\cos\theta + C$$

Since

$$\frac{d\theta}{dt} = 0 \quad \text{when} \quad \theta = 0, \quad C = 24$$

Therefore

$$\frac{d\theta}{dt} = \sqrt{48(1 - \cos\theta)}$$

When $\theta = 90°$, $\omega = \dfrac{d\theta}{dt} = \sqrt{48}$ and $\alpha = \dfrac{d^2\theta}{dt^2} = 24$. The free-body diagram for the bar when $\theta = 90°$ is shown in Fig. 391(b). Hence from equations (1) and (2) we have

$$\Sigma F_n = M\bar{r}\omega^2 \quad \text{or} \quad O_x = \tfrac{64}{32} \times 1 \times 48 \qquad \therefore\ O_x = 96 \text{ lb.}$$
$$\Sigma F_t = M\bar{r}\alpha \quad \text{or} \quad 64 - O_y = \tfrac{64}{32} \times 1 \times 24 \qquad \therefore\ O_y = 16 \text{ lb.}$$

PROBLEMS

625. A solid sphere 15 in. in diameter revolves with an angular velocity of 500 r.p.m. about a fixed axis which passes through its center. What force lying in a diametral plane perpendicular to the axis and acting tangent to the surface will stop the sphere in 5 sec. if friction on the axis is neglected? The weight of the sphere is 500 lb. *Ans.* 40.6 lb.

626. A weight of 30 lb. is suspended from a solid homogeneous cylinder that is mounted on a horizontal shaft, by a weightless cord which is wrapped around the cylinder. The cylinder weighs 193.2 lb. and its radius is 18 in. Bearing friction is 18 lb. and the diameter of the shaft on which the cylinder rotates is 4 in. If the suspended weight has an initial velocity of 10 ft./sec. downwards, what will be its velocity after it has moved 10 ft.? What time is required to move the 10 ft.?

627. What constant twisting moment must be applied to the shaft and balls shown in Fig. 366 (Prob. 600) in order that the shaft may be given an angular velocity of 80 r.p.m. in 4 sec., starting from rest? Treat the balls as particles and neglect the weight of the shaft and rods. *Ans.* 0.426 lb. ft.

PROBLEMS

628. A homogeneous cylinder (Fig. 392) weighs 193.2 lb. and has a diameter of 1 ft. The cylinder rotates with an angular velocity of 120 r.p.m. A frictional force is developed at the surface by the force P which causes the angular velocity to decrease uniformly to 40 r.p.m. in 4 sec. If the coefficient of kinetic friction is 0.1, find the value of P.

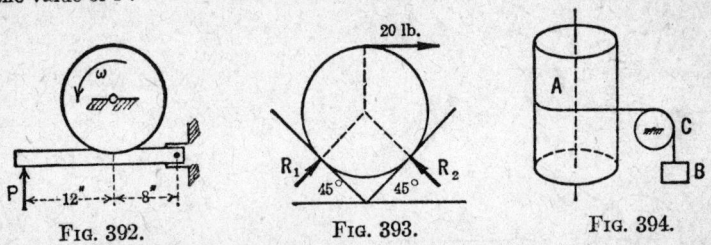

FIG. 392.   FIG. 393.   FIG. 394.

629. A homogeneous cylinder weighing 64.4 lb. and having a radius of 2 ft. rests between two smooth planes, as shown in Fig. 393. A force of 20 lb. perpendicular to the axis of the cylinder is applied as shown. Find the angular acceleration of the cylinder, and the reactions R_1 and R_2 of the planes on the cylinder.

Ans. $\alpha = 10$ rad./sec.^{2}; $R_1 = 31.4$ lb.; $R_2 = 59.7$ lb.

630. In Fig. 394, A is a homogeneous solid cylinder that weighs 322 lb. and has a radius of 2 ft., B is a body that weighs 16.1 lb., and C is a weightless, frictionless pulley. Find the tension in the cord and the angular acceleration of the cylinder.

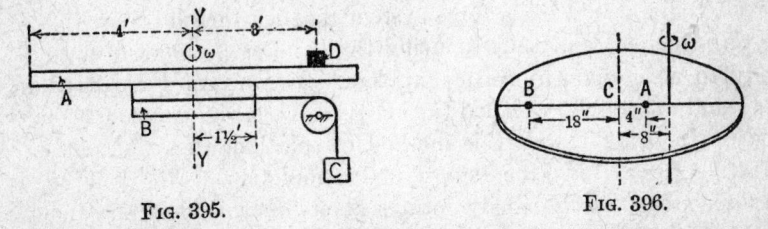

FIG. 395.   FIG. 396.

631. A disk A (Fig. 395) is caused to rotate about the axis YY by a weight C which is attached to a string that passes over a weightless and frictionless pulley and is wrapped around a cylindrical drum B that is attached to the disk. A small weight D is attached to the disk as shown. The weights of A, B, C, and D are 128.8 lb., 32.2 lb., 16.1 lb., and 8.05 lb., respectively. Find (a) the angular acceleration of the disk, (b) the tangential acceleration of D, and (c) the normal acceleration of D, 4 sec. after starting from rest.

Ans. (a) 0.662 rad./sec.^{2}; (b) 1.99 ft./sec.^{2}; (c) 21.1 ft./sec.^{2}

632. In Fig. 396 is shown a circular disk that weighs 24 lb. and has a diameter of 4 ft. The disk rotates at 90 r.p.m. in a horizontal plane about a vertical axis 8 in. from C, the center of the disk. Small bodies weighing 12 lb. and 4 lb. are rigidly attached to the disk at the points A and B, respectively. Find the horizontal force exerted by the axis on the disk. Also find the turning moment that must be applied to the disk to increase its angular velocity uniformly to 120 r.p.m. in 4 sec.

633. The rod BCE (Fig. 397) is made to oscillate by means of the crank AD and link DC. The members are connected by smooth pins at B, C, and D. The rod BCE has a constant cross-section and weighs 16.1 lb. In the position shown its angular velocity, ω, is 60 r.p.m. clockwise, and its angular acceleration, α, is 40 rad./sec.^{2} counter-clockwise. Find the force, P, exerted by the link DC at C, and the reaction, R, of the pin at B on the rod BE.

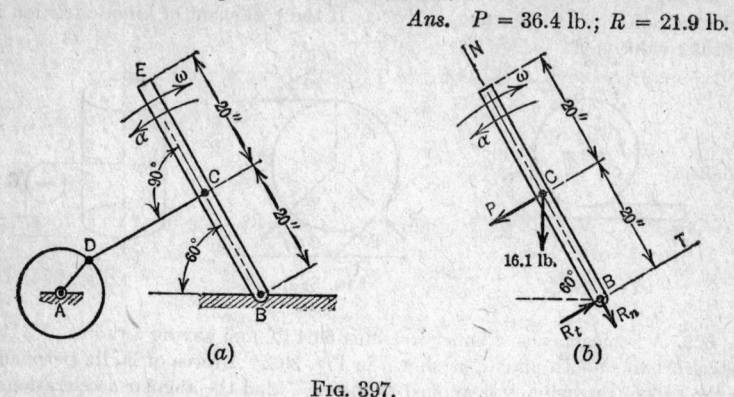

Ans. $P = 36.4$ lb.; $R = 21.9$ lb.

FIG. 397.

112. Second Method of Analysis. Inertia-Force Method.—In some problems dealing with the rotation of a rigid body under the action of an unbalanced force system, it is convenient to assume that the resultant of the effective forces is reversed and acts on the body with the external forces, thereby forming a force system that is in equilibrium (D'Alembert's principle) and thus reducing the kinetics problem of a rotating body to an equivalent statics problem. The reversed resultant force (or resultant couple) is called the inertia force (or inertia couple) for the body. In order to use this method of solution, the resultant of the effective forces must be determined completely. This will be done assuming (1) that the body rotates about an axis that does not pass through its mass-center and (2) that the axis of rotation passes through the mass-center of the body.

I. ROTATION ABOUT AXIS NOT THROUGH MASS-CENTER.—If the body rotates about an axis not through its mass-center, the resultant of the effective forces (and hence also of the external forces), as found in Art. 111, is a force. The components of this resultant force parallel to the n- and t-axes were found to be $M\bar{r}\omega^2$ and $M\bar{r}\alpha$, respectively. The action line of the resultant may be determined by finding the point where it intersects the n-axis. Thus, if in Fig. 398 the resultant of the effective forces be resolved into its components $M\bar{r}\omega^2$ and $M\bar{r}\alpha$ at the point where it intersects the n-axis, the distance, q, from this point to O may be determined from the principle of moments as follows: The sum of the moments of the effective forces about O, as shown in Art. 111, is $I_o\alpha$. Further, the moment of the resultant of the effective forces is the moment of its tangential component, $M\bar{r}\alpha$, only, since the normal component, $M\bar{r}\omega^2$, passes through the center of rotation. Hence, the principle of moments is expressed by the equation

$$M\bar{r}\alpha \cdot q = I_o\alpha.$$

And, since $I_o = Mk_o^2$, in which k_o is the radius of gyration of the body with respect to the axis of rotation, we may write:

$$M\bar{r}\alpha \cdot q = Mk_o^2\alpha,$$

whence
$$q = \frac{k_o^2}{\bar{r}}.$$

Therefore, the action line of the resultant of the effective forces intersects the n-axis at a distance $\dfrac{k_o^2}{\bar{r}}$ from the center of rotation, as shown in Fig. 398. And, since the resultant of the external forces is identical with the resultant of the effective forces, the body may be considered to be in equilibrium if the two forces $M\bar{r}\alpha$ and $M\bar{r}\omega^2$, having the action lines as determined above and shown in Fig. 398, but *reversed in sense*,

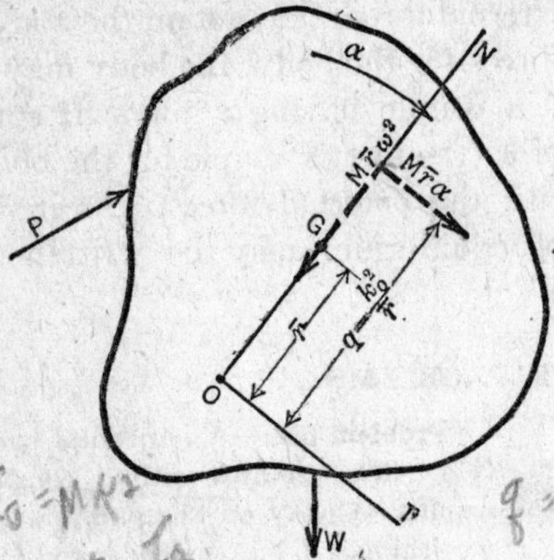

FIG. 398. 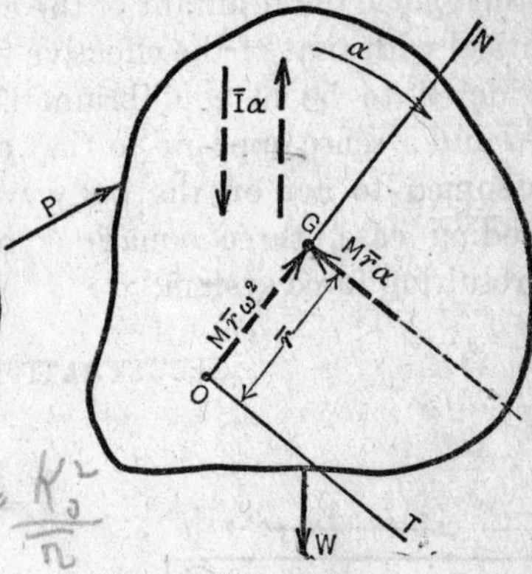 FIG. 399.

are assumed to act on the body with the external forces. Hence, for the force system thus formed, we may write three equations of equilibrium.

It is sometimes more convenient to replace the resultant of the effective forces by an equal parallel force through the mass-center and a couple. It can easily be shown that the moment of this couple is $\bar{I}\alpha$; thus the force $M\bar{r}\alpha$ may be resolved (Art. 18) into an equal parallel force through G and a couple whose moment is

$$M\bar{r}\alpha(q - \bar{r}) = (Mk_o^2 - M\bar{r}^2)\alpha = \bar{I}\alpha.$$

Hence if the inertia couple $\bar{I}\alpha$ and the inertia forces $M\bar{r}\omega^2$ and $M\bar{r}\alpha$, as shown in Fig. 399, be added to the external forces acting on the body, the body will be in equilibrium.

Centrifugal Force.—The n-component, $M\bar{r}\omega^2$, of the inertia force for the body is called the *centrifugal force* for the body. If the body is rotating at a constant angular velocity ($\alpha = 0$), then the centrifugal force is the total inertia force for the body. The nature of this so-called force is frequently misunderstood; the centrifugal force for a body is *not an actual force* exerted on the body by some other body but is a force which if assumed to act on the body in addition to the actual forces acting on the body would hold the body in equilibrium, assuming the body to have a constant angular velocity.

II. ROTATION ABOUT AXIS THROUGH MASS-CENTER.—If the body rotates about an axis that passes through its mass-center, $\bar{r} = 0$ and hence each of the components, $M\bar{r}\alpha$ and $M\bar{r}\omega^2$, of the resultant of the effective forces is zero. Therefore, the resultant is not a force. And, since the effective forces have a moment, the value of which is $\bar{I}\alpha$, the resultant is a couple of moment $\bar{I}\alpha$. The sense of the resultant couple is, of course, the same as that of α, the angular acceleration of the body. Further, since the resultant of the external forces that act on the body is identical with that of the effective forces for the body, the body may be considered to be in equilibrium if a couple having a moment equal to $\bar{I}\alpha$ and a sense opposite to that of α (the inertia couple for the body) is assumed to act on the body with the external forces. As in the preceding case, three equations of equilibrium may be written for the resulting force system.

ILLUSTRATIVE PROBLEMS

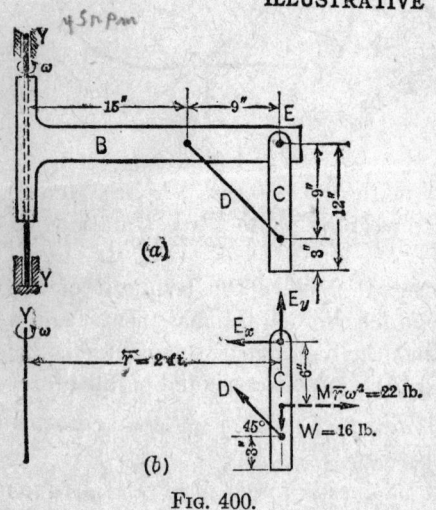

Problem 634.—A horizontal bar B (Fig. 400a) rotates with a constant angular velocity of 45 r.p.m. about a vertical axis YY. A slender rod C, of constant cross-section, having a length of 12 in. and a weight of 16 lb. is attached to the rotating bar by means of a smooth pin at E, and is held in a vertical position by a weightless cord D. Find the tension in D and the magnitude of the reaction of the pin at E on the rod C.

Solution.—A free-body diagram of the rod C is shown in Fig. 400(b). The rod has a motion of rotation about the vertical axis YY under the influence of three forces W, D, and the pin pressure at E (the components of the pin pressure being denoted by E_x and E_y).

If the reversed resultant of the effective forces (inertia force) for the rod is assumed to act on the rod with W, D, E_x, and E_y, the rod may be considered to be in equilibrium. The inertia force is $M\bar{r}\omega^2$, since $\alpha = 0$ and hence $M\bar{r}\alpha = 0$. Its magnitude is

$$M\bar{r}\omega^2 = \frac{16}{32.2} \times 2 \times \left(\frac{45 \times 2\pi}{60}\right)^2 = 22.0 \text{ lb.}$$

The action line of $M\bar{r}\omega^2$ passes through the mass-center of the rod. Thus, the forces W, D, E_x, E_y, and $M\bar{r}\omega^2$, as shown in the free-body diagram, would hold the rod in equilibrium. Using the three equations of equilibrium, we have:

$$\Sigma F_x = 22 - E_x - D \cos 45° = 0,$$
$$\Sigma F_y = E_y + D \cos 45° - 16 = 0,$$
$$\Sigma M_E = 22 \times 6 - D \times 9 \cos 45° = 0.$$

The solution of these equations gives the following results:

$$D = 20.7 \text{ lb.} \qquad E_x = 7.33 \text{ lb.,} \qquad E_y = 1.33 \text{ lb.,} \qquad E = 7.45 \text{ lb.}$$

Problem 635.—Hoop Tension in Flywheel.—Let it be required to find the stress (often called hoop tension) in the rim of a rotating flywheel in terms of the rim velocity v and the weight of the material per unit volume. Assume that the rim is thin and that the effect of the spokes may be neglected.

Solution.—In Fig. 401 is represented one-half of the rim of a flywheel. As the wheel rotates, each half of the rim tends to separate from the other half and is prevented from doing so by the stresses P, P which are developed in the rim. The inertia force for the half of the rim is $M\bar{r}\omega^2$ and it acts through the mass-center of the half-rim. And, since the inertia force is in equilibrium with the external forces (P, P) which act on the half-rim, the following equation of equilibrium may be written:

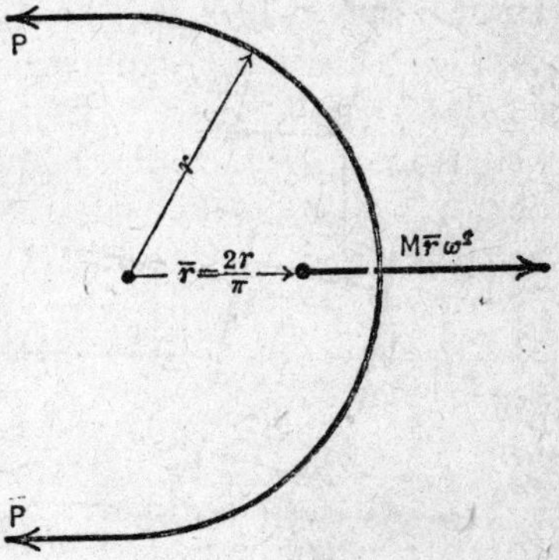

$$2P = M\bar{r}\omega^2 = \frac{W}{g}\bar{r}\omega^2,$$

Fig. 401.

in which W is the weight of the half-rim. Now if the thickness of the rim is small in comparison with the mean radius r, the mass-center of the rim may be considered to coincide with the centroid of the semi-circular arc, and hence $\bar{r} = \dfrac{2r}{\pi}$ (Prob. 332). Whence

$$P = \frac{1}{2} \frac{W}{g} \times \frac{2r}{\pi} \omega^2 = \frac{Wr\omega^2}{g\pi}.$$

The stress, s, per unit of area of the rim cross-section is $s = \dfrac{P}{a}$, in which a is the area of the cross-section. Therefore

$$s = \frac{W}{g} \times \frac{r}{\pi} \times \frac{\omega^2}{a} = \frac{\pi r a k}{g} \times \frac{r}{\pi} \times \frac{\omega^2}{a} = \frac{kr^2\omega^2}{g},$$

in which k is the weight of the material per unit volume. Or, since the velocity, v, of the mid-points of the rim is equal to ωr, the expression for s may be written in the form

$$s = \frac{kv^2}{g}.$$

The units in which s is expressed are pounds per square foot if k is expressed in pounds per cubic foot, r in feet, g in feet per second per second, and ω in radians per second. It will be noted, therefore, that the intensity of stress, s, developed in the rim of a rotating wheel, if the rim is thin and the effect of the spokes is neglected, varies directly as the square of the linear speed of the rim.

Problem 636.—Superelevation of Railroad Track.—When a locomotive or car travels around a curve on a *level* track a horizontal force (called flange pressure) is exerted on the wheels by the rails. Let it be required to find the distance (called superelevation) that the outer rail must be raised above the inner rail to reduce the flange pressure to zero. This superelevation may be expressed in terms of the speed of the car, the radius of the curve, and the distance between the rails.

Solution.—In Fig. 402, the pressures of the rails are R_1 and R_2, θ being such an angle that the flange pressure is zero when the car is moving with a certain speed v. The resultant of R_1 and R_2 will be denoted by R. W is the weight of the car, and r is the radius of the curve around which the car is traveling. Since the mass-center of the car travels in a horizontal plane, the inertia force $Mr\omega^2$ is horizontal and its action line passes through the center of gravity, G, of the car, as shown. Since the inertia force is in equilibrium with the external forces, the three forces W, $Mr\omega^2$, and R form a concurrent system in equilibrium. Therefore, we may write:

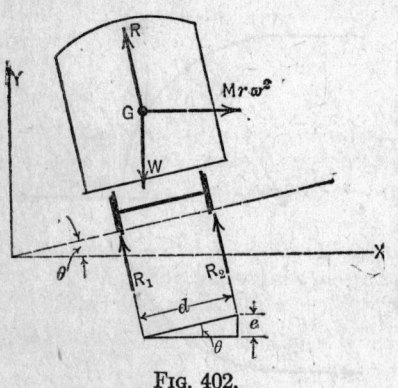

$$\Sigma F_x = 0, \quad \text{or} \quad R \sin \theta = \frac{W}{g}\frac{v^2}{r},$$

$$\Sigma F_y = 0, \quad \text{or} \quad R \cos \theta = W.$$

Fig. 402.

And, by dividing the first of these equations by the second, the resulting equation is $\tan \theta = \frac{v^2}{gr}$. Now for small angles the sine and the tangent of the angle are approximately the same. But from Fig. 402, $\sin \theta = \frac{e}{d}$, in which d is the distance between the action lines of the rail pressures (usually taken as 4.9 ft.). Therefore $\tan \theta = \frac{e}{d} = \frac{v^2}{gr}$. Hence, if v is expressed in feet per second, g in feet per second per second, and d and r in feet, the superelevation (in feet) is found from the equation

$$e = \frac{v^2 d}{gr}.$$

In order to indicate common values of the superelevation, the values used on one particular steam railroad are given in the following table:

SUPERELEVATION OF OUTER RAIL IN INCHES

Degree* of Curve	Speed in Miles per Hour			
	30	45	60	75
1	$\tfrac{3}{8}$	$1\tfrac{1}{8}$	2	$3\tfrac{1}{8}$
2	$\tfrac{7}{8}$	$2\tfrac{1}{8}$	4	$6\tfrac{1}{2}$
3	$1\tfrac{1}{4}$	$3\tfrac{1}{8}$	6	$9\tfrac{3}{4}$
4	$1\tfrac{5}{8}$	$4\tfrac{1}{4}$	8	
5	2	$5\tfrac{1}{4}$		

* A one-degree curve is a curve (circle) in which a 100-ft. chord is subtended by a central angle of one degree. In a two-degree curve a chord of 100 ft. is subtended by a central angle of two degrees, and so on.

PROBLEMS

637. A common rule limits the peripheral speed of cast-iron flywheels or pulleys to 6000 ft./min. (Sometimes stated 1 mi./min.) Calculate the tensile unit-stress in the rim corresponding to this speed, assuming that the effect of the spokes may be neglected. Assume the weight of cast iron to be 450 lb./cu. ft.
Ans. 970 lb./sq. in.

638. Calculate the greatest number of revolutions per minute at which a thin cast-iron hoop 4 ft. in diameter can rotate without bursting. Assume that the maximum tensile strength of the cast iron is 20,000 lb./sq. in. and that the material weighs 450 lb./cu. ft.

639. The radius of a railroad curve is 1800 ft. What must be the superelevation of the outer rail in order to make the flange pressure zero when the speed of a car around the curve is 50 mi./hr.? *Ans.* $e = 5.45$ in.

640. Do the superelevations given in the table in Prob. 636 reduce the flange pressure to zero for the speeds specified? Test several values.

641. A small body is placed on a rough horizontal disk which rotates about a vertical axis. If the distance of the body from the axis is 9 in. and the coefficient of friction between the body and disk is $\tfrac{2}{3}$, find (1) the greatest angular velocity and (2) the greatest angular acceleration the disk can have without causing the body to slide. *Ans.* $\omega = 5.35$ rad./sec.; $\alpha = 28.6$ rad./sec.^{2}

642. A homogeneous thin circular disk having a weight of 64 lb. and a diameter of 4 ft. rotates about a horizontal shaft, perpendicular to the disk and passing through its center, with a constant angular velocity of 10 rad./sec. A small weight of 8 lb. is rigidly attached to the disk at a distance of 1 ft. from the center. When the weight is vertically above the shaft, find the force exerted by the shaft on the disk.

643. The bar AC (Fig. 403) together with the frame to which it is pinned rotates with a constant angular velocity of 30 r.p.m. about the vertical axis YY. The weight of AC is 16.1 lb. and the weight of CD may be neglected. Find the stress in CD and the horizontal component of the pressure of the pin at B on the bar AC.
Ans. $CD = 4.65$ lb.; $B_x = 13.15$ lb.

644. A uniform bar AB (Fig. 404) of length l and mass M rotates about a vertical axis YY with a constant angular velocity, ω. The inertia force for any element of mass dM is $dMx\omega^2$ as indicated. Find the magnitude and line of action

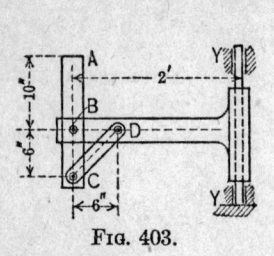

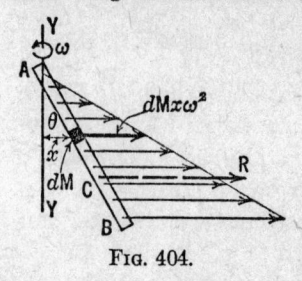

FIG. 403.   FIG. 404.

of the inertia force R for the bar in terms of M, l, θ, and ω. Find also the horizontal and vertical components of the reaction of the axis on the bar.

$$Ans. \quad R = \tfrac{1}{2}Ml\omega^2 \sin \theta; \quad AC = \tfrac{2}{3}l;$$
$$A_x = -\tfrac{1}{2}Ml\omega^2 \sin \theta; \quad A_y = Mg.$$

645. A homogeneous door of constant thickness is 8 ft. high and 4 ft. wide. The door swings on two hinges which are placed at the ends of a vertical edge. When the door swings with a certain constant angular velocity the horizontal component of the reaction at the lower hinge is zero. Find this velocity.

$$Ans. \quad \omega = 2.83 \text{ rad./sec.}$$

646. A disk rotates in a horizontal plane about a vertical axis through its center with a constant angular velocity of 60 r.p.m. A vertical bar which weighs 20 lb. and is 3 ft. long is pivoted at its lower end to the disk at a point 3 ft. from the axis of rotation of the disk. The bar is prevented from rotating about its lower end by a cord which is attached to the upper end of the bar and to the center of rotation of the disk. Find the tension in the cord.

647. A uniform slender rod that is 6 ft. long and weighs 20 lb. is suspended from a horizontal axis at one end and is acted on by a horizontal force of 20 lb. at its midpoint. Determine (a) the resulting angular acceleration, (b) the resulting linear acceleration of the mass-center, and (c) the horizontal reaction of the axis on the rod.

$$Ans. \quad (a) \ 8.05 \text{ rad./sec.}^2; \ (b) \ 24.15 \text{ ft./sec.}^2; \ (c) \ 5 \text{ lb.}$$

648. A door of constant cross-section is 3 ft. wide and weighs 32.2 lb./ft. of width. It swings on its hinges so that its outer edge has a speed of 8 ft./sec. Find the force applied perpendicularly to the door at the outer edge to bring it to rest in a distance of 1 ft. What is the horizontal reaction of the hinges perpendicular to the door while the force is acting?

649. A flywheel used on a punching machine is 8 ft. in diameter and has a rim which weighs 1 ton. Each operation of punching a hole causes the speed of the flywheel to decrease uniformly from 100 r.p.m. to 80 r.p.m. The flywheel has 6 spokes, each 3.5 ft. long. If the time of punching a hole is 0.5 sec., what moment is transmitted from the rim to the hub by each spoke? Assume that the thickness of the rim is small in comparison with the radius of the flywheel and neglect the weight of the hub and spokes.

$$Ans. \quad 607 \text{ lb.-ft.}$$

113. Center of Percussion.

The point P (Fig. 405) on the n-axis, through which the resultant of the effective forces for a rotating rigid

CENTER OF PERCUSSION

body acts, is called the *center of percussion* of the body with respect to the given axis of rotation. Hence, the center of percussion is a point on a line joining the center of rotation and the mass-center, at a distance q from the center of rotation, such that $q = \dfrac{k_o^2}{\bar{r}}$, in which k_o is the radius of gyration of the body about the axis of rotation and $\bar{r}$ is the distance from the axis of rotation to the mass-center of the body.

The physical significance of the center of percussion is suggested in the following illustration. Let a bar (Fig. 405) of weight W be free to rotate about a horizontal axis when a horizontal force, F, is suddenly applied to it. If the force, F, is applied above the center of percussion,

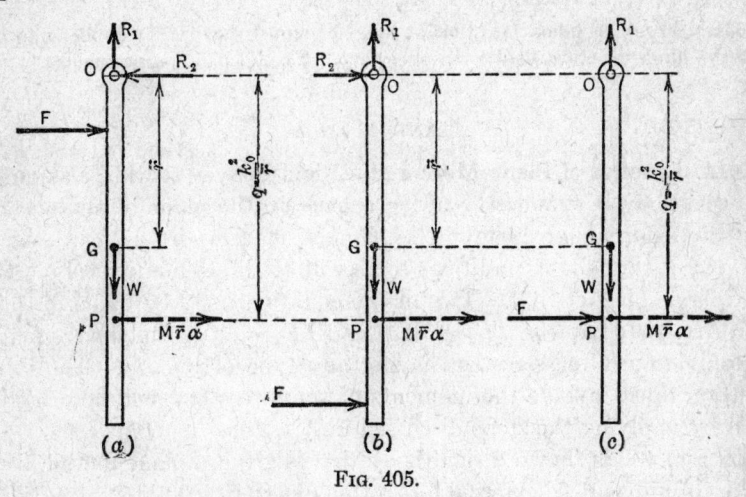

FIG. 405.

as shown in Fig. 405(a), the horizontal reaction, R_2, of the axis of rotation acts towards the left and becomes larger as the force F is applied closer to the axis of rotation. If the bar is struck below the center of percussion, the reaction R_2 acts towards the right, as shown in Fig. 405(b). And if the bar is struck so that the center of percussion is on the action line of the force, as in Fig. 405(c), the horizontal reaction at O is zero, since the action line at F is collinear with the action line of the tangential component, $M\bar{r}\alpha$, of the resultant of the effective forces. It will be noted that the resultant of F and R_2, in each case, is collinear with $M\bar{r}\alpha$, since the component of the resultant of the external forces in any direction is identical with the component of the resultant of the effective forces in the same direction, that is, if $M\bar{r}\alpha$ were reversed and applied to the body as an external force, it would hold F and R_2 in equilibrium.

An excellent illustration of the effect of varying the position of the force F as above discussed is found in batting a baseball. If the ball strikes the bat at the center of percussion (about three-fourths the length of the bat from the end, assuming the axis of rotation at the hands) no reaction perpendicular to the bat is experienced by the batter. If, however, the ball strikes the bat near the end or near the hands, the batter experiences a painful stinging of the hands as a result of the reaction perpendicular to the bat.

PROBLEMS

650. In Prob. 647, at what distance from the axis must the force be applied to cause the horizontal reaction of the axis to be zero? *Ans.* $q = 4$ ft.

651. In Prob. 648, how far from the hinge line must the force be applied in order that the hinge reaction shall have no horizontal component perpendicular to the door?

Plane Motion

114. Kinetics of Plane Motion of a Rigid Body.—It will be assumed that the body is symmetrical with respect to the plane of motion and that the external forces lie in the plane of motion (see note at end of Art. 108). For these conditions there will be three equations of motion as explained in Art. 100. Two of the equations may be taken directly from Art. 109; namely, $\Sigma F_x = M\bar{a}_x$ and $\Sigma F_y = M\bar{a}_y$ which were found to apply to any mass-system having any type of motion. The third equation must involve the moments of the forces and will here be derived by applying the steps discussed in Art. 108.

In Fig. 406 is shown a rigid body that is given a plane motion by a system of unbalanced external forces that act on it. At any instant, the body has an angular velocity ω and an angular acceleration, α. Since the body is rigid the particles of which the body is composed all have the same angular velocity ω and the same angular acceleration α about any axis perpendicular to the plane of motion. The linear velocity and linear acceleration of any particle, however, vary with the position of the particle in the body.

As shown in Art. 96, a plane motion of a rigid body may be considered, at any instant, as a combination of a pure rotation about an axis perpendicular to the plane of motion of the body through any point, O, in the plane of motion, which gives to the body the same angular velocity ω and angular acceleration α that the body has at the instant, and a translation of the body which gives to each particle the same linear velocity and acceleration that the point O has at the instant. Thus the motion of any particle of the body is made up of two component motions, (1) a rotation about O and (2) a motion identical with that of O. Hence,

PLANE MOTION

the acceleration of any particle at a distance, r, from O has a normal component, $a_n = r\omega^2$, and a tangential component, $a_t = r\alpha$, due to the rotation of the body about O, and also an acceleration, a_o, the same as that of O, due to the translation of the body. If now each of these components of the acceleration of the particle is multiplied by the mass of the particle, the components of the effective force for the particle are obtained. These components of the resultant of all the forces acting on

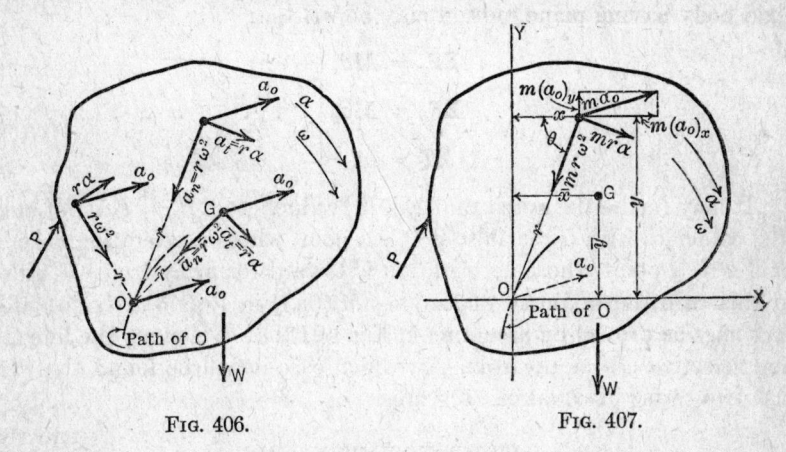

FIG. 406. FIG. 407.

the particle (effective force) are shown in Fig. 407. For convenience ma_o will be resolved into its two components $m(a_o)_x$ and $m(a_o)_y$ as shown in Fig. 407.

The algebraic sum of the moments of the effective forces about O

$$= \Sigma mr\alpha \cdot r + \Sigma m(a_o)_x y - \Sigma m(a_o)_y x$$
$$= \alpha \Sigma mr^2 + (a_o)_x \Sigma my - (a_o)_y \Sigma mx$$
$$= I_o\alpha + M\bar{y}(a_o)_x - M\bar{x}(a_o)_y. \quad \ldots \ldots \quad (1)$$

But the algebraic sum of the moments of the effective forces for all of the particles can also be expressed in terms of the actual forces which include all of the external forces and all of the internal forces (actions and reactions between the particles). Hence

$$(\Sigma T_o)_{\text{external}} + (\Sigma T_o)_{\text{internal}} = I_o\alpha + M\bar{y}(a_o)_x - M\bar{x}(a_o)_y \quad . . \quad (2)$$

But according to Newton's third law, the internal forces occur in pairs of equal, opposite, and collinear forces and hence $(\Sigma T_o)_{\text{internal}} = 0$. Therefore if ΣT_o refers to external forces only, the above equation becomes

$$\Sigma T_o = I_o\alpha + M\bar{y}(a_o)_x - M\bar{x}(a_o)_y \quad \ldots \ldots \quad (3)$$

As already noted, the center, O, about which the assumed rotation takes place and about which the moments of the forces are taken may be any point in the plane of motion of the body. Thus, if the mass-center is selected for the center about which moments are taken, that is, if O coincides with G (Fig. 407), then, in Eq. (3), $\bar{x}$ and $\bar{y}$ are zero; a_o becomes $\bar{a}$; I_o becomes $\bar{I}$; and ΣT_o becomes $\Sigma \bar{T}$. Hence the right-hand member of Eq. (3) reduces to one term, $\bar{I}\alpha$. Thus the equations of motion for a rigid body having plane motion may be written:

$$\left. \begin{array}{l} \Sigma F_x = M\bar{a}_x \\ \Sigma F_y = M\bar{a}_y \\ \Sigma \bar{T} = \bar{I}\alpha \end{array} \right\} \quad \ldots \ldots \ldots \quad (4)$$

It may further be noted that Eq. (3) reduces to $\Sigma T_o = I_o \alpha$, not only if O coincides with G, but also if O is a point whose acceleration is zero, or if O is a point whose acceleration is toward (or away from) G, since in this case the quantity $M\bar{y}(a_o)_x - M\bar{x}(a_o)_y$ in Eq. (3) is zero; this fact may be proved by assuming in Fig. 407 that a_o is along the line OG and selecting OG as the x-axis, in which case it will be found that the last two terms in equation (3) vanish.

ILLUSTRATIVE PROBLEMS

Problem 652.—A homogeneous cylinder which is 3 ft. in diameter and which weighs 805 lb. rolls, without slipping, down an inclined plane that makes an angle of 30° with the horizontal (Fig. 408). The mass-center of the cylinder has an initial velocity $\bar{v}_0 = 50$ ft./sec. Find (1) the acceleration of the mass-center, (2) the magnitude of the friction force, and (3) the velocity, $\bar{v}$, of the mass-center at the end of 10 sec.

Solution.—The cylinder has plane motion under the action of three forces, F, N, and W, as shown in Fig. 408. Let the x- and y-axes be chosen as shown in the figure. The equations of motion are,

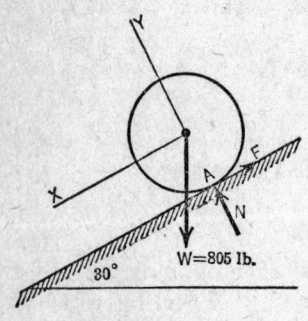

Fig. 408.

$\Sigma F_x = M\bar{a}_x$ . . . (1), $\quad \Sigma F_y = M\bar{a}_y$ . . . (2), $\quad \Sigma \bar{T} = \bar{I}\alpha$ . . . (3)

From (1),
$$805 \sin 30° - F = \frac{805}{32.2} \bar{a}_x. \quad \ldots \ldots \ldots \quad (4)$$

From (2),
$$-805 \cos 30° + N = 0, \text{ since } \bar{a}_y = 0. \quad \ldots \ldots \quad (5)$$

From (3),
$$\frac{3}{2} F = \frac{1}{2} \times \frac{805}{32.2} \left(\frac{3}{2}\right)^2 \alpha. \quad \ldots \ldots \quad (6)$$

ILLUSTRATIVE PROBLEMS

Four unknown quantities are involved in these three equations and hence another equation is needed. From the kinematics of the problem (see Prob. 537), we obtain the equation

$$\bar{a}_x = \bar{a} = r\alpha = \tfrac{3}{2}\alpha. \quad \ldots \ldots \ldots \quad (7)$$

By substituting the value of α from (7) in (6) and solving for F, we obtain the equation

$$F = \frac{25}{2}\bar{a}.$$

Substituting this value of F in (4), we obtain

$$\bar{a}_x = \bar{a} = 10.73 \text{ ft./sec.}^2 \quad \therefore F = \frac{25}{2} \times 10.73 = 134.1 \text{ lb.}$$

Since the mass-center moves with uniformly accelerated rectilinear motion, we may use the equation

$$\bar{v} = \bar{v}_o + \bar{a}t,$$

Hence

$$\bar{v} = 50 + 10.73 \times 10 = 157.3 \text{ ft./sec.}$$

Problem 653.—At what height, h, should the cushion on a billiard table (Fig. 409a) be placed so that the billiard ball on rebounding from the cushion will start off without causing any friction on the table? *Ans.* $h = \tfrac{7}{5}r$.

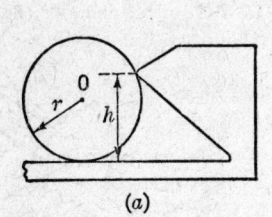

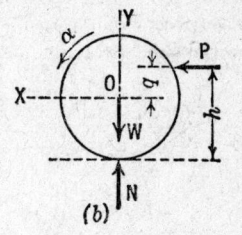

FIG. 409.

Solution.—The free-body diagram for the ball for the conditions of motion imposed in the problem is shown in Fig. 409(b). The ball has plane motion; hence the equations of motion are

$$\Sigma F_x = M\bar{a}_x \ldots (1), \quad \Sigma F_y = M\bar{a}_y \ldots (2), \quad \Sigma \overline{T} = \overline{I}\alpha. \ldots (3)$$

Applying these equations in the order stated, we have

$$P = \frac{W}{g}\bar{a}_x \qquad N - W = 0 \qquad Pq = \frac{2}{5}\frac{W}{g}r^2\alpha = \frac{2}{5}\frac{W}{g}r^2\frac{\bar{a}_x}{r}$$

From the first and third of these equations, we obtain the following equation

$$\frac{W}{g}\bar{a}_x q = \frac{2}{5}\frac{W}{g}r\bar{a}_x$$

Hence

$$q = \tfrac{2}{5}r \quad \text{and} \quad h = \tfrac{7}{5}r.$$

If the cushion is placed higher than this value of h, the friction of the table on the ball will be to the left in Fig. 409(b), and if it is placed lower the friction will be to the right.

PROBLEMS

654. A homogeneous solid sphere rolls without slipping down a rough plane which is inclined at an angle θ with the horizontal. Show that the acceleration of the center of the sphere is $5/7\, g \sin \theta$, and that the ratio of the friction to the normal pressure must be not less than $2/7 \tan \theta$ to prevent the sphere from slipping.

655. A hollow cylinder weighing 32 lb. rolls, without slipping, on a horizontal plane when acted on by a horizontal force of 16 lb. whose action line passes through the mass-center of the cylinder and is perpendicular to its axis. If the acceleration of the mass-center is 9 ft./sec.^{2}, find, in terms of the outer radius r, the radius of gyration of the cylinder with respect to its axis. Also find the frictional force developed.

656. A homogeneous cylinder is placed on the horizontal floor of a car so that it is free to roll in the direction of the track. The friction is sufficient to prevent slipping. If the car is given an acceleration of 3 ft./sec.^{2} in the direction of the track, what will be the acceleration of the center of the cylinder relative to the track?

Ans. $a = 1$ ft./sec.^{2}

657. A homogeneous cylinder weighing W lb. and having a radius of r ft. rolls, without slipping, on a horizontal surface when acted on by a horizontal force of $\tfrac{1}{2}W$ lb. whose action line is $\tfrac{1}{2}r$ ft. above the surface, as shown in Fig. 410; the force is exerted by a string wrapped around a groove in the central plane of the cylinder. Find the acceleration of the mass-center of the cylinder.

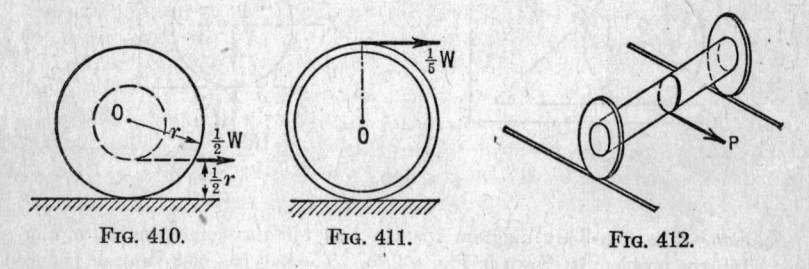

FIG. 410.   FIG. 411.   FIG. 412.

658. A thin cylinder whose thickness may be neglected weighs W lb. It rolls, without slipping, on a horizontal surface when acted on by a horizontal force of $\tfrac{1}{5}W$ lb. applied to the top, as shown in Fig. 411. Find the acceleration of the center of the cylinder, and the frictional force between the cylinder and plane.

Ans. $a = 6.44$ ft./sec.^{2}; $F = 0$.

659. A homogeneous sphere rolls down a plane inclined at an angle θ with the horizontal. If the coefficient of friction for the sphere and plane is $1/7$, what is the maximum value of θ that will allow the sphere to roll without slipping?

660. Two solid cylindrical disks are keyed to an axle as shown in Fig. 412. A string is wrapped around the axle in its central plane, and a force, P, is exerted by the string in a direction parallel to the plane on which the disks roll and tangent to the under surface of the axle. Each disk weighs 20 lb. and is 2 ft. in diameter. The axle is 6 in. in diameter and weighs 40 lb. The magnitude of the force P is 8 lb. Will the disks and axle roll forward or backward? Find the acceleration of the central axis of the disks and axle. *Ans.* $a = 1.91$ ft./sec.^{2}

PROBLEMS   269

661. If the string in the preceding problem is wrapped around the axle in the opposite direction so that the force P is tangent to the top of the axle, what is the acceleration of the central axis of the disks and axle?

662. A homogeneous sphere having a weight of 100 lb. and a radius of r ft. is placed on a horizontal surface. A horizontal force of 20 lb. is applied to the sphere, the action line of the force being $\frac{1}{2}r$ ft. from the surface. The coefficient of friction for the sphere and surface is $\frac{1}{10}$. (a) Find the linear acceleration of the center of the sphere. (b) Find the angular acceleration of the sphere. (c) What type of motion does the sphere have?   Ans. $a = 3.22$ ft./sec.^{2}; $\alpha = 0$; Translation.

663. A homogeneous sphere and a homogeneous cylinder start from rest at the top of an inclined plane and roll without slipping to the bottom of the plane. Which will reach the bottom in the shorter time?

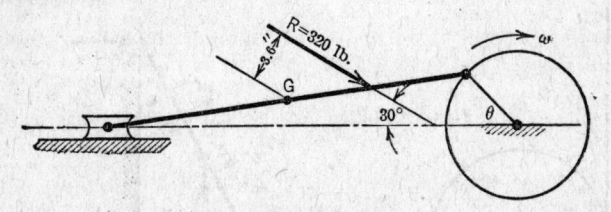

FIG. 413.

664. The resultant, R, of all forces acting on the connecting rod (Fig. 413) is 320 lb. and its action line is located as shown. If the connecting rod is 30 in. long and weighs 80 lb., what is the linear acceleration of the mass-center of the rod and the angular acceleration of the rod, assuming the rod to be of constant cross-section?
    Ans. $\bar{a} = 129$ ft./sec.^{2}; $\alpha = 74.2$ rad./sec.^{2}

665. A solid sphere having a radius of 8 in. and a weight of 161 lb. is made to roll up a rough inclined plane (Fig. 414) by means of a flexible cord, one end of which is attached to an axis through the center of the sphere. The cord passes over a smooth peg and has attached to its other end a suspended body B which weighs 100 lb. Find the acceleration of the body B and the tension in the cord.

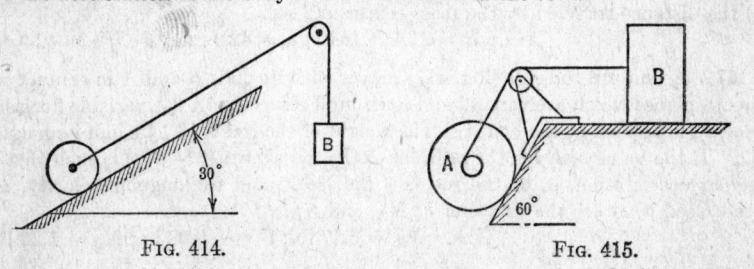

FIG. 414.   FIG. 415.

666. In Fig. 415, A is a body consisting of two cylindrical disks having a radius of 8 in. connected by an axle having a radius of 2 in. (similar to the arrangement in Fig. 412). The weight of A is 40 lb. and the radius of gyration about the axis of the axle is 5 in. A cord wrapped around the axle passes over a smooth, weightless pulley and is attached to a body B that weighs 60 lb. The coefficient of friction between B and the horizontal plane is 0.2. If A rolls, without slipping, down the inclined plane, find the tension in the cord and the acceleration of B.
    Ans. $T = 21.86$ lb.; $a = 5.29$ ft./sec.^{2}

FORCE, MASS, AND ACCELERATION

667. A plane 12 ft. square with two of its sides horizontal makes an angle of 30° with the horizontal. A homogeneous cylinder rolls, without slipping, along one of the diagonals. If the cylinder starts from rest at the upper corner what will be the velocity of its mass-center when it reaches the lower corner?

668. A homogeneous sphere rolls down a plane that makes an angle of 45° with the horizontal. If the coefficient of friction between the sphere and plane is 0.2 will the sphere roll without slipping? *Ans.* No.

669. A homogeneous sphere having a weight of 64 lb. and a radius of 1 ft. rolls, without slipping, on a smooth horizontal plane when acted on by a horizontal force of 16 lb. Find the distance from the plane to the action line of the force.

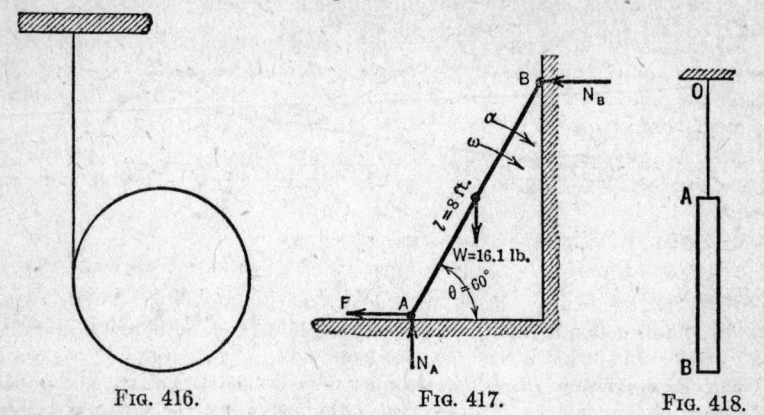

FIG. 416.   FIG. 417.   FIG. 418.

670. A homogeneous cylinder 1 ft. in diameter has a flexible cord wrapped around its central plane. One end of the cord is attached to a fixed plane as shown in Fig. 416. The cord is taut when the cylinder is allowed to fall. Find (a) the acceleration of the mass-center, (b) the angular acceleration of the cylinder, and (c) the distance traveled by the mass-center in 2 sec.

Ans. $\bar{a} = 21.4$ ft./sec.^{2}; $\alpha = 42.9$ rad./sec.^{2}; $s = 42.9$ ft.

671. A uniform rod AB (Fig. 417) moves with its ends B and A in contact with smooth planes which are vertical and horizontal respectively. A variable horizontal force, F, is applied at the end A. The weight of the rod is 16.1 lb. and its length is 8 ft. If the value of F for the position of the rod shown ($\theta = 60°$) is such that the angular acceleration, α, of the rod is 3 rad./sec.^{2}, and the angular velocity, ω, is 2 rad./sec., what are the values of F, N_A, and N_B?

Ans. $N_A = 6.17$ lb.; $F = -0.03$ lb.; $N_B = 1.22$ lb.

672. In Fig. 418, AB is a uniform slender rod 3 ft. long that is suspended from O by a flexible cord OA 2 ft. long. The weight of the bar is 16.1 lb. When a horizontal force P is applied to the bar the initial linear acceleration of the mass-center is 8 ft./sec.^{2} horizontally to the right and the angular acceleration is 4 rad./sec.^{2} counter-clockwise. Find the magnitude, line of action, and sense of P.

Ans. $P = 4$ lb. to right and 1.875 ft. below A.

REVIEW QUESTIONS AND PROBLEMS

673. Complete the following statement: The equations of motion for a body are the equations expressing the relations between the following three factors or quantities:

674. Define: (a) weight of a body, (b) mass of a body.

675. Is the following definition correct? The engineer's unit of mass, called a slug, is the mass of a body that is given an acceleration of 1 ft./sec.^{2} by a 1-lb. force.

676. What is the weight of a body having a mass of 1 slug? How many units of mass (slugs) in a body weighing W lb.?

677. State Newton's second law of motion.

When attempting to compare the weights of two small bodies (pebbles, say) a person instinctively jounces or shakes the bodies in his hands. Why does this enable the person to obtain a better estimate of the relative weights than he could by merely supporting the bodies in his hands?

678. In analyzing the motion of a body by use of Newton's laws of motion, why is the body considered to be made up of particles? Define effective force for a particle.

679. State Newton's third law of motion.

Let A and B be two bodies between which there are mutual actions; if A is a freely falling body and its weight is one of the two (mutual) actions, what body is B?

680. Explain briefly the four steps followed in obtaining the equations of motion for a body.

681. Point out and correct the error in the following statement: The principle of motion of the mass-center states that if the resultant of all the external forces acting on any body is a force, its magnitude is equal to the product of the mass of the body and the acceleration of the mass-center, $\bar{a}$, of the body, and it acts through the mass-center in the direction of $\bar{a}$.

682. Write the three equations of motion for a rigid body having each of the following types of motion: (a) translation, (b) rotation about an axis not passing through the mass-center, and (c) plane motion.

683. (a) State D'Alembert's principle. (b) Define inertia force for a body. (c) Explain the inertia-force method of solving kinetics problems. (d) What is meant by the term "centrifugal force"; is it an actual force exerted by one body on another body?

684. Specify the magnitude, sense, and action line of the inertia force for a translating rigid body of mass M having an acceleration a.

685. If a rigid body rotates about a fixed axis with an angular acceleration, under what conditions will the resultant of the external forces acting on the body be (a) a force, (b) a couple?

686. Prove that the resultant of the effective forces (and hence also of the external forces) for a rigid body rotating about a fixed axis not through the mass-center intersects the line connecting the mass-center and center of rotation at a distance $\dfrac{k_o^2}{\bar{r}}$ from the axis of rotation.

687. A rigid body of mass M is given a plane motion by an unbalanced force system, the acceleration of the mass-center being denoted by $\bar{a}$. What are the magnitude and direction of the resultant of the external forces acting on the body? Does this force act through the mass-center?

688. A rigid body has plane motion: (*a*) If the acceleration, $\bar{a}$, of the mass-center is zero and the angular acceleration, α, of the body is not zero, what can be said about the resultant of the forces acting on the body?   (*b*) If α is zero and $\bar{a}$ is not zero, what can be said?

689. Steam is shut off when a train running at a speed of 30 mi./hr. reaches a 0.4 per cent down-grade. What will be the velocity of the train after 100 sec. if the train resistance is 10 lb./ton?   *Ans.* $v = 27.8$ mi./hr.

690. A man weighing 150 lb. leaves his room by way of a window which is 50 ft. above the ground. He has a rope that is long enough to reach to the ground but it can support a force only of 125 lb. What is the least velocity with which he can reach the ground?   *Ans.* $v = 23.2$ ft./sec.

691. Two strings pass over a smooth cylindrical fixed drum whose axis is horizontal. On one side of the drum the strings are attached to a 50-lb. weight; on the other side one string is attached to a 40-lb. weight and the other string to a 30-lb. weight. Find the acceleration of the weights and the tension in each of the strings during motion.   *Ans.* $T_{30} = 25$ lb.; $T_{40} = 33.3$ lb.; $a = 5.37$ ft./sec.^{2}

692. A door is hung on a track as shown in Fig. 419. The coefficient of friction for each of the shoes (*A* and *B*) and the track is ¼. The door weighs 300 lb. What force *P* is required to give the door an acceleration of 4 ft./sec.^{2}? Find the vertical reactions of the shoes on the track.

Ans. $P = 112$ lb.; $R_A = 43.9$ lb.; $R_B = 256$ lb.

FIG. 419.   FIG. 420.

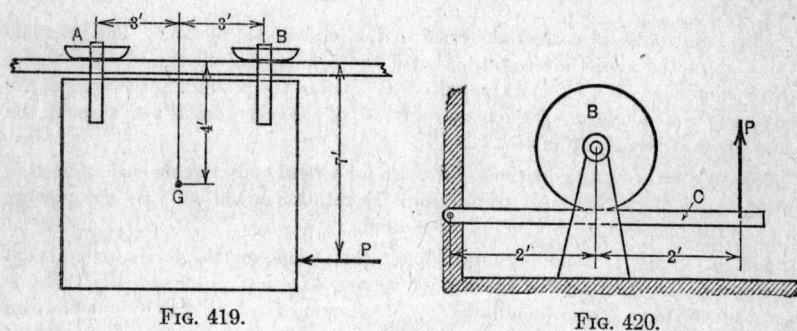

693. The drum *B* (Fig. 420) is rotating with an angular velocity $\omega = 120$ r.p.m. when the brake *C* is applied. The drum is a solid cylinder and has a radius of 10 in. Its weight is 2000 lb. If the coefficient of brake friction is 0.2, what force, *P*, is required to reduce the angular velocity of the drum to 30 r.p.m. in 3 sec.? Neglect axle friction. Find also the horizontal and vertical components of the reaction of the axle on the drum.   *Ans.* $P = 203$ lb.

694. A flat-topped boat having a weight of 300 lb. and a length of 12 ft. is resting in still water. A man weighing 150 lb. stands at one end of the boat. The man starts to run with a speed increasing at the rate of 10 ft./sec. each second. When he reaches the other end of the boat he jumps. Assuming that the water is a perfect (frictionless) fluid, what is the acceleration of the mass-center of the boat and man (considered as one body) before the man starts to run? While he is running on the boat? After he jumps from the boat but before he strikes the water? What is the acceleration of the boat while the man is running on it?

695. Two spheres A and B (Fig. 421) connected by a light slender rod revolve in a horizontal plane about an axle fixed in the top of a vertical post which supports the two bodies. A weighs 4 lb. and B weighs 12 lb. The spheres rotate with an angular velocity of 80 r.p.m. What horizontal force acts on the post tending to bend the post? The mass of the rod may be neglected. Solve by considering A, B, and the rod as a single mass-system. *Ans.* $R = 14.5$ lb.

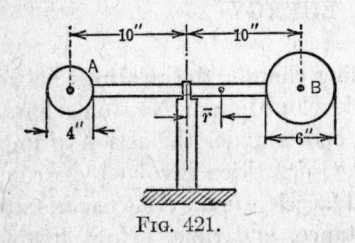

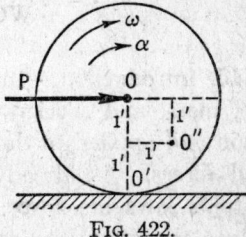

Fig. 421.   Fig. 422.

696. A circular disk (Fig. 422) weighs 100 lb. and is 4 ft. in diameter. The disk rolls to the right on a straight horizontal track. The angular velocity of the disk is 2 rad./sec. and the angular acceleration is 4 rad./sec.^{2} Find the horizontal force P required to produce this motion. Solve in three ways, using the points O, O', and O'' as moment-centers in the moment equation. The acceleration of O' is toward the mass-center and the acceleration of O'' is zero. *Ans.* $P = 37.3$ lb.

697. A solid wooden disk 10 ft. in diameter rotates in a horizontal plane about its geometric axis. Two small bodies each weighing 50 lb. are attached to the disk at a radius of 4 ft. from the axis of rotation so that the radii make an angle of 90°. If the disk rotates at 40 r.p.m. what is the resultant horizontal pull on the axis? Solve by two methods. *Ans.* 154 lb.

698. In Fig. 423, A represents a frame which revolves about a vertical axis at a constant angular velocity $\omega = 40$ r.p.m. A bar, B, is attached to the frame at E by means of a smooth pin. At the end of B a spherical ball, C, is fastened. B weighs 20 lb. and is 16 in. long. C weighs 8 lb. and is 4 in. in diameter. Find the reaction of the pin at E and of the frame at F, on the bar.

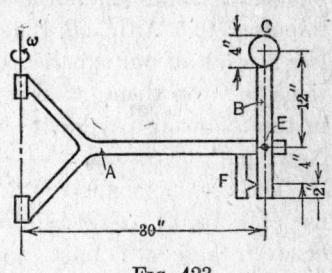

Fig. 423.

Ans. $E = 89.0$ lb., $\theta_x = 161° 40'$; $F = 46.3$.

CHAPTER IX

WORK AND ENERGY

115. Introduction.—In the preceding chapter the relations between force, mass, and acceleration were developed from Newton's laws of motion and applied to the motion of bodies under the action of unbalanced forces. As already noted, the quantities involved *directly* in Newton's laws are force, mass, and acceleration. But, acceleration involves the quantities velocity, distance, and time. Now, in many problems in engineering, it is convenient to use certain other quantities, the more important of which are: work, power, energy, impulse, and momentum. The expression for each of these quantities is a combination of some of the six quantities (force, mass, acceleration, velocity, distance, and time) which are involved in Newton's laws of motion. Thus, force and distance combine to measure work; force, distance, and time combine to measure power; mass and velocity combine to measure momentum and kinetic energy; force and time combine to measure impulse, etc. Although the conceptions of these quantities are more or less a result of our experience with physical phenomena, the exact relations between them, as expressed in certain principles to be developed in the following pages, are based on the definite fundamental laws of Newton.

The present chapter is devoted to a discussion of the meaning and use of work, of energy, and of certain principles that express relations between these two quantities. Although no fundamental physical laws other than those of Newton are used in developing the principles of work and energy, nevertheless, the method of analysis which makes use of work and energy, possesses certain advantages over the method which makes use directly of force, mass, and acceleration, even in certain types of problems which involve only rigid bodies having rather simple types of motion such as translation, rotation, and plane motion. And, in dealing with non-rigid bodies having unordered motion, that is, motion in which the particles of the mass system (body) do not follow definite known paths, the principles of energy are of particular importance. In fact, the study of the behavior of non-rigid bodies in general, such as water, steam, gas, and air is largely based on the principles of energy and, hence, these principles play an important part in hydraulics, thermodynamics, etc.

§ 1. WORK AND POWER

116. Work Defined.—A force does work on a body if the body on which the force acts moves so that the displacement of the point of application of the force has a component in the direction of the force. The amount of work done by a constant force whose point of application has a rectilinear displacement is the product of the force and the component of the displacement of its application point in the direction of the force. The work may also be expressed as the product of the component of the force in the direction of the displacement of its application point and the displacement. The component of the force in the direction of the displacement of its application point is often called the *working component*. And the component of the displacement in the direction of the force is called the *effective displacement*.

117. Algebraic Expressions for Work Done by a Force.—The mathematical expression for the work, w, done by a force, F, in a displacement, s, of its application point depends on the way the force varies during the displacement. Several important special cases are considered here.

I. The force is constant in magnitude and in direction and agrees in direction with the displacement as, for example, the force exerted in lifting a body vertically upward with a uniform acceleration. The amount of work done is

$$w = F \cdot s.$$

II. The force is constant in magnitude and in direction but does not agree in direction with the displacement (Fig. 424). The amount of work done is

$$w = F \cos \theta \cdot s = F_t \cdot s,$$

in which $F \cos \theta$ is denoted by F_t since $F \cos \theta$ is tangent to the path of the point of application.

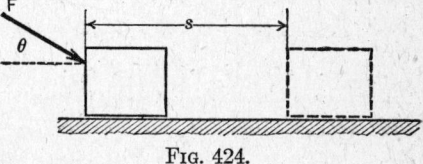

FIG. 424.

III. The force varies in magnitude but not in direction, and the direction agrees with that of the displacement, as, for example, the force exerted in compressing a helical spring or the steam pressure against the piston of a steam engine after cut-off. Thus, in compressing a spring, the force corresponding to any position, s, is F (Fig. 425), and this force may be assumed to remain constant in an infinitesimal displacement, ds. Hence, according to case I, the work done by the force F in the displacement ds is $dw = Fds$, and the total work done on the spring, as F varies from its initial to its final value, is

$$w = \int_{s_1}^{s_2} Fds = F_{av} \cdot \Delta s,$$

where F_{av} is the space-average value of the force in the displacement Δs or $s_2 - s_1$. In order to evaluate the integral by the method of calculus, F must be expressed in terms of s. That is, the manner in which F varies with s must be known.

IV. The force varies in magnitude and in direction, as, for example, the pressure of the connecting rod on the crank pin of an engine (Fig. 426). The expression for the work done by the force is found by the same method as was used in case III except that the tangential component of the force must be used. Hence

$$w = \int_{s_1}^{s_2} F_t ds.$$

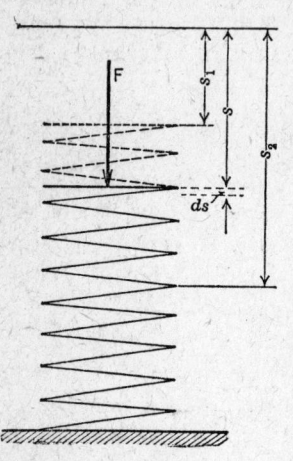

Fig. 425.

This expression applies whether the displacement is along a circular path or not. But when the displacement takes place in a circular

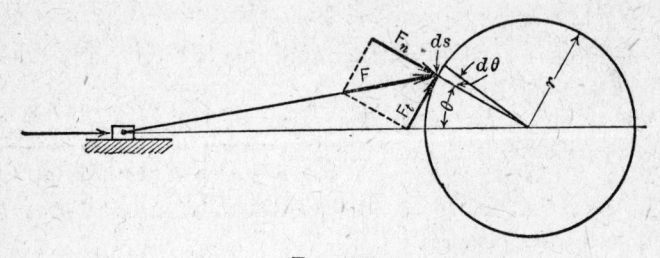

Fig. 426.

path the elemental displacement ds is expressed by the equation $ds = rd\theta$. Whence

$$w = \int_{s_1}^{s_2} F_t ds = \int_{s_1}^{s_2} F_t r d\theta = \int_{\theta_1}^{\theta_2} T d\theta,$$

in which T is the torque or moment of the force about the center of the circular path. And if the torque remains constant during an angular displacement, $\theta = \theta_2 - \theta_1$, then

$$w = T \int_{\theta_1}^{\theta_2} d\theta = T(\theta_2 - \theta_1) = T \cdot \theta.$$

Thus, in one revolution, the work done by the force F having a moment T about the center of the circular path is $w = T \cdot 2\pi$. And if n revolutions occur per unit of time, then the work done per unit of time is $w = T \cdot 2\pi n$.

118. Work Done by a Couple.—In Fig. 427, the couple whose moment is $F \cdot 2r$ turns through an angle $d\theta$ during which displacement the forces F of the couple may be assumed to be constant. The work done by the forces of the couple is $2Fds$ or $2Frd\theta$. But $F \cdot 2r$ is the moment of the couple. Therefore, the work done by the couple in the angular displacement $d\theta$ is the product of the moment, T, of the couple and the angular displacement, $d\theta$, of the couple. Further, if the angular displacement of the couple is $\theta = \theta_2 - \theta_1$, then the work done is

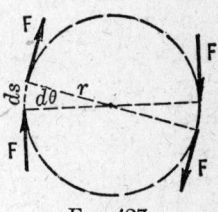

Fig. 427.

$$w = \int_{\theta_1}^{\theta_2} T d\theta.$$

If the moment of the couple remains constant during the angular displacement θ, the work done by the couple is $w = T\theta$.

119. Work a Scalar Quantity. Sign and Units of Work.—Work is a scalar quantity. Thus the work done by one force may be added (algebraically) to the work done by another force regardless of the directions of the forces or of the displacements of their points of application. And the work done on one body of a system may be added (algebraically) to the work done on the other bodies of the system in order to obtain the total work done on the system, regardless of the manner in which the bodies move.

It is convenient to regard the work done by a force as having sign. Work is positive when the working component of the force and the displacement of its application point agree in sense, and work is negative when the working component and the displacement are opposite in sense. Thus, a force which retards the motion of a body does negative work on the body.

The unit of work is the work done by a unit force acting through a unit distance and hence depends on the units used for force and distance.

Thus, the more common units for work in the gravitational (engineer's) system of units are the foot-pound, inch-pound, meter-kilogram, etc. No one-term names are given to the units of work in the gravitational system of units. The common units of work in the absolute system of units are the dyne-centimeter, which is called an erg, and the joule, which is 10^7 ergs. For large units of work the horse-power-hour and the kilowatt-hour are used. For a definition of these units see Art. 122.

120. Graphical Representation and Calculation of Work.—In calculating the work done by a variable force, by the calculus method, the working component, F_t, of the force must be expressed in terms of the displacement s. If it is impossible to express F_t in terms of s, or if, when possible, the expression for F_t is complex and difficult to use, the relation between F_t and s may be expressed graphically by means of a graph or curve, and the work done may be found from the graphical diagram as follows: If values of F_t and s are plotted on a pair of rectangular axes for all positions of the application point of the force F, the curve joining the plotted points is called a tangential-force-space ($F_t - s$) curve (Fig. 428). In most problems, only a sufficient number of values of F_t are plotted to make it possible to draw a reliable F_t–s curve, values of F_t being plotted more frequently when the value of F_t is changing the more rapidly. The work done by a variable force F as shown in Art. 117 is $w = \int_{s_1}^{s_2} F_t ds$. But $F_t ds$ represents an elemental part of the area (Fig. 428) between the F_t–s curve and the s-axis. And the total area under the F_t–s curve between any two ordinates corresponding to abscissas s_1 and s_2 is

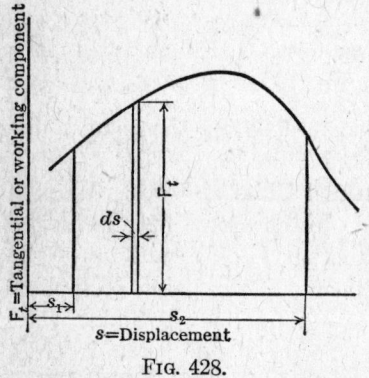

$$\text{area} = \int_{s_1}^{s_2} F_t ds.$$

FIG. 428.

Therefore, the work done by a force in any displacement s is represented by the area under the tangential-force-space curve between the ordinates at s_1 and s_2. This diagram is called a work diagram. In determining the amount of work represented by the work diagram, the scales used in plotting the F_t–s curve must be considered. Thus, if ordinates are plotted to a scale of 1 in. = 50 lb. and abscissas to the scale of 1 in. = 5 ft., then each square inch of area under the F_t–s curve represents 250 ft.-lb. of work.

Since the area of a work diagram equals the product of the average ordinate and the base, the work done by a force equals the (space) average value of the tangential (working) component of the force and the length of the path described by the application point.

The area of the work diagram may be found by means of a planimeter or by dividing the area into small strips and applying Simpson's rule. Or, in some cases, less exact methods may be employed in estimating the area.

121. Work Done on a Body by a Force System.—So far, the work done on a body by a single force or by a couple has been considered. In general, however, a body is acted on by a force system, and, in order to find the work done on the body in any displacement, the work done by the whole force system must be found. The work done by a force system is the algebraic sum of the works done by the forces of the system, and in general is not equal to the work done by the resultant of the system. Thus if two equal, opposite, and collinear forces F, F be applied at the ends of a helical spring causing the spring to stretch as the magnitude of the forces F, F increases, the work done by the forces in stretching the spring is the product of the average value of F and the increase in the length of the spring, although the resultant of the two forces F, F is at all times equal to zero.

If the spring in the above discussion be replaced by a rigid stationary bar and two equal, opposite, and collinear forces F, F be applied along the axis of the bar, it is obvious that the work done by the two forces is zero, regardless of the manner in which the magnitude of the two equal forces may vary during the time they act on the bar, since the point of application of each force does not move. If the bar is moved in any way while the two equal, opposite, and collinear forces are acting on it, it can likewise be shown that the work done by the forces is zero, assuming as before that the bar is rigid, that is, that the distance between the points of application of the forces remains constant. Hence an important proposition may be stated as follows: *The work done by two forces which at all times are equal, opposite, and collinear is zero provided the distance between the points of application of the forces remains constant.* This proposition is true regardless of the displacements of the points of application of the forces or the manner in which the magnitude of the two equal forces varies during the displacement.

This principle will be found to be of particular importance in the discussion of the principle of work and energy for a rigid body (Art. 131). For in a rigid body the distance between any two particles remains constant and, by Newton's third law, the forces that the two particles exert on each other are equal, opposite, and collinear and hence the work done by each such pair of forces in any displacement of the body is zero.

Therefore in any displacement of a rigid body the work done by the internal forces is zero.

Although it is not *always* possible to find the work done by a force system acting on a body by finding the work done by the resultant of the system, as stated above, it is *sometimes* possible to do so. Thus, the work done by the earth-pulls on the particles of a body (weights of the particles) in any displacement of the body is found to be equal to the work done by the resultant of the weights of the particles, that is, by the weight of the body. This may be formally stated in the following proposition: *The work done by the weight of a body in any displacement of the body is equal to the product of the weight of the body and the vertical component of displacement of the center of gravity of the body.*

ILLUSTRATIVE PROBLEMS

Problem 699.—A helical spring (Fig. 429) having a modulus of 200 lb./in. is compressed $s = 4$ in. by an axial load. How much work is done by the (variable) load in compressing the spring?

Solution.—If P_y denotes the force corresponding to any compression, y, of the spring, then, from case III, Art. 117, we have

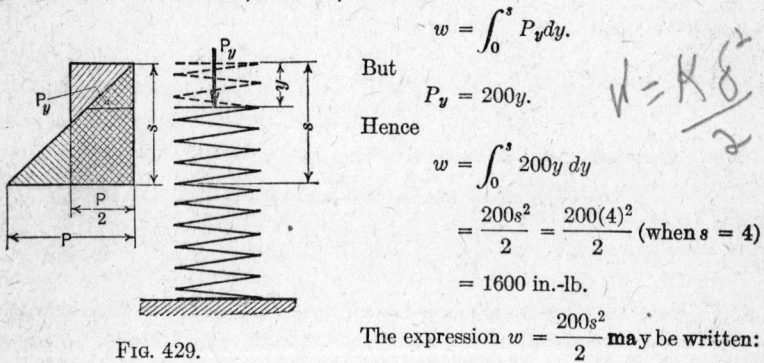

$$w = \int_0^s P_y dy.$$

But

$$P_y = 200y.$$

Hence

$$w = \int_0^s 200y\, dy$$

$$= \frac{200s^2}{2} = \frac{200(4)^2}{2} \text{ (when } s = 4\text{)}$$

$$= 1600 \text{ in.-lb.}$$

Fig. 429.

The expression $w = \dfrac{200s^2}{2}$ may be written:

$$w = \frac{200s}{2} \times s = \frac{P}{2} \times s = \text{area of triangular work diagram}$$

= average force times total displacement
= area of rectangular diagram having the same area as the triangular diagram.

Problem 700.—The component F_t of the crank-pin pressure F in Fig. 426 is called the tangential effort. The tangential-effort diagram for a steam engine (similar to Fig. 430) is drawn to the following scales: 1 in. of ordinate = 24 lb./sq. in. of piston area and 1 in. of abscissa = a 30°-arc of the crank-pin circle. The area under the curve is found to be 11.5 sq. in. Find the work done on the crank-pin per square inch of the piston area per stroke (one-half revolution), if the crank length is 7.5 in. Also find the total work done per stroke, the diameter of the piston being 14 in.

Solution.—A 30°-arc of the crank-pin circle = 3.92 in.

ILLUSTRATIVE PROBLEMS

1 sq. in. of the work diagram = 24 × 3.92 = 94.2 in.-lb. Work done per stroke per square inch of piston = 94.2 × 11.5 = 1083 in.-lb. = 90.2 ft.-lb.

$$\text{Total work per stroke} = 90.2 \times \frac{\pi \times (14)^2}{4} = 13{,}900 \text{ ft.-lb.}$$

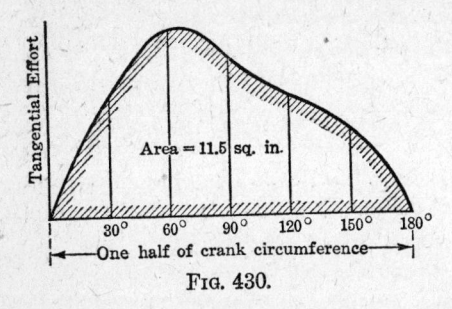

FIG. 430.

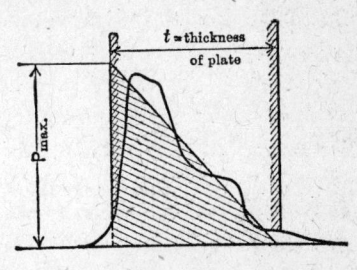

FIG. 431.

Problem 701.—In the design of punching machines (see Fig. 454) it is important to know how much work is done in punching a hole in a plate. Tests show that the work-diagram for steel is approximately of the form shown by the heavy curved line in Fig. 431. This diagram may be assumed, without serious error, to be equal to the triangular work-diagram in which the maximum pressure P corresponds to a shearing strength in the steel plate of 60,000 lb./sq. in. Find the work done in punching a $\frac{7}{8}$-in. hole in a $\frac{5}{8}$-in. steel plate.

Solution.—P_{max} = shearing area × 60,000 = πdt × 60,000
$$= \pi \times \tfrac{7}{8} \times \tfrac{5}{8} \times 60{,}000 = 103{,}000 \text{ lb.}$$

The work done in punching the hole, assuming a triangular work diagram, is

$$w = \text{average pressure times thickness of plate}$$

$$= \frac{P_{max}}{2} \times t = \frac{103{,}000}{2} \times \frac{5}{8} = 32{,}200 \text{ in.-lb.}$$

Problem 702.—A solid cylinder of radius r ft. and of weight W lb. rolls a distance s down an inclined plane without slipping. Find the work done on the cylinder while it is rolling down the plane if the plane makes an angle ϕ with the horizontal (Fig. 432).

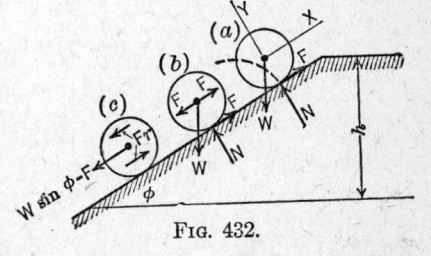

Solution.—The forces acting on the cylinder as shown in Fig. 432(a) are the weight W, the normal pressure N, and the friction F. By introducing two equal and opposite forces F, F at the mass-center (Fig. 432b), and then resolving W into x- and y-components, the original three forces may be resolved into a force, $W \sin \phi - F$, and a couple, Fr, as shown in Fig. 432(c). The work done, then, in a displacement $\bar{s}$ of its mass-center, is

FIG. 432.

$$w = (W \sin \phi - F)\bar{s} + Fr \cdot \theta.$$

But the displacement, $\bar{s}$, of the mass-center equals the length, s, of the plane. And $s = r\theta$, in which θ is the angular displacement of the cylinder. That is,

$$\bar{s} = s = r\theta.$$

Whence
$$w = W \sin\phi \cdot s - Fs + Fs$$
$$= W \sin\phi \cdot s \text{ ft.-lb.}$$

Thus, it will be noted that F does no work, for, if there is no slipping, the point of application of F moves perpendicular to F. Likewise N does no work since its point of application has no displacement in the direction of the force. Therefore, the work done on the body is the work done by W. But the work done by W is Wh (Art. 121), and from the diagram it will be noted that $h = s \sin\phi$. Hence the work done on the body is $w = Ws \sin\phi$, which agrees with the result found above.

PROBLEMS

703. An automobile that weighs 3500 lb. coasts a distance of 300 ft. up a grade of 1 ft. in 50 ft. The total frictional resistance parallel to the road is 0.08 of the weight of the automobile. Find the total work done on the automobile while it is traveling the 300 ft. *Ans.* $w = -105{,}000$ ft.-lb.

704. How much work is done by the draw-bar pull of an engine in pulling a train of 40 cars, each weighing 40 tons, at a constant speed of 30 mi./hr. up a 1 per cent grade a distance of 1 mi.? Assume the train resistance to be 6 lb./ton of weight.

705. A box weighing 80 lb. is pulled up an inclined plane by a force, P, of 60 lb. as shown in Fig. 433. The coefficient of friction is $\frac{1}{4}$. Find the work done by each force acting on the box if it moves 20 ft. Find the total work done on the box.
Ans. 42.8 ft.-lb.

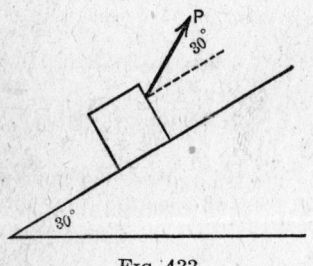

Fig. 433. 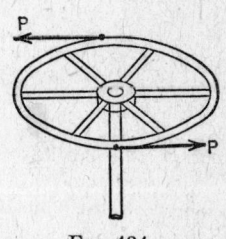   Fig. 434.

706. Two forces P, P (Fig. 434) exert a constant turning moment on the hand-wheel of a large valve. The wheel is 18 in. in diameter. How much work is done in closing the valve if 8 revolutions of the hand-wheel are required and each force has a magnitude of 20 lb.?

707. The steam indicator card (Fig. 435) is drawn to the following scales: 1 in. of ordinate = 100 lb./sq. in. and 1 in. of abscissa = 5 in. of the stroke of the piston. The area of the indicator card is found to be 2.5 sq. in. and the length of the diagram is 3 in. (stroke = 15 in.). The diameter of the piston is 14 in. Find the work done per stroke by the steam on the piston. What is the average steam pressure in pounds per square inch (mean effective pressure) which will do the same amount of work? *Ans.* $w = 16{,}000$ ft.-lb.

708. The screw of the bracket clamp (Fig. 436) moves vertically 1 in. when the hand-wheel is turned 4 revolutions. A helical spring having a modulus of 200 lb./in. is compressed by turning the hand-wheel. The average frictional moment of the screw is 20 in.-lb. What is the average turning moment applied to the hand-wheel in compressing the spring 3 in.?

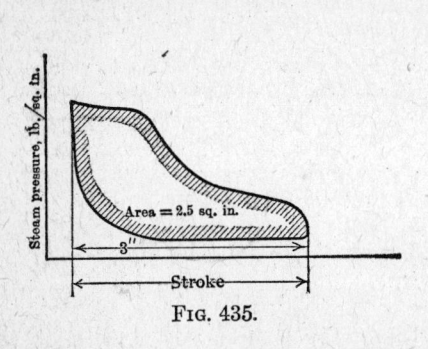

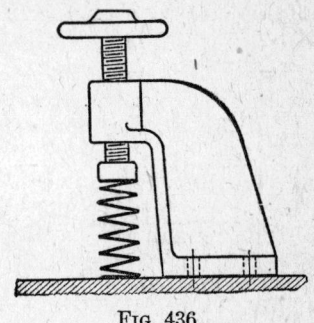

FIG. 435.

FIG. 436.

709. A standpipe 60 ft. high and 6 ft. in diameter is filled with water that is pumped from a pond whose level is 40 ft. below the bottom of the standpipe. The frictional resistance of the water in passing through the pipe is equivalent to an additional lift of 10 ft. How much work is done by the pump in filling the standpipe?
Ans. $w = 8,485,700$ ft.-lb.

710. In Fig. 437 the body A is moved along a smooth horizontal plane by means of a constant force $P = 10$ lb. applied at the end of a cord connected to A and passing over a small peg B. Find the work done on A by the cord while A is displaced 10 ft., assuming no friction between B and the cord.

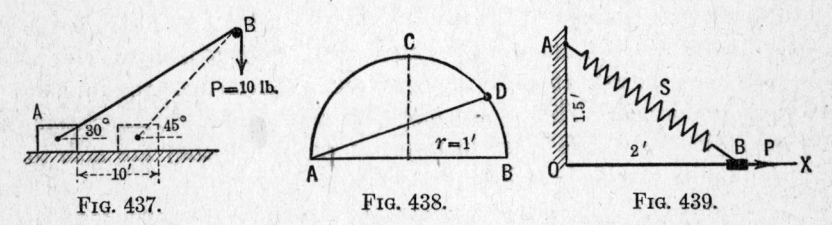

FIG. 437.   FIG. 438.   FIG. 439.

711. In Fig. 438, D is a small body that slides on the semicircular track BCA. AD is an elastic spring attached to the track at A. The unstretched length of the spring is 1 ft. and the modulus of the spring is 5 lb./in. Find the work done on D by the spring as D moves from B to C.   *Ans.* $w = 24.8$ ft.-lb.

712. A spring S (Fig. 439) is attached at A to a fixed vertical plane and to a block B that slides on a smooth horizontal rod OX. The unstretched length of the spring is 1.5 ft. and the modulus of the spring is 60 lb./ft. How much work is done by the spring on B as B is moved 2 ft. from O by the force P?

713. A rope which weighs 5 lb. per foot and which is 500 ft. long is suspended by one end from a drum. How many foot-pounds of work must be done to wind up 200 ft. of the rope?   *Ans.* $w = 400,000$ ft.-lb.

714. Determine the work done by all forces acting on the hollow cylinder shown in Fig. 411 (Prob. 658) during a displacement of s ft. of the center of the cylinder. Express in terms of W and s.

715. Two blocks A and B in Fig. 440 are connected by a spring whose unstretched length is 4 ft. and whose modulus is 100 lb./ft. How much work is done on the spring as the blocks are moved from the position indicated by the dotted line to the position shown in the figure? *Ans.* $w = 117.5$ ft.-lb.

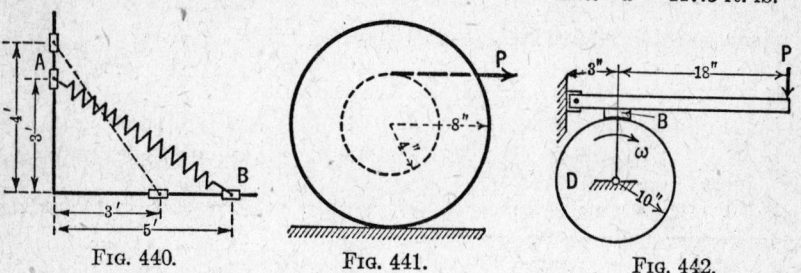

FIG. 440.   FIG. 441.   FIG. 442.

716. A cylinder having a radius of 8 in. has a groove of 4-in. radius cut in its midsection (Fig. 441). A string is wrapped around the cylinder in the groove and a horizontal force P of 10 lb. is applied to the end of the string. The cylinder rolls without slipping on the horizontal surface. Find the work done on the cylinder while its center travels a distance of 6 ft.

717. In Fig. 442 the force P applied at the end of a brake lever is 20 lb. The coefficient of friction for the brake shoe B and drum D is 0.40. The drum is rotating when the brake is applied. Find the work done on the drum while it makes 10 revolutions. Assume the friction of the drum axle in its bearing is negligible.
Ans. $w = 2930$ ft.-lb.

122. Power Defined.—The term *power* as used in mechanics is defined as the rate of doing work. The use or function of many machines depends upon the rate at which they do work as well as upon the amount of work performed. Thus, some machines such as electric generators, steam engines, etc., are rated in terms of the power they are able to develop under specified conditions of service.

If the rate of doing work is constant, the power, P, developed may be defined by the expression $P = \dfrac{w}{t}$, in which w is the work done in time t. If the rate of doing work varies, the power at any instant may be defined by the expression $P = \dfrac{dw}{dt}$.

Units of Power.—Power, like work, is a scalar quantity. The unit of power may be any unit of work per unit of time. Thus, in the gravitational system of units, the foot-pound per second (ft.-lb./sec.) and kilogram-meter per second are common units, whereas in the absolute system, the dyne-centimeter per second (erg/sec.) or joule per second are in common use.

In many problems in engineering, however, it is more convenient to use a larger unit of power than those mentioned above. In the gravitational system of units these larger units are the British or American horse-power (h.p.) and the *force de cheval* or Continental horse-power. They are defined as follows:

One British or American horse-power = 550 ft.-lb./sec.
= 33,000 ft.-lb./min.

One Continental horse-power = 75 kilogram-meters per second
= 4500 kilogram-meters per minute.

And in the absolute system, the larger units are the watt and kilowatt, which are defined as follows:

One watt = 10^7 ergs per second.

One kilowatt = 1000 watts.

The watt and kilowatt are used extensively in electrical engineering. They may be converted into British horse-power by means of the relations

One horse-power = 746 watts.

One kilowatt = 1.34 horse-power.

And, for approximate computations, it is convenient to use 1 horse-power = 3/4 kilowatt or 1 kilowatt = 4/3 horse-power.

For expressing very large quantities of work, the units used are the horse-power-hour (h.p.-hr.) and the kilowatt-hour (kw.-hr.). A horse-power-hour is the work done in one hour at a constant rate of one horse-power. Thus:

One horse-power-hour = 33,000 × 60 = 1,980,000 ft.-lb.

Similarly, one kilowatt-hour = 1.34 × 1,980,000 = 2,650,000 ft.-lb.

123. Special Equations for Power.—If a force, F, remains constant in a given displacement of its application point and acts in the direction of the displacement, as, for example, the draw-bar pull of a locomotive, the work done in one unit of time is Fv, in which v is the velocity of the application point, that is, the distance moved through in one unit of time. Hence, if F is expressed in pounds and v in feet per second, the horse-power developed by the force (or the body exerting the force) is

$$h.p. = \frac{Fv}{550}.$$

If the velocity varies, the above equation expresses the horse-power at the instant the velocity is v. If the force does not act in the direction of the displacement of its application point, the working component of the force must be used in the above equation. And, if the force agrees in direction with the displacement but varies in magnitude, as, for example, the pressure of the steam against the piston of a steam engine or the tangential effort against the crank pin, then the value of F (or F_t) at any instant may be used to obtain the power at that instant. However, the average power during a given cycle (or many cycles) of operations is generally more useful than the instantaneous power. Thus, in the case of a steam engine, the average horse-power is expressed by

$$h.p. = \frac{2\,Plan}{33,000},$$

in which P is the mean effective pressure (lb/sq. in.), a is the piston area (sq. in.), l is the length of stroke (ft.), and n is the number of revolutions per minute (r.p.m.). For Pa is the average force (lb.) which acts through a distance $l \cdot 2n$ (ft.) per minute, the number of strokes per minute being $2n$ in a double-acting engine, and hence the work (ft.-lb.) done per minute (power) is $Pa \cdot l \cdot 2n$ and the horse-power is as given above.

If a couple having a constant moment, T, acts through a given angular displacement of θ radians, the work done is $T \cdot \theta$ (Art. 118). And, if the couple turns through ω radians per unit of time, the work done per unit of time is $T\omega$. Hence, if the moment of the couple is expressed in pound-feet and ω in radians per second, the horse-power developed by the couple is

$$h.p. = \frac{T\omega}{550}.$$

If the angular velocity is not constant, the above equation expresses the horse-power at the instant at which the velocity is ω. But in most cases the average horse-power during a given cycle of operations is of more use than the instantaneous value.

PROBLEMS

718. Niagara Falls is approximately 200 ft. high and the rate of discharge is about 280,000 cu. ft. per sec. Compute the horse-power that could be developed if no energy were lost.

719. A locomotive exerts a constant draw-bar pull of 35,000 lb. while increasing the speed of a train from 30 to 45 mi./hr. What horse-power does the engine develop (*a*) at the beginning of the period; (*b*) at the end of the period? What is the average horse-power during the period?

Ans. (*a*) 2800 h.p.; (*b*) 4200 h.p.; (*c*) 3500 h.p.

720. A man in turning the crank on the winch of a crane was found to exert the forces shown in Fig. 443 at the positions indicated. Plot (freehand) carefully a tangential-effort diagram, the crank (radius) being 15 in. long. Estimate from the diagram the mean tangential effort and calculate the mean horse-power developed by the man assuming that he turns the crank at a constant speed of 40 r.p.m.

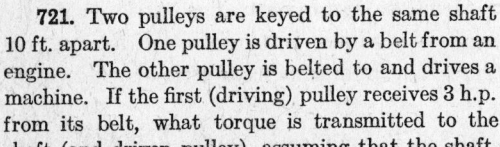

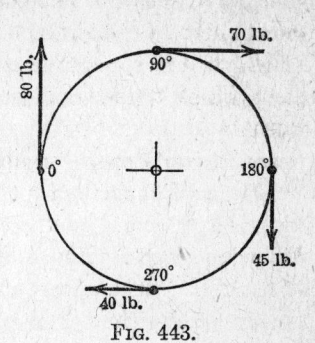

FIG. 443.

721. Two pulleys are keyed to the same shaft 10 ft. apart. One pulley is driven by a belt from an engine. The other pulley is belted to and drives a machine. If the first (driving) pulley receives 3 h.p. from its belt, what torque is transmitted to the shaft (and driven pulley), assuming that the shaft rotates at a constant speed of 150 r.p.m.? *Ans.* 105 lb.-ft.

722. A pump driven by a 3-h.p. motor discharges 200,000 cu. ft. of water from one reservoir to another (higher) reservoir whose water level is 20 ft. above that of the lower reservoir. If the overall efficiency of the whole installation is 80 per cent, how long does it take to pump the water?

723. What indicated horse-power will the engine referred to in Prob. 707 develop if it operates at a constant speed of 250 r.p.m. and is double acting?

Ans. 243 h.p.

724. A generator develops 500 kw. and delivers 450 kw. to a machine shop. A price of 4 cents per kilowatt-hour is paid. Does the machine shop pay for power or for work? What is the cost to the machine shop per day of 8 hours?

725. A certain machine requires 5 h.p. for its operation. If the machine is in use 6 hr. per day, how many foot-pounds of work are delivered to the machine in one day?

726. If the efficiency of the pump referred to in Prob. 709 is 60 per cent and the time required to fill the standpipe is 30 min., what horse-power must be delivered to the pump?

727. In Prob. 704, what horse-power is developed by the draw-bar pull of the engine? *Ans.* 3330 h.p.

728. A shaft transmits a turning moment of 120 lb.-ft. from a pulley keyed at one end to another pulley keyed at the other end. The shaft and pulleys rotate at 120 r.p.m. What horse-power does the shaft transmit from the driving pulley to the driven pulley?

§ 2. Energy

124. Energy Defined.—The *energy* of a body is the capacity of the body for doing work. Work may be considered to be done by forces, as in the preceding section, or, since forces are exerted by bodies, work may also be considered to be done by the bodies which exert the forces, the work being done by virtue of the energy which the bodies possess. A body may have the capacity to do work (possess energy) due to a variety of conditions or states of the body. Thus, energy may be classified as mechanical energy, heat or thermal energy, chemical energy, electrical energy, etc., depending on the state or condition of the body by virtue of which it is capable of doing work. Our knowledge of all the conditions which render bodies capable of doing work is far from complete, but experience shows that any of the forms of energy may, under the proper conditions, be transformed into other forms.

Mechanical energy is of particular importance in connection with the kinetics of bodies and is therefore considered at some length in the following pages. The other forms of energy are discussed briefly in Art. 129. Mechanical energy is divided into *potential energy*, or energy of position or configuration, and *kinetic energy* or energy of motion.

From the definition of energy it follows that energy, like work, is a scalar quantity. Thus, the energy of any mass-system is the sum of the energies of the various particles of the system regardless of the directions of motion of the particles.

The units of energy are the same as the units of work discussed in the preceding section.

125. Potential Energy.—The potential energy of a body is the capacity of the body for doing work due to the configuration of the body; that is, to the relative positions of the particles of the body. Thus a compressed spring, and the compressed steam in a boiler, are capable of doing work by virtue of the relative positions (configuration) of their particles. Likewise, a system of bodies may possess potential energy by virtue of the relative positions of the bodies. Thus, the water above a mill dam is said to possess potential energy since it is capable of driving a water wheel. Strictly speaking, however, the energy is possessed not by the water alone but by the system consisting of the earth and the water. But, since the earth is usually regarded as being fixed, it is convenient to regard the water as possessing the energy.

The potential energy of a body may be defined quantitatively as the amount of work which a body is capable of doing against forces, in passing from the given position or configuration to some standard position or configuration, assuming that no other change in the state or condition of the body takes place. This definition, however, does not lead to a definite quantity for the potential energy of the body for a given configuration, unless the work done by the body (mass-system) depends only on the initial and final configuration of the mass-system and not at all on the paths described by the parts of the system while coming to the standard state. Mass-systems for which this condition is fulfilled are called conservative mass-systems, and the force system which acts on such a mass-system while its potential state changes is called a conservative force system.

The potential energy of conservative systems, only, will be considered herein since, in most kinetics problems which involve non-conservative systems, the kinetic energy of the system is of greater importance in the solution of the problems. The most common case of a non-conservative system is that in which the mass-system does work against frictional forces, such as sliding and journal friction and the friction of the particles developed in deforming an inelastic body. Conservative mass-systems occur frequently in engineering problems. In fact any rigid body under the action of a force system in which friction does not occur (or may be considered negligible) is a conservative system, provided, of course, that no change in the state or condition of the body except that of configuration takes place. A common example of a conservative system is that of the earth and an elevated body (whether rigid or not). The work done on the body in any displacement is equal to the earth-pull (weight) of the body times the vertical displacement of the center of gravity of the body (Art. 121), regardless of the intermediate positions occupied by the body in moving from one position to another position. Another example is that of an elastic body, for, if the body is elastic, the energy possessed by the body when in a given strained condition, that is, for a given configuration of its particles, is the same regardless of the relative displacements of the particles which occurred while being put in the given strained condition. The standard configuration may be arbitrarily chosen, but, for convenience, it is so chosen that the potential energy of the body is positive or zero. Thus, in the case of the earth and an elevated body the earth is considered fixed and the standard configuration occurs when the body is in contact with the earth. A discussion of the mathematical test for a conservative system is beyond the scope of this book.

PROBLEMS

729. A helical spring whose weight is 20 lb. and whose modulus is 200 lb. per in. is compressed 3 in. at sea level by applying forces to its ends by means of a clamp. What is its potential energy, considering its unstrained condition at sea level as the standard configuration? If this compressed spring is now taken to the top of a tower 100 ft. above sea level what will be the potential energy of the spring?

Ans. $E_p = 75$ ft.-lb; $E_p = 2075$ ft.-lb.

730. A flexible, weightless cord passes over a fixed cylinder whose axis is horizontal. From the ends of the cord are suspended two bodies weighing 20 lb. and 30 lb. The standard configuration of the system consisting of the cord and two bodies will be assumed to occur when the bodies are at the same level. What will be the potential energy of the system if the configuration is changed by allowing the 30-lb. body to descend 2 ft. and the 20-lb. body to ascend the same distance?

731. A body B weighing 60 lb. is attached by a flexible string to a spring S (Fig. 444). The pulley over which the string passes is weightless and frictionless. The spring has a modulus of 40 lb./in. If a force P of 50 lb. is gradually applied to B, what is the change in the potential energy (a) of the spring; and (b) of the spring and body B considered as one system?

Ans. (a) $\Delta E_p = 106$ in.-lb.; (b) $\Delta E_p = 31$ in.-lb.

732. Water is supplied to a Pelton water-wheel from a lake whose surface is 800 ft. above the wheel. The water striking the blades of the wheel discharges through a nozzle, the amount of water discharged per second being 3.5 cu. ft. The wheel drives an electric generator. If 10 per cent of the energy of the water flowing through the conduit is lost and if the efficiencies of the water-wheel and generator are 80 per cent and 90 per cent, respectively, how much power (in kilowatts) is delivered to the switchboard?

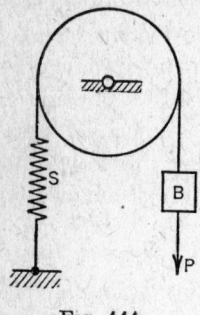

Fig. 444.

126. Kinetic Energy.—The kinetic energy of a body is its capacity for doing work due to its motion. Thus, by virtue of its kinetic energy, a body is capable of doing work against forces which change its motion. For example, a jet of water does work on a tangential water-wheel; a steam forging hammer does work on the material which is deformed by the hammer; the rotating flywheel on a punching machine does work in punching the hole in the metal plate, etc.

The kinetic energy of a body at any instant may be defined quantitatively as the amount of work that the body is capable of doing against forces which destroy its motion, that is, which bring it to a state of rest. The expression for the kinetic energy of a body (mass-system) should, therefore, contain a quantity (velocity) which is a measure of the motion of the body and also a quantity (mass, moment of inertia, etc.) which is a measure of the (kinetic) property of the body that has an influence in governing its change of motion. The "velocity of a mass-system," however, is, in general, an indefinite and meaningless phrase since in general the velocities of the various parts of a system are not the same. Hence, an expression for the kinetic energy of a particle is first obtained and, since energy is a scalar quantity, the kinetic energy of a system of particles (mass-system) is the arithmetic sum of the kinetic energies of the particles. However, the expression for the kinetic energy of a particle is of considerable importance in itself since in many problems a physical body may be regarded as a particle without introducing serious errors.

127. Kinetic Energy of a Particle.

—In Fig. 445, let P be a particle of mass m in a body (assumed rigid for convenience only) which moves so that P travels from position P' to P'', along the path shown, while its velocity decreases from v at P' to zero at P'' due to the forces against which the particle does work. The work done on the particle by the forces (which form a concurrent system) is equal to the work done by their resultant R. Or,

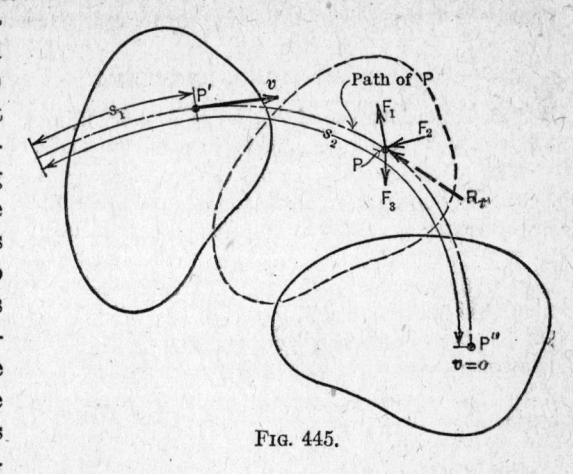

Fig. 445.

$w = \int_{s_1}^{s_2} R_t ds$. But, by definition, the kinetic energy, E_k, of the particle is the work which the particle does against the forces. Hence, the defining equation for the kinetic energy of a particle is

$$E_k = -w = -\int_{s_1}^{s_2} R_t ds.$$

This expression may be transformed so that E_k is expressed in terms of m and v by means of the following relations:

$$R_t = ma_t, \quad a_t = \frac{dv}{dt}, \quad \text{and} \quad \frac{ds}{dt} = v.$$

Thus

$$E_k = -\int_{s_1}^{s_2} R_t ds = -\int_{s_1}^{s_2} ma_t ds = -\int_{s_1}^{s_2} m \frac{dv}{dt} ds$$
$$= -\int_{s_1}^{s_2} m \frac{ds}{dt} dv = -\int_{v}^{0} mv dv = \tfrac{1}{2} mv^2.$$

Therefore, the kinetic energy of a particle of mass m having a velocity v is equal to $\tfrac{1}{2}mv^2$. That is,

$$E_k = \tfrac{1}{2}mv^2 = \frac{1}{2}\frac{W}{g}v^2.$$

Units.—If W is expressed in pounds, g in feet per second per second, and v in feet per second, E_k will be expressed in foot-pounds. Thus, energy is expressed in the same units as is work.

PROBLEMS

733. By making use of Eq. (4) of Art. 85, prove that the kinetic energy of a particle having uniformly accelerated rectilinear motion is $\frac{1}{2}mv^2$.

734. A baseball weighing 5½ oz. is thrown vertically downward with an initial velocity of 40 ft./sec. from the top of a tower 100 ft. above the ground. Find the kinetic energy of the ball when it reaches the ground. *Ans.* $E_k = 42.8$ ft.-lb.

735. The German long-range gun which shelled Paris from a distance of approximately 76 miles was 118 ft. long. The muzzle velocity of the projectile was not far from 5000 ft./sec. The diameter of the projectile was 8.15 in. and its weight was 264 lb. It attained a height of about 24 miles, was in flight about 3 min., and reached Paris with a velocity of about 2300 ft./sec. (For a description of the gun see Journal A.S.M.E., Feb., 1920.) Neglecting the energy due to the rotation of the projectile, calculate the kinetic energy of the projectile as it left the gun, and also its energy at the end of its flight. Find the loss of kinetic energy per second during the flight.

736. A steel ball weighing 1 lb. is attached to one end of a wire 3 ft. long and is rotated about the other end with an angular velocity of 120 r.p.m. What is the kinetic energy of the ball? *Ans.* $E_k = 22.0$ ft.-lb.

737. A pulley 4 ft. in diameter has attached to its rim two small pieces of metal at opposite ends of a diameter. If each piece of metal weighs ½ lb., what is the kinetic energy of the two pieces of metal when the pulley is rotating at 200 r.p.m.?

128. Kinetic Energy of a Body.—Since energy is a scalar quantity the kinetic energy of a body (whether rigid or not) is the arithmetic sum of the kinetic energies of its particles. Hence, for any mass-system,

$$E_k = \Sigma \tfrac{1}{2} mv^2.$$

It is convenient, however, to express the kinetic energy of a *rigid* body in terms of the mass (or some other kinetic property such as moment of inertia) of the *whole* body, and either the linear velocity of some particular point in the body (as, for example, the mass-center) or the angular velocity of the whole body. Thus, for rigid bodies having the special motions of translation, rotation, and plane motion the expressions for the kinetic energy are found as follows:

I. Translation of a Rigid Body.—All parts of the body have the same velocity at any instant whether the motion is rectilinear translation or curvilinear translation, that is, v in the last equation is constant. Hence

$$E_k = \Sigma \tfrac{1}{2} mv^2 = \tfrac{1}{2} v^2 \Sigma m.$$

But Σm is the mass of the body and may be denoted by M. Therefore

$$E_k = \tfrac{1}{2} M v^2.$$

KINETIC ENERGY OF A BODY

II. Rotation of a Rigid Body.—The angular velocities of all particles are the same at any instant, that is, the angular velocity ω of any particle with respect to the center of rotation is the angular velocity of the body. The linear velocity, v, of any particle, P, of mass m, at a distance, r, from the axis of rotation, O, (Fig. 446) is equal to $r\omega$. Hence the kinetic energy of the body is

$$E_k = \Sigma \tfrac{1}{2} mv^2 = \tfrac{1}{2}\Sigma m(\omega r)^2 = \tfrac{1}{2}\omega^2 \Sigma mr^2.$$

But Σmr^2 is the moment of inertia of the body with respect to the axis of rotation and is denoted by I_o. Thus, $I_o = \Sigma mr^2$. Therefore

$$E_k = \tfrac{1}{2} I_o \omega^2.$$

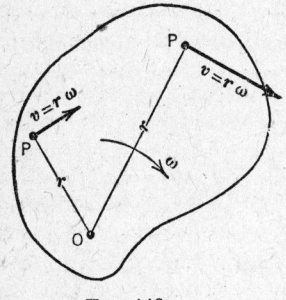

FIG. 446. 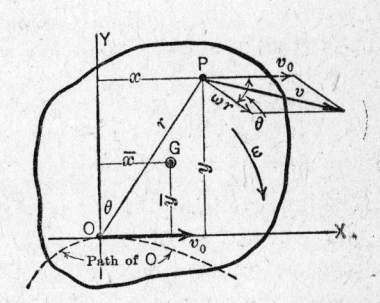   FIG. 447.

III. Plane Motion of a Rigid Body.—As shown in Art. 96, the motion of the body at any instant may be considered to be a combination of a rotation about an axis through any point, O, in the plane of motion with the angular velocity, ω, of the body and a translation defined by the motion of O. Hence the velocity, v, of any particle P of mass m (Fig. 447) is the resultant of the velocity, ωr, which P is given by the rotation about O, and the velocity, v_o, which is given to all particles by the translation. And, since the body is rigid, the velocity ωr has a direction perpendicular to r. Thus

$$v^2 = (\omega r)^2 + v_o^2 + 2v_o \omega r \cos \theta.$$

In Fig. 447, let O be the origin and, for simplicity, let the x-axis have the same direction as v_o. The kinetic energy of the body may then be found in terms of the mass of the whole body, the angular velocity of the body, and the linear velocity of one point (in this case the point O) in the body as follows:

$$\begin{aligned}E_k = \Sigma \tfrac{1}{2} mv^2 &= \tfrac{1}{2}\Sigma m(\omega^2 r^2 + v_o^2 + 2v_o \omega r \cos \theta) \\ &= \tfrac{1}{2}\Sigma m \omega^2 r^2 + \tfrac{1}{2}\Sigma m v_o^2 + \Sigma m v_o \omega r \cos \theta \\ &= \tfrac{1}{2}\omega^2 \Sigma mr^2 + \tfrac{1}{2} v_o^2 \Sigma m + \omega v_o \Sigma mr \cos \theta.\end{aligned}$$

But Σmr^2 is the moment of inertia of the body with respect to the axis through O from which r is measured. Thus $\Sigma mr^2 = I_o$. Further, $r\cos\theta = y$, whence $\Sigma mr\cos\theta = \Sigma my = M\bar{y}$, in which M is the mass of the body and $\bar{y}$ is the distance of the mass-center from the x-axis. Therefore

$$E_k = \tfrac{1}{2}I_o\omega^2 + \tfrac{1}{2}Mv_o^2 + M\bar{y}\omega v_o \quad \ldots \ldots \quad (1)$$

provided that the directions of the x- and y-axes and ω are chosen as in Fig. 447. Now since the point O is any point in the plane of motion it may be chosen at the mass-center. That is, the motion of the body may be resolved into a rotation about an axis through the mass-center and a translation defined by the motion of the mass-center. If the point O is taken as the mass-center, then, $\bar{y} = 0$, I_o becomes $\bar{I}$, and v_o becomes $\bar{v}$. Hence the kinetic energy is given by the expression

$$E_k = \tfrac{1}{2}\bar{I}\omega^2 + \tfrac{1}{2}M\bar{v}^2. \quad \ldots \ldots \ldots \quad (2)$$

It is important to note that, although plane motion of a rigid body may be resolved, at any instant, into a rotation about an axis through *any* point in the plane of motion and a translation defined by the motion of that point, it does *not* follow that the kinetic energy of the body at the given instant is the kinetic energy due to the rotation plus the kinetic energy due to the translation, *unless* the assumed rotation is about an axis through the mass-center of the body and the translation is defined by the motion of the mass-center.

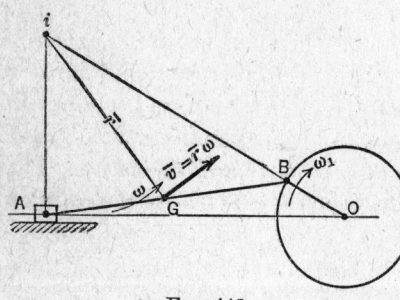

Fig. 448.

Alternative Method. — Plane motion of a rigid body may be considered to be a pure rotation about the instantaneous axis of rotation (Art. 97), and hence if O in Eq. (1) is taken as the instantaneous center i, v_o becomes zero and I_o becomes I_i and thus the expression for E_k becomes,

$$E_k = \tfrac{1}{2}I_i\omega^2 \quad \ldots \ldots \ldots \quad (3)$$

This expression for E_k may be shown to be equivalent to the expression in Eq. (2). Thus the E_k of the connecting rod shown in Fig. 448 is

$$E_k = \tfrac{1}{2}I_i\omega^2 = \tfrac{1}{2}(\bar{I} + M\bar{r}^2)\omega^2 = \tfrac{1}{2}\bar{I}\omega^2 + \tfrac{1}{2}M\bar{v}^2.$$

PROBLEMS

738. Find the kinetic energy of the rocker arm AD (Fig. 449) from the following data: $OB = 10$ in.; $OA = 3$ ft.; angular velocity of crank $OB = 50$ r.p.m.; $\theta = 30°$; length of rod $AD = 4.5$ ft.; and the weight of the rod is 22.7 lb.

Ans. $E_k = 4.95$ ft.-lb.

739. The rod BCD (Fig. 450) is caused to oscillate by the crank OA and connecting rod AC. The crank is 4 in. long and rotates at 90 r.p.m. What is the kinetic energy of the rod BCD and the small weight E in the position shown? The rod is of uniform cross-section and weighs 20 lb., and E weighs 4 lb.

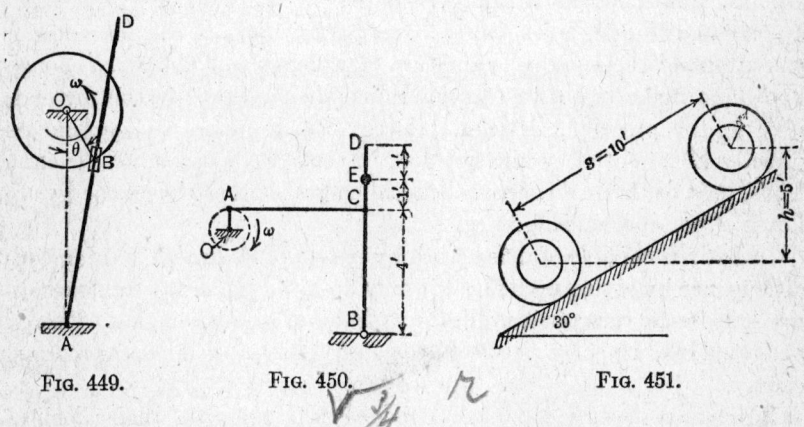

FIG. 449.   FIG. 450.   FIG. 451.

740. A hollow cylinder whose outer radius is r and whose radius of gyration with respect to its geometrical axis is $\sqrt{3/4}\,r$ starts from rest and rolls without slipping down a plane inclined 30° with the horizontal (Fig. 451). The weight of the cylinder is 20 lb. (a) Find the velocity of the mass-center and the kinetic energy of the cylinder when it has rolled a distance $s = 10$ ft. (b) If the cylinder were allowed to fall vertically from rest what would be the velocity of the mass-center and the kinetic energy when it has fallen a distance $h = 5$ ft.?

Ans. (a) $\bar{v} = 13.5$ ft./sec., $E_k = 100$ ft.-lb.; (b) $\bar{v} = 17.9$ ft./sec., $E_k = 100$ ft.-lb.

741. A car weighing 1000 lb. is mounted on four cylindrical disk wheels each of which weighs 100 lb., the total weight of car and wheels being 1400 lb. The diameter of each wheel is 18 in. When the car is traveling on a straight track at 30 mi./hr. what is the ratio of the kinetic energy of the wheels alone to the kinetic energy of the car and wheels? Disregard the weight of the axles.

742. A slender rod, similar to the spoke of a flywheel, is 3 ft. long and rotates about an axis through one end at a constant speed of 120 r.p.m. The rod weighs 50 lb. Find the kinetic energy which the rod possesses. *Ans.* $E_k = 368$ ft.-lb.

743. Two spherical bodies each weighing 20 lb. are connected by a slender rod and revolve at 90 r.p.m. in a horizontal plane about a vertical axis located midway between the two bodies. The center of each ball is 10 in. from the axis. The diameter of each ball is 4 in. The weight of the rod is 6 lb. Find the kinetic energy of the system.

744. The winding drum of a mine hoist is 14 ft. in diameter, its radius of gyration is 6 ft., and its weight is 7 tons. A cage weighing 6 tons is raised by it. When the cage is rising at the rate of 40 ft./sec. what is the kinetic energy of the system?

Ans. $E_k = 554{,}000$ ft.-lb.

745. A homogeneous sphere weighing 48.3 lb. rolls without slipping on a horizontal surface. The velocity of the center of the sphere is 10 ft./sec. Determine the kinetic energy of the sphere by making use, in addition to the other necessary quantities, of the moment of inertia of the sphere about an axis through (*a*) the lower end of the vertical diameter, (*b*) the mass center, and (*c*) the upper end of the vertical diameter.

129. Non-mechanical Energy.

—Experience shows that some bodies are capable of doing work (possess energy) by virtue of certain states or conditions of their parts, the nature of which is not definitely enough known to make it possible to determine their energy by the methods used in the preceding articles. Energy which cannot be determined directly as potential or kinetic energy is called *non-mechanical* energy. Thus, heat or thermal energy, chemical energy, and electrical energy are forms of non-mechanical energy.

A body is capable of doing work by reason of its heated state or condition since by giving up its heat it may do work, under favorable conditions, as in the case of steam in the cylinder of a steam engine. Energy possessed by a body by virtue of its heated state is called heat or thermal energy.

Certain bodies are capable of doing work by reason of their chemical state or condition. Thus, carbon (coal) and oxygen combine and produce heat which as noted above may in turn do work. Energy possessed by bodies due to the state of their chemical elements is called chemical energy.

Some bodies are capable of doing work by virtue of their electrical state or condition. Thus, a copper wire on an armature moving in a field of force may develop electric current which in turn may do work in driving a motor. Or, a charged condenser may do work as its electrical condition changes, etc. Energy which arises out of the electrical conditions of bodies is called electrical energy.

Any one of these, so-called, special forms of energy may be converted, under favorable conditions, into mechanical energy, and there is considerable evidence to indicate that all energy is mechanical energy. Thus, according to this view, the heat energy of a body could be determined as kinetic energy if the motions of the individual particles were known. And, certain forms of chemical and electrical energy could be determined as potential energy if the molecular forces were definitely known. Therefore, the energy possessed by bodies by virtue of special states of their molecular structure are considered as non-mechanical forms of energy, not because these special forms are necessarily different from mechanical energy, but because the energy cannot be determined directly as mechanical energy, and, therefore, has to be transformed into mechanical energy and then measured. Thus, one unit of heat energy, the British thermal unit (B.t.u.), has a definite mechanical equivalent which carefully made experiments have shown to be

$$1 \text{ B.t.u.} = 778 \text{ ft.-lb.}$$

However, the lack of knowledge of the molecular structure and conditions by virtue of which bodies possess energy does not prevent the application of certain principles of energy to such conditions. In fact, the outstanding feature concerning energy is that certain general principles of energy, such as principles of the conservation of energy and of degradation of energy, etc., are the basis upon which our knowledge of the behavior of non-rigid bodies, in general, is built and thus they furnish a method of approach to problems for which the principles of force, mass, and acceleration are inadequate. They are of special importance, therefore, in the study of hydraulics, thermodynamics, electrodynamics, physical chemistry, etc.

In the following section certain principles concerning mechanical energy are developed and applied to the motion of bodies (mainly rigid) in which the motions of the particles are definitely known. And even though the principles of force, mass, and acceleration may be used for many of the problems considered, nevertheless, it will be noted that even for rigid bodies the principles of work and energy are of great importance in many kinetics problems as met in engineering practice.

§ 3. Principle of Work and Energy

130. Preliminary.—As stated in Art. 99, in order to deal with the main problem in kinetics, a relation is found between the forces acting on the body, the kinetic properties (mass, moment of inertia, etc.) of the body, and the change of motion (involving acceleration, velocity, distance, etc.) of the body. This may be done by determining the relation between the work done by the forces acting on the body and the kinetic energy of the body, since work and kinetic energy involve quantities in terms of which the three factors in the kinetics problem as mentioned above are expressed. And since, in general, the motions of all particles of a body are not the same, the principle of work and kinetic energy will be developed for a particle first and then extended to the motion of a body. However, as already noted, in many problems the body may be regarded as a particle without introducing serious errors.

WORK AND ENERGY

131. Principle of Work and Kinetic Energy.—*I. For a Particle.*—In Fig. 452 let A' and A'' be two positions of a body, the motion of which changes due to the unbalanced forces (F_1, F_2, F_3, and F_4) which act on it. The body is assumed, for convenience, to be composed of small cubes of different materials rigidly attached (glued together), each cube being regarded as a particle of the body. Let P be one of the particles which describes the path shown in the figure as the particle moves from P' to P'' while its velocity changes from v_1 to v_2 due to the unbalanced (concurrent) forces which act on it. Let the resultant of the forces acting on P be denoted by R and its component tangent to the path of P be denoted by R_t. It will be noted that some of the particles (cubes) have their velocities changed (are accelerated) by forces exerted only by other particles of the body (internal forces) whereas other particles are acted on both by internal and by external forces.

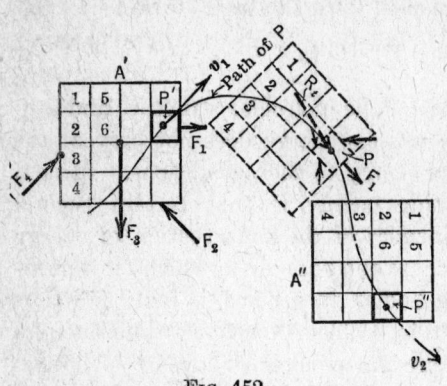

Fig. 452.

The work done by the forces acting on the particle as it moves along its path from P' to P'' is $w = \int_{s_1}^{s_2} R_t ds$ but $R_t ds$ may be expressed in terms of the mass, m, and velocity, v, of the particle by means of the relations:

$$R_t = ma_t, \quad a_t = \frac{dv}{dt}, \quad \text{and} \quad v = \frac{ds}{dt}.$$

Hence

$$w = \int_{s_1}^{s_2} R_t ds = \int_{s_1}^{s_2} ma_t ds = \int_{s_1}^{s_2} m \frac{dv}{dt} ds$$

$$= \int_{v_1}^{v_2} m \frac{ds}{dt} dv = \int_{v_1}^{v_2} mv\, dv = \tfrac{1}{2}mv_2{}^2 - \tfrac{1}{2}mv_1{}^2$$

$$= \Delta E_k = \text{change in kinetic energy of the particle.}$$

Therefore, *the work done by the forces acting on a particle of a body (whether rigid or not) during any displacement is equal to the change in the kinetic energy of the particle in the same displacement.* Or, expressed in the form of an equation,

$$w = \Delta E_k = \tfrac{1}{2}mv_2{}^2 - \tfrac{1}{2}mv_1{}^2.$$

PRINCIPLE OF WORK AND KINETIC ENERGY

II. For a System of Particles.—The principle of work and kinetic energy for a system of particles (body) may now be derived. Since work and energy are scalar quantities, the work done on a body is the algebraic sum of the works done on all the particles. And the change in the kinetic energy of the body is the algebraic sum of the changes in the kinetic energies of all the particles. But the work done by all the forces acting on all the particles equals the work done by the external forces which act on the body (w_e) plus the work done by the internal forces of the body (w_i). Thus, by writing the above equation for each particle and adding both sides of the equations, the resulting equation is

$$w_e + w_i = \tfrac{1}{2}\Sigma mv_2^2 - \tfrac{1}{2}\Sigma mv_1^2 = \Delta E_k.$$

That is, *the work done on a system of particles (whether rigid or not) by all of the external and internal forces in any displacement of the system is equal to the change in the kinetic energy of the system in the same displacement.*

III. For a Rigid Body.—The principle may now be expressed for the special case of a rigid body, for, as pointed out in Art. 121, the internal forces in any mass-system occur in pairs of equal opposite and collinear forces whether the body is rigid or not, but the work done by these forces is zero, in general, only if the application points of each pair of forces remain a fixed distance apart, which is the case in a rigid body. Hence, for a rigid body, $w_i = 0$. Therefore

$$w_e = \Delta E_k.$$

That is, *the work done by the external forces acting on a rigid body in any displacement is equal to the change in the kinetic energy of the body in the same displacement.*

Although an absolutely rigid body does not exist in nature, the work done by the external forces in causing the relative displacements of the particles in physical bodies is usually negligible in comparison with the work done by the forces in causing the displacement of the body as a whole.

Application of Principle to Special Cases of Motion of Rigid Bodies.—By making use of the expressions developed in Art. 128, the principle of work and kinetic energy may be expressed for important special cases of motion of *rigid* bodies as follows:

I. Translation.
$$w_e = \tfrac{1}{2}M(v_2^2 - v_1^2).$$

II. Rotation.
$$w_e = \tfrac{1}{2}I_o(\omega_2^2 - \omega_1^2).$$

III. Plane Motion.
$$w_e = \tfrac{1}{2}M(\bar{v}_2^2 - \bar{v}_1^2) + \tfrac{1}{2}\bar{I}(\omega_2^2 - \omega_1^2).$$

300   WORK AND ENERGY

Units.—If the pound, foot, and second be arbitrarily selected as the units of force, length, and time, respectively, as is usually done in the engineer's system of units (Art. 103), then w_e will be expressed in foot-pounds and kinetic energy will likewise be expressed in foot-pounds, the mass of the body $\left(M = \dfrac{W}{g}\right)$ being expressed in slugs.

ILLUSTRATIVE PROBLEMS

Problem 746.—An engine capable of exerting a maximum draw-bar pull of 51,000 lb. is used on a certain railroad having small grades to draw freight trains having a maximum weight of 2000 tons, the average weight of a freight car with its cargo being about 45 tons. The train resistance per ton of weight varies with the car weight and with the speed. If an average value of 8 lb./ton is used and the engine pulls a 2000-ton train while going up a ½ per cent grade, how far will the train travel while its velocity is increasing from 15 to 30 mi./hr.? How long will it take?

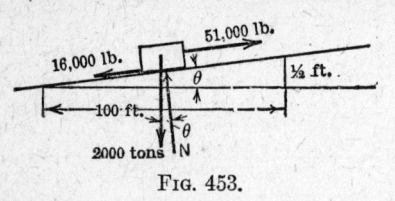

Fig. 453.

Solution.—The forces acting on the train are shown in the free-body diagram (Fig. 453). The angle θ (exaggerated in the diagram) for a ½ per cent grade is so small that $\tan \theta$ may be considered to be equal to $\sin \theta$. Hence, $\sin \theta = \dfrac{1}{200}$.

$$w_e = \Delta E_k = \tfrac{1}{2} M(v_2{}^2 - v_1{}^2),$$

$$\left(51{,}000 - 16{,}000 - \dfrac{2000 \times 2000}{200}\right) s = \dfrac{1}{2} \dfrac{2000 \times 2000}{32.2} (\overline{44}^2 - \overline{22}^2)$$

$$15{,}000 s = 62{,}200 \times 1452, \quad \therefore \ s = 6020 \text{ ft.}$$

But

$$s = \dfrac{v_1 + v_2}{2} \times t, \quad \therefore \ 6020 = \dfrac{22 + 44}{2} \times t.$$

Whence

$$t = 182.5 \text{ sec.} = 3.04 \text{ min.}$$

Problem 747.—The punching and shearing machine shown in Fig. 454 has a capacity for punching a 2½-in. hole in a ½-in. steel plate. The pinion shaft (and flywheel) is driven at 220 r.p.m. from a counter-shaft by means of a belt drive to the tight pulley on the pinion shaft. Each operation of punching a hole (punching cycle) causes a fluctuation (decrease) in the speed of the flywheel. The "coefficient of speed fluctuation" is 0.8, that is, the speed of the flywheel decreases 20 per cent in each punching cycle. If the work done in punching the hole is all supplied by the flywheel, what moment of inertia should the flywheel have? What is the moment of inertia of the flywheel on the machine as actually designed (as shown in Fig. 454), neglecting the material in the hub and spokes? If the difference in the belt tensions, $T_2 - T_1$, is 286 lb. and the pinion shaft turns through an angle of 230° while the hole

ILLUSTRATIVE PROBLEMS

is being punched, how much work is done on the shaft (and flywheel) by the belt while the hole is being punched? The diameter of the pulley is 22 in.

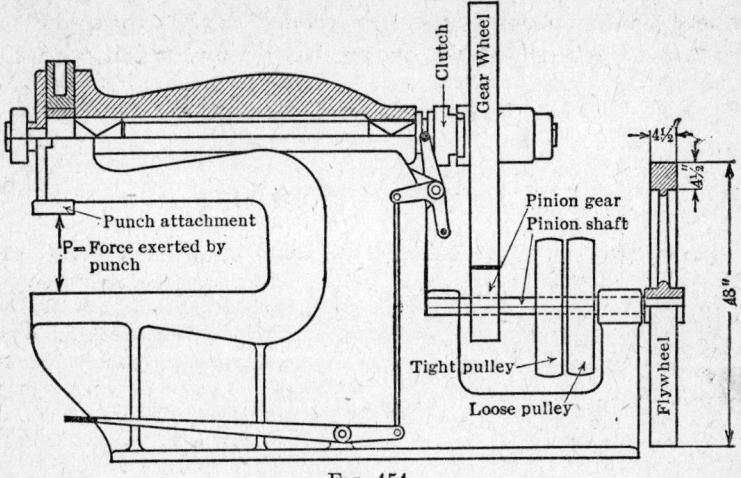

FIG. 454.

Solution.—The maximum value of the force P required to punch the hole, using 60,000 lb./sq. in. for the ultimate shearing strength of the material of the plate, is

$$P = \pi d \times t \times 60,000$$
$$= \pi \times \tfrac{5}{2} \times \tfrac{1}{2} \times 60,000 = 235,500 \text{ lb.}$$

The work done in punching the hole, assuming a triangular work diagram (see Prob. 701), is

$$w = \frac{P}{2} \times \frac{1}{2} = \frac{235,500}{4} = 58,875 \text{ in.-lb.}$$

$$= 4900 \text{ ft.-lb., which is supplied by the flywheel.}$$

For the flywheel we have then

$$w_e = \Delta E_k = \tfrac{1}{2} \bar{I}(\omega_2^2 - \omega_1^2).$$

$$4900 = \tfrac{1}{2} \bar{I} \left[\left(\frac{220 \times 2\pi}{60} \right)^2 - \left(0.8 \times \frac{220 \times 2\pi}{60} \right)^2 \right] = 95.5 \bar{I}.$$

Whence

$$\bar{I} = 51.3 \text{ slug-ft.}^2$$

Hence, the moment of inertia of the flywheel should be 51.3 slug-ft.[2] in order that the speed be decreased not more than 20 per cent. Assuming the flywheel to be made of cast iron which weighs 450 lb./cu. ft., the moment of inertia of the flywheel as actually designed, neglecting hub and spokes, is

$$\bar{I} = \tfrac{1}{2} M(r_2^2 + r_1^2). \quad \text{(See Prob. 993.)}$$

$$= \frac{1}{2} \times \frac{\pi}{32.2} \left[2^2 - \left(\frac{19.5}{12} \right)^2 \right] \times \frac{4.5}{12} \times 450 \times \left[2^2 + \left(\frac{19.5}{12} \right)^2 \right]$$

$$= \frac{1}{2} \frac{\pi}{32.2} \times 1.36 \times 0.375 \times 450 \times 6.64 = 74.3 \text{ slug-ft.}^2$$

The work done on the flywheel while the hole is being punched is

$$w = \Sigma T \cdot \theta = 286 \times \frac{11}{12} \times 230 \times \frac{\pi}{180} = 1050 \text{ ft.-lb.}$$

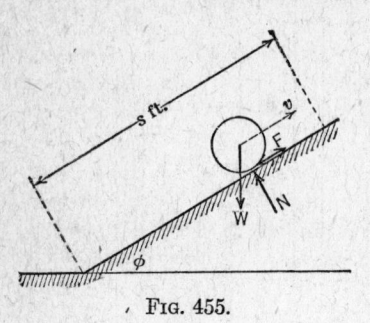

Problem 748.—A solid homogeneous cylinder rolls up an inclined plane without slipping (Fig. 455). The weight of the cylinder is 120 lb. and its diameter is 3 ft. If the angle, ϕ, of inclination of the plane is 15° and the velocity of the center of the cylinder is 20 ft./sec. just as it comes in contact with the incline, how far up the plane will the cylinder roll?

Solution.—The forces acting on the cylinder while rolling up the plane are shown in Fig. 455. And the work done by the forces, as was shown in Prob. 702, is $W \sin \phi \cdot s$. Thus

FIG. 455.

$$w_e = \Delta E_k,$$

Or
$$-W \sin \phi \cdot s = \tfrac{1}{2}(M\bar{v}_2{}^2 + \bar{I}\omega_2{}^2) - \tfrac{1}{2}(M\bar{v}_1{}^2 + \bar{I}\omega_1{}^2).$$

Also
$$W \sin \phi \cdot s = \tfrac{1}{2}(M\bar{v}_1{}^2 + \bar{I}\omega_1{}^2), \text{ since } \bar{v}_2 \text{ and } \omega_2 \text{ are zero.}$$

Hence
$$\bar{v} = r\omega = 1.5\omega.$$

$$120 \times 0.2588 \times s = \frac{1}{2}\frac{120}{32.2}(20)^2 + \frac{1}{2}\left(\frac{1}{2}\frac{120}{32.2} \times \overline{1.5}^2\right)\left(\frac{20}{1.5}\right)^2.$$

Whence
$$s = \frac{746 + 372}{31.1} = 36 \text{ ft.}$$

PROBLEMS

749. A bullet fired with a velocity of 1000 ft./sec. penetrates a block of wood to a depth of 12 in. If the bullet were fired through a board of the same wood 2 in. thick, find its velocity after passing through the board. Assume the resistance of the wood to the bullet to be constant. *Ans.* $v = 913$ ft./sec.

750. A body weighing 80 lb. is projected along a rough horizontal plane with a velocity of 8 ft./sec. It comes to rest in a distance of 10 ft. Find the coefficient of kinetic friction.

751. An automobile which weighs W lb. is moving at the rate of 30 mi./hr. when it comes to the foot of a hill. Power is then shut off. The slope of the hill is 1 ft. in 50 ft. How far will the machine coast up the hill if the total frictional resistance (parallel to the road) is $0.08W$? *Ans.* $s = 301$ ft.

752. A box slides from rest 10 ft. down a plane inclined 30° to the horizontal. After reaching the bottom of the plane the box moves on a horizontal floor. If the coefficient of friction between the box and plane and between the box and floor is 0.3, how far will the box move on the floor before coming to rest?

753. A bullet that weighs 1 oz. is moving with a velocity of 2000 ft./sec. when it strikes a plank normally and passes through it. The velocity on leaving the plank is 1200 ft./sec. If the average resistance to penetration is 5000 lb., how thick is the plank? *Ans.* $t = 5.96$ in.

754. A weight of 8.05 lb. is placed on a horizontal plane and touches one end of a horizontal spring whose other end is in contact with a vertical wall. The weight is moved toward the wall, compressing the spring 6 in. The spring is then released causing the weight to be projected away from the wall. The modulus of the spring is 2 lb./in. and the kinetic friction between weight and plane is 1 lb. What is the velocity of the weight when the spring regains its normal length? If the spring is stopped at that time, how much farther will the body move before coming to rest?

755. A body B (Fig. 456) that weighs W lb. falls from rest through a distance h of 2 ft. and strikes a helical spring whose modulus is 40 lb./in. If the maximum compression s of the spring is 6 in., what is the value of W? Neglect the mass of the spring. *Ans.* $W = 24$ lb.

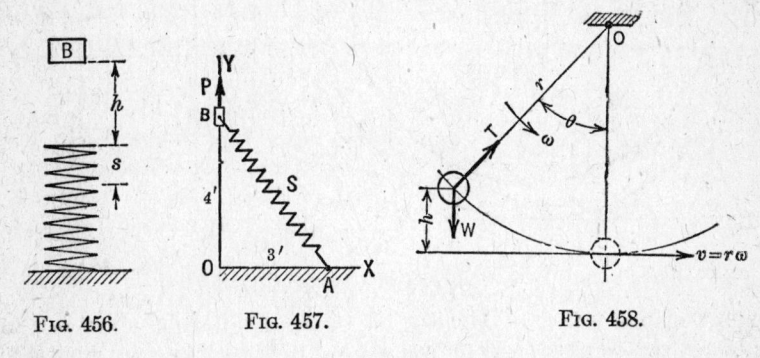

FIG. 456.   FIG. 457.   FIG. 458.

756. A block B (Fig. 457) that weighs 16.1 lb. slides without friction along a vertical rod OY. A spring S, whose unstretched length is 3 ft., is attached to B and to the stationary plane OX at A as shown. If a constant vertical force P of 50 lb. is exerted on B, what will be the velocity of B after a displacement of 4 ft., assuming that B starts from rest at O? The modulus of the spring is 20 lb./ft. Disregard the mass of the spring.

757. A simple pendulum (Fig. 458) consists of a cord having a length, r, of 4 ft. and a bob (assumed to be a particle) having a weight, W, of 6 lb. The pendulum is displaced an angle, θ, of 60°. What will be the velocity, v, of the bob when in its lowest position, if air resistance is neglected? Note that the pull T of the cord on the bob does no work. *Ans.* $v = 11.36$ ft./sec.

758. A shearing machine has 3 h.p. delivered to it by the belt. Every two seconds an operation occurs which requires seven-eighths of all the energy supplied during the two seconds; the other one-eighth of the energy is required to overcome the friction of the machine. During each operation the speed of the flywheel decreases from 120 to 80 r.p.m. Assuming that the work done in shearing is done by the flywheel, what should be the moment of inertia of the flywheel? If the weight of the flywheel is 400 lb. what is its radius of gyration?

759. The flywheel shown in Fig. 459 is made of cast iron which weighs 450 lb./cu. ft. If the turning moment exerted by the shaft to which the flywheel is keyed delivers 5 h.p. to the flywheel for 1 min., what will be the angular velocity of the wheel at the end of this period assuming that the wheel starts from rest? Solve, (a) neglecting the hub and spokes, and (b) neglecting the hub and assuming the spokes to have a constant cross-section equal to the mean cross-section and to extend from the center of the shaft to the rim.

Ans. (a) $\omega = 892$ r.p.m.; (b) $\omega = 862$ r.p.m.

Fig. 459.

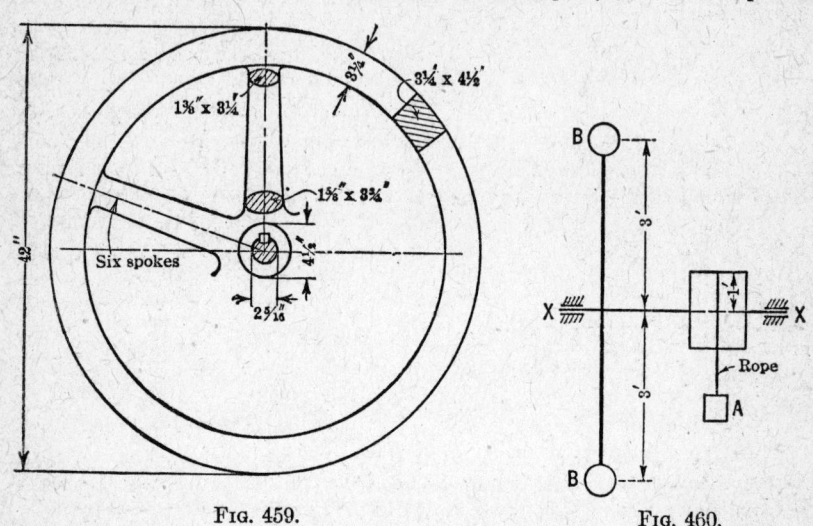

Fig. 460.

760. Two steel balls B, B (Fig. 460) are connected by a rigid slender rod that rotates in a vertical plane about the axis XX and turns a light wooden drum about the same axis. The drum in turn lifts the weight A by means of a rope that is wound around the drum. Each ball is 4 in. in diameter and weighs 8.05 lb. If the rod is given an angular velocity of 100 r.p.m., what is the weight of A if it is lifted 20 ft. while the rod and balls are coming to rest? Neglect the mass of the drum and of the rod and also neglect all frictional forces.

761. If the flywheel shown in Fig. 459 is used on the punching machine shown in Fig. 454 and the punching machine is required to do the same amount of work (4900 ft.-lb.) in punching a hole as was found in Prob. 747, what will be its speed after punching the hole? The speed of the flywheel before the hole is punched is 220 r.p.m., as stated in Prob. 747. Neglect the hub and spokes in determining the moment of inertia of the flywheel. Assume the weight of cast iron to be 450 lb./cu. ft.

Ans. 157 r.p.m.

762. Water flows through a conduit that is 7.76 mi. long and has a cross-section of 100 sq. ft. The velocity of the water is 10 ft./sec. Find the kinetic energy of the water. Discuss what would probably happen if a valve at the lower end of the conduit were closed rather suddenly.

763. A train weighing 500 tons is drawn on a horizontal track by an engine whose draw-bar pull varies with the speed so that it always develops 200 h.p. How many seconds does it take to pull the train 1000 ft. starting from rest? How much work is done on the train by the draw-bar pull? Neglect train resistance.

Ans. $t = 68$ sec.; $w = 7{,}480{,}000$ ft.-lb.

PROBLEMS

764. The vertical bar in Fig. 461 is 4 ft. long and weighs 80 lb. The bar is displaced slightly from the position shown and rotates about O. When it comes to a horizontal position it strikes the two springs shown and continues to rotate until the spring S_1 is compressed ½ in. The springs have the same modulus. Find the modulus of the springs. Assume the bar to be rigid and of constant cross-section.

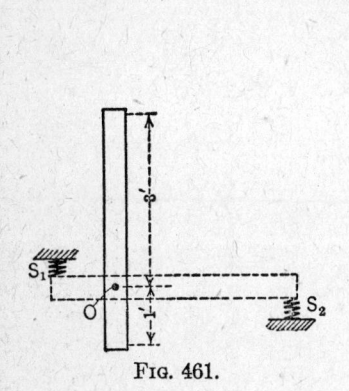

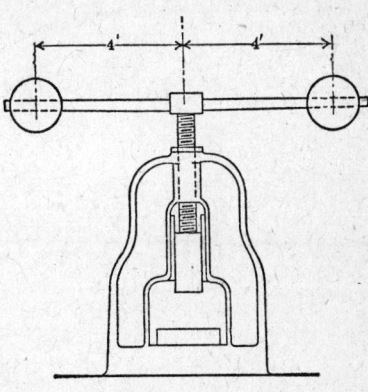

FIG. 461.

FIG. 462.

765. The hand-operated screw press shown in Fig. 462 is used for embossing, lettering dies, punching thin plates, etc. The diameter of the screw is 2½ in. The screw has triple threads with a pitch of 2½ in. Each ball weighs 100 lb. and the diameter of each ball is 9 in. If the balls are revolved at 60 r.p.m., what is the maximum size (diameter) of hole that can be punched in a ¼-in. steel plate, assuming the shearing strength of the steel to be 60,000 lb./sq. in. and the efficiency of the screw to be 15 per cent. Also assume the work diagram for punching the hole to be triangular. (See Prob. 701.) *Ans.* $d = 0.60$ in.

766. A sphere rotates about an axis through its center. Its speed is increased from 600 rad./min. to 90 rad./sec. while it turns through 10 revolutions. If the moment of inertia of the sphere with respect to the axis of rotation is 20 slug-ft.^{2}, find the moment of the couple acting on the sphere.

767. A generator driven by a hydraulic turbine has a speed of 600 r.p.m. and delivers 1000 h.p. An additional load of 200 h.p. is put on the generator. If 2 sec. elapse before the governor can act, what must be the moment of inertia of the rotating parts in order that the decrease in speed shall be 1 per cent?
Ans. $I = 5600$ slug-ft.^{2}

768. A homogeneous sphere rolls, without slipping, up a plane inclined 45° to the horizontal. If the initial velocity of the center of the sphere is 40 ft./sec., how far will the sphere roll before coming to rest?

769. A car weighing 966 lb. is mounted on four cylindrical disk wheels. Each wheel weighs 161 lb. and has a diameter of 4 ft. (The total weight of the car and wheels is 1610 lb.) If the car travels on a straight horizontal track with a velocity of 20 ft./sec., what force parallel to the track is required to stop the car in a distance of 100 ft.? Assume that the wheels do not skid. *Ans.* $P = 120$ lb.

770. A solid cylinder weighing 500 lb. is rolled up an inclined plane by means of a descending weight *B* (Fig. 463). The diameter of the cylinder is 4 ft. The pulley over which the rope runs is assumed to be frictionless and weightless. Body *B* weighs 300 lb. If the cylinder starts from rest at the bottom of the incline, with what velocity will its center reach the top?

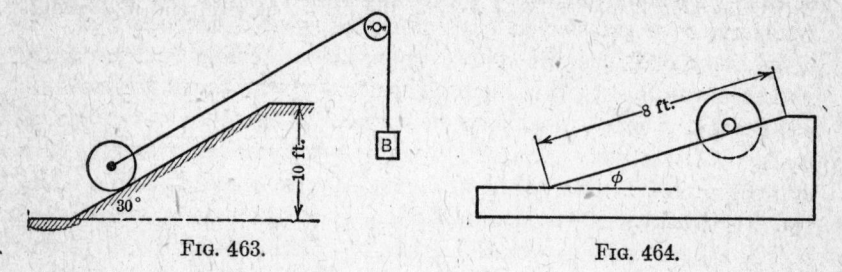

FIG. 463.   FIG. 464.

771. A solid disk 18 in. in diameter is mounted on a shaft 4 in. in diameter (Fig. 464). The shaft rolls, without slipping, on two inclined tracks. The disk weighs 120 lb. and the weight of the shaft may be neglected. The angle of inclination, ϕ, is 15°, and the incline is 8 ft. long. If the disk starts from rest at the top, what will be the velocity of its center at the bottom of the incline?

Ans. $v = 3.46$ ft./sec.

772. A hollow steel cylinder with an outside radius of 1 ft. and an inside radius of 6 in. weighs 966 lb. The cylinder rolls with its axis horizontal and without slipping up a plane making an angle of 30° with the horizontal. If the initial velocity of the mass-center of the cylinder is 10 ft./sec. up the plane, what will be the velocity of the mass-center when it has reached a position 10 ft. down the plane from the initial position?

773. A solid sphere 1 ft. in diameter and weighing 100 lb. rolls down the inside of a thin-walled hollow cylinder whose radius is 6 ft., the axis of the cylinder being horizontal. In its initial position the line from the center of the sphere perpendicular to the axis of the cylinder makes an angle of 60° with the vertical. If the sphere starts from rest, find its kinetic energy and the velocity of its center when it is in its lowest position.

Ans. $E_k = 275$ ft.-lb.; $\bar{v} = 11.24$ ft./sec.

774. A plane 10 ft. square with two edges horizontal makes an angle of 30° with the horizontal. A solid steel cylinder weighing 100 lb. and having a radius of 6 in. rolls without slipping along one of the diagonals. If the cylinder starts from rest at the upper corner what is its kinetic energy and the velocity of its center when it reaches the lower corner?

132. Conservation of Energy.

—One of the greatest achievements of the nineteenth century was the recognition and statement of the principle of the conservation of energy. Like Newton's laws of motion it is an inductive generalization from observation of, and experience with, physical phenomena. The principle states that in any change of the state or condition of an isolated material system the total amount of energy of the system remains constant. By an isolated system is meant one on which no bodies external to the system have any effect. Hence, an isolated system neither gives nor receives energy. Thus, the distribution of energy within the isolated system may be altered and the various forms of energy changed into other forms but the total amount of energy remains constant. Or, as sometimes stated, energy may be transformed or transferred but cannot be created or destroyed. As noted in Art. 129, the principle of conservation of energy is of particular importance in the study of material systems which possess non-mechanical energy, although it is also of much value in the study of mechanical energy. Although an isolated system does not exist in nature, certain systems approach closely thereto, as, for example, the earth and a falling body, provided that the action (and reaction) between the earth and body is large compared with the resistance of the air and the attractions of other bodies on the falling body. Again, although external forces act on a system of bodies, the work done by the forces may be zero (or negligible) as in the case of a simple swinging pendulum and the earth in which the pull of the string on the bob is always normal to the displacement of its application point and the effect of the air is negligible.

§ 4. Efficiency. Dissipation of Energy

133. Efficiency Defined.—The efficiency of a machine, as, for example, a steam engine, an electrical motor, a chain hoist, a jack screw, etc., is the ratio of the energy output of the machine in a given period of time to the energy input in the same period, provided that no energy is stored in the machine which becomes available at a later period. By input is meant the amount of energy received by the machine, a portion of which is transformed or transmitted into the work for which the machine is designed. The work done or energy delivered by the machine is called the output. Thus, denoting efficiency by e, we have

$$e = \frac{\text{energy output}}{\text{energy input}} \quad \text{or} \quad e = \frac{\text{power output}}{\text{power input}}.$$

As already noted, in the transformation and transference of energy (which is the main function of many machines), some of the energy always takes the form of a lower grade of energy (heat energy) and thereby becomes unavailable for the particular process for which the machine is used. The amount of energy which thus miscarries or leaks out in the process is spoken of by various names, such as lost energy (or lost work), energy leak, dissipated energy, etc. Since dissipation of energy occurs with every physical process, the output is always less than the input and, therefore, the efficiency is always less than unity.

The efficiency as defined above is the over-all efficiency of the machine. Certain parts of the machine, however, may have their individual efficiencies; and the over-all efficiency is the product of the efficiencies of the several elements of the machine.

134. Dissipation of Energy.—The work done against frictional forces is the most frequent cause of dissipation of energy in machines. Energy dissipated in doing work against frictional forces is transformed into heat energy. Electrical resistance in connection with electrical machinery also causes a loss of available energy by developing heat. The work done against friction is, in some machines, a necessary evil to be reduced to a minimum, as in the case of prime movers, bearings, teeth of gears, etc.; whereas, in other machines or machine elements, the main object of the machine is to dissipate all the energy received by the machine, as in the case of friction brakes and absorption dynamometers.

135. A Simple Dynamometer. Prony Brake.—A simple dynamometer, commonly called a prony brake, is shown in Fig. 465. A is a flanged pulley keyed to a rotating shaft. The power transmitted by the shaft is not only dissipated or absorbed but is also measured by the brake. B, B are bearing blocks against which the pulley develops a frictional resistance, the magnitude of which is varied by adjusting the nuts C, C. D is the frame or beam with its end E resting on the platform of a weighing scale. When the pulley is running, the beam develops an additional pressure on the platform, due to the friction of the pulley on the bearing blocks. The work lost in friction and the power developed by the shaft may be found as follows:

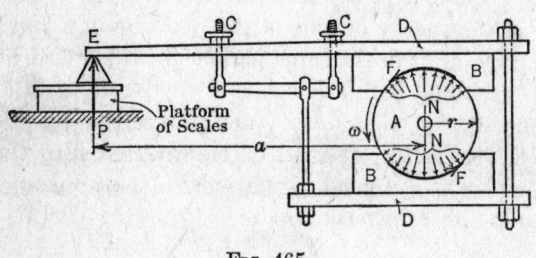

Fig. 465.

It will be assumed that the scales are adjusted to read zero when the beam rests on the platform and the pulley is not running. Thus, the scale reading is a measure of the pressure, P, at E due to the friction developed on the bearing blocks when the pulley is running. Since the brake frame is in equilibrium under the action of the forces, N, P, and F (F denotes the total frictional force on the two blocks), the sum of the moments of P and F about the axis of the shaft must equal zero. Or

$$Fr = Pa.$$

And the work done by the frictional moment Fr in 1 sec. is

$$w_f = Fr\omega = Pa\omega,$$

in which ω is expressed in radians per second. And, since $\omega = \dfrac{2\pi n}{60}$ where n is the number of revolutions per minute (r.p.m.) of the shaft and pulley, the expression for w_f becomes

$$w_f = \frac{2\pi Pan}{60} = \frac{\pi Pan}{30}.$$

If P is expressed in pounds and a in feet, then w_f will be expressed in foot-pounds, and the horse-power developed by the frictional moment (and hence by the shaft) is

$$h.p. = \frac{\pi Pan}{30 \times 550} = \frac{\pi Pan}{16,500}.$$

This expression may be simplified if the dynamometer is constructed so that a has a special value. It should be remembered that the scale reading should not be used for the value of P unless the scales are adjusted to read zero when the pulley is not running.

PROBLEMS

775. What force, P, is required to raise a load, Q, of 200 lb. by means of the differential chain hoist shown in Fig. 466 if $e = 30$ per cent, $r_2 = 8$ in., and $r_1 = 4$ in.?
Ans. $P = 167$ lb.

776. The dynamometer shown in Fig. 467 was devised by Lord Kelvin in connection with the laying of the Atlantic cable for braking the cable drum as the cable was laid out. If it is used in the test of a steam engine, find the horse-power absorbed, using the following data: $W = 400$ lb.; speed of engine = 150 r.p.m.; $r = 4$ ft.; reading of spring balance is 85 lb. *Ans.* 36 h.p.

777. In a test of a jackscrew (see Fig. 210) with a screw 1.5 in. in diameter and a pitch of $\frac{1}{3}$ in., it was found that a pull of 72 lb. at the end of a 15-in. lever was required to raise a load of 2400 lb. when no lubricant was used, and a pull of 63 lb. when an oil lubricant was used. What is the efficiency of the jack for each case?
Ans. $e = 11.8$ per cent; $e = 13.5$ per cent.

778. The band brake described in Prob. 293 allows a certain load to lower at a constant speed such that the brake sheaves rotate at 120 r.p.m., in a counter-clockwise direction. What horse-power is absorbed by the brake?

779. An automobile when traveling at a speed of 50 mi./hr. delivers to the transmission shaft 80 h.p. If the efficiency in transmitting the power from the engine to the rear wheels is 80 per cent, what is the propelling force (tractive effort) developed?
Ans. $F = 480$ lb.

780. A jet of water 2 in. in diameter having a velocity of 150 ft./sec. impinges against the buckets of a tangential water-wheel. If the efficiency of the wheel is

90 per cent, what horse-power is delivered by the wheel? Assume the weight of water to be 62.4 lb./cu. ft.

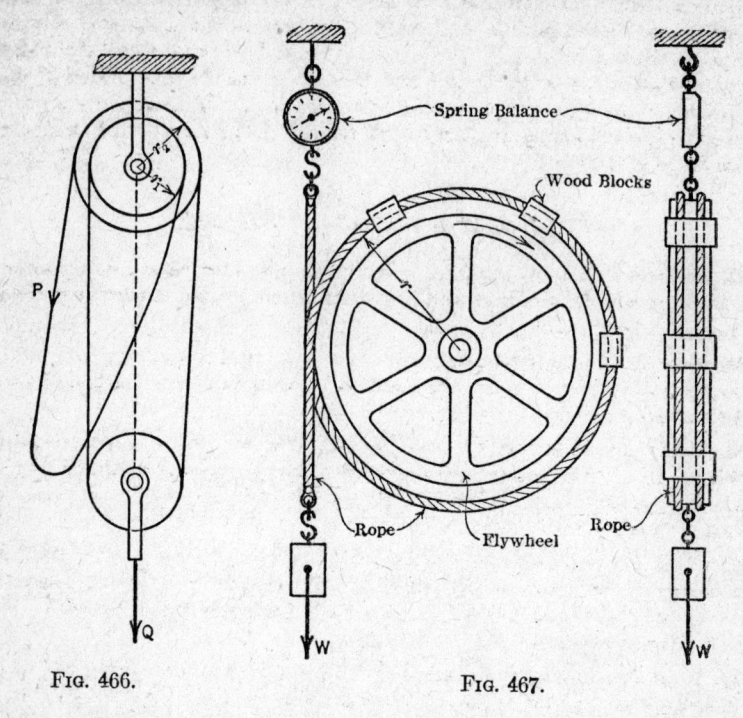

Fig. 466.

Fig. 467.

781. In the band brake shown in Fig. 468 the scale S indicates a force of 120 lb. when $P = 20$ lb. and when the drum D is rotating at 150 r.p.m. What horse-power is being developed by the motor that turns the shaft on which the drum is keyed?

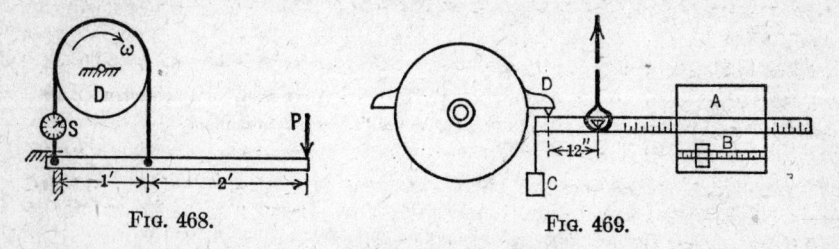

Fig. 468.

Fig. 469.

782. Figure 469 represents one form of a dynamometer. A cast-iron disk keyed to the shaft rotates inside the drum as the shaft turns. The disk rotates in a water-tight compartment between two copper plates that are attached to the drum, and pressure of the copper plates against the disk is produced by water from the city mains which fills the spaces between the copper plates and the ends of the drum. The narrow spaces between the disk and the copper plates are filled with oil. As the shaft (and disk) rotates, the drum (due to the friction developed on the copper plates) tends to turn, causing a pressure at D on the scale beam, which is balanced by the poise weights A and B. The weight of A and B together is 150 lb., and that of B alone is 3.5 lb. The divisions on the large scale are 1 in., and those on the small scale are 0.4 in. When both A and B are set at zero on the scales they are just balanced by the weight of C. If, in order to maintain balance when the disk is rotating, A is set at the tenth division and B is set at the fifteenth division, what is the pressure of the dynamometer on the scale beam at D, and what horse-power is developed by the shaft when rotating at 240 r.p.m.? The distance from the center of the shaft to D is 18 in. *Ans.* 8.69 h.p.

REVIEW QUESTIONS AND PROBLEMS

783. Define work done by any force (a) in words, (b) as a mathematical expression. Write an expression for the work done by a couple in terms of the moment of the couple.

784. Show that the following statement is correct. In lifting a body that weighs 3960 lb. vertically upwards a distance of 100 ft., the work done on the body by the lifting force is 0.2 h.p.-hr.

785. Define kinetic energy of a particle (a) in words, (b) as a mathematical expression. Using this mathematical expression, show that the kinetic energy of the particle is $\frac{1}{2}mv^2$. Assuming that the engineer's system of units is used, what are the units of m and v, and of $\frac{1}{2}mv^2$?

786. Point out and correct the errors in the following demonstration that the kinetic energy of a rotating rigid body is $\frac{1}{2}I\omega^2$: E_k for a particle is $\frac{1}{2}mv^2$. Therefore E_k for the whole body is $\frac{1}{2}Mv^2$. But $v = r\omega$. Hence, $\frac{1}{2}Mv^2 = \frac{1}{2}Mr^2\omega^2$. But $Mr^2 = I_o$; therefore, $E_k = \frac{1}{2}I_o\omega^2$.

787. If the kinetic energy of a rigid body having plane motion is expressed as the sum of two terms ($\frac{1}{2}Mv_o^2 + \frac{1}{2}I\omega^2$), what point in the body must be selected as the point O?

788. The following equation expresses the principle of work and kinetic energy as applying to a non-rigid mass-system $w_e + w_i = \Delta E_k$. Explain why w_i becomes zero for a rigid body. State in words the principle of work and kinetic energy for a rigid body.

789. State the conditions to which the equation $w_e = \frac{1}{2}M(v_2^2 - v_1^2)$ applies.

790. What is the greatest speed at which a motor capable of delivering 10 kw. can lift an elevator weighing 1000 lb., frictional forces being neglected.
Ans. $v = 7.37$ ft./sec.

791. A small sphere weighing 4 lb. is suspended by a string 6 ft. long and swings as a pendulum. As the sphere passes through its lowest position its velocity is 10 ft./sec. How far vertically above its lowest position does it rise?
Ans. $h = 1.55$ ft.

792. A body weighing 16.1 lb. is projected up a smooth plane making an angle of 30° with the horizontal with an initial velocity of 20 ft./sec. After moving 4 ft. the body strikes axially a helical spring, which is fixed at its upper end, and compresses it 3 in. Find the modulus of the spring.
Ans. Modulus = 176 lb./in.

793. In Fig. 470 the pulley B which has a diameter of 20 in. is keyed to the shaft of a motor that is rotating at 90 r.p.m. The weight of A is 10 lb. and the spring

S is stretched 3 in. The modulus of the spring is 20 lb. per in. Calculate the horsepower delivered by the motor to the shaft on which the pulley is keyed.

Ans. 0.72 h.p.

794. A disk D (Fig. 471), weighs 120 lb. and is 4 ft. in diameter. The axle to which it is keyed also carries a drum, B, 10 in. in diameter, to which a friction-band brake (not shown) may be applied. If the disk is rotating at 100 r.p.m. when the brake is applied, what is the average frictional force developed on the circumference of the drum if the disk is brought to rest in 20 revolutions? Neglect the mass of the friction drum.

Ans. $F = 7.8$ lb.

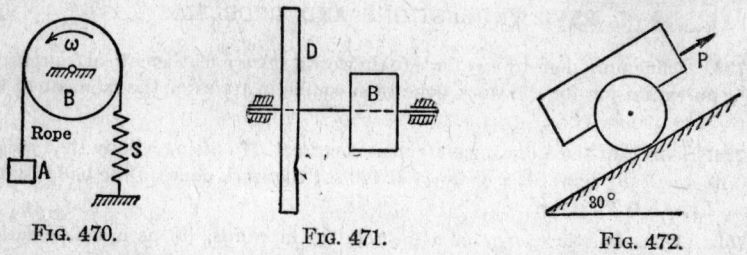

Fig. 470. Fig. 471. Fig. 472.

795. A two-wheeled cart (Fig. 472) weighs 360 lb. including the weight of the wheels; the weight of each disk wheel is 60 lb. and the diameter is 4 ft. What force P parallel to the track is required to give the cart a speed of 15 mi./hr. in a distance of 100 ft., starting from rest?

Ans. $P = 212$ lb.

CHAPTER X

IMPULSE AND MOMENTUM

136. Preliminary.—In Art. 115, the statement was made that impulse is a quantity which involves force and time, and that momentum is a quantity which involves mass and velocity. And the fact was noted that the use of these quantities in the analysis of the motion of bodies requires no fundamental laws in addition to Newton's laws of motion. However, methods which make use of impulse and momentum offer advantages, in certain types of problems, over the methods of work and energy (Chapter IX) and of force, mass, and acceleration (Chapter VIII).

In determining the effect of forces on the motion of bodies, thus far, by the method of force, mass, and acceleration and by the method of work and energy, it has been assumed that the forces have acted on rigid bodies during a definite (comparatively large) interval of time, and when the forces were not constant the manner in which they varied during the period was assumed to be known. To such conditions the methods of impulse and momentum also apply, and in many cases offer a simpler method of solution than the methods previously discussed. Forces sometimes act, however, for a very short (indefinite) interval of time during which the value of the force at any instant is not known. These forces may, nevertheless, produce very appreciable changes in the motion of the body. Such forces are called *impulsive forces*. The principles of impulse and momentum are of special value when considering the motion of bodies under the action of impulsive forces. The bodies upon which impulsive forces act deform under the excessive pressures produced and hence, in determining the motions of bodies under the influence of impulsive forces, the bodies cannot always be assumed to be rigid without introducing appreciable errors. As examples of impulsive forces the following may be mentioned: the force exerted on a projectile due to the explosion of the powder; the action of one billiard ball on another; the force exerted by the ram of a pile driver on the pile; the pressure between two railway cars when making a flying coupling; the action of a steam jet on the blades of a high-speed steam turbine; the pressure exerted by the water in a pipe line on a valve which is closed suddenly.

The purpose of the present chapter is to make clear the conception or meaning of impulse and of momentum, to develop certain principles which express relations between these quantities, and to apply these principles to problems in kinetics.

§ 1. Impulse

137. Impulse and Impact Defined. Units.—The impulse of a constant force is defined as the product of the force and the time interval during which the force acts. Thus, the impulse of a force F is defined by the equation

$$Imp. = F \cdot \Delta t,$$

provided that the force remains constant during the time interval Δt. If the force varies in magnitude but not in direction, the impulse for an indefinitely short period of time dt, is $F \cdot dt$, and, for a time interval $\Delta t = t_2 - t_1$, the impulse is

$$Imp. = \int_{t_1}^{t_2} F dt.$$

In order to evaluate this integral by the method of calculus, F must be expressed in terms of t. The impulse of a force which acts on a body during a very short (indefinite) interval of time is also given by the above expression but, as noted in the preceding article, the impulsive force cannot be expressed in terms of t, since its law of variation is not known, and hence the impulse cannot be determined directly but is found in terms of the change of momentum of the body on which the force acts, as is discussed in the subsequent pages.

The impulse of an impulsive force is sometimes called an *impact*, that is, an impact is a sudden impulse. The term impact, however, is also frequently used as descriptive of the act of collision of bodies. In some problems it is convenient to estimate the time interval of the impulsive force and to express the impact as the product of an average value of the force and an assumed or estimated time interval $\Delta t = t_2 - t_1$. Thus

$$Imp. = \int_{t_1}^{t_2} F dt = F_{av} \cdot \Delta t,$$

in which F_{av} denotes the *time-average* value of the impulsive force which is assumed to act during the time interval Δt. The impulse of a force frequently is called *linear* impulse in contrast with the moment of the impulse which is called *angular* impulse. (See Art. 139.)

Units.—The unit of an impulse is a combination of a unit of force and of time and, hence, is a compound unit. The unit of impulse has no special name. In the gravitational or engineer's system of units (Art. 103) if the pound is selected as the unit of force and the second for the unit of time, the unit of impulse is the pound second (lb. sec.).

138. Components of Linear Impulse.—The impulse of a force, like the force itself, is a directed or vector quantity, the sense and action line of the impulse being the same as that of the force. An impulse of a force, therefore, may be resolved into components and may have a moment with respect to a point or a line. The component, in any direction, of the impulse of a *constant* force is the product of the component of the force in the given direction and the time interval Δt during which the force acts. That is,

$$(Imp.)_x = F_x \cdot \Delta t; \quad (Imp.)_y = F_y \cdot \Delta t, \text{ etc.}$$

And, if the force varies in magnitude or in direction during the time interval $\Delta t = t_2 - t_1$, the components of the impulse are

$$(Imp.)_x = \int_{t_1}^{t_2} F_x dt; \quad (Imp.)_y = \int_{t_1}^{t_2} F_y dt, \text{ etc.}$$

Linear Impulse of a Force System.—The linear impulse, in any direction, of a force system is the algebraic sum of the components, in the given direction, of the impulses of the forces of the system. Thus, for a force system in which the forces are constant, the linear impulse of the force system in any direction x, is

$$(Imp.)_x = \Sigma F_x \cdot \Delta t.$$

Or, if the forces of the system vary during the interval $\Delta t = t_2 - t_1$, then

$$(Imp.)_x = \Sigma \int_{t_1}^{t_2} F_x dt.$$

139. Moment of Impulse. Angular Impulse.—The moment of the impulse of a *constant* force about any point or axis is the product of the moment, T, of the force about the given point or axis, and the time interval, Δt, during which the force acts. The moment of the impulse of a force is also called the *angular impulse* of the force. Thus, the angular impulse of a constant force with respect to an axis O, is defined by the equation

$$(Ang.\ Imp.)_o = T_o \cdot \Delta t,$$

in which T_o is the moment of the force with respect to the axis O.

And, if the force varies in magnitude during the time interval $\Delta t = t_2 - t_1$, the moment of the impulse is expressed by the equation

$$(Ang.\ Imp.)_o = \int_{t_1}^{t_2} T_o dt.$$

Units.—In the gravitational system of units, if the units of force, time, and length are the pound, second, and foot, respectively, the unit of angular impulse is the pound-second-foot (lb.-sec.-ft.).

Angular Impulse of a Force System.—The angular impulse of a force system about any axis is the algebraic sum of the angular impulses of the forces of the system about the given axis. Thus, if the forces of the system are constant, the angular impulse of the system about the axis O is

$$(Ang.\ Imp.)_o = \Sigma T_o \Delta t.$$

And, if the forces vary, the angular impulse of the force system about the axis O, for the time interval $\Delta t = t_2 - t_1$, is expressed by the equation

$$(Ang.\ Imp.)_o = \Sigma \int_{t_1}^{t_2} T_o dt.$$

It should be noted that the linear (and angular) impulse of a constant force, or of a variable force for which the law of variation is known, is not as important a conception in the analysis of the motion of a body as is the impulse of an impulsive force. However, as already noted, even for constant forces which act during a comparatively long time interval, the methods of impulse and momentum may possess advantages over other methods.

PROBLEMS

796. A body weighing 40 lb. slides down an inclined plane in 4 sec. The plane makes an angle of 60° with the horizontal. If the coefficient of friction is 0.2 find the component of the linear impulse of the force system acting on the body parallel to the plane.

797. The linear impulse of the total pressure of the steam on the piston of a steam engine is 4200 lb.-sec. The diameter of the cylinder is 14 in. and the engine runs at 200 r.p.m. Find the average (time average) pressure (in pounds per square inch) of the steam against the piston during one stroke. *Ans.* $p = 182$ lb./in.^{2}

798. A train having a weight of 2000 tons travels up a ½ per cent grade. The draw-bar pull of the engine is 50,000 lb. and the train resistance is 8 lb./ton of weight. If it takes 2 min. to travel up the grade, find the linear impulse of the force system acting on the train for the 2-min. interval.

799. A constant frictional moment of 200 lb.-ft. is applied to a rotating drum by means of a band brake (see Fig. 214). If the moment decreases the angular velocity of the drum uniformly from 90 r.p.m. to 10 r.p.m. while the drum makes 30 revolutions, find the angular impulse of the band brake on the drum.

Ans. 7200 lb.-ft.-sec.

800. A force acts on a body along a fixed straight line, the magnitude and sense of the force being indicated by the ordinate to the graph shown in Fig. 473. Find the impulse of the force for the period of 4 sec. Find the impulse for the first three seconds.

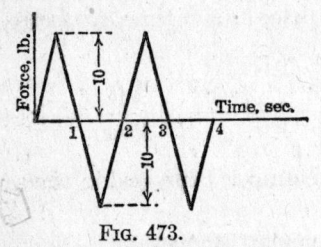

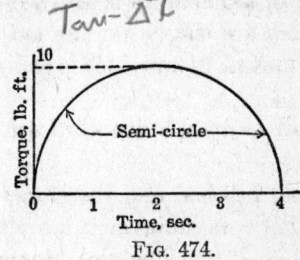

FIG. 473.

FIG. 474.

801. The torque-time curve for a couple that acts on a body is a semi-circle as shown in Fig. 474. What is the angular impulse of the couple for a period of 4 sec.?

Ans. Ang. Imp. = 31.4 lb.-sec. ft.

802. A car coasting on a straight track is brought to rest by bumping into a spring bumper. From a study of the change in the velocity of the car it is found that the impulse of the force exerted on the car by the spring while being compressed is 100,000 lb.-sec. If the time consumed in compressing the spring is ½ sec., what is the time-average value of the force exerted by the spring?

803. A disk is keyed to a shaft and the moment T exerted by the shaft on the disk varies according to the law $T = 2t^2 + 4t$, where T is expressed in pound-feet and t in seconds. Find the angular impulse of the shaft on the disk in the interval $t = 0$ to $t = 4$ sec. *Ans.* Ang. Imp. = 74.7 lb.-sec.-ft.

§ 2. MOMENTUM

140. Momentum of a Particle Defined. Units.—The momentum of a moving particle, at any instant, is defined as the product of the mass of the particle and its velocity at the instant. Thus, the momentum of a particle of mass m moving with velocity v is defined by the equation

$$\text{Mom.} = mv.$$

Momentum, like velocity, is a directed or vector quantity. Furthermore, like force, momentum is represented by a localized vector, that is, it has a definite position line; the direction of the momentum of a particle is the same as that of the velocity of the particle, and its position line passes through the particle.

The momentum of a particle frequently is called *linear* momentum in contrast with the moment of momentum of the particle which is called *angular* momentum.

Units.—The unit of momentum is a combination of a unit of mass and a unit of time, and hence is a compound unit. The unit of momentum has no special name. In the gravitational or engineer's system of units, the unit of mass is a derived unit called a slug, as explained in Art. 103, derived from the units of force, length, and time; hence the unit of momentum is also a derived unit. Thus, if the pound, foot, and second are chosen for the units of force, length, and time, respectively, the unit of momentum is expressed by

$$1 \text{ unit of mass} \times 1 \text{ unit of velocity} = \frac{1 \text{ lb.} \times 1 \text{ sec.}^2}{1 \text{ ft.}} \times \frac{1 \text{ ft.}}{1 \text{ sec.}} = 1 \text{ lb.-sec.}$$

It will be observed, therefore, that momentum is expressed in the same fundamental units as is impulse.

141. Components of Momentum. Angular Momentum.—Since the momentum of a particle is a vector quantity, it may be resolved into components, and, like any localized vector, it has a moment with respect to any point, the moment being defined as the product of the magnitude of the momentum and the perpendicular distance from the position line of the momentum vector to the point or moment-center. The moment of the momentum of a particle is also called the *angular momentum* of the particle. The components of the momentum of a particle of mass m moving with velocity v (Fig. 475), and the angular momentum of the particle with respect to the point O are expressed by the equations:

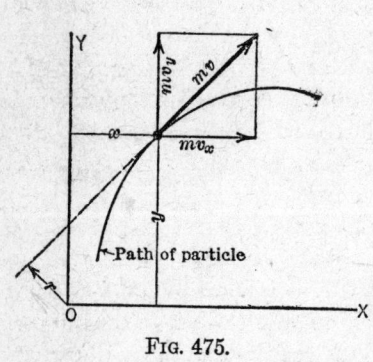

$$(Mom.)_x = (mv)_x = mv_x.$$

$$(Mom.)_y = (mv)_y = mv_y.$$

$$(Ang. Mom.)_o = mv \cdot r, \text{ or}$$

$$(Ang. Mom.)_o = mv_x \cdot y - mv_y \cdot x.$$

The latter expression states that the angular momentum of a particle equals the algebraic sum of the moments of the components of the momentum of the particle.

Fig. 475.

From the expression mvr it is evident that the units of angular momentum are $\text{slug} \cdot \frac{\text{feet}}{\text{seconds}} \text{ feet} = \frac{\text{slug-feet}^2}{\text{seconds}}$, or, if m is expressed in its fundamental units, then the units of mvr are pound-foot-seconds, which are the same as those of angular impulse.

ANGULAR MOMENTUM OF A ROTATING RIGID BODY

142. Linear Momentum of a Body.—The component of the linear momentum, in any direction, of any body (mass-system) is the algebraic sum of the components in the given direction of the momentums of the particles of the body. In general, the momentums of the particles of a body vary in magnitude and in direction. It was shown in Art. 109, however, that the linear momentum of the whole body may be found from the mass of the whole body and the velocity of the mass-center of the body. Likewise the component, in the x-direction, of the linear momentum of the mass-system (Art. 109) is

$$(Mom.)_x = m'v_x' + m''v_x'' + m'''v_x''' + \cdots = M\bar{v}_x$$

A similar equation may be written for the y-component. Thus for **any** mass-system we may write

$$(Mom.)_x = M\bar{v}_x; \quad (Mom.)_y = M\bar{v}_y; \quad \text{and} \quad Mom. = M\bar{v}.$$

That is, *the linear momentum of any moving mass-system is the product of the mass of the whole system and the velocity of the mass-center of the system, and its direction agrees with that of the velocity of the mass-center.*

It should be noted that the linear momentum vector does *not*, in general, pass through the mass-center of the mass-system. If, however, the mass-system is a *rigid* body that has a motion of *translation*, then the linear momentum vector passes through the mass-center of the body. (The proof is left to the student; see Art. 110 for method of proof.)

A general expression could also be obtained for the moment of the linear momentum (angular momentum) of any mass-system having any motion, but it will be found more desirable to derive expressions that apply only to rigid bodies having the special motions of rotation and plane motion.

143. Angular Momentum of a Rotating Rigid Body.—Let Fig. 476 represent a rigid body rotating about a fixed axis through O with an angular velocity ω. The linear velocity of any particle of the body at a distance r from the axis of rotation is $r\omega$, and the linear momentum of the particle of mass m is mv or $mr\omega$ perpendicular to r. Therefore, the moment of momentum of the particle about the axis of rotation is

$$mv \cdot r = mr\omega \cdot r = mr^2\omega,$$

and the algebraic sum of the moments of the momentums of all the particles about the same axis is

$$(Ang.\ Mom.)_o = \Sigma mr^2\omega = \omega \Sigma mr^2,$$

320   IMPULSE AND MOMENTUM

whence
$$(Ang.\ Mom.)_o = I_o\omega,$$

in which I_o is the moment of inertia of the body about the axis of rotation.

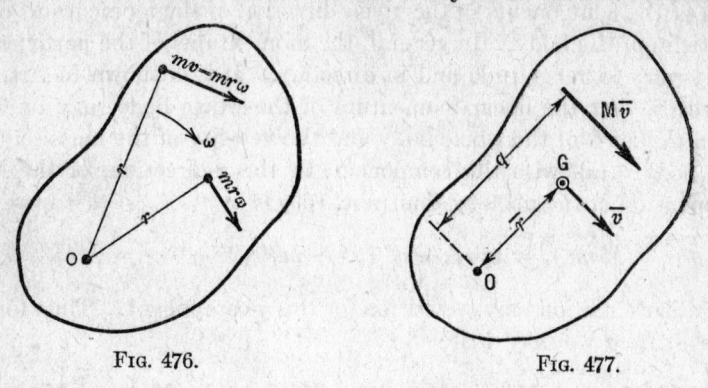

Fig. 476.   Fig. 477.

Position of the Linear Momentum Vector.—The distance, q, from the center of rotation, O, to the linear momentum vector $M\bar{v}$ for a rotating rigid body (Fig. 477) may be found by use of the principle of moments as follows:

$$M\bar{v}q = I_o\omega = Mk_o^2 \frac{\bar{v}}{\bar{r}}, \quad \text{whence,} \quad q = \frac{k_o^2}{\bar{r}}$$

in which k_o is the radius of gyration of the body about the axis of rotation.

144. Angular Momentum of a Rigid Body Having Plane Motion.—Since a plane motion of a rigid body may be considered as a combination of a rotation and a translation (Art. 96), the velocity of any particle P (Fig. 478) is the resultant of a velocity $r\omega$ due to the rotation of the body with angular velocity ω about an axis through any point O perpendicular to the plane of motion, and the velocity v_o due to the translation which gives to each particle the velocity v_o of the point O. Therefore, the components of the momentum of the particle P are $mr\omega$ and mv_o as shown in Fig. 478. And, if $m(v_o)_x$ and $m(v_o)_y$ denote the x- and y-components of mv_o, then the angular momentum of the particle with respect to the axis through O is

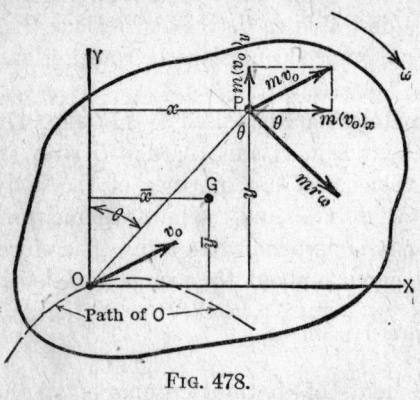

Fig. 478.

$$mr\omega \cdot r + m(v_o)_x \cdot y - m(v_o)_y \cdot x,$$

and the angular momentum for the whole body with respect to the axis through O is

$$(\text{Ang. Mom.})_o = \Sigma mr^2\omega + \Sigma m(v_o)_x y - \Sigma m(v_o)_y x$$
$$= \omega \Sigma mr^2 + (v_o)_x \Sigma my - (v_o)_y \Sigma mx$$
$$= I_o\omega + (v_o)_x M\bar{y} - (v_o)_y M\bar{x}, \quad \ldots \quad (1)$$

where the directions of the x- and y-axes and ω are taken as shown in Fig. 478. If the point O is taken as the mass-center, G, of the body, the above expression reduces to

$$(\text{Ang. Mom.})_{mass\text{-}center} = \bar{I}\omega, \quad \ldots \ldots \quad (2)$$

since $\bar{y}$ and $\bar{x}$ are then equal to zero and I_o becomes $\bar{I}$.

It is important to note that, although plane motion of a rigid body may be considered as a rotation about an axis through any point O in the plane of motion, combined with a translation, Eq. (1) shows that the angular momentum of the body about the axis through O is not equal to $I_o\omega$ unless O is chosen as one of the three following points:

(1) The mass-center of the body, in which case the expression for the angular momentum in Eq. (1) reduces to $I_o\omega$ (or $\bar{I}\omega$), since $\bar{x}$ and $\bar{y}$ are zero as already noted.

(2) The instantaneous center of zero velocity, in which case the expression reduces to $I_o\omega$ since v_o is then zero.

(3) A point whose velocity is directed toward (or away from) the mass-center. To prove this, let v_o in Fig. 478 be directed toward G and, for convenience, let the x-axis be coincident with v_o. The resulting expression for the angular momentum then becomes $I_o\omega$.

Position of the Linear Momentum Vector.—The distance, q, of the linear momentum vector $M\bar{v}$ from O when O has any one of the three positions specified above may be found, as in the case of pure rotation, from the principle of moments. Thus

$$M\bar{v}q = I_o\omega = Mk_o^2\omega. \quad \text{Hence,} \quad q = \frac{k_o^2\omega}{\bar{v}},$$

in which k_o is the radius of gyration of the body about the axis through O.

PROBLEMS

804. A small body (particle) weighing 8 lb. is attached to one end of a string and is made to revolve as a conical pendulum (see Fig. 353). If the body revolves at a distance of 15 in. from the axis with an angular velocity of 90 r.p.m., find (a) the linear momentum of the body, (b) the angular momentum of the body with respect to the axis of rotation.

Ans. (a) Mom. = 2.93 lb.-sec.; (b) Ang. Mom. = 3.66 lb.-ft.-sec.

805. A slender rod rotates in a horizontal plane about a vertical axis through one end of the rod. If the rod is 3 ft. long, weighs 4 lb. per foot, and rotates at 120 r.p.m., find its angular momentum about the axis of rotation.

806. Determine the linear momentum of the rod described in the preceding problem and find the position of the momentum vector.

Ans. Mom. = 7.02 lb.-sec.; $q = 2$ ft.

807. Find the angular momentum, about the axis of rotation, of the flywheel shown on the punching machine in Fig. 454, when the flywheel is rotating at 225 r.p.m. Use the value of I found in Prob. 747.

808. Two small bodies A and B (Fig. 479) move on a circle whose radius is 2 ft. When in the positions shown the velocity of A is 40 ft./sec. and the x-component of the momentum of the system consisting of the two bodies is 5 lb.-sec. The weight of A is 5 lb. and that of B is 8 lb. What is the velocity of B?

Ans. $v_B = 6.89$ ft./sec.

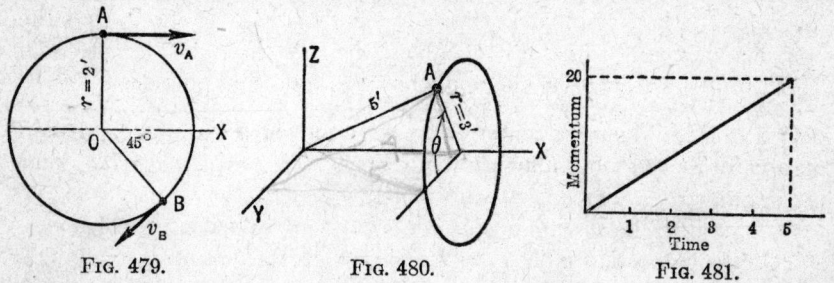

FIG. 479.   FIG. 480.   FIG. 481.

809. A small body A in Fig. 480 weighs 4 lb. and is made to rotate clockwise with a constant angular velocity of 60 r.p.m. in a circular path in a plane parallel to the yz-plane. Calculate the angular momentum of the body with respect to the y-axis in terms of θ, where θ is measured from a line parallel to the y-axis. Draw (freehand) a curve showing approximately the variation of the angular momentum with θ.

810. A small block travels in a straight path along a horizontal plane; its linear momentum varies with time as shown in Fig. 481, in which the momentum is expressed in lb.-sec. units and time in seconds. Describe the motion of the block and calculate the change in linear momentum of the block during the third second.

Ans. Δ Mom. = 4 lb.-sec.

811. A solid cylinder weighing 128.8 lb. rolls, without slipping, down an inclined plane. The linear velocity of the mass-center of the cylinder at a given instant is 30 ft./sec. The diameter of the cylinder is 18 in. Find the angular momentum of the cylinder (a) about an axis through the mass-center perpendicular to the plane of motion, (b) about the instantaneous axis of rotation.

812. A door of uniform thickness and 3-ft. width swings about a vertical axis through one edge with an angular velocity of 2 rad./sec. The door weighs 96.6 lb. Find the angular momentum of the door about the axis of rotation. Also find the magnitude of the linear momentum and the position of the momentum vector.

Ans. Ang. Mom. = 18 lb.-sec.-ft.; Mom. = 9 lb.-sec.; $q = 2$ ft.

813. A homogeneous sphere weighs 322 lb. and has a radius of 1 ft. The sphere rolls, without slipping, on a horizontal plane. If the kinetic energy of the sphere is 700 ft.-lb., what is the angular momentum about an axis through the center of the sphere perpendicular to the plane of motion? Find the linear momentum of the sphere and the position of the momentum vector.

§ 3. Principles of Impulse and Momentum

145. Preliminary.—In order to determine the effect of a force system on the motion of a body, that is, in order to treat the usual problem in kinetics, by means of the quantities impulse and momentum, the relations which exist between the impulse of the force system and the momentum of the body on which the force system acts must be established. These relations are expressed by means of two principles, namely, (1) the principle of linear impulse and linear momentum and (2) the principle of angular impulse and angular momentum.

146. Principle of Linear Impulse and Linear Momentum.—It was stated in Art. 109 that the algebraic sum of the components, in a given direction, of the external forces acting on any body (whether rigid or not) is equal to the mass of the body times the component of the acceleration of the mass-center of the body in the given direction. That is, if x denotes any direction,

$$\Sigma F_x = M\bar{a}_x = M\frac{d\bar{v}_x}{dt} = \frac{d}{dt}(M\bar{v}_x) \quad \ldots \quad (1)$$

And, by integrating this equation, the following equation which expresses the principle of linear impulse and linear momentum is obtained

$$\int_{t_1}^{t_2} \Sigma F_x dt = \int_{\bar{v}'_x}^{\bar{v}''_x} d(M\bar{v}_x).$$

Or

$$\Sigma \int_{t_1}^{t_2} F_x dt = M\bar{v}''_x - M\bar{v}'_x, \quad \ldots \quad (2)$$

in which $\bar{v}''_x$ and $\bar{v}'_x$ are the x-components of the velocity of the mass-center of the body at the end and at the beginning, respectively, of the time interval $t_2 - t_1$. The principle of linear impulse and linear momentum then, as expressed in Eq. (2) may be stated in words as follows: *The algebraic sum of the components, in any direction, of the impulses of the external forces acting on a body during any time interval is equal to the change in the component of the linear momentum of the body in the same direction during the same interval of time*, or, stated in the form of an equation,

$$(Imp.)_x = \Delta(Mom.)_x \quad \ldots \ldots \quad (3)$$

in which x represents any direction.

It should be noted also that equation (1) expresses an important principle which may be stated in words as follows: *The algebraic sum of the components, in any direction, of the external forces acting on any body is equal to the rate of change of the component of the linear momentum of the body in the same direction.*

147. Principle of Angular Impulse and Angular Momentum.—The relation between the angular impulse of the forces acting on a body and the angular momentum of the body will now be found for *rigid* bodies having a motion of rotation or a plane motion.

Rotation of a Rigid Body.—It was shown in Art. 111 that, if a rigid body rotates about a fixed axis, the algebraic sum of the moments of the external forces about the axis of rotation is equal to the product of the moment of inertia of the body about the axis of rotation and the angular acceleration of the body. That is,

$$\Sigma T_o = I_o \alpha = I_o \frac{d\omega}{dt} = \frac{d}{dt}(I_o \omega) \quad \ldots \ldots \quad (1)$$

Now by integrating this equation, the following equation, which expresses the principle of angular impulse and angular momentum for a rigid body rotating about a fixed axis, is obtained:

$$\int_{t_1}^{t_2} \Sigma T_o dt = \int_{\omega_1}^{\omega_2} d(I_o \omega).$$

Or

$$\Sigma \int_{t_1}^{t_2} T_o dt = I_o \omega_2 - I_o \omega_1, \quad \ldots \ldots \quad (2)$$

in which ω_1 and ω_2 are the angular velocities of the body at the beginning and end, respectively, of the time interval $t_2 - t_1$.

The principle expressed by Eq. (2) may be stated as follows: *The algebraic sum of the angular impulses of the external forces acting on a rotating rigid body, about the axis of rotation, for any time interval, is equal to the change of angular momentum of the body about the same axis in the same interval of time.* Or stated in the form of an equation,

$$(Ang. Imp.)_o = \Delta(Ang. Mom.)_o \quad \ldots \ldots \quad (3)$$

It should be noted also that Eq. (1) expresses an important principle which may be stated in words as follows: *The algebraic sum of the* moments of the forces acting on a rotating rigid body about the axis of rotation is equal to the rate of change of the angular momentum of the body about the same axis.

Plane Motion of a Rigid Body.—It was shown in Art. 114 that the equation $\Sigma T_o = I_o \alpha$ also applies to a rigid body having plane motion, provided that the point O is the mass-center of the body. Therefore, Eq. (2) and (3) apply also to a rigid body having plane motion provided that O is the mass-center of the body. Thus the equation $(Ang.\ Imp.)_o = \Delta(Ang.\ Mom.)_o$ becomes $(Ang.\ Imp.)_{mass\text{-}center} = \Delta(Ang.\ Mom.)_{mass\text{-}center}$, and, if the forces acting on the rigid body are constant, this may be written:

$$\Sigma \overline{T} \cdot \Delta t = \overline{I}(\omega_2 - \omega_1)$$

The equation $(Ang.\ Imp.)_o = \Delta(Ang.\ Mom.)_o$, however, is not restricted to the case where O coincides with the mass-center of the body but may be used where O is any point in the plane of motion, as may be shown by starting with the general expression for ΣT_o in equations (1) of Art. 114 instead of starting with the restricted equation $\Sigma T_o = I_o \alpha$. But, as noted in Art. 144, $(Ang.\ Mom.)_o$ is *not* equal to $I_o \omega$ unless O is the mass-center of the body, or the center of zero velocity, or a point whose velocity is directed toward (or away from) the mass-center.

148. Method of Analysis of the Motion of a Body by Means of Impulse and Momentum.—It was noted in Art. 108 that, in the analysis of the motion of any body under the action of an unbalanced force system, relations must be found which involve (1) the forces acting on the body, (2) the kinetic properties of the body, and (3) the kinematic properties of the motion of the body (linear and angular velocity or acceleration, etc.).

Now these three factors are involved in the principles of impulse and momentum. And, as noted in Art. 100, in the analysis of the motion of a body that has a plane motion, three equations are needed. Two of these equations are obtained by expressing the principle of linear impulse and linear momentum with reference to any two rectangular axes in the plane of motion, and the third equation is obtained by expressing the principle of angular impulse and angular momentum with reference to an axis perpendicular to the plane of motion. Thus, the three equations may be written as follows:

$$(Imp.)_x = \Delta(Mom.)_x,$$
$$(Imp.)_y = \Delta(Mom.)_y,$$
$$(Ang.\ Imp.)_o = \Delta(Ang.\ Mom.)_o.$$

IMPULSE AND MOMENTUM

The particular forms of the expressions for the above quantities depend upon the type of forces (whether constant or variable, etc.), the kind of body (whether rigid, etc.), and the type of motion (whether translation, rotation or plane motion).

ILLUSTRATIVE PROBLEMS

Problem 814.—A cylindrical jet of water 1½ in. in diameter impinges on a fixed blade which is inclined at an angle of 30° with the direction of the jet as shown in Fig. 482. The velocity of the jet is 25 ft./sec. Find the horizontal and vertical components of the pressure of the water on the blade (or blade on the water). Assume that the magnitude of the velocity of the jet is not changed by the action of the blade. Also assume that the only force acting on the water while it is in contact with the blade is the pressure of the blade.

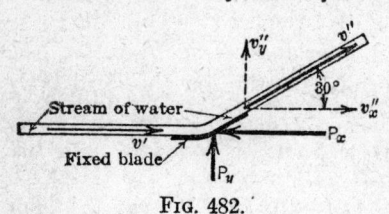

Solution.—Let P_x and P_y be the unknown horizontal and vertical pressures exerted by the blade on the water, these pressures being the cause of the change in the momentum of the water.

The principle of impulse and momentum states that

$$\Sigma F_x \cdot \Delta t = M(v''_x - v'_x), \quad \ldots \ldots \ldots (1)$$

$$\Sigma F_y \cdot \Delta t = M(v''_y - v'_y). \quad \ldots \ldots \ldots (2)$$

Let Δt be taken as any convenient time interval (1 sec., say). Then M is the mass of the water upon which the blade acts in the same time interval.

Taking the direction of the velocity of the impinging water as positive, and the weight of water as 62.5 lb./cu. ft., we have,
From (1),

$$P_x \cdot 1 = \frac{\pi(1.5)^2 \times 25 \times 62.5}{4 \times 144 \times 32.2} (25 - 25 \cos 30°).$$

Whence

$$P_x = 0.594(25 - 21.65) = 1.99 \text{ lb.}$$

From (2),

$$P_y \cdot 1 = 0.594(25 \sin 30° - 0) = 7.43 \text{ lb.}$$

Problem 815.—A cylinder weighing W lb. and having a radius of r ft. rolls, without slipping, up a plane making an angle of 30° with the horizontal. A force of ⅘ W lb. perpendicular to the axis of the cylinder is exerted on the cylinder by means of cords wrapped around short cylindrical projections on the ends of the cylinder as shown in Fig. 483. The radius of the projections is ½r. What is the velocity, $\bar{v}$, of the center of the cylinder 4 sec. after starting from rest?

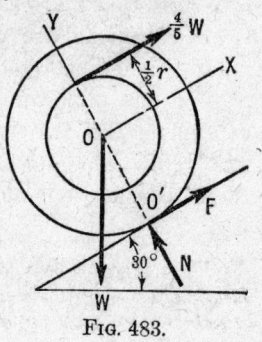

Solution.—The free-body diagram of the cylinder is shown in Fig. 483. From the principles of impulse and momentum we have:

PROBLEMS

$$\Sigma F_x \cdot \Delta t = M(\bar{v}''_x - \bar{v}'_x) \quad \text{or} \quad (\tfrac{4}{5}W - \tfrac{1}{2}W + F)4 = \frac{W}{g}\bar{v}. \quad \ldots \quad (1)$$

$$\Sigma F_y \cdot \Delta t = M(\bar{v}''_y - \bar{v}'_y) \quad \text{or} \quad (N - 0.866W)4 = 0. \quad \ldots \quad (2)$$

$$\Sigma \overline{T} \cdot \Delta t = \overline{I}(\omega_2 - \omega_1) \quad \text{or} \quad (\tfrac{4}{5}W \cdot \tfrac{1}{2}r - Fr)4 = \tfrac{1}{2}\frac{W}{g}r^2\omega_2. \quad \ldots \quad (3)$$

From (3),
$$F = \tfrac{2}{5}W - \tfrac{1}{8}\frac{W}{g}\bar{v}, \quad \text{since } r\omega_2 = \bar{v}.$$

Substituting this value of F in (1) and solving, we find
$$\bar{v} = \tfrac{28}{15}g = 60.1 \text{ ft./sec.}$$

Problem 816.—The wheel in Fig. 484 is rotating with an angular velocity of 120 r.p.m. when the brake shoe A is applied. The force P is increased gradually from 0 to 20 lb. in 5 sec. and then gradually decreased to 0 again as indicated in the force-time diagram in Fig. 484(b). Find the angular velocity of the wheel at the end of 10 sec. The weight of the wheel is 322 lb., its radius of gyration is 1.5 ft., and the coefficient of friction μ between the wheel and brake shoe is 0.3.

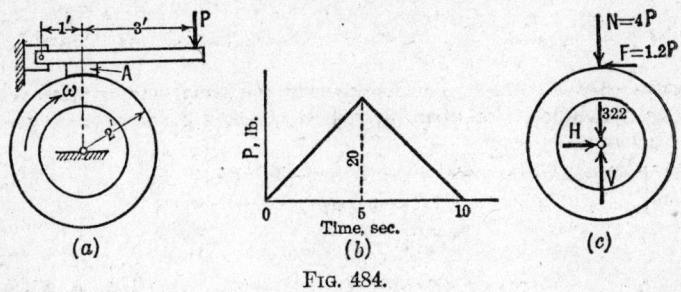

Fig. 484.

Solution.—From the principle of angular impulse and momentum we have
$$\int T\, dt = \Delta(I\omega)$$

where T is the torque acting on the wheel at any time t. From the free-body diagram of the wheel (Fig. 484c) we see that the frictional force $F = \mu N$ at any instant is $1.2P$, the value of the normal pressure N being found by considering the equilibrium of the bar on which P is acting. Hence the torque $T = Fr = 2.4P$. But $P = 4t$. Therefore,

$$2\int_0^5 T\, dt = 2\int_0^5 2.4 \times 4t\, dt = \frac{322}{32.2}\left(\frac{3}{2}\right)^2 (4\pi - \omega_2)$$

$$19.2\left[\frac{t^2}{2}\right]_0^5 = \frac{90}{4}(4\pi - \omega_2)$$

$$\frac{19.2 \times 25}{2} = \frac{90}{4}(4\pi - \omega_2)$$

Hence,
$$\omega_2 = 1.90 \text{ rad./sec.} = 18.15 \text{ r.p.m.}$$

PROBLEMS

817. A jet of water 2 in. in diameter has a velocity of 30 ft./sec. in a horizontal direction. If the jet impinges normally against a fixed vertical plane, what is the pressure of the water on the plane?

818. A 5½-oz. baseball moving horizontally with a velocity of 150 ft./sec. is struck by a bat and is deflected 135° from its original direction as indicated in Fig. 485. If the speed of the ball as it leaves the bat is 130 ft./sec., compute the horizontal and vertical components of the impulse of the bat on the ball. Assuming that the time of contact is $\frac{1}{50}$ sec., determine the average value of the force during the impact.

Ans. $(Imp.)_x = 2.58$ lb.-sec.; $(Imp.)_y = 0.98$ lb.-sec.; $F_{average} = 138$ lb.

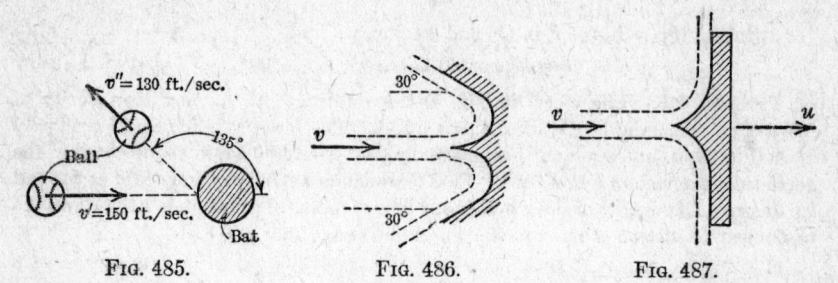

FIG. 485.   FIG. 486.   FIG. 487.

819. A horizontal stream of water having a velocity of 20 ft./sec. strikes a fixed blade as shown in Fig. 486. Assuming that the friction of the water on the blade is negligible find the horizontal force exerted on the blade. The cross-section of the stream is 2 sq. in.

820. A horizontal stream of water having a velocity of 40 ft./sec. strikes a moving blade as shown in Fig. 487. The velocity u of the blade is 10 ft./sec. in the direction of the velocity of the water. The diameter of the stream is $\frac{3}{4}$ in. Find the horizontal force exerted by the water on the blade.   *Ans.* $P = 5.36$ lb.

821. A body slides down a plane inclined 45° with the horizontal. If the coefficient of kinetic friction is 0.2, how many seconds will it take for the velocity of the body to change from 10 ft./sec. to 30 ft./sec.?

822. A certain machine gun fires 350 bullets per minute. If each bullet weighs 1 oz. and the muzzle velocity of the bullets is 2200 ft./sec., what is the average reaction of the gun against its support? Neglect the reaction due to the discharged gases.   *Ans.* $R_{average} = 24.9$ lb.

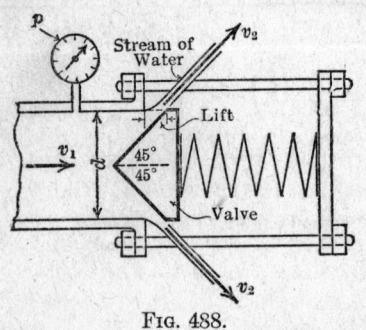

823. In the relief valve shown in Fig. 488 the discharge area is assumed to be equal to the circumference of the pipe times the lift of the valve times cos 45°. The rate of discharge of the water is 2 cu. ft./sec. The diameter, d, of the pipe is 6 in. The "lift" is 0.25 in. The pressure p in the pipe is 30 lb./sq. in. Find the force exerted by the spring on the valve. *Hint*: The force causing the change in the horizontal component of the momentum of the water from Mv_1 to Mv_2 cos 45° is the difference between the pressure on a cross-section of the water in the pipe and the force exerted by the spring.   *Ans.* $P = 650$ lb.

FIG. 488.

824. The table of a planing machine together with the material bolted on it weighs 5 tons. Find the time required to change its velocity from 20 ft./min.

PROBLEMS

(cutting stroke) to 40 ft./min. in the opposite direction (return stroke) if the average force of the pinion on the rack while the velocity is being changed is 200 lb.
Ans. $t = 1.55$ sec.

825. Water flows in a straight pipe with a velocity of 10 ft./sec. The pipe is 4 ft. in diameter and 2 mi. long. Calculate the linear momentum of the water. What would be the effect of closing a valve quickly if the valve is near the discharge end of the pipe? What is the time of closing the valve if the average additional pressure due to closing is 20 lb./sq. in.?

826. An 800-lb. shell is fired from a gun weighing 160,000 lb. with an initial velocity of 1400 ft./sec. What will be the maximum velocity of recoil of the gun? How far will the gun recoil if a constant resistance of 18,000 lb. begins to act immediately after the explosion? *Ans.* $v = 7$ ft./sec.; $s = 6.76$ ft.

827. A flywheel weighing 1288 lb. is keyed to a shaft 4 in. in diameter. The shaft transmits a turning moment of 1200 in.-lb. to the flywheel, thereby increasing its angular velocity from 600 rad./min. to 50 rad./sec. in 10 sec. Find the radius of gyration of the flywheel.

828. The rotating parts of a horizontal-shaft turbine weigh 20 tons and have a radius of gyration of 2 ft. It takes 10 min. for the turbine to come to rest from a speed of 55 r.p.m. under the influence of journal friction alone. The shaft is 12 in. in diameter. What is the average coefficient of friction? *Ans.* $\mu = 0.00238$.

829. A sphere having a weight of 64.4 lb. and a diameter of 30 in. rolls, without slipping, down a plane inclined 30° with the horizontal. What will be the velocity of its center at the end of 5 sec. if the initial velocity of its center is 30 ft./sec.?

830. A homogeneous cylindrical disk (Fig. 489) weighs 128.8 lb. and has a radius of 1 ft. It is mounted so that it rotates in a horizontal plane about a smooth vertical axis at O. A couple of variable moment $T = 8t^3$ is applied to the disk, T being expressed in lb.-ft. and t in sec. If the initial value of ω is 54 rad./sec., how long will it take the disk to come to rest? *Ans.* $t = 3$ sec.

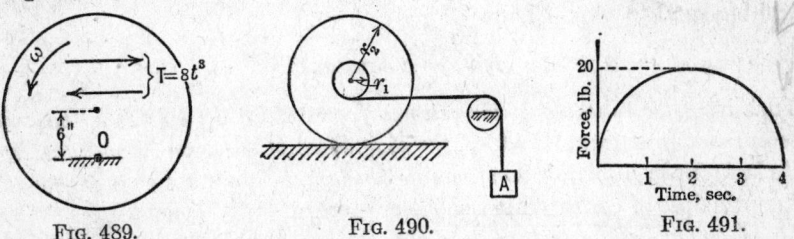

FIG. 489.   FIG. 490.   FIG. 491.

831. The weight of A in Fig. 490 is 20 lb. The string attached to A passes over a smooth peg and wraps around a drum of radius $r_1 = 5$ in. attached to a wheel having a radius $r_2 = 18$ in. The radius of gyration of wheel and drum is 15 in. The wheel rolls without slipping. How many seconds are required for A to acquire a velocity of 10 ft./sec., starting from rest? The weight of the wheel and drum is 64.4 lb. *Ans.* $t = 3.56$ sec.

832. A body rests on a smooth horizontal surface and is acted on by a horizontal force that passes through the mass-center of the body. The weight of the body is 64.4 lb. The force is constant in direction and its magnitude varies as the ordinate to a circle as shown in Fig. 491. Find the linear velocity of the body at the end of 3 sec. *Ans.* $v = 25.3$ ft./sec.

833. A homogeneous cylinder rolls, without slipping, down a plane inclined 30° to the horizontal. Find the velocity of the center of the cylinder 3 sec. after starting from rest.

834. How long will it take the cylinder described in Prob. 670 to acquire an angular velocity of 10 rad./sec., starting from rest?   *Ans.* $t = 0.233$ sec.

835. A homogeneous circular cylinder having a radius of 1 ft. and a weight of 32.2 lb. rests on a horizontal plane, the axis of the cylinder being parallel to the plane. In the plane of symmetry perpendicular to the axis is turned a narrow groove 6 in. deep. A constant horizontal force of 32 lb. is applied through a cord wrapped around the groove, the horizontal portion of the cord being tangent to the groove at its lowest point. If the cylinder rolls without slipping find the velocity of the horizontal portion of the cord at the end of 1.5 sec.

836. A cylinder weighing 96.6 lb. and having a radius of 6 in. is mounted on a horizontal axle whose axis coincides with the axis of the cylinder. A body weighing 32.2 lb. is suspended from a cord wrapped around the cylinder. If the body is allowed to descend from rest, what will its velocity be at the end of 2 sec.? Neglect bearing friction.   *Ans.* $v = 25.8$ ft.

149. Conservation of Momentum.—*I. Linear Momentum.*—As already noted, the principle of linear impulse and linear momentum for the motion of any mass-system under the action of an unbalanced external force system is expressed by the equation

$$(Imp.)_x = \Delta(M\bar{v}_x),$$

in which x represents any direction. Now if the resultant of the forces which act on the body has no component in the x-direction, the impulse of the force system in the x-direction will be zero, and hence $\Delta(M\bar{v}_x)$ will be equal to zero. Thus

$$M\bar{v}_x = a \text{ constant.}$$

That is, *if the resultant of the external forces which act on a body has no component in a given direction, the component of the linear momentum of the body in the given direction remains constant.* This statement expresses the principle of conservation of linear momentum.

II. Angular Momentum.—As already noted, the principle of angular impulse and angular momentum for the motion of any body under the action of an unbalanced external force system is expressed by the equation

$$(Ang.\ Imp.)_o = \Delta(Ang.\ Mom.)_o.$$

Now if the external forces which act on the body have no resultant moment about a given axis, O, the angular impulse of the forces about the same axis will be zero, and hence $\Delta(Ang.\ Mom.)_o$ will be equal to zero. Thus

$$(Ang.\ Mom.)_o = a \text{ constant.}$$

That is, *if the external forces which act on a body have no resultant moment about an axis, the angular momentum of the body with respect to that axis remains constant.* This statement expresses the principle of the conservation of angular momentum.

It was shown in Arts. 143 and 144 that the angular momentum of a body about an axis, O, is expressed by $I_o\omega$ if one of the following conditions is satisfied: (1) The body is rigid and rotates about a fixed axis, the O-axis being taken as the axis of rotation; (2) the body is rigid and has a plane motion and the point O is (a) the mass-center of the body, or (b) the instantaneous center of zero velocity, or (c) a point whose velocity is toward (or away from) the mass-center. Furthermore, $I_o\omega$ also expresses the angular momentum of a non-rigid mass-system that rotates about a fixed axis provided that all parts of the mass-system have the same angular velocity. Thus, if a rod rotates about a fixed axis as bodies slide radially outwards (or inwards) along the rod, the mass-system is not rigid but the angular momentum of the system about the axis, O, of rotation is $I_o\omega$.

Therefore, the principle of conservation of angular momentum *when the above conditions are satisfied*, may be expressed as follows:

$$I_o\omega = \text{a constant.}$$

Thus if I_o decreases, ω must increase, and vice versa. For example a gymnast who leaves the swinging trapeze at the top of a circus tent with a relatively small angular velocity ω (his body being extended) may increase his angular velocity and make several complete turns in midair as he descends in a vertical plane by "doubling up." His moment of inertia is thereby decreased and his angular velocity is increased a sufficient amount to keep $I_o\omega$ constant since no external torque acts on him while he is descending.

ILLUSTRATIVE PROBLEMS

Problem 837.—The weight of the parts of a 3-in. field gun (Fig. 492) which move during recoil is 950 lb. The weight of the projectile is 15 lb. and that of the powder charge is 1.5 lb. The muzzle velocity is 1700 ft./sec. Determine the velocity of free recoil at the time the projectile reaches the end of barrel, assuming that the projectile leaves the gun with a horizontal velocity.

Solution.—Three bodies are to be considered; the projectile, the powder charge, and the recoiling parts of the gun. Since the recoil is free, no horizontal external forces are acting on these three bodies while the projectile is reaching the muzzle of the gun, and hence the linear momentum of the system remains constant. That is, the momentum of the projectile plus the momentum of the gases is equal to the momentum of the recoiling parts. Thus

$$M_p v_p + M_g \bar{v}_g = M_r v_r.$$

332   IMPULSE AND MOMENTUM

The gases (and unburned powder) form a non-rigid body, and hence the velocity $\bar{v}_g$, of the mass-center must be used. It is usually assumed that $\bar{v}_g$ is one-half of the

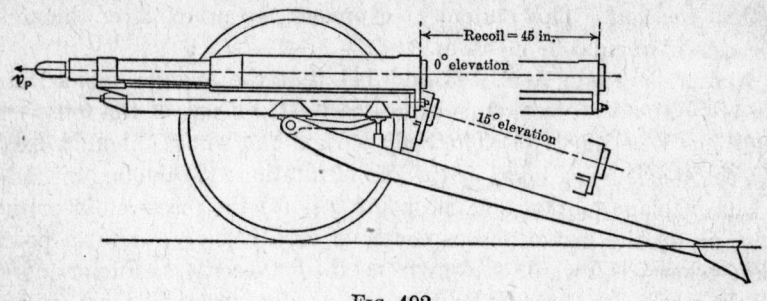

FIG. 492.

velocity of the projectile. Thus, using weights instead of masses since they are proportional, we have

$$15 \times 1700 + 1.5 \times \frac{1700}{2} = 950\, v_r.$$

Hence

$$v_r = \frac{25{,}500 + 1275}{950} = 28.1 \text{ ft./sec.}$$

The velocity of free recoil as the projectile reaches the muzzle of the gun is about 0.7 of the maximum velocity of free recoil. The bore is filled with gases for a short interval after the projectile leaves the gun and these gases continue to exert pressure on the breech and thus to increase the velocity of recoil.

Problem 838.—Two spheres (Fig. 493) are mounted on a light rod on which the spheres may slide without friction. The rod and spheres rotate about the vertical central axis. A string is attached to each sphere and runs over pulleys so that the pull of each string is directed along the rod. Each sphere weighs 8 lb. and is 2½ in. in diameter. When the distance of the center of each sphere from the axis of rotation is 2 ft., the angular velocity of the rod is 60 r.p.m. If the spheres are pulled a distance of 6 in. along the rod toward the axis of rotation what will be the angular velocity of the rod?

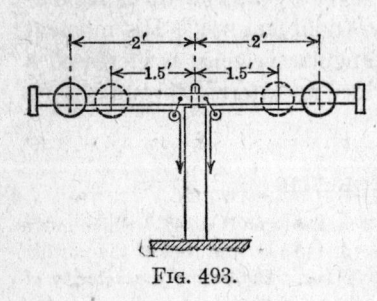

FIG. 493.

Solution.—Since the external forces acting on the spheres have no moment about the axis of rotation, the angular momentum with respect to the axis of rotation remains constant. That is, the angular momentum of the spheres before they are pulled in is equal to their angular momentum after they are pulled in. Whence

$$I_1 \omega_1 = I_2 \omega_2.$$

Little error will be introduced by considering the spheres to be particles and by neglecting the mass of the rod. Thus

$$2M \times (2)^2 \times \frac{60 \times 2\pi}{60} = 2M \times (1.5)^2 \omega_2.$$

Hence

$$\omega_2 = \frac{4 \times 2\pi}{2.25} = 11.15 \text{ rad./sec.} = 106.6 \text{ r.p.m.}$$

Thus it will be noted that, as the moment of inertia of the spheres decreases, their angular velocity must increase. And since the moment of inertia decreases as the square of the distance from the axis of rotation, a relatively small inward movement of the spheres causes a relatively large increase in the angular velocity.

If the pulls of the strings are released when the spheres are at any distance, x (Fig. 494), from the axis of rotation, then no force in the horizontal plane will be acting on either sphere, and hence each sphere will continue with constant speed in a straight line until it strikes the stop at the end of the rod as indicated in Fig. 494. That is, the linear momentum of each sphere remains constant until the stop is hit and then changes from mv to mv_t. The angular momentum of the sphere, however, is the same after the sphere strikes the stop as it was before the sphere struck the stop since no moment is introduced by the pressure of the stop. Thus $mv \cdot x = mv_t \cdot r$.

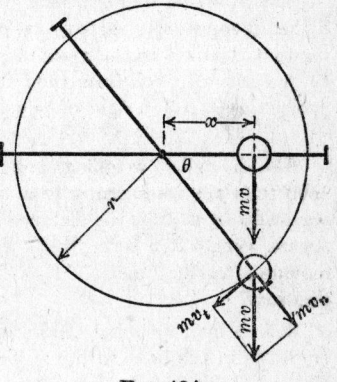

FIG. 494.

PROBLEMS

839. A 2-oz. bullet moving with a velocity of 2000 ft./sec. strikes, centrally, a block of wood which is moving on a smooth horizontal plane in the same direction as the bullet with a velocity of 20 ft./sec. If the block of wood in which the bullet embeds itself weighs 16.8 lb., what is the resulting velocity of the block and bullet?
Ans. $v = 34.6$ ft./sec.

840. Two similar pulleys are running loose on a shaft. One has an angular velocity of 10 r.p.m. and the other a velocity of 30 r.p.m. in the opposite direction. They are suddenly coupled together by means of a friction clutch. What will be the angular velocity of the pulleys after the clutch has ceased to slip? What proportion of the kinetic energy is lost?

841. A disk D and a small body A (Fig. 495) are rotating at 90 r.p.m. about the

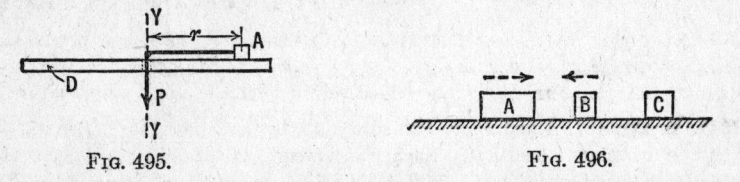

FIG. 495.   FIG. 496.

axis YY. The body A is attached to a string that passes through a small hole at the center of the disk. The distance, r, of A from the axis of rotation is 24 in. and the weight of A is 8 lb. The top surface of the disk is smooth. If by pulling on the string r is decreased to 8 in., what will be the angular velocity of A?

Ans. $\omega = 84.8$ rad./sec. $= 810$ r.p.m.

842. Three bodies A, B, and C (Fig. 496) whose weights are 40 lb., 10 lb., and 20 lb., respectively rest on a smooth horizontal surface. If A is given a velocity of 20 ft./sec. to the right and B a velocity of 10 ft./sec. to the left and C remains at rest until A and B come into contact with it, what will be the final velocity of the three bodies assuming that after coming into contact they remain in contact?

843. A 4.7-in. howitzer field gun rests on a wooden platform. Recoil is checked by heavy ropes attached to stakes driven into the ground in front of the gun. Assuming that the slack in the ropes allows the velocity of free recoil to be developed, find the velocity of recoil from the following data: Weight of gun, 7000 lb.; weight of projectile, 63 lb.; weight of powder charge, 6 lb.; muzzle velocity, 1500 ft./sec.

Ans. $v = 14.1$ ft./sec.

844. A bullet weighing 1 oz. and moving horizontally with a velocity of 1500 ft./sec. strikes centrally a wooden sphere weighing 99 oz. that is suspended vertically by a cord, the distance from the point of suspension to the center of the sphere being 4 ft. With what velocity will the sphere (and embedded bullet) start moving after the impact? How far will the sphere rise vertically above its initial position?

845. A man weighing 150 lb. jumps into the center of a boat that weighs 180 lb. He lands in the boat with a velocity having a horizontal component of 10 ft./sec. The boat is drifting with a velocity of 5 ft./sec. in the same direction. Neglecting the resistance of the water, find the resulting velocity of the boat and man. If it takes ½ sec. for the boat to acquire this resulting velocity, what is the average value of the horizontal force exerted by the man on the boat?

Ans. $v = 7.27$ ft./sec.; $P = 25.4$ lb.

846. A tank partly filled with water rests on a flat-topped car. The car and tank are moving along a straight track at 10 mi./hr. when a stone weighing 200 lb. is dropped vertically into the water. The weight of the car is 400 lb. and that of the tank and water is 300 lb. Neglecting the friction of the car on the track, what is the velocity of the car after the stone has been dropped in the water? If the tank slides on the car for ½ sec. before coming to rest relative to the car, what is the average value of the horizontal force that is exerted by the car on the tank while the velocity of the tank (and car) is being changed?

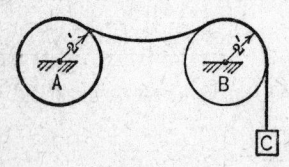

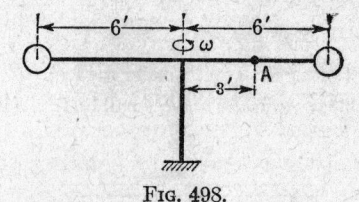

Fig. 497.   Fig. 498.

847. In Fig. 497, A and B are two sprocket wheels mounted on horizontal axles which rest in smooth bearings. Each wheel weighs 20 lb. and has a diameter of 4 ft. and a radius of gyration of 1.75 ft. A body C weighing 10 lb. hangs from a light inextensible chain which passes over the two wheels as shown. C descends from rest and 2 sec. elapse before the slack in the chain is taken up. If the weight of the chain is neglected what will be the angular velocity of the two wheels immediately after the 2-sec. period, assuming that the weight C is detached from the chain just as the chain between the pulleys becomes taut?   Ans. $\omega = 6.37$ rad./sec.

848. Two spherical balls (Fig. 498) connected by a rod rotate about a vertical axis with an angular velocity ω of 30 r.p.m. Each ball weighs 200 lb. and is 1 ft. in diameter. The rod also weighs 200 lb. A man weighing 161 lb. jumps vertically and catches hold of the bar at A. What is the angular velocity of the system after the man catches hold of the bar?

849. A block of wood weighing 20 lb. is suspended by a long string. The block is swinging with a velocity of 40 ft./sec. through its lowest position when a bullet weighing 2 oz. and moving with a horizontal velocity of 2000 ft./sec. strikes the block and is imbedded in it. What will be the velocity of the block and bullet (a) if the velocities of the block and bullet before impact are parallel but opposite in sense? (b) if the velocities are parallel and have the same sense? (c) if the velocities are at right angles?

Ans. (a) $v = 27.4$ ft./sec.; (b) $v = 52.2$ ft./sec.; (c) $v = 41.6$ ft./sec.

150. Impact.—The equations of Art. 148 which express the principles of impulse and momentum apply to the motion of bodies whether the bodies move under the action of impulsive forces or of forces which act during a finite time interval. In fact, as stated in Art. 136, the principles of impulse and momentum are particularly well adapted to the solution of kinetics problems which involve sudden impulses.

The effect of impulsive forces on the motion of a body, in most problems, is so large in comparison with the effect of the other forces which act on the body that the effect of the other forces on the motion of the body, while the impact lasts, may be neglected. The only details of the change in the motion of a body that can be determined, when the change in the motion is caused by impulsive forces, are the initial and final velocities of the body. For, the distance traveled during the impact is indefinitely small; the time interval is also indefinitely small, and hence the acceleration produced is indefinitely large since the change in velocity is a finite quantity. Thus the distance, time, and acceleration are indeterminate. There is, however, a definite (appreciable) change in the velocity, although, as just noted, the manner in which the velocity changes during the period of the impact is unknown and only the initial and final values of the velocity can be determined. Therefore, the momentum of the body at the beginning and at the end of the impact period are definite quantities, and, since these quantities are involved in the principles of impulse and momentum, problems which involve impulsive forces yield to this method of solution although the impulse of the impulsive forces is used and not the forces themselves.

Direct Central Impact.—If two bodies collide and the velocity of each is directed normal to the striking surfaces, the impact is said to be *direct.* If two bodies collide in such a way that the action line of the pressures exerted by the bodies on each other is directed along the line connecting the mass-centers of the two bodies, the impact is said to be *central.*

The period of impact may be divided into two parts: (1) the time of deformation during which the impulsive force is increasing to its maximum value as the two bodies deform, and (2) the time of restitution during which the bodies are separating and partially recovering from the deformation. If the two bodies were perfectly elastic, the period of deformation would be equal to the period of restitution, and the velocity of separation would be equal to the velocity of approach. But, all bodies are more or less inelastic, and hence the velocity of separation is always somewhat less than the velocity of approach.

Coefficient of Restitution.—For direct central impact of two bodies, the ratio of the relative velocity of separation to the relative velocity of approach is defined as the *coefficient of restitution.* Thus, if the velocities before impact are denoted by v_1 and v_2 and after impact by v'_1 and v'_2 and if e denotes the coefficient of restitution, the value of e is defined by the following equation:

$$e = -\frac{v'_2 - v'_1}{v_2 - v_1} \quad \text{or} \quad v'_2 - v'_1 = -e(v_2 - v_1) \quad . \quad . \quad (1)$$

Experiments show that the value of the coefficient of restitution for two spheres in central direct impact depends only on the materials of the two spheres. It is generally assumed that the value of e as found for two spheres of any two materials is the same for other bodies of the same materials whether the impact is central and direct or not. But if the impact is not central and direct, the components of the velocities normal to the impact surfaces must be used in equation (1) instead of the total velocities.

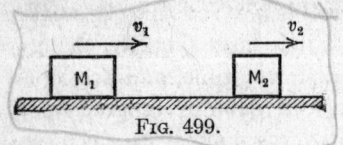

151. Impact of Two Translating Bodies.—*Direct Central Impact.*—In Fig. 499 are represented two translating bodies which collide with direct central impact. It is assumed that the values of

$$M_1, M_2, v_1, v_2, \text{ and } e$$

are known, and it is required to find the values of

$$v, v'_1, v'_2, \int_0^{t_d} P_d dt \quad \text{or} \quad (P_d)_{av} \cdot t_d, \quad \text{and} \quad \int_{t_d}^{t} P_r dt \quad \text{or} \quad (P_r)_{av} \cdot t_r,$$

where v is the velocity of the bodies at the end of the deformation period

t_d, v'_1 and v'_2 are the velocities of the bodies after the impact, and t_r is the restitution period.

Evidently five equations must be found from which the five unknown quantities may be determined. The five equations may be found as follows: From the principle of conservation of linear momentum Eq. (1) and (2) below are obtained. Thus

$$M_1 v_1 + M_2 v_2 = (M_1 + M_2)v \text{ for the period } t_d \quad . \quad . \quad . \quad (1)$$

$$(M_1 + M_2)v = M_1 v'_1 + M_2 v'_2 \text{ for the period } t_r \quad . \quad . \quad (2)$$

And, from Art 150,

$$v'_1 - v'_2 = -e(v_1 - v_2) \quad . \quad . \quad . \quad . \quad . \quad (3)$$

From these three equations the values of v, v'_1, and v'_2 may be found. The impulses for the periods t_d and t_r may now be found by applying the principle of linear impulse and momentum for the periods t_d and t_r, which leads to the following equations:

$$\int_0^{t_d} P_d \, dt = M_1(v - v_1) = M_2(v - v_2), \quad . \quad . \quad . \quad (4)$$

$$\int_{t_d}^{t} P_r \, dt = M_1(v'_1 - v) = M_2(v'_2 - v) \quad . \quad . \quad . \quad (5)$$

PROBLEMS

850. A freight car weighing 40 tons and traveling at a speed of 20 mi./hr. on a straight track overtakes another car weighing 30 tons and traveling on the same track in the same direction at a speed of 15 mi./hr. If the value of e is 0.2, find the velocity of each car after impact and the impulse of each car on the other both for the time of deformation and for the time of restitution.

851. A body weighing 50 lb. moving to the right collides with a 30-lb. body moving to the left. The speed of each body is 15 ft./sec. The impact of the two bodies is direct and central. If the coefficient of restitution is 0.6, find (a) the velocity of each body after impact, (b) the velocity of each body at the end of the deformation period.   *Ans.* $v_1' = -3$ ft./sec., $v_2' = 15$ ft./sec.; $v = 3.75$ ft./sec.

852. A sphere which is at rest is struck directly by another sphere having the same mass and diameter. The velocity of the center of the latter is 20 ft./sec. If the coefficient of restitution is 0.5, find the velocities of the centers of the spheres after impact.

853. A ball drops from rest 16 ft. and strikes a horizontal rigid steel plate. If the ball rebounds 9 ft., what is the coefficient of restitution?   *Ans.* $e = 0.75$.

854. A falling weight of 1000 lb. is used to drive a pile into the ground. If the weight of the pile is 800 lb. and the weight is dropped 20 ft., what will be the depth of penetration of the pile, assuming an average resistance to penetration of 30,000 lb.? Assume the impact between the weight and pile to be perfectly inelastic ($e = 0$).
     Ans. $s = 4.73$ in.

REVIEW QUESTIONS AND PROBLEMS

855. Define linear impulse of a force (a) in words; (b) as a mathematical expression. Is impulse a vector quantity?

856. What is another name for angular impulse of a force? What are the units of angular impulse?

857. Is the linear momentum of a particle a vector quantity? State in words the meaning of $(mv)_x$. What are the units of linear momentum?

858. What is another name for moment of momentum of a particle? What are the units of moment of momentum?

859. Prove that $\Sigma(mv)_x = M\bar{v}_x$, and state in words the meaning of the equation.

860. Where in the body is the position line of the linear momentum vector $M\bar{v}$: (a) for a translating rigid body, (b) for a rotating rigid body?

861. Point out, and correct, the errors in the following demonstration that the angular momentum of a rotating rigid body is $I_o\omega$: The linear momentum of the body is $M\bar{v}$, and the angular momentum of the body about the axis of rotation O is $M\bar{v}\bar{r}$. But $\bar{v} = \bar{r}\omega$, and hence $(Ang.\ Mom.)_o = M\bar{r}^2\omega$. Thus $(Ang.\ Mom.)_o = I_o\omega$, since $M\bar{r}^2 = I_o$.

862. Starting with the equation $\Sigma F_x = M\bar{a}_x$, derive the equation expressing the principle of linear impulse and linear momentum for any mass-system acted on by constant forces.

863. Point out, and correct, the error in the following statement of the principle of conservation of angular momentum: If the forces acting on any body have no resultant moment about a given axis O, then $I_o\omega$ of the body will remain constant.

864. A projectile weighing 2 lb. and moving in a horizontal direction with a velocity of 80 ft./sec. strikes centrally a small box of sand and remains embedded in the sand. The box of sand weighs 18 lb. and is resting on a horizontal plane when the projectile strikes it. The coefficient of friction for the box and plane is 0.20. With what velocity does the box (and projectile) start to move, and how long will it take to come to rest?

Ans. $t = 1.24$ sec.

865. Solve Prob. 815, using O' as the moment-center in applying the principle of angular impulse and momentum.

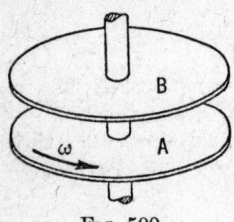

Fig. 500.

866. In Fig. 500, A is a disk keyed to the vertical shaft and rotating with it at 30 r.p.m. The disk B is not keyed to the shaft and is not rotating. If the disk B is allowed to slide down the shaft until it comes in contact with the disk A, what will be the angular velocity of the two disks after slipping between the disks has ceased? Each disk is 4 ft. in diameter and weighs 161 lb. Neglect the mass of the axle. What frictional moment is exerted on B by A if slipping between the disks occurs for 2 sec.? What percentage of the energy of the system is lost?

Ans. $\omega = 1.57$ rad./sec.; $T = 7.85$ lb.-ft.; loss $= 50$ per cent.

867. A cylinder is made to roll, without slipping, on a horizontal plane by the pull, P, on a string that is wound around a groove in the central plane of the cylinder as shown in Fig. 501. The cylinder weighs 64.4 lb. Find the velocity of the center of the cylinder 4 sec. after starting from rest if $P = 10$ lb.

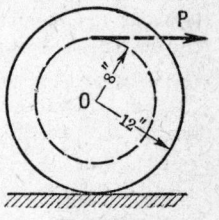

Fig. 501.

Ans. $\bar{v} = 22.2$ ft./sec.

PART IV. SPECIAL TOPICS[1]

CHAPTER XI

MECHANICAL VIBRATIONS

152. Introduction.—A mechanical vibration as met in most engineering problems is a periodic motion, usually of small amplitude, which repeats itself in a definite time interval called the *period* of the vibration; each repetition of the motion is called a *cycle*, and the number of cycles per unit of time is called the *frequency* of vibration.

The prevention of vibration in machine parts and structural members is important in eliminating excessive wear, in reducing repeated stresses that are likely to cause the failure of a member by a progressive fracture called a fatigue failure, and in reducing objectionable noise.

In the analysis of the essential dynamics features of the vibratory motion of a machine member, the member may usually be replaced by a concentrated mass (particle) connected to its supports by one or more weightless springs. The simplest and also the most common type of vibration is a simple harmonic motion. This motion was discussed in Arts. 86 and 107 and the student is advised to read these articles again before proceeding with the next article in which a simple harmonic motion will be analyzed in somewhat greater detail.

A motion, such as a simple harmonic motion, that can be described in terms of a single coordinate is said to have *one degree of freedom*. The vibrations considered here are restricted to this class of motions.

153. Free Vibrations.—Consider the motion of a small rigid body of mass m and weight W (Fig. 502) suspended by an elastic weightless spring from a rigid support. The *spring constant* or *modulus of the spring* (that is, the force required to deflect the end of the spring a unit distance) will be denoted by k, and the static deflection of the end of the spring due to the weight W will be denoted by δ_{st}; hence $k = \dfrac{W}{\delta_{st}}$. It is

---

[1] Each topic or chapter is self contained and may be studied without reference to the preceding topics in Part IV. The topics treated in Part IV are somewhat more advanced than those discussed in Parts I, II, and III, but no additional principles are employed.

assumed that the body is free to move only along a vertical line which will here be taken as the x-axis, x being regarded as positive when measured *downward* from the position of static equilibrium of the body. Let the body be given some initial displacement x_o and, as it is released, let it be given an initial velocity v_o. The body will then oscillate or vibrate with an amplitude A; the forces acting on the body when it has any displacement x are shown in Fig. 502, and by applying the equation of motion $\Sigma F_x = ma_x$ to the body we obtain

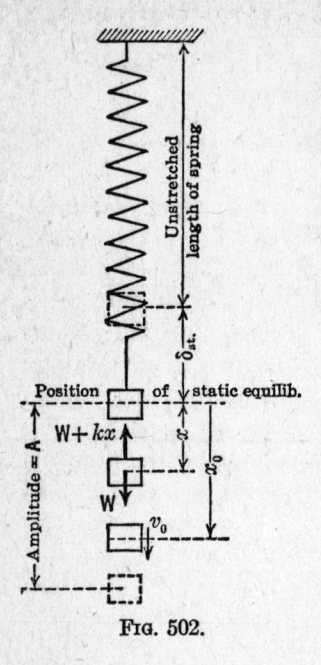

$$W - (W + kx) = ma_x \quad \text{or} \quad \frac{d^2x}{dt^2} = -\frac{k}{m}x. \quad (1)$$

This equation is the defining equation for a simple harmonic motion (Art. 86). Replacing the constant $\dfrac{k}{m}$, for convenience, by p^2 and noting that $W = k\delta_{st}$, we have

Fig. 502.

$$p^2 = \frac{k}{m} = \frac{kg}{W} = \frac{g}{\delta_{st}} \quad \ldots \ldots \quad (2)$$

Hence Eq. (1) may be written

$$\frac{d^2x}{dt^2} = -p^2x \quad \ldots \ldots \ldots \ldots \quad (3)$$

The value of x that satisfies Eq. (3) must be a function of t whose second derivative with respect to t is equal to the original function multiplied by $-p^2$. The functions $x = B \cos pt$ and $x = C \sin pt$ (where B and C are constants) satisfy the equation, as does also their sum. Hence the general solution to Eq. (3) is

$$x = B \cos pt + C \sin pt \quad \ldots \ldots \quad (4)$$

where B and C may be regarded as constants of integration whose values depend on the initial conditions of the motion. The velocity of the body at any instant during the oscillation may be found by differentiating Eq. (4). Thus

$$v = \frac{dx}{dt} = -Bp \sin pt + Cp \cos pt \quad \ldots \quad (5)$$

If the initial conditions of the motion are known, the values of B and C

FREE VIBRATIONS

can now be found. For example, let it be assumed that when $t = 0$, the displacement $x = x_o$ and that the body has an initial velocity $v = v_o$ in the positive (downward) direction. Substituting these values in Eq. (4) and (5), we find that $B = x_o$, and $C = \dfrac{v_o}{p}$. Thus Eq. (4) becomes

$$x = x_o \cos pt + \frac{v_o}{p} \sin pt \quad \ldots \ldots \quad (6)$$

A useful interpretation of Eq. (6) may be made by representing the displacement x as the projection, on the diameter of a circle, of a rotating vector. Thus, in Fig. 503, assume that the vectors $B = x_o$ and $C = \dfrac{v_o}{p}$ rotate, at right angles to each other, about O with an angular velocity p, called the *natural circular frequency* of vibration, and assume also that the vector A which is the resultant of vectors B and C also rotates about O with angular velocity p. It will be noted that the projection of A on the x-axis is $x = B \cos pt + C \sin pt$. The angle which the vector A makes with the x-axis is $pt - \phi$ where ϕ is the angle between the vectors B and A. Thus

$$x = B \cos pt + C \sin pt = A \cos (pt - \phi) \quad \ldots \ldots \quad (7)$$

where

$$A = \sqrt{B^2 + C^2} = \sqrt{x_o^2 + \left(\frac{v_o}{p}\right)^2} = \text{the amplitude of motion} \quad (8)$$

and

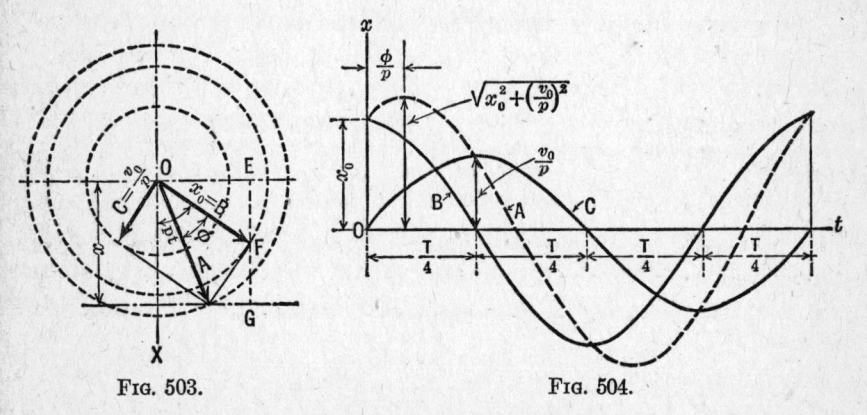

$$\tan \phi = \frac{C}{B} = \frac{v_o}{px_o} \quad \ldots \ldots \ldots \quad (9)$$

FIG. 503.   FIG. 504.

By plotting the x-projections of the vectors B and C as ordinates and time as abscissas the curves shown as B and C in Fig. 504 are obtained.

The displacement x at any time t is obtained by adding algebraically the corresponding ordinates to these two curves, and is plotted as the ordinate to the curve denoted as A in Fig. 504.

Because of the difference in the directions of the vectors in Fig. 503, their maximum projections on the x-axis do not occur at the same time t. Thus the maximum value of the displacement x, which is represented by the maximum ordinate to the curve A, occurs at a time $\dfrac{\phi}{p}$ after the ordinate in curve B attains its maximum value. The angle ϕ is called the *phase angle*.

It will be observed that the simple harmonic motion defined by Eq. (6) or Eq. (7) may be regarded as the resultant of two simple harmonic motions $x = x_o \cos pt$ and $x = \dfrac{v_o}{p} \sin pt$ which have the same frequency but different amplitudes, and which differ in phase by 90°.

Equations (6) and (7) and Fig. 504 show that the oscillatory motion repeats itself whenever the angle pt changes through 2π radians. Therefore the time interval T for each cycle of motion (the period) is $\dfrac{2\pi}{p}$. Thus

$$T = \frac{2\pi}{p} = 2\pi \sqrt{\frac{W}{kg}} = 2\pi \sqrt{\frac{\delta_{st}}{g}} \quad \ldots \ldots \quad (10)$$

The number of cycles per second, called the *frequency*, f, is then

$$f = \frac{1}{T} = \frac{p}{2\pi} = \frac{1}{2\pi} \sqrt{\frac{kg}{W}} = \frac{1}{2\pi} \sqrt{\frac{g}{\delta_{st}}} \quad \ldots \quad (11)$$

By substituting $g = 386$ in./sec.^{2} and expressing δ_{st} in inches we have

$$f = \frac{1}{2\pi} \sqrt{\frac{g}{\delta_{st}}} = 3.127 \sqrt{\frac{1}{\delta_{st}}} \text{ cycles per second} \quad (12)$$

Equations (10) and (11) show that the period and frequency of free vibration of a body depend only on the weight of the body and the stiffness of the string, and are not affected by the initial conditions of the motion. These equations will be found to be applicable to periodic motions of widely different arrangements of elastic members. In other words, Fig. 502 is a conventionalized diagram that can be used with small error to replace many actual motions of bodies that vibrate with small amplitudes.

The motion described above is called a *free* vibration; once started, it continues at constant frequency and amplitude without the aid of externally applied driving or exciting forces. *Damped free vibrations* in which frictional forces cause the amplitude of the motion to decrease with time are discussed in Art. 158. *Forced vibrations* which are maintained by an exciting force that may vary with any frequency are discussed in Art. 159.

Spring Constant.—In a system of vibrating elastic bodies, such as shown in Fig. 505, the vibration of one of the bodies, body M for example, is frequently reduced for convenience to the simple case treated in the preceding discussion by assuming that the body is caused to vibrate with equal frequency by an equivalent spring attached to the body as in Fig. 502. The constant for the equivalent spring is obtained from the spring constants of the several elastic bodies of the system. For this purpose a somewhat more comprehensive definition of spring constant is needed than that used in connection with Fig. 502. The constant of an equivalent spring for any body of a system is the force acting on the body tending to restore it to its equilibrium position when its displacement from the equilibrium position is unity.

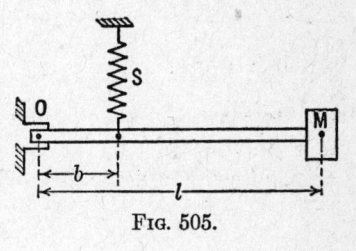

Fig. 505.

To find the equivalent spring constant for M in Fig. 505, let the vertical force that must be applied to the body M to cause it to deflect one inch be denoted by F. Since F is equal (but opposite) to the restoring force, it is equal to the equivalent spring constant. It will be assumed that OM is a rigid weightless rod. The force in the spring S when F is acting on M is found from equilibrium to be $\frac{l}{b}F$. The corresponding deflection of the spring S is $\frac{b}{l}$; and hence the force in the spring is also expressed as $k\frac{b}{l}$, where k is the constant of the spring S. Therefore

$$\frac{l}{b}F = k\frac{b}{l} \quad \text{or} \quad F = \left(\frac{b}{l}\right)^2 k$$

Thus the equivalent spring constant for M is $\left(\frac{b}{l}\right)^2 k$, and hence from Eq. (11) the frequency of vibration is $\frac{1}{2\pi}\frac{b}{l}\sqrt{\frac{kg}{W}}$.

ILLUSTRATIVE PROBLEM

Problem 868.—A body M weighing 150 lb. falls from a height h of 1.5 in. (Fig. 506) upon a helical spring, the modulus of which is 200 lb./in. If the body remains attached to the upper end of the spring; (*a*) determine the frequency of the resulting free vibration; (*b*) write an equation for the displacement of the vibrating body, assuming that $t = 0$ at the instant the weight makes contact with the spring; (*c*) determine the amplitude of motion, and the maximum shortening s of the spring that occurs during the vibration.

Solution.—(*a*) From Eq. (2) the natural circular frequency is

$$p = \sqrt{\frac{kg}{W}} = \sqrt{\frac{200 \times 386}{150}} = 22.7 \text{ rad./sec.}$$

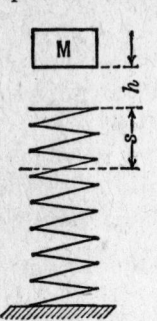

Fig. 506.

and from Eq. (11) the frequency of vibration is

$$f = \frac{p}{2\pi} = \frac{22.7}{6.28} = 3.61 \text{ cycles per sec.}$$

(*b*) At the instant the weight makes contact with the spring the initial conditions for the motion are

$$x_0 = -\delta_{st} = -\frac{150}{200} = -0.75 \text{ in.}$$

$$v_0 = \sqrt{2gh} = \sqrt{2 \times 386 \times 1.5} = 34 \text{ in./sec.}$$

in which the origin of coordinates is at the position of static equilibrium of the body. Hence, from Eq. (6), the displacement at any time t is

$$x = x_0 \cos pt + \frac{v_0}{p} \sin pt = -0.75 \cos 22.7t + 1.5 \sin 22.7t$$

(*c*) From Eq. (8) the amplitude of motion is

$$A = \sqrt{x_0^2 + \left(\frac{v_0}{p}\right)^2} = \sqrt{(0.75)^2 + (1.5)^2} = 1.67 \text{ in.}$$

Therefore the weight vibrates with an amplitude of 1.67 in. about the position of equilibrium and the maximum shortening s of the spring is

$$s = A + \delta_{st} = 1.67 + 0.75 = 2.42 \text{ in.}$$

PROBLEMS

869. A helical spring when supporting a weight of 400 lb. deflects 1 in. If the weight is increased to 1600 lb. and is displaced from its equilibrium position and then released so that it can vibrate freely, what will be the period of vibration?

870. The motor in Fig. 507 weighs 1000 lb. and is mounted on four springs, each having a modulus of 2000 lb./in. Calculate the natural frequency with which the motor will vibrate if given a vertical displacement from its equilibrium position and then released. *Ans.* $f = 8.85$ cycles per sec.

871. In Fig. 508 the body M weighs 40 lb. and the weight of the bell-crank B is negligible. The modulus of the spring S is 20 lb./in. Calculate the equivalent spring constant and determine the frequency of vibration of the system.

Ans. $k = 2.22$ lb./in.; $f = 0.74$ cycles per sec.

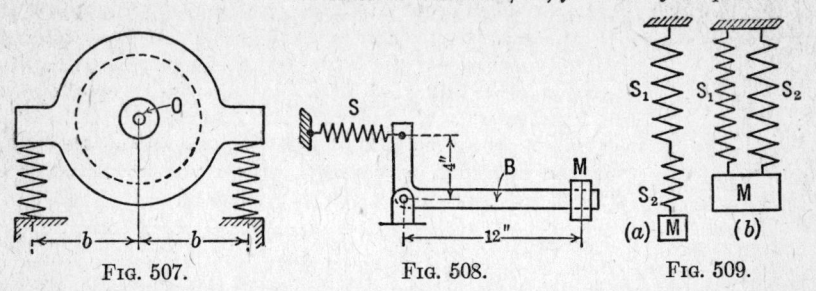

FIG. 507. FIG. 508. FIG. 509.

872. A body M weighing W lb. is suspended from two springs, S_1 and S_2 arranged in series as shown in Fig. 509(a). If the spring constants of the two springs are k_1 and k_2, respectively, show that the equivalent spring constant for the system is $\dfrac{k_1 k_2}{k_1 + k_2}$. If the springs are arranged in parallel as shown in Fig. 509(b) show that the equivalent spring constant is $k_1 + k_2$.

873. Assume that the body in Fig. 502 is raised by a force until the length of the spring is the same as its unstretched length and that the force is then suddenly removed. Write an expression for the displacement x in terms of δ_{st} and the time t after the force is removed. Show that the maximum elongation of the spring is twice as great as the static elongation caused by the weight of the body.

Note: Additional problems will be found after Art. 156.

154. Simple Pendulum.—As a simple application of a free vibration, let it be required to find the period of vibration of small amplitude of a simple pendulum consisting of a particle C (Fig. 510) suspended by a weightless cord of length l from the point O, and allowed to swing in a vertical plane along the path $B'B$. Using the equation of motion $\Sigma T_o = I_o \alpha$, we have

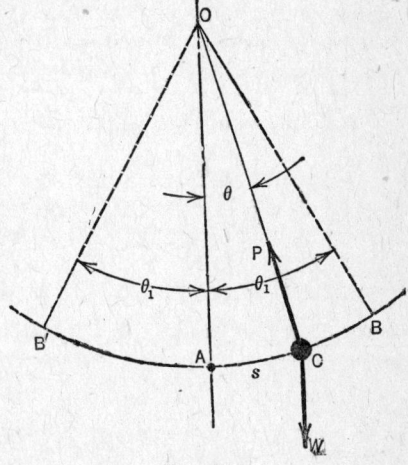

FIG. 510.

$$-Wl \sin\theta = \frac{W}{g} l^2 \frac{d^2\theta}{dt^2} \quad \cdots \cdots \quad (13)$$

and since $\sin\theta = \theta$ approximately, when θ is small, the last equation may be written

$$\frac{d^2\theta}{dt^2} = -\frac{g}{l}\theta \quad \cdots \cdots \quad (14)$$

This equation has the same form as Eq. (3) when $\frac{g}{l}$ is replaced by p^2. Hence the period of vibration, if the amplitude is small, is

$$T = \frac{2\pi}{p} = 2\pi \sqrt{\frac{l}{g}} \quad \ldots \ldots \quad (15)$$

If the amplitude θ_1 is not small enough to permit the assumption that $\sin \theta = \theta$, it can be shown that the period is

$$T = 2\pi \sqrt{\frac{l}{g}} \left[1 + \left(\frac{1}{2}\right)^2 b^2 + \left(\frac{1\cdot 3}{2\cdot 4}\right)^2 b^4 + \left(\frac{1\cdot 3\cdot 5}{2\cdot 4\cdot 6}\right)^2 b^6 + \ldots \right]. \quad (16)$$

where $b = \sin \frac{\theta_1}{2}$.

155. Compound Pendulum.—A physical body of finite dimensions (in contrast to a particle) which oscillates or swings about a horizontal axis is called a compound pendulum. Fig. 511 represents a section of such a pendulum that is free to oscillate about a horizontal axis through O. Let it be required to find the period of vibration for oscillations of small amplitude. Using the equation of motion $\Sigma T_o = I_o \alpha$, we have

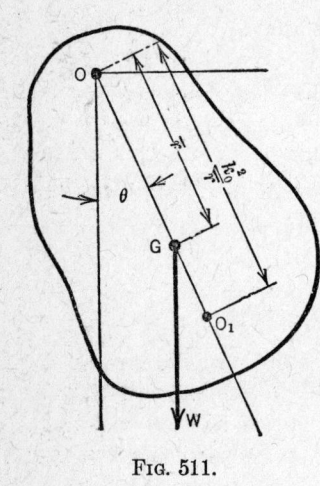

$$-W\bar{r} \sin \theta = \frac{W}{g} k_o^2 \frac{d^2\theta}{dt^2} \quad \ldots \ldots \quad (17)$$

or, if θ is small

$$\frac{d^2\theta}{dt^2} = -\frac{g\bar{r}}{k_o^2} \theta \quad \ldots \ldots \quad (18)$$

Fig. 511.

where k_o is the radius of gyration of the pendulum about the axis of rotation. The last equation is the same in form as Eq. (3) if $\frac{g\bar{r}}{k_o^2}$ is replaced by p^2. Hence the period of the compound pendulum for oscillations of small amplitude is

$$T = \frac{2\pi}{p} = 2\pi \sqrt{\frac{k_o^2}{g\bar{r}}} \quad \ldots \ldots \quad (19)$$

By comparing Eqs. (15) and (19) it is seen that for small amplitudes the period of oscillation of a compound pendulum will be the same as that of a simple pendulum if the length l of the simple pendulum is equal to

$\dfrac{k_o{}^2}{\bar{r}}$ of the compound pendulum. The point O_1 in Fig. 511 is called the *center of oscillation*. It will be noted that the center of oscillation is also the center of percussion (Art. 113). Furthermore, it can be shown that the center of oscillation may be made the center of rotation without changing the period of oscillation. That is, in a compound pendulum the centers of oscillation and suspension are interchangeable.

156. Free Torsional Vibration.—As another application of Eq. (6) let it be required to find the period of vibration (or of oscillation of small amplitude) of a torsional pendulum. In Fig. 512 a disk is rigidly attached to the slender cylindrical rod or shaft of length l. If the disk is given an angular displacement θ, and is then released, the disk will oscillate under the influence of the torque exerted by the rod. The torque is proportional to the angular displacement, provided that the elastic strength of the material is not exceeded, and is opposite in sense to θ. Thus, using the equation of motion $\Sigma T_o = I_o \alpha$, we have

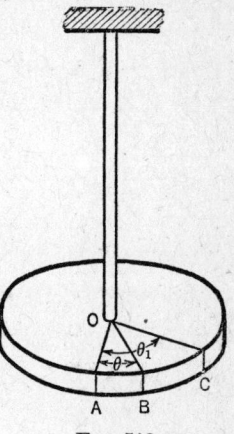

Fig. 512.

$$-k\theta = I_o \dfrac{d^2\theta}{dt^2} \quad \text{or} \quad \dfrac{d^2\theta}{dt^2} = -\dfrac{k}{I_o}\theta \quad \ldots \ldots \quad (20)$$

where k is the torsional spring constant, or the torque required to produce a unit angle of twist of the rod or shaft to which the disk is attached. Eq. (20) is also the equation of motion for free torsional vibrations of many machine parts such as rotors or flywheels in cases where the mass of the shaft is relatively small. Equation (20) has the same form as Eq. (1). Thus the solution is of the same form as Eq. (6) and hence the angular displacement at any time is given by the equation

$$\theta = \theta_o \cos pt + \dfrac{\omega_o}{p} \sin pt \quad \ldots \ldots \quad (21)$$

in which $p = \sqrt{\dfrac{k}{I_o}}$, θ_o is the initial angular displacement, and ω_o is the initial angular velocity of the disk or the value of ω when $t = 0$.

The period of oscillation therefore is

$$T = \dfrac{2\pi}{p} = 2\pi \sqrt{\dfrac{I_o}{k}} \quad \ldots \ldots \quad (22)$$

The torsional spring constant for a cylindrical rod or shaft, as given in books on strength of materials is

$$k = \frac{\pi d^4 G}{32 l} \quad \ldots \ldots \ldots \quad (23)$$

where d is the diameter of the rod, G is the shearing modulus of elasticity of the material of the shaft, and l is the length of the rod. For a cylindrical disk $I_o = \frac{1}{2} \frac{W}{g} r^2$ where r is the radius of the disk, and hence

$$T = 2\pi \sqrt{\frac{16 W r^2 l}{\pi g d^4 G}} \quad \ldots \ldots \quad (24)$$

Two Bodies Connected by Shaft. Nodal Point.—When two heavy masses such as the rotors of a large motor and generator are connected by a relatively small shaft as shown in Fig. 513, torsional vibrations of the system will result if the shaft is given a twist by turning the rotors in opposite directions and then releasing them. Since, after release, there are no external torques acting on the system, the principle of conservation of angular momentum (Art. 149) may be applied. Thus, if I_1 and I_2 are the moments of inertia of the two rotors and ω_1 and ω_2 are their angular velocities at any time, we have

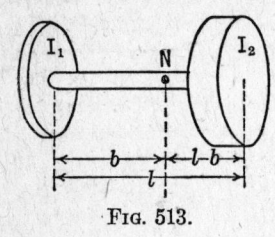

Fig. 513.

$$I_1 \omega_1 + I_2 \omega_2 = 0, \quad \text{or} \quad \omega_1 = -\omega_2 \frac{I_2}{I_1} \quad \ldots \ldots \quad (25)$$

Hence the two bodies rotate in opposite directions during the vibration since their angular velocities are of opposite sign, and there must be a section, N (called the nodal section), of the shaft that remains stationary. Thus, the motion of each body may be considered as that of a torsional pendulum on a shaft which is fixed at N, and the position of this nodal section can be determined since the period of oscillation for each part of the system is the same. From Eq. (22) the period is

$$T = 2\pi \sqrt{\frac{I_1}{k_1}} = 2\pi \sqrt{\frac{I_2}{k_2}} \quad \ldots \ldots \quad (26)$$

where k_1 and k_2 are the torsional spring constants of the two parts of the shaft as divided by the point N. Therefore $\frac{k_2}{k_1} = \frac{I_2}{I_1}$, and by substituting the values of k from Eq. (23) this equation becomes

$$\frac{b}{l-b} = \frac{I_2}{I_1}, \text{ whence } b = \frac{I_2 l}{I_1 + I_2} \quad \ldots \quad (27)$$

By using this value of b for the length of the shaft in Eq. (23) and substituting the resulting value of k_1 in Eq. (26), the period of free torsional vibration for the system in Fig. 513 is found to be

$$T = 2\pi \sqrt{\frac{32 l I_1 I_2}{\pi d^4 G(I_1 + I_2)}} = 2\pi \sqrt{\frac{I_1 I_2 l}{JG(I_1 + I_2)}}. \quad \ldots \quad (28)$$

where J is the polar moment of inertia of the area of the cross-section of the shaft about the axis of the shaft.

PROBLEMS ON FREE VIBRATIONS

874. The disk in Fig. 512 has a weight of 32.2 lb. and a radius of 6 in. A torque of 4000 in.-lb. gives the steel rod to which the disk is attached an angle of twist of 0.04 radian which is the maximum angle of twist the rod can sustain without having its elastic limit exceeded. What will be the frequency of oscillation of the disk assuming the motion of the disk is started by twisting it through an angle less than 0.04 radian and then releasing it without initial velocity? Neglect the mass of the rod. *Ans.* $f = 41.1$ cycles per sec.

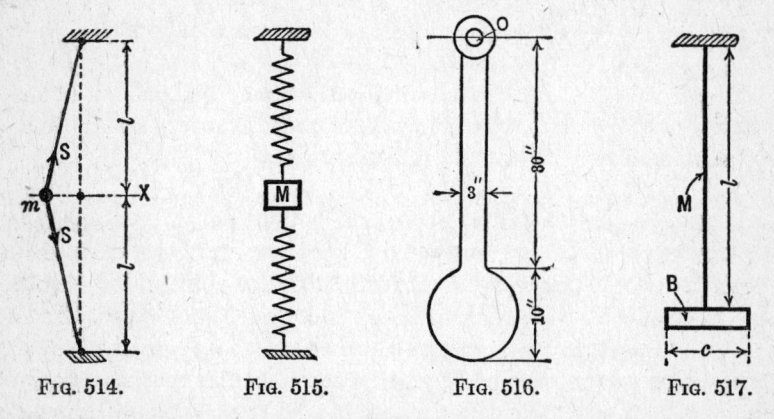

FIG. 514.   FIG. 515.   FIG. 516.   FIG. 517.

875. A small body of mass m and weight W is attached to the center of a tightly stretched weightless elastic wire of length $2l$ (Fig. 514) in which there is a stress S. If the mass is displaced laterally a small distance and then released, show by use of the equation of motion $\Sigma F_x = ma_x$ that the body has a simple harmonic motion and determine the period of vibration. Assume that the increase in stress in the wire due to a small lateral displacement is small in comparison with S and may therefore be neglected.

Ans. $T = 2\pi \sqrt{\dfrac{Wl}{2gS}}$.

876. The body M in Fig. 515 weighs 8 lb. It is given a small vertical displacement from its equilibrium position and then released. The constant for each of the springs is 30 lb./in. Calculate the frequency of the vibration of M, neglecting the mass of the springs. *Ans.* $f = 8.56$ cycles per sec.

877. A steel pendulum consists of a circular disk 10 in. in diameter and 1 in. thick, and a rectangular bar 30 in. long, 3 in. wide, and 1 in. thick, as shown in Fig. 516. If the pendulum oscillates about a horizontal axis through O, what is the period of oscillation? *Ans.* $T = 1.75$ sec.

878. In Fig. 517 a weightless wire M has attached to its lower end a slender rod B of weight W and length c. When B is given a small angular displacement in the horizontal plane and then released, it is observed to oscillate with 3 complete oscillations per sec. If $W = 8$ lb. and $c = 1.5$ ft., what is the torsional spring constant of the wire? *Ans.* $k = 199$ in.-lb./rad.

879. An elevator weighing 10 tons is slowly lowered by a cable whose cross-sectional area is 1.5 sq. in. and whose modulus of elasticity is 20×10^6 lb./in.² When the length of the cable is 112 ft., the hoisting drum is suddenly stopped. If the mass of the cable is neglected, find the frequency of vibration. *Note:* The stretch of a bar or cable caused by a static axial force W, as found in texts on strength of materials is $e = \dfrac{Wl}{aE}$, in which a is the cross-sectional area of the cable, l is the length of the cable, and E is the modulus of elasticity of the cable.
Ans. $f = 3.3$ cycles per sec.

880. A rectangular block floats in water with a depth of immersion d. The cross-sectional area of the block parallel to the water surface is A and the weight of water per unit volume is w. If the block is given a small vertical displacement y from its equilibrium position and then released it will oscillate. If the inertia and friction of the water are neglected, show by applying the equation of motion $\Sigma F_y = ma_y$ that $\dfrac{d^2y}{dt^2} = -\dfrac{g}{d}y$ and hence that the frequency of the oscillation is $f = \dfrac{1}{2\pi}\sqrt{\dfrac{g}{d}}$. In this problem the water is the spring; what is the spring constant?

881. The motor in Fig. 507 is supported by coil springs placed under the four corners of the motor frame. The variable torque on the motor produces a small rocking (angular) vibration of the motor in its supports; the axis of vibration may be assumed for small vibrations to be the same as the axis of rotation, O, of the motor. If the spring constant for each of the four springs is k and the moment of inertia of the motor and frame about O is I_o, show that the natural frequency of the angular vibration is $f = \dfrac{1}{\pi}\sqrt{\dfrac{kb^2}{I_o}}$.

882. A simple pendulum 4 ft. long swings through an angle of 60° (that is, $\theta_1 = 30°$). Find the period of oscillation; (a) by the approximate method and (b) by the exact method. *Ans.* (a) $T = 2.21$ sec.; (b) $T = 2.25$ sec.

883. Find the length of a uniform slender bar having a period of oscillation of 1 sec. when allowed to swing as a compound pendulum about an axis through one end of the bar. *Ans.* $l = 1.22$ ft.

884. Liquid is placed in a U-shaped glass tube (Fig. 518), the total length of the liquid column being l. Pressure is applied to one side of the column depressing it as shown and the pressure is then suddenly released allowing the column of liquid to oscillate. Assuming friction to be negligible, show by applying the equation of motion $\Sigma F_x = ma_x$ to the liquid that $\dfrac{d^2x}{dt^2} = -\dfrac{2g}{l}x$ and that, therefore, the period of vibration is $T = 2\pi\sqrt{\dfrac{l}{2g}}$.

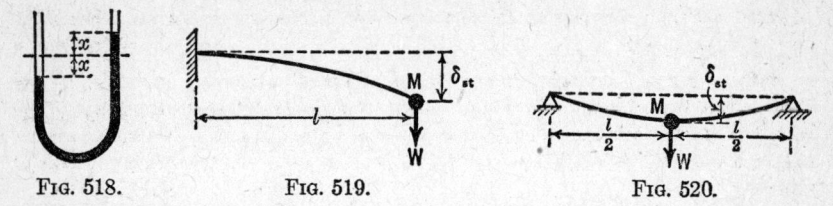

Fig. 518.　　　Fig. 519.　　　Fig. 520.

885. A cantilever beam of constant cross-section (Fig. 519) when supporting a body M of weight W at its free end deflects elastically an amount $\delta_{st} = \dfrac{1}{3}\dfrac{Wl^3}{EI}$ (see any text on strength of materials) in which E is the tensile modulus of elasticity of the material of the beam and I is the moment of inertia of the cross-section of the beam with respect to its horizontal centroidal axis. Show that the period of vibration of M, neglecting the mass of the beam, is $T = 2\pi\sqrt{\dfrac{Wl^3}{3EIg}}$. If the mass of the beam is *not* negligible, it can be shown that only a very small error is introduced in obtaining the period of vibration by neglecting the mass of the beam and assuming that ¼ of the mass (and weight) of the beam is added to that of the body M. If the weight of the beam is ½W, what error (in per cent) is introduced by neglecting the weight of the beam?

886. A simple beam of constant cross-section (Fig. 520) when supporting a body M of weight W at the center of the span deflects elastically an amount $\delta_{st} = \dfrac{1}{48}\dfrac{Wl^3}{EI}$. (See Prob. 885 for meaning of E and I.) Assuming that the mass of the beam is negligible compared to that of M, show that the frequency of vibration of M is $f = \dfrac{1}{2\pi}\sqrt{\dfrac{48EIg}{Wl^3}}$. If the mass of the beam is *not* negligible, it can be shown that only a very small error is introduced in obtaining the period (or frequency) of vibration by neglecting the mass of the beam and assuming that ½ of the mass (and weight) of the beam is added to that of the body M. If the weight of the beam is ¼W, what error (in per cent) is introduced by neglecting the weight of the beam?

887. In Fig. 519 let the body M be suspended from the end of the beam by means of a coiled spring whose constant is k. Find the equivalent spring constant for the system; the spring constant for the beam may be obtained by using the expression for δ_{st} in Prob. 885. Neglect the weight of the beam.　　Ans. $k' = \dfrac{3EIk}{3EI + kl^3}$.

888. The moment of inertia of a body may be found experimentally by allowing the body to oscillate as a compound pendulum and observing the period of oscillation. Show from Eq. (19) that

$$I_o = \dfrac{WT^2\bar{r}}{4\pi^2},$$

in which I_o is the moment of inertia of the body about the center of oscillation, T is the period of a complete oscillation of the body and $\bar{r}$ is the distance from the center of oscillation to the mass-center of the body.

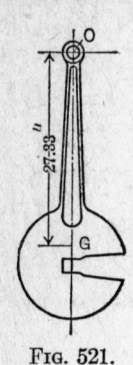

889. The connecting rod of a steam engine weighs 300 lb. and the distance of the center of gravity from the crank-pin is found (by balancing) to be 50 in. When suspended from the crank-pin end and allowed to vibrate as a compound pendulum, it is found to make 30 complete oscillations in 75 sec. Determine the moment of inertia of the rod with respect to the axis of the crank-pin and also with respect to a parallel axis through the center of gravity.

Ans. $I = 198$ slug-ft.^{2}; $\bar{I} = 36.5$ slug-ft.^{2}

890. The pendulum (Fig. 521) of a Charpy impact machine, which is used to determine the resistance of materials to impact, weighs 50.5 lb., and the distance of the center of gravity from the axis of rotation, as determined by balancing, is found to be 27.33 in. When allowed to vibrate about the axis of rotation, the pendulum is observed to make 35 complete oscillations in 61 sec. Find the moment of inertia of the pendulum with respect to the axis of rotation.

Fig. 521.

Ans. $I = 8.85$ slug-ft.^{2}

891. A body M whose weight is W (Fig. 522) is suspended from a cylindrical rotor by means of an inextensible cable. The rotor has a moment of inertia I about its axis of rotation O. The motion of the rotor is restrained by the spring S whose

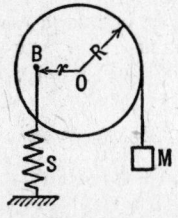

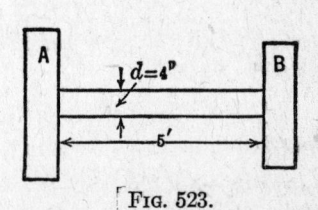

Fig. 522.   Fig. 523.

modulus is k. If M is given a small downward displacement and then is released determine, by use of the equation of motion $\Sigma T_o = I_o \alpha$, the period of vibration.

Ans. $T = 2\pi \sqrt{\dfrac{I_o + \dfrac{W}{g}R^2}{kr^2}}$

892. A Diesel engine whose flywheel and other rotating parts, represented by A in Fig. 523, have a combined moment of inertia of 600 slug-ft.^{2}, drives a generator whose rotor, represented by B, has a moment of inertia of 100 slug-ft.^{2} The steel shaft connecting the engine to the generator is 4 in. in diameter and 5 ft. long. The shearing modulus of elasticity of steel is $G = 12 \times 10^6$ lb./in.^{2} Neglecting the mass of the shaft calculate the natural frequency of torsional vibration of the system.

Ans. $f = 11.1$ cycles per sec.

157. Analysis of Free Vibrations by Principle of Work and Energy.—The principle of work and energy (Art. 131) is frequently useful in determining the natural frequency of free vibration of an elastic system.

As an example, this principle will be applied to the motion of the system shown in Fig. 502. The principle states that during any displacement, x, of the body, the work done on the body is equal to the change in kinetic energy of the body ($w = \Delta E_k$). Thus, referring to Fig. 502, we may write

$$Wx - \left(Wx + \frac{kx^2}{2}\right) = \frac{1}{2}\frac{W}{g}(v_2{}^2 - v_1{}^2) \quad \ldots \quad (29)$$

where v_1 is the velocity at the start and v_2 at the end of the displacement.

It will be noted that in considering the displacement of the body from position $x = 0$ to position $x = x_m = A$, where x_m or A denotes the maximum displacement (amplitude) of the body from its equilibrium position, that v_2 is zero when $x = A$ and that when $x = 0$ the velocity v_1 is the maximum velocity of the body during the vibration which will be denoted by v_m. Hence, Eq. (29) becomes

$$kA^2 = \frac{W}{g} v_m{}^2 \quad \ldots \ldots \ldots \quad (30)$$

If the elastic properties of the spring are not exceeded, the restoring force kx is always directed toward the origin and is proportional to the displacement x, and hence the motion is a simple harmonic motion. Therefore, the displacement may be represented as the ordinate to a sine curve (Art. 86). Hence

$$x = A \sin pt \quad \text{and} \quad v_x = \frac{dx}{dt} = Ap \cos pt \quad \ldots \quad (31)$$

where p has the same meaning as in Art. 153.

From Eq. (31) it is evident that the maximum value of v is $v_m = Ap$, and hence Eq. (30) becomes

$$kA^2 = \frac{W}{g}(Ap)^2 \quad \text{or} \quad p^2 = \frac{kg}{W} \quad \ldots \ldots \quad (32)$$

which agrees with the expression for p in Eq. (2). The method of work and energy is useful in many simple types of problems, and has particular advantages in problems in which the mass of the spring is considered as part of the vibrating system; the method then leads to Rayleigh's method which is discussed in books on vibrations.

ILLUSTRATIVE PROBLEM

Problem 893.—In Fig. 524 is shown a device for measuring the vibrations of ships. The body D is a stiff bar connected to a smooth pin at O, S is a spring whose constant is k, and B is a small body attached to the end of D. The weight of D and B is W and the distance of their center of gravity, G, from O is l. The moment of inertia of D and B about O is I_o. The initial spring tension is such that the bar D is in equilibrium when in a horizontal position. If D is displaced from its equilibrium position and then released, find the period of vibration.

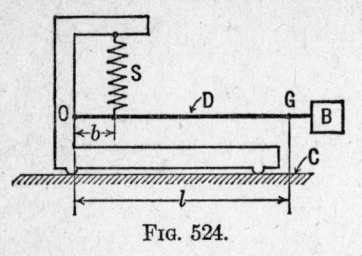

Solution.—When the system is in its equilibrium position the stress in the spring is found from one equation of equilibrium, by taking moments about O, to be $W\dfrac{l}{b}$. If D is given a small angular displacement θ_m downward from its equilibrium position, the increase in length of the spring is $b\theta_m$ and the stress is increased to $W\dfrac{l}{b} + kb\theta_m$. Hence the work done by the spring is

Fig. 524.

$$-\frac{1}{2}\left(W\frac{l}{b} + W\frac{l}{b} + kb\theta_m\right)b\theta_m = -\left(Wl\theta_m + \frac{1}{2}kb^2\theta^2_m\right).$$

And since the work done by the weight of D and B is $Wl\theta_m$, the total work done on D and B is $-\frac{1}{2}kb^2\theta^2_m$. Hence applying the principle of work and energy for the displacement $\theta = 0$ to $\theta = \theta_m$ we have

$$w = \Delta E_k = \tfrac{1}{2}I_o(\omega_2{}^2 - \omega_1{}^2)$$

or

$$-\tfrac{1}{2}kb^2\theta^2{}_m = \tfrac{1}{2}I_o(0 - \omega^2{}_m)$$

where ω_m is the maximum angular velocity of D.

Since the motion is harmonic $\theta = \theta_m \sin pt$, and hence $\omega = \dfrac{d\theta}{dt} = \theta_m p \cos pt$. Thus $\omega_m = \theta_m p$ and the last equation becomes

$$\tfrac{1}{2}kb^2\theta^2{}_m = \tfrac{1}{2}I_o\theta^2{}_m p^2. \quad \text{Whence} \quad p^2 = \frac{kb^2}{I_o}.$$

The period of vibration then is $T = \dfrac{2\pi}{p} = 2\pi\sqrt{\dfrac{I_o}{kb^2}}$.

PROBLEMS

894. In Prob. 893 assume the weight of D to be negligible and the weight of B to be W. Find the period of vibration by the method used in Prob. 893. Check the result by using the equation of motion $\Sigma T_o = I_o \alpha$ and by solving the resulting differential equation. In this problem assume l to be the length of D.

Ans. $T = 2\pi \dfrac{l}{b} \sqrt{\dfrac{W}{kg}}$.

895. If, in Prob. 894, $W = 32$ lb., $l = 30$ in., and $b = 3$ in., what must be the value of the spring constant k to make the period of vibration one second?

896. Determine the frequency of vibration of the pendulum in Fig. 525 which consists of a stiff weightless bar of length l and a small body M whose weight is W. The spring constant for each of the two springs S, S, is k.

Ans. $f = \dfrac{1}{2\pi}\sqrt{\dfrac{g}{l} + \dfrac{2b^2kg}{l^2W}}$.

897. Assume the mass of the rigid bar AB in Fig. 526 to be negligible and the spring constant for the spring S to be k. Calculate (a) the natural frequency of

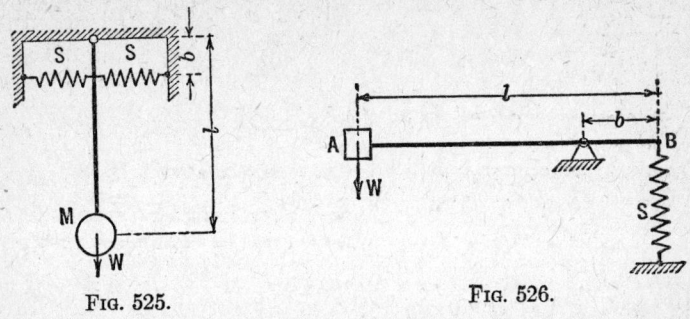

FIG. 525.   FIG. 526.

vibration of the system and (b) the equivalent spring constant K for the system.

Ans. (a) $f = \dfrac{1}{2\pi} \dfrac{b}{l-b} \sqrt{\dfrac{kg}{W}}$; (b) $K = k\left(\dfrac{b}{l-b}\right)^2$.

158. Free Vibration with Viscous Damping.

Free vibrations, that is, vibrations that are not maintained by driving or exciting forces, gradually die out because of the damping due to frictional resistance encountered during motion. In the analysis of vibration problems the damping force developed is usually assumed to be proportional to the velocity of the body and is expressed as $-c\dfrac{dx}{dt}$, where c is called the damping constant. Thus the frictional forces are assumed to be of the type developed by the viscosity of the oil in a dashpot; by assuming a proper damping constant this assumption usually yields satisfactory results even though other types of friction may be damping the motion.

If a frictional force equal to $-c\dfrac{dx}{dt}$ is added to the force system shown in Fig. 502, the force system will be as shown in Fig. 527 and the equation of motion for the resulting damped free vibration may be written as follows:

FIG. 527.

$$\Sigma F_x = ma_x$$

$$W - (W + kx) - c\dfrac{dx}{dt} = \dfrac{W}{g}\dfrac{d^2x}{dt^2}$$

which may be written

$$\dfrac{d^2x}{dt^2} + 2n\dfrac{dx}{dt} + p^2 x = 0 \quad \cdots \cdots \quad (33)$$

where

$$p^2 = \dfrac{kg}{W} \quad \text{and} \quad 2n = \dfrac{cg}{W} = \dfrac{c}{m}$$

An inspection of this equation indicates (as is shown below) that x must be such a function of t that each successive derivative of x with respect to t is equal to the original function times a constant. In a study of differential equations it is found that the function $x = Ce^{st}$ satisfies this condition, where C and s are unknown constants to be determined from the initial conditions of the motion and e is the base of natural logarithms. The truth of this statement is easily shown. Thus, if $x = Ce^{st}$,

$$\frac{dx}{dt} = Cse^{st} \quad \text{and} \quad \frac{d^2x}{dt^2} = Cs^2 e^{st}$$

Hence, if these values of x, $\frac{dx}{dt}$, and $\frac{d^2x}{dt^2}$ are substituted in Eq. (33) the equation becomes

$$(s^2 + 2ns + p^2)Ce^{st} = 0 \quad \ldots \ldots \quad (34)$$

and hence the function $x = Ce^{st}$ satisfies equation (33) if the conditions of the motion are such that

$$s^2 + 2ns + p^2 = 0 \ldots \ldots \ldots (35)$$

Thus there are two values of s that yield a solution of Eq. (33), namely,

$$s_1 = -n + \sqrt{n^2 - p^2} \quad \text{and} \quad s_2 = -n - \sqrt{n^2 - p^2}$$

The general solution of Eq. (33) then is

$$x = C_1 e^{s_1 t} + C_2 e^{s_2 t} \quad \ldots \ldots \quad (36)$$

The damping of the motion, in accordance with this equation results in two different types of motion depending on whether n is greater than p or less than p.

For n greater than p.—If $n > p$ the solution (Eq. 36) does not contain any terms that vary periodically with time. Hence the frictional resistance is so large that the body when displaced does not vibrate, but gradually creeps back to the equilibrium position. When this condition exists the motion is said to be *overdamped*.

For n less than p.—If $n < p$ the expressions for s_1 and s_2 become complex numbers and may be written

and
$$\left.\begin{array}{l} s_1 = -n + i\sqrt{p^2 - n^2} = -n + iq \\ s_2 = -n - i\sqrt{p^2 - n^2} = -n - iq \end{array}\right\} \quad \ldots \quad (37)$$

where

$$i = \sqrt{-1} \quad \text{and} \quad q = \sqrt{p^2 - n^2}.$$

Thus $x = C_1 e^{(-n + iq)t} + C_2 e^{(-n - iq)t} = e^{-nt}(C_1 e^{iqt} + C_2 e^{-iqt})$. (38)

FREE VIBRATION WITH VISCOUS DAMPING

By substituting in Eq. (38) the following mathematical relations, given in texts on calculus and trigonometry,

$$e^{iqt} = \cos qt + i \sin qt, \text{ and } e^{-iqt} = \cos qt - i \sin qt$$

and simplifying, the equation becomes

$$x = e^{-nt}(B \cos qt + D \sin qt) \quad \ldots \ldots \quad (39)$$

in which B and D are constants such that $B = C_1 + C_2$ and $D = i(C_1 - C_2)$, and they are determined from the initial conditions of motion. The expression in parentheses is a periodic function of the same form as Eq. (4) for a free vibration without damping. Hence it represents a vibratory motion with a period

$$T = \frac{2\pi}{q} = \frac{2\pi}{\sqrt{p^2 - n^2}} = \frac{2\pi}{p} \cdot \frac{1}{\sqrt{1 - \left(\dfrac{n}{p}\right)^2}} \quad \ldots \quad (40)$$

For the majority of cases of vibratory motion the ratio $\dfrac{n}{p}$ is less than 0.2, and it will be observed that for these cases the period of the damped free vibration is practically the same as the period of undamped free vibrations. If the initial conditions of the motion are such that $x = x_0$ and $v = 0$ when $t = 0$, Eq. (39) is found, by evaluating the constants B and D, to reduce to

$$x = e^{-nt}(x_0 \cos qt) \quad \ldots \ldots \ldots \quad (41)$$

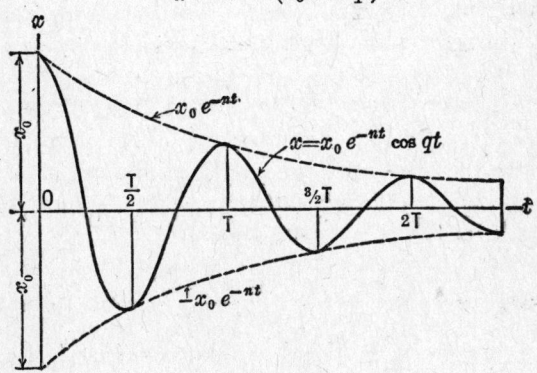

Fig. 528.

The relation between x and t in Eq. (41) is represented graphically by the curve in Fig. 528.

The value of the factor e^{-nt} in Eq. (41) gradually decreases with time and hence the amplitude of each successive oscillation is decreased in the ratio e^{nT} to 1 where $T = \dfrac{2\pi}{q}$ is the period of oscillation. This may be shown as follows: If x_r denotes the amplitude and t the time at the end of r complete cycles and x_{r+1} the amplitude at the end of $r+1$ cycles we have

$$x_r = e^{-nt} x_o \cos qt$$

$$x_{r+1} = e^{-n(t+T)} x_o \cos q \left(t + \frac{2\pi}{q} \right) = e^{-n(t+T)} (x_o \cos qt)$$

Hence

$$\frac{x_r}{x_{r+1}} = \frac{e^{-nt}}{e^{-n(t+T)}} = e^{nT}$$

The logarithm, to base e, of this ratio is $nT = \dfrac{cg}{2W} \cdot \dfrac{2\pi}{q} = \dfrac{\pi c}{mq}$ and is called the *logarithmic decrement*. The logarithmic decrement measures the difference in the logarithms of two consecutive amplitudes of the motion.

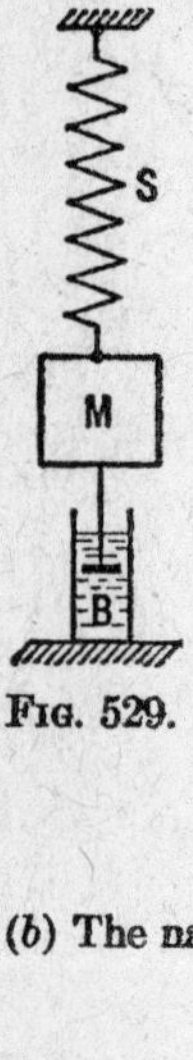

ILLUSTRATIVE PROBLEM

Problem 898.—In Fig. 529 is shown a body M connected to a spring S whose constant is 40 lb./in. M is also connected by a rod to a piston that moves in a dashpot B that is filled with a viscous fluid. The damping force due to the fluid resistance varies directly as the velocity of M and is equal to 50 lb. when $v = 2$ ft./sec. The combined weight, W, of M, the rod, and the piston is 100 lb. Find: (*a*) the damping constant, (*b*) the period of vibration, and (*c*) the logarithmic decrement.

Fig. 529.

Solution.—(*a*) The damping constant is

$$c = \frac{50 \text{ lb.}}{2 \times 12 \text{ in./sec.}} = 2.08 \text{ lb. sec./in.}$$

(*b*) The natural circular frequency is

$$p = \sqrt{\frac{kg}{W}} = \sqrt{\frac{40 \text{ lb./in.} \times 386 \text{ in./sec.}^2}{100 \text{ lb.}}} = 12.4 \text{ rad./sec.}$$

Hence

Therefore

$$n = \frac{cg}{2W} = \frac{2.08 \text{ lb.-sec./in.} \times 386 \text{ in./sec.}^2}{2 \times 100 \text{ lb.}} = 4.02 \text{ rad./sec.}$$

And

$$q = \sqrt{p^2 - n^2} = \sqrt{(12.4)^2 - (4.02)^2} = 11.8 \text{ rad./sec.}$$

$$T = \frac{2\pi}{q} = \frac{2 \times 3.142}{11.8} = 0.532 \text{ sec.}$$

(*c*) The logarithmic decrement is

$$nT = 4.02 \times 0.532 = 2.15.$$

FORCED VIBRATIONS WITHOUT DAMPING

PROBLEMS

899. If the initial amplitude of the motion described in Prob. 898 is 4 in., what is the amplitude at the end of one complete cycle? *Ans.* $x = 0.47$ in.

900. Using the data of Prob. 898, determine the least value of the damping coefficient that will cause an overdamped condition in the motion and hence will prevent a periodic motion. Find also the corresponding value of the damping force when $v = 2$ ft./sec. *Ans.* $c = 6.43$ lb.-sec./in.; $F = 154$ lb.

901. Assume in Prob. 898 that the damping force is 20 lb. when $v = 2$ ft./sec. and that the other data are unchanged. Find the period of vibration and the logarithmic decrement. *Ans.* $T = 0.507$ sec.; $nT = 0.815$.

159. Forced Vibrations without Damping.—The amplitude of a *free* vibration of a body depends only on the starting conditions, whereas a *forced* vibration, which is maintained by an alternating exciting force, has a frequency and an amplitude which are influenced by the frequency and amplitude of the exciting force. A slight eccentricity or lack of balance in rotating machinery may cause exciting forces that develop vibrations of large amplitude.

Two ways in which forced vibrations may be developed are shown in the conventionalized systems in Figs. 530(b) and (d); namely, (I) a

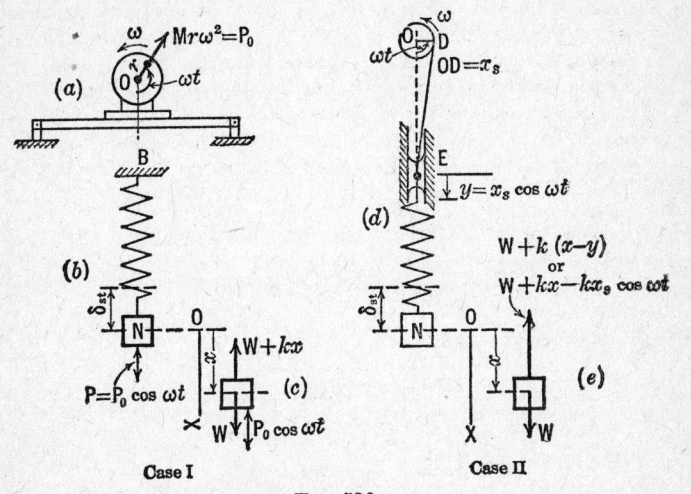

Fig. 530.

force P that varies harmonically with time may be applied directly to the body N of mass m and weight W, as indicated in Fig. 530(b), or (II) the upper end of the spring may be moved vertically with a reciprocating displacement y that is assumed to vary harmonically with time, as indicated in Fig. 530(d). The resulting free-body diagrams for the body N for the two cases are also shown in Figs. 530(c) and (e).

Case I.—The conditions assumed in Case I, for example, could be produced by attaching to an elastic beam (Fig. 530a), a rotor that revolves with an angular velocity ω and that has an unbalanced mass M at a distance r from the axis of rotation, thus causing a rotating unbalanced (centrifugal) force equal to $Mr\omega^2 = P_o$, the vertical component of which is $P_o \cos \omega t$. In this expression of the alternating or exciting force, P_o is the amplitude of the exciting force, and ω is its circular frequency, which in this case is the angular velocity of the rotor. The equation of motion, $\Sigma F_x = ma_x$, for N (Fig. 530b) then may be written

$$W - (W + kx) + P_0 \cos \omega t = m \frac{d^2x}{dt^2} \quad \ldots \quad (42)$$

This equation may be written

$$\frac{d^2x}{dt^2} + p^2 x = \frac{P_0}{m} \cos \omega t \quad \ldots \ldots \quad (43)$$

in which $\dfrac{k}{m} = p^2$.

Case II.—Before Eq. (43) is solved, Case II will be considered. If the displacement, x, in Fig. 530(e) is measured from the position of static equilibrium of the body N when the crosshead, E, is in its middle position, it will be noted that any additional extension of the spring is equal to the difference $(x - y)$ of the displacements of its two ends. The spring force acting on the body N is therefore $W + k(x - y)$. The equation of motion then becomes

$$W - [W + k(x - y)] = m \frac{d^2x}{dt^2}$$

Hence

$$m \frac{d^2x}{dt^2} + kx = ky = kx_s \cos \omega t$$

or

$$\frac{d^2x}{dt^2} + p^2 x = \frac{kx_s}{m} \cos \omega t \quad \ldots \ldots \quad (44)$$

in which x_s is the maximum value of y, that is, the amplitude of motion of the crosshead. This equation is of the same form as Eq. (43) and the two equations are identical if $x_s = \dfrac{P_o}{k}$. It should be noted that the expression $\dfrac{P_o}{k} = x_s$ may be interpreted as the static elongation of the spring which would be produced in Case I by a load P_o. If this substitution is made, Eqs. (43) and (44) are identical.

FORCED VIBRATIONS WITHOUT DAMPING

It is convenient to visualize the forced vibration of the body N as being composed of a combination of a free vibration of the type discussed in Art. 153, plus a new motion caused by the exciting force. Let it be assumed, therefore, that the displacement $x = x_1 + x_2$, where x_1 is the displacement produced by the free vibration and is independent of the exciting force, and x_2 is the additional displacement caused by the exciting force. With this substitution we may assume Eq. (43) to be made up of two parts:

$$(a) \quad \frac{d^2 x_1}{dt^2} + p^2 x_1 = 0 \quad \ldots \ldots \quad (45)$$

$$(b) \quad \frac{d^2 x_2}{dt^2} + p^2 x_2 = \frac{P_o}{m} \cos \omega t \quad \ldots \quad (46)$$

which expressions, when added, give an equation that is equivalent to the original equation. It will be noted that Eq. (45) is of the same form as Eq. (3) and hence the solution for x_1 is of the same form as Eq. (4). Therefore

$$x_1 = B \cos pt + C \sin pt \quad \ldots \ldots \quad (47)$$

It is obvious that a function $x_2 = A \cos \omega t$ will satisfy Eq. (46) if the constant A (the amplitude) is properly selected. Substituting this function in Eq. (46) we have

$$-A\omega^2 \cos \omega t + p^2 A \cos \omega t = \frac{P_o}{m} \cos \omega t$$

or

$$A(p^2 - \omega^2) = \frac{P_o}{m}$$

Therefore

$$A = \frac{P_o}{m(p^2 - \omega^2)} = \frac{P_o}{\frac{k}{p^2}(p^2 - \omega^2)} = \frac{P_o}{k} \frac{1}{1 - \frac{\omega^2}{p^2}} \quad \ldots \quad (48)$$

Thus a solution for the forced vibration becomes

$$x_2 = A \cos \omega t = \frac{P_o}{k} \frac{1}{1 - \frac{\omega^2}{p^2}} \cos \omega t = x_s \frac{1}{1 - \frac{\omega^2}{p^2}} \cos \omega t \quad (49)$$

in which $x_s = \frac{P_o}{k}$.

Hence the complete solution of Eq. (43) is found by combining Eqs. (47) and (49). Thus

$$x = x_1 + x_2 = B \cos pt + C \sin pt + \frac{x_s}{1 - \frac{\omega^2}{p^2}} \cos \omega t \quad \ldots \quad (50)$$

and it can be verified, by substitution, that this solution satisfies Eq. (43) and Eq. (44).

Steady-State Forced Vibration.—In most practical applications the free vibration represented by the expression $B \cos pt + C \sin pt$ in Eq. (50) is transient in nature, being gradually damped out by frictional resistances if the exciting force maintains a constant frequency and amplitude. Thus the final, or *steady-state* forced vibration which the body performs is represented by the solution for x_2 in Eq. (49). Thus it is seen that the displacement x for a steady-state forced vibration is a cosine function whose amplitude depends on the ratio of the impressed circular frequency ω, of the disturbing force, to the natural circular frequency p, for free vibration of the system. The maximum value of x (that is, the amplitude of the forced vibration) is $x_s \dfrac{1}{1 - \left(\dfrac{\omega}{p}\right)^2}$. Denoting this amplitude by A, we have then

$$A = x_s \frac{1}{1 - \left(\dfrac{\omega}{p}\right)^2} = x_s \frac{1}{1 - \left(\dfrac{f_1}{f}\right)^2} \quad \ldots \quad (51)$$

where $f_1 = \dfrac{\omega}{2\pi}$ = frequency of the exciting force in cycles per second; likewise $f = \dfrac{p}{2\pi}$. The ratio $\dfrac{1}{1 - \left(\dfrac{f_1}{f}\right)^2}$ may be interpreted as a *magnification factor*; for example, the force P_o if statically applied would produce a displacement x_s, but when the alternating force varies with a frequency, ω, the actual amplitude A of motion is increased in proportion to this magnification factor. Similarly for the case of Fig. 530(d), if the crank arm OD is revolved very slowly, the body N moves through the same displacement, x_s, as the upper end of the spring; but, when OD revolves with the angular velocity ω, the forced amplitude A of motion of the body is x_s times the magnification factor.

By plotting a curve showing values of the magnification factor as a function of the frequency ratio ω/p, as shown in Fig. 531, a complete picture of the amplitudes developed for steady-state undamped forced vibrations is obtained. It will be noted that if the exciting force alternates slowly (ω/p smaller than $\tfrac{1}{2}$) the amplitudes of motion are only slightly larger than would be obtained if the force were applied statically (that is, $\dfrac{A}{x_s}$ approaches unity). However, for values of ω/p

in the neighborhood of unity, the numerical value of the magnification factor is very large and hence the amplitudes of the forced vibration become dangerously large. When the impressed frequency ω coincides with the natural frequency, p, of free vibration, the system is said to be in *resonance*, and this is a condition which must be avoided in all moving machine parts.

The speed of rotation of a shaft and the rotor attached to it at which resonance occurs is frequently called the *critical speed* for the shaft. In general it is important to know the critical speed of a rotating member so that the speed of operation can be maintained either considerably above or below this dangerous (critical) speed, or so that the member can be designed for an operating speed that will not be too near the critical speed.

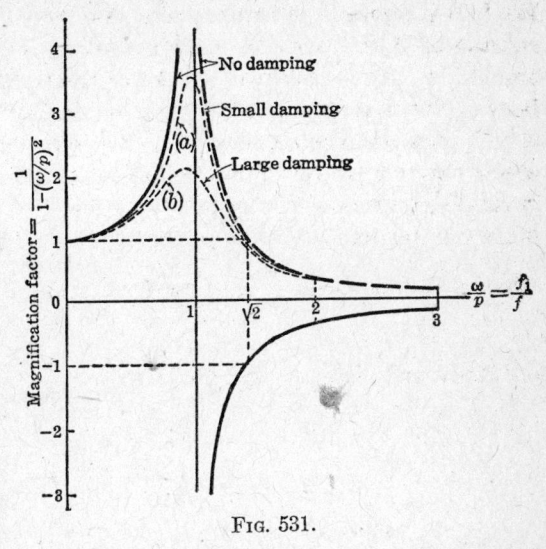

Fig. 531.

For values of ω/p greater than one, the values of $\dfrac{A}{x_s}$ become negative and the exciting force is said to be 180° out of phase with the displacement. Physically this means that the exciting force is pushing upward with its maximum value when the body N is in its lowest position, and the force is always of opposite sense to the displacement. Usually this phase relationship is not of great interest and the magnitude (but not the sign) of the magnification factor may be represented by the ordinate to the dashed line in Fig. 531.

For frequency ratios of ω/p greater than $\sqrt{2}$ the amplitude of forced vibration becomes *less* than would be obtained if P_o were applied statically. In fact, for ratios of ω/p greater than 10, the mass practically stands still in space (its amplitude of motion being less than about 1 per cent of x_s).

Damped Forced Vibrations.—If the above Eqs. (42) to (51) were modified to take into consideration the small damping forces that are always present in actual machines or structures, the magnification factors obtained would differ somewhat from those obtained from Eq. (51) in which damping is neglected. The two dotted curves (a) and (b) in Fig. 531 show the values of magnification factor that would be obtained for a relatively small, and for a relatively large viscous damping coefficient, respectively. The addition of damping does not appreciably affect the amplitudes of motion except near resonance, and the resonant frequency remains practically unchanged. Hence Eq. (51) will also yield satisfactory results for most cases of damped forced vibrations in which the damping is relatively small.

Torsional Forced Vibrations.—Equations the same as those obtained above may be found for *torsional* forced vibrations, except that force is replaced by torque, mass by moment of inertia of mass, and linear displacements, velocities, and accelerations by angular displacements, velocities, and accelerations.

160. Vibration Reduction.—The engineering problem relating to vibration is frequently that of reducing a forced vibration. There are several methods of reducing vibrations, based on the principles discussed in the preceding articles, the more important being:

1. Removal of the exciting force, by balancing.
2. Tuning to avoid resonance.
3. Damping, usually by introducing frictional forces.
4. Isolation, by introducing elastic supports.

1. *Balancing.* A brief discussion of methods of balancing rotating masses is given in the following chapter. There are several widely used machines for determining the dynamic unbalance of rotating parts and the masses that must be added to produce balance, and hence to remove (or greatly reduce) the exciting force.

2. *Tuning.* In order that large amplitudes of vibration may be avoided, machines are frequently designed so that they do not operate at or near the critical speed, the critical speed of a rotating body being identical to its natural frequency of free vibration. This process is called tuning. If the operating speed of a member is at or near the critical or resonant speed, even for a supposedly balanced member, a slight exciting force caused by deviations from assumed conditions will build up large amplitudes of motion. If a member is found to be operating near the resonant speed it may be detuned (I) by changing the frequency of the exciting forces through (a) a change in the speed of rotation, or (b) a change in the number of forced impulses per revolution of the member, as for example a change in the number of jets in a turbine; or (II) by changing the natural frequency of the member by adjusting the relative stiffness and masses of the moving parts.

3. *Damping.* If the operating speeds of an apparatus or machine

that is subjected to forced vibrations involve a wide range of speeds including the resonant speed, damping (caused by introducing frictional forces) is frequently useful in reducing the amplitudes that would occur near the resonant speed. Damping has only a small effect on amplitudes except near the resonant speed, as is indicated in Fig. 531 by the decrease in the magnification factor for a damped forced vibration; the decrease in amplitude produced by the addition of a damping force of considerable magnitude is appreciable only in the neighborhood of the resonant frequency. An automobile that must operate over a wide range of speeds and conditions of road is equipped with shock absorbers as friction dampers which limit the amplitude of resonant vibrations of the body of the car (sprung-weight) induced by road irregularities. Damping caused by the friction in built-up leaf springs as the leaves slip against each other when the spring oscillates plays an important part in reducing the amplitude of resonant vibration of railroad cars on their springs.

On the other hand, the automobile engine is mounted on springs of relatively low modulus, so that the operating speed of the engine is very much above the speed of natural vibration of the assembly of the engine and springs, and hence damping is not needed since resonance does not occur. This method of avoiding resonance is called isolation of the vibration.

4. *Isolation*. When the exciting forces in a forced vibration of a body cannot be eliminated, it is necessary to resort to some method of isolating the vibration so that the periodic force reaction on the foundations or supporting frame is reduced. The usual method of isolation is to use some form of elastic suspension of the vibrating body. The term *transmissibility* is used to denote the ratio of the maximum force actually transmitted to the support through the spring (which is k times the stretch of the spring) to the maximum force that would be transmitted to the support with no elastic suspension; this latter value may be thought of as the amplitude of the exciting force.

The simplest type of spring suspension is indicated in Fig. 532 in which a body B, whose weight is W, is supported by a spring and is given an up and down forced vibration of amplitude A and frequency f_1. The transmissibility, ϵ, of such an undamped isolation mechanism is

$$\epsilon = \frac{\text{max. spring force}}{\text{max. exciting force}} = \frac{kA}{P_o} = \frac{k\left[\dfrac{P_o}{k} \cdot \dfrac{1}{1-\left(\dfrac{f_1}{f}\right)^2}\right]}{P_o} = \frac{1}{1-\left(\dfrac{f_1}{f}\right)^2} = \frac{1}{1-\left(\dfrac{\omega}{p}\right)^2}$$

where f is the natural up and down frequency of vibration of the body B. It will be observed that ϵ is the same as the magnification factor for undamped forced vibration, shown in Fig. 531. In obtaining a value of ϵ its algebraic sign may be neglected, the minus sign merely indicating that the force transmitted to the support is out of phase with the exciting force. It is evident that, to be effective, ϵ must be less than unity, and experience shows that in most cases ϵ should not be greater than 1/10, which means that f should be from 1/3 to 1/4 of f_1.

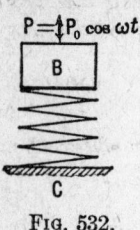

Fig. 532.

Hence if the body B (Fig. 532) represents a machine subjected to a forced vibration, which we desire to isolate by preventing the exciting forces from being transmitted to the supporting structure, Fig. 531 indicates that the ratio $\omega/p \left(= \dfrac{f_1}{f} \right)$ should be made as large as possible, thus making the amplitude of motion approach zero. This is usually accomplished by using a very flexible elastic mounting (spring with a small value of k), in order to make the natural frequency, $p = \sqrt{\dfrac{kg}{W}}$, small compared to ω.

Similarly, to isolate delicate instruments from vibrations which may be present in the framework of a building, they may be placed on a heavy table that is suspended from the ceiling by flexible springs which deflect several inches under the weight of the table. For example, if the elongation of the springs is 2.44 in., the natural frequency of the system is

$$f = 3.127 \sqrt{\dfrac{1}{\delta_{st}}} = \dfrac{3.127}{\sqrt{2.44}} = 2.0 \text{ cycles per sec.}$$

Hence, if the impressed frequency of the vibration of the building is about 20 cycles per second the magnification factor or transmissibility becomes

$$\dfrac{1}{1 - \left(\dfrac{f_1}{f}\right)^2} = \dfrac{1}{1 - \left(\dfrac{20}{2}\right)^2} = \dfrac{1}{99},$$

indicating that the amplitude of motion transmitted to the table is approximately 1% of that present in the building.

ILLUSTRATIVE PROBLEM

Problem 902.—An automobile has main (helical) springs that are compressed 6 in. by the weight of the body of the car. If the axles of the wheels of the automobile are clamped to a test platform and the platform is given a vertical harmonic motion having an amplitude of 1 in. and a frequency of 1 cycle per second, determine the amplitude of the motion of the body of the car, assuming that there are no shock absorbers and hence that the vibration takes place without damping. Find also the maximum shortening of the spring.

Solution.—The frequency of the free vibration is $f = \dfrac{1}{2\pi}\sqrt{\dfrac{g}{\delta_{st}}} = \dfrac{1}{2\pi}\sqrt{\dfrac{386}{6}} = 1.28$ cycles per sec. And since $x_s = 1$ in. and $f_1 = 1$ cycle per sec., the amplitude A of the forced vibration is

$$A = x_s \dfrac{1}{1 - \left(\dfrac{f_1}{f}\right)^2} = 1 \times \dfrac{1}{1 - \left(\dfrac{1}{1.28}\right)^2} = \dfrac{1}{1 - 0.61} = 2.56 \text{ in.}$$

Since the frequency of the impressed motion is below the resonant frequency, the motion of the axles is in phase with the motion of the body of the car, and hence the change in the length of the spring is $2.56 - 1 = 1.56$ in. The maximum shortening of the spring therefore is $1.56 + 6 = 7.56$ in.

PROBLEMS

903. In Prob. 902 assume that the body of the car weighs 2400 lb. and that the axles of the car are acted on by forces, the resultant of which is a vertical force that varies harmonically and has a maximum value of 40 lb. If the length of each cycle is 3 sec., what is the amplitude of the forced vibration? *Ans.* $A = 0.107$ in.

904. A horizontal shaft rotates in bearings at its ends and has keyed to it at the center of its length a disk whose center of mass is 0.01 in. from the axis of the bearings. The weight of the disk is 193 lb. and that of the shaft may be assumed to be negligible. It is found that a static force of 2000 lb. deflects the shaft and disk 0.1 in. (a) Calculate the resonant (or critical) speed of rotation of the shaft. (b) If the speed of rotation is one-half the resonant speed, calculate the amplitude of the steady state forced vibration.

Ans. (a) $\omega = 200$ rad./sec. $= 1910$ r.p.m.; (b) $A = \dfrac{1}{300}$ in.

905. A motor weighing 40 lb. is mounted at the center of a simple beam as shown in Fig. 530(a). The static elastic deflection of the beam caused by the weight of the motor is 0.01 in. A small body M weighing 0.11 lb. is attached to the rotor at a distance r of 4 in. from the shaft. Assuming the weight of the beam to be negligible, determine the amplitude of the forced vibration of the motor when running at 1800 r.p.m. *Ans.* $A = 0.126$ in.

906. A vibrometer (see Fig. 524) having a period of free vibration of 2 sec. is rigidly attached to a body C that has a vertical harmonic vibration with a frequency of one cycle per sec. If the amplitude of the motion of the body B relative to the frame of the vibrometer is 0.5 in., find the amplitude of motion of C. (HINT: The instrument is operating above its resonant frequency and hence the amplitude of the motion of B relative to the frame is the sum of the true amplitude of B and the amplitude of C.) *Ans.* $A_c = \tfrac{3}{8}$ in.

907. The main driving wheels of a locomotive are overbalanced by an excess counterweight of 400 lb. in the wheel at a distance of 15 in. from the axis of rotation. A vertical vibration of the wheel is possible between the locomotive spring (whose stiffness is 15,000 lb./in.) and the track which may be assumed to have a stiffness of 140,000 lb./in. The wheel has a diameter of 72 in. and a total weight (including counterweight) of 8000 lb. Determine the forward speed of the locomotive at which a resonant forced vibration of the wheel would occur. What would be the amplitude of the vertical vibration of the wheel when running at 90 miles per hour? Assume that the wheel does not leave the track.

Ans. $v = 177$ mi./hr.; $A = 0.262$ in.

908. A motor generator set weighing 2000 lb. is mounted on four identical rubber pads placed under the corners of the frame. The speed of the motor is 1200 r.p.m. Determine the maximum allowable spring constant for each pad if the difference in the maximum and minimum values of the force transmitted through the pads to the building is not to exceed $\frac{1}{3}$ of the double amplitude of the vertical force impressed on the set by dynamic unbalance of the rotor. *Ans.* $k = 5120$ lb./in.

CHAPTER XII

BALANCING

161. Need for Balancing.—A moving part of a machine, as a rule, has either a reciprocating motion similar to that of the crosshead of a steam engine or a motion of rotation such as that of the crank shaft of an automobile engine or the rotor of an electric motor. In any case, if the moving parts are accelerated, forces must be supplied to produce the accelerations. If the moving parts are not balanced, the forces which act on the moving masses are transmitted to them from the stationary parts of the machine such as the bearings and the machine frame. And, in supplying these accelerating forces, serious trouble may arise, such as vibrations in automobiles, turbines, etc.; defective commutations in electrical machinery; heavy bearing pressures which cause undue wear; defective work with grinding disks, high-speed drilling machines, etc.; and defective lubrication. It is of great importance, therefore, to properly neutralize or balance these forces in various types of machines.

The moving parts of a machine may be (1) in static or standing balance or (2) in dynamic or running balance. Standing balance exists if the forces which act on the parts, when the parts are not running, are in equilibrium regardless of the positions in which the parts are placed. Dynamic balancing consists in distributing the moving masses, or in introducing additional masses, so that the forces (called kinetic loads) exerted by the masses of the moving system on the stationary parts of the machine are in equilibrium among themselves and hence exert no resultant force on the stationary parts of the machine. The complete balancing of a machine, however, is not always practicable or possible.

The method of balancing rotating masses, only, is here discussed. Furthermore, the shaft on which the rotating parts are mounted is assumed to be rigid. If the elastic deflection of the shaft is considered the rotating masses could be in balance only for one speed of the shaft. For methods of balancing reciprocating masses and for an excellent discussion of the whole subject of the balancing of engines see Dalby's "Balancing of Engines."

162. Balancing of Rotating Masses.—The inertia forces or kinetic loads exerted by the unbalanced rotating masses on the foundations or other stationary parts of machines may be treated, in general, (1) as a system of centrifugal forces or (2) as a system of centrifugal couples or (3) as a combination of the two.

A Single Rotating Mass. Centrifugal Force.—If a shaft (Fig. 533a) rotates at an angular velocity ω and carries a single mass M_1 the center of gravity of which is at the distance r_1 from the axis of rotation, the shaft will be subjected to a kinetic load (which is equal to the centrifugal force of mass M) of magnitude $M_1 r_1 \omega^2$. This kinetic load causes the shaft to exert forces on the bearings which in turn are transmitted to the machine frame. The reactions at the bearings may be eliminated by balancing the rotating mass. This may be done by the addition of

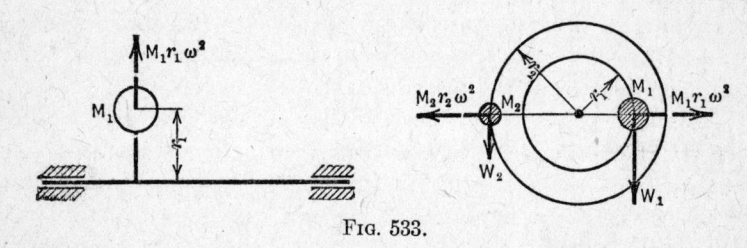

Fig. 533.

a single mass M_2 diametrically opposite to M_1 (Fig. 533b), the center of gravity of M_2 being at a distance r_2 from the axis of rotation, such that

$$M_1 r_1 \omega^2 = M_2 r_2 \omega^2 \quad \text{or} \quad \frac{W_1}{g} r_1 \omega^2 = \frac{W^2}{g} r_2 \omega^2.$$

But, since $\dfrac{\omega^2}{g}$ is a common factor, the conditions for running or dynamic balance may be expressed by the equation

$$W_1 r_1 = W_2 r_2.$$

Now, as is evident from Fig. 533(b), this equation expresses the condition for standing balance also. Thus, a shop method of obtaining approximate running balance with a rotating member, in which the material is substantially in a plane of rotation such as a disk, a pulley, or a flywheel, consists in drilling out material on the heavy side or adding material on the light side until standing balance is obtained.

Two Rotating Masses. Centrifugal Couple.—If a shaft carries two rotating masses M_1 and M_2 in different planes of rotation but in the same axial plane (Fig. 534) and, further, if the centrifugal forces $M_1r_1\omega^2$ and $M_2r_2\omega^2$ exerted on the shaft by the two masses are equal, then the shaft is subjected to an unbalanced centrifugal couple which is resisted by an equal couple exerted by the bearings. Or, if the two rotating masses are to be balanced, two additional masses, M_3 and M_4, must be introduced in the same axial plane (Fig. 534) such that the centrifugal couple $M_3r_3\omega^2 b$ or $M_4r_4\omega^2 b$ which they exert on the shaft is equal and opposite to the centrifugal couple of M_1 and M_2. Hence

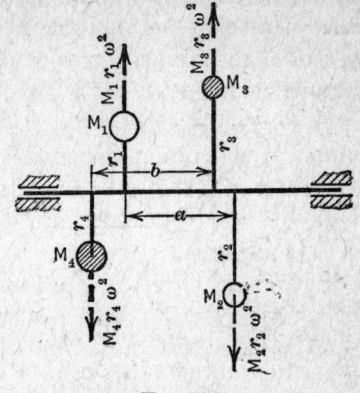

FIG. 534.

$$M_1r_1\omega^2 a = M_3r_3\omega^2 b, \quad \text{or} \quad M_2r_2\omega^2 a = M_4r_4\omega^2 b.$$

And, as before, omitting the common factor $\dfrac{\omega^2}{g}$, we may write

$$W_1r_1 a = W_3r_3 b, \text{ etc.}$$

It will be noted that the shaft when carrying only the two masses M_1 and M_2 is in standing balance but not in running balance.

163. Several Masses in a Single Plane of Rotation.—If several masses M_1, M_2, M_3, etc., lie in the same transverse plane (Fig. 535a), the shaft is subjected to the centrifugal forces

$$M_1r_1\omega^2, M_2r_2\omega^2, M_3r_3\omega^2, \text{ etc.,}$$

which form a concurrent system of forces.

The condition that such a force system shall balance is that the force polygon shall close. That is, the vectors representing the forces $M_1r_1\omega^2, M_2r_2\omega^2, M_3r_3\omega^2$, etc., if laid off in succession, each in its proper direction, shall form a closed polygon. Or, since $Mr\omega^2$ may be written $\dfrac{W}{g}r\omega^2$ and since $\dfrac{\omega^2}{g}$ is a factor common to the expression for each force, the products W_1r_1, W_2r_2, etc., may be used instead of the actual forces. Thus, let the four masses as shown in Fig. 535(a) be a system of masses which rotate in a transverse plane. Suppose that the products W_1r_1, W_2r_2, W_3r_3, and W_4r_4 when laid off as vectors (Fig. 535b) do not form a closed polygon. It is evident then that the four masses are not in running balance. In order to balance the system of masses, a mass, M_o, must be added at a distance, r_o, such that the product $W_o r_o$ is represented both in magnitude and in direction by the closing side, EA, of

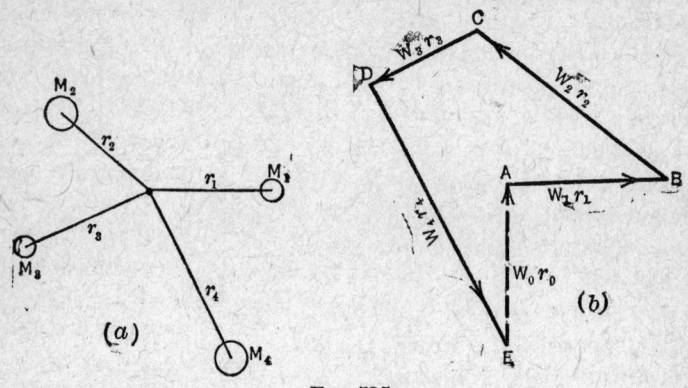

FIG. 535.

the vector polygon. By assuming a convenient value for r_o, a value of M_o may be found. The gap, EA, may be closed, however, by two or more vectors from which two or more masses may be found that will balance the system.

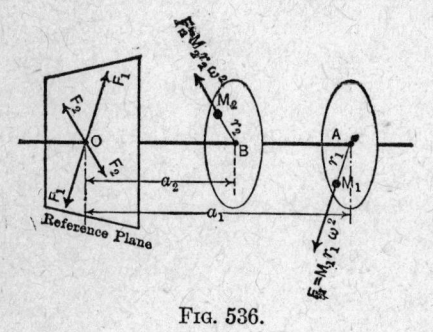

164. Masses in Different Transverse Planes.—In Fig. 536, let the masses M_1 and M_2 be connected with the shaft at A and B, respectively, and through some point, O, of the shaft let a transverse plane, called a reference plane, be chosen. The mass M_1 exerts a kinetic load, F_1, on the shaft such that

$$F_1 = M_1 r_1 \omega^2.$$

Now at O introduce two equal and opposite forces each equal and parallel to F_1. The force F_1 at A and the equal opposite force at O form a couple, C_1, the moment of which is

$$C_1 = M_1 r_1 \omega^2 a_1.$$

Thus the single force F_1 at A is replaced by an equal parallel force at O and the couple C_1. In like manner the single force $F_2 = M_2 r_2 \omega^2$ at B may be replaced by the equal parallel force F_2 in the reference plane and a couple $C_2 = M_2 r_2 \omega^2 a_2$.

MASSES IN DIFFERENT TRANSVERSE PLANES

Thus, the kinetic loads on a shaft exerted by a system of rotating masses may be reduced to a system of concurrent forces in an arbitrarily chosen reference plane and a system of couples which lie in different axial planes. The resultant of the system of concurrent forces, if not balanced, is a single force in the reference plane, and the resultant of the system of couples, if not balanced, is a single couple in some axial plane. Hence, in general, the system of kinetic loads, if not balanced, may be reduced to a single force and a couple. The moment of the couple will, of course, depend on the position chosen for the reference plane.

The conditions then which must be fulfilled to have a system of rotating masses in equilibrium are:

(1) The resultant of the system of concurrent forces must be zero. That is, the force polygon for the forces in the reference plane must close.

(2) The resultant of the system of couples must be zero. That is, the couple polygon must close.

These conditions may be satisfied by the addition of two rotating masses in different transverse planes. Thus, let the shaft (Fig. 537) carry an unbalanced system of rotating masses, M_1, M_2, and M_3, and let the two balancing masses be denoted by M_o and M'_o. Let the

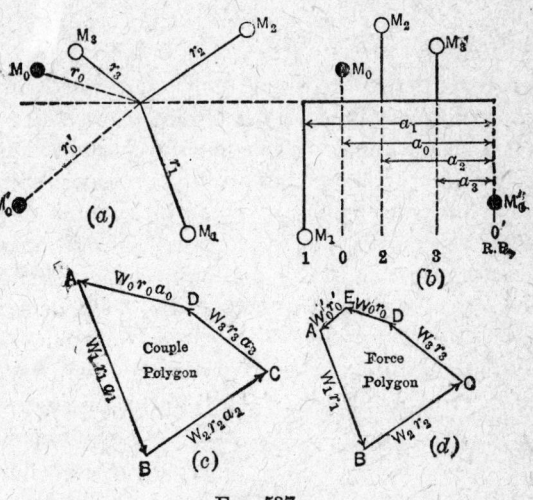

FIG. 537.

transverse planes in which these balancing masses are to lie be chosen arbitrarily but let the plane of one of the masses be chosen as the reference plane. The plane of mass M'_o will here be selected as the reference plane. Let a_o, a_1, a_2, and a_3 denote the respective distances of the masses M_o, M_1, M_2 and M_3 from the reference plane. The couples $W_1 r_1 a_1$, $W_2 r_2 a_2$, etc., may now be calculated (the common factor $\dfrac{\omega^2}{g}$ is omitted in each term for simplicity). The only unknown couple is $W_o r_o a_o$, since the couple $W'_o r'_o a'_o$ is zero owing to the fact that the reference plane was chosen as the plane of M'_o, which makes a'_o equal to zero. By laying off the vectors that represent the known couples as

374   BALANCING

the sides of a polygon, see Art. 17, the closing side determines both the moment of the unknown couple $W_o r_o a_o$ and the axial plane in which it lies. By assigning any convenient value to the moment arm a_o, the product $W_o r_o$ may be found, and by assuming a convenient value for r_o, W_o may be determined and placed in the plane indicated by the closing vector of the couple polygon. Thus, by the addition of the couple $W_o r_o a_o$ condition (2) is satisfied.

Condition (1) may now be satisfied as follows: The kinetic load due to the added mass M_o is replaced by a force in the reference plane and the couple $W_o r_o a_o$ as was done for the kinetic loads due to the original masses. Now, if the products $W_1 r_1$, $W_2 r_2$, etc. (including $W_o r_o$), are laid off as the sides of a polygon, the closing side gives the magnitude and the direction of a product $W'_o r'_o$ for a body W'_o which must be added in the reference plane to balance the system of concurrent forces in the reference plane and thereby satisfy condition (1). By choosing a convenient value for r'_o, the mass M'_o may be determined and the direction of the closing side of the polygon gives the direction of M'_o from the axis of the shaft.

If the couple polygon is formed by drawing the couple vectors perpendicular to the planes of the couples, as explained in Art. 17, and then is turned through 90°, it will be the same as the polygon formed by drawing the couple vectors according to the following rule: Draw the couple vectors parallel to the respective crank directions: outwards for masses on one side of the reference plane; inwards towards the axis for masses on the opposite side of the reference plane.

The vectors of the force polygon are drawn, of course, from the axis outwards parallel to the radii to the masses.

ILLUSTRATIVE PROBLEM

Problem 909.—Three weights W_1, W_2, and W_3 (Fig. 538) which revolve in the planes 1, 2, and 3 are to be balanced by the addition of two weights. Plane 1 is chosen as the plane of one of the weights (W_o), and the plane of the other weight (W'_o) will arbitrarily be taken 1.4 ft. to the right of plane 3 and will be selected as the reference plane. It is required to determine values of W_o and W'_o and the lengths and directions of the corresponding radii for kinetic balance. The accompanying table gives the values of the weights, the lengths and directions of the radii, and the distances from the reference plane.

Solution.—From the given data, the values of the products Wr and Wra for the known weights are calculated and entered in the last two columns of the above table. The couple polygon is then drawn as shown in Fig. 538(c). AB is laid off in the direction of W_1 outwards from the shaft and its length represents to scale the value of the product $W_1 r_1 a_1$ which is 79.2. Next BC is laid off in the direction of W_2 such that its length represents to the same scale $W_2 r_2 a_2$ (62.4). Similarly CD is

ILLUSTRATIVE PROBLEM

laid off to represent $W_3 r_3 a_3$ (25.2). The closing side DA of the polygon represents the product $W_o r_o a_o$ due to the balancing weight W_o in plane 1 (or O). This product

Plane	Weight W (lb.)	Radius r (in.)	Angle θ	Distance from R.P. a (ft.)	Wr (lb.-in.)	Wra (lb.-in.-ft.)
1	2	9	270°	4.4	18	79.2
2	3	8	30°	2.6	24	62.4
3	3	6	150°	1.4	18	25.2
O	(1.36)	(8)	....	4.4	(10.9)	(48.0)
O' (R.P.)	(2.28)	(5)	....	0	(11.4)	....

is found by measuring to be 48.0. Hence

$$W_o r_o = \frac{48.0}{4.4} = 10.9 \text{ lb.-in.}$$

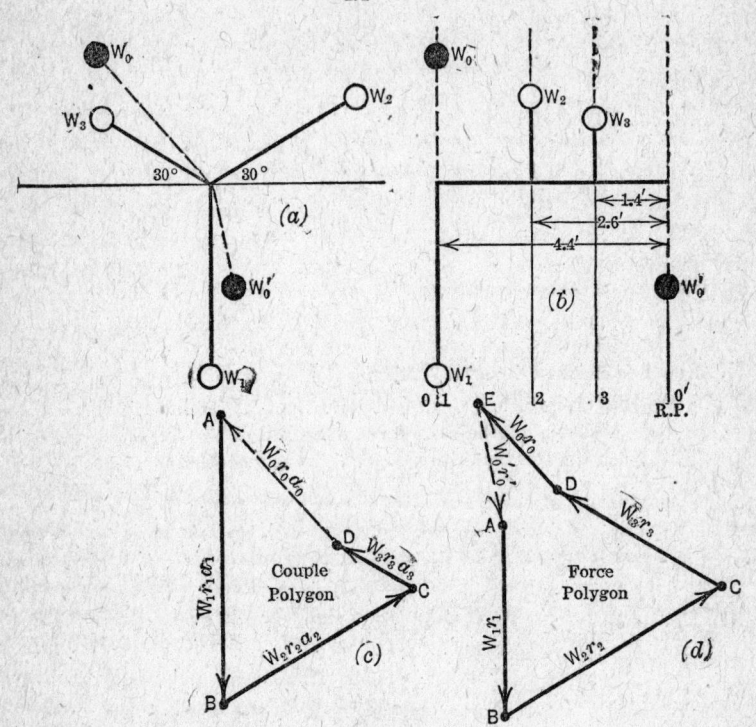

FIG. 538.

This product is now entered in the column of the above table with the other Wr-products. The addition of the weight W_o in the plane 1 at the distance r_o

reduces the resultant couple to zero. There are left, however, the forces in the reference plane, including the force corresponding to the product $W_o r_o$ just found, and these forces will, in general, not be balanced. Now if the vectors corresponding to these Wr-products are laid off in order as in Fig. 538(d), the closing vector EA represents the product $W'_o r'_o$ which by measurement is found to be 11.4. If the values of $W_o r_o$ and $W'_o r'_o$ are divided by assumed values of r_o and r'_o (8 in. and 5 in. respectively) we obtain the values, $W_o = 1.36$ and $W'_o = 2.28$. Hence if weights of 1.36 lb. and 2.28 lb. are placed in planes O and O' at radial distances 8 in. and 5 in., respectively, as indicated in Fig. 538, the system will be in kinetic balance.

PROBLEMS

910. Five bodies are attached to a disk which revolves with constant angular velocity. In the following table are given the weights of the bodies, the angles which the radii from the mass-centers to the axis of rotation make with the x-axis, and the lengths of the radii to the mass-centers. The angles, θ, are measured counter-clockwise from the x-axis.

W	θ	r
5 lb.	45°	18 in.
6 lb.	120°	15 in.
10 lb.	150°	12 in.
4 lb.	240°	12 in.
6 lb.	315°	18 in.

Determine sufficient data for kinetic balance of the system of bodies:
 (a) By the addition of a single weight placed 2 ft. from the axis of rotation.
 (b) By the addition of two weights, one of 2 lb. placed on the y-axis, and the other of 2.25 lb. placed 2 ft. from the axis of rotation.

911. Four bodies are attached to a revolving shaft in different transverse planes. The weights and positions of the bodies are indicated in the following table, the reference plane being the transverse plane in which the mass-center of the 6-lb. body (W_3) lies.

W	θ	r	a
5 lb.	30°	2 ft.	−1 ft.
4 lb.	45°	1½ ft.	2 ft.
6 lb.	150°	1 ft.	0 ft.
4 lb.	240°	2 ft.	½ ft.

The given masses are to be balanced by two masses, one mass to be placed in plane 4 at a radial distance of 1½ ft., and the other to be placed in the reference plane at a radial distance of 2 ft. Find the weights and values of θ for the two masses.

Ans. $W_o = 2.93$ lb.; $W'_o = 4.85$ lb.

912. The crank shaft of a gas engine carries two flywheels A and B, the planes of revolution of which are 3.5 ft. apart. The plane of revolution of the crank is between the flywheels and 1 ft. 7 in. from the plane of A. The crank arms and pin are equivalent to a weight of 108 lb. at a radial distance of 10 in. from the crank shaft and in the plane of revolution of the crank. What weights placed at a radial distance of 2 ft., one in each flywheel, will balance the crank? Solve algebraically.

Ans. $W_A = 24.6$ lb.; $W_B = 20.4$ lb.

CHAPTER XIII

THE GYROSCOPE

165. The Problem Defined.—Gyroscopic motion occurs whenever a body rotates about an axis in the body as the axis (and body) is turned about a second axis, provided that the two axes are not parallel. Thus, the wheels of a locomotive when rounding a curve, or the screw propeller of a ship when the ship is pitching in a rough sea, are given gyroscopic motion. The forces that act on the body in giving it gyroscopic motion may be of considerable importance since under certain conditions they are very undesirable, as, for example, the forces exerted on the propeller of an aeroplane when making a sharp turn. On the other hand, the gyroscope is sometimes used to introduce desirable forces, as, for example, in reducing the rolling of ships.

The gyroscope here considered is a body symmetrical with respect to each of three rectangular axes. The body rotates or spins with constant angular velocity about one of the axes and at the same time turns about one of the other axes with constant angular velocity. Thus, in Fig. 539, let $ABCD$ represent a circular disk which is symmetrical with respect to the three axes x, y, and z. Let the disk rotate or spin with a high constant angular velocity ω about the z-axis and at the same time let the disk turn about the y-axis with the constant angular velocity Ω. The problem to be considered is that of determining the forces which must act on the disk or its axles (axle reactions) in order to maintain this gyroscopic motion.

166. Analysis of Forces in the Gyroscope.—Owing to the two rotations imposed on the disk, a particle, m, at the distance ρ (assumed at the circumference of the disk for convenience) has at any instant, two velocities: (1) a constant velocity $\omega\rho$ in the plane of the disk due to the rotation about the z-axis with angular velocity ω, and (2) the velocity $\Omega\rho \cos \theta$ perpendicular to the disk (parallel to the z-axis) due to the rotation about the y-axis with angular velocity Ω.

The accelerations of the particle m arising from the changes that occur in each of these two velocities due to each of the rotations which are given to the disk will first be investigated, since the effective force for any particle must have components corresponding to the accelerations arising from the change in the magnitude and the change in the direction of each of these two velocities (Theorems I and II, Art. 87, and Newton's second law, Art. 102). And, the effective forces for the particles must be found in order to determine the external forces required to maintain the gyroscopic motion. (Read Art. 108 for the general method of procedure, keeping in mind that gyroscopic motion is not uniplanar motion.)

Changes in Velocities Due to Rotation about Z-axis

(1) *Change in* $\omega\rho$. Since ω is constant, $\omega\rho$ changes in direction only. The resulting acceleration ($\omega^2\rho$) and the corresponding effective force for

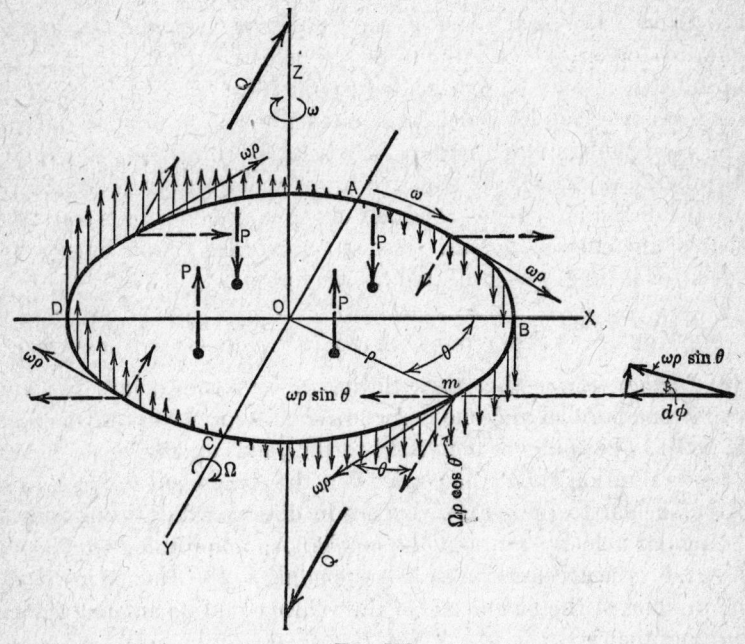

FIG. 539.

the particle are directed towards the center of rotation (towards the z-axis). And, since the body is symmetrical, these effective forces for all the particles form a balanced system; hence, according to D'Alembert's principle, no external forces act on the body by reason of this change in the velocity of the particles.

(2) *Change in* $\Omega\rho \cos\theta$.—In one revolution of the disk about the z-axis, this component of the velocity changes, as follows: It gradually increases in magnitude downwards from zero at A to a maximum at B; it then decreases gradually to zero at C; then increases in the opposite

direction to a maximum at D; and finally decreases to zero again at A. The acceleration, a_1, at any instant then is (Theorem I, Art. 87)

$$a_1 = \frac{d(\Omega \rho \cos \theta)}{dt} = -\Omega \rho \sin \theta \frac{d\theta}{dt} = -\Omega \rho \sin \theta \omega = -\omega \Omega y,$$

in which y is the distance of the particle from the x-axis, and the minus sign indicates that the sense of the acceleration is opposite to that of the velocity for the position of the particle as shown in Fig. 539. Hence, for the position of the particle shown, the direction of $\omega\Omega y$ is upwards. The effective force, corresponding to this acceleration, for any particle in the quadrants OBC and OCD, is an upward force perpendicular to the plane of the disk. And, in the quadrants ODA and OAB, it is a downward force. The resultant of the effective forces for the four quadrants, then, may be represented by the forces P (Fig. 539). These forces form two couples which have moments with respect to only one of the rectangular axes; namely, the x-axis. Further, according to D'Alembert's principle, the effective forces require that external forces act on the disk such that the resultant of the external forces is equivalent to that of the effective forces. Hence, an external couple must act on the disk (or its axles) as indicated by the forces Q (Fig. 539).

Changes in Velocities Due to Rotation about Y-axis

(3) *Change in $\omega\rho$.*—Let the velocity $\omega\rho$ be resolved into two components: one parallel and one perpendicular, respectively, to the y-axis (Fig. 539). The component parallel to the y-axis undergoes no changes due to the rotation about the y-axis; but the component $\omega\rho \sin \theta$, which is perpendicular to the y-axis, changes in direction due to the rotation with angular velocity Ω about the y-axis. And, according to Theorem II of Art. 87, the acceleration a_2 corresponding to this change in velocity is the product of the magnitude of the velocity and its angular velocity of turning, that is,

$$a_2 = \omega\rho \sin \theta \cdot \Omega = \omega\Omega y,$$

and it is directed upwards perpendicular to the plane of the disk. This acceleration, therefore, is equal to a_1 (see above) and has the same direction and sense as that of a_1 for all positions of the particle, as will be observed from a study of Fig. 539. Therefore, external forces which act on the disk as a consequence of the changes in $\omega\rho \sin \theta$ due to the rotation of the disk about the y-axis must constitute a couple exactly the same as that found under (2).

(4) *Change in $\Omega\rho \cos \theta$.*—This velocity changes in direction, only, owing to the rotation about the y-axis with constant angular velocity Ω.

The resulting acceleration, $\Omega^2 \times \rho \cos \theta$ or $\Omega^2 x$, is directed towards the center, on the y-axis, about which the particle is rotating at the instant. The corresponding effective forces for the particles of the whole disk, therefore, form a parallel system in the plane of the disk. But, since the disk is symmetrical with respect to the y-axis, this effective force system is balanced, and hence no external forces act on the disk as a consequence of the changes caused in this velocity by the rotation about the y-axis.

It will be noted, therefore, that if the disk is rotated about the z-axis and at the same time is turned about the y-axis, it will rotate about the x-axis unless an external couple acts on the disk to prevent the rotation. This external couple is called the *gyroscopic couple*.

A simple experiment for demonstrating the existence of the gyroscopic couple may be made by holding a bicycle wheel (dismounted from the frame) with one hand on either end of the projecting (horizontal) axle. If the wheel is spinning in the vertical plane about the axle which is held in the hands, any attempt to turn the axle (and hands) in the horizontal plane will cause the wheel (and hands) to turn about a horizontal axis perpendicular to the axis of the wheel unless the hands exert a couple to prevent this rotation.

167. The Moment of the Gyroscopic Couple.—In the preceding article it was shown that the only accelerations of the particles of the disk which require the action of external forces on the disk are

$$a = a_1 + a_2 = \omega \Omega y + \omega \Omega y$$
$$= 2\omega \Omega y,$$

and that this acceleration for any particle is directed perpendicular to the plane of the disk; upwards in the two quadrants BCD, and downward in the two quadrants DAB.

The force required to produce this acceleration (effective force) of the particle of mass m is

$$F = ma = m \times 2\omega \Omega y,$$

the direction of which agrees with that of a.

The moment of this effective force for the particle, about the x-axis, is

$$F \times y = 2m\omega \Omega y^2,$$

and the sum of the moments of the effective forces for all the particles of the disk is

$$\Sigma 2m\omega \Omega y^2.$$

But since ω and Ω are constant this may be written

$$2\omega \Omega \Sigma m y^2 = 2I_x \omega \Omega,$$

in which I_x is the moment of inertia of the disk with respect to the x-axis.

Now the sum of the moments of the effective forces is equal to the moment of their resultant, but the resultant of the effective forces is a couple, as shown in the preceding article. Further, this resultant couple is equal to the external or gyroscopic couple. Therefore, the moment, C, of the gyroscopic couple is

$$C = 2I_x\omega\Omega.$$

But, since the disk is symmetrical with respect to the x- and y-axes, I_x is equal to I_y. Hence, by making use of the equation of Art. 195, $2I_x$ may be replaced by the moment of inertia of the disk with respect to the axis of spin (z-axis). Therefore, the moment of the gyroscopic couple is

$$C = I\omega\Omega,$$

in which I is the moment of inertia of the disk with respect to the axis of spin.

The following conclusion then may be drawn: If a body is symmetrical with respect to each of two rectangular axes (x and y) and rotates or spins with a constant angular velocity ω about a third axis perpendicular to each of the two axes (the z-axis or axis of spin), a couple having a moment about one of the two axes (the x-axis) is required to maintain an angular velocity, Ω, about the other of the two axes (the y-axis); the moment of the couple is equal to the product of (1) the moment of inertia, I, of the body with respect to the axis of spin (z-axis), (2) the angular velocity, ω, of spin, and (3) the angular velocity, Ω, about the y-axis.

The angular velocity Ω which is maintained by the couple is called the *velocity of precession*, and the corresponding axis (y-axis) is called the *axis of precession*. The axis about which the couple $I\omega\Omega$ tends to rotate the disk (x-axis) is called the *torque axis*. Hence the disk when spinning about the z-axis with angular velocity ω is said to precess about the y-axis when acted on by a couple having a moment of $I\omega\Omega$ about the x-axis.

By referring to Fig. 539, it will be seen that the sense of rotation about the axis of precession (y-axis) is in accordance with the following rule:

> The sense of precession is such as to turn the axis of spin toward the torque axis, that is, the axis of spin tends to become coincident with the torque axis.

In the interpretation of this rule the torque axis must be regarded as that part or end of the x-axis which, considered as a vector drawn outward from the origin, represents the moment or torque of the couple $I\omega\Omega$, and the axis of spin must be regarded as that part or end of the z-axis which, considered as a vector drawn outward from the origin, represents the angular velocity ω about the z-axis.

Thus, if a disk of weight W (Fig. 540) is given an angular velocity ω about the z-axis and then one end of the axis is placed on the vertical post at A, the couple having a moment Wl will cause the disk (and z-axis) to rotate with angular velocity Ω about the axis of the post (y-axis) such that

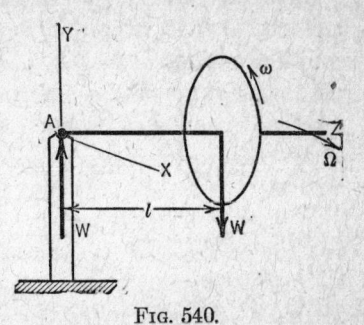

Fig. 540.

$$Wl = I\omega\Omega.$$

Or

$$\Omega = \frac{Wl}{\frac{W}{g}k^2\omega} = \frac{gl}{k^2\omega},$$

in which k is the radius of gyration of the disk with respect to the axis of spin (z-axis). Furthermore, if the sense of ω be as represented in Fig. 540, the sense of precession about the y-axis will be clockwise as viewed from the positive end of the y-axis.

168. Gyroscopic Couple Found by Use of Principle of Impulse and Momentum. *Angular Momentum a Vector Quantity.*—In Chapter X the magnitude, only, of the angular momentum of a body was assumed to change. However, in expressing the principle of angular impulse and angular momentum for a body which moves so that its plane of motion changes in direction (such as the propeller of an aeroplane when making a turn), the angular momentum of the body must be considered as a quantity having direction as well as magnitude, that is, it must be considered to be a vector quantity. The angular momentum of a body may be represented by a vector drawn (1) perpendicular to the plane of motion of the body to indicate the direction of the plane of motion, (2) of such a length that it represents, to some scale, the magnitude of the angular momentum, and (3) with the sense of rotation indicated by an arrow which points in the direction along the vector in which a right-handed screw would advance if given the same sense of rotation as that of the body. Thus, if a disk (Fig. 541) rotates with angular velocity ω_1 about the axis OZ, its angular momentum ($H_1 = I\omega_1$) about the axis of rotation is represented completely by the vector OB. It will be noted that the vector representing the angular momentum may change in length only, in direction only, or both in length and in direction. Thus, in Fig. 541, if the disk is rotated about the axis OY and at the same time the angular velocity about the OZ axis is increased to ω_2, the vector representing the angular momentum ($H_2 = I\omega_2$) of the disk is OC. Furthermore, the change in the angular momentum of a body is represented completely by the change in the angular momentum vector. Thus, in

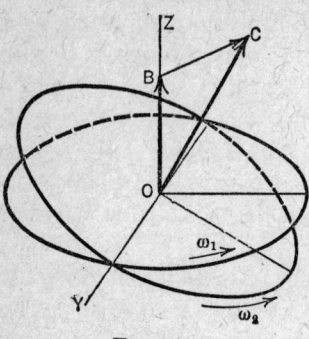

Fig. 541.

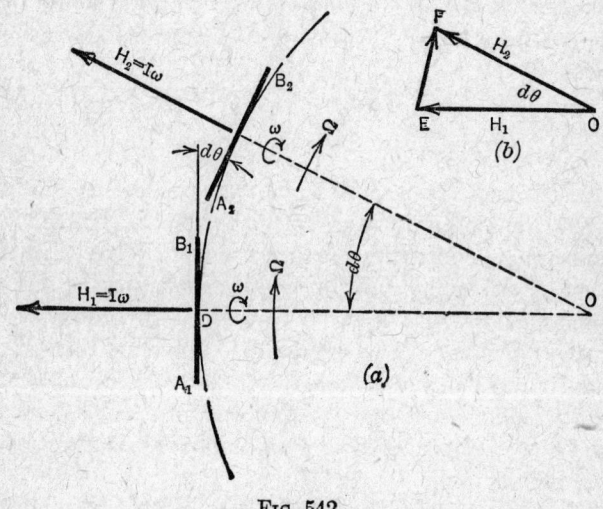

Fig. 542.

Fig. 541 the change in the angular momentum of the disk is represented by the vector BC.

The Gyroscopic Couple.—A disk which rolls round a curved track (Fig. 542a) revolves simultaneously about two rectangular axes and hence it has gyroscopic motion (Art. 165). Gyroscopic motion of a body will here be analyzed briefly by considering the changes in the angular momentum of the body.

MOMENT OF THE GYROSCOPIC COUPLE

In Fig. 542(a) is represented a disk or wheel which rotates with a constant angular velocity ω about its axis (axle) OD as it moves round the curved track with a constant angular velocity Ω. It will be observed that the angular velocity of the disk about an axis through D perpendicular to the paper is also equal to Ω. At a given instant, the disk is in the position A_1B_1 and its angular momentum, H_1, is equal to $I\omega$. After an interval of time dt the disk is in the position A_2B_2 and its angular momentum is H_2, the magnitude of which is also equal to $I\omega$. That is, the angular momentum of the disk ($I\omega$) has changed in direction, only, during the time interval dt.

The change in the angular momentum of the disk from H_1 to H_2 is represented by the vector EF (Fig. 542b) which connects the ends of the vectors H_1 and H_2. Now, since the angle $d\theta$ is small (greatly exaggerated in Fig. 542), the length of DE, that is, the magnitude of the change in the angular momentum, is

$$DE = H_1 d\theta = H_2 d\theta = I\omega d\theta,$$

and the limiting direction of the vector EF as $d\theta$ becomes indefinitely small is perpendicular to H_1. The rate of change of the angular momentum, then, is

$$\frac{I\omega d\theta}{dt} = I\omega\Omega,$$

and the direction of the vector which represents this rate of change of the angular momentum is also perpendicular to H_1. Now a torque or couple is always required to produce a change in the angular momentum of a body; the moment of the couple is equal to the rate of change of the angular momentum of the body (Art. 147); the plane in which it acts is perpendicular to the vector which represents the rate of change of the angular momentum; and the sense of rotation of the couple is such that it would cause a right-handed screw to progress (in the direction of the arrow) along the vector which represents the rate of change of the angular momentum.

Therefore, a couple C must act on the disk in a plane perpendicular to the plane of the disk and to the plane of the paper, with a clockwise sense of rotation (as viewed from behind), the magnitude of the couple being

$$C = I\omega\Omega.$$

It is evident, therefore, that the disk would turn counter-clockwise (outward) unless a couple having a moment equal to $I\omega\Omega$ acted to prevent the turning. This couple is called the gyroscopic couple.

As noted in Art. 165, the forces of the gyroscopic couple frequently cause considerable pressure on the axle of the rotating body as, for example, in the case of the rotor of an electric locomotive when rounding a curve or of the propeller of an aeroplane when making a turn, etc.

If a body (Fig. 543) rotates or spins about the z-axis and a couple Wl having a moment about the x-axis is applied to the body, the body will rotate about the y-axis with an angular velocity Ω unless a couple having a moment about the y-axis acts on the body to prevent the rotation about the y-axis. The angular velocity Ω is called the *velocity of pre-*

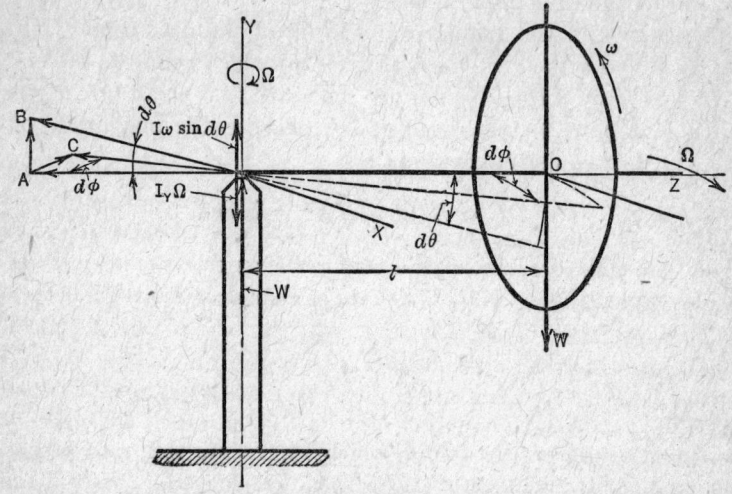

FIG. 543.

cession. It is necessary that the body shall precess in order to develop a resistance to the couple Wl and hence prevent the disk from falling. This fact may be shown by following the changes which occur in the angular momentum about the z-axis. Thus, when the couple Wl (Fig. 543) first acts, the z-axis is turned through an angle $d\theta$ thereby causing a change AB in the angular momentum of the disk. This change requires a couple in the horizontal plane with a clockwise sense as viewed from below. But, since there are no bodies to develop or supply this couple, the disk turns (precesses) in the horizontal plane and thus the necessary couple is developed from the inertia of the disk. As soon as precession starts, however, that is, as soon as the z-axis has turned through the angle $d\phi$, the change AC in the angular momentum is produced. This change requires a couple in the vertical plane (clockwise as viewed by the reader) to prevent the disk and axle from rotating counter-clockwise in the vertical plane. This couple is supplied by the two forces W having a moment Wl. Hence, if the body is allowed to precess about the y-axis with angular velocity Ω, the external couple Wl is resisted by the gyroscopic couple, that is,

$$Wl = I\omega\Omega = \frac{W}{g} k^2 \omega \Omega,$$

from which the velocity of precession is found to be

$$\Omega = \frac{lg}{\omega k^2},$$

in which k is the radius of gyration of the disk with respect to the z-axis.

If precession is prevented, a couple ($C = I\omega\Omega$) must be set up in the horizontal plane, Ω here being the angular velocity, at any instant, produced by Wl, which will be the same whether the disk rotates about the z-axis or not, since no resistance is offered to the external couple unless precession is allowed. This explains why a heavy rotating flywheel or armature on board a ship, with its axis horizontal and athwartship, will offer no more resistance to the rolling of the ship than when it is not rotating. The bearing of the axles, however, must exert a large couple $C = I\omega\Omega$ in a horizontal plane which tends to "nose" the ship around. Ω here represents the angular velocity of roll.

If an external couple is applied in a horizontal plane to increase or hurry the precession, the disk and axle (Fig. 543) will rise, since $I\omega\Omega > Wl$. This principle is employed in the Brennan mono-rail car, the precession being hurried by the rolling of the axle of the revolving flywheels, on a shelf attached to the side of the car. This principle is also used in the "active type" of gyroscope for stabilizing ships. In this case the precession is hurried by means of a precession engine which acts after the ship has rolled a very small amount thus producing a gyroscopic righting-couple sufficient to extinguish the roll. Since the roll is checked in its incipiency, only a small amount of work is done. The stresses produced in the hull of the ship are also small for the same reason, and hence the weight and displacement of the active type of gyroscope likewise may be small.

ILLUSTRATIVE PROBLEM

Problem 913.—The flywheel of an engine on a ship weighs 6000 lb. and has a radius of gyration of 3.75 ft. It is mounted on a horizontal axle which is parallel to the longitudinal axis of the ship, and has a speed of 400 r.p.m. clockwise when viewed from the rear. Find the gyroscopic couple when the ship is turning to the left with an angular velocity of 0.1 rad./sec. What are the axle reactions if the distance between the centers of bearings is 4 ft.?

Solution.—The moment of inertia of the flywheel about the axis of spin is

$$I = \frac{6000}{32.2} \times (3.75)^2 = 2620 \text{ slug-ft.}^2$$

And

$$\omega = \frac{400 \times 2\pi}{60} = 41.9 \text{ rad./sec.}$$

Hence the gyroscopic couple is

$$I\omega\,\Omega = 2620 \times 41.9 \times 0.1 = 10{,}980 \text{ lb.-ft.}$$

In accordance with the rule stated in Art. 167, the vector representing this couple is perpendicular to the axis of the ship and is directed towards the right. The forces constituting the gyroscopic couple are the axle reactions and hence the reaction at the forward bearing is downwards and that at the rear bearing is upwards. Since the distance between centers of bearings is 4 ft., the magnitude of each of these reactions is $10{,}980 \div 4 = 2745$ lb. The effect of the gyroscopic motion, then, is to increase the reaction at the rear bearing and to decrease it at the forward bearing. The reaction at each bearing due to the weight of the flywheel is 3000 lb. Hence the resultant reaction at the rear bearing is $3000 + 2745 = 5745$ lb. and that at the forward bearing is $3000 - 2745 = 255$ lb.

PROBLEMS

914. A disk 4 ft. in diameter (Fig. 544) rolls on a circular track having a radius of 10 ft. The center of the disk has a velocity of 20 ft./sec. The disk is attached to the central axis OY by means of a rod which is collinear with the z-axis about which the disk turns. The disk has a flange similar to that on a car wheel. If the weight of the disk is 450 lb. find the tension, T, in the rod and the pressure, P, of the track against the flange of the wheel. *Ans.* $T = 838$ lb.; $P = 279$ lb.

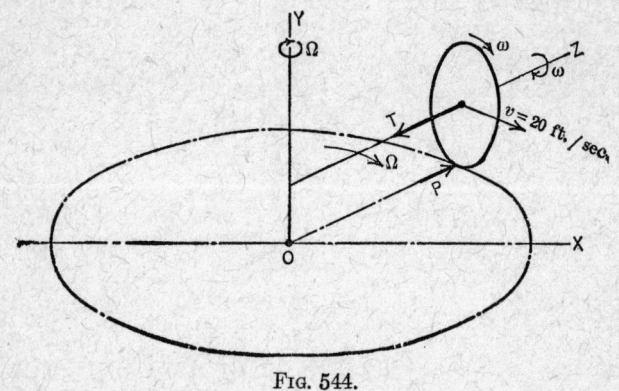

Fig. 544.

915. A circular disk is mounted on a horizontal axle which is free to rotate about a vertical axis as shown in Fig. 540, the distance from the center of the disk to the vertical axis being 2 ft. The radius of the disk is 6 in. and its weight is 10 lb. If the disk rotates about the horizontal axle with a speed of 300 r.p.m., with what velocity will it rotate about the vertical axis? *Ans.* $\Omega = 157$ r.p.m.

916. The propeller of an aeroplane rotates clockwise when viewed from the rear. If the aeroplane turns to the right when moving in a horizontal plane, what will be the effect of the gyroscopic couple?

917. The flywheel of an automobile engine is mounted on a horizontal axle parallel to the longitudinal axis of the automobile. The flywheel rotates counter-clockwise when viewed from the rear. What will be the effect of the gyroscopic couple on (a) the axle reactions of the flywheel, (b) the pressures of the wheels on the road?

CHAPTER XIV

FURTHER STUDY OF THE ACCELERATION OF A POINT

169. Introduction.—In this chapter we shall consider the radial and transverse components of acceleration of a point and also Coriolis' law which in some problems in kinematics offers the simplest method of determining the acceleration of a point. One application of Coriolis' law will be found in Art. 179 of the following chapter, in the analysis of the forces involved in the Rites inertia shaft governor.

170. Transverse and Radial Components of Acceleration.—In addition to the x- and y-components and the n- and t-components of the

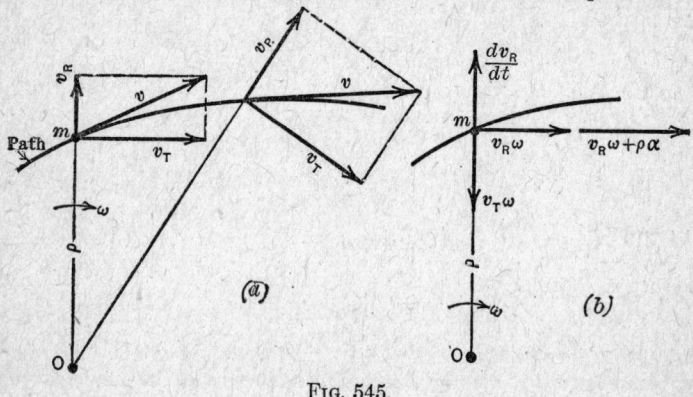

FIG. 545.

acceleration of a particle, the transverse and radial (T and R) components are sometimes convenient to use. The transverse direction is perpendicular to the radius vector drawn from any point taken as the center or pole, and the radial direction is along, or parallel to, the radius vector (Fig. 545).

The T- and R-components may be derived by the application of Theorems I and II of Art. 87. In Fig. 545(a) let m represent a particle moving on a fixed path and let O be any center or pole. The total velocity, v, of the particle may be replaced by the two components v_T and v_R.

Fig. 545(a) indicates that in general at any instant
v_T is changing in magnitude and also in direction, and that
v_R is changing in magnitude and also in direction.

Hence in accordance with Art. 87 there will be four components of the acceleration: two of the type $\frac{dv}{dt}$, and two of the type $v\omega$, as follows (shown in Fig. 545b):

(1) $\frac{dv_R}{dt} = \frac{d}{dt}\left(\frac{d\rho}{dt}\right) = \frac{d^2\rho}{dt^2}$ parallel to v_R, being the rate of change of the magnitude of v_R.

(2) $v_R\omega$ perpendicular to v_R, being the rate of change of v_R due to the change in its direction only.

(3) $\frac{dv_T}{dt} = \frac{d(\omega\rho)}{dt} = \omega\frac{d\rho}{dt} + \rho\frac{d\omega}{dt} = \omega v_R + \rho\alpha$ parallel to v_T, being the rate of change of the magnitude of v_T.

(4) $v_T\omega = \omega^2\rho = \frac{v_T^2}{\rho}$ perpendicular to v_T, being the rate of change of v_T due to a change in its direction only.

The T- and R-components of the total acceleration are then (Fig. 545b),

$$a_T = v_R\omega + (v_R\omega + \rho\alpha) = 2v_R\omega + \rho\alpha = 2\omega\frac{d\rho}{dt} + \rho\frac{d\omega}{dt} = \frac{1}{\rho}\frac{d}{dt}(\rho^2\omega),$$

$$a_R = \frac{dv_R}{dt} - \omega v_T = \frac{d^2\rho}{dt^2} - \rho\omega^2.$$

PROBLEMS

918. A point moves on a circle with varying speed. Show that the expressions for the transverse and radial components of acceleration of the point reduce to the expressions for the tangential and normal components, respectively, of the acceleration when the center of the circle is selected as the pole.

919. A rod rotates in a horizontal plane about a vertical axis through one end of the rod with a constant angular velocity of 2 rad./sec. At the same time a particle moves from the axis of rotation along the rod at a constant rate of 4 ft./sec. Find the magnitude of the linear acceleration of the particle when it is 3 ft. from the axis of rotation.

171. Coriolis' Law.—It is convenient to consider the motion of a point of a body as being generated by a motion of the point along a path (line) as the path moves. Thus, in plane motion of a rigid body, the motion of any point in the body may be considered to be a combination of a motion along a path and a motion due to a translation of the path.

If a point moves along a path as the path is translated, the acceleration of the point is the vector sum of the acceleration relative to the path and the acceleration of the point of the path which is coincident with the point at the instant (or of any point of the path since the path is translated).

If, however, a point moves along a path as the path rotates, the acceleration of the point is obtained as the vector sum of three component accelerations. The relation between these three component accelerations and the total acceleration is expressed by Coriolis' law, which may be derived by use of the theorems of Art. 87 as follows:

In Fig. 546(a) let m represent a particle traveling along a curved path with velocity u, and at the same time let the path rotate about O with angular velocity ω and angular acceleration α. Further let Ω and α' denote the angular velocity and angular acceleration, respectively,

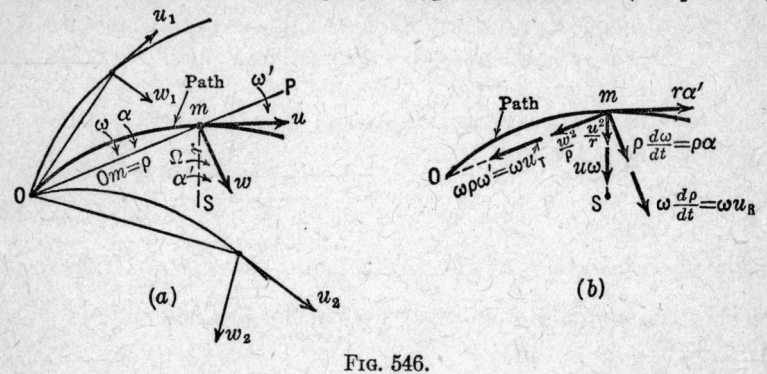

FIG. 546.

that m would have relative to the center of curvature S of the path, if the path were fixed and only the motion of m along the path were considered. The velocity of the particle will then have, at any instant, two components, u and w, u being the velocity along (relative to) the path, and w the velocity of the point on the path which, at the instant, coincides with the particle.

It will be noted from Fig. 546(a) that, as the particle passes from one position to some other position, the velocity u changes in magnitude and also in direction. Likewise w changes in magnitude and also in direction. At any instant, therefore, the acceleration of the particle m will have at least four components. It will be found convenient, however, to consider the change in both u and w to be made up of several parts, as follows:

The change in u from u_1 to u_2 is made up of:

 (1) A change in magnitude, due to an increasing (or decreasing) speed along the path.
 (2) A change in direction, due to the curvature of the path.
 (3) A change in direction, due to the rotation of the path.

The change in w from w_1 to w_2 is made up of:

(4) A change in magnitude, due to the rotation of the path with increasing (or decreasing) angular velocity (assuming ρ to remain constant, that is, considering the particle to be fixed to the path).

(5) A change in direction, due to the rotation of the path (considering the particle fixed to the path).

(6) A change in magnitude, due to the change in length of ρ (assuming the path to be fixed), caused by the movement of the particle along the path.

(7) A change in direction, due to the change in the direction of ρ, caused by the motion of the particle along the path (assuming the path fixed). The change in direction of w is equal to the change in direction of ρ since ρ and w remain at right angles.

At any instant, therefore, the acceleration of m will have seven components, three being of the type $\dfrac{dv}{dt}$, and four of the type $v\omega$. These components (represented in Fig. 546(b)) are expressed as follows:

(1) $\dfrac{du}{dt} = r\alpha'$ parallel to u and having the same sense as u since Ω, the angular velocity, and α', the angular acceleration, of the particle m with respect to the center of curvature, S, of the path were assumed to agree in sense as indicated in Fig. 546(a).

(2) $u\Omega = \Omega^2 r = \dfrac{u^2}{r}$ perpendicular to u, towards S.

(3) $u\omega$ perpendicular to u toward S.

(4) $\dfrac{dw}{dt} = \dfrac{d(\omega\rho)}{dt} = \rho\dfrac{d\omega}{dt} = \rho\alpha$ parallel to w and having the same sense as w, since ω, the angular velocity, and α, the angular acceleration, of the path with respect to O are assumed to agree in sense.

(5) $w\omega = \omega^2\rho = \dfrac{w^2}{\rho}$ perpendicular to w, toward 0.

(6) $\dfrac{d(\omega\rho)}{dt} = \omega\dfrac{d\rho}{dt} = u_R\omega$ parallel to w and having the same sense as w since w is increasing.

(7) $w\omega' = \rho\omega\omega' = u_T\omega$ perpendicular to w toward O, where ω' is the angular velocity of ρ caused by the motion of the particle along the path, assuming the path to be fixed.

The total acceleration of the particle then may be expressed in terms of the seven components shown in Fig. 546(b), grouped as follows:

$$a = \left(r\alpha' \mathrel{+\!\!\!+} \dfrac{u^2}{r}\right) \mathrel{+\!\!\!+} (\rho\alpha \mathrel{+\!\!\!+} \rho\omega^2) \mathrel{+\!\!\!+} u\omega \mathrel{+\!\!\!+} \omega\left(\dfrac{d\rho}{dt} \mathrel{+\!\!\!+} \rho\omega'\right)$$

But $\dfrac{d\rho}{dt}$ and $\rho\omega'$ are the radial and transverse components, respectively, of the velocity u relative to O. Hence the two terms in the last parenthesis may be written $u_R \mathrel{+\!\!\!+} u_T = u$.

Thus the last component in the expression for a becomes $u\omega$ and may be added to the preceding term giving $2\,u\omega$, since both of the components $u\omega$ have the same direction and sense. The expression for a may then be written

$$a = a_r \mathrel{+\!\!\!+} a_m \mathrel{+\!\!\!+} 2u\omega.$$

in which $a_r = r\alpha' \mathrel{+\!\!\!+} \dfrac{u^2}{r}$ and $a_m = \rho\alpha \mathrel{+\!\!\!+} \rho\omega^2$. It will be seen that a_r is the acceleration the particle would have if the path were fixed, and a_m is the acceleration the particle would have if the particle were fixed on the path and moving with the path. The component $2u\omega$ is a vector directed perpendicular to the vector u and its sense may be found by the following rule: Apply the vector representing $2u\omega$ to the end of the vector representing u; then the sense of $2u\omega$ is such that, considered as a force, it would rotate the vector u in the sense of ω, the angular velocity of the path. This equation may be stated in words as follows: If a particle moves on a path as the path rotates, the acceleration of the particle is the geometric or vector sum of (1) the acceleration the particle would have if the path were fixed and the particle moved along the path with velocity u, (2) the acceleration the particle would have if it were fixed on the path and the path rotated with angular velocity ω, and (3) $2u\omega$ called the Coriolis' component or the *compound supplementary acceleration*. This statement is known as *Coriolis'* law.

It will be noted that Coriolis' law reduces to $a = a_r \mathrel{+\!\!\!+} a_m$ if the motion of the path is a translation and hence is in agreement with the analysis of the acceleration of a point of a rigid body that has plane motion as found in Art. 96.

ILLUSTRATIVE PROBLEM

Problem 920.—The circular arc APB (Fig. 547a) represents the vane of a centrifugal pump, P being a particle of water. Find the acceleration of the particle P when it is 12 in. from O, the center of the shaft, if, at that instant, the angular velocity of the wheel is 10 rad./sec. clockwise and its angular acceleration is 50 rad./sec.^{2} clockwise. The tangential velocity of the particle along (relative to) the vane is 10 ft./sec. and the tangential acceleration relative to the vane is 10 ft./sec.^{2} OB makes an angle of 45° with the horizontal and is 18 in. long; OA is 3 in.; and OP is 12 in. The radius of the arc APB is 13¼ in.

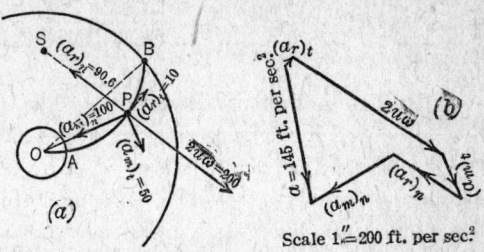

Solution.—By Coriolis' law the total acceleration a is

$$a = a_r +\!\!\!+ a_m +\!\!\!+ 2u\omega;$$

a_r and a_m are found most easily from their t- and n-components. Hence

$$a = (a_r)_t +\!\!\!+ (a_r)_n +\!\!\!+ (a_m)_t +\!\!\!+ (a_m)_n +\!\!\!+ 2u\omega$$

$$= 10 +\!\!\!+ \frac{10^2}{\frac{13\frac{1}{4}}{12}} +\!\!\!+ 50 \times \frac{12}{12} +\!\!\!+ 10^2 \times \frac{12}{12} +\!\!\!+ 2 \times 10 \times 10$$

$$= 10 +\!\!\!+ 90.56 +\!\!\!+ 50 +\!\!\!+ 100 +\!\!\!+ 200,$$

each of the quantities being expressed in feet per second per second. The five components are shown in their proper directions in Fig. 547(a), and the resultant acceleration a as found from the acceleration polygon is shown in Fig. 547(b). By scaling the closing line of the polygon, a is found to be 145 ft./sec.^{2} in the direction shown in Fig. 547(b).

PROBLEMS

921. Solve Prob. 919 by applying Coriolis' law.

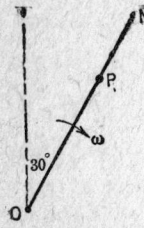

922. Using the data of Prob. 549, find the accelerations of C and D by means of Coriolis' law.

923. Point P (Fig. 548) moves on the rod OM which rotates about the fixed point O. In the given position $OP = 6$ ft.; the velocity along the rod is 5 ft./sec. toward M and is increasing at the rate of 5 ft./sec. each second. The angular velocity of the rod is 2 rad./sec. in a clockwise direction, and is decreasing at the rate of 1.5 rad./sec. each second. Find the acceleration of the point P.

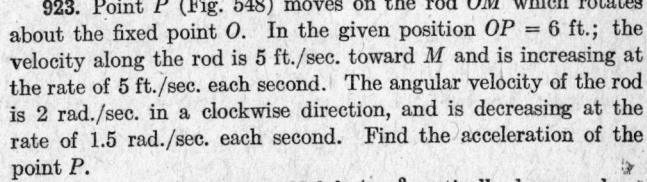

Ans. $a_P = 22.0$ ft./sec.^{2} vertically downwards.

Fig. 548.

CHAPTER XV

GOVERNORS

172. The Action of Governors.—The governor of a steam engine, hydraulic turbine, gas engine, or other motor, automatically regulates the supply of the steam, water, gas, or other fluid, so as to keep the driving force exerted by the working fluid constantly adjusted to the resistance to be overcome. The governor partakes of the motion of the motor so that an increase in the speed of the motor due to a decrease in the load causes a corresponding increase in the speed of the moving parts of the governor, which, in turn, causes, by means of a suitable mechanism, either a decrease in the pressure of the fluid or a decrease in the quantity of fluid delivered to the motor.

The forces which cause the adjustment of the controlling valve, and which are brought into play by the change of motion of the governor parts, depend in the main upon (1) the actual *change* in the speed of the moving parts or (2) the *rate of change* of the speed of the moving parts. Governors in which the governing action depends mainly upon the actual change of speed of the governor parts are called *centrifugal governors* and may be either *pendulum* or *shaft* governors. Governors in which the governing action depends mainly upon the rate of change of speed of the moving parts are called *inertia governors* and are shaft governors. A brief analysis of the forces brought into play by a change in the motion of each of these types of governors will here be made.

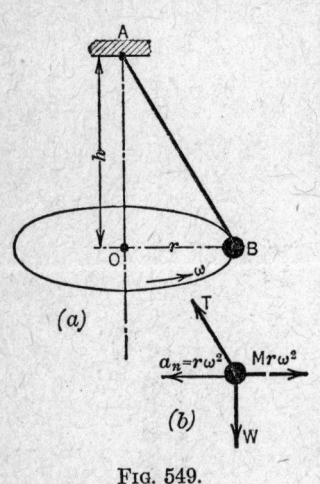

173. The Conical Pendulum.—In Fig. 549(a) a ball of mass M and weight W is held at the end of an arm AB and the ball and arm are caused to rotate about an axis AO with velocity ω. The acceleration of the center of the ball is directed towards O, the center of its circular path, and its magnitude is $r\omega^2$. Hence the force, R, required to produce this acceleration of the ball is

$$R = Mr\omega^2 = \frac{W}{g}r\omega^2.$$

Fig. 549.

THE CONICAL PENDULUM

Now, the accelerating (effective) force R must be the resultant of the external forces which act on the ball. These external forces are the weight, W, and the tension, T, in the arm, as shown in Fig. 549(b). If a force which is equal but opposed to R (the inertia force) is assumed to act with W and T as shown in Fig. 549(b), the three forces will be in equilibrium and hence the sum of their moments with respect to the point A is equal to zero. Thus

$$Wr = \frac{W}{g} r\omega^2 \times h. \quad \text{Therefore} \quad h = \frac{g}{\omega^2},$$

in which ω is expressed in radians per second and g is equal to 32.2 ft./sec.^{2} If the number of revolutions per minute (r.p.m.) is denoted by n, then $\omega = \frac{2\pi n}{60}$. Therefore, h may be expressed (in inches) by the equation

$$h = \frac{35{,}200}{n^2} \quad \ldots \ldots \ldots \quad (1)$$

This equation shows that the height, h, of the cone depends only on the speed of rotation and not upon the weight of the ball nor the length of the arm AB. Now, in the pendulum governor, the governing action depends upon the manner in which h varies with ω. The accompanying table is obtained from equation (1). It will be noted that at low speeds a small change in speed of the ball causes a large change in the height h, whereas at high speed a large change in speed causes only a small change in h. If the conical pendulum is used as a governor as in the simple Watt governor (Fig. 550), it may be made sensitive to small changes in speed either by making h large or by causing the governor to rotate slowly by gear-

n (in r.p.m.)	h (in inches)
20	88.0
40	22.0
60	9.8
80	5.5
100	3.5
150	1.56
200	0.88
300	0.39

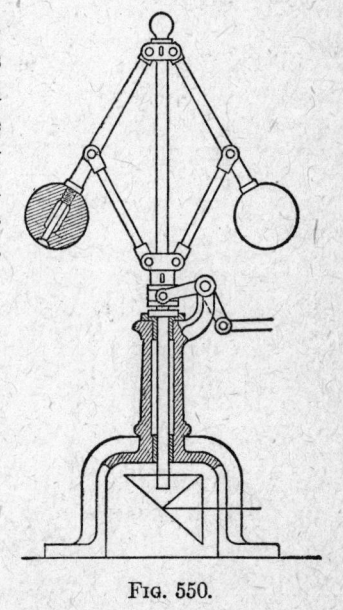

FIG. 550.

ing it down. However, a decrease in the speed of the governor results in a decrease in the energy available to overcome the resistances of the valve which is operated by the governor. In order to make the governor sensitive to small changes in speed without seriously reducing its available energy it may be loaded.

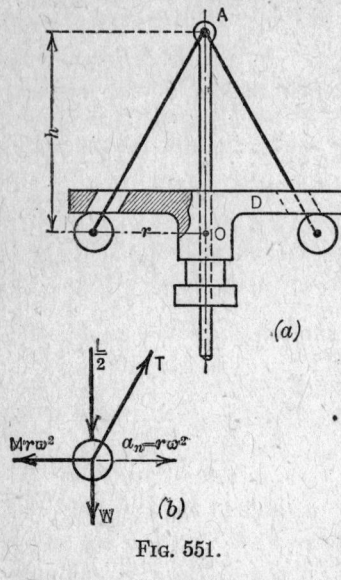

174. The Loaded Governor.—The height h of the conical pendulum may be increased by loading the balls as shown in Fig. 551(a). The disk, D, which rests on the balls (or cylinders) furnishes, by its weight, a vertical external force without influencing the inertia force of the ball or cylinder. If L denotes the weight of the disk (load) then $L/2$ is the load on each ball and the external forces W, $L/2$, and T which act on the ball form, with the reversed effective (inertia) force $Mr\omega^2$, a system in equilibrium as shown in Fig. 551(b). The sum of their moments, therefore, about the point A is equal to zero. Thus

$$\left(W + \frac{L}{2}\right) r = Mr\omega^2 \times h,$$

and by expressing ω in revolutions per minute, h is expressed in inches by the equation

$$h = \frac{W + \dfrac{L}{2}}{W} \times \frac{35{,}200}{n^2}.$$

This equation shows that the addition of the load to the balls of the conical pendulum increases the height h in the ratio of $1 + L/2W$ to 1. For example, if $W = 5$ lb. and $L = 30$ lb., then

$$1 + \frac{L}{2W} = 1 + \frac{30}{2 \times 5} = 4.$$

Thus the height h of the simple conical pendulum corresponding to a speed of 200 r.p.m. is 0.88 in., and when loaded its height becomes $4 \times 0.88 = 3.52$ in.

THE PORTER GOVERNOR

For high rotative speeds, loading must be resorted to in order to increase the change of height for a given change in speed, that is, in order to increase the sensitiveness of the governor.

175. The Porter Governor.—In Fig. 552(a) is shown the Porter loaded governor, in which the load on the conical pendulum is suspended from additional links which are attached to the balls. With this arrangement the load is twice as effective as in the loaded governor discussed in the preceding article, since, for a given rise of the balls, the

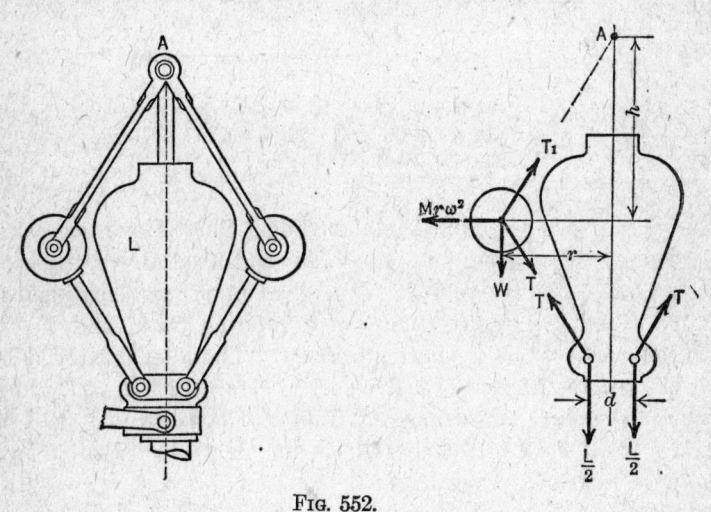

FIG. 552.

load rises twice the distance that the balls rise. If, therefore, L denotes the load, the expression for h (in inches) becomes

$$h = \frac{W + L}{W} \times \frac{35{,}200}{n^2}.$$

Thus, in the above example, for the Porter governor, the height becomes

$$\frac{W + L}{W} \times 0.88 = \frac{5 + 30}{5} \times 0.88 = 6.16 \text{ in.}$$

The student should derive the above equation for h from the analysis of the forces in a manner similar to that used in the preceding two articles. Free-body diagrams for the revolving ball and load are shown in Fig. 552(b).

PROBLEM

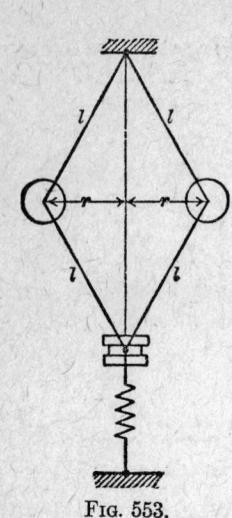

924. A spring-loaded governor is shown in Fig. 553. Let W be the weight (lb.) of each ball; r (ft.) the radius of the path of the balls; l (ft.) the length of each of the four arms; ω the angular velocity in radians per second. When the radius, r, is zero, the tension in the spring is T lb. and the force required to elongate the spring a unit length is Q lb. Show that, if the weight but not the mass of the balls be neglected,

$$\omega^2 = \frac{g[T + 2Q(l - \sqrt{l^2 - r^2})]}{W\sqrt{l^2 - r^2}}.$$

If $W = 3$ lb., $l = 1$ ft., and the balls revolve at 26 rad./sec. when $r = 3$ in., find the tension in the spring, assuming the modulus of the spring to be 58 lb./in.

Ans. $T = 61.0$ lb.

Fig. 553.

176. The Centrifugal Shaft Governor.

In the pendulum governors considered above, the governing action is dependent upon the centrifugal force (inertia force) of a rotating mass, and the same is true for some types of shaft governors. Thus, let a body of mass M be pivoted to the arm of a flywheel as shown in Fig. 554. Let the distance of the center of the mass, G, from the shaft center, S, be denoted by r and let the wheel rotate with an angular velocity ω. The centrifugal or inertia force, then, of the mass M is $Mr\omega^2$. As long as ω remains constant this force has a definite value. To hold it in equilibrium a spring is employed. The moment of the spring tension about the point O must therefore be equal to the moment of $Mr\omega^2$ about the same point (the weight of the body is small in comparison with $Mr\omega^2$ and hence its moment is neglected). If now the angular velocity of the wheel increases to ω' due to a decrease in the load on the engine, assuming the value of r to remain constant, the centrifugal force increases to $Mr\omega'^2$ and the excess force $Mr(\omega'^2 - \omega^2)$ causes the mass to move outwards which in turn changes the time of cut off of the valve and adjusts the amount of the working fluid delivered to the engine.

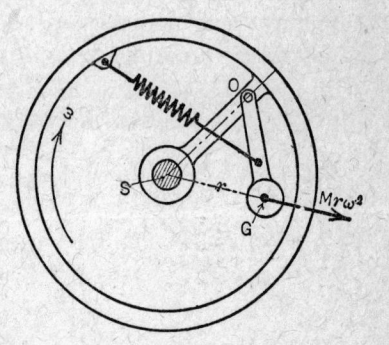

Fig. 554.

THE INERTIA SHAFT GOVERNOR

PROBLEMS

925. What must be the initial tension in the spring and the modulus of the spring so that the weight, A, in the governor shown in Fig. 555 will not leave the inner stop and pass to the outer stop until a speed of 210 r.p.m. is reached? Assume that the weight of A is 16.1 lb., $a = 3$ in., $b = 24$ in., $c = 8$ in., and $d = 16$ in. If the spring should be placed farther from E than 16 in., would A reach the outer stop with the wheel revolving at the same speed that it had when A left the inner stop?

Ans. $T = 242$ lb.; modulus $= 45.4$ lb./in.

926. Given the arrangement as shown in the previous problem, with the following data: $a = 3$ in., $b = 20$ in., $c = 9$ in., $d = 12$ in., modulus of spring $= 50$ lb./in. If the mean speed, n_0, is 200 r.p.m., what must be the weight of A for a coefficient of steadiness, $(n_1 - n_2)/n_0$, of 0.01, where n_1 and n_2 denote the maximum and minimum speeds respectively?

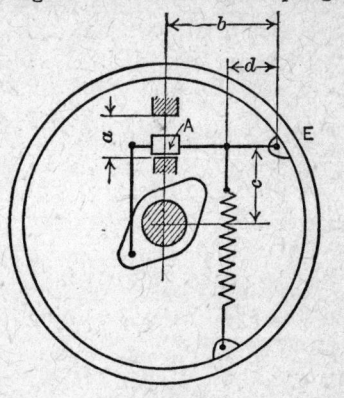

Fig. 555.

Ans. $W = 14.85$ lb.

177. The Inertia Shaft Governor.

As already noted, governors in which the regulating action depends upon a change in the centrifugal force, whether of the pendulum or of the shaft type, are called centrifugal governors. It is important to note that with centrifugal governors there must be an actual change of speed to give a governing action. In the inertia governor, however, the governing action is entirely different.

Thus, in Fig. 556, let a mass M be pivoted to the arm of a flywheel so that the pin, O, passes through the center of mass. The centrifugal force of the mass is balanced by the pin reaction at O and hence the centrifugal force is not involved in the governing action.

In order to show how the forces which cause the governing action arise, let it be assumed first that the wheel of Fig. 556 is standing still and that the mass is turned on the pin, O, with an angular acceleration α. To produce this acceleration a moment, T, is required having a magnitude

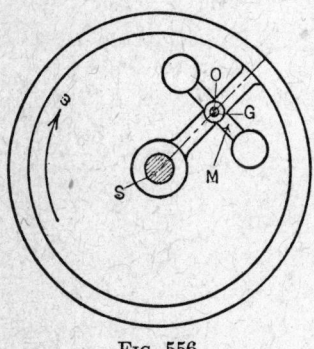

Fig. 556.

$$T = I_o \alpha,$$

in which I_o is the moment of inertia of the mass with respect to the pin O.

Now, if a change in speed of the wheel (and shaft) occurs, due to a change in the load on the motor, each particle in the mass M, by virtue of its inertia, will tend to maintain its linear velocity and hence will turn relative to the wheel about the axis O and thereby cause the valve mechanism to exert forces on the mass, the moment of which about O will be equal to $I_o\alpha$. In this type of governor, therefore, the governing action depends not upon the actual change of speed but upon the rate of change of angular speed, that is, upon the angular acceleration of the wheel or engine shaft. Shaft governors of this type are called inertia governors.

178. Comparison of the Two Types of Governors.—Centrifugal and inertia governors differ in two important particulars. Since, in the centrifugal type, the governing force depends upon the change in the speed there must be an increase (or decrease) in the speed of a definite amount before the governing force is sufficient to move the valve gear against the frictional forces. In the inertia governor, on the other hand, the governing force is proportional to the angular acceleration, and, in general, the angular acceleration of the governing mass is greatest just at the beginning of the change of speed; hence, before the speed of the shaft has changed appreciably, the governor begins to act although the change in the centrifugal force is small. It follows then that the inertia governor acts more quickly and holds the speed within much smaller limits than does the centrifugal governor.

The centrifugal type of governor, however, has one essential property not possessed by the inertia type. The centrifugal force $Mr\omega^2$ varies somewhat for different positions of the balls in Figs. 549, 550, 551, or 552, and of the body in Fig. 554, but for any fixed position it must have a fixed definite value which is determined by the weight of the balls (and load on the balls) in the pendulum governors and by the spring tension in the shaft governor. It follows that, with the governor in a definite position, the speed, ω, of the shaft has a definite value and therefore the speed of the engine is fixed. Thus, if it is determined that the speed shall be 200 r.p.m. and the governor is properly adjusted, the speed cannot vary much from that speed as long as the governor is operative. The speed may sink to 195 r.p.m. under a heavy load or rise to 205 r.p.m. with a light load; but the centrifugal force imposes the average speed of 200 r.p.m., and the engine cannot be made to run at a different average speed without some adjustment of the governor, such as the addition of a weight or an increase in the spring tension.

179. Analysis of Forces in the Rites Inertia Governor.—In the shaft governor known as the Rites inertia governor, a combination of the two governing actions discussed above is effected by means of a single heavy

ANALYSIS OF FORCES IN THE RITES INERTIA GOVERNOR

mass which is pivoted at a point at some distance from the shaft center but not at the center of the mass.

To gain a clear conception of the forces which are developed during the action of a shaft governor of the Rites type, consider the motion of a heavy mass of any form (Fig. 557a) pivoted at a point O which is at a distance e from the shaft center S. The center of gravity, G, of the mass

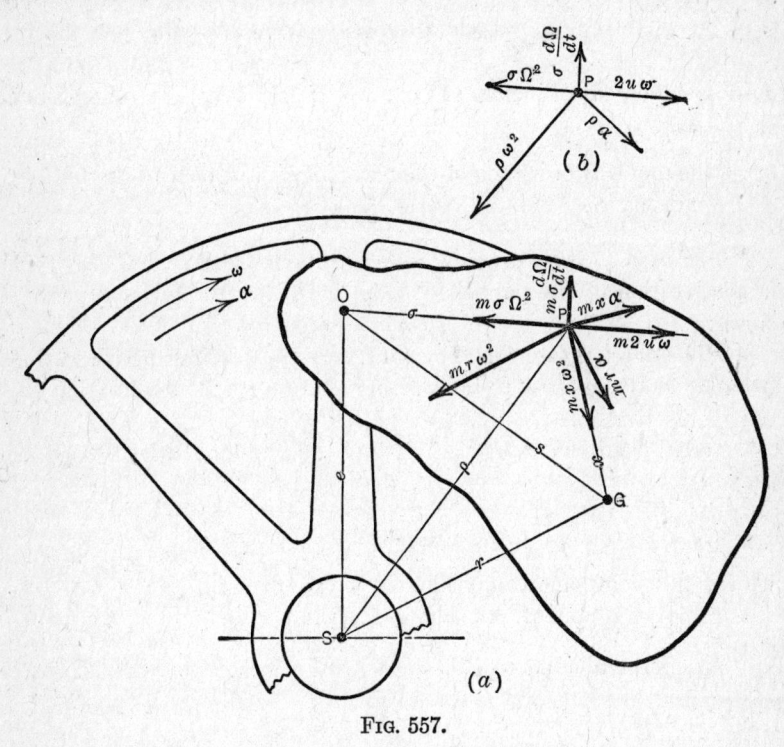

FIG. 557.

is at the fixed distance s from the pivot O and at the distance r from the shaft center S; this latter distance may of course vary. Let any particle, P, of the mass be at the distances σ and ρ from O and S, respectively. The procedure followed in the analysis of the forces in the Rites governor is the same as that used in the analysis of the various kinetics problems in Chapter VIII. The main steps in the procedure are outlined in Art. 108. Let

$M = \dfrac{W}{g}$ = the mass of the body which is pivoted at O;

ω = the angular velocity of the wheel about the shaft center S;

Ω = the angular velocity of the mass M about the pivot O;

$u = \sigma\Omega$ = the linear velocity of P relative to O;

$\alpha = \dfrac{d\omega}{dt}$ = the angular acceleration of the wheel;

$\alpha' = \dfrac{d\Omega}{dt}$ = the angular acceleration of the mass M about O;

I_o = the moment of inertia of the mass M with respect to the pivot O, and

$\bar{I}$ = the moment of inertia of the mass M with respect to the center of gravity G.

Acceleration of Any Particle P.—According to Coriolis' law (Art. 171), the acceleration of the particle P (Fig. 557b) has three components as follows:

(1) The acceleration that P would have considering the wheel to be stationary and the mass to be rotating about O; this acceleration may itself be resolved into:

A radial component $\sigma\Omega^2$ along PO, and a tangential component $\sigma\dfrac{d\Omega}{dt} = \sigma\alpha'$ perpendicular to PO.

(2) The acceleration of that point of the wheel which is coincident with P; this component may likewise be resolved into:

A radial component $\rho\omega^2$ along PS, and a tangential component $\rho\dfrac{d\omega}{dt} = \rho\alpha$ perpendicular to PS.

(3) The acceleration $2u\omega$ along OP.

These components of the acceleration of the point P are shown in Fig. 557(b). No attempt has been made to show the magnitudes of the accelerations by the lengths of the vectors.

It will be found convenient to replace the components $\rho\omega^2$ and $\rho\alpha$ by four other components, parallel and perpendicular, respectively, to the lines SG and PG. These four components may be obtained by direct resolution or by considering the motion of the wheel to be replaced by a rotation and a translation (Art. 96). Thus, at any instant, the rotation of the wheel about its shaft, S, with angular velocity ω and angular acceleration α may be considered as a rotation with the same angular velocity and acceleration about a parallel axis in the wheel which passes through the point G, and a translation of the wheel in a direction perpendicular to SG. The components $\rho\omega^2$ and $\rho\alpha$ which, as found above, were due to the rotation of the wheel about its shaft S will now be replaced by (1) the acceleration of the point P due to the rotation of the wheel about G and (2) the acceleration due to the translation, which is common to all points of the wheel. The accelerations of the point P of the wheel (that is, the point on the wheel which is coincident with the point P of the mass M), then, are

$$x\omega^2 \text{ along } PG$$

and

$$x\frac{d\omega}{dt} = x\alpha \text{ perpendicular to } PG,$$

which are due to the rotation of the wheel about G; and

$$r\omega^2 \text{ parallel to } SG$$

and

$$r\alpha \text{ perpendicular to } SG,$$

which are due to the (curvilinear) translation of the wheel.

Moment of Effective Forces about the Pin O.—The moment of the effective forces for the whole body with respect to the pin O will now be found since the rotation of the mass about the pin O is the cause of the movement of the valve mechanism. And the moment of the effective forces must be found in order to determine the moment of the external forces which are brought into action as a result of this rotation and which are exerted on the valve mechanism. For, by D'Alembert's principle, the sum of the moments of the external forces must be equal to the sum of the moments of the effective forces.

The accelerating or effective force for the particle P of mass m must have a component in the direction of each of the acceleration components, the magnitude of each component of the force being the product of the mass m of the particle and the acceleration component. These seven components of the effective force for the particle are shown in Fig. 557(a), acting at the particle P. The sum of the moments of these forces, for all the particles, about the pin O may be found as follows:

(1) The components $m\sigma\Omega^2$ and $2mu\omega$ are collinear and act through the pin O. The resultant of these components, therefore, for the whole body, is a force which acts through O. The sum of the moments of these components about the point O, then, is equal to zero and hence, these forces have no influence in the problem under discussion. Their only effect is to produce a pin pressure at O.

(2) Consider next the forces $mr\omega^2$. These forces arise from the translation given to the body. All these forces, then, are parallel to SG

and all have the same sense. Therefore, their resultant is a single force (Art. 110) the magnitude of which is

$$\Sigma mr\omega^2 = Mr\omega^2.$$

The line of action of this resultant force passes through G (Art. 110), as shown in Fig. 558. The sum of the moments of the $mr\omega^2$ forces about the pin O (which, of course, is equal to the moment of their resultant), then, is (Fig. 558)

$$Mr\omega^2 \times f.$$

(3) Consider next the $mr\alpha$ forces. These forces also arise from the translatory motion which is given to the wheel (and mass M). All

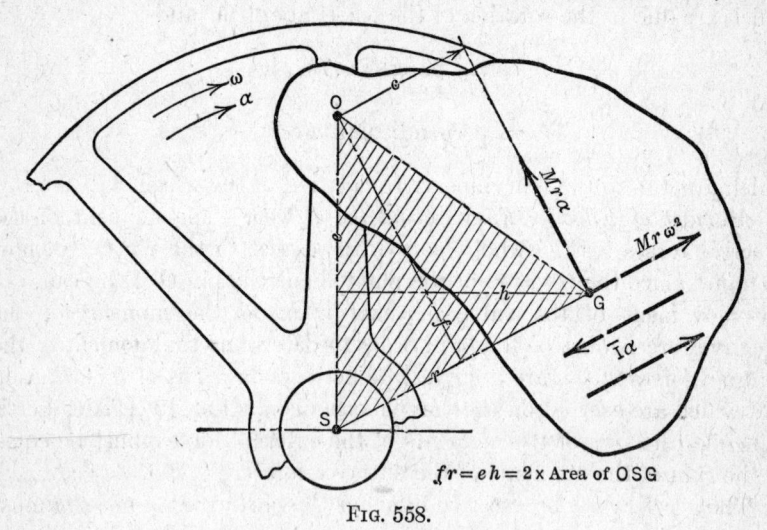

FIG. 558.

these forces then are perpendicular to SG and have the same sense. Their resultant, therefore, is a single force (Art. 110) having a magnitude equal to

$$\Sigma mr\alpha = Mr\alpha.$$

This resultant force also passes through G. The sum of the moments of the $mr\alpha$ forces with respect to the pin O, then, is (Fig. 558)

$$Mr\alpha \times c.$$

(4) The moment of the $mx\omega^2$ forces will be found next. These forces are the normal forces due to the rotation of the wheel (and mass M) about an axis through G. They pass, then, through the axis of rotation, and their resultant, therefore, is a single force having a magni-

tude equal to $M\bar{x}\omega^2$ which acts through G (Art. 23). But G is the mass-center of the mass M, and hence the quantity $M\bar{x}\omega^2$ is equal to zero, since $\bar{x}$, the distance from the mass-center to the axis of rotation, is zero. Therefore, the sum of the moments of the $m x \omega^2$ forces about the pin O is equal to zero.

(5) The $mx\alpha$ forces are the tangential forces which also arise due to the rotation of the wheel (and mass M) about the mass-center G. The resultant of these forces is a couple having a moment equal to $\bar{I}\alpha$ (Art. 111) in which $\bar{I}$ is the moment of inertia of the mass M with respect to the axis through its mass-center. The sum of the moments of the $mx\alpha$ forces, then, with respect to the pin O (or any other moment-center in the plane of motion, Art. 14) is equal to

$$\bar{I}\alpha.$$

(6) Lastly, the $m\sigma\alpha'$ forces will be considered. These forces are the tangential forces which arise due to the rotation of the mass M about the pin O. The sum of their moments, then, about O, the axis of rotation, is (Art. 111)

$$I_o\alpha',$$

in which I_o is the moment of inertia of the mass M with respect to the pin O. This moment, however, for governors as constructed, is small compared with the other moments since α' is small. Therefore, the moment $I_o\alpha'$ will be neglected in the subsequent discussion.

The Moment of the External Forces and the Governing Action.—As noted above, the moments of the external forces must be equal to the sum of the moments of the effective forces. Or, if the effective forces were reversed, external forces would have to act on the body such that they would hold the reversed effective (inertia) forces in equilibrium. Hence, external forces must act on the mass M such that the moments of the external forces will hold in equilibrium the moment (Fig. 558)

$$T_c = Mr\omega^2 f = Meh\omega^2 \quad \cdots \cdots \quad (1)$$

of the centrifugal force, and the moment

$$T_i = Mr\alpha c + \bar{I}\alpha = \alpha(Mrc + \bar{I}) \quad \cdots \quad (2)$$

which is called into action only when the angular acceleration, α, exists.

It will be noted, therefore, that if the angular velocity, ω, of the fly-wheel (and engine) remains constant, that is, if the angular acceleration, α, of the flywheel is equal to zero, the moment ($Meh\omega^2$) of the centrifugal force has a constant magnitude and must be equilibrated by the moment of the spring tension. Further, if ω is constant the only external moment acting on the mass M is the moment of the spring tension since α, and consequently, T_i, is equal to zero. Thus, the moment T_i, unlike the moment T_c, is called into existence only when there is a change in speed of the flywheel, and hence it does not require an opposing moment except that supplied by the resistance of the valve gear as the valve gear adjusts itself to the new speed.

To explain further the governing action in the Rites governor, let it be assumed that the motor is running at a constant mean speed ω_0; the moment $T_c(=Meh\omega^2)$ of the centrifugal force is then just balanced by the moment of the spring tension, which may be denoted by T_s. Now, let the load on the motor be reduced; the excess of the effort over the resistance will cause the moving parts of the motor (flywheel, shaft, etc.) to rotate with an increased speed, ω_1, and the moment T_c will increase from $Meh\omega^2$ to $Meh\omega_1^2$. The difference, $Meh(\omega_1^2 - \omega^2)$, is the excess of the moment of the centrifugal force over that of the spring tension and is available for producing a movement of the governor parts. However, if this difference alone is depended on for moving the valve mechanism, the speed ω_1 must be considerably in excess of the mean speed ω_0 before the governor and attached valve will move. On the other hand, the very instant the change in speed begins, the angular acceleration, α, of the mass M comes into existence and, with it, the unbalanced moment T_i which is available for moving the valve gear. In the ideal governor, therefore, there is needed a moment, T_c, of a centrifugal force which is just sufficient to fix a mean speed ω_0, and a moment, T_i, of considerable magnitude which arises from the rate of change of the angular velocity of the flywheel and which provides for the adjustment of the governor.

Distribution and Position of the Mass M.—An inspection of equation (2) shows that, with a given value of r, the magnitude of the moment T_i depends on M and $\bar{I}$. With a heavy flywheel, α is likely to be small; hence, to make T_i large, either M must be made large or, for a given M, $\bar{I}$ may be made large by constructing the swinging mass M in two parts which are removed a considerable distance from the center of gravity, G, and are joined by a bar. (See Figs. 560 and 561.)

Further, the governing action of the swinging mass will depend largely on the relative position of the points O, S, and G. Thus, in Fig. 559, let a circle be drawn having a diameter equal to OS or e and let the sense of rotation of the shaft be assumed clockwise. As discussed above there are three moments ($Mr\alpha c$, $\bar{I}\alpha$, and $Meh[\omega_1^2 - \omega_0^2]$) which are effective in producing the adjustment of the governor. Now these three moments may or may not have the same sense, depending on the location of the point G. If a counter-clockwise sense is denoted by $+$ and a clockwise sense by $-$, the following table indicates the sense of each of the three moments about O for a location of G in each of the four regions, I, II, III, and IV indicated in Fig. 559.

	I	II	III	IV
$Mrac$	$+$	$-$	$-$	$+$
$\bar{I}\alpha$	$+$	$+$	$+$	$+$
$Meh(\omega_1^2 - \omega_0^2)$	$+$	$-$	$+$	$-$

For the most powerful governing action, the mass-center, G, of the mass M, therefore, should be located in region I. If G is located in region III, the moment T_i becomes equal to $(\bar{I} - Mrc)\alpha$ and this quantity may be positive or negative according as $\bar{I}$ is greater or less than Mrc. With G located in regions II and IV, that is, to the left of the vertical

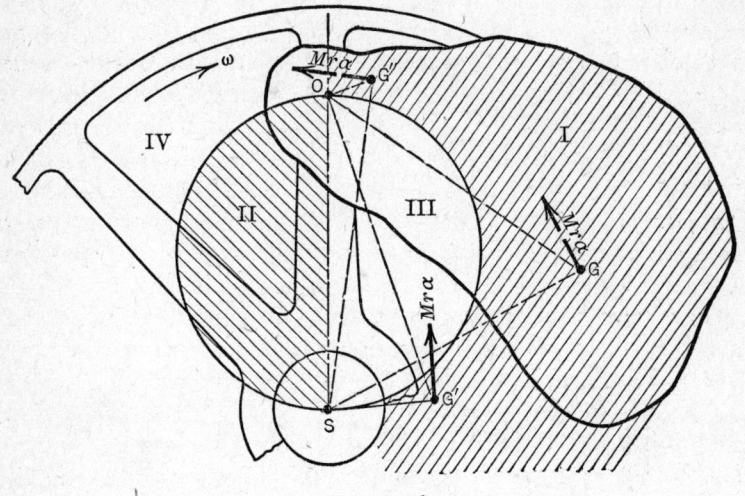

FIG. 559.

diameter, the moment of the centrifugal force and the moment $\bar{I}\alpha$ are opposite in sense. In a governor in which the whole mass is concentrated near to G so that $\bar{I}$ is small, it is permissible to locate G in region IV; with a governor of this type the engine may, therefore, rotate in either direction without changing the governor.

In modern governors of the Rites type $\bar{I}$ is made very large and hence the moment $\bar{I}\alpha$ is very large compared with the moment $Mrc\alpha$. Therefore, in these governors, the mass-center of M may be located on the circle or even in region II if it is desirable to do so in order to decrease the centrifugal moment $Mrc\alpha$ and, in consequence, the size of the spring required.

410 GOVERNORS

From Fig. 559, it will be noted that the moment of the centrifugal force $Mr\omega^2$ is $2M\omega^2$ times the area of the triangle OSG; hence, this moment is directly proportional to the area of the triangle OSG. From this fact, it appears that the size of the spring required varies directly as the area of the triangle OSG; and, to obtain as light a spring as possible, consistent with good regulation, the triangle OSG should be made as small as possible. If G is kept in region I, this object is accomplished by locating G either near to S at G', or near to O at G''' (Fig. 559). In the governors shown in Figs. 560 and 561 it will be noted that G is located near to S.

ILLUSTRATIVE PROBLEM

Problem 927.—In Fig. 560 is shown a Rites inertia governor designed for a 6-h.p. Nagle engine. Experience shows that from 0.5 to 8 ft.-lb. of energy per h.p. should be stored in the governor weight in moving through its arc (work done in stretching the spring). In the design, 5 ft.-lb./h.p. was assumed. Find the inertia weight required and the modulus of the spring from the following data: $OS = e = 3.4$ in.; $h = 1.7$ in.; mean speed = 250 r.p.m.; $l_o = 9.4$ in. = unstretched length of spring; $l_1 = 11$ in. = minimum length of spring; $l_2 = 12.2$ in. = maximum length of spring; $p = 3.8$ in. = moment arm of spring tension.

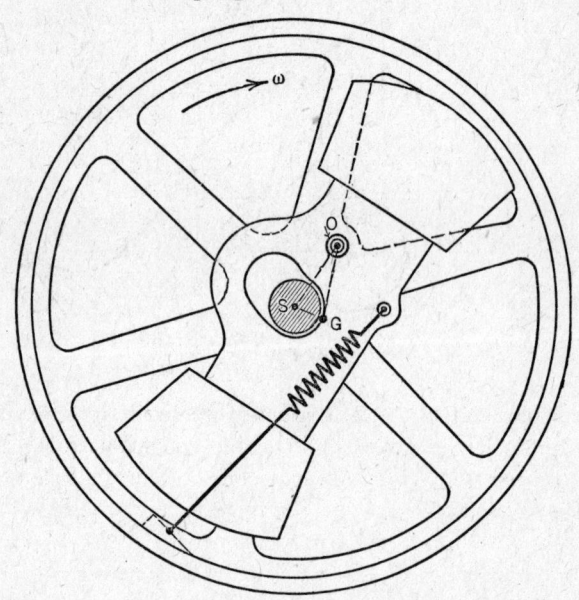

FIG. 560.

Solution.—Since the moment of the centrifugal force (T_c) must equal the moment of the spring tension (T_s) we have the equation

$$T_c = T_s.$$

That is,
$$\frac{W}{g} \cdot \frac{r}{12} \cdot \omega^2 f = T_m \times 3.8,$$

or
$$\frac{W}{g} \frac{\omega^2 he}{12} = T_m \times 3.8 \text{ (since } rf = he\text{)},$$

where T_m denotes the mean value of the spring tension. In order to determine the value of T_m, the work stored in the governor is equated to the work done in stretching the spring. Thus
$$5 \times 6 = T_m \times \frac{12.2 - 11.0}{12}.$$

Hence
$$T_m = 300 \text{ lb.}$$

Using this value of T_m in the above equation, we have
$$\frac{W}{12 \times 32.2} \left(\frac{250 \times 2\pi}{60}\right)^2 \times 1.7 \times 3.4 = 300 \times 3.8.$$

From which
$$W = 111 \text{ lb.}$$

The length of the spring, when the governor is in its mean position, is $\frac{1}{2}(12.2 + 11.0) = 11.6$ in. Hence the modulus of the spring is
$$\frac{300}{11.6 - 9.4} = \frac{300}{2.2} = 136 \text{ lb./in.}$$

PROBLEM

928. In the Rites governor shown in Fig. 561, the inertia weight is 111 lb. and the tension of the spring in mid-position is 500 lb. If $e = 7$ in., $h = 2.6$ in., $r = 3$ in.,

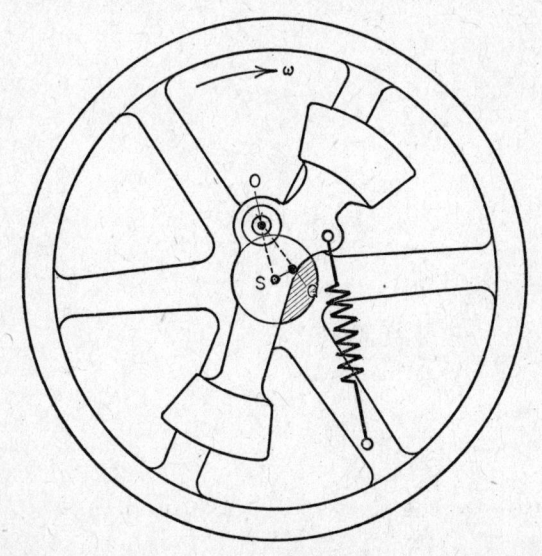

FIG. 561.

and $p = 8.2$ in.; find (a) the normal speed of the engine, that is, the speed when the governor is in mid-position, and (b) the power of the governor in foot-pounds per horse-power if the engine is rated at 50 h.p., assuming that the spring stretches from 20 in. to 22 in. when the governor moves through its whole range.

Ans. $\omega = 268$ r.p.m.; 1.67 ft.-lb./h.p.

APPENDIX

SECOND MOMENT. MOMENT OF INERTIA

§ 1. Moments of Inertia of Areas

180. Moment of Inertia of an Area Defined.—In the analysis of many engineering problems, as, for example, in determining the stresses in a beam, expressions of the form $\int x^2 dA$ are frequently met, in which dA represents an element of an area A, and x is the distance of the element from some axis in, or perpendicular to, the plane of the area, the limits of integration being such that each element of the area is included in the integration. An expression of this form is called the *second moment* of the area or the *moment of inertia* of the area with respect to the given axis. The moment of inertia of an area with respect to an axis may then be defined as the sum of the products obtained by multiplying each element of the area by the square of its distance from the given axis.

The moment of inertia of an area with respect to an axis will be denoted by I for an axis in the plane of the area and by J for an axis perpendicular to the plane of the area. The particular axis about which the moment of inertia is taken will be denoted by subscripts. Thus, the moments of inertia of the area A (Fig. 562) with respect to the x- and y-axes are expressed as follows:

$$I_x = \int y^2 dA, \quad \text{and} \quad I_y = \int x^2 dA.$$

Units and Sign.—Since the moment of inertia of an area is the sum of a number of terms each of which is the product of an area and the square of a distance, the moment of inertia of an area is expressed as a length to the fourth power. If, then, the inch (or foot) be taken as the unit of length, the moment of inertia will be expressed as inches (or feet) to the fourth power (written in.^{4} or

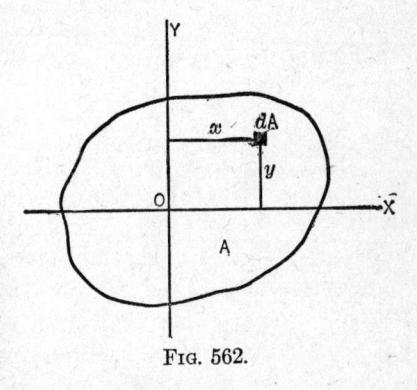

Fig. 562.

413

ft.⁴). Furthermore, the sign of each of the products $x^2 dA$ is always positive since x^2 is always positive, whether x is positive or negative, and dA is essentially positive. Therefore the moment of inertia, or second moment, of an area is always positive. In this respect it differs from the first moment of an area, which may be positive, negative, or zero, depending on the position of the moment axis.

181. Polar Moment of Inertia.—The moment of inertia of an area with respect to a line perpendicular to the plane of the area is called the *polar moment of inertia* of the area and, as noted in Art. 180, will be denoted by J. Thus the polar moment of inertia, with respect to the z-axis, of an area in the xy-plane (Fig. 563) may be expressed as follows:

$$J_z = \int r^2 dA = \int (x^2 + y^2) dA$$
$$= \int x^2 dA + \int y^2 dA.$$

Fig. 563.

Therefore

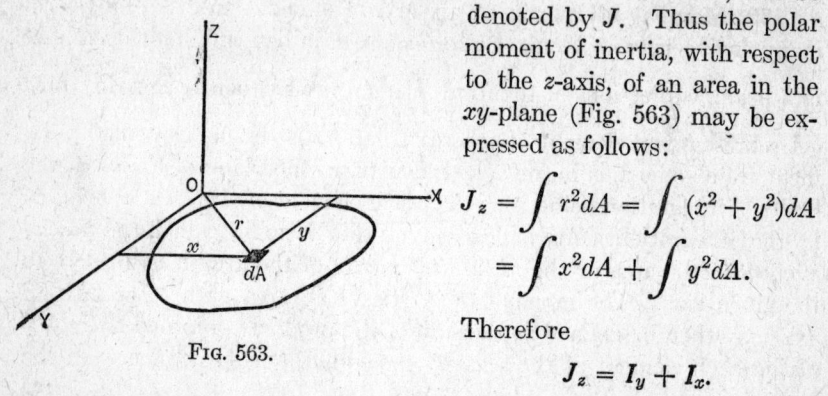

$$J_z = I_y + I_x.$$

Hence the following proposition may be stated:

The polar moment of inertia of an area with respect to any axis is equal to the sum of the moments of inertia of the area with respect to any two rectangular axes in the plane of the area which intersect on the given polar axis.

182. Radius of Gyration.—Since the moment of inertia of an area is dimensionally a length to the fourth power, it may be expressed as the product of the total area, A, and the square of a distance, k. Thus:

$$I_x = \int y^2 dA = A k_x^2, \text{ and } J_z = \int r^2 dA = A k_z^2.$$

The distance k is called the radius of gyration of the area with respect to the axis, the subscript denoting the axis with respect to which the moment of inertia is taken. The radius of gyration of an area with respect to an axis, then, may be regarded as the distance from the axis at which the area may be conceived to be concentrated and have the same moment of inertia with respect to the axis as does the actual (or distributed) area.

From the equation $I_y = \int x^2 dA = A k_y^2$, it will be noted that k_y^2, the square of the radius of gyration with respect to the y-axis, is the mean of the squares of the distances, from the y-axis, of the equal elements of area into which the given area may be divided, and that it is *not* the square of the mean of these distances. The mean distance ($\bar{x}$) of the elements of area from the y-axis is the centroidal distance as discussed in Chapter V. Hence $A\bar{x}^2$ does *not* represent the moment of inertia of an area with respect to the y-axis. In other words, the mean of the squares of various lengths is *not* equal to the square of the mean of these lengths.

183. Parallel-Axis Theorem for Areas.—If the moment of inertia of an area with respect to a centroidal axis in the plane of the area is known, the moment of inertia with respect to any parallel axis in the plane may be determined, without integrating, by means of a proposition which may be established as follows: In Fig. 564 let YY be any axis through the centroid, C, of an area and let $Y'Y'$ be any axis parallel to YY and at a distance d therefrom. Furthermore, let the moment of inertia of the area with respect to the axis YY be denoted by $\bar{I}$ and the moment of inertia with respect to $Y'Y'$ by I. By definition, then,

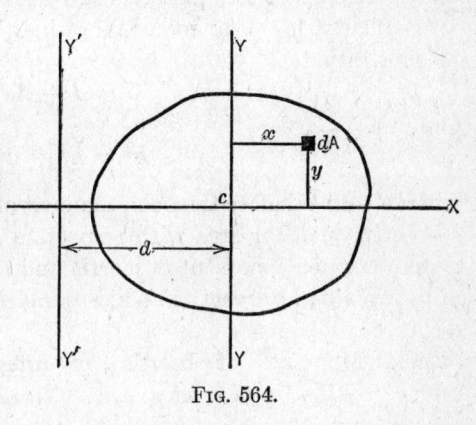

Fig. 564.

$$I = \int (x+d)^2 dA$$

$$= \int x^2 dA + 2d \int x dA + d^2 \int dA$$

Therefore

$$I = \bar{I} + Ad^2 \quad \text{since} \int x dA = A\bar{x} = 0.$$

Hence the following proposition may be stated:

The moment of inertia of an area with respect to any axis in the plane of the area is equal to the moment of inertia of the area with respect to a parallel centroidal axis plus the product of the area and the square of the distance between the two axes. This proposition is called the *parallel-axis theorem.*

A corresponding relation exists between the radii of gyration of the area with respect to two parallel axes, one of which passes through the centroid of the area. For, by replacing I by Ak^2 and $\bar{I}$ by $A\bar{k}^2$, the above equation becomes

$$Ak^2 = A\bar{k}^2 + Ad^2.$$

Whence

$$k^2 = \bar{k}^2 + d^2,$$

where k denotes the radius of gyration of the area with respect to any axis in the plane of the area and $\bar{k}$ denotes the radius of gyration of the area with respect to a parallel centroidal axis.

Similarly, for polar moments of inertia and radii of gyration, it can be shown that

$$J = \bar{J} + Ad^2,$$

and

$$k^2 = \bar{k}^2 + d^2,$$

where $\bar{J}$ and $\bar{k}$ denote the polar moment of inertia and radius of gyration, respectively, of the area with respect to a centroidal axis, and J and k denote the polar moment of inertia and radius of gyration, respectively, of the area with respect to an axis parallel to the centroidal axis and at a distance d therefrom.

184. Moments of Inertia by Integration.—In determining the moment of inertia of a plane area with respect to a line, from the equations of Art. 180, it is possible to select the element of area in various ways and to express the area of the element in terms of either cartesian or polar coordinates. Furthermore, the integral may be either a single or double integral, depending on the way in which the element of area is selected; the limits of integration are determined, of course, from the boundary curve of the area. In any case, however, the elementary area must be taken so that:

(1) All points in the element are equally distant from the axis with respect to which the moment of inertia is to be found, otherwise the distance x in the expression $x^2 dA$ would be indefinite. Or so that

(2) The moment of inertia of the element, with respect to the axis about which the moment of inertia of the whole area is to be found, is known; the moment of inertia of the area is then found by summing up the moments of inertia of the elements. Or so that

(3) The centroid of the element is known and also the moment of inertia of the element with respect to an axis which passes through the centroid of the element and is parallel to the given axis; the moment of inertia of the element may then be expressed by means of the parallel-axis theorem.

The moments of inertia of some of the simple areas will now be found in the following illustrative problems.

ILLUSTRATIVE PROBLEMS

Problem 929.—Determine the moment of inertia of a rectangle, in terms of its base b and altitude h, with respect to (a) a centroidal axis parallel to the base and (b) an axis coinciding with the base.

Solution.—(a) **Centroidal Axis.**—The element of area will be selected in accordance with rule (1) above, as indicated in Fig. 565. The moment of inertia of the rectangular area with respect to the centroidal axis, then, is

$$\bar{I}_x = \int y^2 dA = \int_{-\frac{h}{2}}^{+\frac{h}{2}} y^2 b\, dy = \frac{1}{12} bh^3.$$

(b) **Axis Coinciding with the Base.**—The student should show by integration that the moment of the rectangular area about an axis coincident with the base is $I_b = \frac{1}{3}bh^3$ and should check the result by use of the parallel-axis theorem.

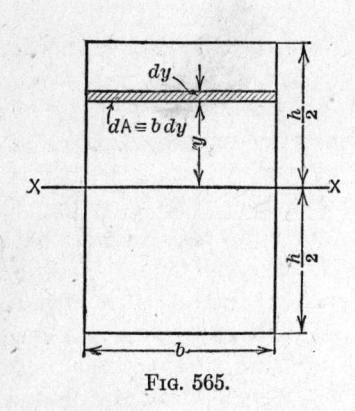

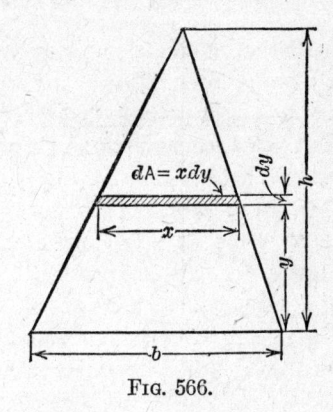

Fig. 565.   Fig. 566.

Problem 930.—Determine the moment of inertia of a triangle, in terms of its base b and altitude h, with respect to (a) an axis coinciding with its base and (b) a centroidal axis parallel to the base.

Solution.—(a) **Axis Coinciding with the Base.**—The elementary area will be selected as shown in Fig. 566. The moment of inertia of the area of the triangle with respect to the base, then, is

$$I_b = \int y^2 dA = \int y^2 x\, dy.$$

But, from similar triangles,

$$\frac{x}{b} = \frac{h-y}{h} \quad \text{or} \quad x = \frac{b}{h}(h-y).$$

Therefore

$$I_b = \frac{b}{h} \int_0^h y^2 (h-y) dy = \frac{1}{12} bh^3.$$

(b) **Centroidal Axis Parallel to the Base.**—The centroidal axis parallel to the base is at a distance $\frac{1}{3}h$ from the base. (See Prob. 333.) By use of the parallel-axis theorem, the moment of inertia of the triangular area with respect to the centroidal axis is found to be

$$I_x = I_b - A(\tfrac{1}{3}h)^2$$
$$= \tfrac{1}{12}bh^3 - \tfrac{1}{2}bh \times \tfrac{1}{9}h^2 = \frac{1}{36}bh^3.$$

Problem 931.—Determine the moment of inertia of the area of a circle, in terms of its radius r, with respect to an axis coinciding with the diameter: (a) using cartesian coordinates; (b) using polar coordinates.

Solution.—(a) **Cartesian Coordinates.**—The element of area will be selected as shown in Fig. 567. The moment of inertia of the circular area with respect to the diameter, then, is

$$I_x = \int y^2 dA = \int y^2 2x\,dy$$
$$= 2\int_{-r}^{+r} y^2\sqrt{r^2 - y^2}\,dy = \frac{1}{4}\pi r^4.$$

Fig. 567.   Fig. 568.

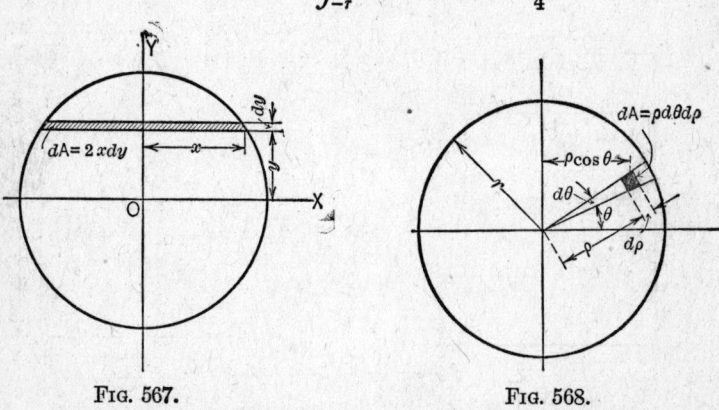

(b) **Polar Coordinates.**—The element of area will be selected as shown in Fig. 568. Hence

$$I_x = \int y^2 dA = \int_0^r \int_0^{2\pi}(\rho\sin\theta)^2 \rho\,d\rho\,d\theta$$
$$= \int_0^r \int_0^{2\pi} \rho^3 \sin^2\theta\,d\theta\,d\rho = \frac{r^4}{4}\int_0^{2\pi} \sin^2\theta\,d\theta = \frac{r^4}{4}\times \pi = \frac{1}{4}\pi r^4.$$

Problem 932.—Determine the polar moment of inertia of the area of a circle of radius r with respect to a centroidal axis: (a) by integration; (b) by use of the theorem of Art. 181.

Solution.—(a) **By Integration.**—By selecting the element of area as indicated in Fig. 569, the polar moment of inertia of the circular area is

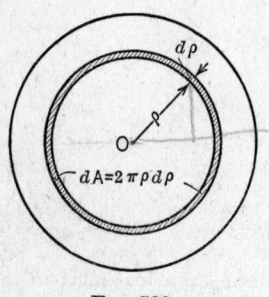

$$J_z = \int \rho^2 dA$$
$$= \int_0^r \rho^2 2\pi\rho\,d\rho = \frac{1}{2}\pi r^4.$$

Fig. 569.

(b) **By Use of Theorem of Art. 181.**—Since I_x and I_y are each equal to $\frac{1}{4}\pi r^4$ (Prob. 931), the polar moment of inertia of the area of the circle is

$$J_z = I_x + I_y$$
$$= \tfrac{1}{4}\pi r^4 + \tfrac{1}{4}\pi r^4 = \tfrac{1}{2}\pi r^4.$$

Problem 933.—Find the moment of inertia, with respect to the x-axis, of the area bounded by the parabola $y^2 = 2x$, and the line $x = 8$ in.

Solution. First Method.—The element of area will be selected in accordance with rule (1) of Art. 184 as indicated in Fig. 570. The moment of inertia of the given area with respect to the x-axis, then, is

$$I_x = \int y^2 dA = 2\int y^2(8-x)dy$$
$$= 2\int_0^4 y^2\left(8 - \frac{y^2}{2}\right)dy = 2\left[\frac{8y^3}{3} - \frac{y^5}{10}\right]_0^4 = 136.5 \text{ in.}^4$$

Second Method.—The elementary area will be selected in accordance with rule (2) of Art. 184 as indicated in Fig. 571. Since each elementary area is a rectangle of

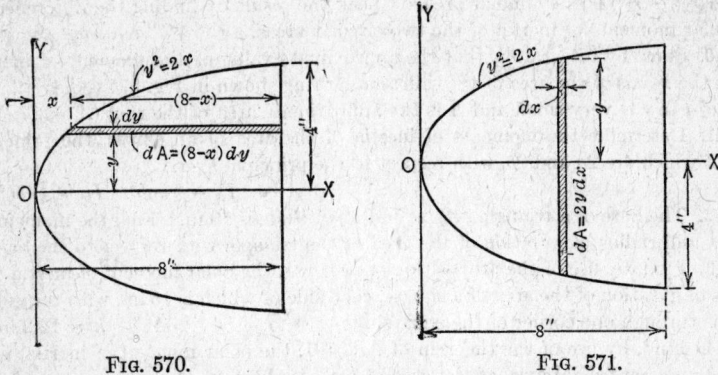

FIG. 570.   FIG. 571.

width dx and height $2y$, the moment of inertia of the element with respect to the x-axis is $\frac{1}{12}dx(2y)^3 = \frac{2}{3}y^3 dx$. (See Prob. 929.) Hence, the moment of inertia of the given area is

$$I_x = \frac{2}{3}\int_0^8 y^3 dx = \frac{2}{3}\int_0^8 (2x)^{3/2}dx$$
$$= \frac{4\sqrt{2}}{3}\int_0^8 x^{3/2}dx = \frac{4\sqrt{2}}{3}\left[\frac{2}{5}x^{5/2}\right]_0^8 = 136.5 \text{ in.}^4$$

PROBLEMS

934. Determine the moment of inertia of the area of a circle, with respect to an axis tangent to the circle, in terms of, r, the radius of the circle; (a) by use of the parallel-axis theorem and (b) by integration.

935. Determine, by use of the theorem of Art. 181, the polar moment of inertia of the area of a rectangle of base b and altitude d with respect to the centroidal axis.

Ans. $\bar{J} = \tfrac{1}{12}bd(b^2 + d^2)$.

936. Find by integration the moment of inertia of the area of a right triangle of base b and altitude h about the base of the triangle. Select the element of area as stated under (2) of Art. 184, using the result of Prob. 929(b).

937. Find the moment of inertia and radius of gyration of a circular area 16 in. in diameter, with respect to a diameter.

938. Find by integration the moment of inertia of a triangular area of base b and altitude h about an axis coinciding with the base. Select the element of area as shown in Fig. 572 in accordance with rule (3) of Art. 184.

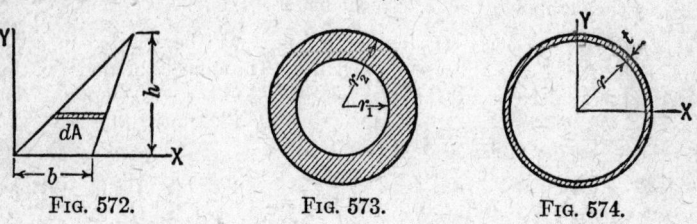

Fig. 572.   Fig. 573.   Fig. 574.

939. Show by integration that the polar moment of inertia of an annular ring (Fig. 573) with respect to a centroidal axis is $J = \frac{1}{2}A(r_1^2 + r_2^2)$ in which $A = \pi(r_2^2 - r_1^2)$ is the annular area. Check the result by finding the difference of the polar moments of inertia of the two circular areas.

940. Show by integration that the approximate value of the moment of inertia about the x-axis of the area of the thin annular ring shown in Fig. 574 is $\frac{1}{2}Ar^2$ if the ratio of t to r is very small and A is the approximate area of the ring ($A = 2\pi rt$).

941. Determine the moments of inertia of the area of an ellipse, the principal axes of which are $2a$ and $2b$, with respect to the principal axes.

Ans. $I_a = \frac{1}{4}\pi ab^3$. $I_b = \frac{1}{4}\pi ba^3$.

942. The base of a triangle is 8 in. and its altitude is 10 in. Find the moment of inertia and radius of gyration of the area of the triangle with respect to the base.

943. Find, by use of the proposition in Art. 181, the polar moment of inertia and radius of gyration of the area of a square, each side of which is 15 in., with respect to an axis through one corner of the square.   Ans. $k = 12.2$ in.

944. Find, by use of the theorem of Art. 181, the polar moment of inertia, with respect to a centroidal axis, of the area of an isosceles triangle having a base b and altitude h.   Ans. $J = \frac{1}{12}bh(\frac{1}{4}b^2 + \frac{1}{3}h^2)$.

945. In Fig. 575 is shown the cross-section of an angle section the area of which is A. The x-axis passes through C, the centroid of the area of the cross-section. Determine the moment of inertia of the area with respect to the x-axis, assuming that the thickness, t, of each leg is so small that the area of each leg may be considered to be concentrated along the longitudinal axis of the leg.

Ans. $I_x = \frac{1}{24}Al^2$.

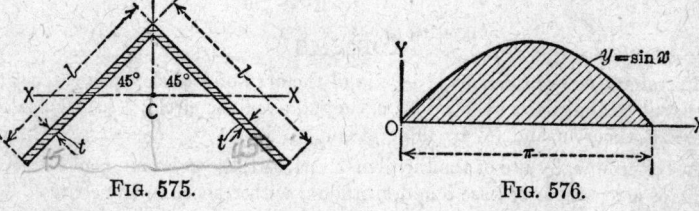

Fig. 575.   Fig. 576.

946. Find the moments of inertia with respect to the x- and y-axes of the shaded area shown in Fig. 576.   Ans. $I_x = 0.444$; $I_y = 5.86$.

947. In Fig. 271, the first moments with respect to the x-axis of the areas A and B are equal. (See Prob. 405.) Find the second moment of each of the two areas with respect to the x-axis.   *Ans.* $I_x = \frac{1}{5}ab^3$; $I_x = \frac{2}{15}ab^3$.

948. Determine by integration the polar moment of inertia of a sector of a circular area about an axis passing through the center of the circle. Assume the radius of the circle to be r and the central angle of the sector to be 2α.

185. Moments of Inertia of Composite Areas.

When a composite area can be divided into a number of simple areas, such as triangles, rectangles, and circles, for which the moments of inertia are known, the moment of inertia of the entire area may be obtained by finding the sum of the moments of inertia of the several areas. Likewise, the moment of inertia of the part of an area that remains after one or more simple areas are removed may be found by subtracting, from the moment of inertia of the total area, the sum of the moments of inertia of the several parts removed.

ILLUSTRATIVE PROBLEMS

Problem 949.—Locate the horizontal centroidal axis, XX, of the T-section shown in Fig. 577, and find the moment of inertia of the area with respect to this centroidal axis.

Solution. First Method.—The distance, $\bar{y}$, of the centroid of the area from the axis X_1X_1 may be found from the equation

$$A\bar{y} = \Sigma(ay_0).$$

Thus

$$\bar{y} = \frac{12 \times 7 + 12 \times 3}{12 + 12} = 5 \text{ in.}$$

The moment of inertia with respect to the XX axis is the sum of the moments of inertia of the three parts a_1, a_2, and a_3, with respect to that axis. Thus,

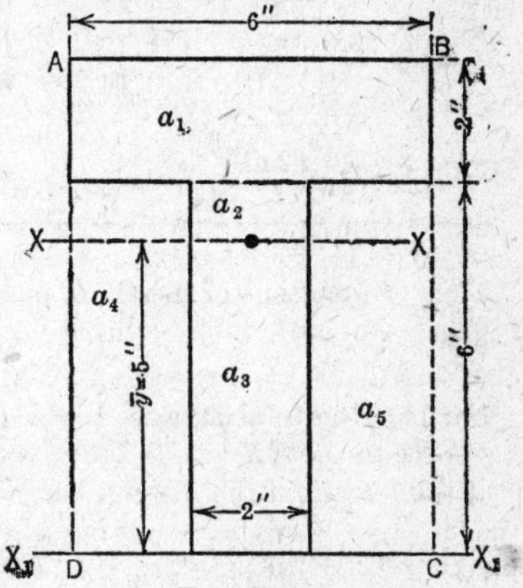

Fig. 577.

$$\bar{I}_x = \tfrac{1}{12} \times 6 \times (2)^3 + 12 \times (2)^2 + \tfrac{1}{3} \times 2 \times (1)^3 + \tfrac{1}{3} \times 2 \times (5)^3$$
$$= 4 + 48 + 0.67 + 83.33 = 136 \text{ in.}^4$$

Second Method.—The moment of inertia of the T-section may also be determined as follows: First find the moment of inertia of the T-section with respect to the axis X_1X_1 by subtracting the moments of inertia of the parts a_4 and a_5 from the moment of inertia of the rectangular area $ABCD$ and then find $\bar{I}_x$ for the T-section by use of the parallel-axis theorem. Thus, the moment of inertia, I_{x_1}, of the T-section with respect to the X_1X_1 axis is

$$\bar{I}_{x_1} = \tfrac{1}{3} \times 6 \times (8)^3 - 2 \times \tfrac{1}{3} \times 2 \times (6)^3 = 736 \text{ in.}^4,$$

and

$$\bar{I}_x = I_{x_1} - Ad^2 = 736 - 24 \times (5)^2 = 136 \text{ in.}^4$$

Problem 950.—Find the moment of inertia of the channel section shown in Fig. 578, with respect to the line XX. Find also the moment of inertia with respect to the parallel centroidal axis.

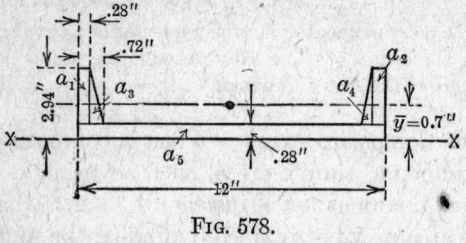

Solution.—The area may be divided into triangles and rectangles as shown in the figure. The values used in the solution may be put in tabular form as shown below, where a denotes the area of any part, y_o the distance of the centroid of the part from the line XX, I_o the moment of inertia of the part with respect to its own centroidal axis parallel to XX, and I'_x the moment of inertia of the part with respect to the axis XX.

Part	a	y_o	ay_o	I_o	ay_o^2	$I'_x = I_o + ay_o^2$
a_1	0.745	1.61	1.20	0.44	1.93	2.37
a_2	0.745	1.61	1.20	0.44	1.93	2.37
a_3	0.585	1.17	0.68	0.23	0.80	1.03
a_4	0.585	1.17	0.68	0.23	0.80	1.03
a_5	3.360	0.14	0.47	0.02	0.07	0.09
	6.02 in.^{2}		4.23 in.^{3}			6.89 in.^{4}

Thus the moment of inertia I_x of the area with respect to the XX axis is

$$I_x = \Sigma I'_x = 6.89 \text{ in.}^4$$

Further, the total area is $A = \Sigma a = 6.02$ in.^{2}, and the moment of the area with respect to the XX axis is $\Sigma(ay_o) = 4.23$ in.^{3} Hence the distance $\bar{y}$, of the centroid of the area from the XX axis is

$$\bar{y} = \frac{\Sigma(ay_o)}{A} = \frac{4.23}{6.02} = 0.70 \text{ in.}$$

Therefore, the moment of inertia with respect to a line through the centroid and parallel to XX is given by the equation

$$\bar{I}_x = I_x - Ad^2 = 6.89 - 6.02 \times (0.70)^2 = 3.94 \text{ in.}^4$$

PROBLEMS

951. A wooden column is built up of four 2-in. by 8-in planks as shown in Fig. 579. Find the moment of inertia of the cross-section with respect to the centroidal axis XX. *Ans.* $I_x = 981$ in.^{4}

952. Find the moment of inertia of the angle section (Fig. 580) with respect to each of the centroidal axes parallel to the two legs of the angle.

PROBLEMS

953. In Fig. 581 is shown the cross-section of a standard $3\frac{1}{4}$-in. by 5-in. Z-bar (fillets are neglected). Find the moments of inertia of the section with respect to the centroidal axes XX and YY. *Ans.* $I_y = 19.2$ in.^{4}; $I_y = 9.04$ in.^{4}

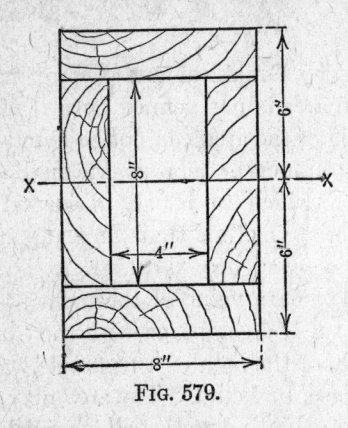

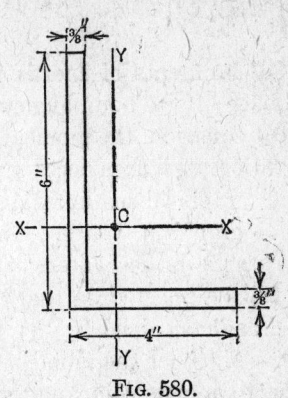

FIG. 579.

FIG. 580.

954. In Fig. 582 is represented a 16-in. circular plate in which there are drilled five 2-in. holes and one 4-in. hole as shown. Find the moment of inertia of the area of the holes with respect to the XX axis and also with respect to the YY axis.
Ans. $I_x = 252$ in.^{4}; $I_y = 224$ in.^{4}

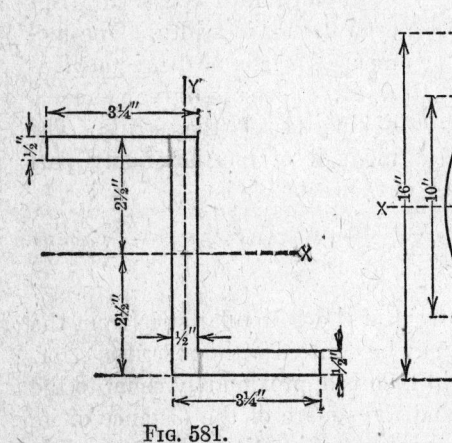

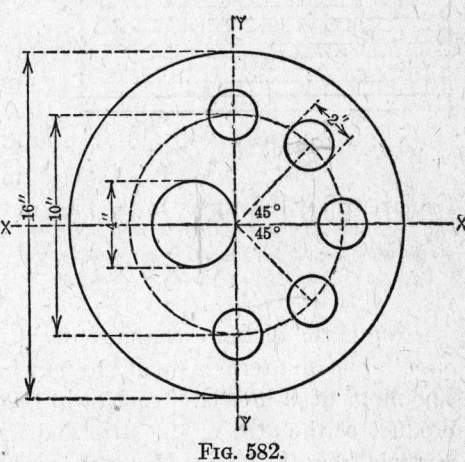

FIG. 581.

FIG. 582.

955. Find the moment of inertia, about the x-axis, of the shaded area in Fig. 252. (See Prob. 347.) *Ans.* $I_x = 852$ in.^{4}

956. Determine the moment of inertia of the area shown in Fig. 255 about the y-axis.

957. From a square area 10 in. on a side is cut a triangular area of 25 sq. in., the base of the triangle being parallel to one of the diagonals of the square. Find, with respect to this diagonal, the moment of inertia of the remaining area.
Ans. $I = 449$ in.^{4}

958. From the area of an equilateral triangle each side of which is 12 in. long is cut the largest possible circular area. Find the moment of inertia of the remaining area with respect to an axis passing through the centroid of the triangle and parallel to one side. *Ans.* $I = 261$ in.^{4}

186. Moments of Inertia of Areas by Graphical and Approximate Methods.

—If the bounding curve of an area is not defined by a mathematical equation, the moment of inertia of the area can not be found by integration. It is then necessary to use graphical or approximate methods. Several graphical methods are available which are usually discussed in texts on graphical statics. An approximate method that can be applied to any area is here described. For convenience, however, a simple area will be selected so that the approximate value of the moment of inertia as determined by this method may be compared with the exact value. Thus, let the moment of inertia of the area of a rectangle, with respect to an axis coinciding with its base, be found. The area may be divided into any convenient number of equal narrow strips parallel to the base, as shown in Fig. 583. (The narrower the strips the more closely will the result agree with the exact result.) Let the area be divided into ten such strips each 0.2 in. in width. The moment of inertia of the rectangle is equal to the sum of the moments of inertia of the strips. The moment of inertia of any particular strip with respect to the base of the rectangle is

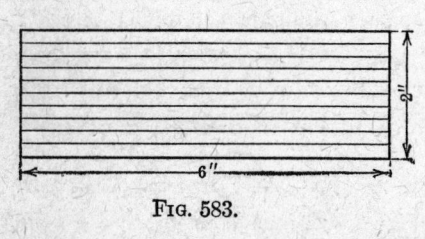

Fig. 583.

$$\tfrac{1}{12} \times 6 \times (\tfrac{1}{5})^3 + 6 \times \tfrac{1}{5} \times y^2,$$

where y is the distance of the centroid of the particular strip from the base. The first term is small and may be omitted without serious error. The moment of inertia of each strip then is approximately equal to the product of the area of the strip and the square of the distance of its centroid from the base. Hence the moment of inertia of the rectangle is

$I = \tfrac{6}{5}(.1^2 + .3^2 + .5^2 + .7^2 + .9^2 + \overline{1.1}^2 + \overline{1.3}^2 + \overline{1.5}^2 + \overline{1.7}^2 + \overline{1.9}^2)$

$= \tfrac{6}{5} \times 13.3 = 15.96$ in.^{4}

According to Prob. 929, the exact value is

$I = \tfrac{1}{3}bh^3 = \tfrac{1}{3} \times 6 \times 2^3 = 16$ in.^{4}

187. Product of Inertia Defined.

If the moments of inertia of an area with respect to any two rectangular axes are known, the moment of inertia with respect to any other axis through the point of intersection of the two axes may frequently be obtained most easily in terms of the moments of inertia of the area with respect to the two rectangular axes and an expression of the form $\int xy\,dA$ in which dA is an element of the given area and x and y are the coordinates of the element with respect to the two rectangular axes. This expression is called the *product of inertia* of the area with respect to the axes and is denoted by I_{xy}. Hence, the product of inertia of an area with respect to any two rectangular axes may be defined as the sum of the products obtained by multiplying each element of area by the product of the two coordinates of the element with respect to the two rectangular axes. That is,

$$I_{xy} = \int xy\,dA.$$

The dimension of product of inertia of an area, like that of moment of inertia of an area, is length to the fourth power and is therefore expressed as in.^{4}, ft.^{4}, etc. Unlike moment of inertia, however, the product of inertia of an area is not always positive, but may be negative or may be zero.

188. Axes of Symmetry.

The product of inertia of an area with respect to two rectangular axes is zero if either one of the axes is an axis of symmetry. This follows from the fact that for each product $xy\,dA$ for an element on one side of the axis of symmetry there is an equal product of opposite sign for the corresponding element on the other side of the axis, and hence the expression $\int xy\,dA$ equals zero.

ILLUSTRATIVE PROBLEM

Problem 959.—Find, in terms of the radius r, the product of inertia of the area of the quadrant of a circle (Fig. 584a) with respect to the x- and y-axes.

Solution. First Method.—Let the elementary area be selected as shown in Fig. 584(a), and expressed in terms of rectangular coordinates.

$$I_{xy} = \int_0^r \int_0^{\sqrt{r^2-x^2}} xy\,dx\,dy = \int_0^r x\left[\frac{y^2}{2}\right]_0^{\sqrt{r^2-x^2}} dx.$$

$$= \int_0^r \frac{x(r^2-x^2)}{2}\,dx = \frac{1}{2}\left[\frac{r^2 x^2}{2} - \frac{x^4}{4}\right]_0^r = \frac{1}{8}r^4.$$

Second Method.—Let the elementary area be selected as shown in Fig. 584(b), and expressed in terms of polar coordinates.

$$I_{xy} = \int_0^r \int_0^{\frac{\pi}{2}} \rho \cos\theta \cdot \rho \sin\theta \cdot \rho d\rho d\theta$$

$$= \frac{r^4}{4} \int_0^{\frac{\pi}{2}} \cos\theta \sin\theta d\theta = \frac{r^4}{4} \left[\frac{\sin^2\theta}{2} \right]_0^{\frac{\pi}{2}}$$

$$= \frac{1}{8} r^4.$$

Fig. 584.

PROBLEMS

960. Find the product of inertia of the area of a rectangle, having a base b and altitude h, with respect to two adjacent sides. *Ans.* $I_{xy} = \pm \frac{1}{4} b^2 h^2$.

961. The altitude of a right triangle is h and the base is b. Find the product of inertia of the area of the triangle with respect to axes coinciding with the base and altitude. *Ans.* $I_{xy} = \pm \frac{1}{24} b^2 h^2$.

962. Find the product of inertia, with respect to the coordinate axes, of the area bounded by the parabola $y^2 = ax$, the line $x = b$, and the x-axis. *Ans.* $I_{xy} = \frac{1}{6} ab^3$.

963. Find the product of inertia, with respect to the coordinate axes, of the area bounded by the curve $y = x^3$, the line $x = a$, and the x-axis.

964. Find the product of inertia, with respect to the coordinate axes, of the area of the triangle bounded by the line $y = \frac{h}{b} x$, the line $x = b$, and the x-axis.
Ans. $I_{xy} = \frac{1}{8} h^2 b^2$.

189. Parallel-Axis Theorem for Products of Inertia.

When the product of inertia of an area is known for any pair of rectangular axes passing through the centroid of the area, the product of inertia of the area with respect to any set of parallel axes may be determined without integrating. Thus, in Fig. 585, $X'X'$ and $Y'Y'$ are axes which pass through the centroid, C, of the area; XX and YY are parallel axes passing through the point O. The coordinates of C with respect to XX and YY are denoted by $\bar{x}$ and $\bar{y}$. If the product of inertia of the area with respect to XX and YY be denoted by I_{xy} and the product of inertia with respect to $X'X'$ and $Y'Y'$ be denoted by $\bar{I}_{xy}$, then, by definition,

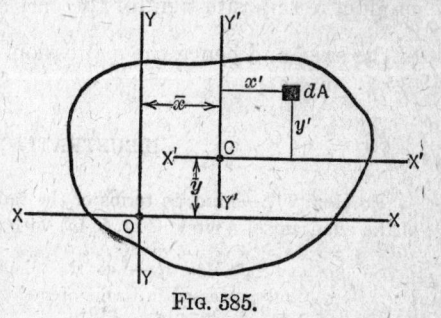

Fig. 585.

$$I_{xy} = \int (x' + \bar{x})(y' + \bar{y}) dA$$

$$= \int x'y' dA + \bar{x}\bar{y} \int dA + \bar{y} \int x' dA + \bar{x} \int y' dA.$$

Since each of the last two integrals is the first moment of the area with respect to a centroidal axis, each integral is equal to zero. The equation then becomes

$$I_{xy} = \bar{I}_{xy} + A\bar{x}\bar{y}.$$

That is, *the product of inertia of any area with respect to any pair of rectangular axes in its plane is equal to the product of inertia of the area with respect to a pair of parallel centroidal axes plus the product of the area and the coordinates of the centroid of the area with respect to the given pair of axes.*

ILLUSTRATIVE PROBLEM

Problem 965.—Find the product of inertia of the area shown in Fig. 586 with respect to the x- and y-axes.

Solution.—The area may be divided into rectangles a_1 and a_2 as shown. Using the formula $I_{xy} = \bar{I}_{xy} + A\bar{x}\bar{y}$ we have, for the area a_1,

$$I_{xy} = 0 + 12 \times 1 \times 3 = 36 \text{ in.}^4,$$

and for area a_2,

$$I_{xy} = 0 + 4 \times 3 \times 1 = 12 \text{ in.}^4$$

Hence, for the entire area,

$$I_{xy} = 36 + 12 = 48 \text{ in.}^4$$

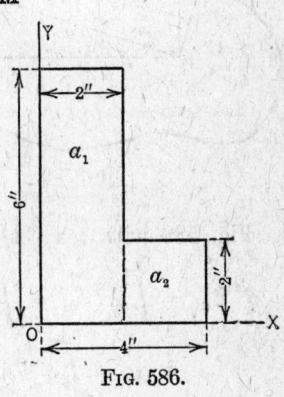

Fig. 586.

PROBLEMS

966. Find the product of inertia of the area shown in Fig. 587 with respect to the x- and y-axes.

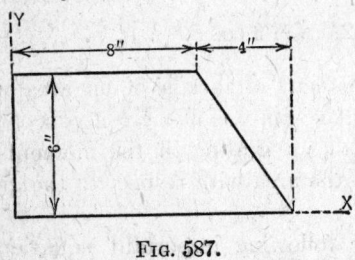

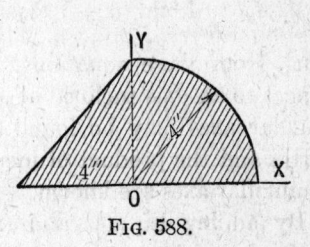

Fig. 587.

Fig. 588.

967. Find the product of inertia of the area shown in Fig. 588 with respect to the coordinate axes. *Ans.* $I_{xy} = 21.3 \text{ in.}^4$

968. Find the product of inertia of the area of a right triangle of base b and altitude h with respect to axes through the centroid of the triangle parallel to the base and altitude. *Ans.* $\bar{I}_{xy} = \pm \frac{1}{72}b^2h^2.$

969. Find the product of inertia of the area of the quadrant of a circle shown in Fig. 584 with respect to axes through the centroid of the area parallel to the coordinate axes. *Ans.* $\bar{I}_{xy} = -0.0164r^4.$

190. Moments of Inertia with Respect to Inclined Axes.

—The moments of inertia of an area with respect to different lines or axes (in the plane of the area) which pass through a given point are in general unequal. The determination of the moment of inertia of an area by the method of integration is comparatively simple for certain axes but rather difficult for other axes. Equations (1) and (2) below make it possible to determine the moment of inertia with respect to *any* line passing through a given point in the area in terms of the moments of inertia and product of inertia of the area with respect to two rectangular axes passing through the point. The equations may be derived as follows: The moment of inertia of the area shown in Fig. 589 with respect to OX' is expressed by the equation

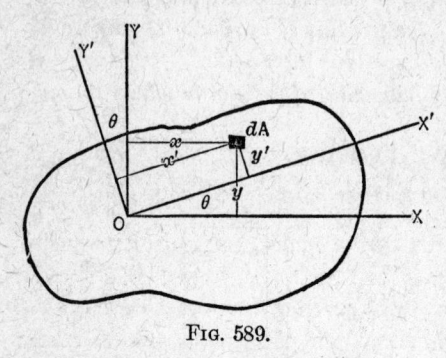

FIG. 589.

$$I_{x'} = \int y'^2 dA = \int (y \cos \theta - x \sin \theta)^2 dA$$

$$= \cos^2 \theta \int y^2 dA + \sin^2 \theta \int x^2 dA - 2 \sin \theta \cos \theta \int xy dA$$

$$I_{x'} = I_x \cos^2 \theta + I_y \sin^2 \theta - 2I_{xy} \sin \theta \cos \theta. \quad \ldots \ldots \quad (1)$$

In a similar manner the following equation may be derived:

$$I_{y'} = I_x \sin^2 \theta + I_y \cos^2 \theta + 2I_{xy} \sin \theta \cos \theta. \quad \ldots \ldots \quad (2)$$

Thus, from these equations, the moment of inertia of an area with respect to an axis inclined at an angle θ with one of a given pair of rectangular axes may be found, without integrating, if the moments of inertia and the product of inertia of the area with respect to the given rectangular axes are known.

By adding Eq. (1) and (2) the following important equation is obtained:

$$I_{x'} + I_{y'} = I_x + I_y. \quad \ldots \ldots \ldots \quad (3)$$

That is, the sum of the moments of inertia of an area with respect to all pairs of rectangular axes having a common point of intersection is constant. It should be noted also that each side of Eq. (3) is equal to the polar moment of inertia of the area with respect to an axis passing through the point (Art. 181).

PRINCIPAL AXES

Axes for Which the Product of Inertia is Zero.—It may be shown that through any point in an area there is one set of rectangular axes for which the product of inertia is zero. Thus from Fig. 589,

$$I_{x'y'} = \int x'y' dA = \int (x\cos\theta + y\sin\theta)(y\cos\theta - x\sin\theta)dA$$

$$= (\cos^2\theta - \sin^2\theta)\int xy\, dA + \cos\theta\sin\theta \int (y^2 - x^2)dA$$

$$= I_{xy}\cos 2\theta + \tfrac{1}{2}(I_x - I_y)\sin 2\theta.$$

Hence

$$I_{x'y'} = 0 \text{ when } \tan 2\theta = \frac{2I_{xy}}{I_y - I_x}.$$

191. Principal Axes.—In the analysis of many engineering problems the moment of inertia of an area must be found with respect to a certain axis called a principal axis. A *principal axis of inertia* of an area, for a given point in the area, is an axis about which the moment of inertia of the area is either greater or less than for any other axis passing through the given point. It can be proved that through any point in an area two rectangular axes can be drawn for which the moments of inertia of the area are greater and less, respectively, than for any other axes through the point. There are then two principal axes of inertia of an area for any point in the area. Furthermore, it can be shown that axes for which the product of inertia is zero are principal axes. And, since the product of inertia of an area is zero for axes of symmetry it follows that axes of symmetry are principal axes. The above statements may be demonstrated as follows:

The direction of the principal axes may be determined from equation (1) of Art. 190, which may be written in the form

$$I_{x'} = I_x \frac{1 + \cos 2\theta}{2} + I_y \frac{1 - \cos 2\theta}{2} - I_{xy}\sin 2\theta$$

$$= \frac{I_x + I_y}{2} + \frac{I_x - I_y}{2}\cos 2\theta - I_{xy}\sin 2\theta.$$

The value of θ which will make $I_{x'}$ have a maximum or a minimum value may be found by equating the first derivative of $I_{x'}$ with respect to θ to zero. Thus

$$\frac{dI_{x'}}{d\theta} = \sin 2\theta(I_y - I_x) - 2I_{xy}\cos 2\theta = 0,$$

whence

$$\tan 2\theta = \frac{2I_{xy}}{I_y - I_x}.$$

SECOND MOMENT. MOMENT OF INERTIA

From this equation two values of 2θ are obtained which differ by 180°, the corresponding values of θ differing by 90°. For one value of θ the value of $I_{x'}$ will be a maximum, and for the other, a minimum. If $I_{xy} = 0$ (which will always be the case if either the x- or y-axis is an axis of symmetry) the value of θ is zero, and hence axes of symmetry are principal axes.

ILLUSTRATIVE PROBLEM

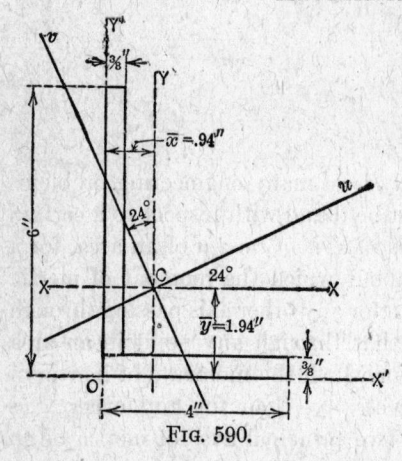

Problem 970.—Find the moments of inertia of the angle section shown in Fig. 590, with respect to principal axes passing through the centroid.

Solution.—The steps in the solution will be made as follows:

(a) The centroid of the area will be located, that is, $\bar{x}$ and $\bar{y}$ will be found.

(b) The moments of inertia and the product of inertia ($\bar{I}_x$, $\bar{I}_y$, and $\bar{I}_{xy}$) with respect to the centroidal x- and y-axes will then be found by the methods discussed in Arts. 185 and 189.

(c) The directions of the principal axes will then be found by use of the equations of Art. 191.

Fig. 590.

(d) The moment of inertia with respect to each of the principal axes, u and v, will then be found by means of Eqs. (1) and (2) of Art. 190.

(a) $\quad \bar{x} = \dfrac{4 \times \frac{3}{8} \times 2 + 5\frac{5}{8} \times \frac{3}{8} \times \frac{3}{16}}{4 \times \frac{3}{8} + 5\frac{5}{8} \times \frac{3}{8}} = \dfrac{3.396}{3.61} = 0.94$ in.

$\quad \bar{y} = \dfrac{4 \times \frac{3}{8} \times \frac{3}{16} + 5\frac{5}{8} \times \frac{3}{8} \times 3\frac{3}{16}}{4 \times \frac{3}{8} + 5\frac{5}{8} \times \frac{3}{8}} = \dfrac{7.01}{3.61} = 1.94$ in.

(b) $\quad \bar{I}_x = \frac{1}{12} \times \frac{3}{8} \times (5\frac{5}{8})^3 + 5\frac{5}{8} \times \frac{3}{8} \times (1\frac{1}{4})^2 + \frac{1}{12} \times 4 \times (\frac{3}{8})^3 + 4 \times \frac{3}{8} \times (1\frac{3}{4})^2$

$\quad\quad = 5.57 + 3.30 + 0.02 + 4.59 = 13.48$ in.^{4}

$\quad \bar{I}_y = \frac{1}{12} \times 5\frac{5}{8} \times (\frac{3}{8})^3 + 5\frac{5}{8} \times \frac{3}{8} \times (\frac{3}{4})^2 + \frac{1}{12} \times \frac{3}{8} \times 4^3 + 4 \times \frac{3}{8} \times (1\frac{1}{16})^2$

$\quad\quad = 0.02 + 1.19 + 2.00 + 1.69 = 4.90$ in.^{4}

To determine $\bar{I}_{xy}$, the value of $I_{x'y'}$ will first be found and then the value of $\bar{I}_{xy}$ may be found by means of the formula in Art 189. Thus

$$I_{x'y'} = \int_{\frac{3}{8}}^{6} \int_{0}^{\frac{3}{8}} xy\,dx\,dy + \int_{0}^{\frac{3}{8}} \int_{0}^{4} xy\,dx\,dy$$

$$= 1.26 + 0.56 = 1.82 \text{ in.}^4$$

Using the formula of Art. 189, we have

$$\bar{I}_{xy} = I_{x'y'} - A\bar{x}\bar{y}$$

$$= 1.82 - 3.61 \times 0.94 \times 1.94 = -4.76 \text{ in.}^4$$

(c) The directions of the principal axes are found from the formula of Art. 191. Thus

$$\tan 2\theta = \frac{2 \times (-4.76)}{4.90 - 13.48} = 1.11,$$

$$\therefore 2\theta = 48° \text{ or } 228°, \quad \theta = 24° \text{ or } 114°.$$

(d) From the formula of Art. 190, the moment of inertia with respect to the axis making an angle of 24° with CX (denoted by u) is

$$I_u = 13.48 \cos^2 24° + 4.90 \sin^2 24° - 2(-4.76) \sin 24° \cos 24°$$
$$= 11.23 + 0.81 + 3.53 = 15.59 \text{ in.}^4$$

Using $\theta = 114°$ and denoting the corresponding axis by v, we have

$$I_v = 13.48 \cos^2 114° + 4.90 \sin^2 114° - 2(-4.76) \sin 114° \cos 114°$$
$$= 2.23 + 4.08 - 3.53 = 2.78 \text{ in.}^4$$

Hence, the principal moments of inertia are 15.59 in.^{4} and 2.78 in.^{4} The corresponding radii of gyration are 2.08 in. and 0.88 in.

PROBLEMS

971. In the Z-section shown in Fig. 591, $\bar{I}_x = 25.32$ in.^{4} and $\bar{I}_y = 9.11$ in.^{4} Find the principal moments of inertia.   *Ans.* 31.3 in.^{4}; 3.09 in.^{4}

972. Show, by use of Eq. (1) of Art. 190, that the moment of inertia of the area of a square is constant for all axes in the plane of the area which pass through the center.

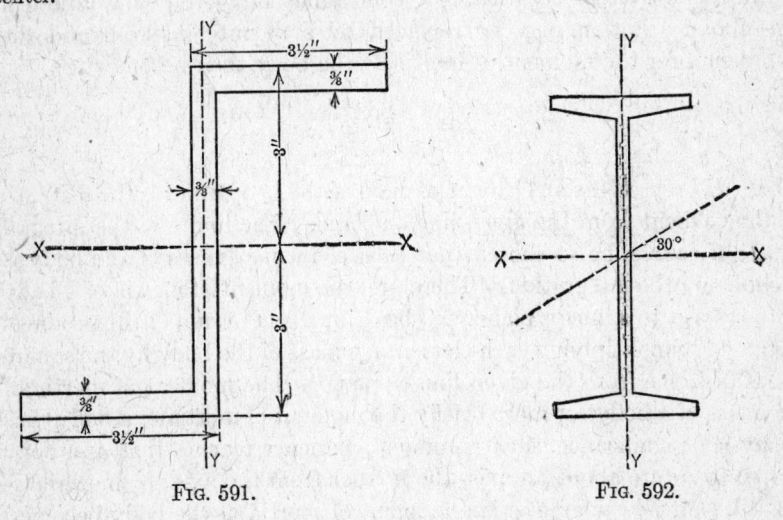

FIG. 591.   FIG. 592.

973. Fig. 592 represents the cross-section of a standard 10-in. 25-lb. I-beam. $\bar{I}_x = 122.1$ in.^{4}, $\bar{I}_y = 6.89$ in.^{4}, and $A = 7.37$ in.^{2} Find the moment of inertia and radius of gyration of the section with respect to a line making an angle of 30° with the x-axis.   *Ans.* $I = 93.3$ in.^{4}; $k = 3.56$ in.

974. Find the moment of inertia of the area shown in Fig. 586 about an axis passing through O and making an angle of 60° with the x-axis.
Ans. $I_{x'} = 35.8$ in.^{4}

§ 2. Moments of Inertia of Bodies

192. Moment of Inertia of Mass Defined.—In the analysis of the motion of a body, the body is frequently regarded as a system of particles, and expressions are met in the analysis which involve the mass of a particle and the square of its distance from a line or plane. This product is called the *second moment* of the mass of the particle or more frequently the *moment of inertia of the mass* of the particle (or briefly the moment of inertia of the particle) with respect to the line or plane. The moment of inertia of a system of particles (mass-system or body) with respect to a line or plane is the sum of the moments of inertia of the particles with respect to the given line or plane. Thus, if the masses of the particles of a system are denoted by m_1, m_2, $m_3 \ldots$, and the distances of the particles from a given line are denoted by r_1, r_2, $r_3 \ldots$, the moment of inertia of the system may be expressed as follows:

$$I = m_1 r_1^2 + m_2 r_2^2 + m_3 r_3^2 + \cdots$$
$$= \Sigma m r^2.$$

If the mass system constitutes a continuous body the summation in the above equation may be replaced by a definite integral, and the expression for the moment of inertia of the body then becomes

$$I = \int r^2 dM,$$

where dM represents an element of mass of the body and r is the distance of the element from the given line or plane. The limits of the integral must, of course, be so chosen that each element of mass of the body is included in the integration. Therefore, the moment of inertia of a body with respect to a line or plane may be defined as the sum of the products obtained by multiplying each elementary mass of the body by the square of its distance from the given line or plane. The moment of inertia of the mass of a body (or more briefly the moment of inertia of a body) has a physical significance, since common experience teaches that, if a body is free to rotate about an axis, the farther from the axis the material is placed, that is, the greater the moment of inertia of the body becomes, the greater is the moment of the forces required to produce a given angular acceleration of the body. Thus, if a rod is free to rotate about a vertical axis and carries two spheres which may be moved along the rod, experience shows that the farther from the axis the spheres are placed the greater is the torque required to produce a definite angular acceleration.

Units.—No special one-term name has been given to the unit of moment of inertia of a body, hence the units of mass and length used are specified. Thus, if the *mass* of a body is expressed in pounds and the dimensions of the body are expressed in feet, the moment of inertia of the body is expressed in pound-foot^2 units (written lb.-ft.^{2}). In engineering problems, however, the pound is generally used as the *unit of force,* in which case the unit of mass is g (32.2) times the mass of 1 lb. and is called a *slug.* (See Art. 103.) Therefore, the moment of inertia of a body, in engineering problems, is expressed in slug-ft.^{2} units.

193. Radius of Gyration.—It is frequently convenient to express the moment of inertia of a body in terms of factors one of which is the mass of the whole body. Since each term in the expression for moment of inertia as defined above is one dimension in mass and two dimensions in length, the moment of inertia of a body may be expressed as the product of the mass, M, of the whole body and the square of a length. This length is defined as the *radius of gyration* of the body and will be denoted by k. Thus, the moment of inertia, I, of a body with respect to a given line or plane may be expressed by the product Mk^2, and hence

$$I = Mk^2 \quad \text{or} \quad k = \sqrt{\frac{I}{M}}.$$

The radius of gyration of a body with respect to any axis, then, may be regarded as the distance from the axis at which the mass may be conceived to be concentrated and have the same moment of inertia with respect to the axis as does the actual (or distributed) mass.

Viewed differently, the radius of gyration of a body with respect to an axis is a distance such that the square of this distance is the mean of the squares of the distances from the axis of the (equal) elements of mass into which the given body may be divided (*not* the square of the mean of the distances).

194. Parallel-Axis Theorem for Masses.—If the moment of inertia of a body with respect to an axis passing through its mass-center is known, the moment of inertia of the body with respect to any parallel axis may be found, without integrating, by use of the following proposition:

The moment of inertia of a body with respect to any axis is equal to the moment of inertia of the body with respect to a parallel axis through the mass-center of the body plus the product of the mass of the body and the square of the distance between the two axes.

This proposition may be stated in equational form as follows:

$$I = \bar{I} + Md^2,$$

where $\bar{I}$ denotes the moment of inertia of the body with respect to an axis through the mass-center and I denotes the moment of inertia with respect to a parallel axis which is at a distance d from the axis through the mass-center.

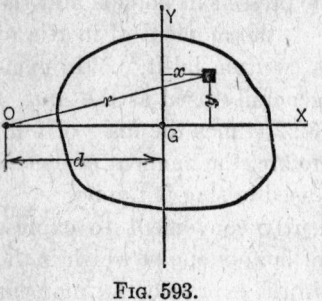

Proof.—Let Fig. 593 represent the cross-section of a body containing the mass-center, G. Furthermore, let the moment of inertia of the body with respect to an axis through G and perpendicular to this section be denoted by $\bar{I}$ and let the moment of inertia with respect to a parallel axis through the point O be denoted by I.

Fig. 593.

The expression for I, then, is

$$I = \int r^2 dM = \int [(x+d)^2 + y^2] dM$$
$$= \int (x^2 + y^2) dM + d^2 \int dM + 2d \int x dM.$$

But

$$\int (x^2 + y^2) dM = \bar{I} \quad \text{and} \quad \int x dM = M\bar{x} = 0.$$

Therefore

$$I = \bar{I} + Md^2.$$

This theorem is frequently called the *parallel-axis theorem* for masses. A similar relation may be found between the radii of gyration with respect to the two axes. Thus, if the radii of gyration with respect to the two parallel axes be denoted by k and $\bar{k}$, the above equation may be written

$$Mk^2 = M\bar{k}^2 + Md^2.$$

Hence

$$k^2 = \bar{k}^2 + d^2.$$

195. Moments of Inertia with Respect to Two Perpendicular Planes.—The determination of the moment of inertia of a body with respect to a line is frequently simplified by making use of the following theorem:

The sum of the moments of inertia of a body with respect to two perpendicular planes is equal to the moment of inertia of the body with respect to the line of intersection of the two planes.

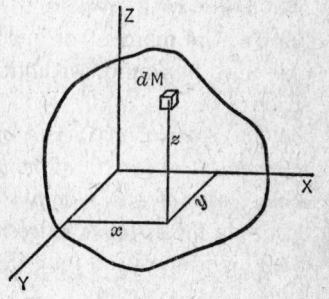

Proof.—If the moment of inertia of the body (Fig. 594) with respect to xy- and xz-

Fig. 594.

planes be denoted by I_{xy} and I_{xz}, respectively, the expressions for the moments of inertia are

$$I_{xy} = \int z^2 dM \quad \text{and} \quad I_{xz} = \int y^2 dM.$$

By adding these two equations the resulting equation is

$$I_{xy} + I_{xz} = \int (z^2 + y^2) dM = I_x.$$

196. Moments of Inertia of Solids by Integration.—In determining the moment of inertia of a body with respect to an axis by the method of integration, the mass of the body may be divided into elements in various ways, and either cartesian or polar coordinates may be used, leading to a single, double, or triple integration, depending on the way the element is chosen. The elements of mass should always be selected, however, so that:

(1) All points in the element are equally distant from the axis (or plane) with respect to which the moment of inertia is to be found, otherwise the distance from the axis to the element would be indefinite. Or, if condition (1) is not satisfied, the element should be selected so that

(2) The moment of inertia of the element with respect to the axis about which the moment of inertia of the body is to be found is known; the moment of inertia of the body is then found by summing up the moments of inertia of the elements. Or so that

(3) The mass-center of the element is known and the moment of inertia of the element with respect to an axis through its mass-center and parallel to the given axis is known, in which case the moment of inertia of the element may be expressed by use of the parallel axis theorem (Art. 194).

The moments of inertia of some of the simpler solids are found in the following problems.

NOTE: The symbol δ will be used in the following pages to denote the density (mass per unit volume) of a body.

ILLUSTRATIVE PROBLEMS

Problem 975.—Determine the moment of inertia of a homogeneous right circular cylinder with respect to its geometrical axis.

Solution.—In accordance with the first of the above rules, the element of mass may be selected as indicated in Fig. 595. The volume of this element is $h\rho d\rho d\theta$, and if the density be denoted by δ, the mass of the element is $\delta h \rho d\rho d\theta$. Hence the expression for the moment of inertia becomes

$$\bar{I} = \int \rho^2 dM = \int_0^r \int_0^{2\pi} \rho^2 \delta h \rho d\rho d\theta$$
$$= \tfrac{1}{2}\pi \delta h r^4 = \tfrac{1}{2}(\pi r^2 h \delta)r^2 = \tfrac{1}{2}Mr^2.$$

Problem 976.—Determine the moment of inertia of a homogeneous sphere with respect to a diameter.

Solution.—The cross-section of the sphere in the xy-plane is shown in Fig. 596. In accordance with the second rule above, the element of volume may be taken as a thin circular lamina included between two planes parallel to the xz-plane, as shown in cross-section. This element, then, may be regarded as a circular cylinder of radius x and altitude dy. The mass of the elemental cylinder is $\delta\pi x^2 dy$, and its moment of inertia with respect to the y-axis is $\tfrac{1}{2}\delta\pi x^4 dy$ (Prob. 975). Hence, the moment of inertia of the entire sphere with respect to the y-axis is

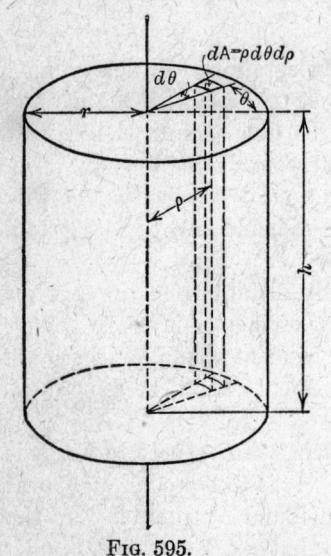

$$\bar{I} = \tfrac{1}{2}\delta\pi \int_{-r}^{+r} x^4 dy$$
$$= \tfrac{1}{2}\delta\pi \int_{-r}^{+r} (r^2 - y^2)^2 dy$$
$$= \tfrac{8}{15}\delta\pi r^5$$
$$= \tfrac{2}{5}(\tfrac{4}{3}\delta\pi r^3)r^2$$
$$= \frac{2}{5}Mr^2.$$

FIG. 595.

Problem 977.—Show that the moment of inertia of a homogeneous thin circular lamina, with respect to an axis through the mass-center, parallel to the bases of

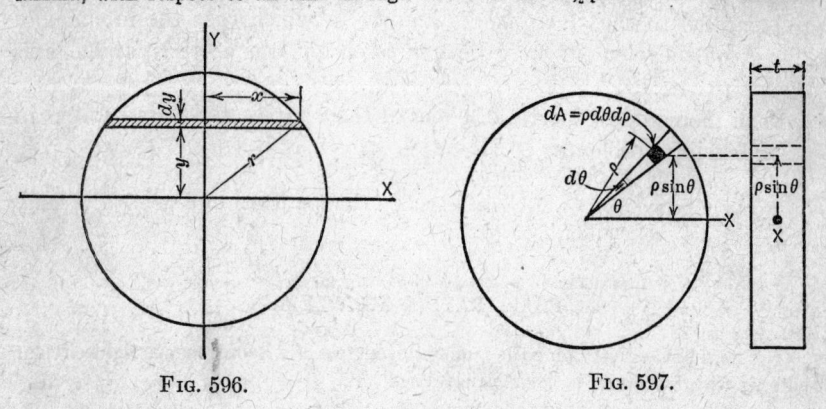

FIG. 596.   FIG. 597.

the lamina, is approximately $\tfrac{1}{4}Mr^2$, in which M is the mass of the lamina and r is the radius.

Solution.—A top view and an end view of the lamina are shown in Fig. 597. The element of volume will be taken as a prism of altitude t and cross-section $\rho d\rho d\theta$, as indicated in the figure. The mass of the element is $\delta t\rho d\rho d\theta$. Now if the thickness t is relatively small, all points in any elementary prism are approximately at the same distance ($y = \rho \sin \theta$) from the x-axis except for those prisms which are near the axis, and these prisms contribute little to the moment of inertia of the lamina with respect to the x-axis. Thus, the moment of inertia of the lamina with respect to an axis through its mass-center parallel to the bases of the lamina is approximately

$$I_x = \int_0^r \int_0^{2\pi} \delta t \rho^3 \sin^2 \theta d\rho d\theta$$
$$= \tfrac{1}{4}\delta t \pi r^4 = \tfrac{1}{4}(\delta t \pi r^2)r^2 = \frac{1}{4}Mr^2.$$

It should be noted that the smaller the value of t becomes, the closer is the approximation. The above expression is also a close approximation to the moment of inertia of the lamina with respect to a diameter of either base of the lamina.

Problem 978.—Determine the moment of inertia of a homogeneous right circular cone with respect to a diameter of the base.

Solution.—In accordance with the third of the above rules the element of volume may be taken as a thin cylindrical lamina parallel to the base, as indicated in Fig. 598. The mass of this element is $\delta \pi x^2 dz$, and its moment of inertia with respect to its centroidal axis parallel to the x-axis is $\tfrac{1}{4}\delta \pi x^4 dz$. (See Prob. 977.) The moment of inertia with respect to the x-axis, according to the parallel axis theorem (Art. 194), is $\tfrac{1}{4}\delta \pi x^4 dz + \delta \pi x^2 z^2 dz$. Hence the moment of inertia of the entire cone with respect to the x-axis is

$$I_x = \int_0^h \tfrac{1}{4}\delta \pi x^4 dz + \int_0^h \delta \pi x^2 z^2 dz.$$

From similar triangles, $x = \dfrac{r}{h}(h - z)$.

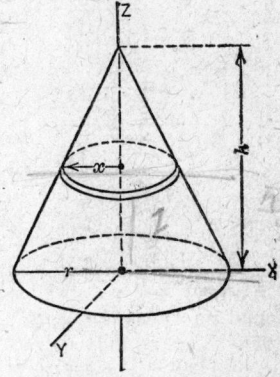

Fig. 598.

Hence

$$I_x = \tfrac{1}{4}\delta \pi \frac{r^4}{h^4}\int_0^h (h-z)^4 dz + \delta \pi \frac{r^2}{h^2}\int_0^h z^2(h-z)^2 dz$$
$$= \tfrac{1}{20}\delta \pi h r^4 + \tfrac{1}{30}\delta \pi r^2 h^3 = \tfrac{1}{3}\delta \pi r^2 h(\tfrac{3}{20}r^2 + \tfrac{1}{10}h^2)$$
$$= M(\tfrac{3}{20}r^2 + \tfrac{1}{10}h^2) = \frac{1}{20}M(3r^2 + 2h^2).$$

Problem 979.—Determine the moment of inertia of a homogeneous right circular cylinder with respect to a diameter of one of the bases.

Solution. First Method.—In accordance with the third of the above rules, the element of volume may be taken as a thin circular lamina parallel to the base as indicated in Fig. 599. The mass of the element is $\delta \pi r^2 dz$ and the moment of inertia of the element with respect to a centroidal axis parallel to the x-axis, as found in the preceding problem, is $\tfrac{1}{4}\delta \pi r^4 dz$. The moment of inertia of the element with respect to the x-axis, then, as found by the parallel axis theorem (Art. 194), is

$$\tfrac{1}{4}\delta \pi r^4 dz + \delta \pi r^2 z^2 dz.$$

Hence the moment of inertia of the entire cylinder with respect to the x-axis is

$$I = \int_0^h \tfrac{1}{4}\delta\pi r^4 dz + \int_0^h \delta\pi r^2 z^2 dz$$
$$= \tfrac{1}{4}\delta\pi r^4 h + \tfrac{1}{3}\delta\pi r^2 h^3 = \tfrac{1}{12}\delta\pi r^2 h(3r^2 + 4h^2)$$
$$= \frac{1}{12} M(3r^2 + 4h^2).$$

FIG. 599.   FIG. 600.

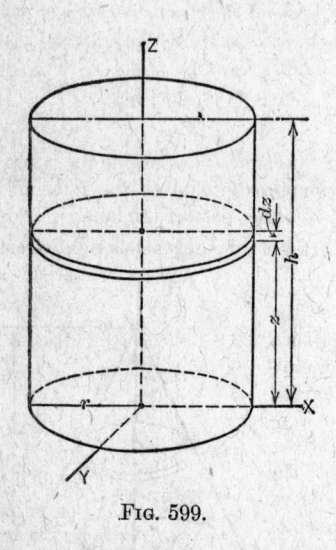

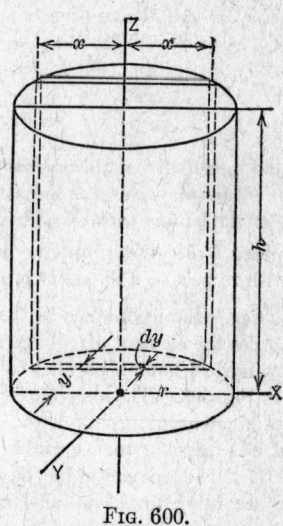

Second Method.—The moment of inertia with respect to the x-axis may also be found by adding the moments of inertia with respect to the xy- and xz-planes (Art. 195). Thus, in Fig. 600,

$$I_x = I_{xy} + I_{xz}.$$

The moment of inertia with respect to the end (xy) plane is

$$I_{xy} = \tfrac{1}{3}Mh^2. \quad \text{(See Prob. 988)}$$

To find the moment of inertia with respect to the xz-plane an element of mass may be selected as indicated in Fig. 600. Thus

$$I_{xz} = \int y^2 dM = \int_{-r}^{+r} y^2(\delta h 2x dy)$$
$$= 2\delta h \int_{-r}^{+r} y^2 \sqrt{r^2 - y^2} dy = \tfrac{1}{4}\delta h \pi r^4 = \tfrac{1}{4}Mr^2.$$

Therefore

$$I_x = \tfrac{1}{3}Mh^2 + \tfrac{1}{4}Mr^2 = \frac{1}{12}M(3r^2 + 4h^2).$$

PROBLEMS

980. A solid of revolution is generated by rotating about the x-axis the area bounded by the parabola $y^2 = ax$, the line $x = b$, and the x-axis. A homogeneous body has the same form as the solid so generated. Find the moment of inertia of the body about its axis of symmetry.

981. Determine the moment of inertia of a steel cylinder 6 in. in diameter and 12 in. high, about its geometric axis. Assume the weight of steel to be 490 lb./cu. ft.

982. Show that the moment of inertia of a homogeneous slender rod with respect to an axis through the mid-point of the rod and perpendicular to the rod is approximately $\frac{1}{12}Ml^2$.

983. Determine the moment of inertia of a homogeneous rectangular parallelopiped with respect to a central axis parallel to an edge, selecting the element of mass as indicated in Fig. 601. *Ans.* $I_z = \frac{1}{12}M(a^2 + b^2)$.

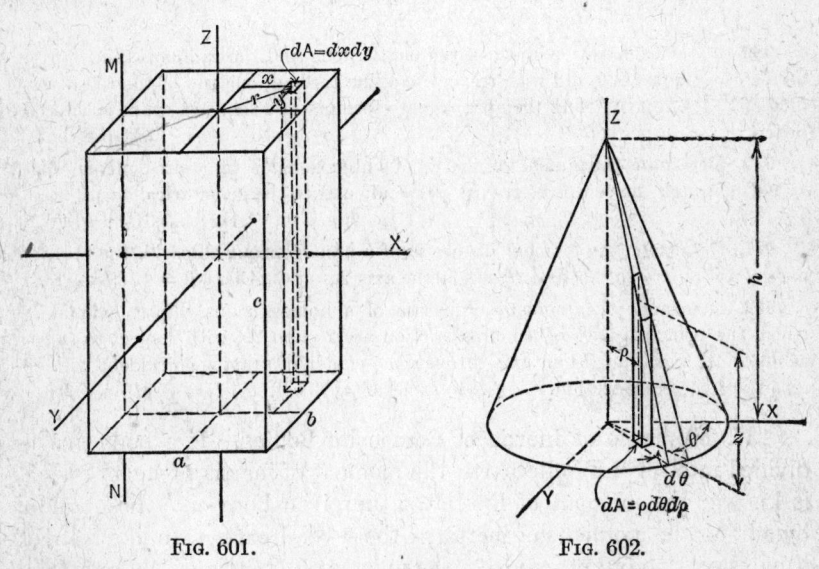

Fig. 601.   Fig. 602.

984. Determine the moment of inertia of a homogeneous right circular cone about its geometrical axis, selecting the element of mass as indicated in Fig. 602.
Ans. $I_z = \frac{3}{10}Mr^2$.

985. Find, by the parallel-axis theorem, the moment of inertia of the parallelopiped in Fig. 601 about the axis MN.

986. Determine the moment of inertia of a sphere with respect to a central axis if the density at any point varies directly as the distance of the point from a central plane perpendicular to the axis. *Ans.* $I = \frac{1}{3}Mr^2$.

987. Find the moment of inertia, with respect to a central axis, of a cast-iron sphere 10 in. in diameter. Assume the weight of cast iron to be 450 lb/cu. ft.
Ans. $I = 0.296$ slug-ft.^{2}

988. Show that the moment of inertia of a homogeneous right prism (Fig. 603) having a cross-section of any shape, with respect to a *plane* coinciding with one of the bases of the prism, is $I = \frac{1}{3}Ml^2$, in which M is the mass of the rod and l is the length of the rod. Furthermore, show that for a *slender* rod the above expression represents, with slight error, the moment of inertia of the rod with respect to an *axis* passing through one end of the rod and perpendicular to the rod.

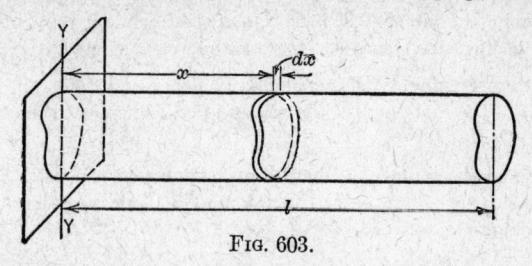

FIG. 603.

989. A homogeneous cylindrical rod is 2 ft. long and the radius is 2 in. If the moment of inertia is found with respect to a line through one end of the rod perpendicular to its axis by using the approximate formula of Prob. 988, what is the error in the result, in per cent? *Ans.* 0.52 per cent.

990. Determine the moment of inertia of a homogeneous right circular cone about an axis through the center of gravity perpendicular to the geometrical axis.
$$\text{Ans. } \tfrac{3}{20}M(r^2 + \tfrac{1}{4}h^2).$$

991. Determine the moment of inertia of a homogeneous ellipsoid, the principal axes of which are $2a$, $2b$, and $2c$, about the axis $2a$. *Ans.* $I = \tfrac{1}{5}M(b^2 + c^2)$.

992. Determine the moment of inertia of a homogeneous elliptic cylinder, in which the principal axes of the cross-section are $2a$ and $2b$, with respect to (a) the geometrical axis, and (b) an axis through the center of gravity coincident with the axis $2a$ of the cross-section. *Ans.* (a) $I = \tfrac{1}{4}M(a^2 + b^2)$; (b) $I = \tfrac{1}{12}M(h^2 + 3b^2)$.

197. Moments of Inertia of Composite Bodies.

If a body can be divided into several finite parts, the moment of inertia of each of which is known, the moment of inertia of the given body may be obtained by adding the moments of inertia of the several parts. In like manner, if parts of a body are removed, the moment of inertia of the remaining part may be obtained by subtracting from the moment of inertia of the original body the sum of the moments of inertia of the parts removed.

ILLUSTRATIVE PROBLEMS

Problem 993.—Determine the moment of inertia of a homogeneous, hollow, circular cylinder with respect to its geometric axis, in terms of its mass M and its inner and outer radii, r_1 and r_2.

Solution.—Let I_2 and M_2 denote the moment of inertia and the mass of a solid cylinder of radius r_2 and let I_1 and M_1 have similar meanings for the cylinder of radius r_1 which is removed. Then

$$I = I_2 - I_1 = \tfrac{1}{2}M_2 r_2^2 - \tfrac{1}{2}M_1 r_1^2$$
$$= \tfrac{1}{2}\delta\pi r_2^4 h - \tfrac{1}{2}\delta\pi r_1^4 h = \tfrac{1}{2}\delta\pi h(r_2^4 - r_1^4)$$
$$= \tfrac{1}{2}\delta\pi h(r_2^2 - r_1^2)(r_2^2 + r_1^2) = \tfrac{1}{2}M(r_1^2 + r_2^2).$$

Problem 994.—Determine the moment of inertia of the cast-iron flywheel shown in Fig. 604 with respect to the axis of rotation. Assume the weight of cast iron to be 450 lb./cu. ft.

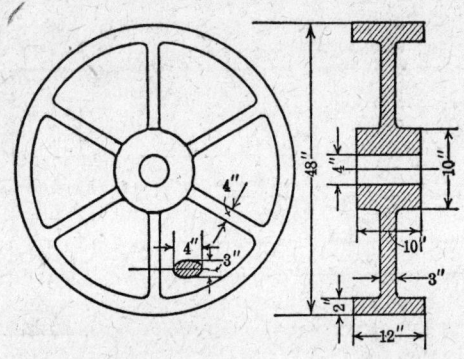

FIG. 604.

Solution.—The rim and hub are hollow cylinders and the spokes may be regarded as slender rods.

The weight of the rim $= \pi\left[\left(\dfrac{24}{12}\right)^2 - \left(\dfrac{22}{12}\right)^2\right] \times \dfrac{12}{12} \times 450 = 903$ lb.

The weight of the hub $= \pi\left[\left(\dfrac{5}{12}\right)^2 - \left(\dfrac{2}{12}\right)^2\right] \times \dfrac{10}{12} \times 450 = 172$ lb.

The weight of each spoke $= \pi \times \dfrac{1.5}{12} \times \dfrac{2}{12} \times \dfrac{17}{12} \times 450 = 41.7$ lb.

For the rim, $\quad I = \dfrac{1}{2}\dfrac{903}{32.2}\left[\left(\dfrac{24}{12}\right)^2 + \left(\dfrac{22}{12}\right)^2\right] = 102.3$ slug-ft.^{2}

For the hub, $\quad I = \dfrac{1}{2} \times \dfrac{172}{32.2}\left[\left(\dfrac{5}{12}\right)^2 + \left(\dfrac{2}{12}\right)^2\right] = 0.54$ slug-ft.^{2}

For the spokes, $\quad I = 6 \times \left[\dfrac{1}{12} \times \dfrac{41.7}{32.2} \times \left(\dfrac{17}{12}\right)^2 + \dfrac{41.7}{32.2} \times \left(\dfrac{13.5}{12}\right)^2\right] = 11.1$ slug-ft.^{2}

Hence the moment of inertia of the flywheel is

$$I = 102.3 + 0.54 + 11.1 = 113.9 \text{ slug-ft.}^2$$

PROBLEMS

995. Determine the moment of inertia of the frustum of a homogeneous right circular cone with respect to the geometrical axis, the radii of the bases being r_2 and r_1.

Ans. $I = \dfrac{3}{10} M \dfrac{r_2^5 - r_1^5}{r_2^3 - r_1^3}$.

996. The head of the mallet shown in Fig. 605 is a rectangular parallelopiped and the handle is a right circular cylinder. If the weight of the material is $\frac{1}{4}$ lb./cu. in., find the moment of inertia of the mallet with respect to the line YY.

Ans. $I = 3.81$ slug-ft.^{2}

997. The wheel shown in Fig. 606 is made of cast iron and has a solid web. Determine the moment of inertia of the wheel with respect to the axis of rotation. Assume the weight of cast iron to be 450 lb./cu. ft.

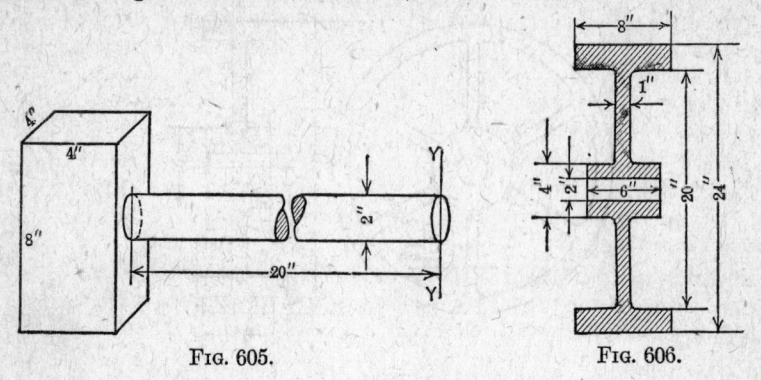

FIG. 605.   FIG. 606.

998. From a round steel disk which is 20 in. in diameter and 4 in. thick are bored four holes, each 4 in. in diameter. The axes of the holes are parallel to the geometric axis of the disk and 5 in. therefrom. Find the moment of inertia of the remainder of the disk with respect to its geometric axis, assuming the weight of steel to be 490 lb./cu. ft.   *Ans.* $I = 3.51$ slug-ft.^{2}

999. Two spheres are connected by a horizontal rod and are free to rotate about a vertical axis midway between the spheres. The diameter of each sphere is 9 in., the distance between their centers is 2 ft., and the diameter of the rod is 2 in. Find the moment of inertia of the rod and spheres with respect to the axis of rotation. Assume that the rod and spheres are made of cast iron which weighs 450 lb./cu. ft.

1000. A wood block has a rectangular cross-section 8 in. by 10 in. and a height of 2 ft. A cylindrical hole 2 in. in diameter is cut from the block, the axis of the hole being parallel to the longitudinal centroidal axis of the block. The distance between the two axes is 3 in. The wood weighs 40 lb./cu. ft. Find the moment of inertia of the remaining portion of the block with respect to the longitudinal axis of the original block.   *Ans.* $I = 0.128$ slug-ft.^{2}

1001. In Fig. 607, a sphere A is attached to a cylinder B by a slender rod C. The weights of A, B, and C are 96.6 lb., 64.4 lb., and 32.2 lb., respectively. Calculate the moment of inertia of the whole body about the axis YY.

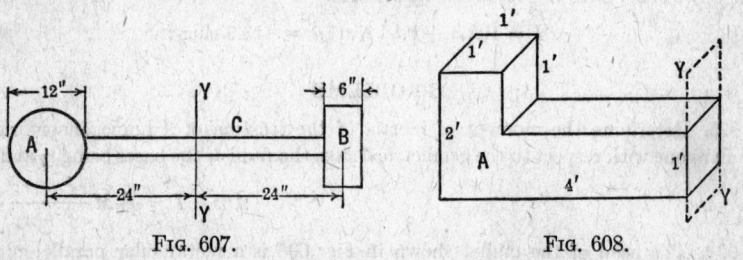

FIG. 607.   FIG. 608.

1002. In Fig. 608, A is a wooden block. Calculate the moment of inertia of the block with respect to the plane YY, assuming the weight of wood to be 40 lb./cu. ft.
    Ans. $I = 41.8$ slug-ft.^{2}

1003. A slender rod 8 ft. long rotates about an axis perpendicular to the rod 2 ft. from one end. The rod weighs 20 lb. Find the moment of inertia of the rod about the axis of rotation.

1004. Two spheres each weighing 16.1 lb. and having a diameter of 8 in. are connected by a cylindrical rod 16 in. long and 4 in. in diameter, the distance between the centers of the spheres being 24 in. The rod weighs 0.25 lb./cu. in. Find the moment of inertia of the spheres and rod with respect to an axis perpendicular to the rod and midway between the spheres. *Ans.* $I = 1.27$ slug-ft.^{2}

1005. A right circular cone has an altitude of 16 in. and a base of radius 4 in. Its weight is 0.20 lb./cu. in. Find the moment of inertia of the cone with respect to a line that is parallel to its geometric axis and passes through a point on the circumference of the base.

1006. The density at any point of a right circular cylinder varies directly as the distance of the point from the geometric axis. Derive the expression for the moment of inertia of the cylinder with respect to the geometric axis. *Ans.* $\bar{I} = \tfrac{3}{5}Mr^2$.

198. Moments of Inertia of Bodies by Experimental Methods.—

If a body is irregular in shape, the moment of inertia cannot be found by methods of integration, since it is impossible to determine the limits of the integral. The moments of inertia of such bodies may be determined experimentally, however, by methods which make use of the laws of motion of a pendulum (Art. 155).

REVIEW PROBLEMS AND QUESTIONS

MOMENT OF INERTIA OF AREAS

1007. Define the moment of inertia of an area with respect to a line (*a*) in a word statement and (*b*) as a mathematical expression.

1008. What are the dimensions of the moment of inertia of an area? Can the moment of inertia of an area be zero or negative? Explain.

1009. Complete the following statement: The radius of gyration of an area with respect to an axis may be thought of as a distance from the axis at which the area may be considered to be concentrated. . . .

1010. Correct the following statement: The radius of gyration of an area with respect to an axis is equal to the square of the quotient found by dividing the moment of inertia of the area about the given axis by the area.

1011. Prove and give a word statement of the formula $J_z = I_x + I_y$.

1012. State and prove the parallel-axis theorem for areas.

1013. In deriving, by the calculus method, an expression for the moment of inertia of an area about a line, what are the three general ways of selecting the element of area?

1014. Determine by integration the moment of inertia of a quadrant of a circle of radius r about one of the bounding radii. Then by the parallel-axis theorem find the moment of inertia about a parallel axis through the centroid of the area.

Ans. $I = \tfrac{1}{16}\pi r^4$; $\bar{I} = 0.055 r^4$.

444   SECOND MOMENT. MOMENT OF INERTIA

1015. Determine the position of the centroid, O, of the shaded area shown in Fig. 609 and then find the moment of inertia of the area about the x-axis.

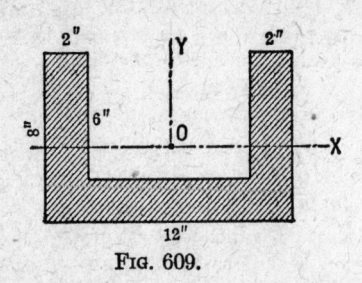

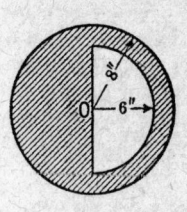

Ans. $I_x = 272$ in.^{4}

FIG. 609.

FIG. 610.

1016. In Fig. 610 a semi-circular area is removed from a circular area. Calculate the polar moment of inertia of the remaining (shaded) area with respect to an axis passing through O. Ans. $J = 5420$ in.^{4}

1017. Calculate, without integrating, the moment of inertia of the shaded area in Fig. 588 with respect to the y-axis. Ans. $I_y = 71.6$ in.^{4}

PRODUCT OF INERTIA AND PRINCIPAL AXES FOR AREAS

1018. Define the product of inertia of an area (a) in a word statement and (b) as a mathematical expression.

1019. Can the product of inertia of an area be zero or negative? What are the dimensions of the product of inertia of an area?

1020. Is the following statement correct: The product of inertia of an area with respect to two rectangular axes is zero if either, or both, of the axes is an axis of symmetry? Give reasons for your answer.

1021. State in words and prove the parallel-axis theorem for the product of inertia of an area.

1022. Explain all the terms in the formula

$$I_{x'} = I_x \cos^2 \theta + I_y \sin^2 \theta - 2I_{xy} \sin \theta \cos \theta.$$

1023. Interpret the formula $I_{x'} + I_{y'} = I_x + I_y$.

1024. Define a principal axis of inertia of an area.

1025. An axis of symmetry is always a principal axis. Is a principal axis always an axis of symmetry? Explain.

1026. Are the following statements correct: (a) If the product of inertia of an area with respect to a set of rectangular axes is zero, the axes are principal axes; (b) any two rectangular axes one of which is an axis of symmetry are principal axes?

MOMENT OF INERTIA OF BODIES

1027. Define the moment of inertia of a body with respect to a line or plane (a) in a word statement and (b) as a mathematical expression.

1028. What are the dimensions of the moment of inertia of a mass?

1029. Point out and correct the error in the following statement: **The moment**

of inertia of a mass with respect to a line or plane is the product of the mass and the square of the distance of the mass-center from the line or plane.

1030. Criticize the following statement: The radius of gyration of a body with respect to a line or plane is the distance from the line or plane at which the mass of the body may be considered to be concentrated.

1031. State in words and prove the parallel-axis theorem for the moment of inertia of a mass.

1032. In determining by integration an expression for the moment of inertia of a mass, what are the three general methods of selecting the element of mass?

1033. Find, by integration, the moment of inertia of one half a right circular cylinder with respect to a plane containing the central longitudinal axis of the cylinder. Express in terms of M, the mass of the half-cylinder, and r, the radius of the cylinder. *Ans.* $I = \tfrac{1}{4}Mr^2$

1034. The body shown in Fig. 611 consists of a cylinder A that weighs 96.6 lb. and a slender rod B that weighs 16.1 lb. Calculate the moment of inertia of the body about the axis YY. *Ans.* $I = 12.63$ slug-ft.^{2}

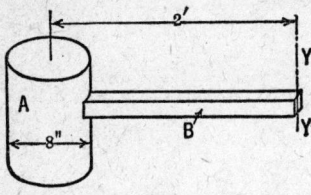

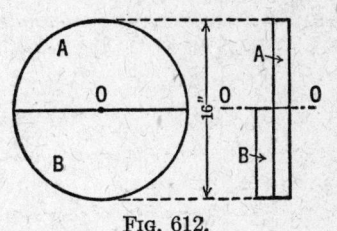

FIG. 611.   FIG. 612.

1035. In Fig. 612, a circular disk A has its mass increased by the addition of a semi-circular disk B. The weight of A is 100 lb. What is the weight of B if the moment of inertia about an axis through O perpendicular to the disk is increased 50 per cent by the addition of B? *Ans.* $W_B = 50$ lb.

1036. Calculate the moment of inertia of a sphere having a radius of 6 in. and a weight of 64.4 lb. about a line tangent to the sphere. *Ans.* $I = 0.7$ slug-ft.^{2}

1037. The dimensions of a rectangular parallelopiped are 4 in. by 4 in. by 18 in. and the weight of the parallelopiped is 16.1 lb. Calculate the moment of inertia of the parallelopiped with respect to a central axis perpendicular to one 4 in. × 18 in. face; (*a*) by the approximate formula (see Prob. 982), and (*b*) by the exact formula (see Prob. 983). *Ans.* $I = 0.0937$ slug-ft.^{2}; $I = 0.0984$ slug-ft.^{2}

INDEX

The numbers refer to pages

Acceleration, angular, 192, 193
— components of, 190, 196, 390
— linear, 177, 178, 194
— of gravity, 4
— radial and transverse, 390
— relative, 203
— tangential and normal, 190
— time curve, 179
— uniform circular, 193
— — rectilinear, 182
Amplitude, 187, 340
Angle of friction, 123
— — repose, 124
Angular acceleration, 192, 194
— displacement, 166
— impulse, 315
— momentum, 317, 318, 319, 320, 323, 330, 383
— velocity, 169, 172
Anti-resultant, 7

Balancing, 369
— of rotating masses, 370
Bow's notation, 6, 41

Cables, 104
Catenary, 107
Center of gravity, 147
— — — by experiment, 162
— — oscillation, 347
— — percussion, 262
— — pressure, 159
— — rotation, 207
Centrifugal couple, 370
— force, 258
Centroids, 146
— by graphical method, 161
— — integration, 148
— of composite figures and bodies, 153
Circular frequency, 341

Coefficient of friction, 122
— — restitution, 336
— — rolling resistance, 141
Composition, defined, 7
— of couples, 58, 60
Compound pendulum, 346
Conservation of energy, 306
— — momentum, 330
Coriolis, 391
Couple, 7, 19
— characteristics of, 20
— gyroscopic, 381, 383, 384
— moment of, 19
— transformations of, 21
— vector representation of, 23
Cycle, 339

D'Alembert's principle, 238
Damped free vibrations, 343
Dimensional equations, 29
Displacement, angular, 166
— components of, 167
— linear, 165, 166
— relative, 199
— time curve, 169
Dynamics, 2
Dynamometer, 308
Dyne, 225

Effective force, 237
Efficiency, 307
Energy, 287
— conservation of, 306
— dissipation of, 308
— kinetic, 290, 292
— non-mechanical, 296
— of a body, 298
— — — particle, 291
— potential, 288

INDEX

Equations of motion, defined, 221
— — — for a particle, 225
— — — — plane motion, 266
— — — — rotation, 250
— — — — translation, 243
Equilibrant, 7
Equilibrium, 7, 64
— algebraic conditions of, 65
— diagrams, 64
— equations of, 64
— graphical conditions of, 65
— of collinear forces, 70
— — coplanar, concurrent forces, 71
— — coplanar, parallel forces, 78
— — coplanar, non-concurrent, non-parallel forces, 83
— — non-coplanar, concurrent forces, 111
— — non-coplanar, parallel forces, 114
— — non-coplanar, non-concurrent, non-parallel forces, 116
— — of three forces, 72
Erg, 278

First moment, 144
Flywheel, stresses in, 259
Force, 1, 3
— characteristics of, 4
— component of, 7
— conception of, 3
— effective, 237
— external effect of, 3
— inertia, 231, 244, 256
— internal effect of, 3
— measure of, 4
— moment of, 15
— polygon, 40
— proportional to displacement, 232
— resolution of, 11, 21
— units of, 4
— vector representation of, 5
Forced vibrations, 343, 359, 363, 364
Forces, classification of, 6
— composition of, 7
— impulsive, 313
— resultant of a system of, 7, 34
— system of, 7
— triangle of, 8
Free-body diagram, 66, 67

Free vibrations, 232, 339, 347
— — by work and energy, 352
— — with viscous damping, 355
Frequency, 187, 339
Friction, defined, 121
— angle of, 123
— belt, 136
— coefficient of, 122
— laws of, 124
— limiting, 122
— pivot, 132
— rolling, 141
Funicular polygon, 41

Geepound, 224
Governors, 396
— centrifugal shaft, 400
— inertia shaft, 401
— loaded, 398
— Porter, 399
— Rites' inertia, 402
Guldinus, theorems of, 157
Gyroscope, 378
— analysis of forces in, 378
— axis of precession of, 382
— velocity of precession of, 382
Gyroscopic couple, 381, 383, 384

Harmonic motion, 186
Hoop tension, 259
Horse-power, 285
— -hour, 285

Impact, 314, 335, 336
Impulse, 313, 314
— angular, 315
— components of, 315
— linear, 314
— moment of, 315
Impulse and momentum, principles of, 323, 324
Inertia, defined, 222
— couple, 257, 258
— forces, 231, 244, 256
— moment of, 413, 432
— product of, 425
Instantaneous center, 215

Joule, 278

Kilowatt, 285
— hour, 285

INDEX

449

Kinematics, 2, 164
Kinetic energy, 287, 298
— — of a body having plane motion, 293
— — — — — — rotation, 293
— — — — — — translation, 292
— — — — particle, 291
Kinetics, 2, 220, 237

Magnification factor. 362
Mass, 144, 222
Mass-center, 147
— motion of, 239
Mechanical vibrations, 339
Moment-arm, 15, 20
Moment-center, 15, 84
Moment of a couple, 19
— — — force, 15
— — inertia, 413, 432
— — — about inclined axes, 428
— — — by experiment, 443
— — — of composite areas, 421
— — — — — bodies, 440
— — — by graphical methods, 424
— — — — integration, 416, 435
— — — parallel axis, theorem for, 415, 433
— — — about perpendicular planes, 434
— — — polar, 414
— — — principal axes of, 429
Momentum, 317
— angular, 317, 318, 319, 320, 323, 330, 383
— — a vector quantity, 383
— components of, 318
— conservation of, 330
— linear, 317, 330
— moment of (see angular momentum)
Motion curves, 169, 179
— curvilinear, 165
— gyroscopic, 378
— Newton's laws of, 220, 223
— of a projectile, 183
— — mass-center, 239
— — rigid bodies, 206
— rectilinear, 165, 178
— relative, 199
— simple harmonic, 186
— uniformly accelerated circular, 193
— — rectilinear, 182

Newton's laws of motion, 220, 223
Nodal point, 348
Normal pressure, 121

Pappus, theorems of, 157
Parabolic cable, 104
Parallelogram law, 7
Particle, 164
— equations of motion for, 225
— kinetic energy of, 291
Pendulum, compound, 346
— conical, 397
— simple, 345
— torsion, 347
Period of oscillation or vibration, 339, 346, 347
Phase angle, 342
Pivot friction, 132
Plane motion, 208, 264
Polar moment of inertia, 414
Pole of force polygon, 41
Potential energy, 288
Power, 284
— special equations for, 285
Precession, axis of, 382
— velocity of, 382
Principal axis, 429
Principle of impulse and momentum, 323, 324
— — moments, 17, 43, 49
— — transmissibility, 4
— — work and energy, 297
Product of inertia, 425
— — — parallel-axis, theorem for, 426
Projectile, motion of, 183
Prony brake, 308

Radius of gyration, 414, 433
Rays of force polygon, 41
Reaction, types of, 67
Relative motion, 199
Resolution, 7
— of a force, 11, 21
— directions of, 84
Resonance, 363
Resultant of a force system, 7, 34
— — a system of couples, 58
— — collinear forces, 34
— — coplanar, concurrent forces, 35
— — coplanar, parallel forces, 39

Resultant of coplanar, non-concurrent, non-parallel forces, 48
— — non-coplanar, concurrent forces, 53
— — non-coplanar, parallel forces, 55
— — non-coplanar, non-concurrent, non-parallel forces, 61
Reversed effective force, 244
Rigid body, 2
Rolling resistance, 140
Rotation, 207, 249

Scalar quantity, 5
Screw, 134
Second moment, 413, 432
Slug, 224
Space diagram, 6
Speed, 167
Spring constant, 233, 339, 343
Statically indeterminate force system, 64
Statics, 2
Steady-state forced vibration, 362
Stresses in trusses, 95
String polygon, 40, 41
Superelevation of railroad track, 260

Translation, 206, 242
Triangle law, 8
Trusses, analysis of, 95
— graphical analysis of, 101
— method of joints, 96
— — — sections, 96
Two-force members, 71

Units, absolute system of, 225
— gravitational system of, 224
— kinetic system of, 224

Varignon's theorem, 17
Vector, 5
— addition and subtraction, 164
— diagram, 5, 41
— quantity, 5
Velocity, angular, 169, 172
— components of, 174
— linear, 167, 172
— relative, 201
— time curve, 169, 179
Vibration, amplitude of, 187, 340
— damped, 343, 355, 363
— forced, 343, 359, 363, 364
— free, 232, 339, 347, 352, 355
— frequency of, 187, 339
— period of, 339, 346, 347

Watt, 285
Work, 275
— done by force system, 277
— — in punching hole in plate, 281
— expressions for, 275
— graphical representation of, 278
— units of, 277
— and energy, principle of, 297